Allied Wartime Diplomacy

Allied

NEW YORK · JOHN WILEY & SONS, INC.
London · Chapman & Hall, Ltd.

EDWARD J. ROZEK

Department of Political Science
University of Colorado
Boulder

Wartime Diplomacy

A PATTERN IN POLAND

27730

To George and Sarah Stewart

who gave me a home and a new
country when I lost mine.

Foreword

This study of one of the most important and most neglected aspects of American foreign policy leading up to the concluding phases of the war and the peace settlements might have been called, in a spirit of bitterness, "The Betrayal of Poland." But it is not treated in a spirit of bitterness in spite of the fact that Professor Rozek, who has served this country in many valuable ways and is a most loyal American citizen, must, from his own wartime experiences and participation in the Polish combat forces, feel some of the stirrings that would move any patriot of Polish origins. Why not? Resignation and despair are not necessarily proof of objectivity or even wisdom. Written under the direction of Professor Merle Fainsod, who shares my high esteem for the finished work, this study shows, despite the author's personal involvement in the events, something of the schooling in objectivity and scholarly restraint that marks Professor Fainsod's own work. Professor Rozek's book is the more effective for that reason. It is a prime piece of documentation and analysis for all who would probe the brutal reality of Soviet policy, neither a riddle nor an enigma to those with eyes to see.

The story it tells is, of course, written to show the London Polish government's efforts to win and keep Polish freedom. Taken largely from the indicated Polish sources, set in their proper context, this work sketches the historical background and traces Soviet policy with great insight. But these sources, thoroughly sifted and set forth against the background of the others that are relevant, make available in a form not previously accessible to the student and scholar the twisting and turning of both British and American policy. This policy, taken up at the crucial points of 1939 and 1944 especially, was confronted by the dilemma of how to honor the British commitments to Poland without laying down a direct challenge to the declared intentions of the Soviet Union. These commitments included not only those given at the outbreak of the war in 1939 but the assurances given at the time of the invasion of Poland by the Soviet Union in 1941 that Britain would not recognize "any territorial changes which have been effected in Poland since August, 1939." The puppet "Lublin government" of hand-picked and Communist-controlled figures was intended, as the Moscow broadcasts flatly declared, to assure that "the London clique will be wiped out." By being forced into a coalition with the Lublin government, the London government-in-exile was indeed wiped out, and Mikolajczyk barely escaped with his life.

This mosaic of the changes in attitude and the unwillingness of the principal powers engaged in the defeat of Germany from the West to look beyond the unconditional surrender of Germany and attempt to restore freedom for all of Europe forms a part of a much larger pattern. In Yugoslavia the same commitments had not been given to the Yugoslav patriots who were sacrificed to Tito and the Communists there. But the moral was the same: the Western Powers, certainly Britain and the United States, seemed either unwilling or unable, or both, to attempt a genuine implementation of the Atlantic Charter. They certainly were in no frame of mind to challenge the practical supremacy of the Soviet Union dictating to governments controlled by Moscow in what were rapidly to become obvious "satellites."

In his detailed and scrupulous examination of the existing documentary evidence, Professor Rozek reveals facts which, if shocking, are nonetheless educational. The decisions, or the lack of decisions, leading up to Allied concessions to the Soviet Union might be explained on these grounds, namely, that once the occupation of Poland by Soviet troops had been facilitated and after the revealing brutality with which the Polish uprising in Warsaw was most cynically left to Nazi liquidation, "realistic" Allied statesmanship accepted a *fait accompli* and sacrificed the forces which would have been able to restore a free Poland to the mere hope of future agreement and a peaceful world. Yet the brutal and ruthless Soviet habit of brushing aside protests and treaty rights might, if Poland's fate had served its purpose as a warning, have prevented wishful thinking after 1944 as to getting on with Moscow through concessions intended "to relax tensions."

Retrospectively perhaps nothing short of a willingness to take the risk of lengthening the war and sacrificing more British and American lives in the conquest of the Nazis was open to Churchill and Roosevelt after two cardinal decisions had been taken. The first of these was the limitation of the war objectives of the only real powers involved on the Western side to the ambiguous Casablanca formula of "unconditional surrender," which in practice tied the hands of the United States for any freedom of action. The second surrender of Allied freedom on the part of the West was the Lend-Lease assistance limited only by logistic access to Russia, which, through trucks and Allied logistic support and transport through the available open ports and across the Caucasus, freed the Soviet armies to anticipate the West in a military occupation of and hold on Eastern Europe. An attack through the "soft underbelly of Europe," following the World War I route that broke Germany's back in 1918 by cutting its Roumanian oil supply off, was already made impossible because Russia could anticipate such an attack by the speed of the movement of its armies aided by Lend-Lease trucks and rolling stock. The Allied aim in World War II appeared to be only to finish off the war as rapidly as possible with the least sacrifice of British and American manpower. This meant turning over East Europe to the Soviets.

It is apparent from the study of now-available memoirs and documents and reports on the series of conferences that, in effect, Roosevelt and Churchill had given up any thought of limiting the power designs of the Soviet Union in the occupation of Berlin and East Europe, certainly as early as the Quebec Conference. They reasoned, whether from a mistaken view of the ultimate designs of the Soviet Union or from a sense of the limits of their own powers, that they should contain the Soviet Union within its own boundaries or work out really joint occupation (such as the token regime in Berlin), that no guarantees were possible beyond the Soviet promise of free elections. How much faith they put in this Soviet promise no one but the participants was probably in a position to say, and they were not likely to be frank on this subject. Both Roosevelt and Churchill had to deal with the demand to "bring the boys home."

This is, therefore, a fit subject for a tragedy and the prelude to the subsequent tragedies which have been unfolded in the enslavement not only of Poland, but of the other nations of the Baltic and Eastern Europe. It leaves a Poland smoldering, yet compromised by the Soviet "gift" (abetted by Churchill) of German territory in the West to make up for the rape of Eastern Poland by a new Russian partition.

It is not in that light, however, that this study has been written, but as an objective recounting from documents of undeniable authenticity of *when*, *where*, and *how* this Allied policy that left the Soviets in complete control of Poland was worked out.

There is such a thing as *raison d'état*. There is always a necessity in high politics for a choice of evils. But in the light of the event it may today be doubted whether it was not in our power to have forestalled this outcome had we better understood what was its price or what was in store. On the other hand, to have had this understanding perhaps was beyond the compass of our statesmen or their hopes of securing support from their war-weary people. Once again the wearier and the warier partner, Britain, may have controlled the main decision, though the onus of the failure will have to be borne, too, by the stronger partner, the United States. Roosevelt and Churchill may have had in mind the failure of Woodrow Wilson to carry the United States into the Tripartite Agreement to enforce the peace after World War I, as they were undoubtedly influenced in adopting unconditional surrender by the classic mistake of misapplying the lessons of a previous war under quite different conditions of world power arrangements.

Of course this volume views only a part of a very complex whole. It does serve, however, to fill in rather definitively, and from sources heretofore not available, a segment of the story that has not yet been adequately told. Professor Rozek has done this with fidelity and genuine scholarship. He has, therefore, made a most important contribution to the understanding of what has brought our present world to a state far more parlous than anything with which Hitler confronted us. Not the least danger comes from a Poland on the brink of revolt against Moscow's armies. But perhaps the poison of this love of freedom may prove a contagion more dangerous to totalitarianism at home (the Soviet Union) than the other dangers of a new conflagration in the fantastic world of nuclear destruction. This is a subject, however, not for scholarly analysis, or for wild surmise, but for steadfast faith in the triumph of freedom and reason, and for prayer.

No one can read this work with detachment, I believe, without drawing one moral: The road of appeasement to Moscow leads not to relaxing by good will and faith the tensions, Moscow-made, but to surrender and to slavery.

WILLIAM Y. ELLIOTT
Leroy Professor of History and Government
Harvard University

Cambridge, Massachusetts
August, 1957

Preface

This book was written in response to Professor Merle Fainsod's suggestion that a documented study of Soviet foreign policy would be of great help to the student of the Soviet Union. In these pages the Soviet conquest of Poland will be examined and thoroughly documented to illustrate both the complex strategy and tactics used by Soviet leaders and the role played by circumstances and events outside the Soviet sphere in contributing to the success of their foreign policy.

Since a government's foreign policy does not operate in a vacuum but is by definition related to the current situation and policies of other states, and since it is constantly affected in any one area by the decisions of its opposite numbers in other areas, a study of Soviet-Polish relations between 1939 and 1947 necessarily must be concerned with the foreign policies of Great Britain and the United States insofar as they touched on the common problems of Poland and the Soviet Union in that period.

The fact that, in the rivalries between states, a given country can score important diplomatic gains or losses according to the vigilance or complacency of other states makes it clear that to maintain her advantageous position abroad and at home, a nation can and should candidly examine her past mistakes both to avoid their repetition and to frame positive policies which will not jeopardize the achievements of the past. To minimize or explain away such errors to satisfy the claims of partisan politics or of national pride is to do a grave disservice to the long-range interests of such a nation.

In the present unarmed phase of the conflict between the communist and the non-communist worlds, a more thorough knowledge and a deeper understanding of Soviet performances, as contrasted with their verbal professions, is necessary to the survival of Western civilization and to the unhampered growth of freedom in the non-Western part of the world. I hope that the present study may be a contribution, however modest, toward this knowledge and this understanding.

This work was made possible through the kindness of Mr. Stanislaw Mikolajczyk, the former Prime Minister of Poland, who generously allowed me unrestricted access to the official documents of the Polish Government in his possession, and to his private files. I am equally grateful for the numerous and lengthy conversations—often prolonged into the early hours of morning—in which Mr. Mikolajczyk elaborated upon the documents and recalled his personal observations and judgments of the events with which this study is concerned. These conversations were invaluable in guiding me in the use of the documents. Mr. Mikolajczyk, now several years removed from his experience of those dramatic events which led to the present condition of Poland, was willing to open his files in order that Soviet methods of subversion and conquest should be better understood. I am honored by Mr. Mikolajczyk's trust that I would present the story as objectively as I knew how.

It is with particular pleasure that I acknowledge the invaluable suggestions and constructive criticisms of Professor Merle Fainsod throughout the period of writing and research. Professor Bruce C. Hopper's kindly suggestions and comments were greatly appreciated, as were those of Professor Adam B. Ulam. I wish to express my deep gratitude to Professor William Y. Elliott for his constant encouragement and continued help, which made this work possible. I also acknowledge with deep gratitude the generous help rendered by Mr. Marc Gutwirth and Mr. Peter K. Obloblin which saved me from many pitfalls in the English language. The extraordinary quality of Mr. Gutwirth's mind and heart inspired and sustained me for many years, during a difficult period in my life.

Last, but not least, I am profoundly grateful to my wife, who not only typed all of the numerous drafts, but also made many substantive suggestions and was a constant source of encouragement throughout my work.

Finally, a word of explanation about the original documents. These were either in the Polish or Russian language and required translation. These translations are mine. I have kept as close to the original wording as the rules of English grammar permit. The maps and charts in this edition were lent me by Mr. Mikolajczyk. They are photographs of the originals used in his various negotiations.

It is hoped that the length and abundance of the documents is justified, not only because of their pertinence to the subject matter, but because most of them are not as yet available anywhere else. Although the sources herein quoted are only a selection from a much larger file, I have seen fit to make many quotations *in extenso* to meet the conceivable objection that the implied criticism of aspects of past Allied policies is arbitrary and not founded on documentary evidence. If the reader will bear with this presentation, it is hoped that he will appreciate this endeavor to comply with the standards of truth and scholarship.

EDWARD J. ROZEK

Boulder, Colorado
July, 1957

Contents

List of Maps
and Charts

Strategy and Tactics
of Soviet Foreign Policy

The study of the strategy and tactics of Soviet foreign policy is one of the most perplexing riddles for those who seek to explain its long-range objectives. As will be shown, its ultimate goal is the elimination of what the Soviets call the capitalistic world and the establishment of Soviet world domination in its place. But, since their aim requires the destruction of those fundamental values in Western society which assert the dignity of man and challenge the arbitrary powers of society and the state, what is at stake is not so much the issue of "capitalism" as the survival of Western civilization itself. If this civilization is to survive such a systematic long-range offensive from the communists, it needs to supplement its inherent strength with an endeavor to understand the nature of this implacable threat and to find counter measures which can effectively match and check Soviet actions.

The Soviets were among the first to realize the inadequacy of Marx's utopian assumptions that capitalism could not survive the inevitable victory of the "proletariat." They became convinced that the downfall of capitalism required more than the automatic operation of Marx's historical materialism, and they therefore applied themselves to the task of building an effective machine to help accelerate this downfall.

In the earlier stages of the development of the Soviet Union, the Bolsheviks had no clear conception of the state policy needed to help bring about the communist goal which was "historically inevitable." But, as time went by, the ever-present aim of their activities (the destruction of their opponents *and* world supremacy) came to be more vividly defined and the methods to achieve that goal perfected. They believed that their ideology embodied the purpose of all collective efforts, that, in fact, the ideology was a statement of such purposes. It was, they held, the ultimate justification for the existence of both the Soviet individual and his community.

The greatest immediate tasks which they set themselves were to train efficient revolutionaries, to create a strong party, and to set up a powerful state. These were to be stepping stones towards the achievement of the distant goal.

In the beginnings of the Soviet State, its leaders hoped that a series of revolutions would bring about the downfall of the international capitalist system. But soon bitter experience convinced the rulers in the Kremlin that revolutionary forces abroad were not powerful enough to do this and that they would have to be supplemented by the activities of the Soviet State if world communism was to be promoted in the future. A series of unplanned events led Stalin to assign to the Soviet Union the same role in the constellation of states which Marx assigned to the working class in an individual capitalist society. This meant that the burden of weakening and destroying the non-communist states would rest on the shoulders of the Soviet State. Since the strength of the Soviet Union was not yet sufficient to achieve that objective (let alone the greater objective of victorious world communism) through direct use of military force, it was only logical that the task of waging political and economic warfare against capitalism should be entrusted to Soviet foreign policy and its strategic diplomacy.

The Soviets' aim is to achieve not so much world communism as the destruction of capitalism, which is expected to be achieved by a skillful application of strategy and tactics.

The duty of tactics is primarily as follows: While guided by the indications of strategy and drawing on the experience of the revolutionary struggle of the workers of all countries, it must be determined by the forms and methods of fighting that are most closely in accord with the concrete situation of the struggle at the given moment.[1]

Since the original Marxist theory did not prescribe the exact tactical measures to be taken for the execution of strategic goals, the self-appointed disciples of Marx in each generation are therefore "free" to determine the methods for executing the "will of history" by exempting it from the yoke of inevitability.

The choice of tactics was, however, determined by empirical necessity as understood by the actors of the drama. Finally, tactics would merge into strategy. All of this, in practice, amounts to extreme opportunism or expediency successfully developed in the field of diplomacy and revolutionary policies. In each case, Marxian assumptions and prescriptions are invoked to give justification, motivation, and "grace" to the actions taken. Since all these rationalizations are performed in the name of the Marxian goal which still lies in the distant and indefinite future, and since no proof to the contrary can be derived from an unfulfilled future, a judgment of Soviet acts in terms of their allegiance to communism strongly tends to confirm the practical adequacy of their strategy. The success of their foreign policy testifies to this. The destruction of capitalism seems to be closer to, not further from, realization than it was prior to World War II.

Every other system that does not conform to communism is considered to be an enemy of the Soviet Union. The Soviets constantly emphasize the conviction that the U.S.S.R. is surrounded by a hostile world. This argument, in turn, serves as a justification for the strong, coercive measures used to force people to greater sacrifices. Theoretically, these sacrifices were for "defensive" purposes, but in practice they became a prerequisite for the attainment of the ultimate goal in a strategically chosen time. Whether this goal is attained by "defensive" or "offensive" measures is a matter of complete indifference to the Soviets. An absence of "forces hostile" to the Soviet Union would make it extremely difficult to justify and explain to the people of the U.S.S.R. the totalitarian internal policies inherent in such a system. An enemy, imaginary or real, is essential for the Kremlin's expansionist policies, for it is on this scapegoat that the Kremlin relies to divert and channel the inevitable hostilities of its population.

As early as 1925 Stalin identified the United States as the chief imperialistic nation in the world.

The predominant financial exploiter of the world, and, therefore, the most influential creditor, is the United States. Britain is no more than the Chief Assistant of that Country.[2]

The Soviets maintain that European capitalists, in order to obtain new markets for their surplus products and increase their profits to repay their debts to the United States were forced to plot the conquest of the U.S.S.R., and, in order to do this, were driven to exploit their domestic proletariats. By these actions they tried to suppress the growth of the revolutionary movement against this American-caused exploitation.

On March 10, 1939 in his report to the Central Committee of the Eighteenth Congress of the Communist Party of the Soviet Union, Stalin maintained that the United States tried to turn the Axis against the Soviet Union.[3] After the end of World War II, Stalin accused Churchill and the United States of setting up an anti-Soviet bloc.[4] He conveniently forgot the *coups d'état* in Rumania and Czechoslovakia, the war in Greece, the violation of the Yalta obligations to hold free elections in Eastern Europe and in the Balkans. It was after consideration and analysis of these aggressions and violations that the West was led to take appropriate measures for its protection. Since the end of World War II, the United States has been and is considered as the main opponent of communism because of her strength and because of her successful resistance to Soviet expansion since 1947.

Yet, while branding Western leaders as aggressive, Stalin distinguished the "people" as a separate entity and expressed his deep friendship for the latter, no doubt hoping to drive a wedge between the people and their elected rulers. The whole phenomenon illustrates a fundamental concept in the strategy of Soviet foreign policy.

The Soviets supplemented the theory of class war with the notion of the "inevitability" of the war of nations, and the Soviets decided to put the main emphasis on the war of states and subordinate class war to the strategy of international war. To be successful, that is, to emerge victorious from the struggle of states for power, for world domination, is thus the ultimate aim of the Soviet version of Marxism, and belief in its fulfillment is the chief basis for their allegiance to it. Thus, in this war of states, the Soviet State will play a decisive role and represent the culminating stage of a whole process of historical development.

From an analysis of Bolshevik behavior from 1917 to the present, one cannot escape the conclusion that the temporary departures from ultimate Marxian objectives were only "detours" of varying length and significance, but that in the end, they joined the general pattern of striving to achieve the prescribed goal: the expansion of the Soviet power over the ruins of capitalism. At no time, however, did they forget that the interest of the Soviet State will serve as a means to their ultimate aim.

If the interest of the Soviet State were an end in itself, there have been many occasions when the Soviets could have profited more by establishing lasting and friendly relations than by provoking hostilities.

Throughout the existence of their State, the Soviets have remained consistent in their verbal profession of Marxist ideals and in their acceptance of a Marxist interpretation of politics, vigorously justifying their opportunism and their flexibility of tactics to achieve the final goal. The successors of Stalin have adhered to this pattern no less than he.

In the ultimate analysis, the meaning of Soviet foreign policy can be understood only in terms of their belief in the inevitability of the collapse of capitalism and the advent of Soviet victory. Every effort is made to keep that assumption alive and to achieve its realization. The belief in the incompatibility of these two systems and the inevitability of Western defeat generates the psychological strength necessary for the vigilance of the Soviet bloc and the predatory tendency to take every advantage of Western mistakes or complacency.

Knowing that the Western Powers are fundamentally interested in global peace and that in order to preserve it they would be willing to satisfy (at least partly) Soviet demands in a specific area of the world, the Bolsheviks resolved to attain their goal piecemeal. By posing as a formidable opponent, by making excessive demands at almost regular intervals, by generating pressures engendering the fear of war, and by extracting concessions profitable only to themselves, the Soviets managed to seize objective after objective from their adversaries. Skillful use of these techniques combined with other more organic factors increased the political and military stature of the Soviet Union from a position of insignificance in 1917 to one of great power in 1957.

Given the dual role of the Soviet Union as a headquarters of world communism and as a major military power, the strategy and tactics of the latter in dealing with other states are their most effective means of advancing the aims of the former. The successes of their foreign policy can be largely explained by the mobility with which they switch back and forth between the revolutionary tactics of foreign infiltration and the traditional diplomatic and military pressures of Machiavellian power politics.

As the history of the Soviet Union makes clear, the social, economic, and political disruptions which follow in the wake of war provide the Soviet Union with the most favorable opportunities to practice their versatile arts of paralyzing resistance and seizing control wherever they can by whatsoever means they can find.

The Second World War again gave them a highly favorable opportunity to use the resources of their diplomacy, their followers abroad, the Red Army, and the secret police towards consolidating their power at home and vastly extending their influence abroad.

Western appreciation for the outstanding contribution of the Soviet armed forces made to defeat German power provided the Soviets with an opportunity to secure the political fruits of war for themselves and, by the same token, to deny these to the West.

In the scheme of Soviet war and post-war objectives was their determination to establish control over Eastern Europe. To do this, the Soviets felt bound to conquer Poland. The following pages will attempt to document exactly how this was achieved.

Notes

[1] *Strategy and Tactics of the Proletarian Revolution*, New York, International Publishers, 1936, pp. 28–29.

[2] Joseph Stalin, *Leninism*, New York, International Publishers, 1928, p. 359.

[3] *Leninism, Selected Writings*, New York, International Publishers, 1945, pp. 438–442.

[4] *Information Bulletin*, Washington, Embassy of the U.S.S.R., March 19, 1946, Vol. VI, p. 225.

Historical Background
of Soviet-Polish Relations

From 1917 to September 1939

1. The Setting

Although we have no detailed individual case study which would illustrate *all* the principles involved in the strategy and tactics of Soviet foreign policy, a study of the relations between the Soviet Union and Poland between the years 1939 and 1947 may serve as a *partial* illustration of these principles. This is so because Soviet-Polish relations in that period reflected the relationships which existed between the Soviet Union and the two major Western Powers, namely, Great Britain and the United States; thus Soviet-Polish relations are to be understood within the broader framework of Soviet foreign policy specifically, and allied wartime diplomacy generally.

The extension of Soviet power over Poland in these years was preceded by the most ruthless diplomatic maneuvering and by the use of force. The actions of the secret police and Communist Party activity in laying the foundation for their seizure of the country continued to terrorize the people despite the known opposition of the rest of the world. In subsequent chapters an attempt will be made to determine: first, how the fundamental strategy of Soviet foreign policy was able to overcome such apparently overwhelming odds; and second,

7

how this policy was applied by the Soviets to Poland in the period 1939–1947. For it must appear more than curious to all thinking men that a power on the very brink of physical destruction by its Nazi foes was nevertheless able to achieve all of its major objectives, while its apparently stronger allies were able to salvage only a few second-best objectives from a war in which all odds were in their favor. How did this happen? And, more important, what were the reasons for it?

In the last analysis the Soviet conquest of Poland was achieved with the tacit consent of the Western Powers, despite the fact that it was a geo-political extension of communist power *vis-à-vis* the Western democracies and therefore directly contrary to their best interests. It was a strategic step, well camouflaged by the Soviet Union, in the course of its efforts to weaken the Western World. Apparently the significance of this step was completely misunderstood by Western leaders at the time. One could say that it marks the beginning of what was later called the Cold War against the free world.

Further examination will show that the stage for the tragedy which befell the Polish people and subsequently affected the West was set long before World War II by circumstances partly determined by geography and partly by history, poor Polish leadership, insufficient interest among the Western Powers in that troublesome part of Europe, and the ambitious expansionist policies of the Nazis and the Soviets. By placing Poland between Germany and Russia, it appears that Providence wanted to punish the Polish Nation through the subsequent follies of its leaders. The thousand-year-old struggles of Poland with Germany and Russia produced a frame of mind in Polish leaders whereby the very idea of political compromise was synonymous with national betrayal. They therefore rejected the notion of compromise from the realm of desirable political action. This state of mind also induced reverent admiration for the supreme sacrifices which each generation of Poles had to lay down at the altar of the Polish State in the continual struggle with Poland's giant neighbors. Coincidentally, the best works of literature appeared during and after the long partition of Poland; their main theme was the heroic struggle by the Polish Nation against foreign oppression. The pen entered the ranks of combat when the sword had weakened. It was in that spirit of admiration for sacrifice that the post World War I generation of Poles took over the reins of power in an independent Poland. Thanks mainly to the widespread acceptance of President Wilson's Thirteenth Point, Poland was re-established as an independent nation. Long years of life under foreign occupation were not helpful to the creation of the qualities of mind and character which are needed to establish the Western type of democracy for which the Poles longed. The military leaders who had shown their valor in the underground before and during the First World War felt that it was only logical for them to take over political power in the independent Poland for which they had so bravely fought. The grateful nation did not resist their claims because heroic military activity was traditionally identified with political wisdom. That military bravery did not necessarily imply the qualities of political wisdom and leadership required for the growth of a real democracy was not realized in the nation. The fear of Germany and of the Soviet Union was a powerful ally of those in power as well as a justification for their authoritarian measures.

Painful experiences under these political conditions and the gradual political enlightenment of the Polish people slowly began to produce new political symptoms, promising that Poland might eventually join those nations in which law, justice, and real freedom are conditions for man's self-fulfillment and where the state is the servant of its citizens. Yet the reaction abroad to these authoritarian leanings (often exaggerated) within the frame of the Polish Republic produced a certain Western disapproval not only of the Polish Government but also of the Polish Nation as such. This attitude proved to be very costly to all concerned when the future of Poland was decided after World War II.

The stand which the two most powerful European countries, France and England, took towards Poland was always a by-product of their attitude towards Germany, or the Soviet Union, or both. Poland was played off against one or the other according to the shifting fortunes of the two under the Balance of Power system. The attitude of France and England towards Poland was never based on feelings of genuine friendship or sympathetic understanding. The various treaties signed by these two countries with Poland were based on calculated self-interest. Polish leadership, on the other hand, either did not want to understand the real meaning of these treaties or else was unable to do so. It continually assumed that Poland had genuinely altruistic friends in the West. This incapacity eventually led to tragic consequences for Poland. The only mitigating factor for the Polish leadership's incapacity to understand the British and French attitudes was the desire of both the communists and the Nazis to exploit any isolation or weakness of Poland, and this they did with consummate skill. The dilemma presented to Poland was so great that it would take a series of volumes and a corps of dedicated historians to explain it so that future generations in Poland and elsewhere could better under-

stand the tragedy and the events which led up to it between the two
world wars in that part of Europe, and might be helped to avoid such
far-reaching misunderstandings. In justice to the victims of this
tragedy, at least, such a study would be a fitting tribute to their
memory.

Soviet-Polish relations in the inter-war period were marked by a
number of formal declarations and treaties.

On March 14, 1917 the Bolsheviks issued a special proclamation to
the Polish Nation condemning one hundred and fifty years of Tsarist
occupation and explicitly supporting Poland's right to complete independence and self-determination.[1]

This proclamation was in the nature of a reward to Poles such as
Jozef Pilsudski, Tomasz Arciszewski, and many others who collaborated with Lenin against their common foe, the Tsar of Russia.

On August 28, 1918 the Council of People's Commissars issued
decree No. 698, signed by Lenin himself, which, in paragraph 3,
stated:

All treaties and pacts concluded by the government of Tsarist Russia
with the Prussian Kingdom and the Austro-Hungarian Empire which refer
to the partition of Poland, are henceforth annulled as contradictory to the
principles of self-determination of nations and to the revolutionary sense of
justice held by the Russian people, who recognize the inalienable rights of
the Polish nation to independence and unity. Hence, those acts are irrevo-
cably annulled.[2]

The Commissar for Minorities at that time was Joseph Stalin. His
signature, too, appears at the bottom of the decree.

By that act, the Soviet Government recognized Poland's right to all
the territories which had belonged to her prior to the first partition
of Poland in 1772. The Russian-Polish frontier, however, was not
fixed until two and a half years after that declaration.

In the meantime a fluid and chaotic condition prevailed in the western territories of the Soviet Union.

The Western Powers, and particularly France, used Poland and the
other small East European states as a *cordon sanitaire* in order to
isolate the Soviet Union and to protect themselves from the undesirable
consequences of the professed Soviet ambition to set Europe aflame.

Although the Polish Government would have been glad to see the
Western Powers determined to oppose the rise of Soviet power
directly and effectively, it began to negotiate on its own with the
Soviets concerning the conclusion of the peace. These negotiations
failed. Because the Soviet negotiations were backed by a mass concentration of Soviet troops on the Polish front, the confidence of the

Poles in the sincerity of Soviet good faith was weakened. They began a full-scale resumption of military operations (which had already lasted in varying degrees of intensity for a year). On April 28, 1920 Pilsudski began an offensive against the Red Army.

On May 6, 1920 Polish legions reached Kiev, but soon afterwards the Red Armies of Tukhachevsky and Budenny began to push them back towards Warsaw. What had been known as a defensive war against Pilsudski was for a brief time transformed by the military success of the Red Army into a revolutionary crusade. The Bolsheviks established a Polish "provisional government" (with Felix Dzierziński [Dzerzhinsky], later to gain notoriety as the head of the Cheka, as one of its prominent members) behind the Red Army lines and attempted to set up local Soviets as they went along.

Local Polish support was not forthcoming as expected, however, and the cruel behavior of the Red Army unified national sentiment behind Pilsudski. The rural population was more loyal to the appeal of the peasant leader Wincenty Witos than to communist slogans.[3] Tukhachevsky issued a proclamation which stated that the Red Army was marching through Warsaw, Berlin, and Paris to London.[4]

Prior to the launching of his offensive, Pilsudski reached an agreement with the Ukrainian leader, Petlura, which signified a future union of Poland and the Ukraine. Pilsudski's political conception of the federation of Poland and the Ukraine met with criticism from Allied statesmen, with the sole exception of Winston Churchill. This unfavorable attitude seriously affected the decision reached at the Spa Conference of July 10, 1920 when the Curzon Line first was proposed by the British Foreign Minister.

The conference of the Supreme Council at Spa, to which Polish delegates addressed a request on July 6, 1920 for military assistance or peace mediation, assembled in the most unfavorable atmosphere possible for Poland. France, interested in upholding Poland more than anyone else, was under the incapable government of Millerand and became vague and indecisive in its policies and actions. The initiative, meanwhile, passed to the British Government which was at that time indifferent to the fate of Poland and anxious only to avoid the international complications which would follow her collapse. In the meantime, Allied intervention necessitated either direct material assistance, for which Poland had asked on July 6, or diplomatic mediation.

The Allies were reluctant to give material aid, and diplomatic intervention would demand contact with Soviet authorities. Such contact would be equivalent to a certain form of recognition of that regime. To this France was opposed; in her eyes only General

Wrangel represented Russia, and any diplomatic conversations with the Soviets would mean the abandonment of previous policy. Under these circumstances Millerand left all the initiative to Lloyd George who, since May 1920, had conducted conversations with the Soviet delegates Krassin and Kamenev.

It must be added that since America had retired from European affairs and had refused to ratify the guarantee pact, France was dependent on Britain's good will in forcing Germany to obey the clauses of the Treaty. The Spa Conference was summoned in order to break Germany's sabotage in supplies of reparation coal, and in this respect it produced the desired result. *"Nui ne pouvait à Spa obtenir plus ni payer moins cher,"* writes Jacques Bardoux in his book *De Paris a Spa.* *"M. Millerand est revenu aux meilleurs traditions de la méthode diplomatique."* [5]

The Polish delegates who came to Spa met with understanding and friendliness on the part of the Italian Foreign Minister, Count Sforza, to whom, if one is to believe Tommasini, Poland owed certain concessions with regard to Eastern Galicia.[6]

The conditions imposed on Poland by the Principal Powers in the agreement signed on July 10 were exceedingly rigid. They contained the following clauses:

The Polish Government agrees:

(a) That an armistice shall be signed without delay and the Polish Army withdrawn to the line provisionally laid down by the Peace Conference of November 8, 1919 as the eastern boundary within which Poland was entitled to establish a Polish administration, whereas the Soviet armies shall stand at a distance of 50 kilometers eastward of that line. Wilno shall without delay be relinquished to Lithuania and excluded from the zone occupied by the Red Army during the armistice. In Eastern Galicia both armies shall stand on the line fixed at the date of the signature of the armistice, after which each army shall withdraw 10 kilometers in order to create a neutral zone.

(b) That as soon as possible thereafter a conference sitting under the auspices of the Peace Conference should assemble in London to be attended by representatives of Soviet Russia, Poland, Lithuania, Latvia, and Finland, with the object of negotiating a final peace between Russia and its neighboring states; representatives of Eastern Galicia would also be invited to London to state their case for the purpose of this conference.

(c) To the acceptance of the decision of the Supreme Council regarding Lithuanian frontiers, the settlement of the question of Eastern Galicia, of Teschen, and of the future Polish treaty with Danzig.

In the event of Poland's acceptance of the above terms the British Government shall immediately send a similar proposal to Soviet Russia and should she refuse an armistice the Allies shall give Poland all aid, particularly in war material, as far as would be possible in view of their own exhaustion and heavy obligations undertaken elsewhere. This aid would be given in order to enable the Polish nation to defend its independence.[7]

As this agreement shows, the armistice line was to correspond in the north with that of December 8, 1919, while on the territory of Eastern Galicia it was to run along the front reached on the cessation of hostilities. At the time of the signature of the agreement, that is, until the last days of July, Polish troops stood on the River Zbrucz (thus occupying the whole of Eastern Galicia) in view of which clause (c) of the above agreement had great significance. Although the agreement stated that the Principal Powers were to take the final decision regarding Eastern Galicia, whose representatives were to be present at the Peace Conference with the Soviets, the fact that the province was left under Polish and not under Soviet occupation could have been understood as recognition of Polish rights to that territory.

With respect to eastern territories in general, nevertheless, the decision of the Spa Conference was undoubtedly unfavorable to Poland.

Following Poland's agreement with the Principal Powers, which was the price she had to pay for material assistance, a cable signed by Lord Curzon was sent on July 11, 1920 to the Soviet Government. There was in its contents, however, a discrepancy with respect to the agreement concluded with Poland on the previous day. That discrepancy lay specifically in the description of the armistice line to which Poland had agreed. The British telegram, after a short introduction emphasizing the belief of the British Government in the peaceful intentions of the Soviets, laid down the following proposals:

(a) That an immediate armistice be signed between Poland and Soviet Russia whereby hostilities shall be suspended. The terms of this armistice should provide on the one hand that the Polish Army shall immediately withdraw to the line provisionally laid down last year by the Peace Conference as the eastern boundary within which Poland was entitled to establish a Polish administration. This line runs approximately as follows: Grodno, Vapovka, Nemirow, Brest-Litovsk, Dorogusk, Uscilug, east of Hrubieszow, Krylov, and thence west to Rawa Ruska, east of Przemysl to the Carpathians. North of Grodno the line which will be held by the Lithuanians will run along the railway running from Grodno to Vilna and thence to Dvinsk. On the other hand, the armistice should provide that the armies of Soviet Russia should stand at a distance of 50 kilometers to the east of this line; in Eastern Galicia each army will stand on the line which they occupy at the date of the signature of the armistice.

(b) That as soon as possible thereafter a conference sitting under the auspices of the Peace Conference should assemble in London to be attended by representatives of Soviet Russia, Poland, Lithuania, Latvia, Finland with the object of negotiating a final peace between Russia and its neighboring states; representatives of Eastern Galicia would also be invited to London to state their case for the purpose of this conference. Great Britain will place no restriction on the representatives which Russia may nominate, provided that they undertake, while in Great Britain, not to interfere in the politics or the internal affairs of the British Empire or to indulge in propaganda. . . . The British Government would be glad of an immediate reply to this telegram, for the Polish Government has asked for the intervention of the Allies, and if time is lost a situation may develop which will make the conclusion of lasting peace far more difficult in Eastern Europe. Further, while the British Government has bound itself to give no assistance to Poland for any purpose hostile to Russia, it is also bound under the Covenant of the League of Nations to defend the integrity and independence of Poland within its legitimate ethnographic frontiers. If, therefore, Soviet Russia, despite its repeated declarations accepting the independence of Poland, will not be content with the withdrawal of the Polish armies from Russian soil on the condition of a mutual armistice, but intends to take action hostile to Poland in its own territory, the British Government and its Allies would feel bound to assist the Polish nation to defend its existence with all the means at their disposal. The Polish Government has declared its willingness to make peace with Soviet Russia and to initiate negotiations for an armistice on a basis of the conditions set out above if directly it is informed that Soviet Russia also agrees. The British Government, therefore, would be glad of a reply within a week as to whether Soviet Russia is prepared to accept the aforesaid proposal for putting an end to further unnecessary bloodshed and giving peace to Europe.[8]

At the same time the British Government suggested that a separate agreement be signed with General Wrangel.

The discrepancy between the content of the agreement of July 10, i.e., between the decision of the Supreme Council and Lord Curzon's telegram, lay in the first sentence of paragraph (a), whereby the provisional frontier of December 8, 1919 was suggested as an armistice line but described in inexact terms: in the south, on the territory of Eastern Galacia, the former "Botha Line" was added. The so-conceived armistice line would leave the city of Lwów and the greater part of Eastern Galicia on the Russian side. Such an intention was not, however, in conformity with the last sentence of paragraph (a) of the agreement of July 10 which stipulated that in Eastern Galicia each army would stand on the line which they occupied at the date of the signature of the armistice. This clause clearly meant that Eastern Galicia was not intended to come under Soviet occupation and that the proposed armistice line would run, in its southern sector, near the eastern frontier of that province.

The lack of precision in the description of the "provisional frontier" of December 8, 1919 would not be easy to explain if it were not for the specific tendencies of the people who inspired the Curzon Line. Lord Curzon himself had little to do with that line, as the well-informed author, Harold Nicolson, states in his book.[9] The same British experts who played an important role in elaborating the "Botha Line" of November 21, 1919 and the line of December 8, 1919 were the actual authors of the Curzon Line. They had their own conception of the eastern Polish frontier which they proposed to settle according to allegedly "ethnographic" principles set up in an arbitrary way and not altogether in accord with the actual census of the Polish population in the eastern territories. They may have desired to prepare and influence the decision of the Supreme Council regarding Eastern Galicia by a reminder of the line of demarcation of 1919 (Botha Line) through a combination of that line with the other one of December 8. (See map on page 347.)

The London *Times* of July 15, 1920 published a map, supplied, no doubt, by British experts, on which the Curzon Line was drawn along the Botha Line as stipulated in Lord Curzon's telegram, as if the clause regarding Eastern Galicia were non-existent.

That line was in fact to run along the Rivers Bug and Zbrucz and was to serve merely as a boundary during an armistice. Neither the agreement of July 10 nor Lord Curzon's telegram of July 11 contained any stipulation that it was to become the Soviet-Polish frontier. Reference to a boundary occurred only later in Lord Curzon's further note acknowledging Soviet readiness to grant Poland "a frontier no less favorable than the ethnographic one suggested previously by the Supreme Council."

The myth which arose round the Curzon Line resulted in an erroneous interpretation both as regards its position (on the territory of Eastern Galicia) and its character. As an armistice line in 1920, it was not accepted by Poland and would have remained in diplomatic archives entirely were it not for the fact that this myth was maintained in certain British circles, which attempted to give it a significance quite at variance with the facts.

In any case, the proposed armistice line failed because the Soviet Government in its note of July 17, 1920 rejected the proposals of mediation and of peace settlement in Europe by a general conference of Powers put forward by Great Britain.

On July 17, 1920 Chicherin rejected the Curzon proposals, stating:

In regard to peace with Poland, the Soviet Government considers it necessary to take into account, besides the interest and aspiration of the Russian working masses, only the interest and aspiration of the Polish working masses, and consequently it considers it possible to reach peace with Poland solely by direct negotiations. . . . The Soviet Government categorically rejects the claim of any outside grouping of Powers to take

on themselves the part of supreme arbiters of the fate of other peoples.
. . . At the same time the Soviet Government announces its readiness to
agree to a territorial frontier more favorable to the Polish Nation than that
indicated by the Supreme Council in December last, and which is again
proposed by the British Government in its ultimatum of 12 July (the
Curzon Line). The Soviet Government cannot refrain from calling attention to the fact that to a certain extent this frontier was drawn up by the
Supreme Council under the influence of counter-revolutionary Russian elements, adherents of the bourgeoisie and the landlords, and that, for example, in the Kholm (Chelm) district the decision of the Supreme Council
clearly reflects the influence of those counter-revolutionary elements and
follows the anti-Polish policy of Tsarism and of the imperialist White
Russian bourgeoisie.[10]

Instead, in their note, the Soviet Government consented to conclude
peace with Poland by way of direct negotiations and at the same time
declared its readiness to grant Poland a frontier much more favorable
than the Curzon Line.

On October 8, 1920 Lenin, while speaking at a meeting of workers
in the leather industry said:

The Poles forced war on us, and we know that it was not the Polish
landlords or Polish capitalists who played the chief part in that, for Poland's
situation then, as now, was desperate. It went into this adventure from
desperation. But the chief thing pushing the Poles into war with us was,
of course, the power of international capital, in the first place French capital. It has come out that hundreds of French officers served and are now
serving in the Polish Army, that all the arms, all the money, and military
assistance in general, were given to Poland by France. These were the
conditions in which the war started. It was a new attempt by the Allies to
destroy the Soviet Republic. . . . If Poland had become Soviet, if the
Warsaw workers had received from Russia the help they expected and
welcomed, the Versailles Treaty would have been shattered, and the entire
international system built up by the victors would have been destroyed.
France would not then have had a buffer separating Germany from Soviet
Russia. It would not have had a battering-ram against the Soviet Republic.
It would have had no hope of getting back its milliards. . . .
While the Red Armies reached the Polish frontier, their victorious offensive caused an unprecedented political crisis. The essential thing in this
crisis was that the English Government threatened to declare war on us; it
said: "If you go further, we shall make war on you, we shall send our navy
against you," but the English workers said that they would not permit
such a war.[11]

The British Government responded to the Soviet note of July 17,
1920 with a second note of Lord Curzon (July 20, 1920) in which it
was stated that Great Britain and her Allies would give Poland "every
assistance" if "despite the Polish Government's armistice proposals the
Soviet troops advanced any further." The same note also acknowl-

edged Soviet readiness to grant Poland a frontier no less favorable than the ethnographic one proposed by the Supreme Council.[12]

The Polish Government agreed to direct negotiations with Russia and sent an appropriate proposal in a note of July 22, 1920. The negotiations began, and soon afterwards military events favored Poland. In consequence, a frontier was fixed by the Riga Treaty which obliterated all memory of the Curzon Line, and which was, as the Soviets had said, more favorable to Poland than the Curzon Line.

On August 16, 1920 Pilsudski's armies defeated the Red Army on the outskirts of Warsaw. The first attempt to Sovietize Central Europe or to establish a "friendly government" failed, but only for the time being. Both Poland and the Soviet Union were exhausted by years of war, and both desired peace. On March 18, 1921 the Treaty of Riga was signed between the Soviet Union and Poland.

Article 2 of the Treaty delimited the actual frontiers.

Article 3 stated:

Russia and the Ukraine abandon all rights and claims to the territories situated to the West of the frontier laid down by Article 2 of the present Treaty. Poland, on the other hand, abandons in favor of the Ukraine and of White Russia all rights and claims to the territory situated to the East of this frontier.[13]

The Treaty of Riga was not imposed on the Soviet Union; it was a settlement based on compromise. It established permanent frontiers which ran between the Curzon and Borisov lines. Mutual respect for the political and territorial sovereignty of both parties and non-interference in each other's internal affairs were pledged.

By this Treaty Poland abandoned her claims to some 300,000 square kilometers or 120,000 square miles which had belonged to her before the 1772 partition. Soviet official quarters recognized without reservation the conciliatory character of the Riga Treaty. Before its conclusion, they suggested several times to Poland the possibility of a border line which would reach even farther east than the one fixed by the Treaty of Riga.

Not only was the Treaty of Riga signed by delegates of the Russian Soviet Republic (RSFSR), who were at the same time acting in the name of the White Russian (Byelorussian) Republic, but it was also signed by the authorized delegates of the Ukrainian Soviet Republic. After having signed the Treaty, the head of the Soviet delegation, Joffe, made a speech in which he said:

It must be stated that both during the period when blood was still being shed and the clangor of war was heard at the front, and during the later period in more peaceful circumstances, the sincere desire for peace and the tact shown by the Polish delegation, and in particular by its respected chairman, were extremely helpful both for the conduct of negotiations and for the achievement of a satisfactory settlement. On behalf of the Russo-Ukrainian delegation I wish, in closing, to express my gratitude for this to the Polish delegation and in particular to its chairman.[14]

Significant evidence is also contained in the *Great Soviet Encyclopedia*. In the 1940 edition, Vol. XLVI, page 247, is found the following statement about the Soviet-Polish frontiers established by the Riga Treaty:

In accordance with its provisions, Poland kept Galicia and a part of White Russia. However, the new Soviet-Polish frontier was far less advantageous for the White Poles than the one which was proposed to Poland by the Soviet Government on April 1920; the frontier determined after the Soviet-Polish war runs 50 to 100 kilometers to the West of the line which was suggested at the beginning of the war. This means that Soviet Russia emerged victorious even from this struggle against the forces of counter-revolution.

The frontiers drawn by the Treaty of Riga were recognized on March 15, 1923 by the Conference of Ambassadors of the Principal Allied Powers in accordance with Article 87 of the Versailles Treaty, which authorized these Powers to fix Poland's eastern boundaries. At that time Lord Curzon was still Foreign Secretary of Great Britain. The Government of the United States recognized the frontiers of the Riga Treaty three weeks later, on April 5, 1923.

The Soviets were forced to abandon, at least for the time being, their desire to set Europe afire with revolution. Instead, the doctrine of socialism in one country was launched in order to build up the strength of the Soviet State, which would then later pursue, more successfully and through other means, the temporarily postponed objectives. In order to assure non-interference in Soviet affairs from outside during this critical build-up period, the Bolsheviks invented a new slogan for their foreign policy; namely, peaceful co-existence with the capitalist countries. Within the framework of that policy of temporary alliances, Soviet-Polish relations remained normal, at least on the surface. The basis for this new Soviet policy was set by the Fifteenth and Sixteenth Congresses of the Communist Party of the Soviet Union held in December 1927 and in April 1929, respectively. They decided to embark on a "peace policy" in order to weaken or destroy their Western neighbors. A particularly energetic effort was made to improve relations with Poland, which the Kremlin considered to be an outpost of French imperialism.

On February 9, 1929 a protocol was signed in Moscow by the representatives of Estonia, Latvia, Poland, Rumania, and the Soviet Union for the immediate enforcement of the Treaty of Paris (The Briand-Kellogg Pact), which renounced war as an instrument of national policy.

On July 25, 1932 a pact of non-aggression between Poland and the Soviet Union was signed in Moscow. Article I stated:

The two Contracting Parties, recording that they have renounced war as an instrument of national policy in their mutual relations, reciprocally undertake to refrain from taking any aggressive action against or invading the territories of the other Parties, either alone or in conjunction with other Powers.

Any act of violence attacking the integrity and inviolability of the territory or the political independence of the other Contracting Parties shall be regarded as contrary to the undertakings contained in the present Article, even if such acts are committed without declaration of war and avoid all possible warlike manifestations.

ARTICLE II

Should one of the Contracting Parties be attacked by a third State or by a group of other States, the other Contracting Party undertakes not to give aid or assistance, either directly or indirectly, to the aggressor State during the whole period of the conflict.[15]

It was to be valid for three years. On May 5, 1934 this Pact was extended until December 31, 1945.[16]

Prior to the extension of the Non-Aggression Pact, both Poland and the U.S.S.R. took part in the Convention for the Definition of Aggression, signed in London on July 3, 1933. It stated that:

. . . the aggressor in an international conflict shall . . . be that State which is the first to commit any of the following actions:

1. Declaration of war upon another State.
2. Invasion by its armed forces, with or without a declaration of war, of the territory of another State.

No political, military, economic, or other consideration may serve as an excuse or justification for the aggression.[17]

This Definition of Aggression, to which the Soviet Government was a party, acquired particular significance to the student of Soviet foreign policy in September 1939.

When France and Britain rejected Pilsudski's proposal to organize a preventive war against Hitler, Poland was forced to sign a non-aggression pact with Germany in January 1934. This in turn led to a cooling off in Polish relations with France and the Soviet Union. The situation was aggravated even more when Poland refused to participate in the Eastern Security Pact (the Eastern Locarno) on the grounds that it would antagonize Hitler. Poland also refused to join any power arrangement against the Soviet Union. On November

9, 1937 the Polish Foreign Minister sent the following instructions to all Polish diplomatic missions abroad:

So far, no proposal to join the Italo-German-Japanese Protocol (Anti-Comintern Pact) has been received by Poland. In any case, Poland could not be a party to that Protocol in view of her special position as neighbor of the U.S.S.R., as well as her objection in principle to the formation of any bloc.

If inquiries are made on this subject please reply in the above sense.[18]

In November 1938 a series of conferences was held by the Polish Ambassador in Moscow with Litvinov. At the end of these conferences, the following joint communiqué was issued on November 26, 1938.

A series of conversations recently held between the U.S.S.R. People's Commissar for Foreign Affairs, M. Litvinov, and the Polish Ambassador in Moscow, M. Grzybowski, has led to the following statement:

1. Relations between the Polish Republic and the Union of Soviet Socialist Republics are and will continue to be based to the fullest extent on all the existing Agreements, including the Polish-Soviet Pact of Non-Aggression dated July 25, 1932. This Pact, concluded for three years and extended on May 5, 1934 for a further period ending December 31, 1945 has a basis wide enough to guarantee the inviolability of peaceful relations between the two States.

2. Both Governments are favorable to the extension of their commercial relations.

3. Both Governments agree that it is necessary to settle a number of current and longstanding matters which have arisen in connection with the various agreements in force, and, in particular, to dispose of the various frontier incidents which have lately been occurring.[19]

On February 19, 1939 a commercial treaty, which was intended to reinforce the improved diplomatic relations, was signed between the two countries. These relations were soon to be endangered by Stalin's analysis of the international situation. On March 10, 1939 Stalin said, "We stand for peace and the strengthening of business relations with all countries." [20] At the same time, after warning the Western democracies that the Soviet Union would not fight their battles, the Soviet leader said:

The war is being waged by aggressor states, who in every way infringe upon the interests of the non-aggressive States, primarily England, France, and the United States, while the latter draw back and retreat, making concession after concession to the aggressors. . . . To what are we to attribute the systematic concessions made by these States to the aggressor? . . . The bourgeois politicians know, of course, that the first imperialist World War led to the victory of the revolution in one of the largest countries. They are afraid that the second imperialist world war may also lead to the victory of the revolution in one or several countries.[21]

The speech was looked upon by Western observers as mere rhetoric. This was a crucial juncture in the skillful maneuvers of Soviet foreign policy which opened its doors to both sides—to Hitler and to the West. On August 23, 1939, while signing the Non-Aggression Treaty with Ribbentrop, Molotov observed that ". . . it has been Stalin who through his speech of March of this year, which had been well understood in Germany, had brought about the reversal in political relations." [22]

On April 14, 1939 the French Government submitted to Moscow a suggested text for a joint declaration.

In case France and Great Britain should find themselves at war with Germany as the result of action taken by them to bring help to Rumania and Poland following upon unprovoked aggression against the latter, the U.S.S.R. would at once come to their aid. In case the U.S.S.R. should find itself in a state of war with Germany as the result of action taken by it to bring help to Rumania or Poland, following upon unprovoked aggression against the latter, France and Great Britain would at once come to its aid. The three Governments shall enter into discussions without delay on the forms of this assistance and take all measures to assure its full efficiency.[23]

On April 15, 1939 Sir William Seed, the British Ambassador in Moscow, handed to Litvinov a British proposal almost identical to the French, with an additional request to the U.S.S.R. to guarantee the frontiers of Poland and Rumania.

On April 17, Litvinov gave the British Ambassador a counterproposal to the effect that a three power pact should be concluded between the U.S.S.R., Britain, and France, including the formation of a military convention pledging the three powers to guarantee the independence of all States between the Baltic and the Black seas.[24] This was promptly turned down by Chamberlain. Britain objected to the terms which would have given the right to any one of the three signatories to initiate military action in the defense of any state included between the Baltic and the Black seas which fell under the heel of an aggressor. London wished the pact to be invoked only after Britain and France had intervened.

Poland was also reluctant to accept the Soviet guarantee. England, on the other hand, while not wishing to alienate the U.S.S.R. in the event that hostilities should break out, still did not wish to press demands upon Poland or Rumania nor did she wish to compromise the British position by allying herself with the Bolshevik menace against the Anti-Comintern Powers.

While negotiating with the West, Stalin did not fail, at the same time, to establish contacts with Germany. Apparently a decision was made in the Kremlin that a treaty with Hitler would be preferable to that with the Western Powers.

On May 3, 1939 Litvinov disappeared from his position of influence as Commissar of Foreign Affairs, and on May 5 Molotov replaced him as Foreign Commissar. The Polish Ambassador, Grzybowski, reporting subsequently to his Minister, stated:

> Today we realize that the Soviets' imperialistic plans must have been already sufficiently formulated for them to retain a final and decisive understanding with Chancellor Hitler as a trump card in their policy of instigation of war. It is obvious that such an understanding could not be negotiated by M. Litvinov.[25]

On May 7 Molotov warmly complimented Ambassador Grzybowski on Beck's speech two days before (that Poland would not succumb to the German threats) and emphasized especially how much he had been impressed by his words on national honor. Then he talked about the conversations between the Soviet Union, Great Britain, and France. Ambassador Grzybowski stated that Poland viewed those conversations with sympathetic understanding. He also added that Poland had adopted a pacific and loyal attitude to all her neighbors and that only clearly aggressive acts committed by any one of them could modify that attitude.[26]

On May 9 the Deputy Foreign Commissar of Russia, Potemkin, arrived in Warsaw and saw the Polish Foreign Minister, Beck. On May 13, in a message to the Polish Embassy in Paris, Beck wrote:

> The conversations with M. Potemkin during his stay in Warsaw on the 10th of May have made it clear that the Soviet Government takes an understanding attitude of our point of view with regard to Polish-Soviet relations, which are now developing quite normally.
>
> The Soviets realize that the Polish Government is not prepared to enter into any agreement with either one of Poland's great neighbors against the other, and understands the advantages to them of this attitude.
>
> M. Potemkin also stated that in the event of an armed conflict between Poland and Germany the Soviets would adopt *"une attitude bienveillante"* towards us.
>
> As M. Potemkin himself indicated, his statements were made in accordance with special instructions which the Soviet Government sent to Warsaw for him.[27]

Upon his return to Moscow, Potemkin recapitulated those conversations to Ambassador Grzybowski and stressed with satisfaction Beck's declaration that in the event of war with Germany, Poland would inevitably rely on the Soviets.

About the middle of May Grzybowski sent to Molotov a résumé on the Polish attitude towards the Soviet Union in which he stated that

Polish adoption of a more definite attitude would be conditioned by the results of the Anglo-French-Soviet negotiations. He emphasized the complete loyalty of Poland in its relations with the Soviet Union. In the event of conflict, Poland would by no means reject specified forms of Soviet aid but considered it premature to determine them definitely. He added that Poland also considered it premature to open bilateral negotiations with the Soviets before the Anglo-French-Soviet negotiations had achieved results. Molotov apparently made no objections whatsoever to this.[28]

In terms of subsequent events, it seems that these Soviet probings of the Poles were intended to gauge the degree of their determination to resist Hitler's demands and to reassure the Kremlin that, on the one hand, their overtures in Berlin would not be superfluous and, on the other hand, that their attitude towards Britain and France would have greater bargaining strength.

On May 17 Astakhov, the Soviet Chargé d'Affaires in Berlin, told the German Foreign Office that "there were no conflicts in foreign policy between Germany and the Soviet Union, and that, therefore, there was no reason for enmity between the two countries. . . ." To substantiate his opinion concerning the possibility of a change in German-Soviet relations, Astakhov repeatedly referred to Italy and stressed that the Duce, even after the creation of the Axis, had implied that there were no obstacles to a normal development of the political and economic relations between the Soviet Union and Italy.[29]

On May 20 Molotov told German Ambassador Schulenburg that "the Soviet Government could only agree to a resumption of the (trade) negotiations if the necessary political basis for them had been constructed." [30]

On May 27 a new Anglo-French proposal was made to Molotov but, as before, Britain and France refused to commit themselves as to whether they would aid the U.S.S.R. in the event that the nation sought to guarantee the territories of Latvia, Lithuania, and Estonia.

On May 30 the State Secretary in the German Foreign Office, Weizsäcker, had another meeting with the Soviet Chargé d'Affaires, Astakhov. Reporting about it in an official memorandum, he recorded:

> I reminded the Chargé of certain conversations which he, himself, had conducted in the Office and above all of the statements of his Ambassador, now absent from Berlin, who told me in the middle of April of the possibility of a normalization and even further improvement of German-Russian political relations. . . .
> The Chargé, who had followed the talk attentively and had contributed to it a number of remarks not mentioned here, stated in conclusion that

the ideological barrier between Moscow and Berlin was in reality created by us.

Before our treaty with Poland we had rejected a Russian offer of alliance and until recently there had been little comprehension here of the Russian thesis that foreign and domestic policy did not have to interfere with each other. He believed that his Government had not wavered in this viewpoint and was still faithful to it today.[31]

This memorandum reveals a few significant facts:

1. That the Soviets approached the Nazis before the exchange of the various proposals between Britain, France, and the Soviet Union took place. The most charitable view of this conduct rests on the presumption that they thus intended to strengthen their bargaining position.

2. That even before the Nazi-Polish Treaty of 1934, they were willing to conclude an alliance with Hitler although publicly they were advocating disarmament and collective security.

Astakhov and Weizsäcker had reached sufficient accord by May 30 to begin a discussion of political topics. On that same day, Weizsäcker telegraphed to Schulenburg in Moscow that the German Government had now decided to undertake definite negotiations with the Soviet Government.[32]

On May 31, 1939, speaking to the Supreme Council of the U.S.S.R., Molotov stated:

. . . We stand for the cause of peace, and for an end being put to the development of aggression. . . . As is known, a special communiqué was published in February last, concerning the development of good neighborly relations between the U.S.S.R. and Poland. A certain general improvement is now noticeable in our relations with Poland. Furthermore, the Trade Agreement concluded in March with Poland may considerably increase the trade turnover between the U.S.S.R. and Poland. . . .[33]

In early June the Soviet Government replied to the Anglo-French proposals of May 27, stating that only a pact of mutual assistance between France, Britain, and Russia which effectively guaranteed the territories of Latvia, Estonia, and Finland, as well as Poland, Rumania, Turkey, Greece, and Belgium, would now be acceptable. This dilatory tactic was striking in its imaginative originality; by positing unattainable conditions the Soviets in effect increased the time required for negotiations (by, for example, their spontaneous addition of Belgium to the list) and thus postponed the conclusion of any real agreement.

The lengthy and complex discussions held by the English, French, and Soviet diplomats in Moscow during June and July and supplemented in August by military negotiations ended in a deadlock when no agreement on a definition of "indirect aggression" was reached. The Strang Mission, which was dispatched to Moscow when the failure of the previous missions was apparent and when the British Foreign Office began to hear more frequent reports of Soviet-Nazi discussions, failed to resolve the block caused by the definition of indirect aggression. The Soviets preferred a loose interpretation of the words, which would mean that any change of government in any guaranteed Eastern European country could be understood as creating a cause for intervention. This interpretation would naturally give the U.S.S.R. the chance they sought to control the timetable, in that they would be able to initiate a war at the slightest provocation by Germany. When they failed to agree to such a definition, Moscow then accused the British and the French of inventing artificial stumbling blocks.

In the meantime, beginning in June, the Soviets made a series of offers to Poland to supply her with armament materials, but these were always accompanied by unacceptable conditions. The Soviets never ceased to urge Poland to resist the German demands. Whenever the Poles raised the question of accelerating the transit negotiations, it was turned down under various pretexts. Potemkin assured Ambassador Grzybowski that, obviously, everything would change in the event of a conflict, and that in such an event the Poles could count on the transit.[34]

In his final report, Ambassador Grzybowski recalled:

. . . So long as the Anglo-French-Soviet negotiations lasted it was almost impossible for us to go beyond a waiting attitude. We felt no optimism whatever in regard to the result of these negotiations. It was difficult to expect that the Soviets would do anything in the direction of preventing a conflict or even of rendering its outbreak difficult. We observed rather that their tactics aimed at the exact opposite.[35]

On August 7 Strang was recalled to London, and on August 11 the Anglo-French military missions arrived in Moscow. From the beginning of the military negotiations the Soviets insisted on the right to enter not only Rumania and Poland but also the Baltic States in order to forestall aggression. On the 17th of August these negotiations were adjourned while an effort was made, principally by France, to have Poland accede to the Russian demands.

Poland remained unmoved by French pressure, owing to an underestimation of the strength of the German Army and an overestimation of her own military strength, and also on the strength of the positive turn in the Anglo-Polish negotiations which were going on in London.[36]

On August 23 Ribbentrop arrived in Moscow and signed the Nazi-Soviet Treaty, thus removing the world's last vestige of doubt concerning the reality of the Nazi-Soviet rapprochement.

The Secret Additional Protocol signed by Molotov and Ribbentrop, together with the Treaty, dealt largely with Poland's fate. Article II of that Protocol stated:

> In the event of a territorial and political rearrangement of the areas belonging to the Polish State, the spheres of influence of Germany and the U.S.S.R. shall be bounded approximately by the line of the rivers Narev, Vistula, and San.
> The question of whether the interests of both parties make desirable the maintenance of an independent Polish State and how such a State should be bounded can only be definitely determined in the course of further political developments.
> In any event, both Governments will resolve this question by means of a friendly agreement.[37]

On August 25 London and Warsaw announced the conclusion of an Anglo-Polish Treaty of Mutual Assistance committing Britain to a war which, unknown to them, was less than a week away. The British decision was motivated not by any specific sympathy for Poland, but by the final realization that a struggle for a redivision of Europe was on, that the traditional balance of power was just about to be upset, and that the struggle for the integrity of the British Isles had to be fought outside the British Isles. The British were certain that the "romantic" Poles would fight and, by so doing, would at least weaken the impact of the German war machine on the West. Thus Poland's resistance would buy a certain amount of the time needed by the Western Powers to arm themselves and temporarily divert from the West the full force of the German Armies.

The news emanating from Berlin and London about the conversations between the British Ambassador and Hitler prompted the Soviets to issue a warning to Berlin. On August 27 the Commissar for War, Voroshilov, answering a question during a press interview, stated that the supply of raw materials to Poland in the event of conflict was a "commercial matter." [38]

The Ribbentrop-Molotov Pact was a considerable victory for Moscow. It granted the Kremlin a sphere of influence which extended over Finland, Estonia, and Latvia. The new common boundary with Germany was established in Poland and any future adjustments were to be settled by peaceful means. The Soviet interest in Bessarabia was also recognized. Of greatest importance was the fact that there was no stipulation anywhere that the provisions of the treaty should apply only in event of a defensive war. Hence, Germany was in effect encouraged into a war with Poland.

The reasons for the Nazi-Soviet rapprochement were numerous. First, the Soviets thought that Britain and France were not particularly anxious to reach an agreement with Moscow and to pay the demanded price. Second, Moscow realized that the nations of Eastern Europe were prepared to deny a passage to Russian troops indefinitely and that Russia could no longer tolerate the possibility of a German advance to her frontier—especially in the region of Leningrad. Third, Moscow realized that the partition of Poland would place Germany at war with England and France, consequently rendering it inexpedient for Hitler to proceed further eastward until the Western Powers had been disposed of. The Kremlin intended to make the maximum use of the time so cheaply purchased. The Soviet's strategic frontier was about to be improved, once the terms of the treaty were exploited. With these temporary benefits Stalin decided to pave the way for Hitler's showdown with the West. Contrary to popular interpretation, and the confusion among the various Communist Parties of Europe, the Ribbentrop-Molotov Pact was not a departure from the ideologically motivated policy. Had Stalin thought purely in terms of power politics, he would have had to think primarily of the security of the Soviet State, and the safest way to provide that security would have been to accept the Anglo-French offers and to ally himself with them. He knew that the Soviet Union could join the Anglo-French Bloc at any time; there was, therefore, no hurry. He also knew that Hitler was interested (for a different reason) in the destruction of the Western capitalist countries. Stalin shared this goal with Hitler, for ideological reasons. It seems that on the basis of primarily ideological considerations he had decided to give Hitler the green light to destroy the West. Stalin expected that the British and the French armies would give a "good account of themselves," which would exhaust both sides so much, economically and militarily, that the Red Army—strengthened by that time—might exploit that result. Furthermore, war is always a favorable and rewarding arena for the communists.

It is obvious that Stalin did not foresee the sequence of events which followed, but his ability to take risks, and his taking this one in particular, was rewarded handsomely in 1945. The power politics consideration was undoubtedly an important factor. However, the risk that Stalin would have had to face Germany in case Hitler's victory over the West materialized sooner than expected could have been overcome by an ideologically motivated zeal alone. It is an ideological rather than a power politics consideration to use one ideological enemy to destroy another.

It appears that the security of the Soviet State was risked for the realization of the ideologically prescribed goal. This phase of extreme flexibility and concurrent intransigence of Soviet diplomatic strategy cannot be explained satisfactorily in any other way.

Had Stalin known the price which the Soviet Union would subsequently have to pay, as well as the results of the Second World War —which he helped considerably to precipitate—it still seems that he would have done exactly the same. From the point of view of the communist and Soviet objectives, the Kremlin's strategy proved to be successful. The full significance of the Nazi-Soviet Pact to the Soviets and to the West acquires clearer meaning against the background of events which followed.

Germany, having reached an understanding with the Soviet Union, was quick to seize the initiative while the British and the French were in confusion, and on September 1, 1939 Hitler's armies invaded Poland. The whole Polish nation stood up against them, paying an extraordinarily high price for its decision not to succumb to the temptations[39] or the threats offered by Hitler.

Notes

[1] *Pravda*, March 16, 1917.

[2] *Soviet Documents on Foreign Policy* (ed.), Jane Degras, London, Oxford University Press, 1951, Vol. I, p. 98.

[3] *Ibid.*, p. 189.

[4] Louis Fisher, *Soviets in World Affairs* (2 vols.), Princeton University Press, 1952, Vol. I, pp. 268–270.

[5] Jacques Bardoux, *De Paris à Spa, La Bataille Diplomatique Pour La Paix Francaise* (From Paris to Spa, The Diplomatic Battle for the Peace of France, Paris, F. Alcan, 1921, pp. 206–207.

[6] Francesco Tommasini, *Odrodzenie Polski*, Warszawa, Nak. F. Hoesicka, 1928, p. 124.

[7] Kazimierz Wladyslaw Kumaniecki, *Odbudowa Państwowości Polskiej, Najwazniejsze Dokumenty 1912—Styczen 1924*, Kraków, Ksiegarnia Powszechna, 1924, pp. 291–292.

[8] The author used the official documents of the Polish Government now in possession of Mr. Stanislaw Mikolajczyk, former Prime Minister of Poland, hence-

forth to be referred to as Poland, *Official Government Documents,* by volume and document: Vol. II, Doc. 1.

[9] Harold Nicolson, *Curzon: The Last Phase, 1919–1925,* Boston, Houghton Mifflin Company, 1934, p. 204.

[10] *Soviet Documents on Foreign Policy,* Vol. I, pp. 194–197.

[11] *Ibid.,* p. 217.

[12] Kumaniecki, *op. cit.,* p. 302.

[13] *The Polish White Book,* Official Documents 1933–1939, published by the authority of the Polish Government, London, Hutchinson & Company (publishers), Ltd., pp. 164–165.

[14] *Soviet Documents on Foreign Policy,* Vol. I, pp. 242–244.

[15] *The Polish White Book,* pp. 170–172.

[16] *Ibid.,* pp. 179–180.

[17] *Ibid.,* pp. 172–175.

[18] *Ibid.,* p. 181.

[19] *Ibid.,* pp. 181–182.

[20] *Soviet Documents on Foreign Policy,* Vol. III, p. 321.

[21] *Ibid.,* p. 318.

[22] United States, Department of State, *Nazi-Soviet Relations, 1939–1941,* Department of State Publication No. 3023, Washington, U. S. Government Printing Office, 1948, p. 76.

[23] Georges Bonnet, *Défense de la Paix: De Washington au Quai d'Orsay,* Geneva, Bournin, 1946, p. 180.

[24] *The Polish White Book,* p. 208.

[25] *Ibid.,* p. 207.

[26] *Ibid.,* p. 208.

[27] *Ibid.,* p. 183.

[28] *Ibid.,* p. 208.

[29] *Nazi-Soviet Relations, 1939–1941,* p. 5.

[30] *Ibid.,* p. 6.

[31] *Ibid.,* pp. 12–15.

[32] *Ibid.,* p. 15.

[33] *The Polish White Book,* pp. 183–184.

[34] *Ibid.,* pp. 208–209.

[35] *Ibid.,* p. 209.

[36] The Polish delegation was headed by Dr. W. W. Kulski.

[37] *Nazi-Soviet Relations, 1939–1941,* p. 78.

[38] *Soviet Documents on Foreign Policy,* Vol. III, p. 362.

[39] The last Nazi attempt to gain Polish collaboration in their designs on Russia was made by Hermann Göring to Beck during the hunting party in the Bialowieza Forest Preserve in January 1939. Beck declined that invitation, too. The Polish Government might have chosen to collaborate with Hitler and to share in the "New Order" at the expense of Russia. Instead, they kept their loyalties to Britain and to France and decided to oppose the Nazi war machine unaided.

From 1933 onwards, during the Polish-German conversations, the Germans expressed a strong anti-Soviet bias. Communist Russia was regarded as a grave menace to Europe, and above all to Germany. As early as 1935 Field Marshal Göring proposed a common Polish-German policy against the Soviets. This was rejected by Marshal Pilsudski. Periodically Göring would renew the same proposals and offered the Ukraine in return for Polish support of an anti-Soviet stand. Each time these offers were rejected.

Toward the end of October 1938 Ribbentrop, for the last time, demanded among other things a joint Polish-German policy in the East and met with Polish refusal.

The Polish White Book, p. 216.

The Fourth Partition of Poland

1. From Hostility to Alliance: September 1939 to July 1941

If Soviet strategy was to succeed, Germany had to become involved in war with Britain and France, while the Soviet Union remained neutral. Hitler, of course, wanted the Soviets to go to war against Britain, and France simultaneously with Germany. Britain and France were not yet at war with Germany, so Stalin hesitated. On September 2, 1939 the Soviet Ambassador, Sharanov, called on Beck and asked him why Poland was not negotiating with the Soviets regarding supplies, since the "Voroshilov interview has opened up the possibility of getting them."[1] Accordingly, Beck instructed his Ambassador in Moscow to investigate the possibilities. On the same day Ambassador Grzybowski received instructions to give the Soviets official notification of the German aggression and the resulting state of war between Poland and Germany. On the third he was received by Molotov.

He (Molotov) did not question our statement that it was a case of unprovoked aggression committed without a previous declaration of war, by a surprise attack during negotiations. He agreed in recognizing Germany as the aggressor. He asked whether we counted on the intervention of Great Britain and France, and whether we expected any time-limit on such intervention. I told him that I had no official information, but I anticipated their declarations of war to follow a day later, on the 4th.

M. Molotov smiled sceptically. "Well, we shall see, Monsieur l'Ambassador. . . ."[2]

Berlin began to press Moscow to occupy her zone of Poland. This was obviously a move to commit the U.S.S.R. on the Nazi side of the large war. It failed. Molotov replied on September 5 that "In our view, the time is not yet ripe. . . . It seems to us that precipitancy might cause harm and draw the other side closer together."[3]

The Polish Ambassador had a great deal of difficulty in getting to see Molotov. On September 8, when Molotov saw him at last, he referred to previous Soviet official statements and Marshal Voroshilov's interview and expressed Poland's willingness to buy additional raw materials. Molotov answered that Marshal Voroshilov's interview had been made public in totally different circumstances. Marshal Voroshilov did not and could not know that the intervention of Britain and France would follow. The situation had now radically changed. "Poland," said Molotov, "is now synonymous with England, so far as we are concerned." The Soviet Union was compelled to safeguard its own interests first and foremost and thus to remain outside the conflict.[4] It had now succeeded in embroiling Germany with the West, while it was still neutral. The only issue left was the division of the loot in Poland with Hitler. Under the logic of these circumstances, unknown to Poland, Poland could not possibly expect any Soviet aid.

The Polish Ambassador then passed to the transit question, by referring to former Soviet declarations, and asked what facilities could be granted to Poland in this sphere. Molotov answered that he was afraid the transit of military materials would be in contradiction with the Pact of Non-Aggression concluded with Germany. At the end of the conversation, Molotov stated that all he had said was in reference to present conditions but that circumstances might change. He repeated the phrase "in present conditions" several times.[5]

Three days later the Soviet Ambassador in Poland visited the Deputy Foreign Minister, Szembek, in Krzemieniec (Southeast Poland), to inform him that he and his family were departing for the Soviet frontier for the purpose of getting in touch with Moscow by telephone which he was

. . . unable to do from Krzemieniec. He intends to return the day after tomorrow, or, if he is summoned to Moscow, in a week's time. The Ambassador emphasized that we shall be able to get medical supplies from the Soviets.[6]

He never came back.

The next day, *Pravda* published a leading article violently attacking the condition of the minorities in eastern Poland. It stressed the point that the fate of these minorities could not be a matter of indifference to the Soviet public. The lack of military action on the part of Britain and France and the rapid movement of the German Armies helped Stalin to overcome his previous doubts about the fulfillment of his obligations to Hitler.

On September 14 Schulenburg reported to Berlin:

Molotov summoned me today at 4:00 p.m. and stated that the Red Army had reached a state of preparedness sooner than anticipated. Soviet action could therefore take place sooner than he had assumed at our last conversation (several weeks before). For the political motivation of Soviet action (the collapse of Poland and the protection of Russian "minorities") it was of the greatest importance not to take action until the governmental center of Poland, the city of Warsaw, had fallen. Molotov therefore asked that he be informed as nearly as possible as to when the capture of Warsaw could be counted on.

. . . I would direct your attention to today's article in *Pravda*, carried by D.N.B., which will be followed by a similar article in *Izvestia* tomorrow. The articles serve [to prepare] the political motivation mentioned by Molotov for Soviet intervention.[7]

The Polish Nation now began to fear a Soviet "stab in the back." On September 17 at 3:00 A.M. Ambassador Grzybowski was summoned by Potemkin to the *Narkomindel* to be informed of an important statement to his Government. Potemkin slowly read the following text of a note signed by Molotov, to the Polish Government:

The Polish-German war has revealed the internal bankruptcy of the Polish State. In the course of ten days' hostilities Poland has lost all her industrial areas and cultural centers. Warsaw no longer exists as the capital of Poland. The Polish Government has disintegrated, and no longer shows any sign of life. This means that the Polish State and its Government have, in fact, ceased to exist. Therefore, the Agreement concluded between the U.S.S.R. and Poland has ceased to operate. Left to her own devices and bereft of leadership, Poland has become a suitable field for all manner of hazards and surprises, which may constitute a threat to the U.S.S.R. For these reasons, the Soviet Government, which hitherto has preserved neutrality, cannot any longer observe a neutral attitude towards these facts.

The Soviet Government further cannot view with indifference the fact that the kindred Ukrainians and White Russian people, who live on Polish territory and who are at the mercy of fate, are left defenseless.

In these circumstances, the Soviet Government has directed the High Command of the Red Army to order the troops to cross the frontier and to take under their protection the life and property of the populations of Western Ukraine and Western White Russia. At the same time, the Soviet Government proposes to take all measures to extricate the Polish people from the unfortunate war into which they were dragged by their unwise leaders, and to enable them to live a peaceful life.[8]

Reporting on that event, Ambassador Grzybowski stated:

When he had finished I told him at once that I refused to take the contents of the note into cognizance. I refused to communicate it to my Government, and expressed the most categorical protest against its contents and form.

I protested against the unilateral abrogation of existing and binding agreements. None of the arguments intended to justify the transformation of those agreements into "scraps of paper" would withstand criticism. According to my information the heads of the Polish State and of the Government were within the territory of the Republic. The functioning of the Government was by the nature of things restricted by the state of war. "You will not demand that at such a time the Minister of Agriculture should carry out agricultural reforms?" The sovereignty of the State existed so long as a single regular soldier was still fighting. "You will not maintain that the Polish soldiers are no longer fighting?"

That which the note said about the position of the minorities within our borders was nonsense. All the minorities, including the Jews, had not only given expression of their loyalty, but were actively proving it by their complete solidarity with Poland in her struggle against Germanism. "More than once in our conversations," I told him "you have appealed to Slavonic solidarity. At our side at this moment not only Ukrainians and White Russians, but also Czech and Slovak legions are fighting the Germans. Where is your Slavonic solidarity?

"So many times has the U.S.S.R. indignantly condemned and stigmatized the Germans' perfidy. The note which you have read to me would signify that you had taken the same road.

"During the Great War the territories of Serbia and Belgium were occupied, but it entered no one's head to regard their obligations to these States as non-existent on that account. Napoleon was once in Moscow, but so long as Kutuzov's army existed it was considered that Russia existed."

M. Potemkin tried to explain that my historic responsibility would be very great if I refused to accept a document of such importance. I said, "Monsieur le Commissaire, if I agreed to communicate the contents of the note to my Government it would be not only a proof that I had no respect for my Government, but it would also be a proof that I had lost all respect for the Soviet Government. I understand that I am in duty bound to inform my Government of the aggression probably already committed, but I will do no more than that. But I still hope that your Government will restrain the Red Army from invasion, and will not stab us in the back at the moment of our struggle against the Germans." [9]

At 5:00 A.M. on September 17 Grzybowski sent a telegram *en claire* which reached the Polish Ministry for Foreign Affairs at 11:00 A.M. At 6:00 A.M. the Red Army crossed the Polish eastern frontier along its entire length. The insignificant number of Polish troops left on

that border offered resistance but soon was overcome by dispropor-
tionately larger Soviet military formations. The Polish Government
protested to Moscow and instructed their Ambassador to demand passports for himself and his diplomatic staff.

This Soviet aggression, disguised under the pretext of helping their
"unfortunate brethren" (Ukrainians and Byelorussians), resembled
previous such Nazi justifications. By that act, the Soviet Government
violated the Polish-Soviet Pact of Non-Aggression concluded in Moscow on July 25, 1932 in which both parties mutually undertook to
abstain from all aggressive action or from attack against each other.
Moreover, by the Protocol signed in Moscow on May 5, 1934, the
above Pact of Non-Aggression was prolonged until December 31, 1945.
The Soviet Government also violated the Convention concluded in
London on July 3, 1933 in which the Soviet Union and Poland, together with the other signatories, agreed on a definition of aggression,
which stamped as an act of aggression any encroachment upon the
territory of one contracting party by the armed forces of the other,
and further agreed that no consideration of a political, military, economic, or any other order could in any circumstances serve as a pretext or excuse for committing an act of aggression. That the Treaty
of Riga was also violated is equally obvious.

The westward march of the Red Army was accompanied by Soviet
propaganda spread in Poland to the effect that the Soviets were coming as allies rather than as invaders. Confusion was mixed with fear
of war. The absence of an official explanation from the Polish Government through the conventional media of communication, which
were by then disrupted, did not dispel the Soviet assurances of good
intentions. It was rather Soviet acts which dispelled any such illusions.

Molotov admitted that all was not peaceful friendship when he said:

As the Red Army advanced through these districts there were serious
encounters in some places between our troops and the Polish troops, and
consequently there were casualties. These casualties were as follows: On
the White Russian front, counting both officers and men of the Red Army,
there were 246 killed and 503 wounded, or a total of 749. On the Ukrainian front there were 491 officers and men killed, and 1,359 wounded, or a
total of 1,850. Thus, the total casualties of the Red Army were 737 killed
and 1,862 wounded, or a total of 2,599.

As for our war trophies in Poland, they consist of over 900 guns, over
10,000 machine guns, over 300,000 rifles, over 150 million rifle cartridges,
over one million artillery shells, about 300 aeroplanes, etc. The territory
which has passed to the U.S.S.R. is equal in area to a large European
State.[10]

On September 20 Schulenburg reported:

Molotov stated to me today that the Soviet Government now considered the time ripe for it, jointly with the German Government, to establish definitively the structure of the Polish area. In this regard, Molotov hinted that the original inclination entertained by the Soviet Government and Stalin personally, to permit the existence of a residual Poland had given way to the inclination to partition Poland along the Pissa-Narev-Vistula-San line. The Soviet Government wishes to commence negotiations on this matter at once, and to conduct them in Moscow, since such negotiations must be conducted on the Soviet side by persons in the highest position of authority, who cannot leave the Soviet Union.[11]

A joint communiqué was issued in Moscow on September 22 which publicly affirmed the demarcation line agreed upon in the Secret Protocol attached to the Non-Aggression Treaty of August 23. In conformity with that agreement, those German troops which by that time found themselves in Eastern Poland, withdrew to their predetermined zone.

On September 25 Stalin stated the following to Schulenburg:

In the final settlement of the Polish question anything that in the future might create friction between Germany and the Soviet Union must be avoided. From this point of view, he considered it wrong to leave an independently run Polish State. He proposed the following: From the territory to the east of the demarcation line, all the Province of Lublin and that portion of the Province of Warsaw which extends to the Bug should be added to our share. In return, we should waive our claim to Lithuania.[12]

Hitler accepted that proposal and on September 28 Ribbentrop and Molotov signed the Boundary and Friendship Treaty, including one confidential and two secret supplementary protocols which established the demarcation line along the four rivers proposed by Stalin. The Soviet Union found itself in possession of a large part of indisputably Polish territory. The two signatories further agreed to exchange their nationals living on the opposite sides of the demarcation line and pledged themselves to "restore peace and order" and not to "tolerate in their territories any Polish agitation which affects the territories of the other party." [13]

On September 28, 1939 a joint declaration of the Soviet and German Governments stated:

. . . Having finally settled by the treaty signed today the questions arising from the dissolution of the Polish State, and having thereby created a firm foundation for a lasting peace in Eastern Europe, in mutual agreement we express the opinion that the liquidation of the present war . . . will be of interest to all nations. [If war continues] it will be established . . .

that England and France bear the responsibility for the continuation of the war, and in the event of a continuation of the war the Governments of Germany and the U.S.S.R. will consult each other on the necessary measures.[14]

The fourth partition of Poland by the Soviet Union went beyond the Curzon Line, paralleled almost exactly the line of the third partition of Poland, and, in addition, gained for the Soviet Union the territory of Eastern Galicia which had never been permanently occupied even by Tsarist Armies.

2. The Soviet Share of the Fourth Partition

The portion of Polish territory which the Soviet Union occupied in September and October of 1939 constituted in area 51% of the entire Polish territory, covering 77,586 square miles. It was inhabited by about 13,200,000 people consisting of the following groups, according to an estimate made in the year 1939 and based on their respective mother tongues.

Poles	5,274,000	39.9%
Ukrainians	4,529,000	34.4%
Byelorussians	1,123,000	8.5%
Jews	1,109,000	8.5%
Russians	134,000	1.0%
Germans	89,000	0.7%
Lithuanians	84,000	0.6%
Czechs	35,000	0.3%
Other nationalities	822,000	6.2%

Of the last group, 802,000 described themselves as speaking the local dialect of Polesie.[15]

Those eastern provinces of Poland taken over by the Soviets provided 50% of Poland's forests, 63% of the total Polish oil output, 90% of the natural gas production, one of Europe's richest potassium mines, unique deposits of phosphates and ozocerites, and half of the output of Poland's quarries, including those most important for road building. Moreover, these eastern provinces possessed 42% of Poland's waterpower, and they were also the chief source of flax, hemp, maize, and tobacco.

In the same area large and medium-sized landed property (above 50 hectares or 125 acres) amounted to only about 15% of the total arable land in 1939 (in England, e.g., landed estates of over 125 acres amount to 25%).[16]

Occupation of these territories by the Red Army disrupted local

economic life considerably. On September 18 the Polish President and
the Government crossed the Rumanian border and relinquished their
authority in favor of Raczkiewicz as the President and Sikorski as
Prime Minister. On September 28 the gallant garrison of Warsaw surrendered. On September 30 the Polish Government protested against
the German-Soviet agreement of September 28, 1939, and their diplomatic representatives abroad presented that protest to the respective
governments to which they were accredited. In the protest it was
stated:

> Poland will never recognize this act of violence, and, strong in the
> justice of her cause, she will not cease to struggle for the day when, her
> territory liberated from the invaders, her legitimate rights will be estab-
> lished in their entirety.[17]

This conviction of right was to be the guiding force for the Poles
in their subsequent dealings with the Soviets.

It is of interest to note what happened to Ambassador Grzybowski
after he received instructions from his Government to leave the Soviet
Union, because his experiences were to prove typical of those encountered by many others later. The Soviets declined his request to transfer the protection of his Embassy to a third power on the ground that
the Polish State no longer existed, and thus they refused recognition
of the customary diplomatic privileges to the personnel of the Embassy. Only upon the intervention of Nazi Ambassador Schulenburg
did Molotov state that *"les usages diplomatiques"* would be respected.
On September 30 the Counselor of the Embassy, Matusinski, was summoned to the Soviet Foreign Office, ostensibly to agree to the final
details of his departure. He went at once, with two chauffeurs and
accompanied by two police cars. From that moment all three van-
ished without trace. The Italian Ambassador, Rosso, who had already
done more than anyone else to help the Poles, intervened with Potemkin, who replied that he had no information as to their whereabouts,
but pointed out that since Matusinski had lost his diplomatic privileges,
he could have been called to account by the Soviet authorities if it had
appeared that he had committed some crime against the Soviet Union.
Ambassador Rosso replied that he saw no possibility of that, for
until September 18 Matusinski had enjoyed full diplomatic privileges,
while from that day he had been, in fact, interned and could have
committed no crime whatsoever.

Ambassador Grzybowski decided to inform the Soviet Government,
through Rosso, that he would not leave Moscow so long as Matusinski
was not set free and to demand a formulation of the charges against

him. In response, Molotov informed Schulenburg, most categorically, that the Soviet authorities had no information whatever as to the place of residence and the fate of Matusinski.

I assure you, said Molotov, that he is not in our hands. I am myself personally making investigations in order to clear up this affair. To hold up the Ambassador's departure on this account is pointless, and I cannot agree to it.[18]

In view of the obvious intention of the Soviets to avoid formulating any charges against Matusinski, Grzybowski concluded that there was really nothing to wait for, since one could no longer expect him to be found. On October 11, 1939 the personnel of the Polish Embassy crossed the Finnish border in a sealed train.

From the moment the Red Army took over the eastern half of Poland, the Soviets began to lay the foundation for their rule of the people of that territory. A fundamental cornerstone of their policy was the mass deportation of all "anti-Soviet elements" in cattle cars to Asiatic and Arctic Russia. Regarded as "anti-Soviet elements," and so treated, were administrative officials, police, judges, lawyers, members of Parliament, prominent members of political parties, non-communist non-political societies, clubs, and the Red Cross; civil servants not included above, retired military officers, officers in the reserve, priests, tradesmen, landowners, hotel and restaurant owners, clerks of the local Chambers of Commerce, and any class of person engaged in trade or correspondence with foreign countries—the latter definition extending even to stamp collectors and Esperantists—were also deported. Many artisans, peasants, and laborers (both agricultural and industrial), were banished too, so that, in effect, no Polish element was spared. The families of these unfortunate people were also banished. In many cases they were separated, wives from husbands, and children from parents. Besides individuals, the deportation of the inhabitants of whole villages and whole districts of the major towns was carried out.[19]

On September 17, 1940 *Red Star* reported that 181,000 men and over 9,000 officers had been taken prisoner. It is not known exactly how many civilians were deported, but it is known from subsequent statistics, compiled by the Polish Embassy (established in 1941) in Moscow, that it was well over one million.

Mass executions, especially of judges, policemen, and army officers took place, and the extermination of the intelligentsia proceeded apace. Besides these acts of violence, the Soviet occupation authorities began forcibly to introduce the communist system. They ordered instruction to be given in communist ideology and limited instruction in Polish to three hours a week. They banned the teaching of universal history and replaced native teachers with Russian teachers.

These acts were accompanied by appropriate steps taken to undermine family life and morality. Children were invited to denounce their parents; adolescents were encouraged to enter into free sexual intercourse. This was necessary so that everyone would in some way be compromised in police records and thus be subject to immediate arrest at any time. The Soviet theory was, of course, to destroy all actual or potential leadership in order to be able to communize and victimize the less articulate mass of the population as they pleased. By degrading the victims in their own eyes, by removing whatever hopes remained of ameliorating their condition, and by making the population dependent for the very necessities of their life on their communist masters, the Soviets hoped to ease their problems of government and to enforce the passive submission of the population. But first it was necessary to lower the population's standards to approximate those of the Soviet way of life.

An eyewitness report, typical of the procedures followed in other areas, described the process of arrests and terror as well as the Soviet behavior in Wolyn (Volhynia) in February 1940.

First of all the Soviets arrested the retired military men and the forestry personnel as the most probable conspirators and partisans. The process of arrest was as follows: A team of NKVD men, together with one or two local agents, would enter a house and superficially conduct a search, only to subsequently inform the head of the household that the whole family (children, women, the old and the sick, if any) would be transported *"v druguyu oblast"* where he could work at his profession. They were allowed to take 50 kilograms of luggage and were given fifteen minutes to get ready. In most cases the NKVD did not permit them to select the most necessary items or to take valuable papers, documents, etc. It all depended on the NKVD. As soon as the arrested family was out of the house a horde of communists would run in to steal whatever caught their fancy. Soon after, Soviet military trucks would take away the furniture and everything movable. The arrested family was put on horse-driven carts and driven to the nearest railroad station. The temperature was 35°C below zero. After being put into overcrowded cattle cars (dirty and odious), they had to wait several days for the departure. Brutal guards kept order. The journey to the east lasted eleven days. The arrested did not receive water or food for days, and the cold and dirt killed a substantial portion. The remainder arrived at a small railroad station, Shabrychshy, located in the forest. They were then loaded into hundreds of sleds (from the nearest *kolkhozes*) and driven for twenty-three kilometers into the heart of the wilderness of the Poldnevitsa forest. The temperature was about 45°C below zero. Here on marshy land they found dirty, gloomy, and cold barracks with rows of double bunks and a multitude of cockroaches. The families were assigned to the barracks on the basis of one square meter per person. The conditions were matched only by the brutality of the NKVD guards and inspectors who greeted the newly arrived in such a manner. "Forget about your Poland. . . . We shall never release you from here. . . . You will die like those cockroaches." Then they began to offend our religious feelings. We were forbidden to sing religious songs and to display crucifixes. When the NKVD inspector, Kovrygin, found one he tore it from the wall, threw it on the floor, stepped on it and then cast it into a pile of rubbish. They forced us to work on Sundays and holidays and made sarcastic remarks about the exhausted individuals. One mother in our barracks who was sitting by her child, suffering from typhoid fever, was forcibly removed to spend three days in solitary confinement for a previous minor "offense." While dragging her away from her child, inspector Svortsov shouted "*nichevo, umriot rebionok i bez tebya pokhoronim.*" When the senior inspector, Goriunov, addressed the deported he assured us that we would never see Poland again. The Soviet-German Soyuz would see to that. France was defeated and in two weeks England would be destroyed. "*Nie pomozhet vam eta staraya bezzubaya Amerika nastayaschshezhiy bankrot.*" We were deprived of any objective news or information. We were told only what the NKVD wanted to tell us.

Our job consisted of cutting trees. We were badly dressed, undernourished, and not experienced in that work. Everybody, women, school children, and the sick were forced to do that job. Absence or tardiness were punished by a court martial for "*proguly.*" The guilty were thrown into a jail and fined.

Our extremely poor earnings were shamefully cut by 30% or 50% by our guards. For months we were given only a portion of the promised wages and no final payment was ever made. In order to get a piece of badly baked bread or to buy a jar of watery soup in a "canteen," children had to spend long hours in a line, in sub-zero temperature. The older, teen-age children from about fourteen to sixteen years of age, were used to clean the latrines or dig out new ones. Most of the deported had to sell everything they could spare, i.e., clothes, shoes, linen, watches, and so on in order to buy food.

The state of health was lamentable. For over 2,000 deportees there was only one unqualified feldscher (veterinary), who was lazy and unclean. He would play an accordion prior to and during the birth of children. About March, a great number of people developed pneumonia, typhus, and dysentery. In the absence of medical care, death took a heavy toll. When the death rate reached 25%, the NKVD got one woman doctor to care for the sick.

In many families only the small children were left alive and those were taken to *detprintov* (orphanages). In other families children were the first to die.

In the fall, 300 inmates were transferred to Shabrychshy and 600 to Vologda Oblast. For the remainder, several new barracks were built. This somewhat eased living conditions.[20]

This story is typical of the experiences which the arrested and deported went through. Those who remained behind were subjected to a different method of Soviet rule.

In the domain of spiritual life, religion was banned from schools. About 4,000 churches and convents, Catholic and Orthodox, as well as synagogues, were converted into movie houses, garages, restaurants, communist clubs, and atheistic museums. Anti-religious blasphemous posters were displayed; the clergy, executed or deported; and theological colleges, closed.[21]

It was a period of unilateral action on the part of the Soviet Union about which the Polish Government was in no position to do anything but protest. Protests had no value so far as the hundreds of thousands of innocent people arrested, executed, and terrorized were concerned.

Meanwhile, Stalin decided officially to incorporate those "liberated brothers," the Ukrainians and the Byelorussians, into the Soviet Union. On October 6, Marshal Timoshenko, later to be the Soviet Commander-in-Chief of the "Western Front" ordered an election to be held on October 22 for "Popular Assemblies." The Soviet military authorities were going to conduct the elections. There were no attempts to inform the electorate of the purpose of these assemblies. In Lwów (Lvov), the Municipal Council announced that the assemblies were to decide the future status of Eastern Galicia. The Western Byelorussians were going to determine the fate of their territory.

The electorate, as a whole, remained unaware of the purpose of the elections. They had no voice in the nomination of the candidates they were to vote for; most of them, as a matter of fact, came from Russia. In Krzemieniec, in Wolyn (Volhynia) the candidates were Molotov and Marshal Voroshilov. In other districts Ponomarenko and various other Soviet leaders were nominated.[22]

The entire area was divided into constituent districts, with a single candidate running in each district. Candidates were agreed upon in advance by the Party, the military representatives, and the local temporary administration. Agitators were imported from the Soviet Union. The elections were to be supervised by a joint effort of the Red Army and the NKVD.

The majority control in the local electoral committees was usually in the hands of the Soviet officials. According to *Izvestia* (October 11, 1939) the Lwów committee, for the so-called "Western Ukraine" included seven Red Army or NKVD officers (Bergman, Gorbatenko, Grulenko, Gryshchuk, Lukin, Matsko, and Yeremenko), the Chairman of the Supreme Soviet of the Ukraine, Grechukha, and a Soviet-

Ukrainian writer, Korneychuk, the total strength of the committee being seventeen. According to *Pravda* (October 11, 1939), among the twelve members of the Bialystok committee for the so-called "Western Byelorussia" there were: the Chairman of the Supreme Soviet of Byelorussia, Natalevich; two deputies of the same Soviet, Mrs. Grekova and Pankov; and at least three Red Army or NKVD officers, Gaysin, Karkeyev, and Spasov. According to *Pravda* (October 22, 1939), 100,000 agitators were brought from the U.S.S.R. to Western Byelorussia in order to urge the electorate to vote "properly." The same issue of *Pravda* reported that out of 921 candidates in "Western Byelorussia" there were only 110 Poles, although the Poles in this area made up 40% of the population. In the "Western Ukraine," where Poles formed 36.2% of the populace, there were only 402 Polish candidates out of a total of 1,500. The votes were counted secretly by regional committee, and the electorate had no means of checking the count.

The electors were allowed to vote only for the one candidate whose name was on the ballot, and they were watched so that they should not cross out the name or write some remark. Many Russian soldiers voted. Agents of the Secret Police called at the houses of the electors to warn them of the consequences of abstention from voting. In some constituencies polling was preceded by numerous arrests; many men fled. There were numerous cases where secret police and troops rounded up constituents and escorted them to the polling stations.

In Lwów, where the size of the city made even these measures impossible, only 44% of the voting population cast ballots. The Soviet authorities ordered a new poll, but it was never held.

The established figures of the result of the elections were:

In Western Ukraine (Eastern Galicia and Wolyń) of 4,776,275 electors, 4,433,997 voted—93%.

In Western Byelorussia (Polesie and parts of the Wilno (Vilna) district) of 2,763,191 electors 2,672,280 voted—97%.[23]

The figures for individual constituencies in these areas were not published. Out of 1,495 candidates for Western Ukraine, 1,484 were elected. They were formed into two "National Assemblies" which, not by ballot but by a show of hands, unanimously resolved:

1. That "Western Ukraine" and "Western Byelorussia" pass into the hands of the working class.
2. That "Western Ukraine" and "Western Byelorussia" be "admitted" to the Soviet Union.
3. That the big estates be confiscated.
4. That the banks and industries be nationalized.
5. That homage be paid to "The Great Stalin."

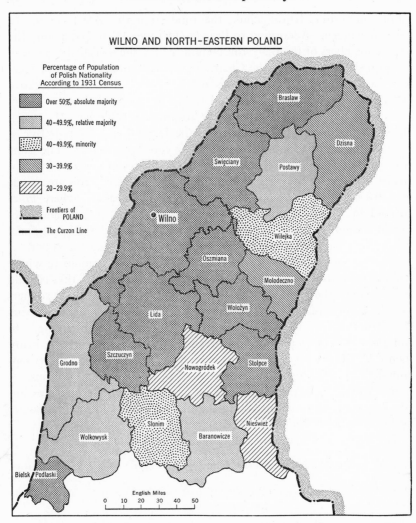

WILNO AND NORTH-EASTERN POLAND

Percentage of Population
of Polish Nationality
According to 1931 Census

- Over 50%, absolute majority
- 40-49.9%, relative majority
- 40-49.9%, minority
- 30-39.9%
- 20-29.9%
- Frontiers of POLAND
- The Curzon Line

Braslaw
Dzisna
Swięciany
Postawy
Wilno
Wilejka
Oszmiana
Molodeczno
Wolożyn
Lida
Grodno
Szczuczyn
Nowogródek
Stolpce
Slonim
Nieśwież
Baranowicze
Wolkowysk
Bielsk Podlaski

English Miles
0 10 20 30 40 50

A petition was sent to the Supreme Soviet of the U.S.S.R. to incorporate Western Byelorussia and the Western Ukraine into the Soviet Union. The Supreme Soviet graciously complied with this request which illustrated the "spontaneous will" of the people. On November 1 and 2 the Supreme Soviet issued decrees which incorporated those territories into the U.S.S.R. A few years later, when the Polish Government was presented with those acts of *faits accomplis*, it was never able to shake Soviet confidence in their legal validity. This entire farce violated Article 43 of the Fourth Hague Convention

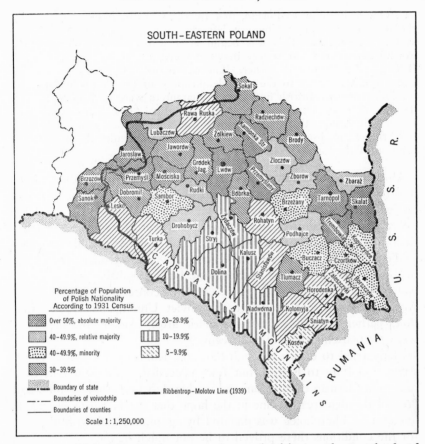

SOUTH-EASTERN POLAND

Percentage of Population
of Polish Nationality
According to 1931 Census

Over 50%, absolute majority   20-29.9%

40-49.9%, relative majority   10-19.9%

40-49.9%, minority   5-9.9%

30-39.9%

Boundary of state

Boundaries of voivodship   Ribbentrop-Molotov Line (1939)

Boundaries of counties

Scale 1:1,250,000

of 1907, which forbade the occupying authorities to change the legal
system existing in the territories under their jurisdiction.[24]

At the time of the election the Polish Government in exile sent the
following note to all Polish diplomatic missions abroad to be presented to their accredited governments:

The Polish Government has just learned that on Polish territory temporarily occupied by the U.S.S.R. a plebiscite is to be held to ascertain
the will of the population on the question of the transfer of such territory
to the U.S.S.R.

The Polish Government hereby declares that the holding of such a
plebiscite in areas under military occupation is contrary to international
law. Therefore, they will consider it as null and void, and in no case
will they recognize it as having legal force.[25]

Speaking to the Fifth (extraordinary) Session of the Supreme Soviet
on the subject of the partition of Poland and Soviet foreign relations,
Molotov, on October 31, 1939 stated:

. . . One swift blow to Poland, first by the German Army and then by the Red Army, and nothing was left of this ugly offspring of the Versailles Treaty. . . . This was begun as a war between Germany and Poland and turned into a war between Germany on the one hand, and Britain and France on the other. The war between Germany and Poland ended quickly owing to the utter bankruptcy of the Polish leaders. As we know, neither British nor French guarantees were of help to Poland. To this day, in fact, nobody knows what these "guarantees" were. . . . Everybody realizes that there can be no question of restoring old Poland. It is, therefore, absurd to continue the present war under the flag of restoration of the former Polish State.[26]

More waves of arrest, deportation, and liquidation on the spot of mostly innocent people marked a further step in the consolidation of Soviet power. From September 17, 1939 to June 1941, 1,692,000 Poles, Jews, Ukrainians, and Byelorussians were forcibly taken from their homes and deported to Russia. This number included 230,000 soldiers and officers of the Polish Army; 990,000 civilians, who were deported because of their "nationalistic bourgeois background"; 250,-000 political "class enemies"; 210,000 Poles conscripted into the Red Army and then sent deep into the Soviet Union; and 12,000 other Poles gathered forcibly from the Baltic area. Among the deportees were 160,000 children and adolescents.[27]

Many tried to escape through Slovakia, Rumania, Hungary, Yugoslavia, and Italy to France, but few succeeded. Some thought they preferred German occupation, and so they left everything behind and crossed the demarcation line in the hope that the Germans would be less cruel. The choice was dictated by ignorance and wishful hope, for the conditions there proved to be not much better.

As the subsequent testimony of Jozef Swiatlo (a high-ranking officer of the Security Police in Communist Poland) indicated, the Soviet NKVD collaborated closely with the Nazi Gestapo in an attempt to wipe out Polish opposition.[28]

The Soviets began to build up a Polish communist organization which had been virtually eliminated because it had lacked efficiency and because it had been infiltrated by the Polish police during the Great Purge of 1936–1938. The Polish Communist Party was dissolved in 1937 by the Comintern. From 1939 on the new Party was under the leadership of Soviet citizens. Later on, this led to considerable friction within the Party, when more nationalistically inclined members of the Party attempted to push forward their leader, W. Gomulka.[29] These internal policies were intended, in part, to prepare the ground for the complete absorption of the eastern territories into the Soviet Union.

A very rapid communization of every aspect of social and political life began to take place. Terror became the substitute for persuasion. The "brotherly intention" of the Soviets to help the "abandoned" Ukrainians and Byelorussians was replaced by oppression, and Ukrainians and Byelorussians, together with Poles, began to comprehend the real nature of Soviet objectives. Their partial and temporary relief was to come on June 22, 1941 when the Wehrmacht overran these territories.

When the more conspicuous "enemies," or potential enemies, of the Soviet administration were forcibly removed to the Soviet Union, the Bolsheviks began to organize the rest of the population in a more elaborate manner. In the first year of the occupation, their policy was definitely anti-Polish and pro-Ukrainian and pro-Byelorussian. Every effort was made to capture the allegiance of the nationalistically minded leaders of these two nationalities. For this reason, the Soviets completely abandoned all anti-religious propaganda, only to revive it later in a more subtle and discreet manner in the press and in public speeches. The main theme in Soviet overtures to these two nationalities was the anti-Ukrainian and anti-Byelorussian attitude of the Poles and the Polish Government prior to 1939. This nationalistic appeal superseded any stress of class conflict or Marxist ideology. For this reason too, the Soviets removed from any position of power and pushed into obscurity in these regions all Jewish communists in order not to antagonize the generally anti-Semitic local nationalists. Their jobs were offered to the former members of the nationalistic organizations which had striven for the political independence of the Ukraine and Byelorussia.

All Poles were removed from positions in any offices, government stores, post offices, etc. Many former white collar workers became manual laborers, porters, or servants of the communists. Many of those who had any valuable articles (in their homes) had to sell them to Soviet officials or Army officers in order to live.

The official language of this area became Ukrainian and Byelorussian, according to the Soviet Republic into which the specific area was incorporated. In the press and in public speeches Poland was referred to as an artificial creation of French and British imperialists, who wanted to use Poland against the Soviet Union. Actually, every effort was made to avoid the word "Polska"; but whenever this was impossible, this name was preceded by *"byvshaya"* (former). In official publications the part of Poland occupied by Germany was called *"Germania."*

Almost all monasteries and convents were closed. The churches were subjected to heavy taxes. Together with the synagogues they had to pay an exceedingly high price for electricity. The ringing of bells was prohibited. Church services and the practice of religion itself were not, however, prohibited. Yet, in rural areas and in the small towns, all Polish books in libraries were burned.

Still there was no official encouragement actively to persecute Poles. The Soviets always rather stressed the point that they had come to liberate Ukrainians, Byelorussians, and Jews, as well as the Polish working masses, from the yoke of Polish *Panów* (landlords, aristocracy, etc.). But this, of course, was only a smoke screen. Behind the slogans of the class conflict, a concept of the persecution of the various nationalities lay hidden. In this connection, a very revealing pamphlet appeared at that time. It was written by Prof. Picheta and entitled, "The Struggle for the Liberation of Western Ukraine and Western Byelorussia." Since Picheta occupied a Chair in the History of Western Slavs and was a member of the Soviet Academy, one is inclined to believe that his views were more than personal. The author presented the whole problem in Marxian terms, maintaining that the struggle of the Ukrainians and the Byelorussians was a struggle of the exploited masses against their capitalistic and fascistic oppressors. Every Ukrainian and Byelorussian peasant was a communist and every Pole a fascist and exploiter. The pamphlet made no mention of the social stratification of the Ukrainian and Byelorussian villages. Not a word could be found about the anti-Jewish policies of the extreme Ukrainian and Byelorussian nationalists prior to 1939.

In the middle of the year 1940 a striking reversal of the anti-Polish attitude took place. This was due to the cooling relations between the Nazis and the Soviets and the consequent possibility of armed conflict. The Soviets wished to prepare public opinion for such an eventuality, and they did this through various lectures and speeches. While the Soviet press was constantly presenting the German-Soviet relations in the best of terms, the speakers at these lectures were admitting that numerous other lectures were being organized to acquaint the public with the real facts of Russo-German relations, which could not be published in the press. Gradually a pro-British element was introduced, whereby Chamberlain was represented as an agent of Hitlerism and Churchill was described as a genuine British patriot. The speakers forecast an anti-Hitler crusade, and the increased sharpness in the tone of these speeches became more conspicuous when Molotov visited Berlin in the winter of 1940. It was believed that an armed conflict between Germany and the Soviet Union was not very far away.

The second reason for abandoning an anti-Polish attitude was the failure of the Soviet effort to capture the allegiance of the Ukrainian nationalists. This was coupled with the extreme inefficiency of the Soviet administration, the result of importing Ukrainians and Russians into these territories to fill all political and social positions of authority. Most of them were very primitive individuals in every sense of the word, without any administrative or organizational sense whatsoever. They had no ideas or knowledge of the social, economic, or political aspects of the new country in which they were to rule. They did not understand the mentality of the local people and, what is more, did not feel it necessary to learn more about it. They relied on several standard Soviet schemes of action which they brought with them and were unable successfully to adjust even these to the situations which confronted them, for the conditions that they found in Poland did not conform with the ready-made patterns with which they had come to rule. Their attitude towards the local people was one of distinct superiority. Even on those occasions when they wanted to appear friendly, they could not help but show that they were better, that they were confidants of Moscow, and that they had power in their hands. Because they had special stores, better supplied by the distributing centers, they antagonized the local population, which was itself deprived of the most essential articles. The instinct of self-preservation in the natives led them to discover that the moral stamina of the new rulers was low, that private contacts meant more than rules, and that they were susceptible to bribes. Furthermore, their prestige was drastically lowered when some of the officials appropriated properties of deportees. No anti-Soviet propaganda could have harmed them so much as their own acts did.[30]

Any comparison of this administration with the Polish administration prior to September 17, 1939 was obviously in favor of the latter. Poles began to acquire a much more respectable position in the eyes of Ukrainians and Byelorussians than their Soviet rulers had intended they should. Numbers of Ukrainians and Byelorussians decided to cross the German frontiers and look for better conditions there. Others escaped from these territories in order to avoid conscription into the Red Army. As a reprisal, the families which they left behind were deported.

The peasants' bitter resentment of the new order reached its peak in the summer of 1940 when the Soviets announced extremely heavy taxes. The tragedy started in early spring when the Soviets began to organize *kolkhozes*. The peasants began to rebel. They attacked posts of the NKVD. Only terror and deportation could calm the antagonized peasantry. These measures were swiftly applied.

The treatment which the Jews received from the Soviets was not much different from that allotted to the Ukrainians and Byelorussians. The elder generation of Jews was definitely anti-Soviet. The younger one was divided in this respect. Many of the elder generation illegally crossed the German frontier in preference to life under Soviet occupation. When in April and May of 1940 German missions arrived in eastern Poland to register the refugees from western Poland for the return to their homes, an overwhelming majority of Jews, as well as Poles, declared their willingness to live under German occupation. The reason for such a drastic decision, besides the hardships under Soviet rule and the desire to join those who had been left behind, was the fear of being left permanently under Soviet rule. They were afraid that once the war was over they would be unable to leave the U.S.S.R., and so they preferred the uncertainty of life under Hitler. The Germans agreed to accept all Poles who were registered but allowed only one transport of Jews, so the latter mingled with the Poles in order to overcome the restriction. Others bribed their way by paying off German guards with money or jewelry. Still others attempted to cross the borders illegally.

Most of those Jews who remained were immediately deported to Siberia and Kazakhstan. It took a long time before their tragic fate under conditions of extreme hardship and suffering became known to the outside world. When it finally did, few in the West were willing to listen, for by then the Soviet Union was the ally of the democracies fighting the Nazis.[31]

3. The Dissolution of the Nazi-Soviet Partnership and Subsequent Polish-Soviet Negotiations

On June 22, when Hitler launched his "Operation Barbarossa," the "Second Imperialistic War" automatically assumed a new significance for the U.S.S.R., because it now became termed the "Great Patriotic War." Hitler's militant totalitarian power, acutely conscious of historical and racial backgrounds, could not tolerate on a common frontier a colossus of a different civilization, having an expansionist foreign policy and a revolutionary ideology. The clash of interests brought about that "inevitable" war.

Between September 17, 1939 and June 22, 1941 the Polish Government in exile, which was recognized by all States except the Soviet and German Governments, could do nothing against the unlawful acts inflicted upon Polish people on their own territory but to send notes of protest to the governments with which it had diplomatic relations. Words of sympathy were all it received in return.

Up to September 1939 the Polish Government was free to adopt any policy towards the Soviet Union which it deemed necessary or right. Between September 1939 and July 1941, Poland had no official diplomatic relations with the Soviet Union. But from June 22, 1941 on Polish foreign policy was subjected to and conditioned by the Anglo-American attitude of loyalty towards the Soviet Union. While the lofty slogans of the Atlantic Charter, the Four Freedoms, and other idealistic pronouncements raised the hopes and cheered the hearts of those who suffered under the Nazis and of those who represented their victims as exiled governments in the free world, the actual policies of the major Allies cast an ugly and ominous shadow of the things to come. The policies which the Western Allies implemented and their subsequent implications for Poland have to be judged in the light of the events which will be set forth in the following pages.

After June 22, 1941 the Soviet Union found herself thrust into the Western camp by Hitler and was recognized by the Western Powers as a full-fledged ally. The Western Allies considered the great size of her territory, of her army, and of her human resources as indispensable for the successful prosecution of the war against Germany.

Although the Soviet Union had no choice but to gratefully accept its inclusion into the Western camp, and although the prospect of her survival was very dim when, in the earlier part of the Nazi-Soviet war, Hitler's Armies were moving more swiftly than they had in 1939 in Poland or in 1940 in Western Europe, yet, the Soviet Union was as determined to dictate its conditions in its diplomatic dealings with the West as if the Western Powers were obliged to reward her for joining them.

This Soviet determination was demonstrated again and again in connection with British efforts to bring about a reconciliation between the Polish and Soviet Governments. It was deemed indispensable for the sake of Allied unity that the two countries, the U.S.S.R. and Poland —both engaged in a mortal struggle against Hitler—should be on friendly terms.

Despite the horrifying messages about Soviet behavior in Poland which were coming to the notice of the Polish Government in exile, Prime Minister Sikorski was prepared to extend his hand in friendship to the Soviets if they found themselves in the Western camp. As early as 1940 when British Ambassador Cripps, then on his way to Moscow, visited him in Paris, Sikorski had a detailed discussion with him on the possibility of re-establishing normal diplomatic relations with the Soviets and asked for any information which might lead to that event. Sikorski understood perfectly well that the Western Allies would never fight for the independence of Poland. Besides, he knew that the Poles were unable to reconcile their problems with the Soviets[32] by themselves. He therefore spared no effort to find a *modus vivendi* with his communist neighbors.

On June 23, 1941, while speaking in a broadcast from the BBC to Poland, Sikorski described the attitude of the Polish Government towards the Nazi-Soviet war, and expressed the hope that the Nazi attack on the U.S.S.R. would bring Soviet-Polish relations back to the condition of the Treaty of Riga signed on March 18, 1921 and that "over a million Poles deported to the U.S.S.R. would be released to join the Allied forces struggling against Hitler's oppression." [33] Two weeks later the Polish Government sent the following note to Foreign Minister Anthony Eden:

The German attack on Russia has again raised the question of the status of eastern Poland. The Soviet Union occupied eastern Poland in accordance with her agreement with Germany on August 23 and the agreement concerning the German-Russian frontier on September 28, 1939. Neither these agreements nor the subsequent Soviet annexations of the territories to the south and north of Poland were recognized by H. M. Government nor by any other government with the exception of Germany and Italy. In attacking Russia, Germany has *ipso facto* broken the terms of her agreement with Russia.[34]

In view of these new circumstances the Polish Prime Minister, appreciating the importance of a settlement between the two countries attacked in turn by Germany, stretched out his hand in friendship to Russia in his speech of June 23, 1941. He proposed a normalization of Soviet-Polish relations on condition that the two countries should return to the terms of the Convention which had bound them before September 1939 and had secured for them twenty years of peace as neighbors. The Prime Minister also demanded the release by Russia of Polish war prisoners and of the many hundreds of thousands of Polish citizens deported to Central Russia.[35]

On July 4, Eden informed Sikorski that he had had a meeting with the Soviet Ambassador, Maisky, during which the latter expressed the readiness of the Soviet Government to begin negotiations with the Polish Government. Whereupon Eden handed Sikorski a résumé of his conversation with Maisky on the same day, which read:

The Soviet Government has been reconsidering its relations with Poland, Czechoslovakia, and Yugoslavia. It has taken the decision to give facilities to all three States to form National Committees in the U.S.S.R. These Committees would have facilities to form national military forces, Polish, Czechoslovak, and Yugoslav. The Soviet Government would undertake to supply arms and equipment to those forces. It followed as a result of this that all Polish prisoners of war in Russian hands would be handed over to the Polish National Committee. Their number was not as large as General Sikorski had told me; he (Maisky) understood that there were only about 20,000. These forces would fight with the Russian armies against the German oppressor.

With regard to Poland, Soviet policy was to favor the establishment of an independent national Polish State. The boundaries of this State would correspond with ethnographical Poland. From this it might follow that certain districts and towns occupied by Russia in 1939 might be returned to Poland. The form of internal government to be set up in Poland was, in the view of the Soviet Government, entirely a matter for the Poles themselves. If General Sikorski and his Government found these statements of policy acceptable, the Soviet Government was prepared to make a treaty with him to form a common front against the German aggression.[36]

After reading the contents of the résumé Sikorski observed that the stated conditions and objectives of the Soviet Union led him to believe that the Soviets showed a tendency to re-establish Panslavism, but this time of a red color. Furthermore, Sikorski stated that Poland could not go along with such unrealistic and harmful ideas. Any Panslavic bloc would only be an annex of the U.S.S.R.

Eden completely agreed with Sikorski's view but stated that he would not use those views in his dealings with the Russians. He would, however, keep them in mind for future reference. Sikorski noted that figures given by Maisky of the number of Poles deported to Russia were false and cited instead those given by *Red Star*, September 17, 1940, that there were around 181,000 former soldiers, 9,000 officers, and many thousands of civilians in various camps in Central Asia. He also rejected the Soviet proposal to create a Polish national committee in Russia on the ground that Poland already had a legal government. Yet, in spite of these objections, and in spite of the discouraging Russian attitude, Sikorski expressed a willingness to enter into negotiation with the Soviets and proposed the following agenda:

1. The Soviet Government will cease to recognize its treaties of August and September 1939 with Germany.

2. The Soviet Government will automatically restore the Polish Embassy in Moscow and will recognize the Ambassador appointed by the Polish Government, who may eventually create a National Committee, but subordinate to the Polish Government. Such a Committee will be concerned with the welfare of the Poles scattered over the Soviet territory.

3. War prisoners and political prisoners will be released from their places of confinement. Out of the released military men and civilians of military age a Sovereign Polish Army may be formed for the struggle against Germany. Such an Army would be subordinate to the Polish Commander-in-Chief in London.[37]

Eden expressed full agreement with Sikorski's agenda and observed that it was not correct for the Soviet Government on the one hand to approach the Polish Government for negotiation and on the other hand to suggest the establishment of a Polish national committee.

On July 5 the first conference between Sikorski and Maisky took place in the British Foreign Office. The following notes of that conference were taken by Sir Alexander Cadogan:

When it came to the question of frontiers, Maisky thought that it would not be profitable at this time to discuss this matter at great length or in detail.

To this General Sikorski replied that he could not accept any departure from the status which existed prior to August 1939. He would not be able eventually to return to his country having agreed to a diminished Poland. Moreover, were he to recognize even implicitly a surrender of Poland to the U.S.S.R. it would make it difficult, if not impossible, to create enthusiasm among the Polish soldiers who are at present in Soviet gaols or concentration camps, or deported under distressing conditions. Monsieur Zaleski (the Polish Foreign Minister) remarked that the Germans who are now trying to form a puppet government in Warsaw are promising Poles a most considerable extension of their eastern boundaries.

M. Maisky said that his Government favored the formation of an independent national Polish State and they agreed further that the regime to be established was the exclusive concern of the Poles, but they would not explicitly recognize the frontiers of 1939. Perhaps, however, it would not be necessary to say that now, and the question might be left open.

General Sikorski explained that prior to the present war there were practically no Soviet nationals in the territories occupied by the Soviet armies in September 1939; moreover, as the U.S.S.R. is not a national State, but a composition of numerous nations ruled by Moscow, she has no grounds to impose strictly ethnographical frontiers on Poland. General Sikorski said that he could agree that this question need not be discussed in detail at present. He could not, however, agree that the Soviet Government should declare that the frontiers of 1939 would *not* be restored.

He (Maisky) then summed up what he understood to be the Polish position mainly:

1. Provided the Soviet Government denounces the two treaties with Germany of August and September 1939, the discussion of frontiers is not material.

2. Return to normal relations between the two Governments and the appointment of a Polish Ambassador in Moscow.

3. A special Polish Army would be formed as a unit on Soviet territory or be transported elsewhere if that were desired. The exact status of the

Polish Army would be similar to that of the Polish forces in the United Kingdom.

4. Poland would then be prepared to collaborate in the common fight against Germany.

5. Polish military and political prisoners were to be liberated.[38]

These proposals Maisky promised to submit to his Government.

On July 11 a second meeting took place in the British Foreign Office between Premier Wladyslaw Sikorski, Foreign Minister August Zaleski, Soviet Ambassador Ivan Maisky, and British Secretary of State Sir Alexander Cadogan. Since the results of this conference proved to be extremely significant to the future development of the Soviet-Polish relations, the whole text is hereby included. The notes were again taken by Sir Alexander Cadogan.

MAISKY. The General position of the Soviet Government as regards the Polish State was that it maintained the point of view previously expressed in favor of the independence of the Polish State within the territorial limits of Polish nationality. This was the Soviet Government's general point of view. It was prepared to accept the Polish suggestion to put aside for the present the question of the frontiers of Poland.

The Soviet Government was prepared also to make a declaration to the effect that the Soviet-German Treaties of 1939 regarding Poland are to be considered as non-existent.

As regards the question of the formation of a Polish National Committee the Soviet Government was animated in making this suggestion by their desire to meet Polish national aspirations; but if the Polish Government finds the creation of such a committee undesirable the Soviet Government does not insist upon it.

The Soviet Government was prepared to resume diplomatic relations with the Polish Government and to receive a Polish representative in Moscow.

The Soviet Government favors the creation of an independent Polish Army on Soviet soil under commanders appointed by the Polish Government in agreement with the Soviet Government. This Army, being part of the forces fighting against Germany, is to be under the general direction of the Soviet High Command.

As regards the Polish prisoners of war, of whom the Polish Government claimed that there were 180,000, 10,000 being officers, the Soviet Government stated that there were only 20,000. The remainder were released as the Soviet Government had not considered it possible to keep these as prisoners of war, and were now dispersed throughout Russia.

This was the message which he had been instructed by his Government to convey to the Polish Government.

SIKORSKI. Reserving the final answer of the Polish Government, he would at once observe that if the Soviet Government renounced the Treaties of 1939 with Germany, this meant, in his view, the return to the legal situation which existed before these Treaties were concluded. He had received the approval of Poles in Poland and the United States for this point of view and could not abandon it without losing that approval.

He would not for a moment say that, at the peace conference, Soviet Russia would not be at liberty to put forward all sorts of pretensions and the Polish Government might also put some forward. But the Polish Government could not recognize the Soviet Government's statement on ethnographical frontiers.

CADOGAN. There was no question of that.

SIKORSKI. According to M. Maisky's declaration the Polish Government should agree that the future Poland was to be an ethnographical one.

MAISKY. No; the Soviet Government did not insist that the Polish Government accept its point of view.

SIKORSKI. It was necessary to underline certain consequences of the Soviet point of view. For example, what would happen if the Polish and Soviet armies marched victoriously into Polish territory? Who would govern this territory, Poles or Russians? He would be satisfied if Monsieur Maisky said that the Poles would govern it.

MAISKY. Suggested that at the moment this question was perhaps a little academic.

SIKORSKI. Repeated that he could not accept the Soviet Government's point of view and wanted to make the Polish point of view clear to the Ambassador.

MAISKY. Repeated that he only wished to state his Government's point of view, about the future limits of the Polish State and did not ask the Polish Government to agree.

SIKORSKI. The Polish Government could not accept a declaration regarding the future Poland such as Monsieur Maisky proposed.

MAISKY. The Soviet Government did not ask for this; it merely stated its point of view.

SIKORSKI. If the Polish Government accepted they would lose the support of Poles abroad. He could not discuss this question. It was not possible that the Soviet Government should make a unilateral declaration on this matter. Any declaration should be bi-lateral and agreed upon by both parties. He had understood M. Stalin to say that Russia had occupied Polish territory by arrangement with Germany in order to gain time. If this were so, it was only natural that M. Stalin should now declare that he had only taken the territory temporarily.

MAISKY. The General had not quoted M. Stalin correctly. The latter had said that his non-aggression Pact with Germany was concluded with the object of allowing time for preparation. He did not say anything about territorial arrangements.

SIKORSKI. If the Soviet Government denounced its Pact with Germany, it should renounce all territorial gains it had got from it.

MAISKY. The important thing seemed to be to reach an agreement now. If they dwelt on general political matters and questions regarding frontiers, they would not get this agreement now. His statement of the Soviet Government's point of view did not mean that this point of view was to be embodied in a document to be agreed upon here and now by the Polish Government. The Soviet Government was ready to leave discussion and agreement on this point for the present.

SIKORSKI. Some declaration would be necessary and he would make proposals in a few days.

MAISKY. It was important to state as soon as possible
1. that the treaties of 1939 were dead,
2. that diplomatic relations should be restored,
3. that the Polish Army should be recruited, and
4. that both Governments agreed to fight against Germany.

SIKORSKI. Two important points would then be lacking.
1. The question of Polish political prisoners in Russia. He did not believe the German assertion that all these had been murdered. There must be some still to be released; all of whom were Polish citizens.
2. The Soviet Government should restore Government and private property which they had taken from occupied Polish territory.

CADOGAN. Could not these points be raised when diplomatic relations had been restored?

SIKORSKI. What were the Ambassador's views on future procedure? Was he authorized to sign an agreement, e.g., a military agreement?

MAISKY. He was not authorized to sign at the moment, but he would seek authorization if they could agree on something.

CADOGAN. It was most important from the point of view of world opinion, particularly in the United States, to conclude a Soviet-Polish Agreement soon. Nothing else done by Monsieur Maisky could have such a good effect. Meanwhile the latter would seek authority from his Government to sign.

SIKORSKI. It was necessary to underline the importance of two points. (1) The question of the Polish Frontier; and (2) that of the prisoners, both prisoners of war and political prisoners.

MAISKY. The suggestion for the conclusion of an agreement on the basis of the four points he had put forward was his own suggestion, and his Government would have to consider an agreement in that form, though they were agreed on the essence.

CADOGAN. To sum up: It was important to try and get an early agreement. Monsieur Maisky had made a personal suggestion of an agreement on the four points. The Secretary of State would try to put them on paper for both Governments to consider. The question of the frontiers was, in his opinion, not one which really remained outstanding, since if the four point agreement was concluded, the Polish point of view was legally safeguarded.

SIKORSKI. It was important to be clear that the Polish Government held by the 1939 frontier and felt that the Poles should take over the administration if the Germans were driven back west of that frontier.

CADOGAN. This question could be discussed later; if the 1939 Treaties fell to the ground, the legal position was clear. The question of political prisoners, however, remained and Monsieur Maisky should try and help to meet the Poles in this problem; e.g., by arranging for its discussion when diplomatic relations were restored.

SIKORSKI. If the Polish and Soviet Governments reached agreement on the lines proposed, the Polish Government could not understand how the question of the political prisoners could not be automatically settled.

MAISKY. The exact views of the Soviet Government on this point were not known, but it might feel difficulty in settling this question by a comprehensive promise to release all prisoners. Perhaps something could be done by a private undertaking, negotiated by the Polish Ambassador in Moscow.

SIKORSKI. The Polish Government could not understand the difficulty of settling this point. They would agree not to publish any agreement about political prisoners, but the Soviet Government ought to be able to appreciate the good impression which the release of those prisoners would make.

MAISKY. The question was a little more complicated than the General thought. For example, suppose that after Russia occupied Polish territory some Pole had committed a political crime for which he had been sentenced? This would not be a question of military operations. The problem was one that might be considered, but was not so simple as that of prisoners of war.

SIKORSKI. This question showed how difficult the frontier question would be. If the Soviet Government did not regard these people as Soviet citizens, their status was regulated by the Hague Conventions. They could only be regarded as having committed political crimes because they remained Polish citizens. It was impossible for the Polish Government to admit the right of the Soviet Government to judge and condemn Polish citizens.

CADOGAN. The General was not asking the Soviet Government to recognize the 1939 frontier as regards the past as well as the present, and to admit that their actions since 1939 in these former Polish territories had been illegal.

SIKORSKI. The Polish Government could not agree to reach an agreement with the Soviet Government at the price of selling the Polish political prisoners.

CADOGAN. The Soviet Government would not want to keep these prisoners for ever. What the Polish Government wanted is that they should be freed in the near future. The Soviet Government ought to be able to give a private assurance to this effect.

MAISKY. The figures which the Polish Government had mentioned were, he thought, exaggerated.

SIKORSKI. The principle of the release of political prisoners should be recognized by the Soviet Government. It was a sacrifice for Poland to ignore the Russian aggression of 1939.

MAISKY. It was not the time to argue about this. Argument could be used to condemn Polish aggression in the past as well as Soviet aggression. He did not wish to dwell upon the past, but to concentrate on the present and future. An agreement between the Soviet and Polish Governments was important from the point of view of public opinion, and something effective should be made public soon. It was therefore desirable to concentrate on the four points and to make other independent arrangements about the political prisoners; and he was prepared to raise with his Government the possibility of a parallel private agreement on this point.

It was agreed by the Polish representatives and the Soviet Ambassador to proceed along these lines. The aim would be to conclude first a political agreement, the draft of which, based on Monsieur Maisky's four points, would be communicated by the Secretary of State to the Polish Government and the Soviet Ambassador; and later a military agreement. In the meanwhile Monsieur Maisky would sound out his Government about the proposed four points agreement and would seek their views about the private agreement regarding the political prisoners.

A further meeting would be held when Monsieur Maisky had received a reply from Moscow.[39]

Subsequently, Zaleski had a conference with Eden to discuss the outcome of the preceding meeting. He recalled:

Eden, with increased impatience, pressed the Poles to reach an agreement, maintaining that such an agreement was indispensable for England in her dealings with the Catholic countries which were suffering from the German and Italian psychosis. Actually, it is more likely that Churchill, in his desire to consolidate a British public opinion which is at this stage partially anti-Soviet, wanted to show that even Poles were willing to go along with the Russians.[40]

Although these meetings were strictly confidential, and although the Polish side was prohibited by Eden from saying anything to the press, The London *Times* and *Daily Telegraph* of July 12, writing about these conferences stated that "satisfactory progress is being made in the conversations now proceeding in London between the Soviet and the Polish Governments. . . ." The Poles concluded that the reason for the British pressure was Churchill's anxiety to reach an agreement in the negotiations which were going on between Cripps and Molotov in Moscow about a British-Soviet treaty.

On July 14, 1941 Polish Ambassador Ciechanowski, reporting to his Government in London about his conference with United States Under Secretary of State, Sumner Welles, wrote, among other items:

The Russian circles in the U.S.A. (particularly Kerensky's group, as well as the Ukrainians and Lithuanians) started an action against the return to the status provided for by the Riga Treaty.

In this connection I was informed that Kerensky's group supposedly sent its representative to the Labor Party in London to ask it to oppose the return to the Riga Treaty which might result out of the Soviet-Polish negotiations. Also, Ukrainians in London are active while the Lithuanians are preparing propaganda in that direction here.

At the last moment I have learned *most confidentially* and privately from the State Department that, according to the information which is coming in from the American Embassy in Moscow, the British Ambassador, Sir Stafford Cripps, is helping to prevent a positive solution of the Soviet-Polish relations by discreetly suggesting to the Soviets that the Soviet Government exploit the present situation in order to get territorial concessions from the Polish Government.[41]

On July 15 Sikorski and Zaleski again met with Eden, who presented them with a British version of the Soviet-Polish treaty which left the problem of frontiers for post-war consideration. Sikorski asked if he could take the text for three hours in order to make the corrections which his Cabinet might feel necessary. Eden refused and told Sikorski and Zaleski to make them on the spot. They did so. Before leaving them, Eden announced, "Whether you want to or not, an agreement with the Soviet Union has to be signed." [42]

On July 16, Sikorski, addressing Polish forces in Scotland, stated that the Poles and the British were in agreement on the problem of frontiers but that Maisky was making difficulties. The same day Eden telephoned Zaleski to inform him that the British Government had decided not to publish this speech in any newspaper appearing in Britain. Various notes and proposals were exchanged between the Polish and the British Governments which did not soften Polish determination to secure a minimum from the Soviets.

On July 19, during a luncheon between Sikorski and Eden, Sikorski was forced to accept the Maisky draft under British pressure. On July 21 the Polish Cabinet put limits to Sikorski's freedom of decision as a protest against this state of affairs, but this had no practical effect. It was not the Polish Cabinet but the British Government which limited Sikorski's freedom of decision. The British submitted Sikorski's concessions to Moscow and a prompt approval of Maisky's draft came back. Sikorski's concessions were made when Eden promised to compensate the Poles for the vagueness of certain points in Maisky's draft, especially the matter of frontiers, by offering a British declaration to the effect that His Majesty's Government did not recognize any territorial changes which took place in Poland since August 1939.

On July 25, when Eden showed Maisky the text of the proposed British declaration to Poland to be published at the conclusion of the Soviet-Polish Treaty, Maisky objected and demanded an additional clause reading: "This declaration does not predetermine a position which Great Britain will adopt towards the future boundaries in Eastern Europe." [43] Eden complied with Maisky's demands and inserted the clause in the declaration. The Poles objected.

Eden attempted to calm the disturbed Poles by saying that he was willing to state in Parliament that Great Britain stood on Churchill's declaration of September 5, 1940 which did not recognize any territorial changes made by force. The Polish representatives replied that it was obvious that the declaration to be made in Parliament or a reservation within the text itself deprived Mr. Eden's declaration to Poland of all its value.

Since Sikorski was not in a position to make any protest, three of his ministers, A. Zaleski, Dr. M. Seyda, and General K. Sosnkowski, resigned in protest. They represented a considerable part of the Polish exiles who did not trust Soviet verbal promises and who believed that this was the only time—when the Soviet Union was under the pressure of Hitler's armies—to get clear and strong guarantees about the frontiers and other disputed matters. They believed that it would be impossible to get any guarantees from the Soviet Union when and if the Red Army began to roll back the Nazis.

Sikorski and the majority of his Cabinet did not believe that a Nazi victory in Russia was possible. He was convinced that the Allies would give maximum support to the Soviets and that if Poland created any roadblock in Allied unity, even morally, her prestige and position would go down. Furthermore, he wanted to show the good will of his Government towards the Soviets, and he trusted Eden's pledge of the British declaration about the inviolability of pre-war frontiers. Above all Sikorski wanted to secure the release of the imprisoned multitudes of Polish citizens in the Soviet Union and to create a Polish army out of them. He wished to use that army in the common struggle against Hitler and to have a considerable armed force at his command at the moment when Hitler would be defeated. He thought that the presence of a strong Polish army in Poland would be the best argument possible towards reaching a better agreement with the Soviets.[44] The Cabinet accepted Sikorski's decision and the President approved it.

It must be stated here that when the British were pressing the Poles for a speedy conclusion of the treaty, they often pointed out that this was indispensable in order not to encourage the Americans to turn away from European problems. Remembering President Wilson's sympathetic attitude toward Poland, and assuming a continued strong American interest in Poland, the Polish Government therefore approached the State Department through its Ambassador, Ciechanowski, and asked if the United States would be willing to guarantee Polish independence. To many Poles, America was not only a refuge for hungry and persecuted people, it was also a source of inspiration and hope to those who looked upon her as the moral champion of mankind. While every other nation could be suspected of compromising moral principles, a majority of Poles fervently believed that the descendants of those who suffered in the Old World would not tolerate the perpetuation of a tyranny from which their forefathers had fled.

On July 30, 1941 the United States Government offered the following guarantee to Poland:

That the Polish Government in accepting the text of the first paragraph of the Polish-Soviet Treaty did not in any way recognize any changes of its pre-war frontiers and does not admit any possibility for any kind of future discussion of the problem of frontiers.[45]

This guarantee came a few hours after the signing of the Pact took place on July 30. The following day the State Department informed Ambassador Ciechanowski that "in view of the successful conclusion of the treaty and its favorable terms to both sides the previous guarantee given by the State Department is superfluous." [46]

The text of the Polish-Soviet Agreement signed in the British Foreign Office provided:

1. The Government of the U.S.S.R. recognizes that the Soviet-German treaties of 1939 relative to territorial changes in Poland have lost their validity. The Government of the Republic of Poland declares that Poland is not bound by any agreement with any third State directed against the U.S.S.R.

2. Diplomatic relations will be restored between the two Governments upon the signature of this agreement, and an exchange of Ambassadors will follow immediately.

3. The two Governments mutually undertake to render one another aid and support of all kinds in the present war against Hitlerite Germany.

4. The Government of the U.S.S.R. expresses its consent to the formation on the territory of the U.S.S.R. of a Polish Army under a Commander appointed by the Polish Government in agreement with the Soviet Government. The Polish Army on the territory of the U.S.S.R. will be subordinated in operational matters to the Supreme Command of the U.S.S.R., at which there will be a representative of the Polish Army. All details as to command, organization, and employment of this force will be settled in a subsequent agreement.

5. This Agreement will come into effect immediately upon its signature and without ratification.

Protocol.—As soon as diplomatic relations are re-established the Government of the U.S.S.R. will grant amnesty to all Polish citizens who are at present deprived of their freedom on the territory of the U.S.S.R., either as prisoners of war or on other adequate grounds.

Secret Protocol.—(1) All types of claims of public as well as of private character will be considered in further negotiations between both Governments.

        (2) This Protocol comes into force simultaneously with the Pact of 30th July 1941.[47]

It was due largely to British efforts and pressure that the Agreement was signed. In accordance with Eden's promise, a British official note was handed to Sikorski. It read as follows:

On the occasion of the signature of the Polish-Soviet Agreement of today, I desire to take this opportunity of informing you that in conformity with the provision of the agreement of mutual assistance between the

United Kingdom and Poland of the 25th of August, 1939 His Majesty's Government in the United Kingdom have entered into no understanding towards the Union of Socialist Soviet Republics which affects the relations between that country and Poland. I also desire to assure you that His Majesty's Government do not recognize any territorial changes which have been effected in Poland since August, 1939.[48]

On August 31 the American Government published the following statement in the press:

Mr. Welles described as gratifying to this Government the Russian-Polish agreement signed in London yesterday. He made clear, in commenting on it at his press conference, however, that he was discussing only general policy, not details. The United States position towards Poland, he pointed out, was made clear immediately after that country was invaded. It was one of not recognizing any change in her status as a free, sovereign, and independent nation. That position, he added, is maintained and continued. His understanding of the Russian-Polish agreement was that it was in line with the United States policy of non-recognition of territory taken by conquest.[49]

Immediately after the signing of the Soviet-Polish treaty, a Parliamentary debate took place in the House of Commons. During this debate Eden was asked by Captain McEwen, Member of Parliament for Berwick and Haddington, whether it was right to assume that as a result of this Soviet-Polish agreement a guarantee of frontiers in Eastern Europe would be undertaken by His Majesty's Government. Eden replied that the exchange of notes between the British and the Polish Governments "does not involve any guarantee of frontiers by His Majesty's Government." [50] It is obvious that *suaviter in modo fortiter in re*, the British Government decided to leave the problem of frontiers open.

Commenting on that treaty, The *Times* of August 1, 1941 in its editorial "Peace and Power" made the following observations:

The Treaty of Vienna of 1815 was realistic and free of abstract principles so characteristic of the Versailles Treaty. . . . Some leadership in Eastern Europe in the future must replace the chaos of the last twenty years. This leadership may be provided either by Germany or Russia. Therefore, the interests of Great Britain and also of the United States demand that the German influences will not overshadow the Russian interests in Eastern Europe—for Britain, together with the United States, should take active part in the future ordering of Europe.

The Soviet Government presumably understood Eden's remarks and the consequent reaction of the British press to mean that Britain would not oppose Soviet demands if a more opportune moment would arise. From that time onwards, the Soviets were most efficient in utilizing the British desire to maintain friendship with the Soviet Union to exert pressure on the Polish Government to comply with Soviet demands. Even at that early stage of the war, the Soviets had managed to convince Britain that friction between Poland and Russia would be due only to Polish stubbornness and not to excessive Russian demands. Poland's sovereignty became a diplomatic "share of stock" for the Western Great Powers, and especially for England, to be bargained away or traded for Soviet loyalty to the Allied cause.

Upon the signing of the Soviet-Polish Treaty a considerable part of the right-wing Polish groups in London and elsewhere became very critical of its terms. They thought that the Soviets did not make any concessions for their attack on Poland and their cruelty to her people. Nevertheless, in spite of the eighteen various notes, proposals, and counterproposals exchanged between the British Foreign Office and the Polish Government about the terms of the treaty, Maisky stuck to his original proposal, and the Soviets got what they wanted. Sikorski attempted to object to the term "amnesty" for the imprisoned and deported because it carried the implication of guilt and asked for a replacement of that word by "released." The British Government, however, would not permit such an apparent trifle to block a bigger result.

In Soviet terminology every worker who takes up arms against the Soviet Union is considered a criminal offender, and therefore only an "amnesty" could excuse him from punishment.

When President Raczkiewicz and numerous other influential politicans and journalists were known to be in disagreement with the treaty, Sikorski felt obliged to justify his decisions. On August 5, speaking to the First and Second Polish Tank Batallions in Blairgowrie, Scotland, he took issue with the critics of his act and stated: "If I had not signed that treaty you soldiers of our Army would have been disarmed today and put either into Labor Battalions or into Internee Camps." [51]

Considering the conditions prevailing at that time, it would be difficult even today to present a satisfactory alternative. The Soviet Union had much more to offer Britain in the struggle against Hitler than did Poland. Moreover, the only unifying element in the precarious relations which were established by that treaty were, ironically enough, Hitler's armies. Yet, in spite of the conspicuous lack of friendship between Poland and the Soviet Union, official relations were established.

Moscow was determined not to relinquish the handsome gains secured for her by the Molotov-Ribbentrop pact. Stalin knew that, together with Britain and the United States, the Soviet Union would be able to defeat Hitler. It was only a matter of time. He decided to use his bargaining power as a member of the new alliance by insisting on the revision of the status quo in Eastern Europe before 1939. He knew that the Western Powers were afraid of a new rapprochement between him and Hitler (however small the chance may have been) and that this would force them to accept his terms. He skillfully played up the rights of the Ukrainians and Byelorussians, which Britain was particularly willing to consider. While Britain was preoccupied with the merits of these nationalistic claims and with the desire to secure the good will of the Soviets, Stalin thought in terms of the long-range strategic interests of the Soviet State which, as the base of world communism, was bound to be mindful of communist objectives which transcend a particular war. From the point of view of the post-war interests of the Soviet Union, his diplomatic strategy proved to be correct. This tri-partite or multi-party method of negotiating a bi-lateral treaty taught him a lesson which he found profitable in future dealings with Poland and other Eastern European nations.

Although the treaty did not mention the problem of frontiers at all, the Polish Government was determined to preserve the inviolability of its 1939 eastern boundaries. Soon after the conclusion of the treaty, Sikorski expressed that view publicly in order to quiet those of his critics who thought that he did not hold that view, and, undoubtedly, also to reassure himself that this was really so, as well as to see what the Soviet reaction would be. He did not have long to wait for a reaction from the latter. On August 3, an editorial in *Izvestia* disputed the accuracy of Sikorski's interpretation of the treaty to mean a return to the terms of the Riga Treaty. With this answer, there was not much that the Poles could do except to form the secret hope that the march of Hitler's armies eastward would humble Moscow, or even defeat the Soviet Union, and that the growing armed strength of the Anglo-Americans would alone destroy Nazism and its New Order.

On July 30 the Soviets appointed the former Ambassador to Vichy, A. E. Bogomolov, as the Ambassador to the Polish Government. On the same day Professor Stanislaw Kot, a member of the Peasant Party and the Minister of Interior in Sikorski's Cabinet, was appointed Ambassador to Moscow by the Polish Government. The urgency of appointing an Ambassador to Moscow was implied in a stipulation by the Protocol of the treaty which said that,

. . . as soon as diplomatic relations are re-established the U.S.S.R. will grant amnesty to all Polish citizens who are at present deprived of their freedom on the territory of the U.S.S.R.

Notes

[1] *The Polish White Book*, p. 187.
[2] *Ibid.*, p. 209.
[3] *Soviet Documents on Foreign Policy*, Vol. III, p. 372.
[4] *The Polish White Book*, p. 188.
[5] *Ibid.*
[6] *Ibid.*
[7] *Nazi-Soviet Relations 1939–1941*, pp. 92–93.
[8] *The Polish White Book*, pp. 189–190.
[9] *Ibid.*, pp. 211–212.
[10] *Soviet Documents on Foreign Policy*, Vol. III, pp. 392–393.
[11] *Nazi-Soviet Relations 1939–1941*, p. 101.
[12] *Ibid.*, pp. 102–103.
[13] *Soviet Documents on Foreign Policy*, Vol. III, p. 380.
[14] *Nazi-Soviet Relations 1939–1941*, pp. 105–107.
[15] H. W. Henderson, *Polish-Soviet Relations*, Perth, Scotland, Munro Press, Ltd., p. 15.
[16] *The Eastern Provinces of Poland*, issued by the Polish Ministry of Preparatory Work Concerning the Peace Conference, London, May 1944, p. 9.
[17] *The Polish White Book*, p. 193.
[18] *Ibid.*, pp. 213–214.
[19] See Appendix 1.
[20] Poland, *Official Government Documents*, Vol. II, Doc. 4.
[21] *Ibid.*, Vol. V, Docs. 10–17.
[22] *Pravda*, October 15, 1939.
[23] Cf. N. Baltiyskiy, *Pol'ska—Nash Sosed* (Poland—Our Neighbor), Voina i Rabochiy Klass, February 1, 1944.
[24] Poland, *Official Government Documents*, Vol. V, Docs. 21–25.
[25] *The Polish White Book*, p. 194.
[26] *Soviet Documents on Foreign Policy*, Vol. III, pp. 388–389.
[27] These figures were compiled by the Polish Embassy in the U.S.S.R. during the period from August 1941 to April 1943 and are based on the testimony of over 18,000 eyewitnesses—Poles who passed through prisons, concentration camps, and forced labor camps in the Soviet Union. This collection is now in the Hoover Library on War, Revolution, and Peace in Stanford, California.
[28] *News from Behind the Iron Curtain*, Vol. IV, No. 3, Free Europe Press, Free Europe Committee, Inc., New York, March 1955, p. 30, contains a summary of Swiatlo's report.
[29] *Ibid.*
[30] Poland, *Official Government Documents*, Vol. XV, Doc. 45.
[31] *Ibid.*, Doc. 47.
See also: Solomon M. Schwartz, *The Jews in the Soviet Union*, Syracuse, New York, Syracuse University Press, 1951.
[32] Stanislaw Kot, *Listy z Rosji do Generala Sikorskiego*, London, 1956, p. 12.
[33] Poland, *Official Government Documents*, Vol. XVII, Doc. 19.
[34] *Ibid.*, Doc. 22.
[35] *Ibid.*, Doc. 23.

[36] *Ibid.*, Doc. 15.

[37] *Ibid.*, Docs. 23–24.

[38] *Ibid.*, Doc. 30.

[39] *Ibid.*, Vol. L, Doc. 5.

[40] *Ibid.*, Doc. 6.

[41] *Ibid.*, Doc. 31 (Report 3/sz-tin-10).

[42] *Ibid.*, Doc. 12.

[43] *Ibid.*, Doc. 16.

[44] Kot, *op. cit.*, pp. 10–14.

[45] Poland, *Official Government Documents*, Vol. L, Doc. 26.

[46] *Ibid.*

[47] *Ibid.*, Doc. 6.

[48] *Ibid.*, Doc. 7.

[49] Jan Ciechanowski, *Defeat in Victory*, Garden City, New York, Doubleday & Company, Inc., 1947, pp. 39–40.

[50] Poland, *Official Government Documents*, Vol. L, Doc. 8.

[51] This writer was one of Sikorski's audience that day.

The Precarious Alliance:
August 1941 to April 1943

1. Attempts to Implement the Terms of the Treaty to Free Poles Imprisoned in the Soviet Union

On August 12, 1941 the decree of the Presidium of the Supreme Soviet granted ". . . amnesty to all Polish citizens presently on Soviet territory who were deprived of freedom either because of being war prisoners or because of other sufficient reasons." [1] Only the results of that decree, namely, the release of hundreds of thousands of mistreated Polish citizens imprisoned in Soviet concentration camps, persuaded the Poles in London to swallow the term "amnesty." Carrying out the "amnesty" was, however, another matter. It was to consume much time and to require constant and often bitter diplomatic proddings.

Immediately after the decree on amnesty was issued, a dozen or so of the most prominent Poles in Soviet hands, among them General Wladyslaw Anders, were released from Soviet prisons. The speed with which Anders was freed was due to Sikorski's decision to name him Commander-in-Chief of the Polish Army which was going to be formed in the U.S.S.R. Others had to wait their turn. Generally speaking, that turn was to come slowly; in many cases, not at all.

According to the terms of the Soviet-Polish Treaty of August 14, a military agreement was signed in Moscow between Soviet General

Alexander Vasilevsky and General Zygmunt Szyszko-Bohusz, which laid the legal basis for the formation of a Polish Army.

On August 22, the Polish Chargé d'Affaires in Moscow delivered a note to Molotov requesting the implementation of the amnesty and asking for permission to establish a mixed Polish-Soviet commission which would supervise the welfare of the released Poles. The same note also requested permission to establish delegates of the Polish Embassy in the various *oblasts* who would care for the freed prisoners.[2] On September 28 Molotov replied in a *pro-memoria* in which he granted these requests and stated that all prisoners were already released from prisons and labor camps.[3]

As could be expected, the reaction of the deportees to the news of the Soviet-Polish treaty was enthusiastic. The following report by Teresa Lipkowska from a labor camp in the Poldnevitsa area is typical of the reactions of Polish internees in general.

When we received the news of the conclusion of the Polish-Soviet Treaty and of the formation of the Polish Army, an indescribable enthusiasm was visible on every face. The people began embracing each other, crying and singing. Everyone, in spite of age or physical condition began getting ready to take an active part in whatever role or place he could be most useful in the common struggle against the Nazis.

The news was received through the Soviet press and radio. We were waiting anxiously for word from the Polish authorities. We wanted to send an enthusiastic telegram to our Government but the Soviets would not allow this. Soon after, the communist agitators were sent into our camp to spread propaganda to the effect that this was a part of the official policy to communize Poland. They were saying that the Red flag would be flying over Warsaw, and that our Army would be completely dependent and subordinated to the Red Army; that the Soviet authorities would decide who would be admitted to our Army, etc. We rejected all this nonsense. Then we heard General Sikorski's broadcast from Moscow. It explained everything. We were waiting for the implementation of the promises. We were getting impatient and then began to worry because the attitude of the Soviet authorities towards us was not changing. There was a marked distinction between official pronouncements of the Soviet leaders and the behavior of their petty officials.

Time was passing by, the arrested people in the prison were not released, the camp authorities were still sentencing people for new terms of confinement, and we were still under NKVD terror. One day a lieutenant of the NKVD arrived from Gorky. He began calling all heads of families for separate interviews. He was urging them to join the Red Army and to apply for Soviet citizenship. He was very critical of Poland. No one accepted his offer. There were dangerous moments during the interrogation. Then he announced the amnesty publicly and asked what our attitude towards the Polish Army was and where we wanted to go. We all gave positive answers: That we would join the Army or wished to be near its place of formation. But the instinct of self-preservation dictated that we should not disperse. So we decided to stay in the camp, to work and to wait for instructions from the Embassy.

After a week we received a certificate of amnesty valid for three months. This gave us some freedom of movement. Twenty-seven persons did not receive that certificate. They were told that it was simply an oversight.

We were informed that each person willing to join the Polish Army had to file an application (zayavtenia) to the Soviet Military Commissar in Sharii with a request to be directed to the Polish Army. The Commissar was going to send it to the Headquarters of the Polish Army, and upon receipt of a reply would call the applicants before the Soviet Drafting Board which would decide the fitness for military service of the volunteers and then make the final decision. In spite of the fact that the Poles were not too happy about that arrangement, over 300 persons filed applications only to learn four weeks later that there would not be any reply. Then, under strong pressure from the Poles, the Soviet authorities permitted the sending of a telegram to the Polish authorities. Such a telegram was dispatched with a post-paid reply, but there was no reply because the Soviet post office did not forward it. The same happened to the written appeal sent by mail.

The local Soviet authorities became more aggressive than before. The moral and material situation of the Poles began to deteriorate rapidly. Wages for work in the forest were stopped. When some of the deportees went into the villages to help pick potatoes in order to get food for their families, they were threatened with expulsion from the barracks and denial of the meager food rations.

Finally, one of the men made his way to Buzuluk, where the Army was forming, and informed the authorities about his camp and conditions there. A few weeks later a representative of the Embassy arrived to register all present.[4]

The Polish Embassy found itself confining all its efforts and attention to collecting and caring for the countless thousands of Poles who were being released from the prisons and labor camps spread over the most northern and far eastern peripheries of the Soviet Union. For this reason a special department, the "Department of Social Welfare," was established at the Embassy and placed under the supervision of Mr. Jan Szczyrek and his deputy, Mr. Emanuel Freyd. The objectives of the Department were:

1. To determine as soon as possible how many people were to be released from confinement.

2. To find out what kind of help they had received from the Soviets and to secure food and shelter for them from the Soviet authorities.

3. To get a list of the names of those released from the Soviet authorities.

4. To sound out Moscow about the possibility of a Soviet loan for the freed Poles.

5. To strive to resettle the liberated persons in the more tolerable regions of the Soviet Union, keeping in mind that:

(a) Those of military age would go to the Polish Army: its combat services or the women's corps.

(b) That specialists and other qualified persons would be placed in the Soviet war industry.

6. To establish a complete file of all Poles in the U.S.S.R.

7. To help dispersed families re-establish contacts with relatives or friends inside the U.S.S.R. or outside.

8. To inform London regularly about the amounts and kinds of needed help which could be sent from San Francisco and from India, and to suggest the most feasible routes of transportation.

9. To establish contact with the International Red Cross to enable the Poles in the U.S.S.R. to get in touch with their nearest relatives in Poland.[5]

Because of the complexity of the problems connected with the activities and objectives of this action, Ambassador Kot asked the Soviet authorities to establish a mixed Soviet-Polish commission which would deal with them. Such a commission was established under K. N. Novikov—who represented the *Narkomindel*—and one Commissar from the NKVD. The Polish side was represented by two members of the Embassy.

The first meeting of the Commission took place on September 9, 1941. The Polish side presented the 9 objectives just mentioned and suggested the following method of implementing them:

1. That the Soviet authorities should issue orders and instructions to local authorities, preferably over the radio, to report immediately the exact address of the given locality (poselok, rayon, oblast) where Polish people resided, to give their numbers, and to note especially the number of children and elders.

2. That the same instructions would include an appeal from the Polish Embassy which should transmit to the Poles the information that:

(a) All able-bodied persons between the ages of seventeen and fifty should proceed immediately to the center of the Polish Army in Buzuluk.

(b) The remainder should not change their residence without special instructions from the Polish Embassy. They should ask for such instructions by telegram.

3. That the places for resettlement should be established, keeping in mind:

(a) The size and capacity of the new places of settlement.

(b) Climatic conditions.

(c) The possibility of local employment for Poles, with the fullest use made of professional talents. The problem of employment would be a help in establishing a net of local citizens' committees under the general supervision and control of the Social Welfare Department of the Embassy.

4. That these local citizens' committees would register all Polish citizens in order to:

(a) Equip them with personal documents of identification.

(b) Execute instructions regarding employment.

(c) Extend care to the disabled and those otherwise incapable of work.

(d) Distribute the expected material help from abroad.

5. That trusted persons or the delegates of the committees should be especially permitted to purchase larger quantities of products from the State stores and they should have freedom of movement in the regions under their care. The price of the articles purchased should correspond to the norms provided for the working people.

6. That in accordance with the social principles of the U.S.S.R., the old, sick, and disabled and those unable to work should be sent to rest homes and to hospitals or medical centers.

7. That the committees should organize, with the help of the Soviet authorities, schools and recreation centers for the children and the youth.

8. That experience had shown that the local authorities refused to provide transportation to Poles who were on their way to new places of residence and also declined to pay fifteen rubles a day for their food and for their railroad tickets. This should be remedied.

9. That the disabled and those unfit for military service should be cared for by the local authorities. The kind of care they should receive should be established by the Mixed Soviet-Polish Commission.

During the subsequent meeting of the Commission, the Soviet side refused to permit the establishment of citizens' committees on the basis that these would be political institutions and, as such, not permissible. The Poles insisted that these committees would be of a strictly social character, but this explanation was not accepted. All the other suggested points were either ignored or answered in a vague manner. The Soviets permitted the broadcast of the Embassy appeal to the Poles, but the point was that nobody in the camps had a radio. They could listen only to what came over the public loud-speakers. The Soviets consequently never submitted a complete list of the released Poles or of their places of residence. The work of the mixed commission itself was suspended; there was nothing that it could do.

According to the information provided by the released Poles, there were numerous camps as yet unaffected by the decree of amnesty. Consequently, on October 13 Ambassador Kot sent the following note to Andrei Y. Vyshinsky, the Deputy People's Commissar for Foreign Affairs.

Mr. Commissar: Referring to the Note of the Chargé d'Affaires *ad interim* of the Republic of Poland addressed to the Commissar for Foreign Affairs, No. 30/41 of August 22, 1941, and the Note Verbale of the Polish Embassy, No. D. 467/41 of September 27, 1941, I have the honor, Mr. Commissar, to inform you of the following:

In both the aforesaid Notes, as in my conversation with you, Mr. Commissar, I emphasized particularly the need for the fulfillment by the Soviet Government of the provisions of the Agreement concluded between the Polish Government and the Soviet Government on July 30, 1941, and of the provisions of the Decree of the Presidium of the Supreme Soviet of the U.S.S.R. of August 12, 1941, concerning the release of Polish citizens from prisons, labor camps, and localities of compulsory residence at the earliest possible date; at least before the coming winter, during which the departure from many of the camps would be most difficult if not altogether impossible. The question of release was also brought up by the Polish delegation at the two meetings of the Mixed Soviet-Polish Commission, where emphasis was laid on the special urgency of this problem.

During my conversation with you, Mr. Commissar, on September 20, I received your assurance that the Soviet authorities would take care that Polish citizens detained in distant northern regions, where the climate is unsuitable for Poles, would be transported to more suitable districts before the winter season set in. During my conversation on October 7, I quoted figures relating to Polish citizens who were still detained in large numbers in camps, and mentioned the fact that certain categories among them had been transferred to very remote northern regions. In spite of repeated Polish requests and the assurances given on behalf of the Soviets, this Embassy has not as yet received the list of localities nor the exact number of Polish citizens released.

Contrary to the assurances that all Polish citizens, except for a small number of individuals suspected, indicted, or convicted of espionage on behalf of Germany, whose names and dossiers up to now have not been communicated to the Embassy, had been set free and that in a small number of cases only was delay caused by purely technical considerations, the Embassy is in possession of information that there are still thousands of Polish citizens in a number of prisons and camps who were not informed of the Agreement concluded on July 30, 1941, or who were informed that the provisions of this Agreement and of the Decree of the Presidium of the Supreme Soviet of the U.S.S.R. of August 12 did not apply to them.

By way of example, may I state that Polish citizens are still being detained in prison at Saratov, Gorky, Balashov, Chelyabinsk, Kizel and in compulsory labor camps in the Maritime Province, in the north-eastern extremity of the Yakut District (near the mouth of the Kolyma on the Arctic Ocean), near Aldan, in the region of Tomsk, Karaganda, in the mines of Karabash (Chelyabinsk District), in the Ivgel camp (Sverdlovsk District), in the Arkhangelsk District, and in the Republic of Komi, along the railway line under construction between Kotlas and Pechora, and at other points.

More detailed information concerning the numbers and condition of these Polish citizens is given in the Annex to the present Note. As will be seen therefrom, the local authorities either did not receive detailed orders concerning the treatment of Polish citizens after the conclusion of the Agreement of July 30, or, in some cases, the local authorities were content to deal with the matter in a purely *pro forma* way [the People's Commissariat of Internal Affairs withdrew police supervision of the 2,000 Polish citizens employed in the mines of Karabash-Voloshynovsky-Rudnik, but left the persons concerned where they were, which actually made their position worse than before] or with a partial execution of the orders issued. It is to be assumed that various considerations have dictated this treatment and in some instances local authorities may have desired to secure for themselves virtually unpaid man-power, whence the tendency to release sometimes elderly, invalid or ailing persons, while the stronger and healthier are retained for compulsory labor.

I have the honor to draw your attention, Mr. Commissar, to another characteristic feature of the conduct of local government authorities towards Polish citizens who are released, or who approach them with the request for employment or for the assignment of a residence. This conduct, without doubt unknown to the Central authorities and which should cease in the interests of good relations between the Polish and Soviet Governments, consists in informing those concerned that the blame for their difficult situation rests with the Polish Government and their representatives in the U.S.S.R. Naturally Polish nationals are not misled by this, but it arouses unnecessary mistrust among the Polish population.

Information issued abroad by the Polish Government, entirely in line with good Polish-Soviet collaboration, is to the effect that Polish citizens in the Union of Soviet Socialist Republics have been liberated from prisons and camps. I presented to you, on the 7th of this month, copies of communiqués issued by the Polish Telegraph Agency in London and New York. The Polish Government is of the opinion that such official information should correspond to the real situation of the Polish population in the U.S.S.R. In the common interests of both Governments, the Polish-Soviet Agreement should be fully carried out so that elements in foreign countries, unfriendly to this collaboration and hostile to the U.S.S.R. should not find a theme for their propaganda in the difficulties of the deported Polish population.

The Polish Government could in no case agree that, as a result of the Agreement of July 30, 1941, the lot of Polish citizens residing in the Union of Soviet Socialist Republics should become worse or that local authorities should carry out its provisions in a manner contrary to the declarations and statements of the representatives of the Soviet Government.

Consequently, in its Note, No. 30/41 of August 22, 1941, the Embassy presented a number of proposals forming a logical whole with a view to the practical solution of the problem of the Polish population in the U.S.S.R., in accordance with the interests of this population and of both Governments. The fact that the suggestions contained in point 2 were only carried out in part, and that points 3 and 4 were left completely unfulfilled, has meant that such Polish citizens as have been released have not been able to improve their living conditions, and that a large number of them have been forced to wander aimlessly and compelled to camp at railway stations or in the open air in the localities newly chosen for their residence. In view of the approaching winter, which in some parts of the Soviet Union has already set in, many of them are threatened with death by starvation. Their position is rendered still worse by the fact that the local authorities not only refuse to carry out the suggestions of the Embassy, but do not even comply with the assurances given by the People's Commissariat for Foreign Affairs contained in the Aide-Memoire of August 28, 1941, with regard to free railway fares, travelling subsidies, subsistence allowances and, most important of all, employment for the persons released.

I also venture to draw your attention, Mr. Commissar, to the fact that the organization of the Polish Army in the U.S.S.R. is not progressing in accordance with the letter and the spirit of the Agreement of July 30, 1941, or with the intentions of the two Governments.

The Supreme Command of the Polish Armed Forces in the U.S.S.R. has vainly waited four weeks for a decision on the formation of further Polish divisions and the designation of the localities in which this formation is to take place. In consequence, numerous Polish citizens reporting for military service and rallying en masse to the Polish Army stream into the two already overcrowded camps, which lack the necessary number of tents, adequate food supplies and medicines. Thus a situation, harmful alike to the troops and to the common cause, is being created. The local administrative authorities very often do not carry out the instructions issued by the Central authorities with regard to questions concerning the Polish Army and create new additional difficulties, as, for instance, by declining to release all Polish citizens, military and reservists, from prisons and camps and in many instances by detaining the more physically fit elements, which reduces the military value of the units already formed. Moreover, considerable numbers of Polish citizens enrolled in the Red Army and subsequently transferred to the so-called labor battalions, have not up to the present been re-directed to the Polish Army.

Thus the Polish contribution to the common struggle against Germany, contrary to the intentions of the Polish and Soviet Governments and to the unanimous will of the Polish citizens, is being weakened to the detriment of the cause of all the Allies.

In the profound belief that the Soviet Government attaches no less importance than the Polish Government to the development of friendly relations between the two States, I have the honor to request you, Mr. Commissar, to take measures to put into full effect all the proposals contained in the Note of the Embassy of August 22, and in particular the immediate release of all Polish citizens from prisons, camps, and localities of compulsory domicile, the friendly treatment of those who are unfit for military service and the acceleration of the decision concerning the formation of further large units of the Polish Army, in accordance with the letter and spirit of the Agreement of July 30, 1941.[6]

On October 16 a similar note was sent by Sikorski to the Soviet Ambassador in London, Bogomolov. On November 14, Bogomolov, replying to it and that of Ambassador Kot, denied all points as being based on misinformation.[7]

In the meantime, the Polish Embassy was informed by its delegates that Polish citizens of Ukrainian, Byelorussian, and Jewish origin who were released from Soviet prisons were being drafted into the Red Army. Upon instructions from London, Ambassador Kot protested to Vyshinsky against this arbitrary and illegal act.

According to information received, the War Commissar for Kazakhstan at Alma-Ata, General Schcherbakov, issued orders that all Polish citizens deported by the Soviet authorities from occupied Polish territory and possessing documents issued to them by these authorities, endorsed to the effect that they are of Ukrainian, Byelorussian, or Jewish origin are to be enrolled in the Red Army if they meet the age and fitness requirements.

After an intervention by the interested parties and by representatives of this Embassy, General Schcherbakov declared that he was acting on instructions from the Central authorities, who are alleged to have directed him to treat as citizens of the U.S.S.R. all citizens of the Republic of Poland of other than Polish origin possessing Soviet passports. Among others the following Polish citizens, despite protests on their part, were among those conscripted and sent, it would seem, to the Far East: Alexander Rothstein, Silberspits, and Kotok.

This same discrimination between Polish citizens according to origin or race, devoid of any impartial basis and contrary to the provisions of the Polish-Soviet Agreement of July 30, 1941, is being practiced by the military authorities in Alma-Ata, who also explain to the Polish citizens reporting to them to settle various formalities connected with their enlistment in the Polish Army in the Union of Soviet Socialist Republics, that they are acting on instructions from the Central authorities. Only Polish citizens of Polish origin are given permits to travel to centers where the Polish Army is being organized, while Polish citizens of Ukrainian and Jewish origin are, it seems, categorically refused permits by the aforementioned authorities.

The Polish Embassy has the honor to request the People's Commissariat for Foreign Affairs to cause instructions to be given to the War Commissar in Kazakhstan to apply impartially to all Polish citizens residing in the area under his authority, the principles deriving from the Polish-Soviet Agreement of July 30, 1941, and the Polish-Soviet Military Agreement of August 14, 1941, which guarantee the right to serve in the Polish Army in the U.S.S.R. to every Polish citizen who is capable of bearing arms.[8]

On December 1, Molotov sent the following reply:

Referring to the fact of the conscription by the Red Army in the Kazakh Soviet Socialist Republic, as Soviet citizens, of citizens of Ukrainian, Byelorussian, and Jewish origin who left the territories of Western Ukraine and Western Byelorussia, the Embassy of the Polish Republic calls in question the existence of a legal basis for this order, considering that it is contrary to the principles of the Soviet-Polish Agreement of July 30, 1941 and the Soviet-Polish Military Agreement of August 14, 1941.

The People's Commissariat cannot agree with this point of view of the Embassy of the Republic of Poland. No foundation to support the point of view expressed in the Note of the Embassy of the Republic of Poland, referred to above, can be found in the Agreement of July 30, or in the Military Agreement of August 14, 1941. In accordance with the Decree of the Presidium of the Supreme Soviet of the U.S.S.R. of November 29, 1939, all citizens of Western districts of the Ukrainian and Byelorussian S.S.R.'s who found themselves on the territory of the said districts on November 1 and 2, 1939, respectively, acquired the citizenship of the U.S.S.R. in accordance with the Citizenship of the Union of Soviet Socialist Republics Act of August 19, 1938. The Soviet Government's readiness to recognize as Polish citizens persons of Polish origin, who resided (until November 1 and 2, 1939) on the aforementioned territory, gives evidence of good will and compliance on the part of the Soviet Government, but can in no case serve as a basis for an analogous recognition of the Polish citizenship of persons of other origin, in particular those of Ukrainian, Byelorussian, or Jewish origin, since the question of the frontiers between the U.S.S.R. and Poland has not been settled and is subject to settlement in the future.[9]

When the difficulties grew beyond manageable proportions, Ambassador Kot asked for an audience with Stalin. This was granted, and on November 14 he was received by Stalin and presented the issues which were causing friction between the two Governments. Stalin promised to remove all the causes of complaint and took that occasion to declare that "I am particularly interested in restoring a free and independent Polish State with an internal political and social system of its own choice." [10]

It took considerable time before the Poles realized that there was a vast difference between Stalin's polite promises and the performance of his subordinates. These latter were often blamed for completely contrary interpretations of his decisions, although actually, as it was found later, they were executing the real intentions of the dictator himself.

This hopeless situation was by-passed by the decision of the Poles to proceed on their own and to salvage what they could of the situation. First of all, they decided to register all Polish citizens. This had to be based on reports from various individuals and from various places where Poles were discovered and which the Embassy managed to reach. It obviously did not embrace every center.

Up to December 15, 1941 it was established that the number of Poles located in various *oblasts* was as listed on page 78.

On the basis of various reports received by the Embassy, it was estimated that between 15% and 20% of this number had died between the time they were taken from Poland and December 1941. These were mainly children, old people, women, and the sick. This indicated and confirmed that over one million Poles had been deported to the U.S.S.R. It was also estimated that as a result of the twenty months of starvation, hard labor, and disease, about 60% of the above number were disabled or unfit for work. This included women and children.

The most difficult problem for the Embassy was to arrive at any reliable estimate of the Poles drafted into the Red Army or into *stroybattalions* (labor battalions) which were under military control. They were not included in the "amnesty" and their fate was most tragic. They were treated worse than Soviet citizens.

The majority of Poles were forced to work in mines and forests

Russian SFSR

Arkhangelsk Oblast	40,000	
Chelyabinsk Oblast	5,000	
Gorky Oblast	5,000	
Kirov Oblast	5,000	
Komi ASSR Oblast	35,000	
Molotov Oblast	7,000	
Mari ASSR Oblast	4,000	
Vologda Oblast	5,000	
Irkutsk Oblast	12,000	
Sverdlovsk Oblast	8,000	
Krasnoyarsk Krai	10,000	
Novosibirsk Oblast	12,000	
Omsk Oblast	3,000	
Altai Oblast	12,000	
Yakut ASSR Oblast	5,000	168,000

Kazakh SSR

Alma-Ata Oblast	10,000	
Akmolinsk Oblast	12,000	
Aktyubinsk Oblast	12,000	
Dzhambul Oblast	30,000	
Kustanai Oblast	10,000	
Pavlodar Oblast	10,000	
South Kazakh Oblast	40,000	
Semipalatinsk Oblast	15,000	139,000

Kirghiz Republic	5,000	
Tadzhik Republic	5,000	
Turkmen Republic	20,000	
Uzbek Republic	80,000	
Others	50,000	160,000

Total		467,000
Military Centers		40,000
Total		507,000

Those deported to Franz Josef Land, the Kolyma area or drafted into the Red Army were estimated to be approximately 300,000

Approximate grand total accounted for 807,000

(*leso-povals*). They were not allowed to work in factories. A considerable portion of them worked on the building of three railroad lines, Arkhangelsk-Byelomorsk, Kotlas-Vorkuta, and Akmolinsk-Kartaly.

Even the "amnesty," when strictly applied to certain numbers of the deported, proved to be a great burden. The NKVD stopped issuing food rations. This forced the freed Poles to look for work, which was not easy to come by; for in the documents issued to them by the NKVD, it was stated that they could not settle in cities of the first or second categories—which meant the large industrial cities. Outside cities in these categories, it was extremely difficult to secure employment or to purchase food. The situation became further complicated when whole masses of people began migrating south to Uzbekistan, Kirghizistan, Tadzhikistan, Turkmenistan, and Kazakhstan (especially to Alma-Ata) in order to escape the approaching winter and to find food. This chaos lasted several weeks, only to be stopped when they were rounded up by the Soviet authorities and transported back to the northern regions. In order to obtain food, the deportees had to sell the last pieces of clothing which they could spare.

These hungry and cold masses of people became an extraordinary problem to the Embassy. For a long time it was not in a position to extend any of the help needed, because the NKVD would not permit it. Only after the exchange of numerous sharply worded notes with the Narkomindel did the Soviets give tacit permission to direct the freed deportees to the former German republic along the Volga. It was subsequently found that this was not feasible, and so the regions of Buzuluk and Totsk were chosen instead. The choice was dictated by the presence of the Polish military camp, which could employ a certain number of the civilians in various services. From that time on, the Soviets provided transportation which consisted of unheated cattle trains not equipped with any food. The journey often lasted over a week, and only the ingenuity of the most energetic passengers and the ordinary human sympathy of natives en route enabled most of them to reach their destination. The weaker ones did not survive.

The tragedy is illustrated by the following reports submitted to the Embassy by reliable individuals:

COL. DR. TORWINSKI, October 10, 1941. Huge waves of Poles are continuously arriving at Novosibirsk from Krasnoyarsk Krai, Irkutsk Oblast, Yakut Republic, etc. They are coming individually, in small or large groups, and then move on further south. Most of them are in a lamentable condition, exhausted, in shabby rags, hungry and without money. They have sold everything that they had to buy railroad tickets for themselves and their families. All of them are under a powerful psychosis to get out as soon as possible and at any price to the south. We have no means to help them. Children are dying in great numbers. Please send help.[11]

DR. STANISLAW KODZ, November 18, 1941, reported from Tashkent: We are swamped with great numbers of sick and dying—particularly children. Every day new transports are arriving. Work on the fields (i.e., in Kagan) is over. We located 7,000 people in the Kolkhozys but more than 6,000 of them are without work. In Farab 4,000 of our people are camping out in the open air without any shelter whatsoever. They are gradually moving south on open barges along the Amu-Darya River. Many of them get wet and the temperature is low. The mortality rate is growing rapidly. Many transports which arrive here from Omsk consist up to 10% of dead bodies. Others faint from hunger.[12]

Similar conditions were reported from numerous other regions.

The vast distances and the imperfect Soviet system of communication were not helpful to the Embassy in extending its aid. Railroads were overworked by military transports. Food was located in governmental stores and could not be given away or sold without a special order. The Embassy attempted to send money by telegraph, but in most cases it took over two weeks before it reached its destination. Consequently, the Ambassador sent his representatives to all the major railroad stations through which Poles were traveling in order to distribute money and bread. In some cases and in certain places the Soviet authorities were helpful, but this was the exception and not the rule.

On November 21, the Soviet authorities decided to evacuate 45,000 Poles back north to Uzbekistan. Jan Kwapinski (a socialist leader and later a member of the Polish Government in London) reported to Kot:

On the night of November 21, in all the kolkhozes and sovhozes where Poles were located, the Soviet authorities issued an order to get ready for departure in fifteen minutes to one hour. No one received any supply of food. Then all were moved to railroad stations: Kiseldipi, Bukhara, Karshi, Guzar, Kiplap, and Kagan. People were exhausted and depressed by the previous weeks and months of the journey south. They were afraid of the northern climate and conditions. But an "ukaz" cannot be changed. They were packed into trains and disappeared without trace.[13]

Then an order was issued by the Soviet authorities to stop all other transports of Poles south. It took several months and considerable pressure before they were resumed and the people shifted to places chosen by Stalin.

The Embassy realized that even with the best organized help it could not save all those who benefited from the amnesty. The undernourished, the sick, and particularly the women and children could not withstand the hardship of the winter.

But at least for those who managed to reach the region of Buzuluk, where the Polish Army was formed, or Kuybyshev, where the Embassy was located after its evacuation from Moscow, their welfare was improved.

An urgent appeal was issued by the Polish Embassy and Government to Britain and to the United States for help, but it was understood that considerable time would elapse before any relief would be available.

With the verbal consent of Vyshinsky, Ambassador Kot developed an extensive scheme to send his delegates to all the republics and *oblasts* where Poles were known to reside. It was decided that the delegates would be located in the capitals of those republics or oblasts. They, in turn, would choose trusted men who would be located in the capitals of the regions, and these would be helped by assistants attached to the actual settlements of the Poles. The prerogatives of these officials were spelled out in a mutual agreement between the Polish Embassy and Vyshinsky.

In the beginning of September this plan was put into operation, and the names of the delegates and their places of assignment were submitted to the Narkomindel. The Embassy was informed that the local Soviet authorities were not only unwilling to extend any help to these representatives but that they even began to ostracize them. They were also informed that no instructions were received from the Narkomindel. Intervention with the latter did not bring immediate results, but the Poles did not give up.

By the beginning of December 1941 the representatives of the Embassy were located in the following republics, krais, oblasts, or regions:

1. Akmolinsk Oblast, Kalininski Region
2. Aktyubinsk Oblast
3. Altai Krai
4. Alma-Ata Oblast
5. Arkhangelsk Oblast
6. Gorky Oblast and Region
7. Irkutsk Oblast, Nizhne-Udinsk Region
8. Irkutsk Oblast, Bodaibo Region
9. Yakut ASSR, Aldai Region
10. Komi ASSR
11. Komi ASSR, Letsk and Pryluzhsk Regions
12. Kirov Oblast, Nagorsk Region
13. North Kazakhstan Oblast, Krasnoarmeysk Region
14. Mari Republic, Gorno Mari Region
15. Novosibirsk Oblast, Tomsk Region
16. Novosibirsk Oblast, Asino Region
17. Novosibirsk Oblast, Zhyryansk Region
18. Novosibirsk Oblast, Suzun Region

19. Pavlodar Oblast, Bayan-Aul Region
20. South Kazakhstan Oblast
21. Semipalatinsk Oblast
22. Semipalatinsk Oblast, Bel-Agatsk Region
23. Semipalatinsk Oblast, Georgevsk Region
24. Semipalatinsk Oblast, Zarma Region
25. Semipalatinsk Oblast, Urdzhar Region
26. Semipalatinsk Oblast, Kokpekty Region
27. Semipalatinsk Oblast, Novoshuldinsk Region
28. Semipalatinsk Oblast, Ayaguz Region
29. Sverdlovsk Oblast, Krasnouralsk Region
30. Sverdlovsk Oblast, Revda Region
31. Tadzhik SSR
32. Uzbek SSR [14]

The Soviet authorities were not too happy about this network of the Embassy. Several delegates, mainly in Sverdlovsk, Arkhangelsk, and Tashkent were confidentially invited to collaborate with the NKVD. When they refused, their usefulness as representatives of the Embassy was finished. The work of others was handicapped by the outright refusal of local authorities to cooperate.

This difficulty was partially overcome when the Embassy sent a team of roving representatives, Prof. M. Hitzman and Dr. R. Szumski, together with an officer of the NKVD. They traveled 8,000 kilometers and brought back very valuable material. Three other teams were dispatched without NKVD representatives (the NKVD was unwilling to appoint any) and this was a cause of protests from the Soviet authorities.

A certain amount of chaos was created when General Anders sent military teams to take over control of the civilian population. The considerable confusion lasted until Ambassador Kot imposed civilian supremacy and confined military activity to its own sphere.

Kot expected a definite improvement in Soviet-Polish relations from an announced visit of Sikorski[15] to Moscow. Sikorski arrived in the beginning of December, and on December 3 he was received by Stalin. Present also at the meeting were Molotov, Kot, Anders, and Molotov's secretary.[16]

SIKORSKI. I am extremely glad that I can greet one of the real makers of modern history, and congratulate you, Mr. President, on the heroism of the Russian Army in the fight with the Germans. As a soldier, I would like to express my admiration for the valiant defense of Moscow led so successfully by you, Mr. President, who himself remained in the capital. Simultaneously I thank you, Mr. President, for the great hospitality which has been extended to me from the very moment I stepped upon Soviet soil.

STALIN. I thank you, Mr. Prime Minister, for what you said and I am very glad to see you in Moscow.

SIKORSKI. I will begin by stating that I have never conducted, and have never agreed with the policy directed against Soviet Russia over the past twenty years. I am, therefore, morally entitled to sign this pact, since it may bring about the final fulfillment of the principles which I have upheld for so long. Furthermore, I have, in this problem so vital for the future, the backing of the Polish nation in our country as well as in all Polish communities abroad, either larger ones such as those in America where four and a half million Poles live, or in Canada and in France where there are six hundred thousand Poles, or in other smaller communities. Opposed to me are those who did not conduct such a policy as mine. I would not want an overly slow realization of this agreement to weaken the policy of rapprochement and of friendly co-existence between our two nations. Whether we have really reached a turning point in history depends upon a complete and loyal realization of this agreement. This, in turn, depends on you, since your decisions are authoritative in this country. Therefore, it is necessary that our agreement be realized, that the chicaneries, annoying our population disappear. . . .

I return, however, to our problem. I confirm in your presence, Mr. President, that your declaration about the amnesty is not being fulfilled. Many of our people, a great number of very prominent men, are still kept in labor camps and in prisons.

STALIN [taking notes]. This is impossible, as the amnesty has referred to all, and all Poles have been released. [The last words are directed toward Molotov. Molotov nods.]

ANDERS [gives details upon request of General Sikorski]. This is not in accordance with the real facts, since we possess the most concrete data that first Jews, then Ukrainians, and finally physically weaker Polish laboring groups were released from the camps. Stronger ones were retained, the local authorities releasing but a small number of them. I have in my armed forces people who have been released but a few weeks ago from such camps, and they confirm that hundreds and even thousands of our countrymen are still retained in each individual camp. Governmental orders are not carried out there, because the commanders of the individual camps, who are responsible for the fulfillment of their plan of production, do not want to lose their best laboring groups, without which the fulfillment of the plan of production might be at times impossible.

MOLOTOV [smiles and nods his head].

ANDERS. These people do not understand the real weight of our common problem, and this is extremely detrimental to our common problem.

STALIN. These people should be taken before the courts.

SIKORSKI. It is not up to us to supply the Soviet Government with accurate lists of names of our people; however, complete lists are in the possession of the commanders of the camps. I have with me a list containing the names of approximately 4,000 officers who were deported by force and who presently still remain in the prisons and labor camps. Even this list is not complete, since it contains only those names which we were able to record from memory. I ordered that checks be made whether they are back in Poland, with which we have steady contact. It has been proven that not one of them is there, and likewise not in our prisoner of war camps in Germany. These people are here. Not one of them has returned.

STALIN. That is impossible, they have escaped.

ANDERS. Where then could they escape?

STALIN. Well, to Manchuria.

ANDERS. It is impossible that all could escape, the more impossible considering the fact that since they have been deported from prisoner of war camps to labor camps and prisons, their correspondence with their families has stopped completely. I know perfectly well, being informed by officers who have already returned even from Kolyma, that there are still a large number of officers remaining there. Many of them are mentioned by name. I know that groups of Poles were already prepared for release and departure, but they were retained at the last moment. I am informed that our people are found even in Novaya Zemlya. The greater number of the officers mentioned in this list I know personally. Among them are commanders and officers of my staff. These people perish and starve there under terrible conditions.

STALIN. Surely they have been released, but have not as yet arrived.

SIKORSKI. Russia is immense and the difficulties are great. Maybe the local authorities did not carry out the orders. Those who arrive after being released confirm that others who remain there just merely exist and labor. And if anyone should succeed in getting beyond the boundaries of Russia, he would surely report to me.

STALIN. I want you to know that the Soviet Government has not the slightest reason to retain even one Pole; I released even Sosnkowski's agents, who attacked us and murdered our people.

ANDERS. However, we received evidence about people whom we know very well, evidence containing names of prisons and numbers of cells in which they are confined. I know the names of many camps in which an extremely large number of Poles have been retained and must continue to labor.

MOLOTOV. We have retained only those, who, after the war, had committed felony, stimulated diversion, set up radio stations, and the like. You will surely not concern yourself about these.

KOT. Certainly not; however, I have asked many times that lists of these people be given us, because people whom I know as ardent patriots and who are absolutely innocent are very often charged with this.

MOLOTOV [nods].

SIKORSKI. Let's not touch the questions which arose during the war. It would be useful now if you, Mr. President, would make a public statement pertaining to this matter, in order to bring about a basic reversal of the situation of the Poles in Soviet Russia. Certainly they are not tourists here, but people taken by force from their homes. They did not come here of their own free will, but were deported and have survived tremendous sufferings.

STALIN. The attitude of the population in the Soviet Union toward the Poles is favorable. Only officials can make mistakes.

ANDERS. It is not only our concern that the officials carry out their orders badly, but it is also our concern that the population should understand that the Poles are gathered in certain places not of their own will. We are particularly interested in good relations with the population.

SIKORSKI. In Kuybyshev I saw a transport of our people which impressed me terribly. It is necessary to give them speedy relief. I classify our people into two groups—those who are able to work and those who are not. The former should be given work under best conditions possible.

STALIN. On the same conditions as Soviet citizens.

SIKORSKI. It does not matter that they be the same, however, simply tolerable ones. The proper use of our people lies in the interest of our joint war efforts. You of course understand, Mr. President, that an expert in building tanks who is now felling trees in a forest, or a distinguished chemist who does physical work on farms is not properly utilized. The second category of our citizens consists of people unfit for work, old men, women, and children, who should all be gathered into places with favorable conditions and climate, so that our Embassy could look after them. From the labor camps everyone should be released at once, while those who were deported and who are living in settlements under tolerable conditions may remain there for the time being. An uncoordinated moving of people back and forth causes only ill feelings, as they find themselves under very severe conditions, and in the end result it may come about that I, by making this pact with you, only did them wrong. People even die of these terrible conditions. Their corpses will heavily influence our future relations. These people must be helped instantly, and it is not worthwhile to bargain over a few million rubles which during the war do not play any part whatsoever. A loan to the Polish Government should be given on a large scale.

It is also necessary that delegates of the Embassy be given permission to enter Polish communities and be granted true and not fictitious rights. As an example, our delegate in Arkhangelsk is not able to give any help to our population, and his work is limited only to the dispatching of transports. He cannot even distribute warm clothing to the Polish population. I am also concerned that a mission of the Embassy should be set up in Vladivostok. The Polish community in America has collected many things for Poles in Russia; however, they make the shipment dependent upon the condition that it be delivered into Polish hands, to delegates of the Embassy.

STALIN. I agree as to the delegates and also as to Vladivostok.

MOLOTOV. I believe it impossible that your people are still in the camps.

ANDERS. Nevertheless, I definitely confirm that they are; I repeat that the strongest are retained because they need workers. The retention of our people serves our joint cause badly.

STALIN. This will be settled. Special orders will be given to the authorities. However it should be understood that we are conducting a war.

SIKORSKI. And you conduct it well.

STALIN. Oh, no, just fairly. Our system of transport was terribly overloaded. We shipped out the wounded, evacuated the population, transferred seventy large factories. We were forced to transfer armed forces back and forth. Your Poles should understand the tremendous difficulties that we had. But it will be better.

SIKORSKI. The Polish population should be located in a province with a better climate.

STALIN. We have to think over what regions can be assigned to the Poles. We regularly deliver grain to Fergana and Uzbekistan, because we produce cotton there and we have even issued special orders prohibiting the raising of grain. From this point of view these territories are not convenient. However, the southern regions of the Semipalatinsk Province would be more adaptable. We can even see how it looks on the map [all rise and approach the map, Stalin points to the map]. Thus, Tashkent, Alma-Ata, and the entire southern Kazakhstan.

KOT. The territories around Barnaul and Novosibirsk would be better for those from the Far East.

STALIN. It is cold there but bread is abundant.

KOT. But where can those be sent who are in the Arkhangelsk Province and in Komi?

STALIN. Also to southern Kazakhstan. [They sit down at the table.]

SIKORSKI. Regarding the loan, I think that one hundred million rubles would settle the case for a long time, if only for the reason that it not cause a bad impression, and so that you would avoid the charge that you make difficulties over such insignificant matters.

MOLOTOV. Of course, we have already given sixty-five million.

KOT. But that was for the armed forces.

SIKORSKI. Hitler taught everyone how, without gold and only through labor, great things can be created. Do not follow, Mr. Commissar, the example of the Western ministers of treasury who in the beginning bargained for every million.

STALIN [nodding]. Good.

SIKORSKI. That is all that I wanted to say about the Polish civilian population. Now I must bring up military matters. Should I speak about the whole problem immediately, or shall we discuss its elements successively?

STALIN. As you wish, General.

SIKORSKI. We Poles do not consider warfare as a symbol but as a true fight.

STALIN [makes a nodding gesture].

ANDERS. We want to fight for Poland's independence here on the continent.

SIKORSKI. In our homeland we have a strong military organization, which I had ordered to remain quiet, because there people are shot for every word. [Stalin nods.] [General Sikorski gives several details pertaining to the methods of fighting of the Polish nation against the Germans.] Our army fights everywhere. In Great Britain we have a corps which needs reinforcements. We possess a navy which performs excellently. We have in action seventeen air force units which are equipped with the most modern English planes, and they fight superbly. Twenty percent of the German Air Force losses in England were caused by Polish pilots.

STALIN. I know that Poles are valiant.

SIKORSKI. If they are well led. Thanks to Providence, and thanks to you, Mr. President, we have here with us General Anders, my best soldier, whose eight stars received for wounds prove his valor. You put him into prison because he wanted to join me. This is a loyal leader, not a politician, who will not allow any of his subordinates to conduct any political activity.

STALIN. The best policy is to fight well. [Turning to Anders.] How long did you stay in prison?

ANDERS. Twenty months.

STALIN. How were you treated?

ANDERS. In Lwów exceptionally badly, in Moscow slightly better. But you, Mr. President, know yourself what "better" means in a prison if one is confined for twenty months.

STALIN. Well, such were the conditions.

SIKORSKI. I have one brigade in Tobruk which will be transferred to Syria and reorganized into a motorized division with two tank battalions. If the need arises I can transfer it here to the East. We have a few navy vessels. When I had decorated the sailors from one submarine which was stationed in Malta and which had sunk an Italian cruiser and a transport ship, the crew of this submarine became so enthusiastic that immediately afterwards the submarine entered a Greek port and, even with a damaged periscope, sank another cruiser and one Greek transport ship. They returned without any losses. The Polish soldier will fight in this manner everywhere, if he is led well. Our homeland is occupied, and we have here the only reserve of our youths. I wish to send to Scotland and Egypt approximately 25,000 as reinforcements. We should form about seven divisions with the rest. This is extremely important for the homeland, which is looking at the Polish Army as a symbol of its resistance and independence. We want to fight, and that is why our armed forces in Scotland will be used as a vanguard for the establishment of a second front, or will be transferred here to the East. In this latter case I would personally take the command. The present difficulties of feeding, equipping and training make me anxiously concerned lest the formations created under such conditions will be completely useless. Instead of sacrificing health and life for the common cause, people merely exist here or perish in vain. The war will be long. Great Britain and the United States disarmed themselves too much, and their war industry, particularly the American, needs much time to achieve full capacity of production. With time, the avalanche of war materials will grow. However, I already have Roosevelt's and Churchill's assurance that they will equip our divisions parallel with yours, without straining the shipment for you, but under the condition that the formation of our armed forces will take place in regions to which supplies can be sent without much trouble. The present state of equipping our divisions is completely inadequate. The divisions under such conditions are incapable of fighting, since they did not receive all of the necessary equipment. General Anders will explain this to you in detail.

ANDERS [explains in detail the state of the equipment received and the entire matter of equipping the Polish armed forces, stressing the insurmountable difficulties which appear every day].

STALIN [inquires about certain details of artillery equipment]. Russia entered the war with divisions each having 15,000 men, which however in practice proved too large. Therefore, we changed over to a type of light divisions having a strength of approximately 11,000 men in each.

SIKORSKI. The conditions under which the Polish forces are now formed are completely inadequate. The soldiers freeze in summer tents, feel the want of food, and are simply doomed to slow extinction. Therefore, I propose that the entire army and all the people eligible for military service be moved, for instance, to Persia where the climate as well as the promised

American and British help would allow these people to recover within a short time and form a strong army which would return here to the front and take over the section assigned to them. This has been settled with Churchill. On my part I am ready to declare that these forces will return to the Russian front, and that they might even be strengthened by several British divisions.

ANDERS [continues to present the situation of the armed forces which are formed at present and confirms that under such conditions of food supplies, housing, sanitation, and of unfavorable climate, the organization of units capable of warfare is completely unfeasible]. This is simply a miserable existence toward which all the efforts of the people are directed, to live and to live very badly! It is, of course, our concern that the Polish Army be prepared for war as soon as possible and fight for Poland with our Allies, which under these conditions is absolutely impossible. Therefore, it is essential to transfer the forces into an area with such conditions of climate, food, and supply, which would allow the whole problem to be solved. Faced with the difficulties in which Russia finds herself, we must take into consideration the facility of Anglo-American shipping. The most adequate area is Persia. All the soldiers and all men capable of military service should locate themselves there. When we take part in fighting, the striking force of our Army should not only be a symbol but it should serve towards the aim, the struggle for Poland, for which we are fighting in the entire world.

SIKORSKI. I hope that the Soviet Government will look with confidence upon my proposition. I am a person who, when I say yes, then I mean yes, when I say no, it means no, and when I say nothing, I either cannot or do not want to tell the truth.

STALIN [expression of excitement and evident displeasure]. I am a person of experience and of age. I know that if you go to Persia you will never return here. I see that England has much to do and needs Polish soldiers.

SIKORSKI. We are united with Great Britain by an alliance which she fulfills loyally. We have full sovereignty in Great Britain. I can even bring a corps from Scotland here, and I am sure that no one in England would trouble me about it. Likewise, I can attach the units stationed at Tobruk to our forces here.

KOT. A Pole fights especially well when he is near his fatherland.

STALIN. Iran is not far from here, but the English may force you to fight against the Germans on Turkish territory, and tomorrow Japan may enter the war.

ANDERS. We want to fight for Poland. We believe that even the strongest air force and navy will not end the war. The battles on the continent will end the war. We all, without exception, love our country and want to enter it first, we want to be ready for fighting as soon as possible, but under the conditions which we now face, it is impossible to prepare ourselves for it.

SIKORSKI. England of today and of the past is heaven and earth. The English now have enough armed forces to defend their Isles, therefore, they have no reason not to allow our corps to leave them.

MOLOTOV [proposes that General Panfilov be called and gives orders to the secretary who is leaving].

ANDERS [explains the difficulties of forming forces, the living conditions in Koltubianka, Tatishchev and Totsk, and the lack of punctuality in the delivery of food, fodder, equipment, tools, and so on]. This is only a miserable existence and months are wasted. Under such conditions it is impossible to form armed forces.

STALIN [angry]. If the Poles do not want to fight, then let them go. We cannot hold back the Poles. If they want to, they may go away.

SIKORSKI. If we had been allowed to organize ourselves, we would be fighting already. But, so much time is wasted here for which we are not to blame. In the areas where our soldiers are now quartered, we still do not have facilities for their training. [An interval of silence.] I, therefore, must ask for another solution.

STALIN. If the Poles do not want to fight here then let them say so, one way or the other. I am sixty-two years old and I know that where an army is formed, there it remains.

SIKORSKI [in a sharper tone]. Then please show me another solution because the proper conditions for organizing of our armed forces are not available here, and I do not want people to perish in vain. I am not presenting an ultimatum, but when there is a severe winter, winds and frost, from which people perish, I cannot look at it and remain silent.

ANDERS. Where I am the freezing temperatures have already fallen to 33° C below zero. The people live in simple tents, the majority without heating stoves, which are not supplied to us in a sufficient number. They awaken in the morning with frozen noses and ears. This is not an organization of armed forces but simply sheer existence.

SIKORSKI. One cannot throw an untrained soldier against the Germans. One cannot be exposed to disgrace. The Polish Army must be well armed and fight as a body.

ANDERS. Even so, I have full admiration for our soldiers as they have never complained, in spite of their extreme sufferings during the past two years and in spite of the horrible conditions under which they now live. Only two weeks ago they had received shoes, until then 60% of them were barefoot. They never received their due share of food, and for a long time were not even paid.

SIKORSKI [emphatically]. You hurt me, Mr. President, by saying that our soldier does not want to fight.

STALIN. I am rough (*grubiy*) and I want to know clearly whether you want to fight or not.

SIKORSKI [emphatically]. That we want to is proven not by words but by facts.

ANDERS. That is why we are organizing, in order to fight here and we understand that we will fight on the continent. According to my calculations I can have 150,000 soldiers; this is equivalent to eight divisions. But we do not have quite two divisions, and the formation is limited to that. We do not receive our due share of food and all promises to complete it are not fulfilled.

STALIN [turning to General Sikorski]. As you wish, Sir.

SIKORSKI. I do not want the matter to be presented in that way. I am still waiting for a new formula and I am ready to accept every just solution.

STALIN [with a shade of irony]. I see that the English are in need of good armed forces.

SIKORSKI. This estimate is not exact. In England they value us, but they do not exploit us. I know Churchill very well, and I know that he wants to do all he can to help Russia.

ANDERS. Sixty percent of my people are from the reserves, but they must recover from two years of hardship and must be retrained. Volunteers likewise are in very bad shape and must undergo proper training, for which time and proper conditions are necessary.

STALIN [angry]. That means that we are savages, and that we can not improve anything. It amounts to this, that a Russian can only oppress a Pole, but is unable to do anything good for him. However, we can do without you. We can give back all of them. We will manage ourselves. We will conquer Poland and then we will give her back to you. But what will people say to this? They will ridicule us all over the world that we are not able to achieve anything here.

SIKORSKI. I did not receive a reply as to where I am to establish an army, so that it could participate in the war but not perish from the horrible climatic conditions. I ask for concrete counter-propositions. I categorically confirm once again that we want to fight for Poland and at your side.

STALIN. When you go to Iran then perhaps you will have to fight in Turkey against the Germans. Tomorrow Japan will enter the war, then against Japan. So as the English will order. Perhaps in Singapore.

ANDERS. It is on the continent that we want to fight the Germans for Poland. Our people have not seen their country for a long time, and no one loves his country as much as the Poles do. From here it is closest to Poland.

SIKORSKI. The patriotism of the Poles does not have to be proven. I confirm that I still have no clear counter-proposition.

STALIN. If you insist—one corps, two to three divisions, may leave. However, if you so desire, I shall assign the place and the means necessary for the forming of seven divisions. I see, however, that the English need Polish soldiers. I, of course, have received Harriman's and Churchill's request to evacuate the Polish Army.

SIKORSKI. The English are not so badly off that the Polish Army formed here would decide their fate. They are slow. However, today they represent a great power. It was I who demanded that Churchill request the evacuation of our armed forces. I will, however, prove my good will; I am ready to leave the army in Russia, if you assign an adequate region for its concentration and if you assure to it equipment and supplies and proper quarters, and so establish adequate conditions for its training.

MOLOTOV. Panfilov is ready. Gentlemen, do you have any objections against Panfilov entering the room? [All nod, and shortly Panfilov, the Deputy Chief of Staff of the Red Army enters the room.] [A conversation, concerning the conditions for the organization of Polish forces, follows with Stalin, General Anders, and General Panfilov; each side brings up various details.]

ANDERS. I confirm categorically that I do not receive the due share of food nor fodder for horses. The divisions have not received their due rations of food, nor articles of equipment so necessary, like stoves for the tents. Several months have passed since I was promised delivery of tractors, but up to this time they have not arrived. All our requests remain without results, and promises from Soviet military authorities remain unfulfilled. I have typhoid fever in my units, and all my begging for a hospital train has been futile. For several months the soldiers have not received any soap, tools for construction, lumber or nails. The soldiers never receive any vegetables. Many additional food products are never delivered. The means of transportation are absolutely inadequate and in very bad shape. A few weeks ago the food rations were suddenly cut from 44,000 to 30,000. In spite of President Stalin's promise to our Ambassador, that rations would be restored to 44,000, up to now it has not been carried out. On the 1st of December the entire camp in Totsk did not receive any food at all. [He enumerates a series of other shortages and lacks of food and supplies.] It does not comply with facts that we did not remind them about it. I myself continuously turned to the Liaison Officer, Colonel Volkovsky, and I myself sent out dispatches and letters. [Panfilov remains silent.] I went after these matters a great deal personally.

STALIN [very sharply to Panfilov]. Who is responsible for this?

PANFILOV. Proper instructions were issued, the orders were given by General Khrulov.

STALIN. When did I give the orders for increasing the number of food rations?

PANFILOV. Two and a half weeks ago.

STALIN. Why then has the order not been carried out up to now? Shall they eat your directives? [This entire part of the conversation is conducted in a very harsh tone by Stalin. Panfilov is standing at attention—turning colors.]

SIKORSKI. Only the extreme difficulties which we are encountering here, and the bad conditions, have compelled me to present the matter in this way.

STALIN. We can give the Polish Army the same conditions as we give the Red Army.

SIKORSKI. Under the conditions existing up to now, not even a corps will be established.

STALIN. I understand that they are bad. Our units are organized under better conditions. I say this sincerely, that if they can give you better conditions in Iran, then as far as we are concerned, we are able to offer only such conditions as we give our Army. Food for our soldiers is better than what the Germans have.

ANDERS. If they will receive all the food which is due a soldier, then I consider it sufficient, but it should be delivered without those continuous shortages which we encounter. I myself must have the opportunity to manage and establish my own stocks and not live from one day to the next; when a transport does not arrive then people often go hungry.

SIKORSKI. I confirm once again our desire for fighting jointly with you against the Germans, our common foe.

STALIN. It seemed to me that the English need your army.

SIKORSKI. No, it was I, seeing what difficulties we have to face here, that requested the English and Americans to move our soldiers to better conditions.

ANDERS [gives detailed explanations about the number of Polish soldiers in the area of the southern territories of Russia, enumerating particular localities. A discussion follows about the places where they are being formed. The names of Uzbekistan, Turkmenistan, and Transcaucasia are mentioned]. I am counting on 150,000 people, that is eight divisions together with the army's maintenance forces. Perhaps there are even more of our people, but among them there are also a great number of Jews who do not want to serve in the army.

STALIN. Jews are poor warriors.

SIKORSKI. Many from among the Jews who reported are speculators or those who have been punished for contraband; they will never make good soldiers. Those I don't need in the Polish Army.

ANDERS. Two hundred Jews deserted from Buzuluk, upon hearing the false report of the bombing of Kuybyshev. More than sixty deserted from the 5th Division a day before the distribution of arms to the soldiers was made public.

STALIN. Yes, Jews are bad warriors.

[A discussion follows among Stalin, Anders, and Panfilov concerning armament and its shortages. Verifications and calculations are made from lists.]

SIKORSKI. When will a new area be assigned to us and when will we learn about the other details pertaining to the organization of forces?

STALIN [deliberates audibly with Panfilov and gives as suggestions names like Uzbekistan, Turkmenistan, and Transcaucasia].[17]

SIKORSKI. After organizing and training, all Polish units should be gathered together as one unit, in order to strike as an army, because only such a force will inspire the imagination of the Polish nation.

STALIN. This will require much time.

ANDERS. No, if everything will be carried out properly then the organization, after the arms are received, will not take much time.

STALIN [touches upon the question of the army, without the organization of corps].

SIKORSKI. Maybe this is better. We will agree with this, only the divisions must then be equipped and armed still more strongly.

STALIN. The organization without corps is better because the commander of the army delegates all the responsibility to the commanders of the corps, when such exist, and the result is such that no one is responsible to anyone. It would be better that your army have simply seven divisions, as it is in ours.

SIKORSKI. I will see to it, that equipment comes to you from abroad in a great volume. With good will this can be done.

STALIN. We will give a part, the English should give the rest. However, the ocean transports do not always arrive on time. They can be late, and this should be kept in mind.

SIKORSKI. I must evacuate 25,000 people from here, because I need them for the air force, navy, and panzer units. Besides that we can set up seven divisions. Here, of course, exist our only human reserves. Do you have sufficient airplanes?

STALIN. There is never a sufficient number of airplanes. As to the quantity we are no worse off than the Germans, regarding the quality we are superior. However, in reference to tanks the situation is much worse.

SIKORSKI. Libya has destroyed a great part of the German Air Force.

STALIN. For the past two months we have not felt the superiority of the German Air Force. They now have very inexperienced pilots, young ones. Their airplanes are relatively slow. And how many airplanes does your Air Force division have?

SIKORSKI. Twenty-seven, eighteen of which are in the first, and nine in the second line.

STALIN. That is equivalent to our Air Force regiment.

SIKORSKI. From England we will be able to send several Air Force divisions for our army. There the people are anxious for that.

STALIN [praises the English airmen who are in Russia].

SIKORSKI. Our airmen have excellent vision and quick orientation.

STALIN. The best and most valiant airmen are Slavs. They act very quickly, because they are a young race which as yet has not been worn out.

SIKORSKI. The present war will make the Anglo-Saxons younger. The British are not the French, who really are already finished.

STALIN. I don't agree with this opinion.

SIKORSKI. Perhaps the lower class is still good, but the upper class does not represent a greater value. [A longer discussion on Petain, Weygand, and others follows.]

STALIN. The Germans are strong, but the Slavs will crush them.

SIKORSKI. I now would like to travel in order to inspect the Army and visit the centers of the civilian population, and later return once again to Moscow, in order to see you again, Mr. President.

STALIN. By all means, I am at your service.

SIKORSKI. Tomorrow I shall speak over the radio on behalf of the nations occupied by the Germans. Commissar Vyshinsky was to have sent you the text of my speech.

STALIN. Yes, I read it. It will be good for the broadcast to take place.

SIKORSKI. I imagine that it will be useful to the world. The broadcast will be received and transmitted also by the BBC and America.

STALIN. I ordered that here your speech be translated into forty languages.

SIKORSKI. I would like you to announce my speech. I make the suggestion that we sign a joint political declaration. I don't insist upon it, of course, but I am leaving its draft with you, Mr. President. [Hands over a draft of the declaration.]

STALIN. Basically, I agree. I will read it and tomorrow we will settle it jointly.

SIKORSKI. And so, of course, I consider the problem of the armed forces as settled in principle. I will be substituted by General Anders in a mixed committee which should be assembled as soon as possible, in order to bring about a final conclusion of these questions. Please appoint your trusted persons for the inspection of the camps.

STALIN. I agree. [He mentions Vyshinsky and Panfilov, asking whether they suit General Sikorski.]

SIKORSKI [replies with approval and bids farewell together with the Ambassador and General Anders. As they are leaving Stalin asks that General Anders remain].

[The conversation between Stalin and General Anders lasts a few minutes. Stalin inquires about his collaboration with Panfilov, to which General Anders stated that this collaboration was proceeding favorably, but that General Panfilov could not accomplish much.]

ANDERS. Now since you, Mr. President, have promised to do away with the difficulties I believe that the forming of the army will be settled properly.

STALIN. I am very sorry that I did not meet you before.

ANDERS. It is not my fault that I was not called to you, Mr. President.

STALIN. I will want to meet you from time to time.

ANDERS. Mr. President, I am always at your disposal to call at your demand.[18]

The above meeting, so promising in its content, did not, as subsequent events showed, resolve any fundamental issues. The differences in objectives and methods disclosed were put aside by Stalin for the time being, to be reviewed later and resolved by different means. The eastward march of Hitler's armies was the major reason why the differences had to be overlooked. The appearance of a unified force had to be preserved.

On December 4 a Declaration of Friendship and Mutual Assistance was signed by Stalin and Sikorski. After pledges to fight were expressed, the declaration went on to say:

Implementing the Treaty concluded on July 30, 1941 both Governments will render each other full military assistance during the war, and troops of the Republic of Poland located on the territory of the Soviet Union will wage war against the German brigands shoulder to shoulder with Soviet troops.

In peacetime, their mutual relations will be based on good-neighborly collaboration, friendship, and reciprocal honest fulfillment of the obligations they have taken upon themselves.[19]

The border question was not settled by this treaty. Sikorski relates that at a banquet given after the conclusion of the treaty Stalin suggested that the boundary be settled between the two men. Sikorski, observing the laws of his country, replied that only the Polish Parliament could discuss the issue. Stalin tried to press the matter further, claiming that he only wanted to change the border, *"chut-chut."* Sikorski refused.[20]

This legally correct but diplomatically unfortunate decision by Sikorski became a subject of much critical discussion among the Poles on the ground that, without violating Polish rights or his own legal prerogatives, Sikorski could have found out the context of Stalin's territorial claims.

2. *First Soviet Steps to Undermine the Polish Government*

When the Polish Government learned from its underground sources that the Soviets had left behind their own agents and organizations in Eastern Poland, Sikorski, while in Moscow, attempted to reach an agreement with General Zhukov which could coordinate the activities of the Polish underground organizations with those of Soviet partisans and parachutist groups operating on Polish territory. Zhukov rejected his proposals.[21]

At the same time, the Commander-in-Chief of the Polish Underground Army had a conference with the representative of the Soviet partisans operating in Poland. He suggested that the Soviet partisans be recognized as self-sufficient units provided that operationally they would be subordinated to the Polish Military High Command operating in Poland, in the same way as the Polish Army, then in the U.S.S.R. was subordinated to the Red Army. He also promised to provide supplies to the Soviet partisans so that they would not need to rely on the villages and would not endanger the latter with reprisals from the Germans. The Soviet reply was: "We are operating under the Red Army, on the territories of the U.S.S.R., and the native people are friendly to us. We shall not be subordinated to anyone else." [22]

When General Sikorski first arrived in Moscow, what seemed to him a very irritating incident later proved to be of great significance. Before he even saw Stalin, he read in an article entitled "Listen, Polish Brethren" in the December 2, 1941 issue of *Izvestia*, that a meeting of the "representatives of the Polish nation" took place in Saratov on November 27. These "representatives" were listed as Wanda Wasilewska, who was the main speaker, Prof. Jakub Parnas, Aleksander Joczys, Julian Bronowicz-Brun, Stefan Jedrychowski, Alexander Korneychuk (who spoke in Ukrainian), Jerzy Putrament, and Wiktor Grosz. Out of these proceedings emerged a "Manifesto to the Polish Nation," the burden of which was to inform Poland that a "Union of Polish Patriots" was formed on Soviet soil. Although Sikorski was furious when he read this article, he realized that it was probably meant as a form of pressure on him and his government, and so he resolved to ignore these "Eastern" tactics and go about his mission undisturbed.[23]

This "Union of Polish Patriots," which was to form the nucleus of the future puppet government at Lublin, was a group of Polish communists and sympathizers headed by the writer and "Colonel" in the Red Army, Wanda Wasilewska[24] (the wife of Alexander Korneychuk, later a deputy foreign minister of the Soviet Union).

The most important members of this organization were Boleslaw Drobner (expelled before the war from the Polish Socialist Party for his communist activities), Stefan Jedrychowski (communist), Aleksander Zawadzki (a colonel of the NKVD), Stanislaw Skrzaszewski (before the war a schoolmaster and a communist), Jerzy Sztachelski (a communist from Wilno), Stanislaw Radkiewicz (a communist organizer in pre-war Poland), and Hilary Minc (a pre-war fellow traveler who later became a communist). Among the original members of the Union of Polish Patriots, there were four Soviet nationals, one collaborator (General Berling), five communists, and one communist sympathizer.[25]

The Polish Communist Party was also re-established at this time under the name of the Polish Workers' Party. This, too, was kept a secret. The founders of the Party were: Boleslaw Bierut (later communist President of Poland), Kazimierz Hardy, Kulesza Lutomski, Mrs. Kwiatkowska, Kotek-Ogroszewski, Szymon Zolna and Wladyslaw Gomulka (subsequently Vice-Premier and Secretary General of the Party).

The staff of the Party was secretly parachuted into Poland to infiltrate the Polish underground, to set up cells for the later seizure of power, to denounce members of the patriotic Underground to the Gestapo, and to set up new, seemingly non-communist, underground groups which were actually under the complete control of the Communist Party. The Kremlin exercised direct control over this group by its agent and Secretary General of the Workers' Party, Marceli Nowotko, who later was liquidated and replaced by another agent, Pawel Finder, also later liquidated.[26]

On the basis of subsequent findings by the Polish Embassy in the U.S.S.R., most of the deported Poles were subjected to communist propaganda. The weaker and exhausted were tempted to collaborate when they were promised comfortable living conditions. A luxurious villa at Malakhovka was given to those who accepted the offer by the NKVD. Once there, they had to sign a written obligation to inform the NKVD about everyone and everything which might interest their new bosses. Out of 14,000 officers only 74 "accepted" this new way of life. The most prominent among them was Lt. Col. Zygmunt Berling, who later became the Commander-in-Chief of the Soviet sponsored and controlled Polish Army which was officially established in 1943. (After his disloyal behavior towards the Soviets during the

Warsaw uprising in 1944—it is reported that he was moved by the tragedy of Warsaw and attempted to lift the siege—he disappeared for the remainder of the war, only to reappear in 1947 as the Chief of the Scientific Institute of the Polish Army.) Among the civilians, the most prominent was Andrzej Witos, who succumbed to pressure by the NKVD to become an informer. The function of this group was to infiltrate Polish settlements in order to create disharmony, distrust, and confusion, which effects were in turn exploited by the Soviet authorities.[27]

All this was done during the so-called "honeymoon" period in Soviet-Polish diplomatic relations. Ambassador Kot was repeatedly assured that the Soviets entertained the most friendly disposition towards the Polish Government and that every effort was being made to fulfill the terms of the Soviet-Polish treaty. Any difficulties in carrying out certain provisions were blamed on and explained away by the fact that the Soviet Union was at war and that everything else had to be subordinated to that overriding consideration.

Although the Polish Government was becoming more and more aware of the growing difficulties concerning its eastern boundaries, there was nothing it could do about this except to provide factual data about the disputed territories and spread them in the United Kingdom and the United States. It believed that when public opinion in the Western democracies was sufficiently informed about the relative merits of the disputed claims, no government would dare to take the side of expediency. The Soviet Government did not ignore this aspect either. On the contrary, and with a much greater degree of experience in presenting its case, with much larger funds at its disposal, and furthermore, with the West's appreciation of its efforts on the eastern front to add credibility to its statements, it proceeded not so much to justify its claims to the eastern part of Poland on moral or historical grounds as to describe Poles as reactionary, imperialistic, intolerant in social and religious matters, and hostile to the Soviet Union. The liberally-minded segment of Western public opinion and administration was inclined to believe, or wanted to believe, that the European tragedy and the immense sufferings undergone by the U.S.S.R. in particular had changed the latter's aggressive intentions. At the same time they were not so sure that the alleged reputation of the Poles was outdated. There was no geo-political compulsion to believe that the Poles had probably undergone a similar change in their mental attitude and orientation as it was hoped and believed that the Soviets had. Sympathy and respect for Polish sacrifices and heroism could not overcome or transcend the partial and fragmentary knowledge of the complex Polish problems and the pre-war shortcomings of the Polish leaders. These various elements could not, therefore, be so readily reconciled with the loyalty and friendship so much needed by this tragic nation. Lip service pronouncements by the Allies were intended to satisfy Polish leaders who were searching for firmer and more reliable symptoms of Western support. But these involved problems will be taken up again in their proper chronological place.

On December 4, the very day Sikorski and Stalin signed the Declaration of Friendship and Mutual Assistance, Ambassador Kot was informed that the NKVD had arrested two Polish Jewish socialist leaders, Henryk Ehrlich and Wiktor Alter. At first Sikorski was angry and informed a representative of the Narkomindel that he had no intention of talking with the Soviet leaders if they behaved in so contemptible a way. Then he realized that this was another method used by Moscow to show their power and to soften him for negotiations. He proceeded with his mission as planned.[28]

The tragedy of these two outstanding leaders of the *Bund* (All Jewish Workers' Union) was, at the same time, a tragedy for the 400,000 Polish Jews[29] who were deported to the U.S.S.R. Like other deportees, many of them perished in the subnormal conditions in which they found themselves. Immediately after the "amnesty" proclamation, the majority of the released Jews wanted to join the Polish Army, but the Soviets had different plans for them. The NKVD tried to create a religious conflict between Jews and Christians by playing upon memories of the intolerant treatment which Jews received in pre-war Poland. This was designed to create friction and chaos. The Soviets wanted to separate the Jews from the Poles and were therefore tempting them to take out U.S.S.R. citizenship. The Jews refused. Then the NKVD agitated for and urged the Jews to file complaints against the Poles in order to show the outside world how intolerant and oppressive the Poles really were.

The extreme right-wing elements in General Anders' army were unintentionally helping the Russians in this operation when they began a move to create special military units of the army which would be composed only of Jews. The Polish Government put a stop to that scheme by issuing an order that Jews had to be treated on an equal basis with other Poles. Faced with such a state of affairs, the Soviets wanted to limit the number of Jews in the Polish Army to a minimum. This they proceeded to achieve through unlawful practices in the Draft Board. The Soviet representatives on the Draft Board insisted that Jews, Ukrainians, and Byelorussians could not be drafted. A great number of Jews decided to appear before the Board as Christians.

When the Soviets discovered this, they proceeded to determine racial origin through physical examinations. The Jews were infuriated. In order to shift their anger from the Soviet authorities, the NKVD began explaining privately to the Jews that their action was in response to Polish requests to keep Jews out of the Polish Army.[30]

This complex and disturbing situation was brought under control by the influence of Ehrlich and Alter, who realized what the Soviet objectives were. Ehrlich and Alter were selected for departure to London as soon as they were released from prison. But because of their lamentable appearance, the NKVD objected to this until they had regained their health after their two years of incarceration. Ambassador Kot decided to shelter them in the Polish Embassy and sought their wise counsel on many vital problems.

On September 24, 1941 both of them submitted the following declaration of the Bund to Ambassador Kot:

Mr. Ambassador. When two years ago the gates of prison were shut behind us, we were representing the biggest political organization in the Polish nation and we enjoyed the confidence of the Jewish masses. We trust that today also, when we received an opportunity to return to an active political and social life, we have the right to speak on behalf of those masses.

Therefore, on this peculiar historical occasion we are obliged to submit to you, Mr. Ambassador, and through you to the Polish nation, our stand on two most important issues of the day—war and peace.

The struggle against Hitler is a struggle by every means; and above all the armed struggle is a duty of all men who detest barbarism and beastliness. This is also a duty of every nation which loves freedom.

As Socialists and as citizens of Poland, so horribly treated by Hitler, we are joining the ranks of those fighting against those under the swastika. As the sons of the Jewish nation, most severely humiliated and tortured by Hitler, we feel a particular duty to take part in this struggle to defend human dignity.

Today, when on the U.S.S.R. soil the new Polish Army is formed for further struggle against Hitler, we are turning to all Jews—Polish citizens who are able to bear arms and who are on U.S.S.R. territories—with the following appeal:

"To Arms! Join the ranks of soldiers who with their blood will redeem the right of Poland to free life, who together with the Allied Armies want to liberate Poland and who would free the world from the nightmare of the brown slavery. Those of us who are not able to take arms should not spare any effort to help the Army to fulfill its obligation to speed up victory!

The participation in the present war for freedom is a duty and a distinguished right. In the name of the Jewish working masses and of the Jewish intelligentsia who honor us with their trust, we declare our readiness to fulfill our obligations and we are demanding an opportunity to use that right.

This much about war. An inseparable part of war is the question of peace and the question of a new Poland. We are ignoring the pre-war mistakes of general Polish policy and, among them, the harm experienced by the Jewish people in Poland. Today we are only stating the conclusions derived from the historical experiences of the recent years:

1. Poland can exist without constant fear of losing her freedom only in a democratic Europe.

2. A free and democratic Europe can rise, exist, and develop in a peaceful environment only after the military defeat of Hitlerism, when the European countries will bravely and boldly attempt social reconstruction which will uproot nationalism, militarism, and fear of new wars which exist in the capitalistic structures.

3. The new social organization of Europe should be accompanied by a new political structure of Europe, which will rest not on antagonism and mutual annihilation of individual countries, but on their common interest and mutual defense against danger.

4. The new Poland should be an active member of the community of nations which will shape the fate of the future Europe in the spirit of political freedom, social justice, and national equality. This means the application of those principles in the internal life of Poland as well as in her relations with the other states and nations.

5. The achievement of these objectives depends on the unity and creative energy of the Polish working masses and on their ability to incorporate into reality their vision of Poland, the true mother of all her inhabitants.

Represented by us, the Jewish people of Poland who are an organic part of the Polish working masses, will not spare any effort to contribute to the building of a New Poland—which will rest on the well-being of her people and on freedom for spiritual development of her citizens.

In accordance with the above we are starting our work in the U.S.S.R.

The lion's share of it will consist of recruiting Jewish deportees for the Polish Army and of welfare work among the civilian population. We intend to work closely with the Polish Embassy, and hope that nothing will stand in the way of harmonious collaboration.[31]

Ambassador Kot accepted their declaration in its totality because all of its postulates were in accord with the policies of the Polish Government in London, which was itself composed of persons critical of the pre-war regime and who intended to right the wrongs.

At the same time, Alter and Ehrlich informed Kot that the NKVD made them a proposition to undertake broadcasts to the United States. The Soviets were anxious to enlist the support of American Jews. Alter and Ehrlich replied that they were quite willing to do so, provided that they would be free to plan and arrange the programs and that, furthermore, these programs would have to be under the general control of the Polish Embassy. This answer discouraged the NKVD from utilizing their readiness to serve.[32] A few days later the NKVD approached them again to suggest the establishment of a Jewish Anti-Hitlerite Committee in the U.S.S.R. which would be composed of Jews from four nationalities—Soviet, Polish, United States, and British. The presidium would be composed of three persons: Ehrlich as Chairman, Alter as Secretary, and Michoels as a Soviet citizen. The purpose of the Committee was to:

1. Urge Jews throughout the world, but mainly in the occupied countries and in the United States, to intensify their fight against the Nazis.

2. Liberate Jews from nationalist oppression in all countries.

3. Truly liberate all Jewish masses from nationalistic oppression, which would be possible only when national life everywhere would be based on social justice. They would direct their energies towards this goal.

4. Propagate in the United States, and in other countries which were not yet formally at war, the idea of the necessity of sending armed help to the U.S.S.R.

5. Send delegates to these countries for this purpose.[33]

Both Ehrlich and Alter accepted this offer in order to speed up the defeat of Hitler and to help the oppressed and hungry.

In the meantime, the Polish Government decided to bring Ehrlich to London so that he might become a member of the National Council. Alter, for the time being, was to work with the Ambassador in the U.S.S.R. and then was to go to the United States, where he planned to start political activities. As soon as Ambassador Kot learned about their re-arrest, several notes of inquiry were dispatched to the Narkomindel asking for an explanation of the reasons for their arrest and demanding their release. All the notes were ignored until March 22, 1942, when the Narkomindel replied that according to Soviet law both Ehrlich and Alter were citizens of the U.S.S.R.[34] The Polish Government protested against this arbitrary decision. Nothing, however, was heard about them until the end of February 1943. At the beginning of March 1943, the Polish Government learned from the American and the British press about their execution. The press of both these countries published excerpts of the letter of the Soviet Ambassador in Washington, addressed to William Green,[35] which maintained that Ehrlich and Alter were sentenced to death by the Soviet authorities and subsequently executed because they were collaborating with the German and Polish intelligence services engaged in subversive activities against the Soviet Union and that they had issued an appeal to the Soviet armed forces to stop fighting and to conclude a peace with Germany.[36]

On March 8, 1943 the Polish Government protested vigorously against the execution of Ehrlich and Alter by Soviet firing squads, stating that

. . . both of them were widely known as outstanding leaders of the Jewish socialist movement in Poland. Furthermore, Mr. Ehrlich was a member of the Executive Committee of the International Workers Union while Alter was a member of the Executive Committee of the International Trade Union. Because of their outstanding contribution to the workers' movement in Poland, the Polish Government had asked that Ehrlich be permitted to leave the U.S.S.R. in order to become a member of the Polish National Council (Parliament) in London and Alter was to work with the Polish Ambassador in Kuybyshev.

Their long struggle against fascism in general and German fascism in particular could not make it possible for them to work secretly for the Germans, as they were accused by the Soviet authorities.

In accordance with the above, the Polish Government firmly rejects the accusations advanced in the letter of the Soviet Ambassador in Washington addressed to Mr. Green, and protests against the execution of the Polish citizens, Henryk Ehrlich and Wiktor Alter.[37]

On March 31 Ambassador Bogomolov sent a reply to the Polish Government in London in which he stated:

> The Soviet Government rejects the Polish protest against the executions of Ehrlich and Alter as baseless. They were sentenced to death because at the time when the Soviet forces were struggling against the attacking Hitler army in 1941 they were conducting hostile activity against the U.S.S.R. including the issuing of appeals to the Soviet forces to stop fighting and to immediately conclude a peace with the Germans.[38]

Apparently the Soviet authorities had come to the conclusion that Ehrlich and Alter were individuals too upright and hardy to compromise their principles or to be willing to forget the treatment which they had suffered in Soviet prisons. Their contacts inside and outside of Poland were too extensive. It was, therefore, decided to dispose of them arbitrarily and to announce it publicly at a time when Soviet military performance was the subject of general admiration. Western public opinion was not informed about the unpleasant aspects of the Soviet behavior. There was nothing else for the Polish Government to do in this and similar matters.

Writing about that problem, Mikolajczyk stated:

> We in London could not raise our voices. Nothing was to be said that would embarrass Stalin. We were told by the British to hold our peace, not only in the face of the arrest of many relief workers, but also despite the fact that hundreds of thousands of Poles were forced to become Russian citizens. Those who resisted were jailed, shot, or sent to slow death in the labor camps. . . .
>
> The picture of Russia became distorted. Ambassador Jan Ciechanowski reported from Washington that pro-Soviet elements had moved into important places in some of the United States war agencies and that any American who attempted to bring up such distasteful matters as, for instance, the cold-blooded murders of the Polish Jewish socialist leaders,

Henryk Ehrlich and Wiktor Alter, was pilloried as a "Fascist Saboteur and German Spy. . . ."

We turned from Churchill to Roosevelt, then back to Churchill. They both were uniformly sympathetic but continued to impose silence upon us, as they were reluctant to inject anything into their relations with Stalin that might displease him. . . . In the echelons beneath Churchill and Roosevelt our position became worse. We were told not to make any move or release any statement that might anger Stalin or give him an opportunity to break off relations with the Polish Government in London. That imposed on us an increasingly unbearable muteness. . . .[39]

The Soviets were fully conscious of this sympathetic attitude and this friendly understanding of their larger problems shown them by their Western Allies and proceeded to take calculated advantage of these attitudes in solving their own somewhat smaller questions. Before the end of 1941, the Polish Embassy was informed that a number of Polish citizens, mainly former judges, lawyers, officers of the Army, civil servants, and police, who at the time they were released from prison found themselves in the Ukraine, were again arrested and then executed on the basis of Article 54, paragraph 13 of the Ukrainian Criminal Law. This particular Article and paragraph state that

. . . those in foreign countries whose occupation or the institution to which they belong may expose the Soviet Union to war or may in any other way endanger the structure of the Soviet State will be punished by death or imprisonment.

The Polish Government filed a protest against this arbitrary procedure. The Soviet officials replied by clarifying the meaning and application of that law.

The Red Star—the symbol of Communism—has five arms. Each stands for one continent of the world. Sooner or later Communism is going to dominate the whole world. Therefore, every person, in spite of his present nationality, is subject to Communist authority. Every act, even of non-Soviet citizens may be and must be punished by the Soviet authorities if that act was committed against the Soviet State in the course of fulfilling one's work in his own country.[40]

In the face of these insurmountable obstacles it was only natural that the Polish Embassy decide to concentrate on helping those people who actually were released. But, in spite of the most extraordinary efforts, the situation of the civilian population continued to be lamentable. The most tragic conditions were found in the south of the U.S.S.R., where the majority of the released Poles came from the north. They had a hard time finding work, and those who managed to obtain some employment found it very difficult physically and badly paid. Although the climate was not so severe as in the north, they had no shelter and their situation consequently became even worse than before. In Uzbekistan itself, approximately 200,000 lived under terrible conditions. Most of them were not housed and were on a starvation diet. This led to outbreaks of typhoid fever and of epidemics of malaria. There was no serum for vaccination, and not even soap. The Embassy asked the Polish legation in Teheran to buy soap for 100,000 rubles. Constant pleading with the Soviets secured their permission to organize orphanages, kindergartens, homes for invalids and old people. Furthermore, the Soviet authorities gave permission to evacuate 500 orphans to India.[41]

One of the thousands of letters sent to the Polish Embassy in Kuybyshev was that of Dr. Wasung from Katta Kurgan—a rather typical letter.

Here in southern Russia I am witnessing a terrifying martyrdom of the Polish nation. These poor people are dying from starvation—yet the price of food goes up. Spotted typhoid (here considered a rather mild disease), small pox, scarlet fever, and a peculiar kind of grippe kill children by the hundreds. All railroad lines and all railroad stations through which our people come from their prisons and labor camps are surrounded by the countless graves of Polish children—victims of "order and harmony." The poverty is unbelievable. Our people are pale and look miserable. If you saw me today, you would not recognize me. I am enclosing my photograph taken in prison. From the 130 kilograms which I used to weigh I now weigh only 75. I am constantly hungry. There is no fat available and flour is very expensive. No one can earn a ruble. They do not want to draft us into the army and so they keep postponing the date when that will begin. Oh! If we could finally leave this cursed land, because I don't know how many of us will survive if this thing will continue for another few months.

I am a doctor in charge of a medical center. The Russians call it "Med-Punkt," but there is nothing in it—not even a hypodermic needle, or the most necessary instruments for first aid, not to speak of medicine. First of all we need vitamins, fats, calcium, biotics because otherwise those children who have survived up till now will soon die. In many transports from the north, a great many mothers have lost all their children because of scarlet fever or small pox. I could describe more problems for you and write about the tragedy of parents and children, but I am so exhausted that I have no strength to do so. When I get a little better I shall put down all those things which I saw—it will be a shocking and disgraceful testimony against the Soviets.

I consider this to be high time to liberate our people from this Babylonian Captivity and to show them at least a ray of the "Promised Land" by taking them out of Soviet territory. I am not asking for anything for myself. I want to work in a hospital as a Polish doctor.

Please speak to General Sikorski for us so that he can take us out of here. Exhausted by prison and a lack of food, we long to return to our country and to our loved ones and we shall obey orders.[42]

From the political point of view, the most disturbing question was the Soviet attempt to impose Soviet citizenship on the Poles who on November 1 and 2, 1939 found themselves in the eastern part of Poland. The Polish Government was not willing to comply with this somewhat tricky Soviet move intended to lay the ground for the incorporation of that territory into the U.S.S.R. Accordingly, the following note was dispatched to the Soviet Government.

(1) Polish legislation is founded on the principle of equality before the law of all citizens, regardless of their origin or race. The Polish Embassy is, also, not aware of any Soviet laws which would introduce or sanction any discrimination or differentiation of this kind.

The Agreement of July 30, 1941 and the Military Agreement of August 14, 1941 do not introduce in any of their provisions relative to Polish citizens (amnesty, military service) the notion of origin or race, and thus they concern all Polish citizens without exception.

In this state of affairs, this Embassy sees no possibility of changing its attitude as expressed in its Note of November 10, 1941 which stated that it was contrary both to the Agreement of July 30, 1941 and the Military Agreement of August 14, 1941 that only Polish citizens of Polish origin should be able to enlist in the Polish Army, while Polish citizens of Ukrainian, Byelorussian, and Jewish origin were enlisted in the Red Army by the War Commissariat in Kazakhstan.

(2) The fact of the possession of Polish citizenship by a given person is regulated by Polish law, in particular by the Polish State Citizenship Act of January 20, 1920. For this reason and for the reasons stated above under paragraph 1., this Embassy has the honor to declare that it finds itself unable to take into cognizance the statement included in the Note of the People's Commissariat for Foreign Affairs of December 1, 1941 to the effect that the Soviet Government is prepared to recognize as Polish citizens only persons of Polish origin from among the persons who found themselves on November 1 and 2, 1939 on the territory of the Republic of Poland temporarily occupied by the military forces of the Soviet Union.

(3) The Citizenship of the Union of Soviet Socialist Republics Act of August 19, 1938 cannot be applied to Polish citizens, for its introduction on the territory of the Polish Republic occupied by the Soviet Union from the latter half of September, 1939 until June or July, 1941 would be contrary to the provisions of the Fourth Hague Convention of 1907.

(4) The Polish Embassy does not connect the matter referred to in Note D. 740/41 of November 10, 1941 with the problem of Polish-Soviet frontiers. The People's Commissariat for Foreign Affairs points out in the Note in question that it does not recognize as Polish citizens persons of Ukrainian, Byelorussian, and Jewish origin who possessed Polish citizenship before November 1-2, 1939, "because the problem of the frontiers between the U.S.S.R. and Poland has not been settled, and is subject to settlement in the future." The Polish Embassy is bound to state that such a thesis

is self-contradictory. Maintaining fully the fundamental attitude expressed above in paragraphs (1)–(3), this Embassy has the honor to point out that such a view would be tantamount to a unilateral settlement by the Soviet Union at the present time of a problem which, in accordance with this same statement of the People's Commissariat for Foreign Affairs, is subject to settlement in the future.[43]

Neither logic nor international law could persuade the Soviets to alter their decision. On January 5, 1942 the Narkomindel replied, rejecting the Polish note and saying:

The Polish view cannot be justified by the provision of the Fourth Hague Convention of 1907 because that provision applies only to the conditions of occupation on enemy territories. Neither from the political nor from the international legal point of view can this be applied to the Western Ukraine and Western Byelorussia because the entrance of the Soviet forces into those territories in the autumn of 1939 was not an occupation but only the inclusion of those territories into the U.S.S.R., and this was the result of the freely expressed will of the people of those regions.[44]

Even if one could accept the dialectically twisted interpretation of the cited provision of the Hague Convention, it was and still is difficult to comprehend what the Soviets meant when they justified the entrance of their forces into these territories by "the freely expressed will of the people of those regions." It must be stated that there was no "election" or any other polling of public opinion on this matter prior to September 17, 1939, when the Red Army crossed its western border.

On January 6, Molotov sent a note to all governments which had diplomatic relations with the U.S.S.R., bringing to their attention the magnitude of German atrocities committed on Soviet territory. It pointed out:

On June 30, the Hitlerite bandits entered the town of Lwów and the following day they organized a mass slaughter. Thirty-two working women of the Lwów clothing works were raped and then killed by German storm troopers. Drunken German soldiers dragged young women and girls in Lwów to the Kosciuszko Park and brutally raped them. According to incomplete data, no less than 6,000 people were shot. . . .[45]

This notification provoked the Polish Government to send a protest to the Narkomindel. After condemning the German autrocities against the helpless civilian population, the note went on to say:

It must have been an oversight to refer to Lwów as a Soviet city, because from the point of view of history and international law, as well as the ethnographical composition of its residents, Lwów was and is a Polish city.[46]

Replying to the above, Molotov stated:

The People's Commissariat considers that it is not right for the Polish Government to refer to Lwów, Brześć, Stanislawow and other cities as being on the territories of the Polish Republic.

Considering that it is impossible to begin a discussion about the historical and legal question as to whom those cities belong to, it is my duty to inform the Polish Embassy that in the future the People's Commissariat for Foreign Affairs will not be able to receive for consideration any note from the Embassy with this kind of statement.[47]

From such Soviet behavior the Poles derived a clear hint of the things to come. The Soviet attitude proved to be a significant move of far-reaching consequence. It was a tactical device to keep that part of Poland which they appropriated in September 1939. The Soviets began to exploit Polish unwillingness to discuss the future Soviet-Polish frontiers by making arbitrary decisions. They also exploited their diplomatic relations with Poland, which prevented the Poles from informing the public opinion of the world about the nature of the difficulties which Poles were encountering in their dealings with the Soviets.

The Polish Government intended to take up the matter with the United States Government in order to enlist its support. But the Western Allies were themselves under Soviet criticism. Stalin, in an Order of the Day, and Litvinov, in a speech to the Overseas Press Club in New York on February 26, attacked the Allies for their inaction, and stated that the Soviet Union exclusively was bearing the entire burden of military operations.

Inspired by Moscow, a score of American writers simultaneously started a well-timed campaign supporting the "ethnographic rights of Soviet Russia to certain territories," openly referring to the defunct Curzon Line. . . .[48]

This was synchronized with Soviet pressure on the British. When in the winter of 1941 Eden visited Moscow in connection with the preparatory work for the conclusion of a Soviet-British treaty, he was presented by Stalin with a request to recognize the Curzon Line as well as Soviet rights to those territories of Finland acquired by force in the Russo-Finnish war of 1940, the entire territories of the three Baltic States, almost half of Poland, and the Rumanian provinces of Northern Bukovina and Bessarabia. Eden excused himself from dealing with this problem, basing his refusal upon his lack of authority. In order not to hinder the conclusion of the Anglo-Soviet treaty, however, he promised to give most careful consideration to that matter.[49] Soon afterwards Soviet propaganda launched a whispering campaign in London and Washington that the Soviet Union might have to conclude some agreement with Hitler. The intention was obvious—to make the Western Powers more responsive to Soviet demands.

It was against this background that the acting Polish Foreign Minister, Edward Raczyński, arrived in Washington in February 1942 to enlist American help. On February 24 he visited Assistant Secretary of State Adolph Berle.

> In the course of the conversation, reports Ambassador Ciechanowski, Raczynski mentioned that he had heard that Eden had been faced in Moscow with definite territorial demands on the part of the Soviets, especially regarding the Baltic. Berle most unexpectedly expressed the prophetic view that Russia would emerge from this war as one of the Great World Powers, and added that he thought that the granting of special demands of so great a Power would probably be inevitable. He also added that it was difficult to conceive that unlimited sovereignty of smaller States, in the pre-war sense of the word, could stand in the way of the natural and inevitable political and economic expansionism of a Great Power. It was then, for the first time, that I heard such an opinion from a high American official.[50]

The next day Raczyński was received by President Roosevelt who, in the course of the conversation, said to him:

> The British Government, through Churchill, had entirely coordinated its view with the American Government on the fundamental principle that the two Governments would not agree to any territorial or political changes during the war.
>
> . . . .
>
> Our apprehensions, writes Ciechanowski, somewhat allayed by the conversation with the President, were again revived when we were informed that the demands which Stalin had presented to Mr. Eden had not been finally rejected by the British Government. On the contrary, London was trying to persuade Washington to agree to participate in the conclusion of a tri-partite agreement which would recognize Soviet territorial demands.[51]

Commenting on Stalin's game of nerves, Hopkins observed that: "In reality Russia has no choice in the matter of selecting her Allies even if she would prefer to cast her lot with Hitler rather than with the Western democracies. Stalin cannot get out of the war. Soviet tactics should be regarded as a means of pressure. Stalin's main aim is to obtain the fullest material aid from us rather than to get territorial or other concessions. However," he added with a broad smile, "it is possible that Britain, unable to invade Western Europe for the time being, hopes to placate Russia by paying her at other people's expense."[52]

Although the United States was unwilling to comply with the Soviet demands, neither was she ready to put things on a clearer footing by stressing that America was determined to abide by her stated policy as frequently stressed by the President in public speeches.

Constant diplomatic pressure by the British was eroding the soundness of these principles and was widening the gap between the stated principles and actual performance. Roosevelt counted on making a personal plea to Stalin for Poland at a meeting planned for the indefinite future, but Stalin kept postponing it.

When General Sikorski visited Washington in March, 1942, he

. . . told the President that he had talked . . . with Churchill and Eden in the course of the last few days. He [Sikorski] feared that the British Government was on the point of giving in to Soviet pressure and of agreeing to their territorial demands in the Baltic States and the Rumanian provinces bordering on Russia.[53]

He made it clear that a permanent acquisition by Russia of the Baltic States and of Bessarabia and Northern Bukovina would threaten Poland with Soviet encirclement in the north and in the south. President Roosevelt assured him that the United States at least continued to respect the principles of the Atlantic Charter and was opposed to territorial settlements for the duration of the war. Roosevelt reaffirmed his determination not to depart from the Atlantic Charter and assured Sikorski that he was very strongly opposing the conclusion of an Anglo-Soviet treaty if that treaty were going to be based on recognition of the Soviet territorial demands.[54]

This did not dispel Sikorski's fear that the British were almost ready to make the requested concessions. Furthermore, he was aware that the Soviets had established at Saratov and then moved to Moscow a "Union of Polish Patriots." This was interpreted by the Polish Government to mean that Soviet plans *vis-à-vis* Poland went beyond territorial claims and that their aim was undoubtedly to extend their ideological and political control over the whole of Poland.

Sikorski's misgivings about the British attitude towards the Soviet claims was justified by Churchill's telegram to President Roosevelt of March 7, in which he said:

The increasing gravity of the war has led me to feel that the principles of the Atlantic Charter ought not to be construed so as to deny Russia the frontiers she occupied when Germany attacked her. . . .[55]

Two days later, in a telegram to Stalin, Churchill stated: "I have sent a message to President Roosevelt urging him to approve our signing the agreement with you about the frontiers of Russia at the end of the war."[56]

Stalin naturally expressed his gratitude for that message. Having Churchill on his side, he proceeded to act more firmly.

President Roosevelt had very definitely stated his position to Churchill, and Mr. Sumner Welles confirmed it to Litvinov, who in turn communicated it to his Government.[57]

Furthermore, Roosevelt wanted to talk directly to the Soviets in order to persuade them to abandon their territorial demands, at least for the duration of the war.[58] For this and other reasons he invited Molotov to come to Washington. Instead, Stalin informed Churchill that "the Soviet Government had decided, in spite of all the obstacles, to send Mr. Molotov to London, in order, by means of personal discussion, to dispose of all matters which stand in the way of the signing of the agreements." [59] Molotov arrived in London on May 22, 1942 and immediately made it plain that the frontier agreements must be settled before a treaty of alliance could be signed. Molotov "even brought up specifically the question of agreeing to the Russian occupation of eastern Poland." [60]

Churchill was motivated by the military situation. The Red Army was the only Allied force fighting Hitler in Europe, and the prospect of the second front was remote. On the other hand, Roosevelt's pressure was strong enough to change the English attitude. It was Ambassador Winant who by his splendid personification of the position of his President and Secretary of State managed to change the British position. As Mr. Hull put it, "we certainly had to give them (the British) hell before we could make them realize it." [61] Eden was forced to reject Soviet demands as incompatible with the Anglo-Polish Agreement of August 1939. Writing about that event, Churchill said:

On May 23, Mr. Eden proposed to substitute for a territorial agreement a general and public Treaty of Alliance for twenty years, omitting all reference to frontiers. By that evening the Russians showed signs of giving way. They were impressed by the solidarity of view of the British and American Governments with which they had been confronted.[62]

The treaty, without any territorial provisions or references, was signed on May 26. In a telegram to Stalin, Churchill stated:

As regards the treaty, he (Molotov) will explain to you the difficulties, which are mainly that we cannot go back on our previous undertakings to Poland, and have to take account of our own and American opinion.[63]

This was a victory of American diplomacy and of the principles of the Atlantic Charter. Poles were greatly relieved and grateful for American moral leadership.

On May 29 Molotov arrived in Washington. Mr. Hull later told Ciechanowski

. . . that during his conversations with Molotov in Washington, when expressing his concern he had alluded to the various incidents created by the Soviet Government in its dealings with the Poles, Molotov had very curtly changed the subject without any discussion.

When the Secretary insisted on the importance for the Allies of obtaining fresh Polish military contingents, Molotov replied that he regarded these matters as purely Soviet-Polish problems, and wished to assure the Secretary that the Soviets were carrying out their obligations.[64]

3. The Soviets Maneuver the Polish Army out of the U.S.S.R.

After Sikorski's departure from Moscow and after his visit to Washington in particular, the Soviets began to create various difficulties for the Poles in the U.S.S.R. New problems arose during the formation of the Polish Army. When Stalin gave promises to Sikorski that an army of 96,000 would be organized, General Anders proceeded rapidly to achieve that goal. Within a few months he had collected 75,000 soldiers. Their upkeep and equipment was going to be provided by the Soviet authorities from their own supplies and those provided by Lend-Lease. Early in 1942, Anders was informed that a food supply could be provided for only 44,000 so that only that number could be kept in the army. Simultaneously, the Embassy learned that a considerable number of Poles were forced into Soviet labor battalions instead of being allowed to join the Polish Army.

On March 18, 1942 at the request of General Anders, Stalin agreed to evacuate every man under Anders' command to Iran except the 44,000 of Anders' Army who would be retained to fight alongside the Red Army.

At the same time, Anders raised the question of the missing officers.

There are still a lot of our people in prisons and labor camps. Men recently released are steadily returning (between 1,000 and 1,500 a day). We still lack our officers who were taken away from Starobelsk, Kozelsk, and Ostashkov. They must still be in your hands. We have collected additional data about them. [He hands over two lists, which were taken by Molotov.] They may have gone astray somewhere. We have traced their stay on the Kolyma.[65]

Stalin replied that he did not know where they were, and switched the conversation to an inquiry as to the whereabouts of Jozef Beck and Edward Smigly-Rydz. This subject of the missing army men did not stop Poles from searching for and inquiring about them; but as the mystery thickened, a suspicion arose that they had been disposed of.

Learning that Stalin had consented to keep a Polish corps of 44,000 in Soviet territory, the Polish Government in London was very pleased. It was thought that if these men would fight side by side with the Red Army and would eventually enter Poland, Stalin would have at least moral difficulties in pursuing his aggressive plans against Poland. The fact that Polish soldiers would march, fight, and even die together with the Soviet soldiers would also have a powerful effect on Western public opinion—which, in the day of the final political settlement between the U.S.S.R. and Poland, would presumably have its weight.

For various reasons, among them the necessity of discussing the political implications of the presence of the Poles on the eastern front, General Anders was summoned to London. There he attempted to persuade Sikorski to remove his army from the U.S.S.R. altogether. Sikorski rejected that suggestion and insisted that the Polish Army remain in the Soviet Union. Shortly afterwards Anders returned to the U.S.S.R., and Sikorski was informed by the British that the Russians had given him permission to transfer the Polish forces and a certain number of civilians into the Middle East. Subsequently 77,000 soldiers and 37,000 civilians—men, women, and children—were allowed to leave Russia. This was only a small fraction of approximately 1,500,000 Poles originally deported to the U.S.S.R.

Thereafter, it was established that General Anders had been informed by General Zhukov that the Soviet authorities would acquiesce to Anders' request to evacuate the Polish Army to the Middle East. Anders had decided on his own, without consulting his Government, to ask for such permission, and the Soviets had readily granted it on July 31, 1942.[66]

Speaking later in London, Anders stated:

> I had to make such a decision against orders from London. I was convinced that that order resulted from a lack of understanding of our situation. The head of the Government was badly informed by the Polish Ambassador in Moscow. Remaining in Russia was contrary to the Polish national interest. The decision to get out of there I took on my own responsibility and God granted that it was a right one.[67]

In terms of saving those who were permitted to leave Russia, that decision undoubtedly was the right one. But from the political point of view, the problem was much more complicated. The presence of the Polish forces in the U.S.S.R. would have been very advantageous to the London Government. It was a political asset of considerable importance, and it is difficult now to speculate on what would have happened if that armed force had remained there and had marched together with the Red Army into Poland.

We shall be on safer ground in analyzing the political aftermath of their departure.

First, Stalin accused the Poles of cowardice. Then he proceeded to organize another Polish Army under Colonel Berling—one of the members of the "Polish Patriots' Union." [68] This army was under the complete control of Soviet authorities. Moreover, its potential military contribution strengthened the position of the "Union of Patriots." This was so because when Anders' Army was forced to wait in the Middle East for an opportunity to disprove Stalin's accusation of its cowardice, a portion of Berling's army took part in the defense of Stalingrad, and this was immediately exploited by the communist propaganda to show that only Poles within the Soviet Union were anxious to fight Hitler's invaders. From that time on, the Union of Polish Patriots ceased to be only a collection of a few individuals with a newspaper, and became a political body which had under its control the future "liberators of Poland." [69]

Stalin's decision to cut his losses of this portion of Polish manpower and make the most of what was left proved to be a master stroke from the point of view of his future plans. Having removed the most important asset from the hands of the London Government, which was also the main pillar of the Soviet-Polish treaty of 1941, he proceeded to set in motion the chain of events which led to the breaking of diplomatic relations.

From the time when Sikorski visited Washington in March 1942, the relationship between the Polish Embassy and the Narkomindel deteriorated. The Soviets began to be suspicious and irritated. All practical matters which concerned the Poles in the U.S.S.R. had been dealt with by the NKVD and General Anders' staff. This was not coincidental but was based on the Soviet's knowledge that the military and the Embassy did not see eye to eye in political matters. It was only natural for the Soviets to play one off against the other in order to drive them further apart. The Army was flattered by the NKVD's amicable attitude towards it. [70]

Consequently, delivery of letters and telegrams to the Embassy was delayed and even stopped. *Agents provocateurs* were sent under various pretexts, mainly to ask for help, shelter, and protection from the Soviet authorities. In some cases, when natural human instinct prompted some official of the Embassy to give them shelter, the NKVD would soon after search the premises of the Embassy and arrest the "culprit." This gave them grounds for accusations and diplomatic threats to the Embassy against the abuse of diplomatic privileges. [71]

Under these circumstances Professor Kot decided that it would be better for the Polish cause if he resigned as ambassador. On August 13 he left Kuybyshev. Within one week after his departure the Soviet authorities liquidated all offices of the representatives of the Embassy in all places where Poles were located. At the same time, they arrested most of the personnel, including those with diplomatic immunity, took their archives and the stores of food and clothing from which the deportees had been supplied. When the Chargé d'Affaires, Michal Sokolnicki, protested to Vyshinsky, he was told that it was established that all those arrested had been spying on the Soviet Union.[72] Neither then nor subsequently did the Soviet authorities provide any factual proof of the accusations. This action by the Soviets against the Polish Embassy abruptly ended the distribution of relief supplies from Britain and the United States among the destitute Polish deportees in camps all over Russia.

Within one month the Polish Army and 37,500 civilians were out of the country, and the role of the Embassy was so limited that for all practical purposes it was left only to receive and send official notes.

This, then, was the Soviet reaction to America's support of Polish rights. The Polish Government attempted to sound out Washington in order to determine what could be done. Ambassador Ciechanowski was assigned to that task.

We discovered what could be done. . . . In view of the importance of maintaining good Polish-Soviet relations and of preserving the united front of the Allies, Mr. Hull considered that only joint diplomatic action of the United States and Britain could succeed in prevailing upon Soviet Russia to change the course of its policy toward Poland. Russia was obtaining considerable Lend-Lease aid from Britain and the United States. Hull was of the opinion that this advantage should be made use of to save the situation from deteriorating beyond remedy.[73]

Hull had arranged for Ciechanowski to see the President who was "bewildered by the state of Soviet-Polish relations." Roosevelt told Ciechanowski that he was aware of Soviet obstinacy and that even the American Ambassador, Standley, had difficulties in seeing Molotov —let alone Stalin—but that he was expecting a lot from Harriman's visit to Moscow. Harriman was being sent as his special representative to discuss war supplies, and he would be instructed to prevail on Stalin to abandon all those "curious decisions and to release the 120 arrested Polish relief officials." [74]

The place of Ambassador Kot in the U.S.S.R. was filled on October 12 by a professional diplomat, Tadeusz Romer. From the beginning, his functions were curtailed.

On August 20, 1942 Ambassador Kot, reporting from Teheran to his Prime Minister, stated:

> Mr. Tabaczynski wrote me from Moscow that Churchill and Harriman refrained from mentioning the Polish question even by one word. This was immediately understood by the Russians to mean that the Anglo-Americans had abandoned us. The American Counselor, Thornstone, a decent man, assured him that Harriman did not receive any instructions to discuss the Polish problem with Stalin. Apparently Ciechanowski was misled. In spite of all difficulties, Churchill should have been obliged, at least morally, to ask for the release of our delegates from prison. He had numerous conversations with Stalin, and was unusually pleased with them. Whatever letters you may receive from him will never be able to remedy what was understood in Moscow, that London and Washington are not interested in the fate of the Poles nor in eventual Soviet withdrawal from the treaty (with us).[75]

There is no mention of this in Sherwood's *Roosevelt and Hopkins* nor in Churchill's *The Hinge of Fate*. Churchill and Harriman were mostly preoccupied with explaining to Stalin why the Second Front could not be established in 1942. It might be that an irritated and annoyed Stalin was not in the mood to be bothered with lesser problems.

The relief work among Poles was subsequently carried out by the NKVD with the help of the people from the "Union of Polish Patriots."

4. Increased Pressure and Katyn: The Soviets Rupture Diplomatic Relations

A new problem was created in Poland by the Soviet partisans. The Polish underground authorities reported to London that the Soviet agents and parachutists operating in Poland were avoiding an open fight against the Germans and that they were not even interested in sabotage, but that, instead, they were robbing, raping, and terrorizing the Polish population. Consequently, the Polish Government was obliged to file a strong protest with Ambassador Bogomolov—a protest which was rejected.[76]

This Soviet move was carefully calculated. Once they realized that the Polish Government in London was gradually becoming a burden to the unity of the Allies—and this was shown by the attitudes of Churchill and Harriman—the Soviets decided to weaken and expose its lack of effectiveness inside Poland and to discredit it before the Polish people. Sikorski reacted by delivering a speech to Poland in which he attacked "foreign agents" for torturing the defenseless population.

On September 4, 1942 the Polish Government sent a note to Ambassador Bogomolov informing him that according to reports received from Warsaw

. . . on the night of August 20-21 the Soviet Air Force bombed that city, and that all the bombs had fallen on the residential district killing 800 people and wounding over 1,000. Radio Moscow, in its broadcast about the second Soviet air raid on Warsaw which took place on September 1-2, stated that the objects of attack were the General Headquarters and the Ministry of Military Affairs. The Polish note pointed out that these two buildings were burned out in 1939 and since then had not been rebuilt, and that in the nearest vicinity the Germans had organized a very densely inhabited Jewish ghetto. It stated, furthermore, that Warsaw was overcrowded with refugees and that there were no military or industrial centers, plus the fact that the Germans were dispersed among the Polish population in order to escape bombardment.[77]

The note suggested that Polish military authorities would be glad to help the Soviet Air Force in selecting important objects for bombardment.

On September 9 Bogomolov informed Raczynski that the Soviet air raid on Warsaw had been successful and went on to say that the Soviet Government could not agree with the information that the result of the Soviet bombardment of Warsaw would be negatively interpreted by the civilian population.[78]

In September 1942 Wendell Willkie, after a lengthy conference with Professor Kot in Teheran during which he became well acquainted with the Polish problems in Russia, arrived in Moscow and on September 23 had an interview with Stalin on behalf of the Poles. Stalin promised Willkie to take a new look at the Polish question and to adopt a positive attitude towards it. He also expressed a willingness to discuss mutual problems with the Poles.[79]

The results were prompt and encouraging. The Soviets released 114 of the arrested delegates of the Polish Embassy but retained the other sixteen who were never released. They permitted the Embassy to carry out the distribution of American relief supplies and this was done through "trusted men." [80]

To the Poles this was a proof that Stalin was quick to exploit the weakness of the Western stand and that he was equally quick to change his policies whenever he met a firm opposition.

The new Ambassador, Tadeusz Romer, was treated with utmost courtesy, but the condition in which the masses of the deportees existed continued to be sad and hopeless. Even the most hopeful and optimistic were broken down by the lack of food and by the cold. The winter conditions cut off numerous places in the north and in Siberia, where Poles were located, from contact with the Polish Embassy. Most of these people were of very humble origin, less experienced in worldly problems, shy and reserved, and therefore more helpless in overcoming the difficulties which separated them from the Embassy. The Ambassador was afraid that before spring came many thousands of them would be dead. He made every effort to save at least the children, but the Soviets rejected the various proposals. An appeal was made to Roosevelt to help evacuate 50,000 children. He responded by asking the South American Union to take 10,000 and by arranging that their maintenance would be provided by the American Red Cross. The Soviets declined that offer by pointing out the difficulties of transporting them.[81]

All diplomatic intercourse between Ambassador Romer and the Soviets was confined to a superficial skimming of the complicated problems. The major problems were held in abeyance or answered in a way which avoided the real issue. The Poles were humbled by the realization that they were powerless in all these matters and that the decisions concerning the lives of millions of their citizens and the future of their country would depend on the constellation of world powers and their good will, or lack of it, towards Poland. The awareness that the Western Powers were anxious not to antagonize the Soviets by opposing their expansionist ambitions encouraged the Soviets to pursue these policies, and this naturally disturbed the Poles. For this reason, Sikorski's Government attempted to intensify its willingness to by-pass silently the disputed issues and to show a maximum amount of good will in order to adjust its relations with Russia. They wished to manifest Polish willingness to let bygones be bygones for the sake of Allied unity and victory over Nazism. They were anxious also to show the Russian people and the Western world that their intentions were of the best. This was also imperative since, in the event that the Poles would not be able to change Soviet designs on Poland, Western public opinion and governments would then at least have no doubts about the causes of friction and would feel a moral obligation to support the professed principles of the Atlantic Charter.

For this reason the Polish Government was anxious to plunge all of its armed forces in the West into battle so that the name of Poland as an uncompromising foe of Hitler would be brought again before the eyes of the world. The underground organizations and the army were instructed to paralyze the German Wehrmacht and its lines of communication leading towards the East in order to help the Eastern Ally. Ambassador Romer prepared a new program for his dealings with the Russians which accommodated almost all their previous objections and submitted a new plan for relief distribution and the proposed personnel to handle it. The Soviets were not impressed with either.

Recognizing the importance of personal contacts in diplomacy, Sikorski arrived again in Washington in the beginning of December 1942. Since his last visit in March, the political atmosphere in Washington had become very positively disposed towards the Russians. As the war progressed, Soviet propaganda intensified its efforts to impress upon America the belief that the successes were being won primarily by the Red Army and that therefore the Russians were entitled to preferential treatment over any other ally.

Sikorski informed the President that he intended to make a second visit to Stalin to resolve Polish-Soviet difficulties, but, he added that he regarded one condition an essential to the success of his venture, namely, that he should have the full support of the President and that Stalin should be made aware of it.

While agreeing that such support was necessary, the President did not think he could express it in any too definite a way at the time. He agreed, however, to give a letter to Sikorski assuring him of the President's support. Sikorski could make use of the letter when talking with Stalin.[82]

Sikorski was anxious to have the wording of the letter as clear as possible with respect to Poland's territorial status, but Roosevelt pointed out that he could not go into "such detail, on account of the declared American policy of not discussing territorial issues during the war." [83]

Sikorski realized immediately that conditions had changed. He feared that American policy was beginning to drift towards the direction of appeasement of Soviet Russia.

He hoped that President Roosevelt would soon succeed in persuading Stalin to meet him. The President had told him how anxious he was for such a meeting. But he doubted if Stalin would risk seeing the President while he was still uncertain of maintaining his initiative and his advantages in such a meeting.[84]

In all conversations with Sikorski, Roosevelt deliberately avoided any discussion of the most essential aspects of Sikorski's visit or of the subjects of the impending meeting between himself and Churchill in Casablanca, which was to take place in January 1943.

The Soviets did not wait for the result of Sikorski's consultations with the Americans. Judging by the previous results of his visit to Washington, they anticipated a revival of American support for Poles. In order to forestall any synchronized American-Polish move, and in complete disregard of international law and its usage, the Soviet Government, on January 16, notified the Polish Embassy that the Western Ukraine and Western Byelorussia were inseparable provinces of the Soviet Union. Furthermore, it decided to regard all Polish deportees still remaining in Russia as citizens of the U.S.S.R. on the basis that they originated from the above-mentioned Soviet territories.[85]

The Polish Government, in reply, reaffirmed its determination not to recognize any changes which occurred in the disputed areas since September 1939.[86]

Some of the people who had been forcibly evacuated were called upon to produce visas proving legal entry into the U.S.S.R. Naturally, they could not possibly have such papers. They thereupon received sentences as high as two years of imprisonment for illegal residence in the U.S.S.R. without proper documents.

Ambassador Ciechanowski discussed this new development with Sumner Welles who, while condemning the Soviet behavior asked, "Am I to understand that the Polish Government is determined not to sacrifice even an inch of its eastern territory?" He was told that without the possibility of consulting its Parliament and finding out what the will of the Polish nation was, the Government in London did not consider itself as having the power to make such a sacrifice.

Roosevelt, upon his return from Casablanca, told Ciechanowski that he considered the Polish-Soviet relations

> . . . so delicate and difficult that, in the circumstances, the Polish Government should not press him for immediate intervention. For various reasons connected with the war situation he did not think he could effectively act at once, but hoped to be able to do so in the very near future. Then Roosevelt told Welles to advise Sikorski and the Polish Government to "keep their shirt on." [87]

The British were sympathetic too but were unwilling actively to take the Polish side. On the contrary, they were broadly hinting that there was no other way to relieve the tension but by making some more concessions to the Soviets.

This was the time of the Stalingrad victory. The Red Army now had tipped not only the military but also the political scales. The Soviets realized that by the time the Western Powers would open a second front the Red Army would have made good headway westward. It might even be able to occupy Poland and present the West with a *fait accompli*. Public opinion in the West was full of respect for Soviet successes. Stalin kept postponing the date to meet the Western leaders—presumably in order not to be tied down by specific plans and commitments until he would be able to negotiate from a position of strength. "I have made five attempts to see this man," exclaimed President Roosevelt, "but he has always eluded me." [88]

On February 19, 1943 Korneychuk wrote an article which appeared in the *Radianska Ukraina* in which he accused Poland of launching an arbitrary claim to Soviet territories.[89]

In accordance with the old and frequently practiced principle of accusing their victims of the crimes which they themselves were committing or were about to perpetrate, the Soviet Government issued on March 1 a very strongly worded declaration accusing the largely powerless Polish Government in London of imperialistic tendencies. They furthermore invoked the protection and sanction of the Atlantic Charter in this charge. For the first time they officially stated that only the Curzon Line could be a just frontier between the two countries.[90]

On March 4 the Polish Government replied:

> Until the conclusion of agreements between the U.S.S.R. and the Third Reich concerning the partition of Polish territories, the Treaty of Riga and its frontier clauses approved in 1923 by the Conference of Ambassadors and by the United States of North America were never called in question by Russia. These Russo-German Agreements were cancelled by the Soviet-Polish Agreement of July 30, 1941. The question of any return to the German-Soviet frontier line of that year requires no further comments.[91]

The British and American leaders were irritated by this firm reply of the Polish Government.

Ambassador Ciechanowski saw President Roosevelt again and suggested issuing an energetic joint American-British note on behalf of Poland. Roosevelt readily replied that he thought this a very good idea and that

> . . . my suggestion appealed to him. . . . Some time later the President told me that, though he deeply regretted it, his advisers—as he put it—had persuaded him "that the moment was ill chosen for such a declaration which might be resented by Stalin." I had been asked by the President to impress upon my Government the necessity of keeping the whole matter strictly secret.[92]

This meant that the Polish Government could not make the facts known to the Western public. The Poles feared that Stalin would take proper advantage of this Western silence. At the same time, Soviet diplomacy and propaganda were greatly increasing their activities in both Anglo-Saxon countries. Fear of a separate Soviet-German peace was handsomely exploited by the Russians. The British were reluctant to have anything to do with the Polish Government except to exchange diplomatic notes.

When, on March 11, Eden arrived in Washington, several appointments were made for Ambassador Ciechanowski to see him. Eden, however, canceled them all under the pretext that he was too busy with other official duties. Instead, Ciechanowski conferred with Sir William Strang, who headed the department at the Foreign Office which dealt with Polish and Soviet affairs. Strang was convinced that joint British-American intervention should be attempted but was of the opinion that it was up to the United States rather than Britain to take the initiative.[93]

According to Ciechanowski, Eden

. . . had used all his very convincing and suave diplomacy to impress upon the American Government and political circles how indispensable it was to continue to apply great caution in dealing with the Soviets, and to avoid so far as possible any too forcible arguments which Stalin might resent and which might result in the loss of this powerful partner, who was bearing the brunt of the war against Germany.[94]

Hopkins recorded Eden's conference with the President which was held on March 15, 1943.

Eden said he thought that Russia would demand very little territory of Poland, possibly up to the "Curzon Line." This would not affect Poland unduly from an economic point of view. Eden said he believed that Stalin wanted a strong Poland, provided the right kind of people were running it, and that (Russian) policy at the Peace Table would depend on this.

The President said it would be difficult to work out geographical boundaries on this basis because, while there might be a liberal government in Poland at the time of the Peace Conference, they might well be thrown out within a week.[95]

. . . .

Then Eden criticized the excessive ambition of the Poles to emerge from the war as the most powerful country in Eastern Europe when Germany and Russia would be weakened. He was critical of Sikorski's plan to federate the European states because the Russians were suspicious of any organizations of states on their flanks.

The President said that, after all, the big powers would have to decide what Poland should have and that he, the President, did not intend to go to the Peace Conference and bargain with Poland or the other small states.[96]

It was apparent that Anglo-American leaders were not going to examine the merits of such a small issue as a territorial dispute between the Soviet Union and Poland. They were preoccupied with the solution of the larger problems, and of those the largest was the question of peace.

On March 16 Hopkins met with Litvinov who told him

. . . that Russia would insist on what he called "her territorial rights on the Polish frontier." He said he did not anticipate any great difficulty with Poland about this although he said Poland would make "outrageous" demands. He felt that Great Britain and the United States should decide what was to be done about Poland and "tell them" rather than ask them.[97]

As events have shown, Litvinov's advice was gradually accepted.

Eden told Hopkins of talks he had had just before leaving London with Maisky. . . . (Maisky) expressed the hope that Eden would make no definite commitments for detailed post-war settlements while in Washington. Eden gave assurances that the talks would be "entirely exploratory." . . . Maisky evidently expressed much the same views as regards Poland. . . . He added that his Government . . . would not look with favor on the reestablishment of the same kind of government as that which had existed in Poland before the war or which had the political coloration of the current Polish Government-in-Exile.[98]

Eden's views fell on fertile ground and were publicly expounded in Walter Lippmann's articles. This unfavorable behavior towards the Poles by her powerful Allies was due not so much to genuine sympathy for the Soviets, as it was to the fear of her unpredictable policies. It was thought that a far-reaching accommodation of the Soviet demands would dispel Soviet distrust of the West. For the Soviets, it presumably meant that if they acted firmly their requests would be granted—or at least not actively opposed.

On March 9 Ambassador Romer complained to Foreign Minister Molotov about new arrests of his personnel in Kirov and Kustanai, where the NKVD had organized meetings of the Embassy delegates and had offered them Soviet passports. When this offer was rejected, all those present, as well as their families, were arrested. Ambassador Romer asked for an explanation and the release of the arrested.

In reply, Molotov stated that,

. . . the Polish authorities must comply with Soviet orders. What do you want? If you don't intend to obey our laws, then we cannot reach any understanding. I see that you don't want to recognize our legislation of November 29, 1939. It seems to me that you intend us to ask every single resident of Western Ukraine and Western Byelorussia which citizenship he wants to have. I want to draw your attention to the fact that this is out of the question. This would be contrary to our Soviet legislation. According to it, the place of birth is meaningless. Any place of residence in Western Ukraine and Western Byelorussia is, however, important.

ROMER. What about the citizenship of the staff of the Polish Embassy?
MOLOTOV. Theoretically I am not excluding the possibility that there
might be a Soviet citizen on your staff, i.e., that you may have somebody
who comes from Bialystok.
ROMER. Do you mean to say that your legislation applies also to my
diplomatic staff? My staff was registered by the People's Commissariat
for Foreign Affairs and recognized as Polish citizens.
MOLOTOV. Our note changes all this.
ROMER. You mean that this even applies to the officials of the Embassy
previously recognized by your office as Polish citizens?
MOLOTOV. The law is the law (*zakon yest zakon*).[99]

Romer concluded that Molotov was unwilling to see any logic, or
to understand the meaning of the issues. As on previous occasions, the
Poles could only protest.

The continually growing tension reached its height in April 1943,
when news of the Katyn massacre was brought into the foreground.
The fate of the missing Polish officers was the subject of endless notes
and conversations between Polish and Soviet authorities. It was
known from the Soviet authorities that the number of Polish officers
taken prisoner was about 9,000, in addition to the 2,000 arrested and
deported during the sovietization of Eastern Poland.[100] It was also
established that they were kept in three large camps and that in April
and May of 1940 they were transferred from those camps to an unknown destination. After the "amnesty," only about 400 of them
were located in the smaller camps and were included in the Polish
Army. On several occasions the Soviets assured Kot and Anders that
all prisoners of war had been set free. All efforts to locate them had
failed.

On April 5, 1943 the *Völkischer Beobachter*, No. 104, announced:

Über 10,000 Offiziere der ehemaligen Polnischen Armee, darunter zahl-
reiche Generäle, die beim militärischen Zusammenbruch ihres staates als
Gefangene in die Hand der Sowjets gefallen waren, sind von den Bol-
schewisten ermordet worden. Das grauenhafte Verbrechen kam zutage
als die Massengräber dieser Opter der GPU Justiz unlängst aufgefunden
wurden: Sie liegen im Wald von Katyn, am Kosegory-Hügel, an der
strasse Smolensk-Witebsk, rund 20 kilometer, westlich von Smolensk un-
weit des Ortes Sofiewka.

The German radio publicly charged the Soviet Government with
the murder of 14,500 Poles in the three camps, and proposed to hold
an international inquiry on the spot as to their fate. The Goebbels
propaganda machine had its heyday in exploiting the discovery for
all it was worth.[101] Poles in London were by nature skeptical of all
German statements, but this discovery of the Katyn atrocities tied up
many of the loose ends of the Polish search for the missing men.

The Polish Underground dispatched its own units to the scene and within four days received confirmation that the graves had been found and about 4,000 bodies had been unearthed.

For three days the Soviets were silent. On April 17 the *Soviet War News*, No. 541, carried the following statement by the Soviet Information Bureau.

In the past two or three days Goebbels' slanderers have been spreading vile fabrications alleging that Soviet authorities effected a mass shooting of Polish Officers in the spring of 1940 in the Smolensk area. In launching this monstrous invention, the German-Fascist scoundrels do not shrink from the most unscrupulous and base lies in their attempt to cover up crimes which, as has now become evident were perpetrated by themselves.

The German-Fascist reports on this subject leave no doubt as to the tragic fate of the former Polish prisoners of war who in 1941 were engaged in construction work in areas west of Smolensk and who, along with many Soviet people, residents of the Smolensk region, fell into the hands of the German-Fascist hangmen in the summer of 1941, after the withdrawal of the Soviet troops from the Smolensk areas.[102]

Sikorski went to Churchill and told him that he had proof that the Soviet Government had murdered those Poles. Writing about that meeting, Churchill stated:

He had a wealth of evidence. I said, "if they are dead nothing you can do will bring them back." He said he could not hold his people and that they had already released all their news to the press.[103]

Accordingly, on April 16 the Polish Minister of National Defense (a former Professor of History at Kraków University) General Marian Kukiel, issued the following announcement:

On September 17, 1940 the official organ of the Red Army, the *Red Star*, stated that during the fighting which took place after September 17, 1939, 181,000 Polish prisoners of war were taken by the Soviets. Of this number, about 10,000 were officers of the regular army and reserve.

According to information in possession of the Polish Government, three large camps of Polish prisoners of war were set up in the U.S.S.R. in November, 1939.

(1) In Kozelsk, east of Smolensk
(2) In Starobelsk, near Kharkov, and
(3) In Ostashkov, near Kalinin, where former Polish police and military police personnel were concentrated.

At the beginning of 1940 the camp authorities informed the prisoners in all three camps that all camps were about to be broken up and that they would be allowed to return to their homes and families. Allegedly for this purpose, lists of places to which individual prisoners wished to go after their release were made.

At that time there were:

(1) In Kozelsk, about 5,000 men, including some 4,500 officers.

(2) In Starobelsk, about 3,920 men, including 100 civilians; the rest were officers, of whom there were some medical officers.

(3) In Ostashkov, about 6,570 men, including some 380 officers.

On April 5, 1940 the breaking up of these camps was begun and groups of 60 to 300 men were removed from them every few days until the middle of May. From Kozelsk they were sent in the direction of Smolensk. About 400 people only were moved from all three camps in June, 1940 to Gryazovetz in the Vologda district.

When, after the conclusion of the Soviet-Polish Treaty of July 30, 1941 and the signing of the Military Agreement of August 14, 1941 the Polish Government proceeded to form the Polish Army in the U.S.S.R., it was expected that the officers from the above-mentioned camps would form the cadres of senior and junior officers of the army in formation. At the end of August, 1941 a group of Polish officers from Gryazovetz arrived to join the Polish units in Buzuluk; not one officer, however, among those deported in the other direction from Kozelsk, Starobelsk, and Ostashkov appeared. In all, therefore, about 8,300 officers were missing, not counting 7,000 N.C.O.'s, soldiers and civilians, who were in those camps when they were broken up.

Ambassador Kot and General Anders, perturbed by this state of affairs, addressed to the competent Soviet authorities inquiries and representations about the fate of the Polish officers from the above-mentioned camps.

In a conversation with Mr. Vyshinsky, People's Commissar for Foreign Affairs, on October 6, 1941, Ambassador Kot asked what had happened to the missing officers. Mr. Vyshinsky answered that all prisoners of war had been freed from the camps and therefore they must be at liberty.

In October and November, in his conversations with Premier Stalin, Mr. Molotov, and Mr. Vyshinsky the Ambassador on various occasions returned to the question of the prisoners of war and insisted upon being supplied with lists of them, such lists having been compiled carefully and in detail by the Soviet Government.

During his visit to Moscow, Prime Minister Sikorski in a conversation with Premier Stalin on December 3, 1941 also intervened for the liberation of all Polish prisoners of war, and not having been supplied by the Soviet authorities with their lists, he handed to Premier Stalin on this occasion an incomplete list of 3,845 Polish officers which their former fellow-prisoners had succeeded in compiling. Premier Stalin assured General Sikorski that the amnesty was of a general and universal character and affected both military and civilians. On March 18, 1942 General Anders handed Premier Stalin a supplementary list of 800 officers. Nevertheless, not one of the officers mentioned in either of these lists has been returned to the Polish Army.

Besides these interventions in Moscow and Kuybyshev, the fate of Polish prisoners of war was the subject of several interviews between Minister Raczynski and Ambassador Bogomolov. On January 28, 1942 Minister Raczynski, in the name of the Polish Government, handed a note to Soviet Ambassador Bogomolov, drawing his attention once again to the painful fact that many thousands of Polish officers had still not been found.

Ambassador Bogomolov informed Minister Raczynski on March 13, 1942 that in accordance with the Decree of the Presidium of the Supreme

Council of the U.S.S.R. of August 12, 1941 and in accordance with the statements of the People's Commissariat for Foreign Affairs of November 8 and 19, 1941 the amnesty had been put into full effect, and that it related both to civilians and to the military.

On May 19, 1942 Ambassador Kot sent the People's Commissariat for Foreign Affairs a Memorandum in which he expressed his regret at the refusal to supply him with a list of prisoners, and his concern as to their fate, emphasizing the high value these officers would have in military operations against Germany.

Neither the Polish Government nor the Polish Embassy in Kuybyshev has ever received an answer as to the whereabouts of the missing officers and other prisoners who have been deported from the three camps mentioned above.

We have become accustomed to the lies of German propaganda and we understand the purpose behind its latest revelations. In view, however, of abundant and detailed German information concerning the discovery of the bodies of many thousands of Polish officers near Smolensk, and the categorical statement that they were murdered by the Soviet authorities in the spring of 1940, the necessity has arisen that the mass graves should be investigated and the facts alleged verified by a competent international body, such as the International Red Cross. The Polish Government has therefore approached this institution with a view to their sending a delegation to the place where the massacre of the Polish prisoners of war is said to have taken place.[104]

Simultaneously, the Polish Government issued a communiqué which summarized and condemned numerous Nazi crimes committed against the Polish people, and went on to say:

> Poland's enormous price in terms of victims and great suffering does not entitle the Germans to advance shameful pretenses of being the defenders of Christian Europe and its culture against Russian "barbarism."
>
> The Polish Government condemns all crimes performed on Polish citizens and denies the right to anyone to exploit them in political games. Whoever is guilty of these atrocities against the Polish nation should be punished.[105]

Three days later the Polish Government requested Ambassador Bogomolov to explain the whereabouts of the prisoners in question.[106]

Pravda on April 19 angrily declared that the Polish Government was "cooperating with the Hitlerite hangmen," that the Polish appeal to the International Red Cross "constituted direct assistance to the enemy in the fabrication of a foul lie which will fill all people of common sense with repugnance. . . ."

The next step in this sequence of events was Maisky's visit to Churchill.

> He brought me a message from Stalin that after the hideous charges which the Polish Government in London had published and sponsored against Russia, of the wholesale murder of the Polish officer prisoners,

the Agreement of 1941 would be immediately denounced. I said I thought the Poles had been unwise to make or lend themselves to such an account, but that I earnestly hoped a blunder of this kind would not entail a breach in their relations with the Soviets.[107]

The Poles were convinced, however, that the Soviets were guilty of this crime. They were prepared for the worst. If the Polish Government in London had chosen any other course of action, it would have been immediately repudiated by all Poles at home and abroad. It had no choice. The repercussions were immediate and drastic.

On April 25, 1943 Molotov delivered the following note to the Polish Ambassador in the U.S.S.R., Romer.

The Soviet Government considers the recent behavior of the Polish Government with regard to the U.S.S.R. as entirely abnormal and violating all regulations and standards of relations between two Allied States. The slanderous campaign hostile to the Soviet Union launched by the German Fascists in connection with the murder of the Polish officers, which they themselves committed in the Smolensk area on territory occupied by German troops, was at once taken up by the Polish Government and is being fanned in every way by the Polish official press.

Far from offering a rebuff to the vile Fascist slander of the U.S.S.R. the Polish Government did not even find it necessary to address to the Soviet Government any inquiry or request for an explanation on this subject.

Having committed a monstrous crime against the Polish officers, the Hitlerite authorities are now staging a farcical investigation, and for this they have made use of certain Polish pro-Fascist elements whom they themselves selected in Occupied Poland, where everything is under Hitler's heel, and where no honest Pole can openly have his say.

For the "investigation" both the Polish Government and the Hitlerite Government invited the International Red Cross, which is compelled, under conditions of a terroristic regime with its gallows and mass extermination of the peaceful population, to take part in this investigation farce staged by Hitler. Clearly such an "investigation" conducted behind the back of the Soviet Government cannot evoke the confidence of people possessing any degree of honesty.

The fact that the hostile campaign against the Soviet Union commenced simultaneously in the German and Polish press, and was conducted along the same lines, leaves no doubt as to the existence of contact and accord in carrying out this hostile campaign between the enemy of the Allies—Hitler—and the Polish Government.

The Soviet Government is aware that this hostile campaign against the Soviet Union is being undertaken by the Polish Government in order to exert pressure upon the Soviet Government by making use of the slanderous Hitlerite fake for the purpose of wresting from it territorial concessions at the expense of the interests of the Soviet Ukraine, Soviet Byelorussia, and Soviet Lithuania.

All these circumstances compel the Soviet Government to recognize that the present Government of Poland, having slid down the path of accord with Hitler's Government, has actually discontinued Allied relations with the U.S.S.R., and has adopted a hostile attitude towards the Soviet Union.

On the strength of the above, the Soviet Government has decided to sever relations with the Polish Government.[108]

The Polish Ambassador, Romer, did not accept that note.

On April 23, the International Red Cross announced from Geneva that it could not undertake any inquiry into the German allegations unless a corresponding invitation to do so was received from the Soviet Government. Since Stalin was obviously not willing to issue a similar invitation to dispel any doubt as to who the guilty party really was, the Poles announced that they regarded their appeal as having lapsed.

Notes

[1] Poland, *Official Government Documents*, Vol. XVII, Docs. 44–45.

[2] *Ibid.*, Docs. 47–49.

[3] *Ibid.*, Doc. 50.

[4] *Ibid.*, Vol. II, Doc. 5.

[5] *Ibid.*, Doc. 1.

[6] *Ibid.*, Vol. XVII, Docs. 51–53.

[7] *Ibid.*, Docs. 59–60.

[8] *Ibid.*, Docs. 58–59.

[9] *Ibid.*, Docs. 77–78.

[10] *Ibid.*, Doc. 68.

[11] *Ibid.*, Vol. II, Doc. 5.

[12] *Ibid.*, Doc. 6.

[13] *Ibid.*, Doc. 17.

[14] *Ibid.*, Doc. 7.

[15] Among other matters to be resolved by his visit, Sikorski wished to sign a pact of mutual friendship and assistance with the U.S.S.R.

[16] Although the transcript of that meeting is of some length, it seems necessary to include it here because it brings out all the major issues which divided the two parties.

[17] These regions proved to have every conceivable disease, such as typhoid, malaria, jaundice, dysentery. From February 1942 to August 1942, 47,411 Poles were infected with various diseases.
Stanislaw Kot, *Listy z Rosji do Generala Sikorskiego*, London, 1956, p. 40.

[18] Poland, *Official Government Documents*, Vol. XVII, Doc. 50.

[19] *Ibid.*, Doc. 51.

[20] Stanislaw Mikolajczyk, *The Rape of Poland: Pattern of Soviet Aggression*, New York, Whittlesey House, 1948, p. 23.

[21] Poland, *Official Government Documents*, Vol. X, Doc. 58.

[22] *Ibid.*, Vol. IV, Doc. 30.

[23] Kot, *op. cit.*, pp. 64–65.

[24] At the end of 1939, under the protection and instruction of the NKVD,

Wanda Wasilewska organized an "Alliance of Former Polish Communists" and a "Union of Former Political Prisoners" which were actually the nucleus of the future Polish Communist Party. Together with Helen Usiyevich she became the editor of a political monthly, *New Horizons*. After the Nazi attack on Russia in June 1941, this publication was discontinued, to be resumed at Kuybyshev on May 5, 1942 as a fortnightly.

[25] Poland, *Official Government Documents*, Vol. XVII, Docs. 4–35.

[26] Jozef Swiatlo, *Za Kulisami Bezpieki i Partji*, New York, Free Europe Press, 1955, p. 15.

[27] Poland, *Official Government Documents*, Vol. IV, Docs. 36–38.

[28] Kot, *op. cit.*, p. 209.

[29] *Ibid.*, p. 136.

[30] *Ibid.*, p. 321.

[31] Poland, *Official Government Documents*, Vol. CLXI, Doc. 7.

[32] *Ibid.*, Doc. 8.

[33] *Ibid.*, Doc. 9.

[34] Kot, *op. cit.*, p. 290.

[35] Then the President of the American Federation of Labor.

[36] Poland, *Official Government Documents*, Vol. XVII, Doc. 280.

[37] *Ibid.*, Docs. 280–281.

[38] *Ibid.*, Doc. 305.

[39] Mikolajczyk, *op. cit.*, pp. 24–26.

[40] Poland, *Official Government Documents*, Vol. CLXI, Doc. 9.

[41] *Ibid.*, Vol. XVII, Doc. 12.

[42] *Ibid.*, Vol. CLXI, Doc. 1a.

[43] *Ibid.*, Vol. XVII, Doc. 52.

[44] *Ibid.*, Doc. 54.

[45] *Ibid.*, Doc. 55.

[46] *Ibid.*, Doc. 56.

[47] *Ibid.*, Doc. 58.

[48] Jan Ciechanowski, *Defeat in Victory*, Garden City, New York, Doubleday & Company, Inc., 1947, p. 92.

[49] Cordell Hull, *The Memoirs of Cordell Hull* (2 vols.), New York, The Macmillan Company, 1948, pp. 1166–1167.

[50] Ciechanowski, *op. cit.*, pp. 93–94.

[51] *Ibid.*, p. 95.

[52] *Ibid.*, p. 96.

[53] *Ibid.*, p. 98.

[54] *Ibid.*, p. 100.

[55] Winston S. Churchill, *The Hinge of Fate*, Boston, Houghton Mifflin Company, 1950, p. 327.

[56] *Ibid.*, p. 328.

[57] Ciechanowski, *op. cit.*, p. 104.

[58] *Ibid.*

[59] Churchill, *op. cit.*, p. 331.

[60] *Ibid.*, p. 332.

[61] Ciechanowski, *op. cit.*, p. 108.

[62] Churchill, *op. cit.*, pp. 335–336.

[63] *Ibid.*, p. 338.

[64] Ciechanowski, *op. cit.*, p. 110.

[65] Poland, *Official Government Documents*, Vol. XVII, Doc. 68.

[66] Kot, *op. cit.*, p. 50.

[67] *Ibid.*, p. 565.

[68] Even before the Polish-Soviet treaty of July 1941 Beria attempted to persuade General Waclaw Przezdziecki, while the latter was still in prison, to form a Polish legion beside the Red Army. His refusal brought upon him more severe treatment. *Ibid.*, p. 94.

[69] Undoubtedly Anders had shared the desire of all the soldiers under his command, as well as that of the civilian population, to get out of the U.S.S.R. as soon as possible. This was only natural. But, according to Prof. Kot, he was also closely connected with the right-wing leaders in London—including President Raczkiewicz—who were the political enemies of Sikorski and who were after his scalp for his too liberal policies towards the U.S.S.R. Therefore, it was hoped that once Anders was outside the Soviet Union and in command of the large military formation he would be able to replace Sikorski. In February of 1943 he sent a confidential letter from the Middle East to President Raczkiewicz asking for the dismissal of Sikorski and his Government. The letter was unanswered, presumably because it was realized that the British would take a dim view of such a performance. *Ibid.*, pp. 72, 428.

[70] *Ibid.*, pp. 255, 338.

[71] *Ibid.*, pp. 154, 541–543.

[72] *Ibid.*, p. 348.

[73] Ciechanowski, *op. cit.*, pp. 110–111.

[74] *Ibid.*, pp. 616–629.

[75] Poland, *Official Government Documents*, Vol. XVII, Doc. 72.

[76] *Ibid.*, Vol. X, Doc. 42.

[77] *Ibid.*, Vol. XVII, Doc. 101.

[78] *Ibid.*, Doc. 105.

[79] *Ibid.*, Doc. 99.

[80] Kot, *op. cit.*, p. 384.

[81] *Ibid.*, p. 383.

[82] Ciechanowski, *op. cit.*, p. 132.

[83] *Ibid.*

[84] *Ibid.*, p. 134.

[85] Poland, *Official Government Documents*, Vol. XVII, Doc. 118.

[86] *Ibid.*, Doc. 119.

[87] Ciechanowski, *op. cit.*, p. 142.

[88] Ciechanowski, *op. cit.*, p. 153.

[89] Poland, *Official Government Documents*, Vol. XVII, Doc. 125.

[90] *Ibid.*, Doc. 126.

[91] *Ibid.*, Doc. 127.

[92] Ciechanowski, *op. cit.*, pp. 145–146.

[93] *Ibid.*, p. 155.

[94] *Ibid.*, p. 156.

[95] Robert E. Sherwood, *Roosevelt and Hopkins*, New York, Harper & Brothers, 1948, p. 709.

[96] *Ibid.*, p. 710.

[97] *Ibid.*, p. 713.

[98] *Ibid.*, pp. 713–714.

[99] Poland, *Official Government Documents*, Vol. XVII, Doc. 130.

[100] A considerable number of these officers were members of the Polish intelligentsia, including university professors, doctors, engineers, and leading citizens who had been mobilized as reservists.

[101] Paul Joseph Goebbels, *The Goebbels Diaries, 1942–1943*, Louis P. Lochner, ed. and trans., Garden City, N. Y., Doubleday & Company, Inc., 1948, pp. 318, 328, 332, 345–348, 487.

[102] Poland, *Official Government Documents*, Vol. XVII, Doc. 135.

[103] Churchill, *op. cit.*, p. 759.

[104] Poland, *Official Government Documents*, Vol. XVII, Doc. 136.

[105] *Ibid.*, Doc. 137.

[106] *Ibid.*, Doc. 138.

[107] Churchill, *op. cit.*, p. 760.

[108] Poland, *Official Government Documents*, Vol. XVII, Doc. 140.

From the Rupture
of Diplomatic Relations
to the Soviet Establishment
of the Lublin Committee

April 1943 to January 1944

1. The Final Outcome of the Katyn Massacres

On April 26, 1943 Ciechanowski called on Sumner Welles.

As I came into his room at the State Department I noticed he was upset. I sensed for the first time a tense atmosphere in my relations with the Under-secretary. He started by saying that he could not understand how the Polish Government could have appealed to the International Red Cross to investigate an accusation made—as he put it—"by the German propaganda machine." How could the Polish Government expect an impartial result from such an investigation? He expressed his deep regret that the Polish Government had taken this course, giving an easy pretext to the Soviets to break relations with Poland.[1]

Ciechanowski explained that in view of the discovery of the mass graves the Polish Government had to ask for an impartial investigation of the corpses in order to determine the date of the crime. Such a request did not prejudice the whole matter.

When the International Red Cross declined the Polish request, the Germans conducted their own investigation, and a committee of experts,[2] drawn from the countries under German occupation, produced a detailed report claiming that upwards of 10,000 bodies had been found in mass graves and that the evidence of documents found on them and the age of the trees planted over the graves showed that the execution dated back to the spring of 1940, when the area was under Soviet control. Subsequently, when the Red Army regained that area, the Soviets appointed a special committee composed of their own men to investigate the bodies.[3] Its report, *The Truth About Katyn*, London, 1944, based on an examination conducted in January 1944, stated that 11,000 Poles were murdered but that only 925 bodies were exhumed and examined. The Soviet report claimed that the Germans were responsible for that crime. But since the Soviets claimed in their communiqué of April 15 that they knew all along that the massacres had been perpetrated by the Germans, the question obviously arises as to why they did not tell the Poles this before, instead of giving a number of either evasive or contradictory answers.[4]

In the German war crimes trials at Nürnberg, the murder of the Poles at Katyn was mentioned in the indictments[5] of Goering and others, who in their defense presented the White Book of the German investigation before the court. Upon examination of the evidence submitted, the Germans were acquitted of this accusation. The ultimate sentence of the Nazi war leaders did not mention Katyn. The Soviet Government never took the opportunity of clearing itself of the accusation against it nor of fastening the guilt conclusively upon the Germans, although it had ample opportunity to do so.

Washington and London were primarily concerned with the preservation of Allied unity. Although they were upset by the great tragedy at Katyn, they were also annoyed that the Poles had appealed to the International Red Cross. The Poles were convinced that if the Americans and the British had been in the same position, they would have behaved in at least the same manner. Both governments were known then and are known now to threaten the use of force for the mistreatment, not to mention murder, of a single of their nationals, let alone 14,000. There was a limit to the price which any self-respecting country could pay for Allied peace and harmony.

2. The Soviets Launch an All-Out Effort to Undermine the Polish Government

On May 4, 1943 Stalin supplied the following answer to two questions submitted to him by the Moscow correspondents of the London *Times* and *The New York Times*.

QUESTION: Does the Government of the U.S.S.R. desire to see a strong and independent Poland after the defeat of Hitlerite Germany?
STALIN: Unquestionably, it does.

QUESTION: On what fundamentals is it your opinion that relations between Poland and the U.S.S.R. should be based after the war?

STALIN: Upon the fundamentals of solid good neighborly relations and mutual respect, or should the Polish people so desire, upon the fundamentals of an alliance providing for mutual assistance against the Germans as the chief enemies of the Soviet Union and Poland.

The British made unofficial inquiries as to whether Sikorski would be willing to dismiss those members of his Cabinet whom the Soviets considered unfriendly to them. The answer was no. The British were under the spell of Stalin's statement that he wanted "a strong and independent Poland" and "a friendly government." The Poles were suspicious of the meaning of the Soviet interpretation of these terms. The British, on the other hand, could not share the Polish fear that the Soviets wanted to dominate Poland and to Sovietize it.

The Soviets did not waste any time in preparing grounds for the establishment of "a strong and independent Poland" with a government friendly to them. Such a government was already being formed.

A convention of so-called Polish Patriots took place in Moscow. Sixty-six delegates, whose names were not disclosed, supposedly represented all "Polish political, democratic, and progressive parties." The convention condemned the Government-in-Exile and promised to fight "hand in hand" with the Red Army for a "democratic and progressive Poland." [6]

Almost simultaneously, a communist-controlled Polish Army came into being in the U.S.S.R. with Berling as its head. Berling's Soviet military superior was Major General Bevzink, while political control was entrusted to Alexander Zawadzki, the NKVD colonel. Recruits for the Army were supplied by compulsory conscription among Polish war prisoners who either had only then been released, or who had not been allowed to leave Russia with the Polish Army of General Anders.

In a relatively short time, the communist agents succeeded in infiltrating several underground organizations, although they were unable to infiltrate the official underground State and the Home Army. [7]

The London Government was continually disturbed and worried by increasingly frequent reports that members of the underground organizations were being denounced to the Gestapo by unknown but presumably communist sources, whereupon mass killings of the underground forces followed. More prominent personnel, including many agents parachuted into Poland by British aircraft, were often met by communist "reception committees" and executed on the spot where they landed. [8]

The communists also created some new organizations which, by name, resembled the existing patriotic underground groups. The better known among them were, the "Polish Workers' Socialist Party," "Committee of National Initiative," "Non-Party Democrats," "The Opposition Group of the Peasant Party," "Sword and Plow," "The People's Guard," and "The People's Militia." Although these groups had only a small following, their existence was widely propagandized, both in underground Poland and abroad. They were presented as genuine, patriotic, non-communist organizations. At the same time, the Union of Polish Patriots was depicted as representing the Polish nation in the U.S.S.R.[8]

The main propaganda weapons of this group were the radio station "Kosciuszko" which broadcast in Polish from the U.S.S.R. and two newspapers, *Nowe Widnokregi* (New Horizons) and *Wolna Polska* (Free Poland). The latter was distributed widely among Poles in Great Britain and Americans of Polish descent in Chicago, Detroit, New York, and other cities. The main theme of the radio and the newspapers was to discredit the London Government and its home organization, to organize Poles outside Poland around the "Union of Patriots," and, above all, to glorify the Soviet Union as the only true friend of Poland.[9]

Whatever damage may have been done to Soviet prestige abroad by the discovery of the Katyn graves was outweighed by the dissolution of the Comintern. This fact was so effectively propagandized that it misled Western public opinion as to the real Soviet objectives. A conviction was growing that there were no real difficulties in the way of achieving a genuine and lasting friendship with the Soviets.

Pertinent information about Washington's attitude towards the Polish-Soviet dispute is provided by Eduard Beneš of Czechoslovakia.

In his *Memoirs*, President Beneš recorded his conversation with Roosevelt in the White House on May 12, 1943.

Then we turned to Poland and the Soviet Union. It was at the moment when the differences between them were reaching their climax and when the Allies—especially Great Britain and the United States—had to take a definite decision in this matter. Millions of American Poles intervened strongly in this dispute and their influence on the forthcoming American presidential election played a great role. From the attitude of Roosevelt, as expressed in the discussion—and even more from the opinions of Harry Hopkins, the personal adviser of Roosevelt, which Hopkins explained to me himself in another talk on the following day—I realized that the United States had already taken a definite attitude; that, essentially, they had accepted the view of the Soviet Union on the question of changing the former eastern frontier of Poland and that, in principle, they agreed that there would have to be an agreement between Poland and the Soviet Union and some cooperation between them. Failing this, the United States was not inclined to support the action Poland was taking at this time. In particular, I came to the conclusion (this was *my* estimate of the outcome of the Washington talks) that the ideas of the London Poles—and, of course, of their Government, too—who believed that the Polish demands against the Soviet Union were supported by the United States, were illusions or pious hopes and that it was a total mistake to think that the influence of the American Poles could work a fundamental change in this regard. State Secretary Sumner Welles formulated this attitude to me on the following day just as definitely.[10]

Besides revealing the American view and attitude at that time towards the Soviet-Polish problem, this reference acquires greater importance in light of the following information provided by Beneš himself.

When preparing in London for the journey to Washington, I sent word to Moscow through Ambassador Bogomolov that it would be well if, before my visit to America, I could know some of the fundamental views of the Soviet Union concerning Germany, France, Poland, and ourselves, too, so that I could give the correct answers to questions on the subject in Washington.[11]

The requested answers were provided in time. The Soviets assured Beneš that the planned treaty which Beneš was negotiating with the Soviets would be based on mutual trust and non-interference in each other's internal affairs. They also extended an invitation to the Polish Government to join in on similar terms.[12]

These, then, were the lines, continued Beneš, on which the conversation with Roosevelt developed concerning all these questions. I told him that I knew what course the Soviet Union intended to take (one friendly to the Czechs and Poles) and realized that this necessitated our accommodating ourselves to its policy. . . .

I told him that after my return to England from America I intended to go immediately to Moscow and conclude a formal agreement with the Soviet Union. I added that I believed Poland, too, should follow a similar policy and should thus enable the three chief Powers to reach final accord in the Polish question.

After some further discussion of these matters Roosevelt expressed his full understanding of this policy.

. . . .

In Washington I found full understanding of our policy vis-à-vis the Soviet Union in my very first conversations and Roosevelt, as well as Cordell Hull and Sumner Welles, agreed to it in principle. Our treaty was regarded by the American Government as typical of what the Soviet Union's other neighbors should do, in time, so as to secure their independence and non-interference in their internal affairs or in their social structure on the side of the Soviet Union.[13]

Beneš, being the head of the most democratic country in Eastern Europe, was highly respected in the West, and his counsel carried considerable weight.

Summing up his last conversation with Roosevelt, held on June 7, 1943 Beneš recorded:

> Roosevelt requests that in my conversations with Stalin in Moscow I should present his views in the matter of the Baltic States. The United States are not able and do not intend to hinder their final annexation to the Soviet Union, but must respect world public opinion and therefore it is a question of finding the form and procedure which will calm public opinion. In the matter of Poland he considers Sikorski to be the best Prime Minister but he does not know what will happen among the Poles themselves. He knows that even Stalin would not personally reject Sikorski. He expects that the final solution will be the Curzon Line somewhat modified in Poland's favor, and the incorporation of East Prussia in Poland. He considers this a just and right compensation which the Poles could and should accept.[14]

At that time the Czechs planned to reach an agreement with the Soviets. One of the conditions which the Soviets put forward was to be the abandonment of the Czech-Polish treaty which was going to lay the basis for a future federation of Eastern Europe. That plan was preceded by a joint declaration providing for close political and economic association between Czechoslovakia and Poland and was signed on November 11, 1940. Another document of a similar nature entitled Joint Polish-Czechoslovak Agreement was signed on January 23, 1942. The closer association was not, however, to come into force until ratified by the parliaments of the two countries. At the last moment before the ratification, the Soviets objected to the whole idea, and consequently the Czechs annulled the whole thing.

Upon his return to London from Washington, President Beneš had a meeting with Mikolajczyk[15] during which the former wanted to broaden the historical perspective of his guest and help him to understand the Soviets.

> Beneš began by saying that the Soviet Union is afraid of another attack from Germany—but she is not imperialistically minded. America will not be involved in European politics. England will not go against Russia because an anti-Soviet policy led to Munich.
>
> Then Beneš said that in February 1942 he began talks with Maisky to whom he presented his views on the future of Czechoslovakia. He told Maisky that before the war there were three socialist movements in

Czechoslovakia: The Czech Parliament had 30 Communists, 30 National-Socialists (Beneš' Party), and 40 Social Democrats. This constituted one-third of the Czech Parliament. Assuming that at the end of this war the number of the Communists in the Parliament might increase by 20, this still would not permit the Communist Party to take over power because the other parties would resist and this would harm Czech-Soviet relations. "So I asked Maisky: what do you prefer, to have Communists in the Czech National Government and move the ideological character of Czechoslovakia to the left, or would you prefer to keep the Communist Party as a revolutionary force. Which would be more profitable for you? The same situation will exist in the other European countries." Maisky replied that the Soviet Union will choose cooperation of the Communist Parties in the National Governments in the neighborly countries and will live with them peacefully. Then I offered them a conclusion of a Czech-Soviet treaty against Germany on the following conditions:

    1. Like the British-Soviet Treaty it would be directed against Germany.

    2. It would guarantee the full independence of Czechoslovakia.

    3. It would contain a provision not to interfere into internal matters of both countries.

    4. It would contain the possibility of a Soviet-Polish-Czech treaty against Germany.

    5. It would contain provisions which will provide the Czechs with help to remove all Germans from Czechoslovak territories.[16]

In regard to Poland, Beneš said that he stood on the 1940 Polish-Czech declaration of mutual collaboration.

Mikolajczyk replied that as far as Poland was concerned, the whole value of these proposals was hanging in the air because of the absence of Soviet-Polish diplomatic relations. He said that this was due to the lack of good will on the part of the Soviets. Presumably the Soviets did not want to be bound to Poland by any obligations; and when they declared themselves to be in favor of an independent Poland, they really had in mind only about half of the 1939 Poland, or Poland as the Seventeenth Republic of the Soviet Union. In such a situation Czechoslovakia would also become a tool of communism.

Beneš said that in his conversation with the Soviets he did not get the impression of Soviet unwillingness to reach an agreement with Poland, and he intended to find out what the Soviet position was during his forthcoming trip to Moscow. Beneš stressed that it was important to him to have good relations between Poland and the Soviet Union because under no conditions would he like to remain alone with the Soviets. His ideal was to have a tri-partite agreement between the Soviet Union, Poland, and Czechoslovakia which would secure peaceful cooperation between these countries, and he also would have liked an Anglo-American guarantee to that effect. The whole thing would be directed against Germany, because otherwise the re-birth of Germany would mean the complete destruction of Czechoslovakia. Beneš also said that before he left for Washington he received Soviet permission to show the whole project to Roosevelt. At that time the White House thought that a Soviet-German rapprochement was possible. He assured Washington that such a possibility was out of the question and that there was a possibility of a Czech-Russian treaty. During the Moscow Conference of the Foreign Ministers this project of the treaty had been approved, and now he would go to Moscow to sign it. Before parting, Beneš expressed the desire to see Mikolajczyk after his return, because he expected to have some news for him.[17]

Having to face such extraordinarily difficult problems and the uncertainty as to the future relations with the Soviets, the Polish Government wanted to extend the Polish-British treaty in order to strengthen their hand in dealing with the Russians.

The British-Polish Treaty of Mutual Assistance of August 25, 1939 had the following clause:

1. The present Agreement shall remain in force for a period of five years.
2. Unless denounced six months before the expiration of this period it shall continue in force, each contracting party having thereafter the right to denounce it at any time by giving six months notice to that effect.

The expiration date was August 25, 1944. On June 15, 1942 the Polish Ambassador, Raczynski, delivered to Eden a memorandum in which the Polish Government suggested an extension of the treaty. On June 29, 1942 Eden officially replied as follows:

On further reflection I feel that it would be preferable to consider this question at a later date. Anglo-Polish relations are now firmly established on the basis of the 1939 Treaty and His Majesty's Government will of course enter into consultation with the Polish Government in good time before this Treaty lapses in August 1944, so that the two Governments may consider how best to maintain and prolong its benefits. I should, however, prefer those consultations to take place when the future is clear, and when the two Governments can also consider *inter alia* how best Anglo-Polish relations can be fitted into a regional or general system of security.[18]

A similar reply was given to the Polish Ambassador by the Foreign Office on February 15, 1943 in answer to another inquiry.

Subsequently it was established that the reason for the British attitude lay in an understanding between Eden and Molotov, reached in May 1942, which stated that neither Great Britain nor the Soviet Union would conclude a bilateral agreement with any continental European country. It was true that the Soviet Government denied that it undertook any such obligations towards the British Government. At the same time, and on the basis of that understanding, the British Foreign Office vetoed the Soviet-Czechoslovak treaty about to be signed. The Soviet Government maintained that it must be a misinterpretation on the part of Eden about the conditions as to where that understanding applied and consequently insisted that the Soviet Union had the right to sign a bilateral treaty with the Czechs.

In connection with the approaching visit of President Beneš to Moscow in late November, where he was to sign the treaty (which was open to other Eastern and Southern European countries), the Poles argued that presumably Eden, while in Moscow, had withdrawn his objections. But, by the same token, Great Britain would be free to extend her treaty with Poland. Therefore they thought that the Polish Government should once again approach the Foreign Office with the same suggestion. If the British responded positively, the benefits to Poland would be great. Obviously if they found another excuse for not doing so, then the Poles would know what the British attitude towards collective security in Eastern Europe really was. This would mean that the extension of the Soviet-Czech treaty to other countries would indicate that the Soviet Union would control that part of Europe, and that the British had given their consent to it. The Poles were anxious to learn the real attitude of Britain to this question in general and to Poland in particular in order to act accordingly. The British gave a negative response.[19]

In the beginning of May Churchill arrived in Washington to discuss the mutual problems of the Allies *vis-à-vis* Hitler, and it was decided to approach Stalin for a meeting of the Big Three. Joseph E. Davies, because of his unquestionable friendship for the Soviets, was sent as the President's special envoy to Stalin to discuss the possibility of a meeting between Roosevelt and Stalin prior to the Big Three meeting.[20] Davies had no authority, however, to go into the merits of any of the issues to be dealt with by them. This applied to Soviet-Polish relations as well as to other issues.[21]

Stalin agreed to meet Roosevelt on July 15. But when he learned about the further postponement of the opening of the Second Front, he accused the Western Allies of deliberate bad faith, recalled Litvinov from Washington and Maisky from London, and postponed indefinitely the Roosevelt-Stalin meeting.[22] The Western Powers became alarmed with the fear of a separate Russo-German armistice.

On June 30 Roosevelt dispatched Harriman to London to secure Churchill's consent to a meeting between the President and Stalin prior to any formal conference of the Big Three. Churchill was resentful of the idea.

He certainly lost no time in doing everything he could to prevent the tete-à-tete. . . . Hardly had Harriman left 10 Downing Street in the early hours of the morning before Churchill was hard at work drafting a message to Roosevelt with a counterproposal for a preliminary conference of the British, Russian, and American Foreign Ministers.[23]

Churchill was afraid that his prestige might suffer, and was also afraid of diplomatic isolation. Roosevelt agreed to the Prime Minister's proposal, and eventually Stalin accepted it also.

The Polish Government in London did not abandon hope that some solution could be found to resolve its conflict with the Soviets. At the beginning of June, Sikorski had asked the British and American Governments to help arrange a meeting between himself and Stalin. The positive British and American responses led to a new and vigorous Soviet press attack on Sikorski, whom they described as a "Fascist." His government was labeled as an "unwitting ally of the Germans."

On July 4, 1943 Sikorski was killed in an airplane accident off Gibraltar.[24] Churchill paid high tribute to the memory of the deceased Premier. Even the Russians spoke of him as a great man. Poland had lost an outstanding and respected leader.

3. Failure of Polish Attempts to Obtain Western Support

On July 14, 1943 Stanislaw Mikolajczyk, Vice-Premier in Sikorski's Cabinet and Speaker of the Polish Parliament-in-Exile, was appointed Prime Minister after his name had been chosen for that post by the Polish underground leaders in Poland. This sturdy, determined, indefatigable fighter for democracy in pre-war Poland, born of Polish peasant stock, was the very personification of a fighting Poland. His new Cabinet represented national unity and was composed of three representatives of the Peasant Party (small farm owners), three members of the Polish Socialist Party, two members of the National Democratic Party, and two of the Christian Labor Party. The Ministries of National Defense and Foreign Affairs were filled by non-party persons.

When Mikolajczyk paid his first official visit to him, Churchill said:

I will fight for the freedom of Poland. I will fight for a strong and independent Poland, and I'll never cease fighting for it.
We'll have many troubles with them (Russians), believe me. But also believe me when I say that I'll always be on your side.[25]

Mikolajczyk trusted Churchill.[26] He pledged himself to continue the foreign policy of Sikorski and promised to work relentlessly for neighborly relations with the Soviet Union.

On October 5, 1943 Mikolajczyk told Eden that his Government was most anxious to re-establish relations with the Soviet Union. For this reason he welcomed news about the forthcoming conference of the three ministers of foreign affairs but, at the same time, he stated that his Government was opposed to discussing the Soviet-Polish frontier at that conference. He stated that he would also welcome the help of the three ministers in re-establishing Soviet-Polish relations.

Eden made a gesture of disappointment, and said that he could not accept this view. In his opinion, he said, the Polish Government should accept the Curzon Line in exchange for German East Prussia and Silesia.

Mikolajczyk replied that he could not accept the Soviet demands because he felt that the Soviets were not genuinely interested in the establishment of friendly relations with Poland.

On the contrary, Moscow is striving to control all of Poland as a stepping stone in their imperialistic plans which embrace not only Europe but various key regions of Asia.

Do you think so? asked Eden.

I am convinced, replied Mikolajczyk, that the Soviet promise to you not to form a rival government in Moscow does not mean much, because they cannot use such a government yet. But when the Soviet armies enter Polish territories, then they will undoubtedly be able to use it. For this reason, we are turning to you and to the Americans with the question whether you consider it possible that the British and American Governments could guarantee our political and territorial integrity and sovereignty, and if so, when?

Eden did not answer Mikolajczyk's queries but questioned his convictions that the Soviet had long-range imperialistic ambitions, particularly in Europe. He then observed that if Mikolajczyk's fears proved to be true, that then "the situation would be really critical."

In Eden's opinion, some of the Soviet moves at that time indicated that the Russians wanted to cooperate with the other Western Powers and that they were curtailing their ambitions. He cited, in his own words, the following examples of such moves:

1. The Mediterranean Commission establishing permanent cooperation between the Three Powers, plus France, came into existence as a result of Soviet initiative.

2. When the Foreign Office approached Moscow with the suggestion to retain on his throne the Italian King, who was not particularly liked in Russia, and to recognize Marshal Badoglio, Stalin sent his consent almost by return mail.

Here Mikolajczyk observed that if the Soviet Government proved to be so cooperative with British policy in Italy, it did so only because of its failure to organize and lead a revolution in Italy in the early stages of the upheavals which preceded the physical presence of Allied forces in Italy.[27]

This topic was dropped in favor of the question of Mikolajczyk's plans, which involved the readiness of the Polish Government to call a general uprising in Poland against the retreating German forces. Such a move would, however, require that operations be synchronized with those of the Soviet Government and the Red Army and this, in turn, required the re-establishment of diplomatic relations with the Soviet Union.

Eden received this proposal with great interest and thought that it might not only interest Stalin but persuade him to establish, once again, diplomatic relations with the Polish Government. Eden then added that such probabilities would depend upon Stalin's appraisal of the effectiveness of the Polish Underground Army.

At parting, Eden said:

Now I know what your position is. You expect a lot from me, but for Soviet concessions you are giving me only one card to play—the readiness to call a mass uprising in Poland. I am not too optimistic about the results. The Polish problem is on our agenda. I don't know what the other side thinks. Even if the Moscow conference will not succeed, it should be remembered that it is only the preparation for the meeting of the three Chiefs of Governments.[28]

Before Eden's departure for Moscow on October 5, 1943 the Polish Government handed him a memorandum in which it was stated:

1. That it had the support of Polish people both within and outside Poland.

2. That it had confidence and trust in Anglo-American policies and their attitude toward Poland.

3. That the Polish Government was ready to re-establish a diplomatic relationship with the Soviet Union without discussion of the frontier question.

4. That such a relationship could be re-established only if the British and the United States Governments would express their firm support of the Polish Government.

5. That the Polish Government was opposed to even temporary occupation of Polish territories by the Red forces.

6. That the Polish Government was opposed to Soviet occupation of any other eastern or southern European State, and that for this reason it looked with coolness at the recently signed Soviet-Czech treaty which tended to include other European countries.

7. That the Polish Government suggested the establishment of an Inter-Allied General Staff Headquarters with the participation of legal

representatives from all occupied countries in order to supervise the liberation of the German-occupied territories.[29]

United States Secretary of State, Cordell Hull, had shown the greatest possible sympathy and understanding of the Polish problem. In his own words, he "was decided to defend the cause of Poland as he would defend the cause of his own country." When asked what had finally determined him to undertake so difficult and dangerous a mission at his age, Mr. Hull replied that, in the final analysis, the situation created by the problem of Poland had determined his decision. He said that he felt he "had to defend it to the end." The Poles were encouraged to be hopeful that the deadlock might be resolved.[30]

Eden, upon his return from Moscow, told Mikolajczyk that during the conference he had told Molotov that the Poles were willing to resume a diplomatic relationship with the U.S.S.R. Molotov replied that this might take place only with a friendly Polish Government. The present one did not, he said, show any sign of good will towards the Soviet Union, and the attitude of the Polish press in London was also hostile. Then he criticized General Sosnkowski, at that time the Commander-in-Chief of the Polish forces, who had previously resigned his cabinet post on the occasion of the signing of the Soviet-Polish agreement of 1941. Molotov also complained about the inactivity of General Anders' Army in the Middle East. He contrasted this with the Polish Patriots' Army of General Berling which was taking an active part in the fighting on the eastern front.

Then Eden said that while he was in Moscow, the Australian Chargé d'Affaires, Keith Officer (who represented Polish affairs after the break in diplomatic relations between Poland and the Soviet Union), told him that if the London Government incorporated a couple of individuals from the Soviet-controlled Union of Patriots, that the Soviets would then be willing to discuss resumption of negotiations. Eden thought that this was an impossible suggestion, while Mikolajczyk stated that in his opinion the Soviets did not really want any Polish Government at all. He then asked Eden what would happen when the Red Army entered Poland and what the British Government proposed to do under the circumstances. Eden replied that he did not know quite what to say but that he was certain that the treatment of any Allied country by the Soviet liberating forces would be different from the treatment accorded enemy countries.[31]

Upon Hull's return from Moscow, Hopkins told Ciechanowski

. . . that from Eden's attitude the Soviets might have concluded that Britain was trying "to ease America out of European problems."

On another occasion Hopkins commented that "the President was worried about the Moscow Conference." [32]

The practical result of the Moscow Conference proved to be a serious blow to the effectiveness of the Polish Underground Movement. It had been previously decided by President Roosevelt that the United States would supply war materials and munitions for guerrilla and sabotage warfare in preparation for an uprising against the Germans when the Red Army entered Poland. The British had agreed to deliver them with their RAF. Apparently the Soviets objected to this at the Moscow Conference.

Now, suddenly, immediately in the wake of the Moscow Conference, our military mission was informed by the Combined Chiefs of Staff that this decision had been revoked. As an explanation it was hinted that the Soviet-Polish tension might make it dangerous to arm our men in Poland and also that the Russians might object.[33]

While in Moscow, Cordell Hull had attempted to impress upon Molotov the urgent necessity of re-establishing diplomatic relations with the Poles, but the Soviets remained adamant in their territorial demands on Poland, and would not agree to renew diplomatic relations until these demands were met.

He (Hull) saw clearly that the Soviets were taking full advantage of their exceptionally favorable military position and were determined to regard this matter as solved in their favor. They resented any outside interference on the part of their Western Allies. . . .

When he raised the question of the presence of Western Allied forces at the side of the Soviet forces in the liberation and occupation of European countries neighboring on Soviet Russia, he met with a very determined show of opposition on the part of the Soviet representative.[34]

On November 15, 1943 Secretary Hull held a press and radio news conference about the Moscow Conference.

The Secretary was asked several questions regarding the matter of just how and in what manner the newly liberated countries would have the right of self-determination. Mr. Hull replied that the application of this principle of self-determination would be left to military people in immediate charge, subject to any particular modification in given cases. He pointed out that there were ten refugee governments in existence, and whether or not these would be restored to power in their countries would be up to their people.

A correspondent asked whether, in carrying out the principles under which each liberated country was to choose its own form of government, it had been agreed that all three Governments should have a share in choosing these principles. The Secretary replied that when Allied military organizations went into a country and liberated it, that following that, the military authorities there would carry out that principle in a practical and reasonable manner, not undertaking to use force in setting up any particular kind of government.[35]

On November 16, Secretary Hull held a second press and radio conference, in which he stated that occupied countries involved in territorial disputes would have to wait until the end of the war for solutions to these disputes. They would not, in the meantime, be considered as fully sovereign governments.[36]

On December 1, 1943 the Polish Government protested to the American Ambassador, Anthony J. Drexel Biddle, Jr., against this policy, arguing that it was contrary to the principles laid down and subscribed to by Churchill and Roosevelt at Quebec, because Poland belonged to the Allied Nations. Poland could not, therefore, consent to being treated as though it were an enemy country, like Italy. If Poland was going to be ruled by the Red Army authorities until the Peace Conference, the Red Army would surely see to it that conditions would be established with a view to a communist victory in any kind of election to determine the future form of Poland's Government.[37] Ambassador Ciechanowski then expressed his critical appraisal of the results of the Conference.

A few days later Eden informed Mikolajczyk that Ambassador Halifax reported from Washington that Cordell Hull was dissatisfied with Ambassador Ciechanowski because of his critical views of the Moscow Conference. Eden was of the opinion that "this does more harm than good for Poland." Mikolajczyk defended the Ambassador by saying that Poland had good reason to be dissatisfied with Hull's position *vis-à-vis* Poland as expressed in the press conferences of November 15 and 16.[38]

The Conference itself had been propagandized in Great Britain and the United States as an enormous success and as a happy prelude to the forthcoming meeting of the Big Three. The full truth was, of course, withheld from the Western people. If, instead of being spoon-fed on propaganda of harmony, the public had been told what really happend in Moscow, the chances are that the indignation it was bound to express against schemes of Soviet expansion would have served Churchill and Roosevelt well in their subsequent dealings with Stalin.

It must be remembered that Soviet troops were approaching the pre-war Polish border at this time. Poles began to fear more than ever that British-American unwillingness to protect Polish rights was to be understood as meaning that their interest in Poland was superficial and that this lack of interest was therefore enabling the Russians to solve the Polish problem in their own way entirely.

4. Soviet Psychological Preparation of the Polish Problem for the Teheran Conference

It was widely known that the heads of the Big Three Powers would meet at some time in the not too distant future. In the meantime the Soviets, realizing the importance of the role of public opinion in the Western world, proceeded to go about influencing it.

In the autumn of 1943, Polish communists in London (under the leadership of Puacz and Lapter) began to recruit members among dissatisfied elements of the exiles and to organize these into the "Union of Progressive Democrats," which had the avowed purpose of discrediting the Polish Government.[39] At the same time, the Polski Zwiazek Postepowy (The Polish Progressive Union) was formed in London. Its chairman, Roman Zawisza, was a former member of the communist International Brigade in Spain. The purpose of this organization, too, was to discredit the London Government and to capture the allegiance of Poles in Great Britain.[40] For this purpose, both organizations established the newspaper, *Polish Tribune*, which undertook to publicize their arguments.

At the same time, the propaganda of the British Anglo-Soviet parliamentary committee grew in intensity and now began to explain the nature of the Soviet-Polish frontier problem (from the Soviet point of view, of course) to the British public.

A Soviet-published English daily, the *Soviet Monitor*, No. 3901, reported:

> At a meeting of Poles held in Toronto, Canada, records an Ottawa correspondent, 1,200 persons present sent greetings to Major General Berling, the Commander of the Polish Corps in the Soviet Union, in which they said, among other things, that Poles residing in Canada greet their brother-soldiers of the Kosciuszko-Dabrowski Divisions.[41]

On November 23, 1943 the Polish Government received the following telegram from its legation in Buenos Aires:

> Owing to the situation, the communist movement here transferred part of their activities to Montevideo. Telegraphic communication between Montevideo and Moscow is very lively. The last orders are: to mobilize the Slav movement; to spread slogans saying that the Polish frontier question has been settled at the Moscow Conference; to seek communist sympathizers among the personnel of the diplomatic missions of the Slav countries willing to defy their Governments at a propitious moment.[42]

The Polish Legation in Buenos Aires further wired London to the effect that:

The organizations of Slav communists in South America are keeping in constant touch with Wanda Wasilewska in Moscow.

At a meeting of the leaders of the Communist Party of Argentina, held in Buenos Aires on the 12th of February, 1943, with the participation of Codovilla (a delegate of the Comintern), the following lines of policy concerning the Polish question were adopted:

1. Inclusion of Byelorussia and the Ukraine into Russia.

2. The entry of Soviet troops into Poland; Polish units formed in Russia should enter as the vanguard together with Soviet Forces.

3. After the entry of the Armed Forces a new Polish Government would be formed and, in view of the war with Germany, mobilization would be proclaimed and the war prosecuted further.

4. The present Polish Government would thus automatically be unable to interfere in Polish matters.[43]

On July 1, 1943 the TASS correspondent in America reported the following declaration, signed by forty-five Americans of Polish descent:

Americans and Poles have a common cause: winning the war and maintaining the peace. . . . These facts are simple and it would seem that all Poles and Americans of Polish descent should make all efforts to realize them. Unfortunately, this is not so. In the last two years propaganda has been conducted among Americans of Polish descent against Allied unity. Lately, this propaganda was intensified in connection with the activities of the "National Committee of Americans of Polish Descent." This is being done to exploit the dispute between Poland and Russia in order to destroy Soviet-American unity. The activity of the Committee conducted among Americans of Polish origin tends to create unfriendly feeling towards the Czechs and distrust towards Great Britain. These activities are inspired either by immigrants closely connected with the pre-war, anti-democratic regime, or by fascistic groups of Poles.

This declaration is directed also against the attempts of some Polish diplomats who aim at the creation of distrust of the U.S.S.R. and the United States. Steps are being taken to persuade the United States to give support to a new reactionary Poland, whose policy will be directed against the Soviet Union. Fortunately, these efforts are not succeeding. Yet they disturb the harmony in the Allied camp and are responsible for the breakdown of Soviet-Polish relations. Furthermore, they create a conviction among the American people that the Polish nation remains under the influence of anti-democratic and fascistic ideas. This conviction puts Americans of Polish descent one step below other Americans in United States public opinion.

Americans of Polish origin are deeply attached to the American democratic way of life. This they share with the majority of the Polish people who proved so many times their attachment to these ideas. . . . At the present time, unfortunately, the Polish nation is compelled to silence by its occupant while the majority of the members of the émigré Government are connected with reactionary and anti-democratic elements.

For these reasons, Americans of Polish origin and Poles residing in the

United States must raise their voices on behalf of their tortured and silenced brothers. We want to tell the world that the Polish nation desires to live according to democratic principles and in peace and collaboration with the Soviet Union, Czechoslovakia, and other neighbors. We believe that in the interest of the Polish nation all anti-democratic, fascistic, and hostile elements to the Soviet Union in the Polish exile Government should be expelled. We appeal to Americans of Polish descent to detach themselves from the poisonous propaganda of the National Committee of Americans of Polish Descent and its supporters, because their activities are beneficial only to the enemies of the United States and of Poland. We call upon them to give complete support to the efforts of President Roosevelt and the American Government, because they are striving to win the war and to secure the peace.[44]

In the middle of November 1943 Soviet propaganda against the Polish Government became more active and grew in volume. Its line of argument was quite consistent. In September and October it broadcast in all directions and through all possible means the news of the formation of the "Kosciuszko" Division in Russia. This, the main point of the propaganda, was intended to suggest to Western public opinion that only those Poles fighting on the Soviet front were the true and proper representatives of occupied Poland.

On November 7, 1943 some 300 delegates of Polish-Americans assembled in Detroit. The subject of their deliberations was identical with the topics and problems dealt with by similar groups in England. The timing and similarity of the subject publicly aired was striking. Among other things, the declaration issued at the end of the Detroit meeting stated:

The present Polish Government is a prisoner of reaction. Reaction dominates its state, diplomatic, and military apparatus. At the present moment the Polish Government does not express the true interests of the Polish people.[45]

Similar reports were coming in from Brazil, the Middle East, and other countries where Poles had found shelter from tyranny.

The objectives of all these declarations were identical—to destroy the already weak prestige of the powerless London Government, and to build up that of the Polish communist Committee. The timing of this upsurge of activity in such dispersed continents was significant. Great ingenuity was used by the communists in achieving their objective. Being the spokesmen for a powerful Ally, while advocating an alternative much more convenient to the Western Allies, they found themselves and their views to be welcome to Western public opinion and enlisted considerable approval of their work.

Such Soviet activities among Polish settlements outside Poland were combined with a systematic struggle against the patriotic elements inside Poland. The latter disturbed the London Government even more than the former. At the end of August, Mikolajczyk received the following report from his representative in Warsaw concerning communist activities in Eastern Poland between July 15 and August 15, 1943.

In Bialystok Province, almost all of the Polish intelligentsia were murdered by communist agents. This policy was applied not only to individuals, but also to whole families regardless of age or sex. It was done systematically, according to a list, in all places simultaneously. In Bialystok itself 1,250 persons were murdered, while in the whole province it was estimated that 6,500 people were liquidated.

In the Wolyn region, the liquidation of Poles proceeds mercilessly. Ukrainians are performing bloody massacres. Poles are prevented from escaping west behind the Molotov-Ribbentrop Line.

In the region of Glebokie, communist partisans are murdering Poles. In the Nowogrodek region partisan groups called "Stalincy" and "Msciciele" (Revengers) are wiping out Poles.

Regular Soviet forces are operating in regions of Baranowicze, Nowogrodek, and Slonim. Their attitude to Poles is hostile.

In the Wolyn region Soviet partisans are collaborating with the Polish bands of Kmicic. From July 11 till the present they murdered all Poles in Kowel, Wlodzimierz, and Horochow counties. Now they have spread to Tarnopol and Lwow provinces. Ukrainians are demanding that Poles leave those territories on pain of death. In Wilno those Poles who survived are deeply distressed. The younger Poles have joined our partisan organizations.[46]

The London Government passed this information on to the British and American Governments, for it could do nothing itself to prevent this slaughter.

On October 16, 1943 the Polish Government received another report from its intelligence service, to the same effect:

Recently, the Soviet authorities have transferred, under various pretexts, about 200 of their agents to Turkey. Their mission is to establish saboteur cells for underground work in Greece, Bulgaria, Rumania, and Poland. They have large financial means. In that group are Greeks, Bulgarians, Rumanians, and Poles who were in Russia. A few days ago the former head of the Comintern—Dimitrov—came to Turkey under a false name. He resides in Ankara as a member of the Soviet Trade Delegation. He has already managed to establish contact with Bulgarian students who are studying there. Soon these agents will be dispatched to their assigned countries.[47]

On November 6, 1943 the underground authorities in Poland reported to London:

The PPR (Polish Workers Party) is uncompromising in its fight against the Polish Government and its representatives in Poland, and calls us reactionary and fascist. The Home Army is represented as an instrument of the Polish Government to enslave the Polish nation as in 1918.

The PPR is striving to create a "People's Army" by a fusion of the People's Guard, Peasant Battalions, and the "Working Intelligentsia." It issued a call on July 28, 1943 to other groups to unite with them. These organizations are going to preserve their present form but will have to operate under a new unified command.

The PPR aims at complete militarization of the whole Underground Movement. They justify this by stressing the proximity of the Red Army to Poland and by the necessity of defense against Polish reaction. Lately the communists have shifted the direction of partisan combat operations from the villages to the cities. This is presumed to be a preparation for a general uprising. They are training new cadres of partisans.

The PPR intensified its activities in various organizations, such as:

1. In their own unions, particularly among the steel, transport, and railway unions.

2. Fascistic committees: Committee of National Initiative and Union of Fighting Youth.

3. Rebuilding of "Hammer and Sickle" organizations and the establishment of special information and administrative units based on the NKVD pattern.

The PPR is not completely homogenous. It has two factions. The right wing objects to total dependence and subordination to the Soviet Union, while the left, or "Lenin's Wing," considers the PPR as too nationalistic an organization. Both factions are afraid to oppose the leadership of the PPR because of the proximity of the Red Army. In the Polish eastern territories the PPR is abandoning its tasks to the Ukrainian and Byelorussian Communist Parties. In the western territories the PPR is collaborating with the German Communist Party.

The PPR has intensified its criticism of Anglo-Saxons, stressing their weakness and pointing out that the only Power which is doing anything is the Soviet Union. They reject all concepts of a federation of Europe and maintain that the only way to provide security for post-war Europe is by close relations with the U.S.S.R.

Direct Soviet propaganda is also being intensified. Moscow is parachuting numerous saboteurs, who are ordering our various organizations to submit to their leadership. Refusal is threatened with sentences of death, to be executed by the approaching Red Army.

The PPR has its task simplified by the growing desire among the Polish masses for radical social reforms.

In spite of the radicalization of the Polish masses, resentment of the Soviets is formidable—but fear of the Red Army is considerable, too.

German repressions and terror are pushing a number of individuals into the ranks of the People's Guard.

Polish underground organizations are reacting against the communists strongly, but their efforts are not always coordinated. The PPR responds by capturing secret stores of ordnance. They then distribute these arms among the population and provoke them into attacking the Wehrmacht. This, in turn, leads to reprisals by the Germans, which the PPR hopes will provoke a general uprising prematurely.[48]

The London Government received well-corroborated evidence regarding the nature of the instructions issued to the communist organizations, to the PPR, and to the commanders of the "People's Guard." Reports concerning the activities of these bodies in a large number of districts in different parts of Poland were also received and carefully collated. These activities consisted, among others, in discovering the identity of the largest possible number of members of the Underground Movement (some of whom were reported to have been thereupon betrayed to the Gestapo), in attacking individual leaders as well as whole detachments of the Secret Army, in killing their officers, and in seizing their arms.

At a meeting of the delegates of the PPR and the commanders of the People's Guard held in the district of Siedlce in July 1943, plans for the liquidation of the leaders of the Polish Underground Movement were discussed. The matter was submitted for decision to the Central Committee of the Polish Workers Party (Communist Party) including instructions that additional exact lists of these leaders should be prepared. During a conference of the delegates of the Polish Workers Party and of the People's Guard held in the district of Krasnystaw, under the chairmanship of Jozef Pobreziak, the names of the leaders of the Polish Underground Movement in the southern districts of the province of Lublin were verified. Similar conferences took place in the provinces of Krakow, Bialystok, Grodno, Plock, Czestochowa, Radom, Konskie, and others.

During the last few months reports have been received of actions taken by detachments of the People's Army against the Polish underground organizations, particularly against the Secret Army, in the districts of Kalisz, Pabianice, Tomaszow, Plock, Radomsk, Starachowice, Skarzysko, Ostrowiec, Czestochowa, Lomza, Ostroleka, Siedlce, Grojec, and Lublin. During September and October 1943, threatening letters were received by leaders of the Underground Movement and officers of the Secret Army in the regions of Podlasie and Polesie, containing the warning: "He who is not with us is against us. Those who are against us shall be destroyed."

During October, reports of a series of active operations by the People's Guard against the Secret Army in the regions of Lancut, Lezajsk, and Zambrow were received. In the district of Lublin during the same month a leaflet which carried the slogan: "Down with the officers, the helpers of Hitler" was circulated in large numbers. It was signed by the local battalion commander of the People's Guard and called upon the population to destroy the leaders of the "reactionary independence organization" and the officers of the Secret Army.

In October, in the region of Grodno, communist detachments proceeded to execute death sentences passed on Poles known to be hostile to communism. In the province of Wilno and Nowogrodek, Soviet Fifth Column detachments are attacking Polish partisan units, and demanding their submission to partisan leadership, and, in case of refusal, destroying them with armed force. A company of the Trans-Niemen battalion of the Secret Army has been destroyed in this way. The officers were executed, while the other ranks were forcibly enrolled in the Soviet detachment.

In Polesie, Soviet Fifth Columns are attempting to evaluate the effectiveness of the Polish Secret Army. Those suspected of belonging to that Army are being invited to conferences alleged to be held in various hiding places in the forests, whereupon all traces of their existence disappear.

On October 4, 1944 the body of the kidnapped Colonel Maczynski was accidentally found, while on December 10, 1943 the officer, Dziedzic, invited to a rendezvous in the forest, disappeared.

In the region of Tarnopol, Lieutenant Bomba, commander of the partisans in the district of Tarnopol, and Lieutenant Drzazga, commander of the partisans in the district of Luck perished in a similar way. The units commanded by these two officers have on several occasions distinguished themselves in action against the Germans. The communists are aware of this fact. Nevertheless, these units were attacked by Soviet detachments.

It is reported from the region of Radomsk that the local Secret Army unit has been destroyed by the Soviet People's Army. Reports received from the regions of Plock, Grojec, Garwolin, Radomsk, Ilza, Ostrow, Opatow, Busk, Kielce, Czestochowa and other regions describe the destruction of units of the Polish Secret Army, the seizure of stores of arms and attacks upon private dwellings by the People's Army. Bulletins issued by the People's Guard reporting the execution of alleged spies and informers coincide with the reports received from regional Polish delegates concerning the liquidation of members of the Polish Secret Army as instanced by the reports concerning the liquidation of the alleged spies in the villages of Okolbudy and Zapusty, etc.[49]

After citing numerous dates, places, and names of individuals or units arrested or destroyed by the communists, the report continues as follows:

Propaganda against Britain is carried on by means of a whispering campaign. The "Voice of Warsaw" of August 20, 1943, No. 52, writes: "The bulk of Anglo-American forces continue to remain not in a state of war but in the stage of preparing for war. The conclusion is obvious—that the question of speeding up the termination of war is not as burning for England and America as for those who engaged all their forces in the struggle. The "Tribune of Liberty" No. 41 of October 1, 1943 writes under the heading "The Second Front": "The ruling circles influencing the policy of England are not in a hurry. The war offers good business conditions for the capitalist magnates who draw enormous profits from it. Moreover, the directors of Allied policy do not mind in the least that the flames from the conflagration of war should be extinguished primarily by the extinction of Soviet soldiers." [50]

The Polish Government discussed this report with its Western Allies, and Mikolajczyk pleaded for a British and American mission to be sent to Poland so that they could see and verify for themselves what the situation there really was. His request was declined on the grounds that it might be interpreted by the Soviets as a lack of confidence in them and, as such, would antagonize Stalin.[51]

In spite of this, the Commander-in-Chief of the Home Army, acting on orders from the London Government, issued instruction on November 20, 1943 to all units, ordering them to cooperate with the approaching Red Army and to extend them hospitality and help in the fight against the Germans. They were instructed, however, to resist any attempted subordination of the units of the Home Army either to the Red Army or to the Berling Corps, should this be offered under the pretext that such subordination was in accordance with the instructions of the Polish Government.[52]

5. Polish Efforts to State Their Case before the Teheran Conference

Almost simultaneously, the Underground leaders who represented all the democratic parties issued a declaration—a blueprint for a future democratic Poland. One of its objectives was to reassure Poland's Eastern Ally that they were determined not to return to the pre-war system of government. This document was transmitted to London and given to Churchill and Roosevelt to strengthen their negotiations with Stalin. It read:

DECLARATION OF THE POLITICAL AGREEMENT BETWEEN THE FOUR
POLITICAL PARTIES FORMING THE POLISH HOME
POLITICAL REPRESENTATION

1. In view of the immensity of the present tasks facing the Polish people, and recognizing that these tasks:

(a) of rebuilding the Polish State;
(b) of establishing frontiers and restoring internal order;
(c) of active cooperation of Poland in the determination of new forms of internal collaboration;

will continue to confront them at the time of the liberation of the country from the occupying enemy forces, the undersigned parties, which represent the main trends of Polish political thought and the vast majority of the politically organized Polish community, have decided to cooperate closely with each other (at least until such time as an official announcement of elections to the constitutional legislative bodies is made), while at the same time observing the program contained in the declaration of the Government. These parties will cooperate in Poland, in the Polish Home Political Representation, in the Council of National Unity and, if possible, in the Council of the Republic, and they will collaborate in complete solidarity with the Delegates of the Polish Government in London.

The above mentioned parties will approach their representatives in London with a united appeal, aiming at a similar observance of collaboration within both the Government and the National Council.

While supporting the Government which represents the collaboration of the parties and accepting their full responsibility for it, the parties are opposed, while this collaboration lasts, to the formation of any other form of government.

2. The parties will ensure that the executive machinery of the Government authorities shall possess not only professional qualifications but also the character of an institution closely bound up with the social and civic factors in the Homeland; and that these shall be free from those elements responsible for the mistakes of the former regime, as well as free from any totalitarian leanings.

3. The parties will give the full support of their organization and propaganda to the Polish Home Army as the recognized organ of national unity which will be decisive in the open struggle for our future. At the same time, they will cooperate in establishing a harmonious collaboration of the civilian and military authorities in preparing for coming action, the successful conclusion of which is the main objective of the entire political, administrative, and military activity.

4. For the present period, for the period of the Peace Negotiations, and for the period immediately following the conclusion of hostilities, the parties accept the following basic principles as a definition of their war aims:

(a) The basic principle of Polish foreign policy should be the cooperation with the Allies based on equality, with a distinct emphasis on self-determination in affairs concerning Poland, her sovereign rights, and the integrity of her territory.

(b) A constant watchfulness concerning Soviet influence, which is becoming increasingly marked in Allied countries, and a ceaseless recalling to their memories of the latent danger in Russian-communist totalitarian peace aims.

(c) The insuring to Poland of a Western and Northern frontier which would guarantee her a wide access to the sea together with the integrity of her Eastern frontiers, as well as suitable indemnities.

(d) The formation of a confederation of states of which the Polish-Czechoslovak union might be the nucleus.

(e) The solution of the problem of national minorities, along the principles of tradition, freedom and equality of rights and obligations.

5. In the period of transition, before the convocation of the legislative assembly which is to be elected according to a new democratic electoral law:

(a) The Republican system of government shall be preserved, and its legal institutions shall not be changed without the approval of the parties.

(b) The composition of the Government of National Unity shall not be altered or supplemented without the approval of the parties.

(c) The existing legislation shall be freed from both the influences of the former regime and those of the Government of occupation, and extended in accordance with the following postulates:

(1) Freedom and equality of rights and obligations to all citizens, and

the establishment of territorial, economic, social and cultural self-government.

(2) Recognition is to be extended to labor as constituting the greatest social value, and the foundation of the economic development and welfare of the country.

(3) During the period of transition, the taking over by the Government, in collaboration with the local social elements of such industrial establishments which, during the period of occupation, were administered by the Germans, as well as of all formerly German and ownerless property and credit institutions; and the taking over by the local Government of public utility installations.

(4) The taking of immediate steps to introduce agrarian reform, with the purpose of creating a re-division of arable lands, which shall ensure the largest possible number of efficient, strong, one-family farms as would guarantee an adequate food supply for the entire nation; in this connection, the confiscation and placing at the disposal of the State of all landed property destined for agrarian reform, the landed property formerly owned by the Germans in particular, will also be accomplished during the period of the lifting of the occupation.

(5) Ensuring the availability of the supply of foodstuffs and of indispensable material for industrial production.

(6) The creation of suitable conditions for the development of cooperatives, which shall be assured their necessary positions in the economic organization of local government and which, within the framework of the planning policy, will be used especially for the production, exchange, and distribution of foodstuffs.

(7) The working out of a plan of financial and monetary policy, and of the post-war reconstruction of the country.

(8) The repatriation of citizens ejected from their homes; i.e., those imprisoned and interned in German and Russian camps and those deported for forced labor; and the liquidation, in accordance with the principles of universal employment, of unemployment in towns and in the country.

6. The above Agreement of the signatory parties shall not stand in the way of the free development of their political ideals and programs, as well as of any propaganda they may undertake in the future. Nevertheless, in all their public statements in the press, the signatories shall be bound to observe the loyalty to each other which is the outcome of their mutual understanding and collaboration.

(signed) THE HOME POLITICAL REPRESENTATION OF POLAND[53]

There has never been any evidence that Roosevelt and Churchill were affected by this document, and others like it, at all. The Polish Government, nevertheless, coninued to offer such evidences of the situation in Poland to the Western leaders and never ceased trying to present the Polish case.

In October 1943, President Roosevelt issued an invitation to Premier Mikolajczyk to visit him in the middle of January, 1944. In view of the approaching Big Three conference, however, Mikolajczyk wanted to present personally the Polish case to both Western leaders before they met with Stalin.

Consequently, on November 19 he asked for an appointment with Churchill prior to the latter's departure for Teheran. Churchill refused to see him. On November 20, Mikolajczyk asked Biddle, the United States Ambassador to Poland, to arrange a visit for him with Roosevelt anywhere between Washington and Teheran in order to be able to brief him on the subject of Poland. This request likewise was turned down. Apparently both Churchill and Roosevelt were afraid that news of such a meeting might leak out and consequently offend Stalin.[54]

Mikolajczyk then decided to present the views of his Government through the following memorandum which was forwarded to both leaders.

In the course of his last conversation with Mr. Eden on October 5, before Mr. Eden's departure for Moscow, the Polish Prime Minister, M. Mikolajczyk, placed before Mr. Eden documents emphasizing the complete confidence which the Polish people in Poland and the Poles abroad place in the policy of the Polish Government. Basing his position on this support, M. Mikolajczyk expressed once more the complete trust placed in Great Britain and the United States by the Polish people and the Polish Government. He appealed for guarantees safeguarding the right of the Allied Polish Government to administer Polish territory immediately after its liberation from German occupation, and he also appealed for guarantees to protect the lives and property of the Polish population when Soviet troops entered Poland. At the same time, he requested British and American intercession to bring about the resumption of Polish-Soviet relations, which, under the present circumstances, had become a matter of particular urgency.

The unwillingness of the Polish Government to enter into discussion on frontier questions is based on the following considerations:

1. Poland, which entered the war in 1939 in defense of her territory, has never given up that fight and has not produced any Quisling, and is therefore fully entitled to expect that she will emerge from this war without loss of territory.

2. The Polish eastern lands, which are the object of Soviet claims, amount to over half of the territory of the Polish Republic. They contain important centers of Polish national life. They are closely bound to Poland by ties of tradition, civilization, and culture. The Polish population which has resided there for centuries forms a relative majority of the population of these lands. On the other hand, the lower density of the population of these areas and their possibilities of economic development furnish Poland with a socially sound means of solving the problems of overpopulation of her western and southern provinces.

3. The Polish Government could not, above all, see its way clear to enter a discussion on the subject of territorial concessions for the reason that

such a discussion in the absence of effective guarantees of Poland's independence and security on the part of Great Britain and the United States would be sure to lead to continual further and ever new demands.

The attribution to Poland of East Prussia, Danzig, Opole Silesia (Upper Silesia) and the straightening and shortening of the Polish western frontier are in any case dictated by the need to provide for the stability of future peace, the disarmament of Germany, and the security of Poland and other countries of Central Europe. The transfer to Poland of these territories cannot, therefore, be fairly treated as an object of compensation for the cession to the U.S.S.R. of Polish eastern lands which do not for the reasons adduced above, represent for the U.S.S.R. a value comparable to that which they have for Poland.

The attempt made to prejudge the fate of Polish eastern territories by means of a "popular vote," organized under Soviet occupation by the Soviet occupying authorities, is without any political or legal value.

It would be equally impossible to obtain a genuine expression of the will of the population inhabiting these territories in view of the ruthless methods applied there today and those which have been applied there in the past by consecutive occupants.

Recalling the confidential memorandum handed over to Mr. Eden before his departure for the Moscow Conference, the Polish Government gives below a main outline of instructions which have been issued recently to the underground organizations in Poland.

A rising in Poland against Germany is being planned to break out at a moment mutually agreed upon with our Allies; either prior to or at the very moment of the entry of Soviet troops into Poland.

In accordance with the principles adopted in Quebec, the Polish Government is entitled to exert sovereign authority over Polish lands as they are liberated from the enemy. Consequently, in case the entry of Soviet troops into Poland takes place after the re-establishment of Polish-Soviet relations, the Polish Government together with the Commander-in-Chief would be anxious, as they have already informed the British Government, to return immediately to Poland and to cooperate there in the further struggle against Germany.

The entry of Soviet troops into Polish territory without previous resumption of Polish-Soviet relations would force the Polish Government to undertake political action against the violation of Polish sovereignty, while the Polish local administration and army in Poland would have to continue to work underground. In that case, the Polish Government foresees the use of measures of self-defense wherever such measures are rendered indispensable by Soviet methods of terror and extermination of Polish citizens.

The Moscow Conference, as it appears from the information offered by Mr. Eden, has not brought the question of the resumption of Polish-Soviet relations closer to a satisfactory conclusion. In the meantime, the situation on the eastern front indicates that Soviet troops may soon be expected to cross the borders of Poland. The Polish Government has, moreover, reasons to fear that under present conditions the life and property of Polish citizens may be exposed to danger after the entry of Soviet troops into Poland and after the imposition of Soviet administration on the country. In that case, desperate reactions on the part of the Polish community may be expected, following such violations of the principles adopted in Quebec assuring to all the United Nations their liberty and their own administration.

The principles foreseen by the Moscow Conference in the case of Italy could by no means be satisfactory for Poland. An administration in Poland by a Commander of Soviet troops, even with the cooperation of British and American liaison officers, would place Poland, an Allied country, on the same level as Italy, an enemy country; in practice it is obvious that the cooperation of a necessarily limited number of British and American liaison officers could not possibly be a safeguard for the interests of the Polish population in the territories occupied by Soviet troops.

In this situation, the Polish Government addresses an urgent appeal to Mr. Churchill to intervene with Marshal Stalin with the view to restoring Polish-Soviet relations, safeguarding the interests of the Polish State, and the life and property of its citizens after the Soviet troops have entered Poland.

Polish airmen, sailors, and soldiers in carrying out the fight against the common enemy must be assured that their families will be restored to them and that they can expect to return to a free and independent Homeland.[55]

Before Eden's departure for Teheran, Mikolajczyk informed him that the Polish Government would have no objections to British exploration of the Polish-Soviet question, but that no decisions on this subject taken without the prior concurrence of the Polish Government would be considered as binding by Poles. Should the Polish Government have to express its view, moreover, it could do so only after consultation with the underground organizations in Poland.[56]

6. The Teheran Conference: Political "Legalization" of the Fourth Partition of Poland

The most revealing and complete presentation of the part of the Conference which dealt with Poland is recorded by Churchill himself. It took place on November 28.

After dinner on this first evening, when we were strolling about the room, I (Churchill) led Stalin to a sofa and suggested that we talk for a little on what was to happen after the war was won.

. . . .

I suggested that we should discuss the Polish question. *He agreed and invited me to begin.* Poland was therefore important to us. *Nothing was more important than the security of the Russian western frontier.* But I had given no pledges about frontiers.

. . . .

Personally I thought Poland might move westward, like soldiers taking two steps "left close." If Poland trod on some German toes, that could not be helped, but there must be a strong Poland.

Stalin said the Polish people had their culture and their language, which must exist. They could not be extirpated.

"Are we to try, I asked, to draw frontier lines?"

"Yes."

"I have no power from Parliament, nor, I believe, has the President, to define any frontier lines. But we might now, in Teheran, see if the three heads of Governments, working in agreement, could form some sort of policy which we could recommend to the Poles and advise them to accept."

We agreed to look at the problem. *Stalin asked whether* it would be without Polish participation. I said "yes," and that *when this was all informally agreed between ourselves, we could go to the Poles later.* . . . Stalin asked whether we thought he was going to swallow Poland up. Eden said he did not know how much the Russians were going to eat. How much would they leave undigested? Stalin said the Russians did not want anything belonging to other people, although they might have a bite at Germany. Eden said that what Poland lost in the East she might gain in the West. Stalin replied that possibly she might, but he did not know. *I then demonstrated with the help of three matches my idea of Poland moving westward. This pleased Stalin,* and on this note our group parted for the moment.[57]

When Poland decided to defend her independence in the course of which millions gave their lives, she never could have dreamed that the object of this sacrifice would be so lightly disposed of in an after dinner conversation between her Allies and especially by the author of the Atlantic Charter himself. For Stalin, it was of the utmost importance that Churchill should accept his territorial demands *vis-à-vis* Poland. It must be noted that the Americans did not participate in this conversation. It was to be expected that Roosevelt would be reluctant to oppose the two of them.

On December 1, Poland was again discussed during an after-luncheon conference. Here again are Churchill's notes:

The President began by saying that he hoped the Polish and Soviet Governments would resume relations, so that any decision taken could be accepted by the Polish Government. But he admitted there were difficulties. Stalin asked with what Government he would have to negotiate. The Polish Government and their friends in Poland were in contact with the Germans. They killed the partisans. Neither the President nor I could have any idea of what was now going on there.

I said that the Polish question was important for us in the United Kingdom. . . . *I reverted to my illustration of the three matches*—Germany, Poland, and the Soviet Union. One of the main objects of the Allies was to achieve the security of the Soviet western frontier, and so to prevent an attack by Germany in the future. Here I reminded Stalin of his mention of the line of the Oder in the West.

Stalin, interrupting, said that previously there had been no mention of re-establishing relations with the Polish Government, but only of determining Poland's frontiers. Today the matter had been put quite differently. Russia, even more than other States, was interested in good relations with Poland, because for her it was a question of the security of her frontiers. Russia was in favor of the reconstruction, development, and expansion of Poland mainly at the expense of Germany. But he separated Poland from the Polish Government in exile. He had broken off relations with the Polish Government in exile, not on account of caprice, but because it had joined with Hitler in slanderous propaganda against Russia. What guarantee was there that this would not happen again? He would like to have a guarantee that the Polish Government in exile would not kill partisans, but, on the contrary, would urge the Poles to fight the Germans and not concern themselves with any machinations. He would welcome any Polish Government which would take such active measures, and he would be glad to renew relations with them. But he was by no means sure that the Polish Government in exile was ever likely to become the kind of Government it ought to be.

Here I said that it would be a great help if round that very table we could learn what were the Russian ideas about the frontiers. I should then put the matter before the Poles and say frankly if I thought the conditions fair. His Majesty's Government, for whom alone I spoke, would like to be able to tell the Poles that the plan was a good one and the best that they were likely to get, and that His Majesty's Government would not argue against it at the peace table. Then we could get on with the President's idea of resuming relations. . . .

Stalin said that that was true, but that the Poles could not be allowed to seize the Ukraine and White Russia territory. That was not fair. According to the 1939 frontier, the soil of the Ukraine and White Russia was returned to the Ukraine and to White Russia. Soviet Russia adhered to the frontiers of 1939, for they appeared to be ethnologically the right ones.

Eden asked if this meant the Ribbentrop-Molotov Line.

"Call it whatever you like," said Stalin.

Molotov remarked that it was generally called the Curzon Line.

"No," said Eden, "there are important differences."

Molotov said there were none.

I then produced a map and showed the Curzon Line and the 1939 line, and indicated also the line of the Oder. Eden said that the south end of the Curzon Line had never been defined in terms.

. . . .

Eden suggested that the Curzon Line was intended to pass to the east of Lvov.

Stalin replied that the line on my map had not been drawn correctly. Lvov should be left on the Russian side and the line should go westward towards Przemysl. Molotov would get a map of the Curzon Line and a description of it. He said that he did not want any Polish population, and that if he found any districts inhabited by Poles he would gladly give it up.

I suggested that the value of the German land was much greater than the Pripet Marshes. It was industrial and it would make a much better Poland. We would like to be able to say to the Poles that the Russians were right, and to tell the Poles that they must agree that they had had a fair deal. If the Poles did not accept, we could not help it. Here I made it clear that I was speaking for the British alone, adding that the President had many Poles in the United States who were his fellow-citizens.

. . . .

I said I liked the picture (Poland between the Curzon Line and the Oder River), and that I would say to the Poles that if they did not accept it, they would be foolish, and I would remind them that but for the Red Army they would have been utterly destroyed. I would point out to them that they had been given a fine place to live in, more than three hundred miles each way.

Stalin said that it would indeed be a large, industrial State.

"And friendly to Russia," I interjected.

Stalin replied that Russia wanted a friendly Poland.

I then, runs the record, said to Mr. Eden, with some emphasis, that I was not going to break my heart about this cession of part of Germany to Poland or about Lvov. Eden said that if Marshal Stalin would take the Curzon and Oder Lines as a basis on which to argue, that might provide a beginning.

At this point Molotov produced the Russian version of the Curzon Line, and the text of a wireless telegram from Lord Curzon giving all the place names. I asked whether Molotov would object to the Poles getting the Oppeln district. He said he did not think so.

I said that the Poles would be wise to take our advice. I was not prepared to make a great squawk about Lvov. Turning to Marshal Stalin, I added that I did not think we were very far apart in principle. Roosevelt asked Stalin whether he thought a transfer of population on a voluntary basis would be possible.

On this we left the Polish discussion.[58]

In the available American record on the Teheran Conference only the following notes refer to Poland:

The conversation turned to the subject of post-war treatment of Germany and the frontiers of Poland. Stalin said that Poland should extend to the Oder and that the Russians would help the Poles to establish their frontier thus far west, but he was not specific about Poland's eastern frontier. . . . Roosevelt felt it necessary to explain to Stalin that there were six or seven million Americans of Polish extraction . . . who had the same rights and the same votes as anyone else and whose opinion must be respected. Stalin said that he understood this, *but he subsequently suggested that some "propaganda work" should be done among these people.*

Later, Churchill and Eden arrived for the final meeting. There was a discussion . . . on the frontiers of Poland in which Roosevelt did not take part; it ended with the evolvement of a formula much like that which was eventually adopted. . . .

He (Roosevelt) believed in his heart that the final words of the Teheran Declaration—"We came here with hope and determination. We leave here friends in fact, in spirit, and in purpose"—were more than mere words. He had disagreed with the two men with whom he had been dealing on various important points. He had found Stalin much tougher than he had expected and at times deliberately discourteous, and Churchill's tireless advocacy of his own strategic concepts had been more than ever taxing to his patience; but there was one fault in these two men which was gloriously conspicuous by its absence, and that fault was hypocrisy. . . . Roosevelt now felt sure that, to use his own term, Stalin was "getatable," despite his bludgeoning tactics and his attitude of cynicism toward such matters as the rights of small nations, and that when Russia could be convinced that her legitimate claims and requirements—such as the right to access to warm water ports—were to be given full recognition, she would prove tractable and cooperative in maintaining the peace of the post-war world.[59]

As far as the Poles were concerned, the Teheran Conference was a new partition of Poland, and Churchill was its main architect. As the record shows, Roosevelt spoke only twice, at the beginning when he hoped that "the Polish and Soviet Governments would resume relations, so that any decision taken could be accepted by the Polish Government," and when, realizing that Churchill supported all Soviet territorial claims, he asked if Stalin would permit a transfer of the population on a voluntary basis. No doubt his desire to preserve the unity of the Big Three was the primary consideration. If Churchill had taken a firm stand in support of Roosevelt's opening remarks, together they could presumably have swayed Stalin from his determination to change not only Poland's frontiers but also her Government.

For Churchill and Roosevelt at Teheran, the question of Poland was one of those unpleasant and unimportant matters which had to be disposed of in order to obtain the Soviet approval of "Overlord"—the operational plans for the Second Front. On the other hand, for Stalin it was a matter of pushing his strategic frontiers westward to serve as a springboard for future Soviet domination of parts of Germany and, if possible, of the whole of Western Europe.

7. Implementation of the Teheran Conference by Both Sides

Prior to Eden's return to London (Churchill was taken ill in Africa and remained there for recuperation), the Poles began to worry when, on December 12, the British censor of the Polish broadcasts over the BBC cut out a paragraph which referred to Lwow and Wilno as Polish cities from an address to Poland delivered by Bishop Radomski, a member of the Polish Parliament in exile. On the same day, the same censor protested against the inclusion in a Polish broadcast of a quotation from the Swedish paper, *Svenska Dag Bladet,* which said that "after the war all territories had to be returned to their owners," as well as another paragraph which stated that "since the Atlantic Charter was mentioned in one of the Teheran documents and approved by Stalin, undoubtedly the principles of the Atlantic Charter will be applied to the Western neighbors of Russia." [60]

The first account that the Polish Government received of the Teheran Conference was given by Eden to Ambassador Raczyński, whom he informed that during the Conference the question of Soviet-Polish diplomatic relations was discussed but that Stalin had bitterly complained over the attitude of the Polish Government in London towards Soviet partisans operating in Poland. Stalin maintained that the actions following this attitude were performed with the full knowledge and consent of the Polish Government—he even suggested that there was a secret Polish-German agreement to destroy the partisans. Eden then said that in Churchill's opinion, as well as in his own, Stalin would not try to destroy or occupy Poland. Stalin insisted on the Curzon Line, but they were determined to compensate Poland for the loss of those territories with German territories up to the Oder-Neisse Line, plus East Prussia. At the end of the conference, Eden spoke, with evident satisfaction and conviction, of the fact that British-Soviet relations were considerably improved since the Teheran Conference. It was Eden's opinion that future prospects were bright. He also informed the Ambassador that he had received voluntary offers of help from many Members of Parliament to support the Polish case, but as he said, "I appreciate their good will but I am afraid of too many helpers." [61]

The next day Eden repeated the same arguments to Mikolajczyk, adding that

. . . the air was filled with suspicion and recrimination. . . . I share the Prime Minister's view that Stalin will not try to annihilate Poland or incorporate it into the Soviet Union. . . . Stalin said at Teheran that he would renew relations with any Polish Government that would declare itself ready to collaborate with the advancing Red Army, fight the Germans, and outline its plans for the impending campaign on Polish soil.

Mikolajczyk replied that prior to Teheran he had delivered Polish plans for collaboration with the Soviet Army to Eden, to the chiefs of staff, and to the Americans. "My Government has complied with these demands in all respects and continues to do so. It seems superfluous to promise to do something we are already doing." [62]

The last remaining hope for the Poles was to appeal to Roosevelt who was, for them, a symbol of justice and fair play. Mikolajczyk told Eden that he could not agree to the Soviet territorial demands and that he was looking forward to his scheduled visit to Washington in January 1944. Eden objected to this planned visit and insisted that Mikolajczyk first see Churchill upon his return from Africa. Eden told the Polish Premier to his face that he would try to postpone Mikolajczyk's Washington appointment. Soon afterwards, Mikolajczyk received a telegram from Roosevelt informing him that Churchill had wired asking for a "personal favor"—to postpone the Mikolajczyk visit—and stating that he had agreed to that "request." [63]

In the middle of December 1943, the United States Ambassador to Poland, Anthony J. Drexel Biddle, Jr., a most devoted friend of the Polish Nation and much beloved by it, came back to Washington. On December 16 he saw Ciechanowski and told him the following:

> He was deeply concerned and disturbed by the trend of events, and what little he had heard of the results of the Moscow and Teheran Conferences had increased his anxiety. . . . He would tell the President, very frankly, he said, that if the legitimate interests of Poland and his hopes that Poland's sovereignty and territorial integrity would be energetically defended by the President were not to be fulfilled, he could no longer remain in his post as United States Ambassador to the Polish Government. He had for many years been so closely knit with Poland in her good days as in all her difficulties, that he knew he could never face the Polish nation if the cause of Poland were to be abandoned by the United States.

Biddle saw the President, and then, writes Ciechanowski:

> A few days later I heard that he had asked to be relieved of his functions as Ambassador to Poland.
> "I have come to the conclusion," he told me, "that I can be more useful to Poland if I get into uniform. . . ."
> His decision depressed me. It proved that Tony Biddle, the honest American, was losing hope that the American Government would press for a just solution of Poland's problems by diplomatic means. [64]

The Polish Government decided not to surrender, but all the cards were stacked against it.

Meanwhile, Soviet propaganda intensified its activities. By means of the press and the radio, aimed both at foreign consumption and at the Polish people, they strove to deprive Poland of the sympathies of public opinion in other Allied countries by constantly repeating the accusation that the Polish underground organization was not carrying on the struggle against the occupying authorities, but that this organization was, on the contrary, fighting "Polish partisans" who were sympathetic to the Soviet Union.

At the same time the increased number of Soviet parachutists into Polish territories were not only not aiding the Polish population, but they were exposing the Poles to bloody German reprisals by their provocative and indecisive actions against the Germans. Moreover, they attempted to undermine Polish public confidence in the leadership of the Polish Underground Movement in order to destroy its cohesion and to weaken its forces. They threatened it with reprisals by the Red Army as soon as the latter entered Polish territories. Those threats were repeated by the "Kosciuszko" radio and the affiliated stations operating on the Soviet side. Both inside and outside Poland non-communist Poles were accused of "fratricide."

Soviet political action took different forms in different parts of the country. In the eastern provinces Soviet agents either acted on the ground of the 1939 *fait accompli*, that is, the "plebiscite" carried out by Soviet occupation authorities prior to Hitler's attack on Russia or else conducted open anti-Polish propaganda among the racially mixed population. Thus, according to a report received by the London Government, a band under Pylypienko (a member of the Town Council of Zhitomir [Zytomierz] in 1939) arrived in the district of Lutsk (Luck) and, instead of engaging the Germans in military operations, organized meetings which passed resolutions demanding union with the Soviets. The Orthodox population, and especially the Orthodox clergy, received written instructions to agitate in favor of Russia on the grounds that the Poles were hostile to the Orthodox religion and would take reprisals against the Orthodox population if they ever returned.[65]

In the central, and even more, in the western provinces, Soviet agents employed different tactics. In these provinces, Russia's claims to the eastern part of Poland were not advanced, but their slogans emphasized the need of friendship with Russia, stating that Russia was the only Power that could liberate Poland from the Nazis, and asserting that both Great Britain and the United States were waging war solely for their own selfish interests and were not interested in Poland. In this respect the Soviet organizations in Poland, and particularly the communist press, were used as instruments for the elucidation of the people. They effectuated the plans of Soviet foreign policy which official Soviet agencies in Russia could not conveniently carry out.

Thus, communist propaganda argued:

. . . the war against the Nazis had become, for England and America, a screen behind which the two Powers are preparing a counter-revolutionary dictatorship of AMGOT [Allied Military Government] in Europe. In the United States, when the forthcoming social crisis will be of unprecedented dimensions and violence, the revolutionary élan of the American proletariat—if timed to coincide with the downfall of Hitler—may yet overpower the counter-revolutionary AMGOT policemen in Europe.

Then it proceeded to call upon Poles to get rid of the effect of Anglo-Saxon propaganda.[66]

Apart from sowing distrust of the Western Powers, the communists aimed at discrediting the Polish Government and its organs in the Home Country. This was synchronized with characteristically bold communist action.

On December 31, 1943 and January 1, 1944 a plenary meeting of the Home National Council (which was established by the PPR) took place in Warsaw. The Home National Council was composed of the PPR, the People's Guard (Communist Youth), and the representatives of the following, seemingly independent, but actually integral, organs of the PPR:

1. The Committee of National Initiative.
2. Scientific Workers' Group.
3. Underground Press.

Besides the suborganizations listed above, the following representatives of PPR-controlled units also entered the Home National Council:

1. The Socialist Activists.
2. Activists of the Peasant Party and Peasant Battalions.
3. Democratic Circle of the Medical Union.
4. Underground Trade Unions.
5. Union of Jewish Workers.

Besides the adoption of the provisional statutes for the National Council and the declaration, the following decrees were issued:

1. Decree concerning the establishment and organization of the People's Army,
2. Decree on the organization of the High Command of the People's Army.

In addition, an agreement was reached about the formula under which greetings were to be sent to the peoples and governments of Allied States. Appeals were made to the Allied Nations for assistance and arms for the Polish soldiers fighting in the Homeland, and to the Polish people concerning self-defense and contributions to the National Fund. Finally, a decree for the punishment of "traitors, denunciators, and persons who collaborated with the occupant of the Polish nation" was issued.

In accordance with the adopted statutes a presidium of the Home National Council was formed which was going to be an executive branch of the Home National Council.

The PPR had a great deal of difficulty in establishing that Council, because it could not find suitable people to fill the "state representation." Consequently, the PPR had to divide itself into numerous sub-groups which, in turn, were named as previously mentioned in order to appear as independent political or social organizations. They felt it was imperative to give the Home National Council at least an appearance of national representation. This step had two purposes: (1) to convince foreign powers that political control rested in the hands of the Home National Council, and (2) to create difficulties for the Polish Government in London.[67] The Polish Government in London interpreted this move as a preparation for the establishment of a rival administration for Poland.

In reply to the Soviet announcement of the establishment in Poland of the Home National Council, twenty-four Polish political and social underground organizations issued the following declaration to the Polish nation:

On the eve of those imminent events which will decide the conclusion of the war and which will demand of Poland a great and harmonious effort, quarters hostile to the Republic are endeavoring to weaken the unity of the Polish nation by spreading chaos and strife.

The Polish Workers Party, an agency of foreign communists, is acting on our soil in a way that is threatening the vital interests of the nation.

Obedient to orders issued from abroad by a foreign government, masking their true aims, misinterpreting the claims of their patrons, and fraudulently exploiting patriotic and national slogans, the communist Polish Workers Party and its agencies such as the "Polish People's Army" declare their readiness to give away the eastern territories of Poland to Russia and oppose the Government which enjoys the confidence of the nation, the army, and their counterparts in the home country.

In their endeavor to weaken and divide the forces of the nation in a decisive phase of the war, the communist agencies have set up a Home National Council and a People's Army Headquarters, and have announced that they will form a temporary Government.

Irrespective of the insignificant forces and negligible importance represented by these fictitious institutions, which are only calculated to make an impression abroad, the activities of the PPR must be condemned as treason against the Polish nation and State.

Only the Polish Government, its Deputy in the homeland, the Commander-in-Chief and the Commander of the Home Army acting on his behalf are entitled to issue the orders for the last phase of the struggle against the enemy.

All political problems will be settled by the nation and not by foreign agents.[68]

Western public opinion was presented only with the glossy side of the Teheran Conference, which led to the implication that the Soviets were loyal and reliable Allies of the West. Certainly their military successes were impressive. It was only natural that those whose losses were smaller felt grateful to the eastern partner who was sustaining such enormous losses for the common cause.

At this point, it is necessary to include the information which was brought back by Beneš from his journey to Moscow. It will be recalled that at the end of November, 1943 Beneš went to confer with the Soviet leaders.

My political discussion with Moscow actually began during my journey from London to the Soviet Union when I was met at Habaniyah Airfield, near Bagdad, by Alexander Korneychuk (Molotov's Deputy in the Commissariat for Foreign Affairs), who came to meet me.[69]

We spent a whole week there because of bad weather over the Caucasus and Southern Russia. While waiting to continue our journey we discussed all the questions I wanted to raise in Moscow: questions about the war, peace, Germany, Hungary, especially Poland and the future Slav policy of the Soviet Union. . . . From what I was told by Korneytchuk, our good friend, a talented writer and a good Ukrainian and Soviet patriot, I judged that we would agree well together in Moscow on every point. Korneytchuk himself prepared notes about our talks for Stalin and Molotov so that when our discussions began in Moscow, both Molotov and Stalin were informed about my view on the chief problems. . . .[70]

My discussion with Stalin was interesting, frank, and sincere. . . . We went cursorily but objectively through all the chief problems. . . . I saw at once that we really would agree—our views were fundamentally identical.

. . . .

The question of Poland was discussed several times in Moscow.[71]

. . . .

The most detailed discussion took place during our joint official visit to the "Bolshoi Theater" . . . and in the long intervals and after the end of the performance, deep into the night we discussed the Polish problems. . . . The Soviet politicians (Stalin, Molotov, etc.) wanted to know my opinion about the state of the London Poles, about the British and American attitudes, on whether any agreement with the London Poles was possible, etc. I told them sincerely what I knew and what I believed.

Then Beneš stressed the necessity of reaching an agreement between the Soviets and Poles as a precaution against a future Munich. He continued:

I would always believe agreement was possible with the present Polish Government in London—at least with some of its leading representatives—even if with the others this seemed hopeless. Those who were followers of Pilsudski—and among the London Poles they had a decisive majority—would never come to an agreement with Moscow. But Prime Minister Mikolajczyk and some others were, in my opinion, sincere democrats and were perhaps convinced that agreement and cooperation with Moscow after the war were necessary for Poland. I therefore urged that Moscow should try once more. . . . I repeated to them . . . my last talk with Mikolajczyk. . . . He recognized that the Poles would have to come to an agreement with the Soviet Union and that they would have to make great concessions in the matter of frontiers. He was only interested in keeping Lwow and a part of Eastern Galicia and in non-interference of the Soviet Union in Polish internal affairs. He wanted to do all he could to renew relations with the Soviet Union and he was ready to go to Moscow. He authorized me to inform official circles in Moscow accordingly.

. . . .

I [was] . . . favorably impressed with this conversation with our hosts at the Bolshoi Theater. In general, the views of the Soviets were to the point, calm, and sincere. As Stalin expressed it, they really wanted an independent and strong Poland.[72]

Beneš was apparently convinced that Stalin was telling the truth.

On December 12, 1943, while signing the treaty with the Soviet Union, they also signed a special "Protocol to the Treaty of Friendship, Mutual Aid and Post-War Cooperation" which contained the so-called "Polish Clause." It read as follows:

In concluding the Treaty of Friendship, Mutual Aid and Post-War Cooperation between the Czechoslovak Republic and the Union of Soviet Socialist Republics, the Contracting Parties agree that if any third country having common frontiers with the Czechoslovak Republic or the Union of Soviet Socialist Republics and having in this war been an object of German aggression, expresses the wish to adhere to this Treaty, it will be given the opportunity to do so after mutual agreement between the Government of the Czechoslovak Republic and the Union of Soviet Socialist Republics and this Treaty, by such adhesion, shall acquire the character of a trilateral treaty.[73]

On his way back to London Beneš was invited to visit Churchill at Marrakesh, which he did on January 4 and 5, 1944.

I told him [Churchill] about my negotiations and impressions and about my views about Soviet-Polish relations. His reaction was very strong and decided. He felt that the Poles should accept what I was bringing Mikolajczyk from Moscow; that when I reached London I should first tell Eden and then Mikolajczyk, and that then in conjunction with Eden I should urge Poles as their friend to decide at once to negotiate with Moscow and to accept Stalin's offer.[74]

At the end of Beneš' visit with Churchill, the latter sent the following account of their talk to President Roosevelt.

Beneš has been here, and is very hopeful about the Russian situation. He may be most useful in trying to make the Poles see reason and in reconciling them to the Russians, whose confidence he has long possessed. He brought a new map with pencil marks by U.J. [Uncle Joe] showing the eastern frontier from Königsberg to the Curzon Line, giving the Poles the

Lomza and Bialystok regions in the north but not Lemberg (Lvov) at the southern end. For their western frontier he offers the line of the Oder, including the major part of Oppeln. This gives the Poles a fine place to live in, more than three hundred miles square, and with two hundred and fifty miles of seaboard on the Baltic. As soon as I get home, I shall go all out with the Polish Government to close with this or something like it, and having closed, they must proclaim themselves as ready to accept the duty of guarding the bulwark of the Oder against further German aggression upon Russia, and also they must back the settlement to the limit. This will be their duty to the Powers of Europe, who will twice have rescued them. If I can get this tidied up early in February, a visit from them to you would clinch matters.[75]

Apparently Churchill underestimated Polish stubbornness. Beneš' willingness to bring about a rapprochement between the Poles and the Soviets was a convenient means to achieve the objectives decided upon in Teheran without revealing that decision to the Poles. Beneš was anxious to perform that task for two reasons, (1) because, being a man of peace, he wanted to secure a Soviet-Polish alliance in order to ensure that the stormy political past of Eastern Europe would be stabilized in the future, and (2) his efforts to bring it about would increase Czech prestige in the eyes of Moscow, London, and Washington.

He shared with Churchill and Roosevelt the misleading image of the Soviet Union as a state dedicated to peaceful objectives (in the Western sense). Behind these peaceful appearances lay a strategically sophisticated plan, ready for immediate implementation.

Encouraged by Churchill, Beneš proceeded to go about his mission.

On January 8th in the presence of Jan Masaryk I discussed the whole matter with Eden who was of the same opinion as Churchill, and I invited Mikolajczyk to come to Aston Abbotts on January 10th. There I summarized my impressions and information from Moscow and the Soviet attitude to Polish matters as formulated to me by Stalin as follows:

(a) Moscow did not exclude negotiations with the new Polish Government in London and would be ready to establish diplomatic relations with it at once. But the present Polish Government would have to be reconstructed and old points at issue (Katyn, a systematic hostile propaganda against the Soviet Union, etc.) would have to be dropped. Moscow was willing to negotiate with Mikolajczyk if he cared to form a new Government, from which unsuitable elements were excluded, and if he would negotiate with Moscow in this spirit.

(b) Moscow could not give way about the Curzon Line but was ready to consent to territorial compensations for Poland at the expense of Germany in full agreement with Poland, Great Britain, and America—Moscow would accept any western line upon which they agreed even if it were the Oder Line.

(c) The eastern frontier of Poland could be moved from the Line on which the Soviet Union had agreed with Germany in 1939, to a "corrected" Curzon Line—that is to say to Lomza, Bialystok, and Przemysl would evidently fall to Poland.

(d) The Soviet-Czechoslovak Treaty was the basis for both countries of their eventual agreement with Poland and also of any future joint guarantee for Poland against Germany. Both countries would loyally work for the conclusion of a tripartite treaty.

(e) The Soviet Union had no thought either of procuring a revolution in Germany or of siding with Germany against the other Allies. In this matter, it would go forward jointly with Great Britain and America, and, of course, also with Czechoslovakia and Poland, and was ready to accept the policy of the territorial weakening of Germany.

(f) The Soviet Union would not interfere in Polish internal affairs and there would be no Bolshevization and no Sovietization.

I felt at the time that my remarks had made a strong impression on Mikolajczyk. It seemed to me that till then no one had been so outspoken to the Poles about these matters.

This conversation with Mikolajczyk was very friendly and frank. Mikolajczyk answered quite openly that he feared he would not be able to persuade the Poles to accept the new Soviet-Polish eastern frontier. If Lwow at least could be saved for Poland! He said he knew the Poles. Even if they made matters still worse for Poland, nobody perhaps could get them to yield voluntarily about the Curzon Line. If only it were possible to shift the Soviet-Polish frontier line further to the East and to combine this with an exchange of populations!

He said that nevertheless he would consider all I had told him and would discuss it with his friends. He personally had a fairly strong position politically. Four parties were wholly with him, in England and at home. *Everything I had told him would be regarded as satisfactory and as an acceptable basis for agreement except the question of the eastern frontier* —as I had put it to him. *This difficulty could probably not be overcome.* The growth of a desire among the Poles for agreement with the Soviet Union was already quite considerable; there was also at present more confidence in the Soviet Union and it was especially recognized *that, in the interest of Poland itself, an agreement should be concluded as soon as possible.* He himself was decidedly in favor of an agreement.

I told him that I had seen Churchill at Marrakesh, that he had urged me to speak to Mikolajczyk and tell him that Churchill thought this was the last chance for an agreement. I had therefore delivered this message and added that Churchill thought the Poles should accept the offer I had brought them. He had asked that Mikolajczyk should perhaps visit Churchill as soon as possible so that they could agree on the next step.

Finally, Mikolajczyk asked me whether I considered the Soviet Union to be full of vigour or exhausted and whether I thought that it would keep up its offensive. I assured him that the offensive would continue and that to count on the exhaustion of the Soviet Union would be a most unwarranted assumption. He told me that he thought so too. He rejected the whole well-known ideology of some Polish officers concerning the present-day Soviet Union and Poland and he was working to ensure that Polish feudalism should fall utterly. He added that in Poland itself feudalism had in reality fallen already and social and economic radicalism were much more advanced in Poland than in the emigration. The new Poland would also be quite different, completely changed in fact from the Poland of Pilsudski and Beck.

I had the impression that Mikolajczyk was convinced of the necessity for immediate negotiations. But it was clear to me that he did not believe he would be able to overcome the objections of the London emigrants and force them to negotiate.[76]

Although Mikolajczyk was most eager to resume negotiations with the Soviets, he was actually less optimistic about the chances of success in this endeavor than the impression he conveyed to Beneš would indicate.[77] He realized that the Soviets were exploiting Beneš's humane character and that Beneš was unwittingly presenting Soviet objectives in a much more favorable light than the Soviets could have managed to do by their own efforts. Beneš' prestige in the West was of the utmost importance to the Soviets in this respect. Mikolajczyk did not have long to wait to realize that his suspicions of Soviet intentions were correct.

While on the diplomatic front the Soviets were putting pressure on Mikolajczyk through Beneš and the British, the Polish communist agents in England were extremely active in attacking the Polish Government from the other side.

The Polish Progressive Club in London issued the following appeal to British public opinion:

Polish democratic circles in Great Britain appeal to the British public opinion not to identify them with the official Polish circles known by their fascist tendencies. We can bring many proofs that the Poles in Great Britain have been divided into two groups for a long time.

The first group consists of some members of the Government, their employees, and the military clique desiring a dictatorial regime in the future Poland. These circles support the extreme reactionary politicians and journalists, giving them financial means for the purpose of publishing many newspapers and founding different organizations. The so-called opposition to these Government papers, strong in words but obedient in deeds, attempt to prove that only the extreme right opposes the present Government in exile.

The existence of a second group, consisting of large democratic social organizations and trade unions is very little known in this country, because they do not possess their own newspapers. The Polish Government divided their paper quota between their own press and the reactionary, right, "opposition."

It is characteristic that the official Polish press refused to print any reports of activities of the democratic organizations, and does not even accept paid advertisements from them. (For example: *Dziennik Polski* and the recently suppressed *Wiadomosci Polskie* refused such advertisements recently.)

There is an official order to boycott these organizations as well as an order prohibiting the sale in Polish shops of pamphlets published by the independent democratic groups. Within this category of organizations comes the Polish Society in London established in 1886, the Council of Poles in Great Britain, the Polish Progressive Club, the Polish section of the International Brigades, the "Free Poland" Library, and some Polish Trade Unions.

The ranks of these organizations consist of Polish war-workers, merchant seamen, disabled soldiers, some professional men, and the majority of the pre-war Polish emigration in England.[78]

It is difficult to estimate the effect of this and similar undertakings. Presumably they were not completely impotent.

On December 22, 1943 the *Soviet Monitor*, No. 4015, in its *Evening Bulletin*, carried the following report under the title, "American Poles Welcome the Teheran Decision."

Over 1,500 Americans of Polish descent, at a meeting organized by the National Council of American-Soviet Friendship in New York, unanimously approved the declarations of the Moscow, Cairo, and Teheran Conferences, states a TASS message from New York and reported by Moscow today. . . .

The resolution adopted by the meeting urged Americans of Polish descent to give President Roosevelt their full support and welcomed the formation of a Polish Army in the U.S.S.R. as the basis of a lasting Soviet-Polish friendship.

In a message of greeting to Wanda Wasilewska, the President of the Union of Polish Patriots, the spokesman of the meeting, said:

"By your struggle to assure friendship and collaboration between the U.S.S.R. and Poland you are contributing to the unity of the United Nations against the forces of Fascism. You are also contributing to the formation of a post-war democratic Poland which will take her rightful place in the family of those liberated nations which have devoted themselves to the struggle for the maintenance of peace. Long live the Union of Polish Patriots!"

The meeting also sent a message to General Berling and the heroic soldiers of the "Kosciuszko" Division, who are fighting shoulder to shoulder with the Red Army for the destruction of the Fascist aggressors and the liberation of Poland. "Fighting alongside the Red Army, on the same battlefield," the message continues, "you are strengthening the inviolable friendship and unity between the Polish people and the peoples of the U.S.S.R."

Messages of greeting were received by the assembled members at the meeting from Mayor La Guardia and numerous Polish organizations in the U.S.S.R. and Canada.

The meeting was addressed by the well-known Polish Professor Lange, of the University of Chicago; by the Catholic Priest and Honorary President of the "Kosciuszko" League, Orlemanski; by the President of the American-Slav Congress, Kazicki; by the Democratic Senator Tunnell of the State of Delaware; and by Mr. Corliss Lamont, President of the Council of American-Soviet Friendship.

.   .   .   .

They criticized the activity of small groups of Polish reactionaries in the United States who are conducting anti-Soviet agitation.[79]

On December 7, 1943 in a press release, Herbert Klimczak, President of the American Polish Trade Union Council of Milwaukee County, sent the following statement, adopted by the American Polish Trade Union Council and signed by union representatives of the Trade Union Council and other leading members of trade unions, to the President of the United States and to Secretary of State Cordell Hull.

It is with satisfaction that the American Polish Trade Union Council greets the history making tripower Teheran Conference as the means of implementing the Moscow agreements for action now and in the post-war world, and is proud to present this statement to the President of the United States and to Secretary of State Cordell Hull as signifying the true sentiments of Americans of Polish descent for the indestructible unity of the United Nations and behind our Commander-in-Chief, President Roosevelt.[80]

The Polish Consul-General in Chicago, Dr. Karol Ripa, reported to his Government that communist activity among Americans of Polish descent was growing rapidly and that its center was located in Detroit. Its purpose was to infiltrate all social and political organizations of Poles in America.

According to the best information (received from Mr. Hetman and others) there are between 6,000 or 7,000 Poles who are members of the Communist Party in the Middle West. Milwaukee alone has about 1,000 of them. These people are absolutely obedient to the Communist Party. They are selected and well-trained. The prospective candidates are closely watched over long periods of time. Only intelligent and promising individuals are accepted as members of the Communist Party. They must have a good reputation in their community. Particular stress is laid on workers. No person who is in financial difficulties, or who is inclined to drink, is accepted.

In return, the Communist Party makes every effort (confidentially) to secure good jobs for its members, which will provide good pay and time for the Party's work. The Communist Party pays its members travel and other official expenses. Only 5% of the total membership are trusted men, and these receive regular pay. The basis of Party activity is the creation of an elite whose mission is to infiltrate all possible fields of the activities of Poles in America. The main objects are Polish sections of the International Workers Union and the Polish section in the local CIO. Recently the Communist Party issued instructions to infiltrate the committees of

Polish parishes. The fewest communist activities are observable in insurance organizations, presumably because they are the most difficult to infiltrate—especially the Zwiazek Narodowy Polski, Zjednoczenie, Zwiazek Polek, and Macierz Polska. Because these organizations are non-political the Communist Party has limited itself to stressing its disinterested services for the general betterment of the working class. It has also instructed its members not to be involved in any way with these organizations.

The main objectives of the Communist Party with respect to the Polish problem is to discredit the Polish Government in London. So far they have met only unorganized opposition. This has encouraged the communists. The second point is to convince American public opinion that Poles in America are a working lot who want to organize themselves into a Labor Union which will speak for all Poles in the United States. For this reason they intend to organize a Congress of Poles in Cleveland, Ohio, in the first month of 1944. The delegates to the Congress will come from the Polish Trade Union, the International Workers Union, and the CIO. The official aim of the Congress will be the organization of Poles to improve the working conditions of Polish labor in America and to support the candidacy of President Roosevelt. Unofficially, it was disclosed that two main points on the agenda were going to be: (1) condemnation of the Polish Government in London, and (2) support for the Polish Patriots in Moscow with its military leader, General Berling.

The political line of their activity is illustrated by the declaration of December 1943 issued by the Polish American Council of Trade Unions and signed by forty-three prominent Polish personalities. This resolution was accepted under the strong pressure of the Kosciuszko Committee in Detroit and copies were sent to President Roosevelt and prominent personalities in the American scene.[81]

This synchronized activity of the communists among the Poles in Britain and the United States appeared to be a well-timed move calculated to discredit the London Government and convince the British and Americans that it had lost popular support among its followers. Uninvited, the Soviets were anxious to help their Western Allies in finding a rationale for a gradual minimization of the symbolic importance of the London Government, which might block the full realization of the Teheran decision. As subsequent events have proven, this was an eventuality likely not to find complete disfavor in the eyes of the British and American Governments at that time.

Official British circles, meanwhile, kept silent on the Polish dilemma. Eden made a speech in the House of Commons during the Foreign Affairs debate on the Teheran Conference in which he omitted this subject altogether. This silence was more expressive than even a speech critical of Poland would have been. The reason for his behavior was explained in the following letter which Alan Graham, M.P., sent to Mikolajczyk on December 20, 1943.

I spent the whole of Tuesday from 12:30 P.M. to 5:30 P.M. and the whole of Wednesday from 12:00 to 5:30 P.M. going without my lunch, in a vain effort to catch the Speaker's eye during the Foreign Affairs Debate in order to make a speech and in the course of it to extract from Eden one word of mention of the Poles—enough to show them that they at least had not been forgotten—because I felt that anything was preferable to this complete silence.

After Eden's speech on the first day I spoke to him privately and complained of his silence, to which he replied, "Well, things weren't too bad for them at Teheran. But the Prime Minister will deal with that question and I prefer to leave it to him to speak about it with his much greater authority. Also Roosevelt doesn't want it mentioned yet, because of the impending American elections!" I still felt that for the sake of Polish morale here something should be said and so I tried to get up and make a speech all during these days. Then, when I saw that I had no chance of getting in before Eden's second and closing speech I went to him again and said: "Do, in your speech, say one word about the Poles, because otherwise their reaction will be very bad and they will probably explode in their newspapers." To this he replied, "Well, they'll be very foolish if they do. I can't speak about them, as I promised the Americans not to." I was bitterly disappointed and think it was a cruel blunder on his part, particularly as we don't know when Churchill will be back. Please understand, however, that I was silent only because in spite of every effort on my part the Speaker did not call me. I felt that you should know all this.[82]

Mikolajczyk was puzzled by the reference, "I promised the Americans not to." It was disturbing because Washington was the only hope left, and this reference of Eden's indicated that the Americans, as well as the British, had abandoned the Poles. Ambassador Ciechanowski was unable to learn anything specific about Teheran from the United States Government to clear up this implication.

At this time, the Polish Government received a penetrating report from Colonel Mitkiewicz, the Military Attaché in the Polish Embassy in Washington, who reported to London as follows:

The Polish Government is criticized for the lack of good relations with the Soviets. The American press gave wide publicity to the speech by the Assistant Secretary of State, A. Berle, who is critical of Poland.

Recently I was informed that if the Polish Government will not reach an agreement with the Soviets, a plan is in preparation to establish a mixed commission composed of Soviets, British, and Americans to find out what will be the situation in Poland when the Soviet troops take over Poland, and then to form a provisional government on the spot. This information comes from a person who is favorably disposed towards Russia. The same person told me that President Roosevelt took with him to Teheran a definite plan about the Soviet-Polish frontier which accepts the Curzon Line, leaving Lwow with Poland.

It might be that all this was told me purposely. Even so, we can at least bargain.

From the press and radio here we have no support whatsoever. We must be very cautious about the friendliness of the Republican and Socialist press because these might be only pre-election tricks to get the Polish vote. One feels that in case the Republicans win and the European situation remains complicated, that the United States may withdraw altogether. . . .

One would be right in saying that only Roosevelt, his closest advisers, all Democrats, and the Armed Forces support active participation in European affairs. Our position in America is as follows:

The weakest Polish point is our defense of the eastern frontier. This is due to the Riga Treaty and the 1941 agreement with the Soviets. While we were unable to gain any support over here, Soviet propaganda, diplomacy, and military missions have been successful in persuading Washington and London that since 1939 the Soviets have been controlling the eastern territories of Poland and, in accordance with the will of the Ukrainian, Byelorussian, and Lithuanian peoples they intend to liberate those territories from the hegemony of Polish nationalism.

I had the opportunity to observe the effectiveness of the Soviet activities over here on the Combined Chiefs of Staff. In my various conversations with high military personnel I was told that the Polish eastern territories are not in the hands of the Polish Army but in those of the Soviet partisans. A similar view was expressed by the O.S.S. (General Donovan's organization), and by G-2 (Army Intelligence).

I fully understand that our situation is unusually dangerous and a decision is very difficult. That is why it seems to me that it is not sufficient to rely only on diplomacy and poor propaganda. This does not correspond with reality. If our aim is to defend the Polish frontier of September 1, 1939 we should try to get the support (if it is not too late) of all our minorities, not by general and vague declarations by various people, but by definite acts of the Polish Government, such as:

1. State clearly and firmly that Ukrainians will get autonomy.

2. Establish an understanding with the Lithuanians, because even if Wilno will remain in Poland, we shall have in nearby Kowno a competitive puppet government of the Soviet Lithuanian Republic.

3. Clear the solution of the Jewish problem, and finally,

4. Remove friction with the Czechs by giving them back Zaolzie (Teschen area).

Such acts may influence the attitude of the minorities towards Poland even if a plebiscite were going to be held. There are substantial settlements of these minorities in the United States and Canada, and they have their political weight. At the present time they are hostile to us. We need their support. Up to now nothing was done whatsoever to make sure that the most powerful Jewish organizations in America would adopt an attitude of at least friendly neutrality towards the Polish question.

We are defending our case badly. We are forgetting that the Western World and Soviet Russia remember only too well the period of 1918–1920. They also remember our national structure from before 1939.

If Poland is going to remain a State with substantial minorities, it is indispensable that the Government should strive to change, or at least to weaken, the unfriendly attitude of the West towards us for the supposed (let us say) bad treatment of the minorities, for lack of tolerance, and for our imperialistic ambitions.

Western public opinion is friendly towards Soviet Russia without understanding it and treats the Soviet Constitution as genuine. This is true particularly because it corresponds with Western wishful thinking and the political expediency of Great Britain as well as the United States.[83]

This analysis of the American scene impressed the Polish Government, for its recommendations seemed to make sense. However, time and other events occupied government activities. Such projects could not be accomplished overnight, and the Poles asked themselves whether, even if these could be put into effect, they really could change the fast-moving wheels of history. Anyhow, the communists were more experienced in this field than were the Poles.

Several new attempts made by the London Government and its Ambassador to get any assurances of help from leading Americans failed. The British position was so clear that the Poles were discouraged from making any further attempts in that direction. The Poles were now diplomatically isolated and left to face their discouraging future alone. The Soviet Government, having contributed so greatly to Poland's diplomatic isolation, now proceeded to confront it with another *fait accompli.*

Notes

[1] Jan Ciechanowski, *Defeat in Victory*, Garden City, New York, Doubleday & Company, Inc., 1947, p. 159.

[2] The commission included Dr. Speleers, a Belgian, of the University of Ghent; Dr. Markov, a Bulgarian, of the University of Sofia; Dr. Tramsen, Denmark, Institute of Medicine, Copenhagen; and Dr. Saxén, Finland, Helsinki University. Dr. Palmieri, Italy, University of Naples; Dr. Miloslavich, Yugoslavia, University of Zagreb; Dr. de Burlet, The Netherlands, University of Groningen; Dr. Hajek, Czechoslovakia, Charles IV University of Prague; Dr. Birkle, Rumania, Institute of Medicine and Criminology, Bucharest; Dr. Naville, Switzerland, University of Geneva; Dr. Subik, Czechoslovakia, Jan Comenius University of Bratislava; Dr. Orsos, Hungary, University of Budapest; and Dr. Costedoat, a medical inspector attached to the Vichy Government.

See also *Report on the Massacre of Polish Officers in Katyn Wood; Facts and Documents*, prepared by Prof. Wiktor Sukiennicki—one of the deportees himself, London, 1946, pp. 11–15.

[3] For Official Soviet Report on Katyn, see Appendix 5.

[4] For a full discussion of the factual material see Stanislaw Mikolajczyk, *The Rape of Poland: Pattern of Soviet Aggression*, New York, Whittlesey House, 1948, pp. 32–38.

[5] Indictment of the German War Criminals Presented to the International

Tribunal at Nürnberg: Count Three—War Crimes Section (c) "Murder and Ill-Treatment of Prisoners of War," Subsection 2.

⁶ Poland, *Official Government Documents*, Vol. XVII, Doc. 141.

⁷ For evidence with respect to the communist efforts to infiltrate and destroy the underground political organizations, see *passim* Stefan Korboński, *W. Imieniu Rzeczypospolitej* . . . , Institut Literacki, Paris, 1954.

⁸ On February 17, 1956 the American news magazine, *U. S. News and World Report*, on page 126 carried a summary of the book entitled *The Great Spy Scandal*, edited by John S. Mather and published by the London *Daily Express*: "In his propaganda work (Guy) Burgess was still involved with secret organizations. The Foreign Office trusted him. He had the job, for example, of removing anti-Russian bias from Poles we were training for sabotage." Burgess worked for the Special Organization Executive of M.I.6, where, the report states, he openly exhibited left-wing attitudes. If it is subsequently proven that he was actively transmitting secret data to the Soviets (for it is known that he was a Soviet agent long before this time), the mystery of who was betraying these men would become clear, for in his job in M.I.6 Burgess dealt with exactly this sort of information. It was no doubt most convenient for the Soviets to have a spy located right in the planning center of the underground organizations.

Colonel Jozef Swiatlo, a former high-ranking official of the communist Security Police in Poland, supplied this author with a wealth of information concerning the friendly collaboration of the communist organizations and the Gestapo. Copies of Swiatlo's report are to be found in the files of the Political Adviser to Radio Free Europe, and a summary of this report can be found in *News from Behind the Iron Curtain*, Vol. IV, No. 3, New York, New York, The Free Europe Press, Free Europe Committee, Inc., March 1955, pp. 30–32. See Poland, *Official Government Documents*, Vol. XVII, Doc. 141a.

⁹ Poland, *Official Government Documents*, Vol. XVII, Doc. 141b.

¹⁰ Eduard Beneš, *Memoirs of Dr. Eduard Beneš*, Boston, Houghton Mifflin Company, 1954, pp. 184–185.

¹¹ *Ibid.*, p. 185.

¹² *Ibid.*, p. 242.

¹³ *Ibid.*, pp. 185–186.

¹⁴ *Ibid.*, p. 195.

¹⁵ In the meantime Sikorski had died and Mikolajczyk had succeeded him.

¹⁶ Poland, *Official Government Documents*, Vol. X, Doc. 25.

¹⁷ *Ibid.*, Doc. 25a.

See also: Beneš, *op. cit.*, p. 264. Apart from his respect for Beneš as a man, Mikolajczyk concluded that the Soviets exploited his trust in them. His mission to Moscow is discussed in another part of his *Memoirs*. It will be cited in the appropriate place in this work.

¹⁸ Poland, *Official Government Documents*, Vol. X, Doc. 20.

¹⁹ *Ibid.*, Doc. 21.

²⁰ Robert E. Sherwood, *Roosevelt and Hopkins*, New York, Harper & Brothers, 1948, pp. 733–734.

²¹ Ciechanowski, *op. cit.*, pp. 170–171.

²² Sherwood, *op. cit.*, p. 734.

²³ *Ibid.*, p. 734.

²⁴ Sikorski was on his way back from an inspection of the Polish Army in the Middle East where a group of ambitious young officers, led by Anders' Aide de

Camp, Captain Klimowski, was preparing for some anti-Sikorski action (presumably with Anders' consent). Kot, *Listy z Rosji do Generala Sikorskiego*, London, 1956, p. 422.

[25] Mikolajczyk, *op. cit.*, p. 41.

[26] Poland, *Official Government Documents*, Vol. XVII, Doc. 146.

[27] *Ibid.*, Vol. X, Doc. 9.

[28] *Ibid.*

[29] *Ibid.*, Doc. 9b.

[30] Ciechanowski, *op. cit.*, p. 221.

[31] Poland, *Officials Government Documents*, Vol. X, Doc. 23.

[32] Sherwood, *op. cit.*, pp. 229–230.

[33] Ciechanowski, *op. cit.*, p. 233.

[34] *Ibid.*, p. 236.

[35] Poland, *Official Government Documents*, Vol. X, Doc. 64 (excerpts from the United States State Department Record).

[36] *Ibid.*, Doc. 64a.

[37] *Ibid.*, Doc. 68.

[38] *Ibid.*, Doc. 43.

[39] *Ibid.*, Vol. XLVIII, Doc. 22.

[40] *Ibid.*, Doc. 41.

[41] *Ibid.*, Doc. 33.

[42] *Ibid.*, Doc. 67.

[43] *Ibid.*, Doc. 67a.

[44] This was signed by the following: Prof. Oskar Lange, University of Chicago; Mr. Osowski, Chairman of the Congress of American Slavs in Michigan; Mr. Nowak, a Michigan State Senator; Prof. Heyman, University of California; Prof. Zlotowski, Vassar College; Mr. Julian Tuwim, poet; Mr. Kaminski, attorney; Mr. Soyda, Vice-President of the Union of Polish Journalists; Prof. Karpinski, University of Michigan; Mr. Zaremba, CIO; Mr. Wisniewski, official of the Polish Veterans Organization in America; and Mr. Arthur Szyk, artist. *Ibid.*, Doc. 19.

[45] *Soviet Monitor*, No. 3882, November 24, 1943. Poland, *Official Government Documents*, Vol. XLVIII, Doc. 34.

[46] *Ibid.*, Doc. 28.

[47] *Ibid.*, Doc. 28.

[48] *Ibid.*, Doc. 27.

[49] *Ibid.*, Vol. III, Docs. 61–72.

[50] *Ibid.*, Doc. 88.

[51] *Ibid.*, Vol. CCXCI, Doc. 330.

[52] *Ibid.*, Vol. IV, Doc. 4.

[53] *Ibid.*, Doc. 5.

[54] *Ibid.*, Vol. X, Docs. 36–38.

[55] *Ibid.*, Doc. 39.

[56] *Ibid.*, Doc. 42.

[57] Winston S. Churchill, *Closing the Ring*, Boston, Houghton Mifflin Company, 1951, pp. 359–362.

[58] Churchill, *op. cit.*, pp. 394–397. [Italics mine.]

[59] Sherwood, *op. cit.*, pp. 782–799. [Italics mine.]

[60] Poland, *Official Government Documents*, Vol. X, Doc. 52.

[61] *Ibid.*, Doc. 54.

[62] *Ibid.*, Doc. 56.

[63] *Ibid.*, Doc. 56c.

[64] Ciechanowski, *op. cit.*, p. 259.

[65] Poland, *Official Government Documents*, Vol. X, Doc. 57.

[66] *Ibid.*, Doc. 57a.

[67] *Ibid.*, Vol. XLVIII, Doc. 720.

[68] *Ibid.*, Vol. III, Doc. 122c.

[69] Korneychuk was the husband of Wanda Wasilewska, the head of the Union of Polish Patriots.

[70] Beneš, *op. cit.*, pp. 259–260.

[71] *Ibid.*, p. 260.

[72] *Ibid.*, pp. 263–265.

[73] *Ibid.*, p. 257.

[74] *Ibid.*, pp. 265–266.

[75] Churchill, *op. cit.*, p. 452.

[76] Beneš, *op. cit.*, pp. 266, 267, and 268. [Italics mine.]

[77] Poland, *Official Government Documents*, Vol. LVI, Doc. 60a.

[78] *Ibid.*, Doc. 61.

[79] *Ibid.*, Vol. XLVIII, Doc. 24.

[80] *Ibid.*, Doc. 44.

[81] *Ibid.*, Doc. 43.

[82] *Ibid.*, Vol. X, Doc. 55.

[83] *Ibid.*, Doc. 58.

The Soviets Transform the Lublin Committee into the Provisional Government of Poland

January 1944 to December 1944

1. Polish Attempts to Re-establish Diplomatic Relations

On January 1, 1944 the Soviet radio announced the establishment of the Lublin Committee with Boleslaw Bierut—a pre-war agent of the NKVD—as its head.

This organization was not yet officially recognized by the Soviet Government. The Polish Government considered it, however, as a further form of pressure upon them to come to speedy terms with Moscow and viewed it as a form of political blackmail.

On January 4 the Red Army crossed the pre-war Polish border. The following day the Polish Government issued the following declaration. Prime Minister Mikolajczyk broadcast it to Poland.

In their victorious struggle against the German invader, the Soviet forces are reported to have crossed the frontier of Poland.

This fact is another proof of the breaking down of the German resistance and it foreshadows the inevitable military defeat of Germany. It fills the Polish nation with the hope that the hour of liberation is drawing near.

Poland was the first nation to take up the German challenge and it has been fighting against the invaders for over four years at a cost of tremendous sacrifice and suffering without producing a single Quisling, and rejecting any form of compromise or collaboration with the aggressor.

The Underground Movement, among its many activities concentrated upon attacking the Germans in their most sensitive spots, upon sabotage in every possible form, and upon the carrying out of many death sentences on German officials whose conduct had been particularly outrageous.

The Polish forces, twice reorganized outside their country, have been fighting ceaselessly in the air, at sea, and on land, side by side with our Allies. There is no front on which Polish blood has not been mingled with the blood of other defenders of freedom; there is no country in the world where Poles did not contribute to furthering the common cause.

The Polish nation is therefore entitled to expect full justice and redress as soon as it will be set free of enemy occupation. The first condition of such justice is the earliest re-establishment of Polish sovereign administration in the liberated territories of the Republic of Poland and the protection of life and property of Polish citizens.

The Polish Government, as the only legal steward and spokesman of the Polish nation, recognized by Poles at home and abroad as well as by Allied and free governments, is conscious of the contribution of Poland to the war and is responsible for the fate of the nation. It affirms its indestructible right to independence confirmed by the principles of the Atlantic Charter, common to all the United Nations, and by binding international treaties. The provisions of those treaties, based on the free agreement of the parties, and not on the enforcement of the will of one side to the detriment of the other, cannot be revised by *faits accomplis*. The conduct of the Polish nation in the course of the present war has proved that it has never recognized and will never recognize solutions imposed by force.

The Polish Government expects that the Soviet Union, sharing its view as to the importance of future friendly relations between the two countries, will not, in the interest of peace and with the view to preventing a German revenge, fail to respect the rights and interests of the Polish Republic and of its citizens.

Acting in that belief, the Polish Government instructed the underground authorities in Poland, on October 27, 1943, to continue and intensify the resistance against the German invaders, to avoid all conflicts with the Soviet armies entering Poland in their battle against the Germans, and to enter into cooperation with the Soviet commanders in the event of the resumption of Polish-Soviet relations.

If a Polish-Soviet agreement such as the one the Polish Government had declared itself willing to conclude, had preceded the crossing of the frontier of Poland by the Soviet forces, such an agreement would have enabled the underground Polish army to coordinate its action against the Germans with the Soviet military authorities. The Polish Government still considers such an arrangement highly desirable.

At this crucial moment, whose importance for the course of the war and for its outcome in Europe is evident to everyone, the Polish Government issues the above declaration confident in a final victory and in the triumph of the just principles for which the United Nations stand.[1]

On the following day, the reaction of the British press to this declaration was divided. The *Manchester Guardian*, the *Times*, the *Daily Telegraph*, and the *Daily Mail* saw in it a demonstration of good will on the part of the Polish Government to reach an agreement with the Soviet Union, while the *Daily Herald* and *Daily Worker* were critical and considered it as proof of Polish obstinacy.

Moscow reacted to that broadcast through its sponsored Radio Kosciuszko. On January 9, at 8:55 P.M. it called Mikolajczyk's address humbug and a provocation of the Polish nation. It asserted that the Polish underground organizations were reactionary and that the only democratic underground organization in Poland which effectively fought the Germans was the People's Guard. They accused the Delegate of the Polish Government inside Poland of encouraging a fight against the Soviets and democracy. Moscow ended its broadcast by stating that "this bankrupt Delegate, as well as the entire London clique, will be wiped out because their policies would lead to a new catastrophe." [2]

Upon analyzing the reactions of the Soviets and of those circles in the West which were critical of Poland, the Polish Government was at a loss as how to give additional proof of its good intentions. It seemed that everything that they could possibly do would be viewed with a jaundiced eye by both the Soviets and the Western critics of Poland. Apparently what both of these audiences wanted to hear was a complete capitulation by the Poles to Soviet demands, and this sort of announcement the Poles were not willing to furnish. What better proof of good intentions was there than to order the Polish underground army to cooperate fully with the advancing Soviet armies? It appeared to the Poles that Soviet arguments were not attempts at rational solutions, but were instead efforts to exploit passions and prejudices in a way harmful to Poland.

On January 11, 1944 TASS announced that it had been authorized by the Soviet Government to announce the following:

On the 5th of January the Declaration of the exiled Polish Government on the question of Soviet-Polish relations was published in London containing a number of incorrect assertions. Among them was the incorrect assertion concerning the Soviet-Polish frontiers.

As is known, the Soviet Constitution has determined the establishment of a Soviet-Polish frontier corresponding with the desires of the population of the Western Ukraine and Western Byelorussia expressed in a plebiscite carried out according to broad democratic principles in 1941. The territories of the Western Ukraine, populated in an overwhelming majority by the Ukrainians, were incorporated into the Soviet Ukraine; while the territories of Western Byelorussia, populated in an overwhelming majority by the Byelorussians, were incorporated into Soviet Byelorussia. The injustice caused by the Riga Treaty of 1921, which was forced upon the Soviet Union, in relation to the Ukrainians inhabiting the Western Ukraine and the Byelorussians inhabiting Western Byelorussia was thus rectified. The entry of the Western Ukraine and Western Byelorussia into the Soviet Union not only did not interfere with the interest of Poland but, on the contrary, created a reliable basis for a firm and permanent friendship between the Polish people and the neighboring Ukrainian, Byelorussian, and Russian peoples.

The Soviet Government repeatedly declared its stand for the establishment of a strong and independent Poland and for friendship between the Soviet Union and Poland. The Soviet Government declares that it is striving for the establishment of friendship between the U.S.S.R. and Poland on the basis of firm good-neighborly relations and mutual respect, and should the Polish people wish it, on the basis of an alliance of mutual assistance against the Germans as the principal enemy of the Soviet Union and Poland. Poland, by adhering to the Soviet-Czechoslovak Treaty of Friendship, Mutual Assistance and Post-War Cooperation, could assist the realization of this task. The successes of the Soviet troops on the Soviet-German front speed up day by day the liberation of the occupied territories of the Soviet Union from the German invaders. The selfless struggle of the Red Army and the fighting operations of our Allies, which are steadily unfolding, bring the end of the Hitler war machine nearer, and bring nearer the liberation of Poland and other nations from the yoke of the German invaders. In this war of liberation the Union of the Polish Patriots in the U.S.S.R. and the Polish Army Corps created by it, operating on the front against the Germans hand in hand with the Red Army, are already fulfilling their gallant task.

Now the opportunity for restoration of Poland as a strong and independent State is opening. But Poland must be reborn not by way of occupation of Ukrainian territories and Byelorussian territories, but by way of returning to Poland those age-old territories taken away from Poland by the Germans. Only thus can the confidence and friendship between Polish, Ukrainian, Byelorussian and Russian peoples be established. The eastern borders of Poland can be fixed by agreement with the Soviet Union.

The Soviet Government does not consider the frontiers of 1939 to be unchangeable. Borders can be corrected in favor of Poland on such lines that the districts in which the Polish population is predominant should be handed over to Poland. In this case the Soviet-Polish border could run approximately along the so-called Curzon Line, adopted in the year 1919 by the Supreme Council of the Allied Powers, and which provides for the incorporation of the Western Ukraine and Western Byelorussia into the Soviet Union.

Poland's western border must be extended through the joining of the age-old lands of Poland taken away from Poland by Germany, without which it is impossible to unite the whole of the Polish people in its own State and with which it will obviously acquire the necessary outlet to the Baltic Sea.

The just striving of the Polish people to complete unity in a strong and independent state must receive recognition and support. The émigré Polish Government, cut off from its people, has proved incapable of establishing friendly relations with the Soviet Union. It has proved equally incapable of organizing an active struggle against the German invaders in

Poland itself. Moreover, with its wrong policy it frequently plays into the hands of the German invaders. At the same time, the interests of Poland and the Soviet Union lie in the establishment of firm friendly relations between our two countries and the unity of the Soviet-Polish peoples in the common struggle against the common outside enemy as the common cause of all Allies requires.[3]

The Polish Government interpreted the Moscow Declaration of January 11, 1944 in the following way. In spite of its form it was not considered as completely negative. The Polish Government reasoned as follows to reach this conclusion. First, the declaration contained a fundamental departure from the previous Soviet stand on the Molotov-Ribbentrop Line. A typical example was the paragraph which stated that the Soviets do not consider the 1939 frontier as unchangeable. Its aggressive tone toward the Polish Government did not, therefore, shut the door completely to the discussion of the eastern frontier.

Another interesting point is that this declaration, in trying to present too many legal rights to the territories in dispute, undermines the validity of its logic and consequently weakens its logical position. Moreover, it is not consistent, but is contradictory. The declaration refers to the Soviet Constitution which supposedly determined the Soviet-Polish frontier, and at the same time it announces that corrections in favor of the Polish Nation may be made. This weakens the arguments of constitutionality. If the Constitution does not stand in the way of making corrections, it should also not stand in the way of a return to the 1939 frontiers. The possibility of "corrections" leaves the question of frontiers open and by this token brings the whole question back into the international forum. So, at any rate, reasoned the Polish Government.

Among the other new elements introduced was the Soviet argument that the Riga Treaty was imposed on the Soviet Union. They never raised this issue before. It would, of course, be easy to destroy that argument by citing the declarations of the Soviet leaders at that time and by referring to the Soviet-Polish Treaty of Non-Aggression of July 28, 1932.

When, on September 17, 1939, the Red Army entered Poland, the Soviet note of that day, handed to Polish Ambassador Grzybowski in Moscow, represented that act as a temporary occupation which was necessitated by the desire to protect life and property in the Western Ukraine and Western Byelorussia. There was no mention then of any territorial rights; only in a general way did they point out even the strategic necessity for the occupation.

Another new element was the argument that the 1939 frontier was unjust to the Soviet Union. This was a strange interpretation, since the most valuable part of the disputed southeastern territories never belonged to either Tsarist Russia or to the Soviet Union.

The Soviet argument that the 1939 plebiscite was a valid basis for the transfer of the territories was most unfounded because this enforced plebiscite was contrary to the Fourth Hague Convention of 1907 of which Russia was a signatory. From the point of view of international law, no legal rights can derive from acts of war. Soviet insistence that the plebiscite was conducted on "broad democratic principles" was contradicted by the official acts of the Soviet Union. When they presented only one list of candidates to the voters, they officially and publicly proved that the plebiscite was not based on any democratic principles at all. The "plebiscite" was conducted under the auspices of the Ukrainian and Byelorussian Military Councils, which never pretended to operate on democratic principles.

Among the criticisms the Soviet declaration leveled against the Polish Government were those which claimed that the Polish Government was unwilling or unable to establish friendly relations with the Soviet Union and that the Polish Government was unwilling or unable to organize the fight against the Germans in Poland. The reference to Katyn was thrown in for good measure. These were obviously willful misinterpretations of the facts, and were so regarded by the Polish Government. The main accusation (i.e., the inability to establish "friendly relations" with the Soviet Union) could be applied only to a Soviet satellite, not to a sovereign nation. The Polish Government could have said the same thing about the Soviet Government in its relations not only with Poland but with Finland, Rumania, and the Baltic States as well. There was, in fact, no European neighbor with whom the Soviets could have then claimed "friendly relations."

This accusation implied that the Soviet Union would recognize only such a Polish Government as would suit it. This was, obviously, contrary to international law. To the minds of the Polish Government, it recalled the days of Repnin and Catherine the Great.

This argument about "friendly relations" implied one of the following. It meant either (1) that the Soviet Union would not negotiate with any independent Polish Government in exile but would deal only with a government chosen by them after the expulsion of the Germans, presumably the Union of Polish Patriots in Moscow or (2) that the Soviet Government was in fact ready to negotiate with the Polish Government in exile, but only a reformed one which would show due friendliness to the Soviet Union by first accepting the various Soviet conditions.

In these respects, the declaration left the Soviet Union with a free hand to do what it pleased.[4]

The British press of January 12 evinced almost unanimous support for the Curzon Line. The foreign correspondents in London received the following official commentary from the Foreign Office on the Soviet Declaration of January 11, 1944. "Though it is controversial, it is considered as a most important contribution towards the final settlement of the dispute." [5]

The British press questioned the legal right of Poland to the territories east of the Curzon Line. Especially outspoken was the London *Times* which continually reiterated that the Poles were a minority in those lands and that they were mainly landlords anyhow. Therefore, by implication, they were oppressors of the non-Polish nationalities and thus unworthy of Western support. Even the *Manchester Guardian*, which was generally friendly to Poland, shared this opinion. The *Spectator* maintained that while Poland had moral and legal rights to those territories, nevertheless Russia had the power on her side, and implied that the greater might of Russia made resistance futile, even if right. There were no symptoms from the British press that any effort at all would be made to defend right against might. Of these newspapers, only the *Daily Herald* shared the views and interpretations of the *Daily Worker* most of the time. On the whole, then, the British press was in agreement with the British Government that Poland should accept the Curzon Line as a basis for the re-establishment of relations with the Soviet Union.

The British and American press were anxious to caution their Governments against playing the role of mediator; they wanted their respective Governments to help the Polish Government with advice. This advice, they all agreed, was to be in the nature of Polish acceptance of the Curzon Line as a basis for negotiations with the Soviet Union. They were of course aware that the Russians wanted to solve these Polish problems directly with the Poles, and did not wish the interference of a third party. The Poles, with their "undemocratic" past, marveled at the strange unison between the official positions of Britain and the United States and the views of their free presses.

On January 11, 1944 Mikolajczyk met Eden and was informed that the Soviet declaration of that day opened a new possibility for reaching an understanding between Poland and Russia. Mikolajczyk doubted this, and complained about the British position and their pressure on the Poles. Then he asked whether the British Government had changed its attitude towards their previous declaration that they did not recognize any territorial changes which took place since September 1, 1939. Eden and Cadogan (who was present) firmly reaffirmed that policy as still valid.

Prior to parting, Eden demanded that the Polish Government show him its reply to the Soviet declaration of January 11 before making a public announcement.[6]

On January 13, 1944 Mikolajczyk brought Eden the text of the Polish reply, which read as follows:

1. The Polish Government has taken cognizance of the declaration of the Soviet Government contained in the TASS communiqué of January 11, 1944 which was issued as a reply to the declaration of the Polish Government of January 5.

2. The Polish Government has repeatedly expressed its sincere desire for a Polish-Soviet agreement on terms which would be just and acceptable to both sides.

3. It cannot, however, recognize unilateral decisions or *faits accomplis*, nor can it recognize the validity of arguments designed to justify the loss by Poland of about half of her territory and more than eleven million of her population.

4. The Soviet communiqué also contains a number of statements which are manifestly untrue in view of the ceaseless struggle against the Germans waged at the heaviest cost by the Polish nation under the direction of the Polish Government. In its earnest anxiety to safeguard the complete solidarity of the United Nations, especially at a decisive stage of their struggle against the common enemy, the Polish Government considers it to be preferable now to refrain from further public discussions.

5. The Polish Government on the other hand is approaching the British and United States Governments with a view to securing, through their intermediaries, the immediate resumption of Polish-Soviet relations suspended in April 1943. Such a resumption would render possible the discussion by the Polish and Soviet Governments, with the participation of the British and American Governments, of all outstanding questions, the settlement of which should lead to friendly and permanent cooperation between Poland and the Soviet Union. The Polish Government believes this to be desirable in the interest of victory and of harmonious relations in post-war Europe.[7]

Eden suggested that point (3) of the Polish proposal should be changed as follows:

With reference to the validity of unilateral decisions or *faits accomplis* the Polish Government's views coincide with those expressed by the British Prime Minister on behalf of the British Government in the House of Commons on September 5, 1940, when he said, "We have not at any time adopted, since this war broke out, the line that nothing could be changed in the territorial structure of various countries. On the other hand, we do not propose to recognize any territorial changes which take place during the war, unless they take place with the free consent and good will of the parties concerned."

Furthermore, Eden insisted on a change of point (5), which would eliminate the sentence stating that resumption of negotiations between Poland and the Soviet Union must be preceded by the re-establishment of the diplomatic relations between the two countries.

No agreement was reached on the text of the reply, and it was decided to postpone its crystallization until the following day.

At their next meeting, Eden read a telegram from Churchill which warned the Polish Government not to reject negotiations

. . . on the basis which gives Poland much more valuable territories than those which will have to be sacrificed. In case the negotiations will fail because of the Polish reply to the Soviet note, he will consider himself relieved from moral obligations which Great Britain has towards Poland.

At the end of the meeting, Eden suggested that the best place for negotiation of these matters would be Moscow.[8]

On January 14, 1944 after a Cabinet meeting, Romer informed the British Ambassador, O'Malley, that the Polish Government had decided to retain the original form of point (3) of the Polish reply and handed him a copy of it. Shortly thereafter Eden discussed that text with the British Cabinet, and at 12:15 P.M. of the same day received Romer in order to hand him the British form of the proposed Polish reply to the Soviet declaration. Romer said that the Polish reply was based on the official decision of the Cabinet and that therefore he could not change it. He asked for British support of it as it stood. Eden refused to give any support. Later that same day, at Eden's request, Mikolajczyk met Eden again and, after a lengthy discussion, accepted the British version of the reply in order, as Eden put it, not to "antagonize" the Russians. In return Eden gave instructions to the Chief of the Press Bureau in the Foreign Office "to have the British press interpret that reply favorably for the Poles." [9]

At 4:00 P.M. Eden received Soviet Ambassador M. Gusev and handed him the text of the Polish declaration stating that the British Government supported it as an opening for negotiations.[10] The text follows:

1. The Polish Government has taken cognizance of the declaration of the Soviet Government contained in the TASS communiqué of the 11th of January, 1944 which was issued as a reply to the declaration of the Polish Government of January 5.

2. The Soviet communiqué contains a number of statements to which a complete answer is afforded by the ceaseless struggle against the Germans waged at the heaviest cost by the Polish nation under the direction of the

Polish Government. In their earnest anxiety to safeguard the complete solidarity of the United Nations, especially at a decisive stage of their struggle against the common enemy, the Polish Government considers it to be preferable now to refrain from further public discussions.

3. While the Polish Government cannot recognize unilateral decisions or accomplished facts, nor the strength of arguments designed to justify far-reaching territorial demands on Poland, it has repeatedly expressed its sincere desire for a Polish-Soviet agreement on terms which would be just and acceptable to both sides.

4. To this end, the Polish Government is approaching the British and United States Governments with a view to securing through their intermediary the discussion by the Polish and Soviet Governments, with the participation of the British and American Governments, of all outstanding questions, the settlement of which should lead to a friendly and permanent cooperation between Poland and the Soviet Union. The Polish Government believes this to be desirable in the interest of the victory of the United Nations and harmonious relations in post-war Europe.[11]

Soon afterward, personnel of the Soviet Embassy in London were heard to make sarcastic remarks about the Polish note delivered by Eden to Gusev on January 14, 1944, saying that it was written by Eden and only translated into Polish. Furthermore, they maintained that Moscow considered such action by the British Foreign Office as a violation of the Teheran Agreement. For that reason, the Soviet reply to that note implicitly advised the British and Americans not to interfere in somebody else's business. The British Foreign Office was astonished by the tone of the Soviet reply.[12]

As Eden had promised, this Polish reply was received with approval by the Anglo-American press and by the press of other Allied nations as well. Even the leftist *New Statesman and Nation* said in its editorial of January 14, 1944 that it could not be denied that the Polish Government was representative, while the *Economist* doubted if the Lublin puppet government could be recognized by the Allies.

On the other hand, the *News Chronicle*, the *Daily Telegraph*, the *Observer*, and the *Sunday Times*, while praising Mikolajczyk's Government, had harsh words to say about "the reactionary groups of Sosnkowski." This latter criticism became a source of worry to the British Government, which was anxious not to give any pretext for the rationalization that perhaps the "Russians have a legitimate right" to criticize the Poles. The question of the Polish eastern frontiers was widely debated in Polish and Allied circles. Under pressure from all sides, the Polish Government was heartened to receive the following telegram from its representative on Polish soil on January 15, 1944.

In connection with the Soviet statement on Polish-Soviet relations, we declare in the name of the whole community in Poland that the only lawful and legitimate representative of the interests of the Polish nation is the Polish Government in London, around which rally all classes and circles of the Polish people, all political parties and groups, with the exception only of insignificant groups sponsored by the Soviets. Under the direction of its Government, the Polish nation has been fighting the Germans relentlessly, even at the time when the Soviets were in alliance with the Third Reich, with whom they partitioned Poland, and when the Soviets assisted Germany in her war against the Allies. The Polish people continue their struggle without interruption, at the cost of enormous sacrifices, in accordance with Poland's interests, and will not consent to be used as a tool for the plans advanced by the Soviets who, again, strive for a new partition of Poland and aim at imposing a communist regime in Poland.

The eastern provinces of Poland which the Soviets in their statement now demand were dominated by them in agreement and cooperation with Germany. The plebiscite carried out in these territories under the terror of Soviet occupation in no way represented the free will of the population. The accusation that the fate of these lands was prejudged by the Soviet Constitution is inconsequential, and contrary to all conceptions of international law. The Polish nation categorically and firmly rejects Soviet aspirations to the eastern provinces of Poland, reaffirms the principle of inviolability of the frontiers established in the Treaty of Riga, and will never agree to a new annexation of any part of Poland.

The Polish nation is determined to defend with all possible means the integrity of the eastern territories of the Republic.

(signed) THE COUNCIL OF NATIONAL UNITY AND THE
GOVERNMENTS PLENIPOTENTIARY IN POLAND.[13]

This message had only internal importance for Poland, but it did not have any material effect on the policies of her Allies. Neither Britain nor the United States took part in the duel of verbal exchanges between the Polish and Soviet Governments.

In reply to the Polish Government's declaration of January 14, 1944 the TASS agency on January 17 announced that it was authorized to publish the following statement:

1. In the Polish declaration the question of the recognition of the Curzon Line as the Soviet-Polish frontier is entirely evaded and ignored. This can only be interpreted as a rejection of the Curzon Line.

2. As regards the Polish Government's proposal for the opening of official negotiations between it and the Soviet Government, the Soviet Government is of the opinion that this proposal aims at misleading public opinion, for it is easy to understand that the Soviet Government is not in a position to enter into official negotiations with a government with which diplomatic relations have been broken. Soviet circles wish it to be borne in mind that it was through the fault of the Polish Government that diplomatic relations with the Polish Government were broken off, as a result

of its active participation in the hostile anti-Soviet slanderous campaign of the German invaders in connection with the alleged murders in Katyn.

3. In the opinion of Soviet circles the above-mentioned circumstances once again demonstrate that the present Polish Government does not desire to establish good-neighborly relations with the Soviet Union.[14]

This reply was intended to provoke the Polish Government into taking an unreasonable stand which, in turn, would convince the Anglo-Americans to recognize new representatives of Poland, from the Union of Patriots, as the legal Polish authority. The Poles were anxious to avoid this pitfall. In the meantime, the Lublin Committee proceeded to implement the Soviet plan of seizing control of Poland.

On January 20 the communists dropped over Warsaw a shower of leaflets in the form of a manifesto urging the establishment of the Council of National Unity, which in turn would form a Provisional Government, appoint the High Military Command of the People's Army, and establish relations with the Soviet Union and other Allies. All political and military underground organizations rejected this manifesto and reaffirmed their loyalty to the London Government.[15]

On the same day, Mikolajczyk and Romer had a conference with Churchill and Eden. Churchill decided to act firmly and harshly with the Poles in the hope that this would be the most successful method in forcing them to accept his point of view as to how to solve the Soviet-Polish dilemma. In a blunt manner Churchill stated that his Government considered the Curzon Line as a just frontier for Poland. The loss of territories east of that line would be compensated by pushing Poland westward up to the Oder Line.

When Mikolajczyk objected to this new arbitrary partition of Poland by one of her Allies without his consent, Churchill angrily retorted that the British guaranteed only the western frontiers of Poland and that neither Britain nor the United States would go to war to defend the eastern frontiers of Poland. Churchill thus made clear that the British guarantee given to the Poles on the occasion of the signing of the Polish-Soviet Pact of July 30, 1941, to the effect that His Majesty's Government would not recognize "any territorial changes which have been effected in Poland since August, 1939" was now invalid. Instead, he promised another British guarantee of Polish frontiers only if Poland agreed to accept the Curzon Line first.

Mikolajczyk attempted to reason with Churchill for Western support of his stand not to yield to the Soviets because, he said, they were not so much interested in the piece of territory as in the complete control of Poland and other countries. The further conversation between Churchill and the Poles went as follows:

CHURCHILL. I want the Polish Government to accept the Curzon Line without Lvov as a basis for negotiations with the Russians. . . . You have to accept this not only as a necessity, *but you have to accept it enthusiastically as well,* for it is a solution of the Polish problem on a grand scale. This is demanded not only in the interest of Poland but also in that of all the United Nations. You will get compensation up to the Oder and East Prussia. The Germans from these territories will have to be completely expelled. Therefore, I ask you to accept that solution *because I consider it as just.* . . . I am telling you this privately but I am ready to say this publicly in Parliament if need be.

MIKOLAJCZYK. In the last declaration of the Polish Government we admitted the possibility of a discussion of the Polish-Soviet frontier. But legal and factual considerations prevent us from accepting in advance the position of the opposite side in the dispute. This would eliminate the chances of negotiation. This cannot be done *a priori.*

CHURCHILL [interrupting]. The latest Soviet reply is brutal and not convincing, but it asks for acceptance of the Curzon Line as a starting point for negotiations.

MIKOLAJCZYK. We are ready to negotiate. We are ready to discuss the Riga Treaty, but we are afraid that no nation could stand such vast movements of its frontiers. The smaller the frontier changes the lesser will be the pain of moving the populations. Besides, a question arises of security, and of the guarantee connected with it.

CHURCHILL. The guarantee will be given to Poland by the Big Powers and, if the necessity arises, Poland will be defended.

MIKOLAJCZYK. The acceptance of the Curzon Line as a starting point will stiffen Soviet territorial demands. This is the most difficult problem for us. It would be easier to deal with this problem from the point of view of nationalities. I mean their exchange. It would be much more proper.

1. We consider the Riga Line as a starting point for negotiations.

2. Poland should come out of this war not smaller than she was in 1939.

3. The solution of the whole problem should be found in an exchange of populations and not of territories.

4. A guarantee of Anglo-Saxon powers is indispensable.

5. It should stress the principle of non-interference of one country into the internal affairs of the other.

I trust that you will not permit the Curzon Line to become the starting point for negotiations.

CHURCHILL. The starting point must be the Curzon Line. We are concerned with the security of Poland and her people. That security can be obtained only through your understanding with the Soviets. The Czechs chose such methods and they don't regret it.

MIKOLAJCZYK. That is true, but the Czechs are in a much happier geographical position.

CHURCHILL. I am ready and feel entitled to influence Stalin. The problem of security for people must be very thoroughly considered. But don't forget the Russian point of view. In 1914 the Russians held Warsaw. They have no claims on Finland, which they held at that time, too. The war cannot be won without Russia. Our bombers alone will not win it.

The Russians also have their good reasons. They suffered much in this war.

MIKOLAJCZYK. Proportionately Poland suffered even more.

CHURCHILL. I don't deny it, and I also remember that you suffered much during the partitions. But there is a great difference between the victors and the vanquished. I don't think that Polish-Soviet friendship is impossible. Russia is undergoing deep evolution. Already today Russian wages in industry are higher than ours. Stalin is distributing thousands of prizes. After the war the Russians will become more conservative.

MIKOLAJCZYK. Wouldn't it be better to solve the Polish-Soviet difficulties now by finding a way to coordinate the activities of our underground organizations with the Soviet partisans in their mutual struggle against the Germans? We proposed this already.

CHURCHILL. I want this from you too. But prior to that an understanding between you and Russia is needed—the Curzon Line leads to that.

To sum up: In my telegram to Stalin I want to say:

1. What the British view on the question of frontiers is.
2. What the Poles are prepared to do.
3. That interference into internal problems is impossible.
4. The necessity of reaching an understanding between the fighting units in Poland.

I consider that speed is essential. I trust that you will bring me a far-reaching report for my telegram. I want complete agreement on the part of the Polish Government. Without it we shall not succeed. I understand that it will be very difficult for you, but in this tragic and decisive moment you must prove worthy of the occasion.

MIKOLAJCZYK. I don't anticipate that it will be possible to persuade the Polish nation to such sacrifices. What will the free nations of the world say? What will the Poles in exile say?

ROMER reminded Churchill that the Polish Army on the Italian front was mainly composed of soldiers who came from the eastern territories and who in 1939-40 were deported to Russia.

MIKOLAJCZYK. The Polish soldier, airman, and sailor who is fighting now must know why he is fighting and he must believe that when the war is over he can return to his home. What if he is told that his home is taken over by the Russians, who had already in 1939-40 deported him and his family to Russia? What will he think of Western pledges, slogans, and declarations of principles?

Churchill was silent.[16]

The meeting of the Polish Cabinet held on that day upheld Mikolajczyk's views as he expressed them to Churchill. It was decided that before answering Churchill's request the Delegate of the Polish Government in Warsaw and the Polish Ambassador in the United States would have to be consulted, in the latter case to find out what the American attitude would be.

On January 27 the Polish Government learned from the correspondents of the Associated Press that the Soviet Government had rejected Cordell Hull's offer to mediate in the Soviet-Polish dispute by saying:

The Soviet Government appreciates the good offer of the United States, but the Soviet Government considers that relations between Russia and Poland have not yet ripened to such a point where American mediation could be utilized.[17]

On January 29, 1944 Minister Plenipotentiary, Wladyslaw W. Kulski, was informed by Mr. Roberts of the British Foreign Office that Churchill had sent the previously discussed telegram to Moscow in exactly the same form as he had presented it to Mikolajczyk.[18]

Accordingly, the Polish Cabinet and the Polish Parliament-in-exile, as well as the Polish press, were unanimous in rejecting both the Soviet demands and the British pressure upon them. Before giving the final answer to Churchill's question as to whether the Poles would accept the Curzon Line, the Polish Foreign Minister, Tadeusz Romer, sent a series of questions to Foreign Minister Anthony Eden in order to have a firmer ground for making a decision. These questions were:

Referring to the conversations that have taken place recently between members of the Polish and British Governments regarding the problem of Polish-Soviet relations, and more particularly, the conversations held with you and with Mr. Churchill on January 13 last and on January 20, I have been instructed to place before you a number of questions, the answers to which cannot fail to have an important bearing on the decisions that the Polish Government is called upon to make in the present situation. The views of His Majesty's Government on several of the questions enumerated below have been expressed in the course of mutual conversations. The Polish Government would, however, be greatly obliged to you if you would confirm that they have been recorded and interpreted correctly.

1. What are the measures that the British Government would be prepared to take in the event of a Polish-Soviet agreement being reached, on the basis of Mr. Churchill's suggestions made to M. Mikolajczyk on January 20, in order to safeguard the independence of Poland and the non-interference by the Soviet Government in Poland's internal affairs? In particular:

(a) Can the British Government assure the taking over by the Polish Government, and authorities appointed by them, of the administration of Polish territory as it is freed from German occupation?

(b) Are His Majesty's Government prepared to secure from the Soviet Government their agreement to the participation of Polish and Allied contingents on an equal footing and in comparable numbers in the occupation of Polish territories (including those that would be attributed to Poland at the expense of Germany), should such an occupation be made necessary by the course of military operations against Germany?

(c) Can they undertake to assure that this territory will be duly evacuated by the occupying troops and authorities as soon as military operations against Germany have come to an end on this front?

2. Is the Polish Government right in expecting:

(a) Formal guarantees by Great Britain and, also, if obtainable, by the United States of America, of the territorial integrity of Poland within her new frontiers, of her political independence, and non-interference in her internal affairs against attempts from any quarter whatsoever?

(b) Should the United States prove unwilling to join in such a guarantee, would Great Britain be willing to undertake it herself?

3. Can the Polish Government receive the assurance that neither of the Three Great Powers represented at the Teheran Conference will claim military, naval, or aerial bases on the territory of Poland or on that which would be allotted to Poland by way of compensation at the expense of Germany?

4. Can the Polish Government take it for granted with regard to territories offered to Poland at the expense of Germany, that:

(a) They comprise, with the full consent of the British, all German territories situated between the river Oder and the Polish-German frontier of 1939, and over and above the whole of Opole Silesia, the territory of the Free City of Danzig, and the entire territory of East Prussia?

(b) Poland's new western frontiers will be definitely fixed at the same time as Poland's eastern frontiers and embodied in one international document enacted on the same basis with the participation and consent of the British, the Soviet, and the American Governments?

(c) It will be stipulated that the arrangement is to be considered permanent and that no ulterior German protests would be entertained?

(d) The German territories allotted to Poland on the basis of this agreement will be formally declared as severed from the German Reich in the terms of the first armistice terminating hostilities between the United Nations and Germany, this surrender being a *sine qua non* condition of the termination of hostilities?

(e) The Three Great Powers represented in the Teheran Conference will undertake to impose upon Germany in the same armistice the duty of accepting on German territory, without undue delay, the entire population of German tongue inhabiting at the moment of the signature of the armistice the territory of Poland within her new frontiers? Will these Powers also undertake to assist Poland in the removal from her territory of unwanted Germans?

5. The Polish Government would, finally, be grateful to the British Government for their views on the means which they would deem proper to assure protection of Polish citizens who are now, or may find themselves at a later date, residing on territories under Soviet authority; are they right in expecting to receive guarantees assuring the repatriation to Poland from the U.S.S.R. of all her citizens entitled thereto? [19]

The British reply to the above was guarded. It stated that before the British Government could give an answer it would have to consult other governments and would have to await an agreement between Poland and the Soviet Union.[20]

Similar questions were sent to President Roosevelt who replied evasively, without any commitments.[21] This sameness in the attitude of both Roosevelt and Churchill appeared to the Poles to be not a mere coincidence.

After a careful analysis of the British and American replies to the above series of questions submitted to them, the Polish Government decided to stand firmly behind what it considered its rights; it did not see any honorable alternative. In accordance with Churchill's request, the following reply was therefore sent to him.

The Polish Government is ready to start conversations with the Soviet Government, with the cooperation of the British and American Governments, on all outstanding questions. We do not exclude frontier discussions relating to the east, west, or north.

The dictatorial demand by the U.S.S.R. that we must agree in advance to the recognition of the Curzon Line as the future Polish frontier cannot be accepted by the Polish Government. The result of conversations concerning frontiers can be realized only after the end of the war.

During war hostilities, we could consent to a *demarcation line* running east of Wilno (Vilna) and Lwow (Lvov). The territory west of this demarcation line, after this territory is freed from German occupation, should be taken over by the Polish Government. The territory east of the demarcation line should go to the administration of the Soviet military authorities, with the full participation of representatives of all Allied Powers.

The Polish Government considers it a duty to state that the intention of incorporation into the Soviet Union of a part of East Prussia with Königsberg is against the interests of the Polish State and painfully restrains her free access to the sea.

Any changes in the Polish Government, or changes relating to the Commander-in-Chief of its armed forces, cannot be dictated by a foreign power.[22]

Churchill was very much irritated by this reply; his hope of "bringing the Poles to their senses" now had to be postponed. His activity and Roosevelt's silence acquired more meaning when, on February 19, 1944 Ambassador Ciechanowski reported secretly to his Government that "a highly placed and absolutely reliable source in Washington" told him:

Churchill personally undertook the solution of the Polish-Soviet quarrel. For this reason he called to London Clark Kerr (the British Ambassador to Moscow, who was in Washington a few weeks ago), to discuss in detail the whole question and handed him a personal letter to Stalin. In that letter Churchill informed Stalin that he was taking the whole matter into his own hands, because he considered the Polish-Soviet conflict as the most important from the point of view of the cooperation of the United Nations. . . .

Furthermore, I had an opportunity to get acquainted with some parts of the messages sent by Prime Minister Churchill to President Roosevelt. Churchill stated that he is not afraid of a prolongation of negotiations with the Soviets about the Polish questions. It was most important that all conflicting problems should be exhausted and solved in the preliminary stage, before Polish-Soviet talks began, so that the meeting may succeed.

"The questions cannot be patched up, they must be solved." He promised President Roosevelt to keep him informed continuously and in detail about all his propositions and progress in the Moscow negotiations. Like Roosevelt, he maintained that he attached the greatest importance to the solution of these problems in the spirit (if possible) of close approximation to the fundamental principles. Personally he expressed the conviction that the Polish-Soviet conflict may be solved positively, and he maintained that he was most eager to solve it.

The most significant for us in this situation is that the externally completely passive attitude of President Roosevelt and the American Government towards our problem is explained by the passages in Churchill's message to the President in which he begs him to leave the whole question to Churchill for solution, and asks the President to take a stand only when Churchill will specifically ask him, and that this stand should have a general form. I was informed that the President did not want to agree to such a proposition but that in the end he accepted it.

Churchill added that negotiations conducted from two places seldom succeed and then only if they are identical. In this case it would be impossible because the United States is unwilling to get into the merits of each conflicting Polish-Soviet question. Churchill reminded Roosevelt of the difficulties which arose in connection with the negotiations with Turkey, and lately with Spain, because there was an unavoidable lack of coordination and the use of different methods of negotiation.

This explains why Roosevelt is postponing the date of the visit of the Polish Prime Minister to Washington and why Roosevelt does not want to be involved in any conversations with us on these matters. I know that Churchill is indeed in almost daily contact with the President about the developments of the Polish question and besides this, the Undersecretary of State told me that the State Department has instructions to keep the President continuously informed about all the details connected with the Polish-Soviet conflict.[23]

This report indicated that the Polish Government was faced with insurmountable difficulties, because this revelation of America's policy of non-intervention removed any hope of being able to modify Churchill's stand by appealing to President Roosevelt.

The hopelessness of the Polish situation looked even darker by the following short report from a friendly Czech, which came into the possession of the Polish Government.

At the end of January 1944, the new Soviet Ambassador to the Czech Government, Lebedev, was asked by the Czech editor, Hronka, what was the real nature of the Soviet-Polish dispute. The Ambassador replied that Stalin had given directives for handling the Polish question as far back as 1941, when Sikorski visited Moscow, and that they were still in force. The main objective was to gain control of all Byelorussians and the Ukrainians —especially the latter. By including them in the U.S.S.R., Stalin wanted to stop all the separatistic tendencies of these two peoples.[24]

Stalin's consistent behavior since 1941 tended to confirm the validity of this information. Lacking Western support, the Poles did not see how they alone could make Stalin change his policy.

The communists continued to enlist the support of a certain number of Americans of Polish descent in order to paralyze the effectiveness of the support given the London Government by the great majority of Polish-Americans.

On January 22, 1944 the Polish Consul General, Heliodor Sztark, in Pittsburgh, Pennsylvania reported that a conference of seventy-five representatives of Trade Unions belonging to the CIO had taken place on January 16 at the Hotel Carter in Cleveland, at which it was decided to organize an "American-Polish League of Labor," and that Mr. Leon Krzycki was chosen as its chairman. The newly organized League was to be a Polish branch of the Political Action Committee of the CIO headed by Sidney Hillman. The initiator of the conference was Sidney Hillman, and therefore a telegram was sent to him by the conference with special thanks for the help extended at that conference.

The main speakers were: Leon Krzycki and Professor O. Lange. Letters were received from the Rev. S. Orlemanski and Mr. Louis Adamic. The speakers and letters attacked the Polish Government in London and stated that "Polish leaders declared war on the President of the United States and Secretary Hull, and that their activities verge on treason." The Soviet Union in general and the Red Army in particular were acclaimed as the true liberators of Poland. Professor Lange suggested the establishment of a Polish-American Committee of Liberation of Poland which would not admit American Poles who were supporters of the London Government and which would have three purposes:

1. To welcome the Red Army and the Polish Army Corps when they began the liberation of Poland.

2. To promise complete support to the Polish nation in utilizing its right for the reconstruction of a truly democratic Poland.

3. To organize short and long-term economic help for the Polish nation.

Professor Lange's proposals were unanimously accepted, and the League chose the following as officers: Chairman, Mr. Leon Krzycki; Executive Secretary, Mr. Albert Krzywonos of Joliet, Illinois; and Secretary-Treasurer, Mr. Jan A. Zaremba. The office would be located in New York on the premises of the Political Action Committee of the CIO.[25]

There was obviously nothing that the Polish Government could do about this development, which indicated that the Soviet attack on the Polish Government was well coordinated with Moscow's policies.

On February 14, 1944 the Polish Government received another report from its representatives in the United States.

In the last few weeks Soviet propaganda among the Americans of Polish descent is growing rapidly in volume and strength. The supporters of Wanda Wasilewska, under the leadership of Lange, Penzik, Arski, Hertz, Rev. Orlemanski, Krzycki, and others, who have at their disposal large financial means, are conducting intense radio propaganda and are organizing a so-called "Kosciuszko League." In that way they have already organized "Polish Radio Hours" in New York, Chicago, Detroit, Cleveland, Buffalo, and other cities during which they are spreading Wanda Wasilewska's ideas. This action creates serious confusion and harm among the American Poles.[26]

In view of this, the Polish Consuls General in New York and in other cities urged the Polish Government to provide a special budget for counter-action. However, since the budget for that year was already fixed, there was not even a chance of designating $12,000 for 1944 to combat that action. The London Government was thus unable, for financial reasons, to present its case to the American public. Instead, it issued the following instructions to its Ambassador in Washington on what steps to take in connection with the forthcoming presidential elections.

Our influence on American Poles should center around helping them to establish an effective organization. By this we do not mean a mechanical efficiency or unification of Poles in America, but rather a reasonable separation of the functions. Poles are almost evenly divided between the Republican and Democratic Parties, and this is very important to us in view of the uncertainty of the results of the coming election.

. . . .

We have to restrain ourselves from any influence on our people as to whom they should support.[27]

The Polish Government was anxious to remove any suspicion that it might try to interfere with United States foreign policy by using its prestige among Americans of Polish descent to influence the presidential elections.

In order to give further proof that Poles were doing everything they could to show good will towards the Soviets, Mikolajczyk handed Churchill on February 6 a copy of the latest instructions issued by the Polish Government and the Commander-in-Chief of the Polish Armed

Forces to the Polish underground organizations inside Poland, which read as follows:

> When the Red Army enters any particular district in Poland the underground organization is to disclose its identity and meet the requirements of the Soviet commander, even in the absence of a resumption of Polish-Soviet relations. The local Polish military commander, accompanied by the local civilian underground authority will meet and declare to the commander of the incoming Soviet troops, that, following the instructions of the Polish Government, to which they remain faithful, they are ready to coordinate their actions in the fight against the common foe.
>
> This weighty decision, taken after consultation with the Polish underground organization, constitutes a further signal proof of good will on the part of the Polish Government.

. . . .

> The Polish Government, in taking this decision was aware of the danger to which the members of the Polish underground organizations and the units of the Secret Army will be exposed at the hands of the incoming Red Army when carrying out their instructions.[28]

Churchill expressed his approval of this order, and said that the Soviets would undoubtedly appreciate this policy. As subsequent events have shown, however, the Soviets did not appreciate this order at all. Politically, it would have been more convenient for them if the Polish Government had not issued such an order, for then the Soviets could have accused it of obstructing an Allied victory in general and the liberation of Poland in particular. In any case, the Soviets were willing to acknowledge the assistance of only the Soviet-sponsored Lublin Committee and the Soviet-controlled Polish Army in the liberation of Poland.

An article appeared in the March 27 issue of *Pravda* under the title: "Third Polish Infantry Division in the U.S.S.R. Ready to Fight" which clearly stated what the Soviets had in mind in this respect.

> This Division has been trained and prepared for fighting on the Soviet-German front. To a considerable extent the Division is composed of Poles who lived in the western regions of the Ukraine, recently liberated by the Red Army from German occupation. Among the men of the Third Division are a number of former members of the underground organizations created by the London émigré Polish Government. These men, however, could not reconcile themselves to the humiliating position in which they were placed by their leaders. This Division was named "Romuld Traugutt." [29]
>
> The guests who arrived to attend the ceremony took their places on a rostrum bedecked with the colors of the U.S.S.R., the United States, Great

Britain, Czechoslovakia, France, and the Yugoslav Army of National Liberation.

Among the guests were . . . representatives of the Military Mission of the United States, headed by General Christ.[30]

. . . .

The Vice-President of the Central Board of the Union of Polish Patriots in the U.S.S.R., Deputy of the former Sejm, Andrzej Witos, addressed the soldiers. He greeted General Berling, the generals, officers, and men of the Polish Army, and the guests. "Polish Army Units together with Red Army troops are already at the gate of Poland," Witos said. "You are marching now into the battle for the freedom of Poland, for the freedom of our people after the example of the Kosciuszko[31] Division from which General Berling's Army grew. What will this new Poland be like? Her frontiers on the east will be established in accord with our great neighbor—the U.S.S.R. . . . In Democratic Poland there will be no oppression and the tradition of her freedom-loving leaders, Kosciuszko and the patron of your Division, Traugutt, will be sacredly revered. The Union of the Polish Patriots in the U.S.S.R. is striving to preserve these traditions and bring them to Poland."

For Poles, Kosciuszko and Traugutt were symbols of a heroic struggle against Tsarist oppression. Now, under their names the Polish units were to march to liberate their country. They wanted to believe that what they were promised would be upheld. And, most probably, Andrzej Witos,[32] who addressed them, believed it too. As the Poles discovered later, the Soviets' use of patriotic and nationalistic symbols and names was part of a policy carefully calculated to exploit nationalistic sentiments for the benefit of the Soviet Union.

On February 16, 1944 another meeting took place between Churchill, Eden, Mikolajczyk, and Romer. Churchill again used all his powers of persuasion, bringing out all Polish faults and contrasting them with the splendid achievements of the Red Army and the promises of the Soviet Government not to interfere in the internal affairs of a free and independent Poland, thus making acceptance of the Soviet territorial demands a more pressing matter. The Polish side resisted Churchill's pressure, explaining that they had no authority to accept the Curzon Line, but they offered to draw a demarcation line east of Wilno and Lwow.

Churchill said that what the Poles offered him would not satisfy Marshal Stalin. He pressed the Polish Government to let him send his message with their good will.

It was no use saying something which would only make the Russians more angry. I do not wish to rush the Poles if they wish for forty-eight hours to consider this new draft—well and good.

But he hoped they could reply by the next night and that any suggestion they might have to make would be on practical lines.

Mikolajczyk again referred to his Cabinet difficulties which were based on the fact that the Poles saw no practical guarantee in return for their concessions. They had not been encouraged by the recent hostile article in *Pravda.*

Eden reminded Mikolajczyk that the British would guarantee this settlement on Russian terms so far as the British could and that Marshal Stalin would not break faith lightly with the British and the United States of America. "It would, in any case, be madness, with the Russian armies advancing, not to make every effort to secure a *modus vivendi.*"

Churchill said that the Poles justly rejoice at the advance of the Russian Armies, dangerous though this might be to them, since it was their only hope of liberation from the Germans. There was no reason to suppose that Russia would repeat the German desire to dominate all Europe.[34]

The Poles resisted all arguments. Churchill then announced that he would make a public statement on the whole matter. Mikolajczyk asked him to omit any reference to Poland if he planned to say unkind words about it, because it would only weaken the Polish position. But Churchill would not listen and refused Mikolajczyk's request.[35]

Various Polish social and political organizations outside Poland learned about the Soviet and British pressure on the Polish Government, so they held meetings and passed resolutions asking the Government to defend to the last the eastern frontiers, and, above all, the rights and the honor of the Polish nation.

2. *Churchill Openly Supports the Soviet Territorial Claim on Poland*

On February 22, speaking in the House of Commons, Churchil declared:

I took the occasion to raise personally with Marshal Stalin the questio of the future of Poland. . . . It was with great pleasure that I heard from Marshal Stalin that he, too, was resolved upon the creation and mainte nance of a strong, integral, independent Poland as one of the leading Power in Europe. He has several times repeated these declarations in public, an I am convinced that they represent the settled policy of the Soviet Unior

I may remind the House that we ourselves have never in the past guarar teed, on behalf of His Majesty's Government, any particular frontier lin to Poland. . . . The British view in 1919 stands expressed in the so-calle "Curzon Line," which attempted to deal, at any rate partially, with th

problem. I have always held the opinion that all questions of territorial settlement and readjustment should stand over until the end of the war, and that the victorious Powers should then arrive at a formal and final agreement governing the articulation of Europe as a whole. That is still the wish of His Majesty's Government.

However, the advance of the Russian armies into Polish regions in which the Polish underground army is active makes it indispensable that some kind of friendly working agreement should be arrived at to govern the war-time conditions and enable all anti-Hitlerite forces to work together with the greatest advantage against the common foe. During the last few weeks the Foreign Secretary and I have labored with the Polish Government in London with the object of establishing a working arrangement upon which the fighting forces can act, and upon which, I trust, an increasing structure of good will and comradeship may be built between Russia and Poland.

I have an intense sympathy for the Poles, that heroic race whose national spirit centuries of misfortune cannot quench, but I also have sympathy with the Russian standpoint. Twice in our lifetime Russia has been violently assaulted by Germany. Many millions of Russians have been slain and vast tracts of Russian soil devastated as a result of repeated German aggression. Russia has the right to reassurance against future attacks from the West, and we are going all the way with her to see that she gets it, not only by the might of her arms but by the approval and assent of the United Nations.

The liberation of Poland may presently be achieved by the Russian armies, after these armies have suffered millions of casualties in breaking the German military machine. I cannot feel that the Russian demand for reassurance about her western frontiers goes beyond the limits of what is reasonable or just. Marshal Stalin and I also agreed upon the need for Poland to obtain compensation at the expense of Germany both in the north and in the west.[36]

Hitler did not waste time in using this speech for propaganda purposes. The German radio began urging the Polish Army which was on the Italian front to stop fighting.

Your land has been delivered into Stalin's hands by Churchill. . . . You have no place to which to return when the war is done. . . .[37]

Inside Poland Governor General Hans Frank broadcast from Katowice to the Polish people: "Stop your senseless resistance! You've been sold out to Moscow." [38]

The *Evening Standard* in London reported as follows on February 23, 1944:[39]

Hitler's bait to Polish anti-communist elements in a final bid to gain help against the Russians has failed, according to reports from Istanbul, says Reuters.

In his two-day talk in Krakow with Poles of various classes, Dr. Hans

Frank, German Governor-General of occupied Poland, is reported to have made the following offer in Hitler's name, in return for assistance:
1. Independence of Poland
2. Return of Galician territories at present outside the General government
3. Liberation of prisoners of war and political prisoners
4. Reopening of secondary schools and universities
It was also proposed to create a Polish army to be equipped and officered by Germans.

This report was later verified by the Polish underground authorities. Radio Budapest on March 23 at 9:40 P.M. argued:

While the Bolsheviks behind Allied backs recognize the Badoglio Government (Italy), at the same time they refuse to negotiate with the Polish Government in exile, maintaining that it does not represent the Polish people.

On the same day, in Rome, Roberto Farinacci observed:

It is not enough to remember the Corridor. It is also important to remember that England had guaranteed the existence of Poland. But as for what Poland really meant to the Anglo-Saxons, it is sufficient to notice that after only four years, and in spite of solemn declarations, Poland was sacrificed for the sake of Russia.[40]

Polish underground organizations reported to London that Churchill's speech came like a thunderbolt to the whole country. Shock was great, and bitterness towards England replaced the previous confidence and hope in her. Soviet propaganda immediately moved to exploit Churchill's statement. While previously only the might of the Red Army gave prestige to their propaganda, now their pronouncements had the support of England as well. Polish determination to resist Soviet demands began to give way to more practical and expedient measures, which might at least preserve the physical aspect of the nation by not actively resisting the Soviet imposition of power.[41]

In view of the effect on Poland of Churchill's speech in the House of Commons, an appeal by the Polish Socialist Party from Poland was sent to Mr. Attlee, which stated:

This protest is provoked by the shock with which we learned about the Prime Minister's speech. We see in it an old Munich ghost and a repudiation of the Atlantic Charter. We believe that your Party will not permit the surrender of Poland to the slavery of Soviet totalitarianism and this gives us hope and courage to continue our fight against the horrible conditions of Hitler's occupation.[42]

Reports from Teheran, where thousands of Poles—ex-prisoners of Russia—were waiting for transportation to other countries, stated that

Churchill's portraits were thrown out from their tents and huts, and a feeling of despair besieged the people.[43]

On February 24, 1944 the Minister of Foreign Affairs, Romer, saw Foreign Minister Eden to express the sorrow of the Polish Government at Churchill's speech in the House of Commons on February 22, in which he supported Soviet territorial demands against Poland. Romer asked why Churchill declined the serious pleas of the Polish Government to omit the Polish question in that speech if he could say nothing favorable about Poland. Eden replied that Churchill's speech was the expression of His Majesty's Government's policy for the information of the British public. Romer interrupted to say that it was a proclamation which would attract the attention of the world and would be utilized by the Soviet Union.

Eden observed that Churchill was anxious to create the best possible impression in Moscow and to suggest the best solution of the Soviet-Polish dispute.

Romer replied that Churchill's tactics would prove disappointing because they would not persuade the Soviets to be compromising, but instead would stiffen them in their determination to get what they wanted. He pointed out that the reaction of the Soviet press to Churchill's speech was such that they greeted it warmly as a symbol of British-Soviet solidarity and expressed the hope that this solidarity would have influence on the Polish Government.

Eden suggested that no importance should be attached to the reaction of the Soviet press. Then Eden added that Churchill's speech was carefully prepared and approved by the whole Cabinet. "Poles have to control their emotions and learn how to subordinate their interests to the common fundamental objectives."

Romer described the difficulties in which the Polish Government found itself after that speech and recalled the various moves made by the Poles to reach a compromise solution with the Soviets, who were adamant in their determination to get the full acceptance of their demands.

Eden remained unmoved by these arguments.[44]

Many British citizens were also reacting vigorously to Churchill's speech. One of the typical letters sent to Churchill read as follows:

I read with profound regret your address to the House incorporating your statement as to the possible solution of the Russo-Polish frontier dispute. Stricken Europe is looking to the United Nations for the liberation of her territories and the restoration of her international status. A mere switch of power from Nazi to Soviet could hardly satisfy a country such as Poland, who has staked all in her gallant stand against the forces of evil, converging from both East and West.

In 1939 Britain pledged assistance to Poland in the event of aggression. By our declaration of the 3rd of September we did associate ourselves with her cause, although we could afford no material support. This declaration of war was made when her western frontiers were overrun by Germany, but no similar declaration was made when on the 17th of September her eastern defenses were stormed by Russia. A delicate question. Our action, if hardly logical, was at least indicative of the realistic trends of British diplomatic machinations.

This first issue, virtually a test case, if not honorably settled will rout any hope we may have of a balance of power in Europe. It will constitute a flagrant disregard by the U.S.S.R. of all treaties ratified by her and a vir-tual admission by Britain of the U.S.S.R. as the supreme power in Europe. A sorry tribute to Britain and to her Empire, which stood alone during those dark and crucial days after the fall of France.

You raised the question in your speech of British approval of the Russo-Polish frontiers. But, surely the guarantee of these frontiers and our fre-quent re-affirmation of our intention to restore them was sufficient indica-tion of our approval of them. The League of Nations set up after the last war was admittedly a failure, but what hope can we have of establishing any similar institution, the existence of which in some form will be essen-tial to safeguard post-war Europe from the disasters of this first part of the twentieth century—if the U.S.S.R. assumes the role of European dictator even before the peace is won?

Let it not be recorded for posterity how the descendant of the glorious Marlborough was diverted from his path of honor and justice by the ruth-less leader of a terror regime, and we can hardly consider that of the Soviet as other than terrorist, when to maintain order it required to detain in cap-tivity twenty millions of its one hundred and eighty millions subjects.

Let it not be said of the one-time invincible Churchill: "Were it not better had he gone down in his glory at Teheran before the pass was sold, rather than live to associate his name and that of the Empire with such ignominy and shame."

(Signed) E. J. CAMBELL.[45]

As the Polish press in England indicated, undoubtedly many Poles would have identified themselves with the spirit and the wording of this communication.

It was rather difficult, however, to sway Churchill from a policy, once he had adopted it. And apparently Churchill was determined to carry out his Teheran commitments loyally.

On February 29, 1944 the British Ministry of Information sent the following note to the higher British clergy and to the BBC.

Sir,

I am directed by the Ministry to send you the following circular letter:

It is often the duty of the good citizens and of the pious Christians to turn a blind eye on the peculiarities of those associated with us.

But the time comes when such peculiarities, while still denied in public, must be taken into account when action by us is called for.

We know the methods of rule employed by the Bolshevik dictator in Russia itself from, for example, the writing and speeches of the Prime Minister himself during the last twenty years. We know how the Red Army behaved in Poland in 1920 and in Finland, Estonia, Latvia, Galicia, and Bessarabia only recently.

We must, therefore, take into account how the Red Army will certainly behave when it overruns Central Europe. Unless precautions are taken, the obviously inevitable horrors which will result will throw an undue strain on public opinion in this country.

We cannot reform the Bolsheviks but we can do our best to save them —and ourselves—from the consequences of their acts. The disclosures of the past quarter of a century will render mere denials unconvincing. The only alternative to denial is to distract public attention from the whole subject.

Experience has shown that the best distraction is atrocity propaganda directed against the enemy. Unfortunately the public is no longer so susceptible as in the days of the "Corpse Factory," the "Mutilated Belgian Babies," and the "Crucified Canadians."

Your cooperation is therefore earnestly sought to distract public attention from the doings of the Red Army by your wholehearted support of various charges against the Germans and Japanese which have been and will be put into circulation by the Ministry.

Your expression of belief in such may convince others.

I am, Sir, Your obedient servant,

(Signed) H. HEWET, ASSISTANT SECRETARY

The Ministry can enter into no correspondence of any kind with regard to this communication which should only be disclosed to responsible persons.[46]

It is unknown how many recipients of this communication complied with the above instructions.

On March 9, 1944 Mr. McLaren, the Head of the Political Desk of the Political Intelligence Department in the British Foreign Office, informed Mr. J. Zaranski, the counselor to the Polish Prime Minister, that he had received a specific order to prepare a series of broadcasts to Poland in Polish and other languages in order to prepare Polish public opinion about the necessity of giving up a considerable part of its eastern territories without mentioning, for the time being, the Curzon Line. These broadcasts were almost ready in the BBC, and they would go on the air without any delay. Upon being informed of this proposal, Mikolajczyk categorically rejected the plan, as a result of which the Foreign Office temporarily abandoned it.[47]

At the same time, the democratic organizations which were fighting the Nazis and suddenly were faced with a new terror, sent an urgent appeal to the peoples of the world through their Government in London, asking for help and implying that they had lost faith in Western leaders.

To the Peoples of the World:

On the eve of the decisive blow of the Allied forces, and of their conclusive battles with the Germans in which, on the side of our Western Allies, Polish forces in Poland and abroad will also play their part, the world should realize the situation of the Polish nation, as it is after four years of German occupation, the part it has been playing in this war, its moral strength, and its aims and its hopes.

We opposed the Hitlerite invader, fully aware of the heavy responsibilities that this would entail, and we do not ask for sympathy when we state the price we paid for our love of freedom. During this war some five million Polish citizens were killed in Poland by the enemy. About three millions were deported for slavery to the East or West. Hundreds of thousands were put into prison or concentration camps where the majority of them have perished already. Many thousands were shot or tortured to death in Gestapo torture chambers. Hundreds of villages were burnt down and razed to the ground, and their inhabitants massacred. There is not one family which could not mourn the death of one of its members; there is not one home that could not grieve over some next of kin.

We have paid this heavy price because we remained true to our country and to the terms of our alliance, and would not accept any form of collaboration with the invader. We remained Poles, citizens of our country, loyal to our Government which, though in exile, has maintained its bonds with the home country. Here, in Poland, we have rebuilt underground all the forms of our public life: an Executive of our Government, an Underground Army, Civil Resistance, a representative body of our political parties, numerous clandestine newspapers, and a secret cultural life. The Home Political Representation, formed a couple of years ago, is composed of the representatives of four main political parties, representing all the strata of society and all the principal trends of Polish political thought, acting on the basis of the sovereignty of the Polish State.

From the very beginning the invaders met these manifestations of our independent political existence and everywhere strove to break us by cruel terroristic methods. We return blow for blow. Though disarmed since the end of 1939, we do everything possible to make the Polish soil insecure for the enemy. Nazi tyrants fall by the hand of the Polish Underground, trains are blown up, detachments of the S.S. and other police formations are being destroyed.

A stubborn, constant, unwavering struggle against the Germans is taking place on the Polish soil. In order to keep down the country, the enemy has to maintain in Poland thousands of soldiers, policemen, and administrative officials necessary for the Eastern Front. This struggle is uneven. The nation, almost defenseless, opposes an enemy armed to the teeth. In consequence, over 14% of the Polish population perished in this struggle. This sacrifice is all the greater when we consider the fact that the enemy persecutes the most active and valuable elements of the nation. Scientists, clergymen, artists, teachers, technicians, officers, intellectual workers of all kinds and the great mass of socially and politically active peasants and workers are the principal victims of the invader. The enemy deals his blows in order to ensure that their consequences will be felt for many years. He applies everywhere the terrible principle of collective responsibility. And seeing how difficult it is to break our resistance, he uses his bestiality to an extent hitherto unknown in the history of the world.

Mass executions, in which two and a half million Jews perished, exceed by their cruelty the darkest legends of ancient times. The extreme sadism of public executions taking place in our country during the last two months has no example in the history of mankind. From October, 1943 the shooting of hostages has been taking place in the streets of Warsaw and many other towns of Poland. There are days when in the streets and public squares of Warsaw alone the Germans shoot 270 men at a time. To heighten the terror, loudspeakers repeat the names of the killed and give long lists of new "hostages" caught in the streets in daily manhunts. Every day large red posters are displayed with new names. In that manner more than five thousand were put to death in a few weeks in Warsaw alone. Besides, prisoners confined in prisons or concentration camps are killed by shots fired from behind or are suffocated in gas chambers by a method that is four years old.

We are fully aware that the Germans are bent if not on the extermination of the whole Polish nation, at least on depriving it of strength and rendering it defenseless. Himmler announces further intensification of the terrorism against Poles: If the Germans are obliged to withdraw from our country, our towns and villages will be razed to the ground by the order of this hangman, and masses of the population, apart from those fit for physical work, are to be destroyed—the intellectual class first of all. This puts us in face of new unspeakable horrors and terrible dangers.

This inhuman crime of exterminating the Polish nation takes place before the eyes of the world. This crime is hanging over our daily life. Our duty is to make it known to the peoples of the world and to make them assist our nation, which is struggling for its existence to the last drop of its blood. We ask you, the peoples of the world, for help in our struggle. We ask you to precipitate the military operations in order to shorten the time which the Germans can use for exterminating us. We ask you to give support to our Government and our Army so that they might return as soon as possible to Poland and take part with the whole nation in the final struggle with the enemy. We ask you to deliver swiftly the arms necessary to the Army fighting in our country (which may be joined tomorrow by all the Poles).

Facing the tragic moment of our history, when our nation is menaced by the loss of new millions of lives, we have the right to appeal to you, peoples of the world, to assure us that our sacrifice will not be in vain, that in the new post-war world the rights and interests of Poland will be respected, and that Poland, which holds the key position between the East and West and for centuries has been opposing the thrust of Prussianism to the East (and defending Western culture and civilization against Eastern barbarism) will not be betrayed by her friends.

We Poles, in face of the most terrible dangers have the right to ask for the assurance:

That our country will not be robbed of its territories;

That no one will have the right to interfere in our internal affairs, and that the rights of our Government, which has the full support of Polish public opinion, will be respected;

That the integrity and independence of the Polish State will be held sacred by the world, regardless of how many of us will still be alive after this war

Such an assurance given by the nations of the world fighting for freedom and justice will strengthen our force in the struggle against the enemies of freedom.

NATIONAL PARTY
POLISH PEASANT PARTY
CHRISTIAN LABOR PARTY
CENTRAL COMMITTEE OF WORKERS' MOVEMENT:
"LIBERTY, EQUALITY, INDEPENDENCE"
POLISH SOCIALIST PARTY
CONSTITUTING THE HOME POLITICAL REPRESENTATION[48]

Mikolajczyk complied with their wishes and forwarded that appeal to the press, to Roosevelt, and to Churchill. There was no reply from Roosevelt and Churchill.

The London Poles were becoming discouraged. There was no hope in obtaining any support from the British Government.

3. The Polish Government Attempts to Present Its Case to Roosevelt

In spite of the discouraging confidential reports from the Polish Ambassador in Washington about the attitude of the American officials towards Poland, Mikolajczyk was indefatigable in his efforts to try to talk with President Roosevelt. As the reader may remember, at the end of October 1943 President Roosevelt sent an invitation to Mikolajczyk asking him to visit in Washington around January 15, 1944. When Mikolajczyk learned that a Teheran meeting of the Big Three was approaching, he asked Churchill if he could see both him and Roosevelt in Cairo, prior to that meeting, in order to present the Polish case. Churchill replied that this would be impossible because it might anger Stalin and he might not come to Teheran. Roosevelt replied that he was well informed about the Polish question so he would prefer to postpone the meeting with Mikolajczyk until March.

After the Teheran Conference, Eden approached Mikolajczyk and requested that he postpone his trip to Washington because Churchill was recuperating in Africa and he wanted to see Mikolajczyk first. Mikolajczyk replied that he had an invitation from the White House and could not decline it. Soon after that Mikolajczyk received a telegram from Roosevelt stating that at Churchill's request he would like to postpone Mikolajczyk's visit to Washington. The BBC announced Mikolajczyk's departure to Washington in a way which was interpreted by Poles as a move to torpedo the whole project. The

German press commented that this trip was the result of differences of opinion between the British and Polish Governments, and that the Poles wanted to appeal to Roosevelt. The pro-Soviet press in America began a campaign of accusations against the Polish Government, suggesting that Mikolajczyk wanted to turn Poles in America against Roosevelt and Britain, and that this constituted interference in the internal affairs of America.

In another round of telegrams Roosevelt agreed to meet Mikolajczyk in the middle of February. This was necessitated by the British insistence on an immediate reply about the Curzon Line. On January 31 Mikolajczyk received a telegram from Roosevelt in which he stated that if the proposed visit would take place as scheduled, in mid-February, it would lead to confusion of public opinion and would be badly interpreted for Poland. He therefore suggested a postponement of that visit. Meanwhile, the German press in Poland was arguing that the British would never permit such a visit.

Mikolajczyk asked the American Chargé d'Affaires, R. E. Schoenfield, if President Roosevelt would be willing to receive another Pole and that, if so, he would resign immediately in that Pole's favor. Schoenfield replied that President Roosevelt liked and respected him but that he felt a visit at this time would harm Poland.

Mikolajczyk concluded that Roosevelt was afraid that on such a visit he would have to say something favorable to the Poles and that this might spoil his friendship with the Russians.

At the same time, Roosevelt was naturally anxious to receive the votes of Polish-Americans in the coming elections. Therefore, it was decided that Churchill would handle the Soviet-Polish situation and, by so doing, would relieve Roosevelt of an unpleasant dilemma. It was presumed that Churchill would break Polish resistance. When the Polish Government, to everyone's surprise, resisted, it was decided to postpone the visit to Washington.[49]

In the middle of March, Mikolajczyk recalled Ambassador Ciechanowski from Washington for consultation. At the end of this consultation he handed him a personal letter to the President. This letter was delivered in Washington on March 25. Because this letter contains an expression of the full gravity of Poland's situation, excerpts are included here:

Owing to circumstances I am temporarily unable personally to present to you my views at this time, so critical for Poland and, indeed, for the problems of peace. . . .

I need hardly stress that the Polish people regard you, Mr. President, and the American people as the trustees of the principles for the triumph of which our United Nations' camp is fighting. . . .

I am fully conscious of the considerations which, for the time being, prevent the United States Government from publicly defining its stand on particular European problems. My urgent desire to pay you a personal visit at this time was not inspired by the intention of appealing to you to do so. . . .

I will not enter into a detailed recapitulation of the course of events relating to the difficulties encountered in our attempts to find a solution of the outstanding differences existing between the Soviet and Polish Governments. . . .

The Polish Government sincerely intends to reach an understanding with the Soviet Government which would allow their fullest and most effective joint action against the common enemy, thus forming a solid basis for postwar neighborly collaboration. . . .

I am sure that you will agree that at this time, when the whole future of mankind is involved, it is imperative to face reality in a spirit of sincerity and truth on which alone the future of international relations and durable peace can be founded. . . .

I am firmly convinced that Nazi totalitarianism and its drive for world mastery shall be destroyed. But will not Poland, and later Europe, be overwhelmed against its will by a new wave of communist totalitarianism? Can the nations condemned to the rule of such a new totalitarianism agree to accept its tyranny?

Never, as far as Poland is concerned.

The masses of Polish small farmers, anxious to build their prosperity not in collective farms but in individual farmsteads, will never agree to it. . . .

The present war has proved that wars cannot be localized. The development of technical means of total war makes it impossible, even for the strongest Power, to win a world war single-handed. The collaboration of all of us is indispensable if autarchic systems are to disappear and nationalisms are to be reduced. Political and economic collaboration must be closer than before to bring about the establishment of the future world order. That is why the coordination of the policy of the Great Powers and their collaboration with the smaller Powers already in the course of the war is so important to the future peace. . . .

The responsibility of the Great Powers will be ever greater inasmuch as they will be called upon to safeguard, apart from their own security, the security of smaller nations, their freedom and especially the freedom of the individual throughout the world.

To achieve this aim, it appears to me essential to realize the full truth of the existing situation.

Unfortunately public opinion is frequently being led to accept entirely false views on Europe, and particularly on Poland.

I fully share the admiration inspired by the heroism of Soviet soldiers fighting in the defense of their country against the German invader. I also appreciate the realism of Marshal Stalin whose word can limit the political aims of world communism.

I am afraid, however, that public opinion may be bitterly disappointed should it discover that the widely publicized social changes and the alleged democratization of the Soviet Union are in fact but a combination of old Russian imperialism with communist totalitarianism which has not abandoned its former ambition for world rule.

Therefore it appears to me wrong to lead public opinion to believe that democracy exists where in reality it does not and cannot exist for a long time, as this is fraught with the danger of causing deep disillusionment and even unhappiness in nations who may be subjected to a rule which, while recognizing the freedom of the State, denies that of the individual.

It may also create disillusionment in business circles which expect freedom of trade relations in the future. The deepest disappointment, however, will be that of the working classes now rightly impressed by the fighting valor of the Soviet people but misled to believe that labor's greatest aspirations and democratic ideals have been achieved in the Soviet Union.

I regard the maintenance of Allied solidarity as essential and imperative in our common fight.

I therefore observe with profound misgivings the activity of German propaganda, hitherto completely disbelieved, which now succeeds in rebuilding German morale—shattered by military defeats—by attempting to prove that the Allies are aiming at a compromise which would open the door of Europe to communism.

It is difficult to estimate how far the declared Soviet intentions toward Poland and the Baltic countries have already influenced the attitude of Turkey and Finland—thus directly affecting military operations. It is likewise difficult to say what consequences it may cause in European countries under German occupation.

One thing is certain—Nazi-occupied Europe was decidedly anti-German and its hope of rapid regeneration after its liberation was justified. The activities of communist agencies brought about disunity and fear of chaos, for these agencies have endeavored to achieve supremacy in every country, less for the purpose of strengthening the struggle against the Germans than for that of establishing communism in the countries concerned.

The concealment of truth on which this situation is based is more detrimental to the Polish nation than to others. Once more I must stress that I am most anxious to preserve Allied unity. History will reveal how, in spite of violent criticisms of the Polish opposition at home and abroad, General Sikorski's and my own Cabinet have refrained from publishing the true facts which would have enlightened public opinion regarding Poland's situation and the methods used by Russia in her dealings, and her intentions as regards my country. We have refrained from publishing such facts, although this is clearly against our interests, because we were anxious to reach an understanding with the U.S.S.R. and to safeguard the unity of the Allies. Our reticence is, however, exploited by Russia, thus placing us in an intolerable position. Thus, the Polish Government, responsible for the welfare of our country, is deprived of the elementary right of defense of its national interests and the right of the weaker to appeal for help to the stronger, in the name of the principles and ideals enunciated by you, Mr. President, in the Atlantic Charter, the Four Freedoms, and many other statements which have won the respect and approval of the entire world. . . .

The accusation that the Polish Government is undemocratic, when in reality it is composed of men who by their origins and by their lifelong struggle for democracy have proved their sincere attachment to democratic ideals, is slanderous. It is a serious wrong to insult the Government which enjoys the confidence of its nation and is its expression, merely because it refused to countenance the cession of eleven millions of its citizens to a country where individual freedom is unknown. Nor can one blame it for refusing to hand over half of its national territory, to agree to the transfer from eastern Poland of at least five million Poles in exchange for the transfer of millions of Germans, or because it apprehends the prospect of a turning tide which within fifty years or so, in accordance with the changing European political situation, may once more cause the shifting of populations on its territory.

It is the greatest insult to accuse the Polish soldiers, who have fought since 1939 in Poland, France, Norway, Africa, and Italy—in the Battle of Britain in the air, and on the Seven Seas—of a lack of fighting spirit. While American and British soldiers are rightly promised employment and better conditions after their return home, the Polish soldiers, airmen, and sailors, who come from eastern Poland, are told that they may never be allowed to return to their homes and their families.

Mr. President, the Polish people . . . cannot understand why its great sacrifices appear to have been forgotten. It does not claim payment or reward, but only justice. It still believes that the rights of the weak will be respected by the powerful.

The Polish nation cannot understand why, in the fifth year of war, it does not receive sufficient armament and supplies for its underground struggle, at a time when Allied mass production of aircraft and weapons has reached a wonderful peak, and the contribution of the Polish Underground Army can be of considerable importance. Poland needs these weapons for its final struggle against the Germans. . . .

In fact the supply of equipment for the Polish Underground Army has been virtually stopped since the autumn of 1943. . . .

Mr. President, your name is revered by every Pole. The Polish nation looks upon you as the champion of the principles which you have proclaimed with such deep faith and conviction, presenting to mankind a vision of human freedom in a better world.

Our people fighting in Poland's Underground Army have lost everything. They lay no value on life. They may not reckon sufficiently with realism, while being threatened with the loss of their last hope of freedom and by the prospect of another enslavement. They have faith in you, Mr. President. I am convinced that their faith will be justified.

At the present moment the situation in Poland can be summed up as follows: As far as the attachment to principles is concerned the Polish nation is united and unfaltering.

Its attitude toward the war is expressed in the following points:

1. Poland is determined to carry on to the end the struggle against the Germans and asks for adequate supplies of arms and equipment for that purpose.

2. The Polish people decided, in full agreement with the Polish Government and on its instructions, that our Underground Army will come out

into the open and offer its collaboration against the Germans to the Soviet armed forces as they enter Poland, even if diplomatic relations between the Polish and Russian Governments are not resumed. The Polish Underground took this decision although it is aware of the dangers resulting from disclosing its organization to the Soviets.

I hope that you will kindly forgive this very frank and long letter at this tragic moment for my country. On behalf of the Polish nation and Government I appeal to you, Mr. President, to do all in your power to prevent the creation in Poland of *faits accomplis;* to safeguard the sovereign rights of the Polish State and of its lawful authorities; to insure the respect and safety of the lives and property of Polish citizens; to safeguard the Polish Underground Army and administration from the dangers that threaten them after their disclosure to the Soviet forces.

I am convinced that in your great wisdom and statesmanship, and realizing that the case of Poland has a direct bearing on the future peace, you will find the best way to give support to her just cause. . . .[50]

The President replied, thanking Mikolajczyk for his courtesy "in explaining in such a frank manner your position and that of your colleagues on the various problems confronting your Cabinet at this time," and invited him for the early part of May.[51]

On April 9, 1944 Mikolajczyk was received by Churchill in the presence of Stettinius and Winant.

During the conversation Churchill stated:

The Polish Government should remove General Sosnkowski or Sosnkowski should understand the problem and should resign as the Commander-in-Chief of the Polish Armed Forces. The Soviets are demanding his ouster.

In reply, Mikolajczyk stated:

The problem of Sosnkowski as Commander-in-Chief is misrepresented. I am certain that if Sosnkowski thought that he, as a person, stood in the way of the good of his country, he would immediately resign. But, from the analysis of the political situation it is obvious that it is not so; that independently of Sosnkowski the Soviets are piling up unacceptable conditions against Poland.

Then Churchill urged Mikolajczyk to go to Washington because, as he put it:

The Soviets pay great attention to Anglo-American public opinion and particularly to American public opinion. So you should even suspect that some elements of the American press may be paid by the Russians. You should present your case in this pre-election time to the American public by speaking at a few public rallies.

You could be absolutely certain that Poland will be independent and because the British and Americans will not permit the loss of Polish independence. We shall not permit Poland to become a satellite country. We cannot stand any tyranny in Europe.

When Mikolajczyk informed Churchill that the Soviets intended to form a government in Lublin as soon as they crossed the Curzon Line, Churchill became highly irritated and categorically stated: "We shall not recognize any government formed in such a manner." [52]

When Churchill was asked what the American attitude was to British mediation between the Soviet and Polish Governments, he replied that he kept Roosevelt constantly informed about those matters and in each case had his full support. But now he would be happy to put all those problems on American shoulders. Then he said:

Your trip to Washington should be a very useful thing. The White House will be anxious not to lose Polish votes in the coming election. I don't think that you will get any definite solution to your problems. It will only increase your prestige and therefore strengthen our hand in negotiations with the Soviets.[53]

This was exactly what Mikolajczyk expected to achieve from his visit to Washington. Secretly he dreamed of reversing the trend of events if only Roosevelt agreed to support him. America had always cast a magic spell over the hearts and minds of Poles.[54]

When the Soviets learned of Mikolajczyk's proposed visit to see President Roosevelt, they became concerned. Prior to Mikolajczyk's journey to Washington, therefore, the Soviet Ambassador, Lebedev, came to tell him that he was asked by Moscow to find out what Mikolajczyk's views on the future of Poland were. Mikolajczyk replied that he thought the problem of frontiers should be left to the peace conference. He informed Lebedev that in spite of the dreadful behavior of the Red Army in Poland the Polish Home Army was genuinely collaborating with the Soviet forces, and he stressed the point that all political and military underground organizations in Poland were ready to join the Soviets in any agreement which would speed up the liberation of Poland. Lebedev said that all these difficulties could now be solved.

Three days later he came back with new instructions from his Government, demanding that President Raczkiewicz; General Sosnkowski, Polish Commander-in-Chief; General Kukiel, Minister of Defense; and former Ambassador Kot, presently the Minister of Information, be dismissed. Furthermore, he insisted that they should be replaced by Poles from Britain and the United States, and that the new Government should denounce the Polish Government which had brought the Katyn murders to the attention of the International Red Cross. Mikolajczyk refused to consider these proposals and dismissed his caller.

Lebedev asked for another conference just before Mikolajczyk's departure for Washington, but Mikolajczyk excused himself, hoping that his visit with Roosevelt would eliminate the consideration of these demands.[55]

To make sure that the Polish Government would not be accused of a lack of good will towards the Soviet Union, it made public on April 4, 1944, its previous instructions to the Underground, hoping that at the same time this would strengthen Mikolajczyk's hand in his talks with the Americans.

The instructions to the Underground Movement in Poland, issued by the Polish Government are such that as soon as the Soviet forces entered the territory of the Polish Republic, the Polish Government, in spite of the difficulties preventing agreement with the Soviet Government decided, with the consent of the underground organization, to order the Polish underground authorities and their military formations to collaborate with the Soviet Army. . . .

The Commander of the Home Army (in Poland) said, in his order of the day to his men, dated January 12, 1944:

"As the front is again within our national boundaries, we not only recognize the right of the Soviet armies entering Poland in pursuit of the Germans to wage war on our territory, but shall support their action within the limit of our means and, in accordance with our national interest, are acting under the orders of the Polish Government and our Commander-in-Chief. We shall not, however, submit to any political pressure designed to subordinate us to alien aims, and deprive us of the freedom to organize our national life in accordance with our own political and social ideals." [56]

The detailed instructions ordered the representatives of the underground civil administration to approach the commanders of the entering Soviet forces and to make the following declaration:

"Acting under the orders of the Polish Government's Delegate we meet, on Polish soil, the forces of the Soviet Union as co-belligerents against the common enemy—Germany—against whom the Polish Republic was the first to wage war in the defense of her own and other nations' independence, and against whom she has been fighting for more than four years together with her Allies.

At the same time, we inform the Soviet armies that there exists in these territories an administration secretly organized by the Polish State during the German occupation.

We expect that the Soviet armies will enable the Polish authorities, during the military operations on Poland's territory, to assure the social and economic welfare of the population, in accordance with international law."

According to the first messages arriving from Poland, Soviet commanders stated that they received assistance everywhere and they praised the fighting spirit and leadership of the Polish Home Army, and that cooperation with the Polish Underground Army has been satisfactory.

Later, reports were received about alarming events behind the Soviet front line, which required elucidation. If they should be confirmed and if they were to be repeated, the Polish underground army might have to discontinue coming into the open. In connection with these events the Polish Government has addressed to the British and American Governments a note requesting their assistance in the prevention of incidents which might render impossible further cooperation and continued common operations against the Germans at this moment, which is decisive for Polish-Soviet relations.

The instructions to come into the open and cooperate in the fighting against the Germans have not been revoked and still remain in force.[57]

In June 1944 Mikolajczyk visited Washington, without any hope of reaching agreement or of signing a treaty, but rather to inform the President about the true facts of the Polish-Soviet dispute as the Polish Government knew them, in the belief that this would encourage Roosevelt to take a favorable position towards Poland. Independently of whether Mikolajczyk's mission succeeded or not, the very fact of his conferring with President Roosevelt was almost certain to increase the prestige of the Polish Government.

On June 11 Mikolajczyk had his first conference with the President. Roosevelt expressed his delight at meeting Mikolajczyk and of being able to discuss the Polish problem with him personally, because, as he put it,

. . . the solution of this question has a direct influence in the general war and post-war situation. . . . I am absolutely convinced and firmly believe that as the result of this war Poland will be free and independent. . . .

At Teheran Stalin impressed me as a realist and he did not appear as an imperialist or communist. He is terribly clever, has a peculiar mentality, likes to joke and is obviously very suspicious. It is not easy to negotiate with Stalin, because if he does not like to get involved in a certain subject he simply lets the matter drop.[58]

Then he proceeded to tell stories (anecdotes) about the Teheran Conference, and informed Mikolajczyk that Stalin had special confidence in himself (i.e., the President) but very little in Churchill.

Speaking about his conversation with Stalin at Teheran with respect to the future of Poland, President Roosevelt stated:

Neither Stalin nor I proposed the Curzon Line as the frontier between Poland and the Soviet Union. It was Churchill who suggested it, and obviously Stalin immediately picked it up and accepted it.

Mikolajczyk was terribly shaken by this information. He could not, for a moment, believe that Churchill, who was continually reasserting his great and undying loyalty and friendship to Poland, could be so treacherous. In his anxiety to please Stalin, Churchill had relieved the Soviet dictator of the necessity to press his own claims. Mikolajczyk could not understand how Churchill could be so immoral as to try to buy Stalin's friendship by giving him half of the territory of a State allied to Britain. But Mikolajczyk did not want to attack Churchill in front of his great friend, President Roosevelt, and so remained silent.[59]   In the subsequent part of the conversation the President criticized Churchill for that stand and described various difficulties which were created for him by it.

Then the President went on to observe that only a general improvement of the diplomatic atmosphere would provide some way out of the deadlock. "It seems that Poles must seek an understanding with the Soviets."

When Mikolajczyk observed that the conditions proposed by the Soviets did not indicate that they really wanted to see Poland free and independent, the President replied:

[that he did not think] that the Soviets are anxious to destroy Poland, anyhow, it would not be possible because they know that the United States Government and the American people would be against that.   On the other hand, some concessions on your part would be very welcome in order to prove that you are anxious to reach an understanding and to work on friendly terms with the Soviet Union.

When Mikolajczyk asked if the President thought that the Poles should accept the Soviet territorial demands and comply with their insistence that the Polish Government should dismiss some of its members, the President replied:

You should avoid any final or definite settlement of the frontiers now. In regard to your second question, it might be desirable to find an opportunity to bring some changes in your Cabinet in order to make an understanding with the Russians possible.

Mikolajczyk agreed with Roosevelt's first suggestion but refused to countenance the second on the ground that this would be the first step of the Soviets' interference into the internal affairs of Poland, and thus a violation of the sovereign rights of the Polish Nation.

Then Roosevelt suggested that Mikolajczyk should have a personal conversation with Stalin or Molotov.   Mikolajczyk replied that it was difficult to arrange such a meeting.   However, if the President could arrange it, he would have to have Roosevelt's support and must enter into such talks without prior acceptance of the Soviet demands.

Upon some reflection, the President observed:

In this political year I cannot approach Stalin with a new initiative about Poland, nor can I offer myself as a mediator.   But it may be possible for me to play a role of a moderator—as it exists in the Presbyterian Church —he is not a minister or a bishop, he can only help to interpret things and help in reaching an understanding.

Mikolajczyk informed Roosevelt that President Beneš offered himself as a mediator because the Russians approached him, and that Mikolajczyk had a good personal relationship with him.

Then Mikolajczyk went on to say that he was ready to go to Moscow if there was any chance of reaching an agreement, but he would not go if this would lead to a more complicated situation which might prove beyond repair.

Roosevelt ended the conversation by informing Mikolajczyk that he was contemplating sending a telegram to Stalin in which he would urge a meeting between Stalin and Mikolajczyk in order to establish a personal contact "of man to man." [60]

The next day Mikolajczyk asked Stettinius whether he thought that the President's suggestion of sending a telegram was something which came from a well-thought-out plan, or whether it had been only a spontaneous inspiration. Stettinius replied that it was only a spontaneous project, which most probably would "fizzle away."

You should be aware that the President is a really sick man. He always has many big ideas, but the condition of his health prevents him from putting them into effect.

Impressed with Stettinius' sincerity, Mikolajczyk asked him what he thought would be the best thing for the Poles to do in that situation. Stettinius replied:

Obviously I cannot give you any official advice. But unofficially, as a true friend of Poland, I can tell you the following things for your consideration. At the present time in our internal pre-election period, and in the existing war conditions outside our shores, the President is in a very difficult situation. Neither Great Britain nor America can take a firmer stand against the Soviet Union. The President is not in a position to give the Polish Government truly effective support. But I am convinced that in the not too distant future, maybe in a month or two, or maybe six months from now, the general situation undoubtedly will change; and when it changes, the whole attitude of the United States to Russia will change completely. If it is only possible for you, Mr. Prime Minister, and for Poland to postpone all these matters and to wait for that moment, I am convinced that you and Poland can rest assured that the United States will come back to her fundamental moral principles—because she cannot abandon them permanently—and, in my opinion, she will then undoubtedly support Poland strongly and successfully.[61]

Mikolajczyk was very much impressed with the frankness and logic of Stettinius' arguments (undoubtedly they reflected his own wishful and prayerful hopes as well), and thought that a new stage in American-Soviet relations was in the making—presumably because of the successes on the Second Front and because of the gradual realization of and resistance to Russian objectives by the Americans.[62]

Before Mikolajczyk's departure for Washington, he was asked by Eden to see Professor Oskar Lange, a former Pole of leftist orientation, who had returned from a several weeks' visit to the Soviet Union, where he had conferred with Stalin and other Soviet leaders. Lange had considerable influence among the left-wing Americans of Polish descent.

At the time when Mikolajczyk was in the United States, Rev. Orlemanski, the left-wing Catholic priest from Massachusetts, and the other intellectual leader of left-wing Polish-Americans, was in the U.S.S.R.

On June 7, 1944 Oskar Lange sent the following telegram to Mikolajczyk in Washington:

> Have just returned from a visit to the Union of Polish Patriots and the Polish Army in the U.S.S.R. Should like to see you before your departure from this country, if agreeable to you.

This telegram was withheld from Mikolajczyk by the Polish Embassy in Washington, but the same request came to Mikolajczyk through Stettinius and Bohlen.

When Mikolajczyk received Lange on June 13, 1944, the latter told him:

> Stalin wants to reach an agreement with Poland because he is afraid of the Germans and does not trust the British. He does not insist on the Curzon Line. He would abandon it but he is afraid of the Ukrainians, Byelorussians, and Lithuanians. He is most anxious to see a change in the composition of the Polish Government.

According to Lange:

> Inside the "Union of Polish Patriots" in the U.S.S.R. are quite a lot of "reactionary" elements—particularly among the former civil servants. A constant fight is going on among them. Neither the "Union of Patriots" nor the pro-Soviet "National Council" brought to the U.S.S.R. wants to accept the Curzon Line. They want to postpone the problem of frontiers, but are anxious to get East Prussia and Silesia.

Lange further explained that most of the people deported to the U.S.S.R. did not want to give away their towns and villages to the U.S.S.R. This opinion was shared by the deported Ukrainians and Byelorussians as well as by the Poles. There were instances when the Ukrainians in the eastern territories of Poland occupied by the U.S.S.R. were pretending to be Polish citizens of Polish nationality in order not to be drafted into the Red Army. General Berling was disliked by the Russians.

Poles in the U.S.S.R. were furious with Churchill's speech which they consider a betrayal of Poland. They do have unquestionable faith, however, in the friendship of the U.S.A.

Speaking to him about Premier Mikolajczyk, Stalin said that although some people consider him a *kulak*, he considered Mikolajczyk a democrat; but he could not say the same about all the Polish socialists in his Cabinet because a few of them were "social-fascists." [63]

On June 15 Professor Lange held a press conference during which he was asked about his visit with Mikolajczyk. Lange replied:

I was talking all the time and Mr. Mikolajczyk was sitting with a poker face, asking many questions, but being obviously unwilling to give me his own opinion.[64]

As a result of this conference Mikolajczyk concluded that Stalin had decided to use Lange as a lever to influence American public opinion and to soften Mikolajczyk's stand.

After sounding out various commentators in Washington—among them Walter Lippmann—Ambassador Ciechanowski reported to Mikolajczyk.

In well-informed circles here it is believed that all the things which Stalin said to Lange, and which Lange told you, were Stalin's gesture to support Roosevelt in the election. All this was cleverly arranged to get American Poles on Roosevelt's side. The Polish question appears to have greater significance in terms of the relationship between the Kremlin and the White House than in terms of Polish-Soviet relations. Stalin tends to postpone the solution of this problem until his armies will approach the center of Poland. It seems that we should do everything we can to reach an agreement before that.

The fact that Lange and Orlemanski went to Moscow responds favorably to Roosevelt's desire to find a formula for a compromise in Polish-Soviet relations. At the same time the presence in Moscow of Father Orlemanski solves (at least partly) Stalin's problem with the Catholics in eastern Poland, annexed by the U.S.S.R. If that mission to Moscow had been aimed at influencing the Vatican, Orlemanski would not have been chosen, but some of the Jesuits would have been selected because they have contacts with Moscow. Therefore, it appears that American initiative was guided by both the coming elections and the short period separating us from the time when the Red Army will be in the heart of Poland.

The fact that the Polish problem became a part of the internal politics of America has no significance for us in the long run. All of Roosevelt's pre-election promises will never be put into effect. When Litvinov arrives in Washington after the election he will immediately sense the weakness of the Polish case over here. According to my American friends, we should not expect interest in the Polish case to last any longer than five or six weeks, and probably even less than that. If we cannot get any formula for a Polish-Soviet agreement or include Poland in one form or another into some European system of security before that time, then our chances will be much worse. The lack of definite results now will cost us the loss of our independence.

We cannot harbor any illusions that the postponement of a decision will help our cause. Whatever we can secure in the next six weeks will be all that we should expect. The Polish case does not lie in the sphere of American interests and for this reason, with the exception of the election period, America will not antagonize its powerful Ally [the Soviet Union] just to help us. This is our only chance to save our freedom. Such an opportunity will never come again.

For this reason, your planned trip to Moscow, in the opinion of my American friends, should not depend on any *a priori* conditions advanced by the Polish Government. Your visit to Moscow, without any conditions attached, even if it will not bring any result, will testify to your good will and that will be much more difficult for American public opinion to ignore than not to go to Moscow at all; which may result if the Russians reject your conditions. The reason is the simple political fact that the future of Poland will be decided not by the Soviets but by American public opinion.

Here, in the opinion of the group known to you—which has the greatest influence on the White House—are two factions. One, which is rather indifferent to Poland, and which can be friendly or sympathetic to us only by an appeal to humanitarian feelings and by private contacts. The other, which is hostile to Poland, states openly that it is better for America if Poland makes more mistakes. The foreign policy of the United States towards Eastern Europe is under the influence of that second group. . . .

As to what extent the other foreign governments are anxious to maintain good relationships with that second influential group, I can illustrate for you by the following examples: Ambassador Halifax never stops trying to secure its favors. There is no audience which he cannot postpone in order to consult with one of the members of that group. He maintains a special group of experts exclusively in order to keep that group informed. In a similar manner, Litvinov twice excused himself from appointments in the State Department in order to personally see some members of that group beforehand. Great Britain and the Soviet Union have excellent intelligence information and therefore appreciate the importance of that group.[65]

Mikolajczyk did not see how the Poles could compete with the Soviets in gaining foreign policy objectives by exploiting various influential personalities close to the President. The dark picture of the Washington scene, as presented by Ciechanowski was, if true, considered by Mikolajczyk as the last nail in the coffin of a free Poland.

While conferring with Undersecretary Stettinius, Mikolajczyk expressed the regret that the Office of War Information, a United States wartime propaganda agency, consistently followed the communist line in its broadcasts to Poland. This obviously hindered the work of the London Government and its underground authorities and helped the Soviet-controlled communist groups.

"If you continue to call Russia a 'democracy,'" Mikolajczyk said, "you may eventually come to regret your statements, and your own people will condemn you for them." Stettinius promised to correct this matter.[65]

During his last meeting with the President, Mikolajczyk was asked to see Stalin. He agreed, and Roosevelt subsequently dispatched a telegram to Stalin asking him to receive Mikolajczyk.

The most tangible result of Mikolajczyk's visit to Washington was the resumption of the delivery of military supplies to the Polish underground organizations which had been previously discontinued at Soviet request.

Before his departure for London, Mikolajczyk was handed a letter by Stettinius from the President which read:

I wish to take this opportunity, just before your departure, to wish you a safe return after your most welcome visit to Washington.

I particularly desire to express to you the pleasure I have had in seeing you again, which enabled me to have most frank, sincere and friendly exchanges of views with you on the many questions which are of mutual interest to us.

I need hardly tell you how much the American people admire the courage and fortitude of the Polish people, who, for almost five years, have borne with brave and stout hearts the cruel hardships of war and oppression. Their steadfast determination to be free again and the indomitable spirit of their fighting men constitute the best pledge that Poland shall reassume her rightful place among the free nations of the world.

The forces of liberation are on the march to certain victory and the establishment of a peace based upon the principles of freedom, democracy, mutual understanding and security for all liberty-loving people.

Permit me to express again how much I appreciated the opportunity of renewing our acquaintance. I feel that such personal exchanges of views cannot but contribute to mutual understanding.[66]

Obviously encouraged by the contents of this letter, Mikolajczyk thus expressed his views when speaking to reporters at the airport before embarking:

I am leaving the United States with full confidence that Poland can count on the support and real friendship of the United States.[67]

Commenting on Prime Minister Mikolajczyk's visit to Washington, Ambassador Ciechanowski reported to his Government as follows:

As a result of information unofficially supplied to the press by governmental circles here, the external impression of the Prime Minister's visit with the President and his friendliness to Poland is widely exploited internally in this pre-election period. On the other hand, because of fear of Soviet displeasure, official circles are anxious to show in the press the lack of any concrete promises made by the United States towards Poland, and they imply that the Polish problem is subordinated to the wider and more important Soviet-American relations. The point is that they want to convince the Soviets that the President did not undertake any new obligations towards Poland or her Prime Minister.[68]

Shortly thereafter, Roosevelt sent his telegram to Stalin asking him to see Mikolajczyk. Stalin answered as follows:

It is necessary to bear in mind that the establishment of cooperation between the Red Army and the Polish Underground is undoubtedly now an essential matter. The solution of the problem of Soviet-Polish relations has a great bearing in this matter.

You are familiar with the point of view of the Soviet Government and its endeavor to see a strong, independent and democratic Poland and good-neighborly Soviet-Polish relations based upon durable friendship.

The Soviet Government sees the most important promise of this in the reorganization of the *émigré* Polish Government which would provide for the participation in it of Polish statesmen in England, as well as Polish statesmen in the U.S.A. and the U.S.S.R., and especially by Polish democratic statesmen in Poland itself, and also in the recognition by the Polish Government of the Curzon Line as the new border between the U.S.S.R. and Poland.

It is necessary to say, however, that from the statement of Mr. Mikolajczyk in Washington, it is not observable that he takes any step forward in this matter. That is why it is difficult for me, at the present moment, to offer any opinion about Mr. Mikolajczyk's trip to Moscow.[69]

Churchill, like Roosevelt, was surprised by Stalin's reply. Upon his arrival in London Mikolajczyk had a meeting with Churchill to discuss the outcome of the Washington talks and asked Churchill for his help in arranging a conference with Stalin for him.

On July 13, 1944 Churchill sent the following telegram to Stalin:

1. M. Mikolajczyk has asked me to suggest to you that he should go to Moscow to discuss the whole situation with you.

2. Without expressing to you at this stage a definite view on the utility to the common effort of this plan, which touches upon matters of primary interest to the Soviet Union, I make the following comments:

(1) I think you will find M. Mikolajczyk congenial and reasonable, and I hope that Russo-Polish relations will get on to a new footing if you meet him face to face.

(2) It is only by this means that military action against Germany by the forces of the resistance movement in Poland can be fully coordinated with the action of the advancing Russian armies. I understand that M. Mikolajczyk has some important plans for immediate wide-scale action to put before you.

(3) While I am not authorized to inform you that M. Mikolajczyk is ready to agree in advance to all that the Soviet Government has asked of Poland, he realizes that he will have to make important concessions, particularly territorial concessions, to you.

3. M. Mikolajczyk assures me that he is in contemplation of a recon-

struction of his Government. The question of personalities will not be allowed to obstruct an agreement. The members of his Government have put their offices at his disposal, though he has told them to carry on for the time being.

4. Besides this, it has already been decided to appoint some new man from Poland as President-substitute in the place of General Sosnkowski. M. Mikolajczyk assures me that it is his intention to make a precise provision by some legislative act for the complete subordination of the office of Commander-in-Chief to the Polish Government.

5. M. Mikolajczyk says that he intends to broaden the basis of his Government by the inclusion of new elements, especially from among Poles in Poland. Precise decisions would, however, have to await the result of his proposed visit to Moscow and contact between Mikolajczyk and the Poles in Russia.[70]

4. The Polish Endeavor to Settle the Dispute Directly with Stalin

Stalin responded promptly by inviting Mikolajczyk to Moscow. After Mikolajczyk left London for Moscow the Soviets peremptorily confronted him with a new *fait accompli*.

The Soviets Form the Lublin Committee. On July 22, 1944 at 8:15 P.M. Radio Moscow announced that the Polish Committee of National Liberation had been formed in Chelm—presumably to make sure that Mikolajczyk would have to take people from Poland into his Government. Moscow desired that her people in Poland should not be omitted from any future Polish Government.

A decisive effort has begun to drive the German invaders out of Poland. In the presence of these historical events, the National Council in the Homeland appoints the Polish Committee for National Liberation as temporary executive authority to direct the fight of the people for liberation, to achieve independence, and to rebuild the Polish State.[71]

On the same day, the National Council issued the following decree:

The Polish National Council has decided:
1. To assume the supreme power over the Polish Army in the U.S.S.R.
2. To unify the People's Army with the Polish Army in the U.S.S.R.
3. That the unified Armies shall be called the Polish Army.
4. To set up the Supreme Command of the Polish Army, which shall include: the Commander-in-Chief, two of his deputies, and two members of the Command.
5. That generals' ranks in the Polish Army shall be granted by the Presidium of the Polish National Council upon the motion of the Supreme Command. The power of granting any other officers' ranks shall be delegated by the Presidium of the Polish National Council to the Supreme Command.
6. That this decree does not prejudice the operational subordination of

the Polish Army to the Supreme Command of the Red Army operating on the Soviet-German front.[72]

This announcement forced the Polish Government to react swiftly and promptly. On July 25, 1944 the Polish Government submitted the following note to Prime Minister Churchill:

On July 22, 1944, at 8:15 P.M., the Moscow radio announced in Polish that a "Polish Committee of National Liberation" has been established in Chelm. The following points of this communiqué deserve special attention:

I. 1. The Committee has been formed in the first large town liberated from German occupation to the West of the frontier line established in the Soviet-German agreements of September 28 and October 4, 1939. Consequently, the town is situated in territory to which the Soviet Union made no claims so far and does not make any claims now. It is significant that on July 22, after the announcement by Radio Moscow of the communiqué concerning the occupation of Chelm issued by Soviet H. C. (High Command), the Polish national anthem was played.

2. The Committee has been formed on territory occupied by Soviet troops. Its formation, therefore, took place with the knowledge of the Soviet authorities of occupation. Moreover, the broadcasting of the communiqué by the official Soviet radio would indicate that the Soviet Government approves of it, although no formal announcement by the competent authorities of the Soviet Union has been made in this matter.

3. While it is true that the Committee has not thus far assumed the title of Government, nevertheless its organization is copied on that of a normal government. Moreover, the Committee, after declaring that the Polish Government in London "and its agency in Poland is a self-styled authority, based on the illegal fascist Constitution of April, 1935," announced that the so-called National Council of the Homeland is "The sole legal source of authority in Poland." Being unable to do so, however, the Committee does not produce any reasons why the so-called National Council should be the sole legal source of authority in Poland. But such an assertion seems to indicate that the Committee and the Council tend to concentrate in their hands full state authority on all Polish territories situated to the west of the line of September 28, 1939, and the so-called National Council is described as the "Provisional Parliament of the Polish Nation." The Committee regards itself as the *de facto*, though provisional, Polish Government. The term "provisional" is applied in another description of the Committee as "the legal and provisional executive authority."

4. The statement of the Committee declaring "the *émigré* Government in London and its agency in Poland" as "illegal" gives rise to fear that the Committee will not only refuse to recognize the Polish Underground Movement, but that it intends to break up that organization and persecute its members, who for nearly five years risked their lives in fighting the German authorities and occupation troops, thereby aiding the war effort of the United Nations.

5. The Committee has also announced its political, economic, and social program as well as its intention to put these programs into effect at once

by taking over authority on the territories gradually occupied by Soviet troops. ("The Polish Committee of National Liberation" is taking over authority on liberated Polish territory.) They also announce their intention to form their own local administrative committees and to reconstruct the entire governmental machinery of the Polish State, including the courts of justice and a citizens' militia.

6. The Committee is composed mostly of communists, either completely unknown to the Polish people or of secondary importance.

II. In view of the above, it cannot be doubted that with the consent of the Soviet Government facts have been accomplished on Polish territory, undisputed by the Soviet Union and indicating its intention to impose on the Polish people an illegal administration which has nothing in common with the will of the nation. All this is happening in contradiction to the repeated assurances of Marshal Stalin that he desires the restoration of an independent Poland. Such moves, enacted on the territory of Poland, especially if the announced intentions of the Polish Committee for National Liberation should be realized, constitute an attempt against the independence of Poland.

III. The Polish Government has the honor to approach the British Government, which guaranteed the independence and vital interests of Poland, with a request that the situation created by unilateral acts accomplished under Soviet occupation, should be jointly considered by the two Governments. The above-mentioned facts should undoubtedly and directly interest the British Government as they make it impossible for the legal Government of Poland, recognized by the British and American Governments, to take over the administration of Polish territories not included in Soviet claims. It was only two months ago that the Prime Minister, Mr. Churchill stated on May 24: " * * * the Polish Government which we recognize and which we have always recognized."

The more officially the Soviet Government treats this matter, the more difficult will it be for them to withdraw from its policy of *faits accomplis.* An immediate *démarche* in Moscow by the British Government seems, therefore, to be indispensable. Moreover, in order to avoid further confusion, it would be highly desirable if the British Government would seize an early public occasion in order to reiterate the Prime Minister's declaration of May 24.

Should the matter in its initial stage be left without an immediate and explicit reaction on the part of the British Government, it may render it considerably more difficult in the future for the British Government to fulfill its obligations towards Poland while maintaining at the same time political collaboration with the Soviet Government, because with the occupation by Soviet troops of further Polish territories the Soviet Government will in all probability engage itself increasingly in a policy the first open manifestation of which is the creation of the Polish Committee of National Liberation.

London, 24 July 1944.

The biographical data on the members of the new Committee was attached.[73]

Subsequent reports indicated that the Soviets had launched a full-scale political offensive, their aim being to force Mikolajczyk to capitulate to Soviet demands or else to eliminate the Polish Government from the political scene.

On July 27, 1944 the London *Evening Standard* published a Reuters telegram concerning details of the Agreement signed in Moscow between the Government of the U.S.S.R. and the Polish Committee of National Liberation.

An agreement has been signed by the Soviet Government and the Polish Committee of National Liberation on relations between the Polish Administration and the Soviet High Command in Poland, Moscow radio announced today.

The ceremony took place in the Kremlin in the presence of Marshal Stalin and for Russia, M. Vyacheslav Molotov, Commissar for Foreign Affairs; M. Andrei Vyshinsky, Vice-Commissar; M. Chkalov, of the Soviet Foreign Commissariat; and Marshal Zhukov.

The Polish Committee of National Liberation was represented by M. Andrzej Witos, Vice-Chairman; M. Edward Morawski, Head of the Foreign Affairs Department; and Dr. Boleslaw Drobner, Director of Press Affairs.

General Michal Rola-Zymierski,[74] the new Commander-in-Chief of the United Polish Armed Forces, was also present.

The Agreement contains ten clauses:

1. Supreme power in the zone of military operations where Red Army units are fighting on Polish territory is, for the period necessary for the conclusion of such operations, vested in the Soviet Commander-in-Chief.

COOPERATION

2. The Polish Committee on Polish liberated territory is to establish a Polish administration in accordance with the Polish constitution, create the machinery for recruiting men for the Polish armed forces, and ensure active cooperation with the Soviet Commander-in-Chief.

3. The Polish military formations being created in the Soviet Union will operate only on Polish territory.

4. Liaison between the Soviet Commander-in-Chief and the Polish Committee of National Liberation will be maintained through a Polish Military Mission.

5. In the area of military operations, liaison between the Polish administration and the Soviet Commander-in-Chief will be maintained through an accredited agent of the Polish Committee of National Liberation.

FULL RESPONSIBILITY

6. As soon as an area of liberated Poland ceases to be a zone of direct military operations, the Polish Committee will assume full responsibility in matters of Civil Government.

7. All Soviet Army men will, while on Polish territory, be under the jurisdiction of the Soviet Command. Polish servicemen will be under Polish military law. Polish military law applies also to civilians, even

where crimes are committed against Soviet citizens, except in zones of military operations.

8. In all zones of operations of Soviet troops and Polish armed forces, the Polish forces will be under the Soviet Commander-in-Chief for operational matters and subordinate to the Polish Command in matters of personnel and internal organization.

9. Questions of finance and supply of both Soviet and Polish troops in Poland will be dealt with in a separate agreement.

10. This agreement comes into force with its signature by the contracting parties.[75]

General Nikolai Alexandrovich Bulganin was appointed the Soviet Plenipotentiary to what was later known as the Lublin Committee.

All this took place while the Polish Prime Minister, with the approval of Churchill and Roosevelt, was flying to Moscow on Stalin's invitation.

On his way to Moscow, Mikolajczyk landed in Cairo in order to meet with Tomasz Arciszewski, the courageous leader of the Polish Socialist Party. He, together with Jozef Retinger, Tadeusz Celt, and two others had been transported there from Poland by aircraft (flown by a Polish military pilot) to give Mikolajczyk an account of the latest situation in the country, so that the Prime Minister would be well prepared for discussion in Moscow.

Upon Mikolajczyk's arrival in Moscow, the British Government, through its Ambassador Sir Archibald Clark Kerr, suggested the following points which would "strengthen" the Polish hand in negotiations with the Russians:

1. The remodeling of the Polish Government so as to exclude certain elements believed here to be reactionary and anti-Soviet.

2. The acceptance of the Curzon Line as a basis for negotiations.

3. Some kind of withdrawal from the suggestion that the killing at Katyn was done by the Russians . . . the easiest way out of this difficulty would be the acceptance of the findings of the Soviet Commission that had enquired into the crime.

4. Some kind of a working arrangement with the Polish Committee of National Liberation.[76]

Mikolajczyk refused to consider these suggestions and was disturbed to discover that the British were on the Soviet side in these issues. This was undoubtedly known by the Soviets and meant that the chances for any reasonable solution were very small, because the Soviets would see no need to compromise.

On July 31, 1944 Mikolajczyk was received by Molotov. Mikolajczyk expressed his willingness to reach an agreement and asked for an appointment with Stalin. Molotov replied that it would be better if Mikolajczyk would see the Lublin representatives who were in Moscow. Mikolajczyk answered that this should not be excluded but that he would prefer to see Stalin first.

Molotov then said that Stalin was preoccupied with military problems and that there would be no possibility of seeing him before three or four days had elapsed. He therefore advised Mikolajczyk to see the Lublin people, because they had better information as to what was going on in Poland. Mikolajczyk said that he had direct information from Poland himself. In the last four weeks three couriers had come to London from Poland, and on his way to Moscow he had met five emissaries in Africa who had just come from Poland a few days before. Molotov side-tracked Mikolajczyk's reply and stated that the Red Armies were ten kilometers from Warsaw.

The meeting ended with Molotov's promise to arrange a meeting with Stalin in three days.[77]

This arrangement to keep the Polish Prime Minister waiting for three days was carefully staged to humiliate him. The insistence for talks with what later came to be known as the Lublin Committee was meant to put the Lublin Committee on an equal footing with the London Government. The Moscow press barely mentioned, on its last pages, the "arrival of the London Poles" while it devoted considerable space on its first pages to the arrival of the Lublin Poles.

The Warsaw Uprising. While Mikolajczyk waited for his appointment with Stalin, the Warsaw uprising began on August 1. The uprising was due to the fact that the Soviet Army was on the outskirts of Warsaw and that the Germans were planning to mobilize and transport all able-bodied persons in Warsaw into their war industries and other related work in Germany before evacuating Warsaw. Furthermore, the Polish Government and the leadership of the Underground Army were anxious to help the approaching Red Army and, by so doing, to prove that their determination to fight the Nazi invaders had not weakened since 1939. In this way they hoped to repudiate the Soviet allegations that the Polish Underground was not only impotent but also indifferent to an Allied victory.

Before his departure for Moscow, Mikolajczyk, after a conference with his Cabinet and General Sosnkowski, the Commander-in-Chief of all the Polish forces, gave a free hand to General Tadeusz Bor-Komorowski to decide whether and when to order the general uprising. This delegation of authority was essential since only the commander on the spot had, at his disposal, all the military information and organizations needed to make such a decision. From the political point of view such an uprising, if decided on the spot, was advantageous.

By the end of July 1944 the mechanized units of the Red Army approached Warsaw's suburbs. The Soviets began urging the people of Warsaw to help them by rising against the Germans.

On July 29, 1944 at 8:15 P.M., the Union of Polish Patriots broadcast the following appeal to the people of Warsaw over the Kosciuszko Station in Moscow:

Fight the Germans. No doubt Warsaw already hears the guns of the battle which is soon to bring her liberation. Those who have never bowed their heads to the Hitlerite power will again, as in 1939, join in battle against the Germans, this time for decisive action. The Polish Army entering Polish territory, trained in the U.S.S.R., is now joined to the People's Army to form the corps of the Polish Armed Forces, the armed force of our nation in its struggle for independence. Its ranks will be joined tomorrow by the sons of Warsaw. They will, together with the Allied Army, pursue the enemy westward, wipe the Hitlerite vermin from the Polish land and strike a mortal blow at the beast of Prussian imperialism. For Warsaw, which did not yield, but fought on, the hour of action has now arrived. The Germans will no doubt try to defend themselves in Warsaw, and add new destruction and more thousands of victims. Our houses and parks, our bridges and railway stations, our factories and our public buildings will be turned into defense positions. They will expose the city to ruin and its inhabitants to death. They will try to take away all the most precious possessions and turn into dust all that they have to leave behind. It is therefore a hundred times more necessary than ever to remember that in the flood of Hitlerite destruction all is lost that is not saved by active effort; that by direct active struggle in the streets of Warsaw, in its houses, factories and stores we not only hasten the moment of final liberation but also save the nation's prosperity and the lives of our brethren.[78]

On July 31 all the high civilian and military authorities of the Underground were gathered in Warsaw to make a decision. They knew that the Nazis were mobilizing men to build fortifications and were mining the city for destruction. If the Underground did not respond to the Soviet appeals, Red propaganda would brand it as a collaborator with the Nazis or would use that negative response to prove to the Americans and to the British that all the talk of the London Government about the Underground was just an invented story. This in turn would enable the Red Army and the NKVD to liquidate them quietly.

Besides these considerations, the Poles, after five years of slavery and torture, were waiting for the opportunity to take revenge on the Nazis. The prospect of immediate Soviet support implied that the whole thing would be over in a very short time.

At 5:00 P.M. on August 1, the uprising in Warsaw began. It was a gesture of welcome to the Soviets. Warsaw was ready to welcome the Red Army to the free capital of an exhausted but undefeated nation. At that point, Soviet guns became silent and the Red offensive came to an abrupt stop.

On August 2, 1944 Prime Minister Churchill made the following declaration concerning Poland in the House of Commons:

> This, in my opinion, is a hopeful moment for Poland, for whose rights and independence we entered the war against Germany. We therefore did our best, my Right Hon. Friend (Eden) and I and others, late into the night, to promote the visit of Mr. Mikolajczyk and other members of his Cabinet to Moscow, where Marshal Stalin was willing to receive them. The President of the United States was also favorable. How could it be otherwise in these matters, considering his deep interest in the Polish question? The Russian Armies now stand before the gates of Warsaw. They bring the liberation of Poland in their hands. They offer freedom, sovereignty, and independence to the Poles. They ask that there should be a Poland friendly to Russia.
>
> This seems to me very reasonable, considering the injuries which Russia has suffered through the Germans marching across Poland to attack her. The Allies would welcome any general rally or fusion of Polish forces, both those who are working with the Western Powers and those who are working with the Soviet. We have several gallant Polish divisions fighting the Germans in our Armies now and there are others who have been fighting in Russia. Let them come together. We desire this union and it would be a marvelous thing if it could be proclaimed, or at least its foundations laid, at the moment when the famous capital of Poland, which so valiantly defended itself against the Germans, has been liberated by the bravery of the Russian Armies.[79]

A few days later the people of Warsaw were shocked to see the withdrawal of the Red Army from the outskirts of the city. The tragedy had begun.

The Germans decided to suppress the uprising in a merciless manner—by five combat divisions. These were commanded by General Stahl and *S.S. Obergruppenführer von dem Bach*. In addition, they soon were reinforced by the Hermann Goering Division rushed up from Italy; the S.S. Totenkopf Division from Rumania, and the S.S. Viking Division, withdrawn from the Lublin front. They used all their power and employed every means to break the resistance of Warsaw.

On August 3, prior to seeing Stalin, Mikolajczyk received the following telegram from his deputy in London.

> The latest reports from Poland describe the attitude to our Underground Army as follows:

1. Everything east of the Curzon Line and the river San is treated as an organic part of the U.S.S.R.

Our units of the Underground Army located in these areas are faced with two alternatives:

(1) complete disarming,

(2) inclusion into the Berling Army.

The Soviet authorities announced a general mobilization. The Commander of the Lwow Province met General Zymierski and afterwards decided to disband his units. His action was supported by our local political circles. We have no further news from the Wilno Province.

2. In the territories west of the Curzon Line the situation is not yet clear. There are sporadic cases of disarmament, but it is difficult yet to establish the pattern.[80]

These facts stimulated Mikolajczyk's determination to clarify the whole situation and, if possible, to reach an agreement.

On the same day, August 3, at 9:00 P.M. Stalin received Mikolajczyk. Stalin began by saying that in the present international situation he considered the liberation of Poland as his duty.

Mikolajczyk, after expressing his appreciation for these professed intentions, proceeded to say:

I introduce myself to you as a peasant and a worker, who through my own efforts achieved a few things in life. As a youngster, I strove with the deepest conviction towards the solidarity of the Slav nations against German expansion. Having lived in western Poland, I know their thinking and ambitions. Now, on behalf of my Government, I want to present you with a program for the solution of our question.

1. The establishment of a firm relationship between the Soviet Union and Poland.

2. The supplementing of the Polish-Soviet Treaty of 1941, with an agreement which will regulate the procedure of taking over the territories liberated by the Red Army. I admit that the latest events (the signing of an agreement between Moscow and Lublin) which took place since I left London somewhat change this problem.

3. I should like to know what you think about the future frontiers between Russia and Poland and I would like to discuss them with you.

4. A time is approaching when Warsaw will be liberated. Since August 1st a struggle is going on between our Underground Army and the Germans. Although they need supplies from outside very badly, they have achieved considerable successes. We are contemplating the organization of a Government in Poland which will be based, as of now, on four political parties, and we intend to include the PPR (Polish Workers' Party) in it as well. We intend to hold a free election. This will provide for changes in the Constitution, for the election of the President, and for the ratification of the new Polish frontiers.

STALIN. Your postulates are important from a political and practical point of view, but you omitted the existence of the Committee of National Liberation. Did you do it purposely? In my opinion one cannot by-pass it. We have just concluded an agreement with them to take over the liberated territories of Poland. Can one not see the importance of that fact?

MIKOLAJCZYK. This must be a misunderstanding, because in my second point I mentioned this new development. I want to inform you that in Warsaw we have a Vice Premier and three Cabinet members of my Government. They are running the underground Government of Poland and I trust that nothing will happen to them when they will soon come out from hiding. One should remember that the four Parties represented in my Government and in the underground organizations which have fought the Germans for the last five years should be permitted to express their will. They are also willing to cooperate with the communists. We are anxious to unify all social and political forces in Poland in order to serve most efficiently the Polish nation.

STALIN. Have you finished?

MIKOLAJCZYK. In broad outlines, yes.

STALIN. Mr. Premier, in order to avoid a misunderstanding, I want to say that the Soviet Government is indifferent to how many parties will be represented in the Polish Government. The point lies elsewhere. The essential thing is that the Soviet Government is anxious that all truly democratic parties in Poland form one bloc as a basis for a new Polish Government. The Soviet Government will support such a solution.

MIKOLAJCZYK. The present Polish Government represents four parties which are truly and sincerely democratic. As an example I want to say that in 1939 we disbanded both Houses of our Parliament and limited the power of the President of the Republic. Now we are striving to establish in Warsaw a reorganized Government based on the broad masses and not necessarily under my leadership.

STALIN. Let us agree what we are talking about. If you are not going to talk about the Committee which is a new power well established in Poland then I shall not talk about it either. If you agree to talk about it, then we can discuss the relationship between the Polish Government in London and the Committee of National Liberation.

MIKOLAJCZYK. I am ready to talk with everybody, and in that way we can clear many problems.

STALIN. As you know, Prime Minister Churchill informed me that you were willing to come to Moscow and he asked me if I would receive you. He expressed the conviction that the main purpose of your trip would be to discuss the unification of all political forces in Poland and he thought that I might be helpful in that matter. I agreed with that and therefore I believe that the problem of mutual relations between the Polish Government and the Committee cannot be ignored in our efforts to find a solution.

MIKOLAJCZYK. I don't want to by-pass it and for this reason I am asking you to arrange that I may go to Warsaw. . . .

STALIN [interrupting]. But there are Germans.

MIKOLAJCZYK. Warsaw will be free any day.

STALIN. God grant that it be so.

MIKOLAJCZYK. Once there, we shall be able to form a new Government.

STALIN. Please remember that the Soviet Government does not recognize the Polish Government, with which it broke off relations. At the same time the Soviet Government maintains relations with the Lublin Committee, and we signed a treaty with it and we are helping it. This should be taken into consideration.

MIKOLAJCZYK. Do you mean to tell me that there is no room in Poland for anybody else besides the Lublin Committee?

STALIN. No. I don't have that in mind, but I believe that before we establish normal relations between ourselves it would be well to end this duplicate source of power—one in London and the other in Chelm. In this I agree with Churchill that it would be well to unite all Poles in order to form one Provisional Government. This should be done by the Poles themselves.

MIKOLAJCZYK. It seems to me that the difference between our two views is smaller than it appears. However, I represent four major political parties while my "friends" from the Committee represent only an insignificant fraction of Polish public opinion. There are no respectable socialists in the Committee. . . .

STALIN [interrupting]. What do you mean by "respectable"?

MIKOLAJCZYK. I mean a politician who in the last five years of war has not changed his political convictions and remained firm in the struggle against the Germans.

STALIN. You have to excuse me, but your criterion of political leaders does not seem to me to be convincing. Poland has been under German occupation for over four years. In that time, new personalities have appeared in Poland and, therefore, it is impossible to refer only to the old authorities. The Peasant Party is not only Witos. The political atmosphere under the occupation has moved towards the left. One has to realize that young men, new leaders, born of the struggle and the sacrifice, have to be reckoned with. Take the Red Army—new people are coming up into responsible positions while the old ones descend into the shadows. Great changes are taking place, and one cannot foresee them *a priori*. You should also look for new people—like Osobka-Morawski and others.

MIKOLAJCZYK. I would like to present to you, Marshal Stalin, new young men who, after the execution of Rataj and Professor Piekalkiewicz, the former Delegates of my Government, are leading the Peasant Party in Poland. Less than a week ago in Cairo I met one of them who was on his way from Poland to London. This young man organized the educational department in our underground organization. Also young women have proved to be extremely able and are coming to the top. All the leadership of our underground organizations is in the hands of a new, young, and dynamic generation, which undoubtedly will lead Poland to a better future when the war is over.

STALIN. When we came to Poland we realized what was going on. I have reports from our military commanders about your Underground Army. What kind of army is it—without artillery, tanks, airforce? They do not even have enough hand weapons. In modern war this is nothing. Those are small partisan units and not regular formations. I hear that the Polish Government instructed these units to chase the Germans out of Warsaw. I don't understand how they can do it. They don't have sufficient strength for that. On the whole, these people do not fight Germans but are hiding themselves in the forests. When one of our commanders asked one of these soldiers who came out of hiding why he was not fighting he replied that for every killed German ten Poles would be executed as a reprisal. There are many stupid people in these units. I am talking about the facts which I have from the best sources. For instance, in the Chelm region the Polish military commander announced a general mobilization of the Polish population between the ages of sixteen to sixty-five. This was a careless and a very dangerous step, because all the people thought that after the expulsion of the Germans the war would be over. Here he ordered a mobilization—and who will take part in the harvest? People were furious because they thought that it must be some provocation. We had to arrest that commander and call off his order. There are others among your people who in public meetings say loudly that the old occupants left but the new arrived. How can we deal with such people?

MOLOTOV. Poles are distributing a mass of literature in the Polish language which spreads hate and resentment of everything that is Soviet. We can show you many of these publications.

MIKOLAJCZYK. It might be true that some irresponsible elements are publishing such literature or expressing themselves in such a manner in public meetings. But all this will disappear if only news will be spread that a new understanding has been reached between Poland and the Soviet Union on the basis of which new Polish authority will rest on a broad coalition of all political parties. Please remember that in all occupied countries Germans found their Quislings, but not in Poland. It is true that the Polish Underground Army does not have artillery, tanks, and an airforce, but in spite of this, they continue to fight the Germans. This is proof of great courage and determination on their side. For five years they have been continuously carrying out sabotage. Recently, on the order of the Polish Government, important centers of communication and factories were destroyed around Lwow. In spite of the absence of Soviet-Polish relations, our people continue to fight the Germans in Wilno and Nowogrodek Provinces. Today I received a telegram with the news that 40,000 men started the Warsaw uprising. They ask for arms supplies on the points which they are controlling. I cannot recall all sabotage carried out by them but they are recorded in the Allied General Headquarters and they may be obtained by the Soviet authorities. Your example about Chelm proves only that Poles were ready to forget the harvest in order to defeat the occupant.

STALIN. From the military point of view this commander of Chelm was crazy. . . . We don't have much evidence that the Home Army has done anything of significance.

MIKOLAJCZYK. Can you help those people by supplying them with arms?

STALIN. We will not permit any action behind our lines. For this reason you have to reach an understanding with the Lublin Committee. We are supporting them. If you don't do it, then nothing will come out of our talk. We cannot tolerate two governments.

MIKOLAJCZYK. We are ready to talk and we don't want two governments.

The discussion becomes rhetorical and fruitless. Then Mikolajczyk asked:

How do you picture the future Polish frontiers?

STALIN. In the following way. In the East the Curzon Line. On the West along the Oder and Neisse rivers, and the bulk of East Prussia on the north.

MIKOLAJCZYK. I am convinced that you don't intend to do injustice to Poland in this historical moment when we have the unusual opportunity to establish permanent good relations between our two countries. Yet to deprive Poland of these centers of Polish culture and tradition, such as Lwow and Wilno, will hurt our people badly.

STALIN. I don't intend to harm the Polish nation and I don't want to harm the Lithuanian and Ukrainian nations. As you know all nations, big or small, have the same rights. Such is our Lenin's ideology. I don't want to harm anybody. Poles, Ukrainians, or Byelorussian Slavs should live in friendship on the basis that one friend does not take the territories of the other friend. This is my view of this matter.

MIKOLAJCZYK. I know the attitude of the Polish people, and therefore I am certain that they would consider such a decision as unjust and harmful. The nation would not understand why they would lose half of Poland when they started war because they did not want to give up the "corridor." Russia has immense territories and does not need more land. We do not want to keep minorities in the frontier of 1939. We are willing to grant separation to those minorities which do not want to be with us. Poles will not understand such injustice.

STALIN. We aren't talking about any injustice.

MIKOLAJCZYK. From the economic point of view we would lose rich oilfields and sources of artificial fertilizer which is so needed for our agriculture. When you talk about the friendship of the Slav nations you cannot treat one of them unjustly.

STALIN. There are certain nationalistic Russian circles which accuse us Bolsheviks of weakening Russia in favor of Poland. They remind us that before 1914 Poland was a part of Russia and now we talk about Polish independence. As you see there will always be accusations, and it is silly to listen to them.

But, Mr. Premier, the Curzon Line was not invented by the Russians or Poles but by Lloyd George, Clemenceau, and Curzon. When they developed that line during the Versailles Conference the Russians were not there. The Curzon Line was the result of objective scientific study and it was a compromise. Not many Russians would be willing to grant Poland Bialystok, but in spite of that fact we will support the Curzon Line, and we are doing so.

MIKOLAJCZYK. As far as I know the Curzon Line did not include Galicia.

STALIN. There is no point discussing it. We were not there.

MIKOLAJCZYK. But the Curzon Line was only a demarcation line from the north to the Russian-Austrian frontier. The Soviet side itself offered a better frontier to Poland. I am certain that if you, Marshal Stalin, forget those documents and take under consideration our wishes you will receive the gratitude of the whole Polish nation and will find in it a faithful ally.

STALIN. I cannot harm the Ukrainians. I am too old to act against my own conscience. Also remember that the Ukrainians ask for the Chelm region. We are against that. We have 1,100,000 Ukrainian soldiers in the Red Army. The most outstanding tank units are Ukrainian, e.g., that of Bondarenko. It is unfortunate, but we cannot harm the Ukrainians.

MIKOLAJCZYK. But you cannot harm the Polish nation which lost over five million people in the fight against the common enemy.

STALIN. You are right, Mr. Premier. I shall never permit any political, economic, or territorial harm to the Polish nation. We work for the liberation of Poland and the Ukraine. If you insist on your conditions there shall never be any harmony between Poles and Ukrainians.

MIKOLAJCZYK. Do you expect to settle the frontier problem just now?

STALIN [slowly, after reflection]. The problem of frontiers can be settled with the new Polish Government. It is up to you and the Lublin Committee to reach an understanding which will unite all Poles. This is the most urgent matter.

MIKOLAJCZYK. I will try. What would you advise me to do now?

STALIN. I think that the two political groups should get together to talk and to reach an understanding. Then we can come to the Soviet-Polish question.

MIKOLAJCZYK. During my conversation with Molotov and according to his suggestion I invited Osobka-Morawski as Chairman of the Committee and Andrzej Witos as Deputy for talks, but it appears that they are in Chelm.

STALIN. We can arrange that they will meet you, either in Kiev or in Moscow. Is it all right with you?

MIKOLAJCZYK. I can talk to anybody and anywhere. For practical reasons I would prefer to do so in Moscow.

[Stalin gave an order to Molotov to arrange that meeting for the day after the next.]

Before parting Mikolajczyk asked Stalin to protect the Underground officers and men who were instructed to reveal themselves to the Red Army.

Stalin assured him that nothing would happen to them.[81]

Complying with Stalin's wishes, on August 6, 1944 Mikolajczyk met with the Lublin representatives, whom he, together with nearly all other Poles, considered as the only edition of Polish Quislings who emerged from World War II, but he had to control his feelings. He began by summarizing his conversation with Stalin and asked whether the Lublin people wished to retain in Poland the cities of Lwow and Wilno—two centers of Polish culture. This would be a basis for reaching a rapprochement. He felt that the social and economic programs of Lublin and London did not differ much and that the question of frontiers was the only one which might divide them. He stated the views of his Government on this subject by saying that they were of the opinion that Poland should not come out of this war with smaller territories. Then he stated that he had no personal ambitions and felt that the people from inside Poland should have a decisive role in governing the country. In his view, the new Government should be based on a coalition of the four main parties, plus the PPR and the Communist Party, if they represented any fragment of society. As soon as possible, a *Sejm* (Parliament) should be elected which would decide the selection of the President. When Warsaw was liberated, all democratic forces should settle the basis for the future cooperation of the political parties. In the field of defense, he felt that a war cabinet should be created to which all armed forces would be subordinated.

He ended by bringing up the Warsaw uprising and appealed to General Zymierski to supply it with arms from the Soviet side. It should be of indifference who ordered the uprising, so long as it was directed against the German occupants.

Wanda Wasilewska stated that she had talked with a person who left Warsaw on August 4 and who said that there was no uprising whatsoever. Mikolajczyk replied that this could easily be verified.

Osobka-Morawski observed that the Lublin Committee was for frontier adjustments *now* so that there would not be any trouble later. Then he proposed to postpone the discussion of frontiers until a later time. The other members of the Lublin delegation upheld the Soviet argument for a frontier along the Curzon Line. When Mikolajczyk asked for a postponement of the frontier issue until the peace conference, Osobka-Morawski rejected it by referring to Churchill's stand on the frontier question and especially to his speech in the House of Commons on February 22, 1944 in which he supported the Soviet claims. Further demands were made by the Lublin delegates to dissolve the Home Army and the London Government. The meeting was adjourned, to be resumed the next day.[82]

On August 7, they met again. Bierut stated that he was willing to have Mikolajczyk as Prime Minister together with Professor Grabski, Mr. Popiel from the Labor Party, and one Socialist (to be selected) from London. The rest of the eighteen-member Cabinet would be staffed by the Lublin Committee.

MIKOLAJCZYK. I am bound by loyalty to the President.

BIERUT. We reject the Constitution of 1935 and we stand on the Constitution of 1921.

MIKOLAJCZYK. I cannot by-pass the President, the Vice Premier, the three members of my Cabinet who are in Warsaw, and the Home Army. They cannot be ignored.

BIERUT. They were not loyal to Poland.

MIKOLAJCZYK. I cannot allow that you should pick and choose among us. It will be better if you will be responsible for the governing of Poland. We differ on the question of frontiers and the composition of the Government. You want to give us only 20% of the portfolios. I cannot accept that. You are exploiting the support of the Soviet Union. I don't exclude the possibility of further talks. I shall try to persuade my colleagues in London to make an effort to reach an understanding. Sooner or later we shall meet.

BIERUT. We have the support of the Soviet Union and we are representing the interests of Poland.

OSOBKA-MORAWSKI said that he had talked with Ambassador Kerr and Harriman. According to him, Kerr spoke ironically about the stupid people who expected a war between Russia and the Western Allies and praised those wise men who did not expect such things. Harriman stated that the cement which united the Three Big Allies was not based on temporary expediency. Neither America nor England would start a war because of the Curzon Line.

WASILEWSKA said that Stalin from the beginning was adamant about Lwow and Wilno and she questioned the wisdom of bringing Anglo-American pressure upon Russia on account of the frontiers.

Then BIERUT again brought up the point that he wished Mikolajczyk to be the Prime Minister.

MIKOLAJCZYK. If I wanted to come to Warsaw would you let me in?

BIERUT. If you come as a friend we shall receive you enthusiastically.

OSOBKA-MORAWSKI. But if you come as our opponent we will certainly imprison you.

BIERUT. Speed is of utmost importance. If we shall not reach an agreement here, we [the Lublin Committee] shall form a government ourselves.[83]

Mikolajczyk was getting discouraged. All the odds were against his Government, but he did not lose hope. In the meantime appeals were coming from Warsaw for help.

August 8, 1944

TOP SECRET

Most urgent telegram from London, from the Chiefs of Staff

We have been asked by General Sosnkowski to communicate to Marshal Stalin the following message from the Soviet Army Captain Kalugin which has been received from G.O.C. Polish Home Army, Warsaw:–Begins:–

I am in personal contact with the commander of the Warsaw Garrison who is leading the heroic partisan fight by the nation against the Hitlerite bandits. After acquainting myself with the general military situation I came to the conclusion that, in spite of the heroism of the Army and the entire Warsaw population there are still needs, which, if made good, would permit a speedier victory over our common foe. These needs are:

Automatic arms ammunition,
Grenades, anti-tank weapons,
Dropping arms on:–

Wilson Square, Invalid Square, Ghetto, Krasinski Square, Zelaiwa (Zelazna) Brama Square, Napoleon Square, Polish Mokotowskie, Koszary Szwolezerow (Cavalry Barracks) in Powisle and Bielany.

Recognition signals: White and red sheets.

The German Air Force is destroying the city and killing the civilian population. Please direct artillery fire on Vistula bridges in the Warsaw area, on Saski Garden, Aleje Jerozolimski, as these are the main channels of movement for the German army. The enemy is bombing from Okecie and Bielany airfields. The heroic population of Warsaw trusts that in a few hours time you will give them armed support. Help me to get in touch with Marshal Rokossovski.[84]

Transmitted through the British War Office, Telegram from London No. 03667—dated August 8, 1944.

1. Further our telegram today subject Captain Kalugin, following is message from officer commanding Garrison Warsaw which he desires to be transmitted through Moscow to Marshal Rokossowski, quote:–

Since August 1st I am fighting the Germans in Warsaw with help from the whole population and military organizations united within Home Army as well as such organizations as Workers' Militia, People's Militia, Polish People's Army, and others who joined us in the fight. We are fighting a strenuous battle. The Germans to ensure channels of retreat for their troops are burning the town and exterminating the population. At present we are still withholding the pressure of a great force of German armoured units and infantry. However, we already feel the scarcity of ammunition and heavy arms and a speedy relief therefore by your armies Marshal is necessary.

I have in my H.Q. a Soviet Officer, Captain Kalugin.[85] Would you forward for his use wireless technical particulars to enable him to communicate with you and in that way make it possible for me to coordinate our action. Unquote.

2. If liaison is to be arranged between Russians and Poles it seems that Captain Kalugin's request for wireless facilities should help. Grateful you put forward appropriate authorities.[86]

Mikolajczyk transmitted these messages to the Soviet authorities, including Stalin himself, pleading with them for help. The Soviets promised to consider them.

On August 9, 1944 at 9:30 P.M. Mikolajczyk was again received by Stalin, whom he told that he had had two meetings with the Lublin representatives. However, since the Soviet Government signed an agreement with the Lublin Committee while Mikolajczyk was on his way from London he did not have the proper authority to deal with this new situation. Therefore, he suggested that he return to London to consult his Cabinet and obtain permission about reaching an agreement. Stalin expressed his satisfaction of such a proposal.

Then MIKOLAJCZYK said:

Did I understand you properly that you favor the unification of all political forces in Poland under one leadership?

STALIN. Absolutely.

MIKOLAJCZYK. You don't plan to have the communists take over the leadership of the Government but you desire that all parties and orientations will be united in that Government?

STALIN. That is exactly my idea.

MIKOLAJCZYK. My task is very difficult because constitutional changes will be involved. We limited the extremes in the Constitution of 1935, but we cannot for the time being abandon it.

STALIN. Can't you reject some part of it?

MIKOLAJCZYK. It was on the basis of that Constitution that we concluded various treaties including the Soviet-Polish Treaty of 1941. I would not be for the preservation of that Constitution if we could find a way to preserve the legality of the head of the State. If we return to the Constitution of 1921 the Presidency will be at stake.

STALIN. Is it not possible to have a temporary Parliament act as a sovereign body? Obviously the Provisional Government can exist without the President. The general election may elect the President.

MIKOLAJCZYK. I hope to find some solution in London.

STALIN. It would be very well.

MIKOLAJCZYK. Now I would ask you for immediate help to Warsaw which has united all the people in a mortal struggle against the Germans.

STALIN. What kind of help do they need?

MIKOLAJCZYK. They need arms . . .

STALIN [in a long exposition listed the numerous strategical reasons why the Red Army could not take Warsaw so quickly as one would want].

MIKOLAJCZYK [quotes telegram of the Soviet Captain Kalugin which asks for help].

STALIN. Can we rely on this information?

MIKOLAJCZYK assured him that this was the true reflection of what was going on.

STALIN replied that if proper contact was established with Warsaw, he would help it.

MIKOLAJCZYK [in parting]. Could you not give me some hopeful word which would cheer up Polish hearts in these difficult times?

STALIN. Don't you attach too much faith to the significance of words? One doesn't have to believe in words. Acts are more important.

MIKOLAJCZYK. I believe in pronouncements which are combined with wisdom and power.

STALIN. I would like to have all Poles understand that the present leaders of Russia differ from the rulers of the Tsarist Russia. They wanted to destroy Poland. People often falsely say that we too have such a goal. We are not conducting the old policy of conquest and destruction of the Slav nations. For this reason we rejected Pan-Slavism in its old meaning. We recognize the equal rights of all Slav nations, particularly those who have become victims of the Second World War. If the present leading Polish political personalities will believe that we want a friendly Polish-Soviet relationship and that we want to change the historical trend of

Polish-Soviet relations, then we will be able to realize our plans. But Poles don't believe in it. [Mikolajczyk protests.] There are among you such individuals who state publicly that the old persecutors—the Germans —are leaving Poland and their place is being taken by new—Soviet—oppression. When such talk stops then friendship between our countries will begin.

MIKOLAJCZYK. Marshal Stalin, now you have the unusual opportunity not only to quiet those unbelievers but to capture Polish hearts by taking into consideration our national interests.

STALIN. In my conviction the Polish nation should not follow Soviet leadership but should go with us hand in hand. The Polish nation has its own ways. These may follow a separate path, but parallel to ours— directed against the Germans and oriented to mutual help between our two countries. It is not our duty to lead the Polish nation nor is it the Polish duty to lead Russia. If our two countries will conclude a treaty then we shall eliminate all the dangers which await us. This is our point of view.

MIKOLAJCZYK. Thank you very much for this statement. I am convinced that the Polish nation will never attempt to impose its power or outlook on anyone.

STALIN. Obviously. A friend never tries to impose anything on another friend.

MIKOLAJCZYK. I agree with what you have just said and I agree that Poland and the Soviet Union should go hand in hand in their own, as well as in the general interest.

STALIN. Poland should also preserve its relations with England and France and its friendship with the United States, so that Polish policy will rest not only on the East but also on the West.

MIKOLAJCZYK. After the defeat of Germany we must be vigilant so that Germany will not regain economic supremacy in Central and Eastern Europe.

STALIN. The Germans will rise again. They are a strong nation. From Bismarck's triumph in 1871, they needed forty years to undertake new aggression. After its failure twenty or twenty-two years of regeneration were sufficient to repeat that once more—this time almost successfully. Now, who knows if after twenty or twenty-five years they will not be once more ready to fight. Yes, Germany is a strong country even though Hitler is weakening it. But the German economic and military staff will survive Hitler. It is our conviction that the danger from Germany may repeat itself. For this reason, the present discussions which are going on in Washington about collective security are so urgent. I am for all possible and impossible repression of Germany. But, in spite of this, they may rise again. Therefore, we have to keep the sword ready. This sword will be a treaty between us and the forces provided by collective security.[87]

After that meeting Mikolajczyk returned to London for consultation with his Cabinet. He was ready to seek in earnest a compromise solution between the Soviet demands and the position of his Cabinet.

But the paramount and immediate problem facing the London Government was to provide help for Warsaw. The British and American Governments were supplied with all pertinent and factual data concerning Warsaw's uprising.

Churchill was anxious to help. On August 4, 1944 he wired Stalin:

At urgent request of Polish Underground Army we are dropping, subject to weather, about sixty tons of equipment and ammunition into the southwest quarter of Warsaw, where it is said a Polish revolt against the Germans is in fierce struggle. They also say that they appeal for Russian aid, which seems to be very near.[88]

The next day Stalin replied:

I have received your message about Warsaw. I think that the information which has been communicated to you by the Poles is greatly exaggerated and does not inspire confidence. One could reach that conclusion even from the fact that the Polish émigrés have already claimed for themselves that they all but captured Vilna with a few stray units of the Home Army, and even announced that on the radio. But that of course does not correspond with the facts. The Home Army of the Poles consists of a few detachments which they incorrectly call divisions. They have neither artillery nor aircraft nor tanks. I cannot imagine how such detachments can capture four tank divisions, among them the Hermann Goering Division.[89]

The Polish Government began to suspect that the Soviets had a political reason for preferring to take Warsaw from German hands, rather than from Poles whose primary allegiance was to the London Government.

On August 13 Mikolajczyk sent an urgent message to Stalin again asking for help.

On August 16 Stalin replied:

I received your letter about Warsaw. I have to inform you that after our conversations, I instructed the Soviet High Command to drop arms in the Warsaw region. In addition, one parachutist was dropped but he could not fulfill his mission because he was killed by the Germans.

Later when I got acquainted with the whole question I was convinced that the Warsaw action, which was undertaken without any knowledge of or consultation with the Soviet High Command, constituted a thoughtless brawl—which results in a pointless loss of its inhabitants. It should be added that the accusation campaign of the Polish press insinuates that the Soviet High Command cheated the people of Warsaw.

For these reasons the Soviet High Command openly decided to have nothing to do with the Warsaw brawl (see announcement of TASS of August 12) because it cannot and should not be responsible in any way for Warsaw's affairs.[90]

The Poles considered this reply as a cold-blooded Soviet rationalization of their political reasons for destroying the underground organization and for discrediting the London Government; yet nothing derogatory could be said publicly for fear of jeopardizing the faint hope that Stalin might be persuaded to send help.

On the same day, August 16, Vyshinsky told the United States Ambassador in Moscow:

The Soviet Government cannot, of course, object to English or American aircraft dropping arms in the region of Warsaw, since this is an American and British affair. But they decidedly object to American or British aircraft, after dropping arms in the region of Warsaw, landing on Soviet territory, since the Soviet Government does not wish to associate itself either directly or indirectly with the adventure in Warsaw.[91]

On August 18, 1944 Mikolajczyk replied to Stalin in the following manner:

Marshal Stalin, I understand that the Soviet High Command is not responsible for Warsaw's uprising; which we know now was premature and therefore could not have been pre-arranged with your forces. If certain elements of the Polish press express their nervousness in connection with this, it is only because they are deeply concerned with the tragic fate of the inhabitants of Warsaw. I can assure you that in the spirit of our friendly talks in Moscow I have done my best to stop this and I would wish to have the same spirit shown in this matter by the Soviet side.

Nevertheless, Mr. Marshal, the Warsaw uprising was ordered by the Commander-in-Chief of the Home Army who had the power to do so at the moment when the Soviet armies were approaching the capital and when the appeals of Radio Moscow were calling the people to armed action. For instance, I have before me a text of the radio appeal broadcast on July 29, at 8:15 P.M. by the Union of Polish Patriots from Moscow. If the people of Warsaw had remained passive until the Soviet armies entered Warsaw would they not have been justly criticized for being neutral? I personally learned about the Warsaw uprising during my visit to Moscow and immediately on August 2 I spoke of it to Foreign Minister Molotov, who assured me at that time that the Soviet armies were ten kilometers from Warsaw. It is also true that independently of the appraisal made of the events, the whole population, despite differences in political views, remained for eighteen days alone in its mortal struggle against the whole might of the German invaders. This was verified by the telegram of Captain Kalugin to you. Finally, it is also a fact that an open struggle against the Germans is spreading to other parts of Poland. These people should be helped not only for their own sakes but also in the interest of lasting Polish-Soviet friendship—which is so important for you, Mr. Marshal, and for me.

Once again I am turning to you, Marshal Stalin, with deep confidence, and I strongly appeal to you to establish contact between the Red Army and fighting Warsaw, and to help her with weapons to bomb the German centers and stop the German bombardments. At the same time I ask you to express your willingness to accommodate American planes which are ready to help Warsaw. I am convinced that you, Mr. Marshal, will show understanding of the weight and urgency of my personal appeal, and that therefore you will contribute to my efforts to improve permanently and fundamentally the political atmosphere between our countries.[92]

Stalin did not reply to this message.

The Polish Government turned to its Western Allies asking them for intervention with Stalin and for their direct help. In the meantime, the Germans issued an ultimatum, announcing that all civilians remaining in the city would be massacred.[93]

President Raczkiewicz sent an appeal to President Roosevelt in which he stated:

I grieve to say that during these fateful days the support, the need of which we have been constantly urging, has not materialized. In this struggle some scores of thousands of half-armed Polish soldiers of the Home force are singlehandedly defying German divisions heavily armed with tanks and strong air support. . . .

I appeal to you, Mr. President, to order the American Air Force in the European Theatre of war to give immediate support to the Garrison of Warsaw by dropping arms and ammunition, bombing objectives held in the Warsaw area by the enemy, and transporting Polish Airborne Units to take part in the fight for their capital.

Any delay in affording help spells disaster to Warsaw. The Polish people could never understand why it should fail now at a moment when the common cause of the United Nations is championed by military power of unexampled strength.[94]

A similar plea was sent to the British Government. In response, on August 18, in a message to Roosevelt, Churchill urged their issuing a strong appeal to Stalin to persuade him to extend his support to Warsaw. Two days later they sent the following joint appeal drafted by Roosevelt.

We are thinking of world opinion if the anti-Nazis in Warsaw are in effect abandoned. We believe that all three of us should do the utmost to save as many of the patriots there as possible. We hope that you will drop immediate supplies and munitions to the patriotic Poles in Warsaw, or will you agree to help our planes in doing it very quickly? We hope you will approve. The time element is of extreme importance.[95]

On August 22 they received the following reply from Stalin:

Sooner or later the truth about the group of criminals who have embarked on the Warsaw adventure in order to seize power will become known to everybody. These people have exploited the good faith of the inhabitants of Warsaw, throwing many, almost unarmed people, against the German guns, tanks, and aircraft. A situation has arisen in which each new day serves not the Poles for the liberation of Warsaw, but the Hitlerites who are inhumanly shooting down the inhabitants of Warsaw.[96]

Stalin refused to help directly or to allow the opening of his airfields to American planes. He was determined to allow the Warsaw Garrison to be destroyed by the Nazis in order to eliminate its influence on future policies.

The British press was silent about the Warsaw tragedy. This led Churchill to send, on August 23, the following note to his Minister of Information:

Is there any stop in the publicity of the facts about the agony of Warsaw, which seems, from the papers, to have been practically suppressed? It is not for us to cast reproaches on the Soviet Government, but surely the facts should be allowed to speak for themselves? There is no need to mention the strange and sinister behavior of the Russians, but is there any reason why the consequences of such behavior should not be made public? [97]

This meant that the German liquidation of the helpless city of Warsaw found its place again on the pages of the British press.

On August 25 Churchill, who was moved by the tragedy of Warsaw, made a courageous suggestion to Roosevelt.

As Stalin's reply evades the definite questions asked and adds nothing to our knowledge, I propose a reply on the following lines:
"We earnestly desire to send U. S. aircraft from England. Is there any reason why the refueling ground assigned to us behind the Russian lines should not be used by them to land on without inquiry as to their activities on the way? . . ."
In the event of his failing to reply to this, my feeling is that we ought to send the planes and see what happens. I cannot believe that they would be ill-treated or detained. Since this was signed I have seen that the Russians are even endeavoring to take away your airfields which are located at Poltava and elsewhere behind their lines. [98]

This time it was Roosevelt who was more mindful of Stalin's sensitive feelings. In reply to Churchill he stated:

I do not consider it would prove advantageous to the long-range general war prospect for me to join with you in the proposed message to Stalin, but I have no objection to your sending such a message if you consider it advisable to do so. In arriving at this conclusion I have taken into consideration Uncle J.'s present attitude towards the relief of the underground forces in Warsaw, as indicated in his message to you and to me, his definite refusal to allow the use by us of Russian airfields for that purpose, and the current American conversations on the subject of the subsequent use of other Russian bases. [99]

Churchill commented in a cryptic manner, "I had hoped that the Americans would support us in a drastic action." [100]

Despite this, the American and British Ambassadors intervened for the Poles in Moscow. Molotov informed them that the statements emanating from the Polish Government in London showed that the uprising was inspired by elements antagonistic to the Soviet Union. Since, Molotov concluded, the Soviet Union did not want "directly or indirectly to associate itself with the Warsaw adventure" it therefore could not lend its help in any form.[101] The Ambassadors did not persist in their efforts, presumably because neither the British nor the American intelligence services had supplied them with first-hand information about the Warsaw situation, and the Ambassadors were reluctant to make use of the reports given them by the Polish Government.

On August 31 General Bor reported to London:

The situation in the city of Warsaw as a whole, after one month of desperate fighting, is practically unchanged. Many German strongholds have been taken but the main ones are still intact. Warsaw is truly a city of ruins and the dead are either buried inside the ruins or alongside of them. The losses among the civilian population are very high. Today the German airforce dropped leaflets in which they stated that unless the fight were stopped at once, they would burn the whole city. There are only ruins left to be burnt. Despite all setbacks, the lack of expected help and the heavy losses, the determination of the people to fight to the last is as firm as ever.[102]

On September 1 Mikolajczyk asked Churchill if anything had been done to help Warsaw. Churchill replied that together with President Roosevelt he had sent a strong telegram to Stalin asking him for cooperation in this matter but that he had received a negative reply. "I could not believe it," said Churchill. Then he had suggested to Roosevelt to confront the Soviets with a *fait accompli* by sending a daytime American mass raid over Warsaw and have them land on the Soviet airfields, but the President could not accept that. Churchill said that he regretted this very much because it was the only right tactic which could successfully have solved the whole problem.[103] Those unsynchronized moods of Churchill and Roosevelt proved to be very costly to the Poles.

On September 2, 1944 the Council of National Unity sent an appeal for help to Churchill, Roosevelt, the Speaker of the House of Commons, the Executive of the Labor Party, the American Congress, and the International Red Cross. On September 9 a similar appeal was sent by the Mayor of Warsaw to the Lord Mayor of London and to the Mayor of New York City.[104] None of these efforts had any practical effect whatsoever.

While the struggle for the survival of Warsaw was going on, the Polish Government was not neglecting its effort to reach political accord with Moscow. Mikolajczyk's Cabinet, as well as its political representatives in Poland, realized that they had to put aside the problem of frontiers and try to save the future independence of the country. They were prepared for a compromise.

Writing about that phase of Soviet-Polish relations, Churchill recorded:

On September 1, I received the Polish Premier, Mikolajczyk, on his return from Moscow. I had little comfort to offer. He told me that he was prepared to propose a political settlement with the Lublin Committee, offering them fourteen seats in a combined government. These proposals were debated under fire by the representatives of the Polish Underground in Warsaw itself. The suggestion was accepted unanimously. Most of those who took part in these decisions were tried a year later for "treason" before a Soviet court in Moscow.[105]

On September 4 Churchill's Cabinet met to consider the fate of Warsaw. According to Churchill himself:

I do not remember any occasion when such deep anger was shown by all our members, Tory, Labour, and Liberals alike. I should have liked to say "We are sending our aeroplanes to land in your territory, after delivering supplies to Warsaw. If you do not treat them properly all convoys will be stopped from this moment by us." [106]

Reasons of broad strategy persuaded him not to do so. Instead, Churchill sent a message to Roosevelt:

The War Cabinet are deeply disturbed at the position in Warsaw and at the far-reaching effect on future relations with Russia of Stalin's refusal of airfield facilities.

Moreover, as you know, Mikolajczyk has sent his proposals to the Polish Committee of Liberation for a political settlement. I am afraid that the fall of Warsaw will not destroy any hope of progress, but will fatally undermine the position of Mikolajczyk himself.[107]

At this same time, a balanced but determined request was sent by Churchill to Stalin urging him to reconsider his stand.

The next day Roosevelt answered Churchill as follows:

Replying to your telegram, I am informed by my Office of Military Intelligence that the fighting Poles have departed from Warsaw and that the Germans are now in full control.

The problem of relief for the Poles in Warsaw has therefore, unfortunately, been solved by delay and by German action, and there now appears to be nothing we can do to assist them.[108]

This misinformation was soon corrected by the reports of continuous fighting in Warsaw, which was to last for another month. Their hope for help did not die, and they kept knocking at the doors of every power in the West.

On September 4, 1944 the women of Warsaw sent the following appeal to the Pope:

Most Holy Father, we Polish women in Warsaw are inspired with sentiments of profound patriotism and devotion for our country. For three weeks, while defending our fortress, we have lacked food and medicine. Warsaw is in ruins. The Germans are killing the wounded in hospitals. They are making women and children march in front of them in order to protect their tanks. There is no exaggeration in reports of children who are fighting and destroying tanks with bottles of petrol. We mothers see our sons dying for freedom and the Fatherland. Our husbands, our sons, and our brothers are not considered by the enemy to be combatants. Holy Father, no one is helping us. The Russian armies which have been for three weeks at the gates of Warsaw have not advanced a step. The aid coming to us from Great Britain is insufficient. The world is ignorant of our fight. God alone is with us. Holy Father, Vicar of Christ, if you can hear us, bless us Polish women who are fighting for the Church and for freedom.[109]

On September 5 Eden informed Mikolajczyk that the previous day Churchill had sent a telegram to Stalin which contained an appeal on behalf of the British War Cabinet to change his attitude towards Warsaw and to withdraw his objection against the American request to land on Soviet airfields. Another telegram had been sent to Roosevelt renewing the suggestion to organize an American mass flight over Warsaw and then land on Soviet airfields without prior Soviet consent to do so. Churchill wanted to share the full responsibility for such an act.

Mikolajczyk presented the hopeless situation of Warsaw and, in view of the fact that he could not do much to help it, decided to resign. At this point Eden pressed him not to do so and confidentially stated that Churchill had left for Quebec where he would meet Roosevelt. Before leaving, he had anticipated such an action by Mikolajczyk and charged Eden not to allow this to happen, "because we will not support any other head of the Polish Government. Although during the next peace conference he will not abandon his interest in Poland, now he will not support any other Premier." Furthermore, Eden stated that Mikolajczyk's resignation would leave a wide open field for Moscow to do what they wished in Poland.[110]

Under these circumstances, Mikolajczyk decided to stay and intensify his effort to get Western support.

On September 6 the Polish Government received the following telegram from Warsaw.

Warsaw has lost all hope of help from Allied air deliveries or from a Soviet advance which would liberate the city. The inhabitants of Warsaw now pin their faith on the capitulation of Germany because of their fear of destructive war operations on German soil. This may seem rather paradoxical in view of the proximity of the Red Forces, but it should be borne in mind that the population of Warsaw has been informed for more than a month that the Russians are at the gates of the city. The city is being systematically destroyed by high explosives and incendiary fire, district by district, so that little remains intact.[111]

On September 10 the Polish Government again appealed to Roosevelt and Churchill for help to Warsaw.

On September 12 Roosevelt replied:

I want to assure you that we are taking every possible step to bring Allied assistance as speedily as possible to the Warsaw Garrison. I realize fully the urgent importance of this matter.[112]

Churchill replied in a similar tone.

On September 10 Mikolajczyk was informed by Attlee that:

The Soviet Government stated that if the American and British Governments are convinced about the effectiveness of the air raids, then the Soviet Government will not oppose granting the privilege to the Allied planes to land on Soviet airfields, provided that a plan of such operations will be submitted to the Soviet authorities and will be agreed upon.[113]

This proved that when Churchill and Roosevelt were united and stood their ground that Stalin would change his rigid intransigence.

On September 12 a message from General Bor (the Commander-in-Chief of the Home Army) was delivered to the Soviet Ambassador in London, Lebedev, with the request to deliver it via Moscow to Marshal Rokossovsky. In it Bor was asking for assistance and a co-ordination of their efforts.[114]

Simultaneously, Roosevelt and Churchill pressed Stalin hard for Soviet help to Warsaw. Finally, Stalin yielded and agreed, in the latter part of September, to the proposed aerial shuttle operations. Two British and one American mission took part. About 37% of the supplies dropped, including food, ammunition, and medicine were accounted for.[115]

The American and British examples prompted the Soviets to do the same and they dropped some supplies, but their containers were defective for aerial delivery and almost all the contents were damaged when they hit the ground.

Valuable as this Western Allied help was for the defenders of the city, it came too late to change the military situation, which by that time was hopeless. The heroic city was approaching the end of its agony. Undoubtedly the Soviets were well aware of this fact, for on September 21 Warsaw reported that the Headquarters of the Polish

Army had finally established direct contact with the Soviet forces on the east bank of the Vistula. "Liaison is carried out by two officers who landed in Warsaw by parachute." [116]

Rokossovsky dispatched small units of Berling's Army to cross the Vistula, and they established bridgeheads from which they began shelling the city. But soon an overwhelming German force compelled them to withdraw.

On September 29 Premier Mikolajczyk sent a telegram to Marshal Stalin through the good offices of Prime Minister Churchill.

To MARSHAL STALIN, *Moscow.*
YOUR EXCELLENCY: After 60 days of relentless fighting against the common enemy the defenders of Warsaw have reached the limit of human endurance. General Bor reports that after the fall of the southern sector of resistance Warsaw can hold only for several days more. At this extreme hour of need I appeal to you, Marshal, to issue orders for immediate operations which would relieve the Garrison of Warsaw and result in the liberation of the capital. General Bor has addressed the same appeal to Marshal Rokossovsky.[117]

There was no reply to this message. The Soviets realized that the resistance would come to a quick end.

One of the last broadcasts from Warsaw was picked up in London:

This is the stark truth. We were treated worse than Hitler's satellites, worse than Italy, Rumania, Finland. May God, Who is just, pass judgment on the terrible injustice suffered by the Polish nation and may He punish accordingly all those who are guilty.

Your heroes are the soldiers whose only weapons against tanks, planes, and guns were their revolvers and bottles filled with petrol. Your heroes are the women who tended the wounded and carried messages under fire, who cooked in bombed and ruined cellars to feed children and adults, and who soothed and comforted the dying. Your heroes are the children who went on quietly playing among the smoldering ruins. These are the people of Warsaw.

Immortal is the nation that can muster such universal heroism. For those who have died have conquered, and those who live on will fight on, will conquer and again bear witness that Poland lives when the Poles live.[118]

On October 2, 1944 the heroic Garrison of Warsaw laid down its arms. The Germans were exhausted too. The dead could not challenge the laurels of victory which Rokossovsky's Army was soon to claim.

After sixty-two days of heroic effort the time came when no more could be done. Of the 40,000 members of the Polish Underground force which fought in Warsaw 15,000 were dead. Out of a population of a million nearly 250,000 were killed or wounded. The German Army, in its effort to squelch the uprising suffered the loss of 10,000 killed, 9,000 wounded, and 7,000 missing. The proportions of killed to wounded attested to the hand-to-hand character of the fighting.

The Poles who survived were taken away by the Germans, first into open air camps west of Warsaw where, without food or shelter, they spent several days. Then most of them were taken west into labor units.

Another report received by the Polish Government from Warsaw was most tragic in content:

The population, forcibly evacuated from Warsaw, is receiving no help whatsoever. The people are in a state of utter exhaustion. Among them are many sick and wounded. There are no drugs and no medical aid. People who are seriously ill are lying by the roadside in the cold. Hundreds of thousands camp in the open fields without food or shelter. Families are being separated.

The Germans have arrested all men between the ages of sixteen and forty and are deporting them in the direction of the Reich. Transports are leaving every day. Some go straight to the notorious death camp of Oswiecim (Auschwitz). Up to October 14, 12,000 people from Warsaw were sent to Oswiecim. Their fate was death. On October 7 the Germans began the mass murder of Polish prisoners in Oswiecim in stationary and mobile gas chambers of the type fitted on lorries. The lorries packed with people drive to Maczki, a place thirty miles north of Oswiecim. There the gas chambers are put in operation.

The Moscow radio unceasingly shouted: "Traitors! They surrendered to the Germans! . . ." [119]

On October 3 Mikolajczyk sent the following message to Churchill and to Ambassador Winant.

This is sad news which I have to impart to you today. In the last days the Germans have intensified their attacks against the Polish centers of resistance in Warsaw. German aircraft and artillery have again been very active. On the other hand, the Soviet Army, after a frustrated attempt to cross the Vistula, has stopped all activity. In those circumstances the center of the city—the last bastion of resistance—with 260,000 civilians, apart from the Home Army, has been compelled to cease further fighting after the last round of ammunition had been fired and the last supplies of food exhausted. Large numbers of wounded are dying in cellars without medical assistance. At 8:00 P.M., October 2, military operations in Warsaw stopped.

The cessation of hostilities in Warsaw has, however, by no means affected the activities of the Home Army, fighting the Germans in other districts of Poland. [120]

The communists set their propaganda machine into motion to distort the truth and to give their own version of the facts. On October 5, Radio Lublin, controlled by the National Liberation Committee, gave its version of the Warsaw uprising:

In the last days of July the routed German armies were trailing westward, and we felt liberation from the Nazi jackboot was near. The People's Army was speedily completing its preparation for open action against the enemy's rear. The operations were to start when coordination with the Red Army Command had been secured. Into those preparations the insurgent action started by the command of the Homeland Army in Warsaw crashed like a bolt from the blue. The uprising came without any understanding with us and at an ill-chosen moment. Nevertheless, the People's Army realized that large masses of the population were already involved and therefore decided to fight wherever it happened to be. From the very beginning of the uprising, the People's Army mobilized its formations. The Homeland Army Command, however, looked upon this initiative with misgivings and tried to belittle its part in the uprising by thwarting all operational plans proposed by it. At one time, for instance, the People's Army suggested that every effort should be made to establish liaison between the groups fighting in separate parts of the town. The Homeland Army Command made this impossible, and refused the People's Army access to such means of inter-communication as they held in their own hands. Despite all these obstacles the People's Army played a distinguished part in the fighting for Warsaw. From September 13 onwards the Red Army supplied us with arms, ammunition and food . . . their help was exceedingly effective. Every night their planes came over and dropped food, arms, and ammunition. Independently of this the formation (Red Army) on the other bank of the Vistula gave us very efficient artillery, air, and anti-aircraft support.

The tactics and behavior of the Home Army through all this were strange indeed. . . .

When the surrender was announced . . . the only formation to disobey this order was the People's Army. . . . We found soon that the strength of the German defenses had been grossly exaggerated . . . the command of the Home Army willfully and deliberately delivered us into German hands. . . . In the light of these facts there can be but one epithet in the minds of upright soldiers for the bankrupts who were the authors of these deeds and for their leader General Bor: They are traitors.[121]

On October 6 in another broadcast from Lublin, further accusations were heaped on Polish leaders responsible for the Warsaw uprising.

The Red Army Command was not alone in being surprised at the sudden beginning of the Warsaw uprising. A good many of the Homeland Army units were equally taken aback. The prevalent note from the outset was one of confusion. . . . The only people who were evidently not taken by surprise were the Germans. It was, therefore, glaringly obvious from the beginning that the uprising was a political maneuver intended to place new trump cards in the hands of Raczkiewicz's clique.[122]

Although the patriotic underground organizations were not equipped to challenge the communist propaganda, the people of Poland knew what the real facts were.

Even before the plight of the Polish Home Army in Warsaw, a revealing debate took place in the British Parliament, which showed that Churchill's cold-blooded policy towards Russia and Poland was not affected at all by the heroic attempt of Warsaw to move the hearts of Western leaders.

During the debate in the House of Commons, on September 28, 1944, Churchill stated:

> Marshal Stalin has repeatedly declared himself in favor of a strong and friendly Poland, sovereign and independent. In this, our great Eastern Ally is in the fullest accord with His Majesty's Government and also, judging from American public statements, in the fullest accord with the United States. . . .
>
> Everything in our power has been and will be done to achieve, both in the letter and in the spirit, the declared purposes toward Poland of the Three Great Allies.
>
> Territorial changes on the frontiers of Poland there will have to be. Russia has the right to our support in this matter, because it is the Russian armies which alone can deliver Poland from the German talons; and after all the Russian people have suffered at the hands of Germany they are entitled to save the frontiers and to have a friendly neighbor on their western flank. . . .[123]

The traditional British sense of fair play was shown in the subsequent discussions. During the debate which followed, Lord Dunglass (Lanard) observed:

> Russia operates under a code of ethics which is by no means the same as our own. . . . Let me give examples. When the British Government say: "We will promise to restore an independent and free Poland," they mean it in the unqualified sense of the word; but when Marshal Stalin says: "We will restore your independence and freedom," he says in the name of the Russian Government, to Poland: "Yes, you may have your independence but Russia will dictate your frontiers, and you may have your freedom but Russia will choose your Government and, by implication will control your policy." These are two different interpretations and we must face them. . . . Unless we face (this) fact . . . there will stretch before us a long vista of political difficulty, misunderstanding and disillusion.[124]

Sir A. Southby (Epsom):

> May I remind the House that after the Russo-Polish war of 1920 it was we who suggested to the Poles that they should retire behind what is now called the Curzon Line, but that it was the Soviet Government who refused to accept the mediation of the Great Powers and insisted upon negotiating direct with Poland alone? As a result of those negotiations the Treaty of Riga was signed in March, 1921. Article 3 of that Treaty said: "Russia and the Ukraine abandoned all rights and claims to the west of the frontier."
>
> On 15 March 1923, a representative Conference of Ambassadors passed

a resolution recognizing the eastern boundaries of Poland as set out in the Treaty of Riga, and that resolution was assented to by the United States of America on the 25th of April, 1925.

In May 1939 the Polish Foreign Minister received from the Soviet Vice-Commissar for Foreign Affairs an assurance that in the event of war between Poland and Germany, Russia would adopt an attitude of benevolence towards the Poles. That event took place, and on 17 September, 1939 Russian troops invaded Poland. Eleven days later what is called the Ribbentrop-Molotov agreement was published under which each of the signatories took approximately half of Poland. Anyone who reads *The Times*, as most people do, and observes the way in which the Polish case is played down, must marvel at the change which seems to have come over that paper's point of view. This is what *The Times* said on 30 September 1939 when writing of the Nazi-Soviet pact announced two days before:

The Allied pledge to Poland stood irrefragable, fortified, if that be possible, by the valour of the Poles themselves.

It went on to speak of:

. . . freedom and independence for the Polish nation within the frontiers as unchallengeable as that which Germany violated on 1st September,

It was not long before Germany turned on Russia, as the result of which the Soviet Government on 30th July, 1941 renounced the Ribbentrop-Molotov agreement. Nothing could have been more categorical than the admission of the Soviet Government that the terms of agreement with Germany regarding territorial changes in Poland had lost their force. On the same day, our Foreign Secretary declared specifically that we did not recognize any territorial changes made in Poland since 1939. The following day a similar declaration was made by Mr. Sumner Welles on behalf of the United States Government. In January 1943 it became clear that the Soviet Government intended to insist upon a Russo-Polish frontier, in effect the one laid down in the Ribbentrop-Molotov agreement which the Soviets had themselves renounced on 30th July, 1941. These are historical facts.

Russia's desire for a rectification of her frontier is quite understandable, but that rectification must take place by agreement and not by force. We could agree to the so-called Curzon Line only if the Polish Government and the Polish people agreed to it of their own free will and not under coercion.

Dare anyone deny that the Poles have scrupulously discharged all their obligations in the war against Germany?

. . . Answering the questions in the House on January 26 this year, the Foreign Secretary reaffirmed the statement which was made by the Prime Minister on 5th September, 1940, namely, that we should not recognize any territorial changes which had taken place during the war unless they took place with the free consent and good will of the parties concerned. He also reaffirmed the categorical note which he had addressed to the late General Sikorski after the signature of the Russo-Polish agreement in 1941.

. . . I cannot believe that I was the only person in the House on 22nd of February this year who felt some disquiet when I heard him say:

> I cannot feel that the Russian demand for a reassurance about her western frontiers goes beyond the limits of what is reasonable and just. (Official Report, 22nd February 1944, Vol. 397, c. 698.)

The Russo-Polish frontier which the Soviet Government now seeks to establish is the same frontier established by force in 1939. The British Government, in September 1939 said regarding Poland:

> This attack made upon an Ally at a moment when she is prostrate in the face of the overwhelming forces brought against her by Germany cannot, in the view of His Majesty's Government be justified by the arguments put forward by the Soviet Government.

That was endorsed two days later by the right honorable gentleman, the Member for Wakefield (Mr. Greenwood), speaking for the party opposite, who said:

> There can be no doubt that the justification of it was a justification which reasonable people who had seen, as we have seen, previous acts of aggression, could not accept for one moment. (Official Report, 20th September 1939, Vol. 351, c. 984.) [125]

Sir A. Southby continued:

On August 1st the heroic Poles rose against their German oppressors. It has been most unfairly suggested in some quarters that the rising was premature and unauthorized, but the fact is that the local commanders acted in accordance with general instructions which had been submitted both to President Roosevelt and to the Prime Minister, and the Polish Prime Minister has stated that on 31st of July he also informed M. Molotov. Quite apart from that, for months past both the Soviet-sponsored wireless Station, Kosciuszko, and in the broadcasts by the Union of Polish Patriots, appeals were being made for an armed revolt against the Germans in Poland, and attacks were being made on General Bor, who commands the Polish Army in Warsaw, on the ground of his alleged inactivity. In June the Moscow radio said that it was generally believed that the time had come. On 29th July a direct appeal was made by wireless to the Patriot forces to the effect that direct armed action in the streets of Warsaw would hasten the time of final liberation. On 30th July another appeal went out by the wireless. It said:

> Warsaw shakes from the roar of guns. The Soviet armies are pushing forward and are nearing Praga. The Germans, when pushed out of Praga, will attempt to hold Warsaw and will try to destroy everything. People of Warsaw to arms! Attack the Germans! Assist the Red Army in crossing the Vistula!

Two days later General Bor and his men went into action. Nobody could deny that the rising benefited the advancing Red Army, because it delayed the passage of German reinforcements on their way to the front. . . . Surely one would have imagined that every effort would then have been made to assist the Poles in Warsaw. What they needed was arms, ammunition, and food, and yet in spite of frantic appeals from General Bor and from the Polish Prime Minister and Government in London they were left to their own resources. . . .

Two questions demand an answer. First, we have been told repeatedly that Russia has virtual command of the air on the Eastern Front. Why, then, should General Bor have to write on 5th August that German bombers were active and were operating with no interference from the Russian Air Force? Why were Russian machines not dropping the arms and ammunition that Warsaw needed? It may well be that other military considerations were of so urgent a nature that no Soviet machine could be spared, but if that be true, then the second question arises. Why did our machines have to fly this immensely long flight instead of being allowed to use Russian airfields which must have been in reasonably close proximity to Warsaw? They were denied the right to land on Russian aerodromes until fairly recently.

. . . I believe that the future of the world lies in an understanding between the Soviet Government, ourselves, and the United States, but I believe with all my heart and soul, that you will never get on with the Soviet Government unless there is plain speaking between them and us, and that no useful purpose is served by denying justice to Poland because you wish to put down the soft pedal with the Soviet Government.

. . . On 29th August the R.A.F. did a 2,000 mile flight in bad weather in order to assist the Russian army by bombing the Baltic ports of Stettin and Königsberg, and the operation cost us forty-one aircraft. If we could do this to help our Russian Ally, surely they could have found some machines to fly the infinitely shorter distance which would have brought help to Warsaw. I have tried to state the Polish case moderately and fairly. It deserves, in justice, to be stated. What we do as regards Poland will color the opinion of the whole of Europe so far as Britain is concerned when the war is over.[126]

While Sir A. Southby was speaking, communist and fellow-traveler M.P.'s condemned him for sowing disharmony in the Allied camp.

On September 29, 1944 Churchill asked Mikolajczyk if he was pleased with his speech of the day before in the House of Commons. Mikolajczyk replied, "No," because it weakened the Polish case in the crucial moment prior to resumption of negotiations with the Soviets. "You have conveyed an impression that a weak Poland endangers a powerful Russia and did you not think that it may be just the opposite?"

After giving only evasive answers Churchill asked, "Did you finally get rid of General Sosnkowski as Commander-in-Chief of the Polish Armed Forces?" When Mikolajczyk replied in the affirmative[127] Churchill was visibly pleased and stated that he attached a great deal of weight to this because of Soviet-Polish relations. Then he went on to say that he was delighted that on that day Moscow's press had published in full the section about Poland from his speech to the House of Commons the day before.[128]

The Soviet military authority and the NKVD continued to liquidate the members of the Home Army and the Polish administrative authorities who followed the instructions of the Polish Government and disclosed themselves to the incoming Soviet forces and offered their cooperation.

The Polish Government continued to receive reports of the treatment of the Home Army and the underground government by the Soviets. Generally, the same pattern emerged in nearly every district, with minor deviations, due to local peculiarities. This pattern developed as follows. When the Red Army combat units entered an area, the Home Army revealed its existence to the commanders involved and coordinated combat operations with them. Since the assistance of the Home Army was of considerable (and in many cases of decisive) importance, relations with the Soviet units were correct, courteous, and sometimes even friendly. This was not true in all cases, however; sometimes the Red Army would deliberately let the units of the Home Army be liquidated by the Germans. When the combat troops moved westward, however, the relationships changed radically. First, the Soviets ordered the disarming and disbanding of Polish military units, in some cases of units as large as divisions. Next, the commanding officers and their staffs were arrested. This was often accomplished by luring these men into conferences under false pretexts. Then the officers would usually be shipped to concentration camps located either in the U.S.S.R. or in Poland. In many cases the unit commanders were shot or hanged. The remaining officers, N.C.O.'s, and other men would then be grouped into two classes. Some were arrested, and of these a number were executed, while the remainder were sent to concentration camps, usually being beaten along the way. The group set at liberty was told to register for mobilization in the local areas, with the threat that those who failed to comply with this would be considered as deserters and prosecuted as such in military courts. This threat was carried out in many cases. By and large, however, the policy was to enroll this second group into the ranks of Berling's Soviet-controlled Polish Army.

Soviet treatment of the civilian population followed a similar pattern. Those people who had assisted the Home Army were subjected to various forms of terror, often being arrested. Officials of the underground government, especially mayors, were arrested by the NKVD as soon as they revealed their status. People who possessed weapons of any sort were arrested and prosecuted. The NKVD concentrated its prisoners in the notorious Nazi death-factory at Majdanek, often beating and otherwise maltreating its prisoners. After this series of arrests, that part of the population which was considered physically fit was recruited into the Berling Army. Both men and women were affected by this mobilization. Needless to say, the Home Army protested against these actions and called on their Allies to protect them from the Red terror by sending over liaison officers and military missions. The Home Army was bitter, worried by London's silence, and wanted to tell the world of its desperate straits.

It was obvious that the Soviets were eliminating the Home Army as an organized force and taking steps to liquidate or nullify all actual or potential anti-communist leadership. Separating this leadership from the masses of people, they could then subject the latter to their will without anyone being able to deny them. The Communist Party wanted to seize all power, and by using the Red Army and the NKVD it was able to destroy the Home Army and to eliminate all possible leadership. Meanwhile the London Government could do nothing to prevent this brutal Soviet behavior towards a supposed ally.[129]

5. The Polish Government Offers a Compromise Solution

In spite of these Soviet acts of atrocity, the Polish Government had not ceased to do its utmost to reach an understanding with them which could effectively put an end to this deplorable state of affairs and deliberately avoided any public discussion of the above-cited acts and others. Yet they realized that by keeping silent they would only encourage the Soviets in the continuation of such illegal acts and that this silence, furthermore, might be regarded as a tacit form of acquiescence in these acts. For this reason the Polish Government brought them to the notice of its Western Allies and asked that no unilateral territorial changes made by the Soviets be recognized by them as legally binding.

The United States and British Governments received the information of Soviet atrocities but were at a loss as to what could be done.

In order to show further evidence of its conciliatory attitude, the Polish Government offered the Soviets the following new proposal which was submitted to, and approved by, the underground organizations in Poland.

After the liberation of the capital of Poland the Polish Government will be reconstructed on the following lines.

The parties mentioned below will, in equal strength, form the basis of the Government: The Peasant Party, the National Party, the Polish Socialist Party, the Christian Labor Party, and the Polish Workers' (Communist) Party.

The possibility of joining the Government by representatives of the Fascist-minded and non-democratic political groups, also by those responsible for the pre-September 1939 system of government, is ruled out.

Agreement between the Prime Minister and the political parties concerning the choice of candidates for the Government from amongst these Parties will take place in Warsaw, and thereafter the President of the Republic will, on the motion of the Prime Minister, appoint a new Government.

The program of the Government will rest on the following: The Government will bring about the resumption of diplomatic relations between Poland and the U.S.S.R.

The Government will immediately proceed to take over the administration of the liberated Polish lands and prepare the taking over of the new areas to be surrendered by Germany. To this end the Government will conclude with the Soviet Government an agreement with a view to defining the forms of collaboration with the Red Army in the military sphere. This agreement will be modelled on, and carried out in the spirit of, agreements concluded by the Allied Powers with the governments of the liberated countries of Western Europe. The Government will assure order in the rear of the Soviet Army.

All foreign troops will be withdrawn from Polish territories on the cessation of hostilities.

The Government will, as soon as possible, arrange for the elections to the Constitutional Diet as well as for elections to the local government authorities on the basis of a decree providing for universal, equal, direct, secret, and proportional suffrage. Elections will take place as soon as normal conditions are established in the country.

The new democratic constitution will be passed immediately after the convocation of the Constitutional Diet. A new President of the Republic will be elected on the basis of this constitution.

The Government will undertake the carrying out of social reforms based on the declarations of principles made during the period of occupation by the representatives of the nation in the Homeland and by the Polish Government abroad. In particular, the agricultural reforms will be enacted without delay.

Until the convocation of the Constitutional Diet a National Council will be appointed to assist the Government as an advisory body. It will be composed of representatives of the aforesaid five political Parties, each of which will be represented by equal numbers. Smaller democratic political groups may also be represented on a correspondingly lesser scale.

The Government will bring about an agreement with the Soviet Government with a view to the joint prosecution of the war against Germany and the laying of foundations for a durable Polish-Soviet friendship after the war, based on a Polish-Soviet alliance aiming at close political and economic collaboration between Poland and the U.S.S.R., while respecting the principle of the sovereignty of both states and of the mutual obligation of non-interference in the internal affairs of the other states. It will be the object of all the alliances to devote constant care to the elimination of all German influence in Central Europe and the prevention of the possibility of renewed German aggression.

This object will also be served by the alliance between Poland and Great Britain and France, by the conclusion of a Polish-Czechoslovakian alliance, and by the maintenance of the closest ties of friendship between Poland and the United States of America.

Poland would expect fully to participate in the planning for the safeguarding of peace by a system of general security of peace-loving nations, and also to take part in the occupation of Germany, especially of her eastern territories adjacent to the future western boundaries of Poland.

With regard to the settlement of the frontiers of Poland, the Polish Government will act on the following principles agreed upon with the Soviet Government in the spirit of friendship and the respect of the fundamental interests of the Polish nation.

Poland, which has made so many sacrifices in this war and is the only country under German occupation that produced no Quisling, cannot emerge from this war diminished in territory. In the east the main centers of Polish cultural life and the sources of raw materials indispensable to the economic life of the country shall remain within Polish boundaries.

A final settlement of the Polish-Soviet frontier on the basis of these principles will be made by the Constitutional Diet in accordance with democratic principles.

All Germans will be removed from the territories incorporated into Poland in the north and the west by mutual Soviet-Polish cooperation.

Questions of citizenship and repatriation will be duly settled. Polish citizens who have been interned, arrested, or deported both in Poland and on territories of the U.S.S.R. will immediately be released by the Soviet authorities who will assist in their repatriation.

A voluntary exchange of the Polish, White Russian, and Ukrainian populations will be carried out.

The prosecution of the war and the general direction of all matters concerning the Polish Armed Forces will pass into the hands of the Polish Government, who will form to this end a war cabinet. The latter will, in particular, be cognizant of the following matters:

(a) problems connected with the general prosecution of war;
(b) Polish-Soviet military collaboration;
(c) Polish-British military collaboration;
(d) military cooperation between Poland and other Allied nations;
(e) unification of all Armed Forces of the Polish Republic.

The discussions of the war cabinet may be attended apart from Ministers appointed by the Council of Ministers, by the Chief of the General Staff, and, if necessary, by the chiefs of the services and the commanders of individual groups of the Polish Armed Forces.

The Polish Armed Forces will operate under Polish Command; in the eastern zone of operations under Soviet Supreme Operational Command; in other theaters of war under the Supreme Operational Command of the respective area.[130]

These proposals were submitted to the Soviet, British, and American governments. Churchill and Roosevelt favored the plan but the Soviets kept silent. Subsequently, when asked what the Russian answer was, Lebedev replied, "It was turned over to the Lublin Committee. Since there is no answer it must be held unsatisfactory." [131] By this tactic the Soviets intended to give the impression that the conflict did not involve the Soviet Union and Poland but that the real problem was a quarrel between two rival Polish governments.

Churchill felt it was now up to him to bring about a solution to this and other thorny problems.

The arrangement which I made with the President in the summer (1944) to divide our responsibilities for looking after particular countries affected by the movements of the armies had tided us over the three months for which our agreement ran. But as the autumn drew on everything in Eastern Europe became more intense. I felt the need of another personal meeting with Stalin, whom I had not seen since Teheran, and with whom, in spite of the Warsaw tragedy, I felt new links since the successful opening of "Overlord." [132]

Churchill had decided to see Stalin. Writing to Roosevelt about his proposed subjects of discussion in Moscow he said:

Of course the bulk of our business will be about the Poles; but you and I think so much alike about this that I do not need any special guidance as to your views.[133]

Churchill asked the President whether Harriman might take part in the forthcoming discussions, and Roosevelt agreed. Churchill thanked Roosevelt for that and said:

I am glad that Averell should sit in at all principal conferences, but you would not, I am sure, wish to preclude private tete-a-tetes between me and U.J. (Uncle Joe) or Anthony and Molotov, as it is often under such conditions that the best progress is made.[134]

On October 9, 1944 Churchill arrived in Moscow. The same day he obtained permission from Stalin to invite Mikolajczyk, Romer (the Foreign Secretary), and Grabski (whom Churchill called, "a grey-bearded and aged academician of much charm and quality"), to Moscow at once.

Churchill telephoned Mikolajczyk:

I made it clear that a refusal to come to take part in the conversations would amount to a definite rejection of our advice and would relieve us from further responsibility towards the London Polish Government.[135]

Mikolajczyk's Journey to Moscow. Exactly ten days after the collapse of the Warsaw uprising, Mikolajczyk arrived in Moscow. At the same time, the Lublin Poles, B. Bierut, E. Osobka-Morawski, and others also arrived from Poland. According to the Polish official record:

The first conference in Moscow on Polish subjects took place on Friday, October 13, 1944 from 5:00 to 7:50 P.M. in the Spiridonovka Palace of the People's Commissariat for Foreign Affairs.

Those present were:

The Soviet Delegation: Marshal Stalin, Foreign Commissar Molotov, Soviet Ambassador in London, Gusev, interpreter Pavlov, and two secretaries.

The British Delegation: Prime Minister Churchill, Foreign Secretary Eden, British Ambassador in Moscow Clark Kerr, and an interpreter.

The Polish Delegation: Premier Mikolajczyk, Foreign Minister Romer, Chairman of the National Council Grabski, interpreter Mniszek.

American Observer: United States Ambassador in Moscow Harriman, and a Secretary of the United States Embassy.

The conference was opened at 5:10 by Molotov who acted as unofficial chairman. He mentioned those present, including "our Polish guests" whose names he referred to without their official titles. He pointed to Premier Mikolajczyk as the initiator of the conference and suggested that therefore he should be first to put forward his point of view.

Mikolajczyk thanked Stalin and Molotov for their hospitality and expressed his gratitude to Churchill for not forgetting us (the London Government) although he was so far away.

He began his speech by describing the Polish Memorandum which in his opinion was the best solution of the Polish-Soviet difficulties. He emphasized that he took into account the fact that the Soviet Government had signed an agreement with the Polish Committee of National Liberation on the day before the Polish Delegation had arrived in Moscow for the first time, and the prestige of the Government which had signed it.

The Memorandum dealt with the fundamental problems; the international relations between Poland and the U.S.S.R. and the Polish internal situation. When asked by Molotov, Mikolajczyk explained that he was speaking of the Memorandum of the Polish Government of August 29, delivered in London to Ambassador Lebedev. It was my intention—he continued—for the whole Polish nation thus to take part, as it were, in the understanding with Russia.

He then proceeded to describe in brief the Memorandum point by point. At the first point which dealt with the formation of a new Government after the liberation of Warsaw, Stalin intervened that the text which was received by the Soviet Government speaks of the liberation of Poland and not her capital. This was probably a cypher mistake made by the Soviet Embassy in London, because Eden confirmed that he had the correct text. Churchill solved the difficulty by suggesting that this discrepancy should be noted and that Premier Mikolajczyk should continue.

When reference was made to the evacuation of Polish territory by the Soviet Forces as soon as hostilities have ended, Churchill inquired whether it had been taken into consideration to secure lines of communication for the Soviet Forces, which will be occupying Germany. Mikolajczyk replied in the affirmative.

He ended his long speech by emphasizing that the Memorandum was sent to the Polish underground authorities and approved unanimously by all political parties.

STALIN asked whether political parties existed in Poland under German occupation, and when Mikolajczyk replied in the affirmative, he inquired whether the approval of the parties was obtained on the basis of a published document and whether meetings and public conferences were convened in this connection.

MIKOLAJCZYK explained that the decision of the parties had to be taken in the course of the heaviest fighting for Warsaw, and that the Memorandum was not published in full but a detailed précis was given by the Premier in a press interview.

STALIN expressed his doubts concerning such methods of approval, to which

MIKOLAJCZYK replied: I know that Marshal Stalin, before he became the great leader of his nation, knew how to contact his followers in the underground effectively in a similar way.

STALIN. Excuse me, my practice at the time when we were hiding underground from political persecution was entirely different. During that period we held six conferences, six congresses, twelve meetings, and twenty to twenty-five conferences of the Central Committee of the Party where the program was approved.

MIKOLAJCZYK. I always looked with great admiration to these methods of underground warfare and today it is with the same admiration that I treat the five years of work and combat and methods of liaison of my friends and colleagues of the Underground. I want once more to emphasize that in my opinion and in the opinion of other members of the Polish Government our Memorandum is the best way of uniting all the forces of the nation in a program of Polish-Soviet friendship and cooperation.

CHURCHILL suggests that either now or later there should be a discussion on the verbal comments laid before the Soviet Ambassador together with the Memorandum which, in his opinion, throws an interesting light on its contents.

MIKOLAJCZYK is under the impression that he had included this aspect in his analysis of the Memorandum.

STALIN stated that he had not received the commentaries in question and asked for details.

GRABSKI [in Russian]. When I was presenting, on instructions of the Polish Government, the Memorandum to Lebedev for further transmission to Moscow, I made some verbal comments on its subject, which evidently interested him because he called a stenographer, with my consent, who took them down in shorthand.

In particular I spoke of the necessity of the new Government in Poland being appointed by the Polish President. So long as the greater part of Poland is occupied by the Germans, there is no legal means of changing the Constitution or of electing a President.

The Constitution of 1935 is by no means dear to us. Many of us, including myself, opposed it vehemently just as we did the Pilsudskiites.

The person of the President is not of importance in this connection; he has, as a matter of fact, recently changed his successor.

What is of importance, however, is the legal procedure which is to facilitate a Polish-Soviet agreement. I also spoke of the importance of cooperation between our two nations not only during the war but also, and especially after it, when Central Europe will have to be made safe from the danger of a German revenge.

CHURCHILL. I can thus see that these verbal comments were a development of the Memorandum itself which in my understanding, provides a basis for a compromise between the Polish Government and the Committee of National Liberation. For example, the fact that the Polish Workers' Party is to be included among the five parties which are to form the future Government in Poland does not, surely, imply an intention to diminish the Committee's part in such a Government.

MIKOLAJCZYK. I am a realist. I realize that the fusion of the Government and the Committee would be impossible. One has therefore to go deeper and to seek support among the political parties.

The Polish Government is based on the four principal parties. The Committee, I believe, is based on one, although it claims to have a wider basis. It would be useless to quarrel about it. It will suffice to base the Government on the five principal parties each of which would receive a fifth of the ministries, as suggested by the Memorandum.

CHURCHILL. That is not how I understood the matter. I thought that it would be necessary to seek a more equal proportion between the Government and the Committee. We could now fix the numerical ratio.

I imagined that the general agreement for which we are now working would be concluded between the Polish and Soviet Governments, while its application would be arranged between the Polish Government and the Committee of Liberation.

I also understood that Premier Mikolajczyk and his colleagues would be prepared to discuss the problem of a new constitution with the Soviet Government and with the Committee. I say this because I think that the Memorandum is only the basis for discussion.

I should like to know whether I have understood M. Mikolajczyk correctly.

MIKOLAJCZYK. The actual state of affairs is such: The Soviet Government has concluded an agreement with the Committee. The Polish Government is recognized by the British, American and other Governments. These discrepancies should be brought to a common denominator.

The memorandum envisages the participation in a new Government of the representatives of both parties. Thus a new Government would be constituted which would be recognized by all of the three principal powers.

CHURCHILL. So the Memorandum is the best basis for discussion.

MIKOLAJCZYK. The Memorandum is the best solution that we have been able to find.

STALIN. In my opinion the Polish Memorandum has two important defects which may make an understanding impossible.

The first of them is that it ignores the Committee of National Liberation. How can one ignore such a fact, and how can one close one's eyes on reality? Mr. Mikolajczyk should know that the Committee is carrying out an important task in liberated Poland. Recently there took place three conferences of the Socialist and Peasant parties in the course of which important practical problems were discussed and the opinion of the Liberation Committee was taken into account. Whoever ignores these facts is against an understanding.

An analysis of the present situation on the Polish sector shows that there is either no Government in Poland or else that there are two, which amounts to the same thing. For this reason a Government must be formed on the basis of a compromise between the two authorities which claim to be the Government.

Another defect of the Memorandum is that it does not settle the problem of the eastern frontiers of Poland on the basis of the Curzon Line. If you want to have relations with the Soviet Government, you can only do it by recognizing the Curzon Line as the principle.

On the other hand, what I find that is good in the Memorandum is the scheme which it contains for future Polish-Soviet relations. That part of the Memorandum merits the approval of everybody who desires good relations between Poland and the U.S.S.R. It is a matter, however, which concerns the future, but we must also consider the present.

A weak point in the Memorandum is its treatment of the constitution of which Professor Grabski has spoken. Personally, I think that the Polish Constitution of 1921 is better than the Constitution of 1935. But this should not be an obstacle in the way to improving Polish-Soviet relations. In the long run it is an internal Polish problem.

CHURCHILL. I see a gleam of hope in what Marshal Stalin has just said, because I understand that the Polish Government desires a friendly understanding with the Committee and the Memorandum is no obstacle in its way.

As regards the frontier problems, I must declare on behalf of the British Government that the sacrifices made by the Soviet Union in the course of the war against Germany and its effort toward liberating Poland entitle it, in our opinion, to a western frontier along the Curzon Line. I said so several times to my Polish friends in the course of last year.

I also understand that the Allies will be continuing the struggle against Germany in order to obtain in return for the Polish concession in the East an equal balance [Mr. Churchill first said "full compensation" and then corrected himself] in the form of territories in the North and in the West, in East Prussia and in Silesia including a good seacoast, an excellent port in Danzig and valuable raw materials in Silesia.

It will be a great country, not quite the same as the one designed at Versailles but constituting a real and solid structure in which the Polish nation will be able to live and develop in security, prosperity, and freedom. Britain attaches the greatest importance to this problem. If I were to take part in the Peace Conference, that is if I should still enjoy the confidence of the Government and of the Parliament, I should use the very same arguments.

MIKOLAJCZYK. Marshal Stalin stated that our Memorandum ignored the existence of the Committee of National Liberation. To a certain extent this is true, but to a certain extent it is not.

Please bear in mind that during five years the Polish Government has struggled to create quite a substantial army, navy, and air force which have fought with distinction on all the fronts of the West, the South, and on distant seas.

STALIN. That I appreciate.

MIKOLAJCZYK. For five years the Polish Government has also been organizing an underground army in Poland. But you, Marshal Stalin, ignore this particular Government and recognize the Committee.

STALIN. I do not ignore it as far as a compromise is concerned. And the Memorandum makes no mention of the Committee at all.

MIKOLAJCZYK. Because it goes down to the very foundations on which both the Government and the Committee are based. I should also like to quote certain details over which the press has been silent but which were broadcast by the Lublin radio and which concerned the meetings referred to by Marshal Stalin.

Among the names which were cited in this connection there was not one which belonged to anyone who I know for certain is at present in those parts. For example the Conference of the Peasant Party mentioned Bartnicki, who only joined the party recently, and Antoniuk, of whom no one had ever heard before. The Conference sent greetings and telegrams which every one here would agree to sign; they contained a message of welcome to the Red Army who are coming as liberators and they expressed the desire for a free Poland, free to settle her own fate.

CHURCHILL. I can't understand anything.

STALIN. Mr. Mikolajczyk evidently wants to deny that the Conferences took place in Lublin.

MIKOLAJCZYK. Not at all.

STALIN. That is good.

MIKOLAJCZYK quotes a telegram which he himself received from a Conference of the Peasant Party in Lublin.

STALIN. This information was publicly denied.

CHURCHILL. I think that we have more important things to discuss.

MIKOLAJCZYK. I agree, but I want to add one observation. On the liberated Polish territory, good things and bad things are happening.

STALIN. I think that is the case everywhere. [Smiles among those present.]

MIKOLAJCZYK. I think it would be better if we did not receive telegrams about arrests and deportations. [Stalin is silent.]

And now as regards the Curzon Line. In this matter I disagree both with Premier Churchill and with Marshal Stalin. I cannot decide this problem, for the decision lies with the Polish nation: you would form a very bad opinion of me were I to agree to ceding 40% of the territory of Poland and five million Poles. Were I to concede, it would seem that what the Polish soldier and the soldier of the Home Army was shedding his blood for the politician has sold.

STALIN. It is Ukrainian territory and a non-Polish population which is in question.

MIKOLAJCZYK. The population of the whole territory amounts to eleven million. The soldiers of the Polish Army and of the Polish Home Army are fighting in the hope that they will return to their homes which I am asked to give away.

Were I to do so, I should lose all the confidence I enjoy. It would not serve the Polish-Soviet understanding well, and it is for that understanding that I am working.

STALIN. But you do not seem to notice that a million and a half Ukrainians are fighting for these territories in the ranks of the Red Army. The Ukraine and White Russia have suffered for this reason even more than Poland. Mr. Mikolajczyk does not think of this. He would like to incorporate these territories, and by that he proves that he is an imperialist.

MIKOLAJCZYK. I bow my head before the heroism of the Soviet soldiers, but, as a Pole I remember above all else that Poland has lost 5,000,000 men murdered by the Germans in the course of this war.

CHURCHILL. We recognize Poland's sufferings but in order to bring them to an end a new Government will have to be created which would receive the recognition of all the principal United Powers. If that is not done, further suffering and sacrifices will not be avoided.

STALIN. Quite correct.

CHURCHILL. What should be done, then?

MIKOLAJCZYK. I think that the solution lies in an understanding between the three principal powers and in a generous conciliatory gesture on the part of the Soviet Union. If I am asked to cede 40% of our territory and not to demand guarantees of our independence, then * * *

STALIN [interrupts]. Who is it that threatens the independence of Poland? Is it perhaps the Soviet Union?

MIKOLAJCZYK. I ask for full independence for the return of all Poles to Poland and for free work for everybody.

CHURCHILL. I thought that we had come to an agreement regarding the return of the population and its exchange.

STALIN. Of course.

MIKOLAJCZYK. But the facts are different. All the Governments of the liberated countries of Europe were able to return with the one exception of the Polish Government.

CHURCHILL. It is the result of the absence of the understanding for which we are now working. And as a matter of fact not all Governments have as yet returned to their countries. Heavy and hard fighting is still in progress, and will still be for some time on all the European fronts.

I had hoped that Mr. Mikolajczyk would have been in a position to state that he recognizes the fact that the British Government support the Soviet Government in their proposals concerning the new eastern frontiers of Poland. The Poles may deplore this, but it is an important fact. We do not ask Mr. Mikolajczyk to come forward with the initiative for a Polish recognition of the new frontiers, but to consider that this is a matter of a new home for the Polish nation.

As far as I understand him Marshal Stalin desires, just as we and our American friends do, a sovereign, strong and independent Poland and of course friendly towards the Soviet Union, although I admit that such feelings cannot be in practice unanimous.

STALIN [interrupts]. Quite true. The Russians not only say so but are actually helping towards this end.

CHURCHILL. Were we not to reach an understanding in respect of the frontiers, I should not be in a position to maintain my efforts any further.

I feel it is Russia's attitude that Poland should again rise free, independent and sovereign, and that this is her attitude not because she feels strong but because she considers that she is right.

But no Government could suffer an unfriendly attitude on the part of a neighbor if it had been through what Russia has in this war. [Stalin nods in approval.]

I really do not know what would be the best solution to this problem. Perhaps Mr. Mikolajczyk could make a statement concerning the frontiers which would be acceptable to the Soviet Government, but I am afraid that in such a case he would be denounced in the following day by the Polish public opinion which supports him. He could perhaps state that for practical purposes the Polish Government accepts the frontier solution but that they reserve the right to appeal in this matter at the Peace Conference. I do not know whether this would be acceptable to both parties.

MIKOLAJCZYK. Some time ago I suggested a line of demarcation but I did not imagine that today we were to undertake a new partition of Poland.

STALIN. I am against a partition of Poland, but you, on your part want to carry out a partition of the Ukraine and of White Russia.

MIKOLAJCZYK. I have heard public declarations concerning the partition of Poland but I have so far heard nothing of a partition of Germany.

CHURCHILL [after having whispered something to Eden]. We have discussed this and the problem of Germany was to be settled here but we avoided any publicity which would only have the result of stiffening resistance.

MOLOTOV. Quite correct.

CHURCHILL. I do not wish to avoid replying to this question. I only appeal to Mr. Mikolajczyk to make a great effort on his part to help the British Government in their endeavour.

Though badly prepared, Britain came into the war to save the Polish nation from destruction. I think that our duty will have been fulfilled if as a result of this war a great, free, sovereign and independent Poland will arise and will take the whole nation under its wing.

Our attitude is as follows: The Curzon Line, as the eastern frontier of Poland and in the West and in the North a change of frontiers for Poland's benefit. I do not think in this state of affairs it would be in the interest of the Polish Government to estrange themselves from the British Government.

In the course of this war we were a hair's breadth from defeat: a sword hung over our necks. We have therefore the right to ask the Poles for a great gesture in the interest of European peace. [He turns to Premier Mikolajczyk.] I hope that you will not hold against me these unpleasant but frank words which I have spoken with the best of intentions.

MIKOLAJCZYK. I have already heard so many unpleasant things in the course of this war that one more will not let me lose my balance.

MOLOTOV. I should like to add a few words about what was discussed in Teheran on the subject of Poland. All those who took part are here today with the exception of President Roosevelt. I should like to repeat what he declared and if I am inexact I hope that the other witnesses will correct me.

I can quite well remember that President Roosevelt said that he fully agreed to the Curzon Line and that he considered it to be a just frontier between Poland and the Soviet Union; he thought, however, that for the time being it would be advisable not to give publicity to his view. We can therefore draw the conclusion that the Curzon Line corresponds not only with the attitude of the Soviet Government, but it has also the concurrence of all of the three Great Powers. I wanted to emphasize this as Mr. Mikolajczyk referred to the attitude of the three Powers.

MIKOLAJCZYK. And may I learn what was decided in Teheran with regard to the western frontiers of Poland?

MOLOTOV. The opinion was that the line of the Oder was just. I do not remember anybody objecting.

CHURCHILL. I also agreed.

EDEN. The formula in Teheran was that the new frontier of Poland in the West would go as far towards the Oder as the Poles would wish. [All concur.]

CHURCHILL. In East Prussia, the territories earmarked for Poland extend to the west and south of Königsberg. Would a new united Polish Government accept the Curzon Line, on these conditions, as the *de facto* eastern frontier with the reservation that the matter will be settled finally at the Peace Conference? I must add that I have not yet had the opportunity to discuss this suggestion with the Soviet Government.

MIKOLAJCZYK. I have no authority to make such a declaration.

CHURCHILL. I have not in mind a solemn declaration but a working formula. I do not want to expose Mr. Mikolajczyk to an immediate denunciation by Polish public opinion, but all the same I think that such a settlement would best help to create a united Polish Government.

MIKOLAJCZYK. Even the Committee of National Liberation has recently announced publicly that they have not lost hope that Lwow may be saved for Poland—and I am asked to be put into a worse condition by being made to agree to the Curzon Line.

STALIN. We do not use Ukrainian soil for barter. The rumor you quoted is without foundation.

CHURCHILL. My attitude should not be given such a ruthless interpretation as the Poles have given it. Danzig is certainly not worth less to Poland than Lwow. Does not Marshal Stalin think that it would be better now to interrupt our discussion and to give the Poles time to think the matter over?

STALIN. I should only like to declare that we Russians also speak of including in Poland not only Danzig but also Stettin.

CHURCHILL. Of course.

STALIN. We have all sympathy for this project.

CHURCHILL. So has the British Government. [He turns to Premier Mikolajczyk.]

Please consider this in all seriousness. The problems are to us of the greatest importance:

1. Acceptance of the Curzon Line as the *de facto* eastern frontier of Poland with the right of a final discussion of the matter at the Peace Conference; and

2. A friendly agreement with the Committee of National Liberation on the subject of forming a united Polish Government which in time could undergo such modifications as circumstances would require.

I think this would be the best solution in this final phase of the war. If before taking a decision Mr. Mikolajczyk would like to talk to me or Mr. Eden, we are of course at his disposal.

On my part I consider these two matters as the most important.

ROMER. Are we to understand that Mr. Churchill's suggestion has also the support of the Soviet Government?

STALIN [who has been standing for some time while all the others were sitting]. In order that the whole matter may be quite clear and that there may be no doubts, I want to state categorically that the Soviet Government cannot accept Premier Churchill's formula concerning the Curzon Line. [Churchill makes a gesture of disappointment and helplessness.]

I must add the following correction, as far as we are concerned, to this formula:

The Curzon Line must be accepted as the future Polish-Soviet frontier. One cannot keep changing the frontier, for the social and economic organizations are different here and different in Poland. We have collective farms which we introduce in all our lands, and Poland has the system of private property in land. If in these conditions we start questioning to whom certain territories belong, it will only increase the suffering of the population.

That is why, just as in the case of Rumania and Finland, we aim at determining a definite frontier with Poland. This is a source of surprise among many of our foreign friends but it is, in our opinion, the only just solution of the problem in view of the difference of our economic systems.

With the rest of Premier Churchill's statement I fully agree.

I repeat once more: The Curzon Line as the basis of the frontier. In its definite delimitation I agree, of course, to certain corrections for local reasons, which may move the frontier three or four [he corrects himself], six or seven miles one way or the other.

MIKOLAJCZYK. May we be told what is actually considered as the Curzon Line?

CHURCHILL. We shall let you have a map showing it.

MIKOLAJCZYK. Is the Curzon Line identical to the demarcation line introduced in 1939?

STALIN. No, not by any means. The Curzon Line gives you Bialystok, Lomza, and Przemysl.

Thus ended the conference.[136]

The Poles anticipated what Stalin's position would be, but they did not expect that Churchill would be pressing them so hard to surrender to Stalin's demands. They had come prepared to reach a compromise solution, but Churchill's attitude eliminated all chances of reaching an agreement.

Churchill decided to act swiftly and presented Mikolajczyk with a British draft of an understanding in the Polish problem in Moscow, which read as follows:

In view of the declaration made to them in Moscow by the Soviet Government and His Majesty's Government, the Polish Government accept and undertake to recommend to its Parliament the Curzon Line as defined by those Governments as the basis for the frontier of Poland and the Union of Soviet Socialist Republics, subject to their right to discuss minor adjustments at the armistice or peace conference and provided that the necessary measures be taken for the transfer of all persons wishing to change their allegiance in accordance with their freely expressed wishes, and provided that the free city of Danzig, the regions of East Prussia west and south of Königsberg, Oppeln-Silesia, and the lands desired by Poland to the east of the line of the Oder be added to Poland and their possession guaranteed by the Government of the Union of Soviet Socialist Republics and His Majesty's Government. It is also understood that the German populations of the said regions shall be repatriated to Germany and that all Poles in Germany shall at their wishes be repatriated to Poland.

It is agreed that a united Polish Government will be at once set up in the territory already liberated by Russian arms.

The Soviet Government takes this occasion of reaffirming their unchanging policy of supporting the establishment within the territorial limits set forth of a sovereign independent Poland, free in every way to manage its own affairs and to make a treaty of durable friendship and mutual aid with a Polish Government established on an anti-fascist and democratic basis.

The treaty and relationships established with other United Nations will be unaffected by this settlement, all parties to which declare again their implacable resolve to wage war against the Nazi tyranny until it has surrendered unconditionally.[137]

Mikolajczyk refused to accept the above draft.

On October 13 at 10:00 P.M. Churchill had an opportunity to meet members of the so-called Lublin Committee.

It was soon plain that the Lublin Poles were mere pawns of Russia. They had learned and rehearsed their parts so carefully that even their masters evidently felt they were overdoing it. For instance, Mr. Bierut, the leader, spoke in these terms: "We are here to demand on behalf of Poland that Lwow shall belong to Russia. This is the will of the Polish people." When this had been translated from Polish into English and Russian I looked at Stalin and saw an understanding twinkle in his expressive eyes, as much as to say, "What about that for our Soviet teaching!" The lengthy contribution of another Lublin leader, Osobka-Morawski, was equally depressing. Mr. Eden formed the worst opinion of the three Lublin Poles.[138]

Yet, prior to the next meeting with Stalin, Churchill decided to break Mikolajczyk's resistance to accept Soviet terms. For this reason arrangements were made for a conference of Prime Minister Mikolajczyk with Prime Minister Churchill at the British Embassy in Moscow, held on October 14, 1944, from 11:30 A.M. to 2:00 P.M.

Present:
On the British side:
Prime Minister Churchill

Foreign Minister Eden
Ambassador Clark Kerr
Oliver Harvey
Denis Allen

On the Polish side:
Prime Minister Mikolajczyk
Foreign Minister Romer
Professor Grabski
J. Zaranski

Before the arrival of Prime Minister Churchill, Foreign Minister Eden briefly summarized the events of the sitting held last night. Osobka-Morawski made a propaganda speech on the economic and social "benefits" brought to Poland by the Committee. He dwelt mainly upon the land reform, stating that the principles of the land reform were based on individual ownership system. Prime Minister Mikolajczyk explained the true situation.

Then Mr. Eden reiterated Stalin's declaration that Stalin is not interested in the Polish Constitution and for that reason the difficulties in this matter will appear less than was previously anticipated. Finally, Mr. Eden informed [them] that he had received a document from Mr. Osobka-Morawski which Mr. Osobka-Morawski defined as directives of the Polish Government for the people, instructing them about behavior toward the Committee and the Soviet authorities. Mr. Eden handed this document over to Mr. Mikolajczyk after some hesitation. The Prime Minister, after reading it, remarked that these directives seemed to him quite reasonable and just.

Eden made it known that, following Churchill's instructions Ambassador Clark Kerr notified Stalin of Churchill's desire of holding a conference with him tête-à-tête on Poland and this conference would take place probably at four o'clock P.M.. The Polish position should be explained before this conference takes place.

Prime Minister Churchill arrived at 11:45 A.M. and started expounding his view.

This is the crisis in the fortunes of Poland. No such opportunity will ever return and the damage done would be irreparable if we lose today the chance of agreement. Everything hinges on one thing: the eastern frontier of Poland. If this is settled and announced, in one or two sentences, then agreement can be reached easily. How near we came at the beginning of the year! If you had come to an agreement with the Russians at that time, you would not have had those other people today. They are going to be a frightful nuisance to you. They will build up a rival Government and gradually take over authority in Poland. Fighting will begin with the Russians siding with the rival Government. I shall tell Parliament what I have agreed with Stalin and what His Majesty's Government's attitude is. When you have a victorious army behind you, there is quite enough to make a show, especially when the others will be liquidated. They have unlimited means to do this. Therefore you must never leave Russia, but must go to Poland and form a united Government there. Our relations with Russia are much better than they have ever been. I talked to General Anders, the other day, to whom I took great liking. He entertains the hope that after the defeat of Germany the Russians will be beaten. This is crazy, you cannot defeat the Russians.

I beg you to settle upon the frontier question. You must take responsibilities. If you reach a formula with me I'll go to Stalin at 4:00 P.M.

What else is there beside the frontier question? It means compensation in the west and the disentanglement of populations. If you agree on the frontier then the Russians will withdraw their support from the Committee. When I criticized the Lublin Poles last night, Stalin on many occasions supported me. You are really dealing with Russia. The word "basis" is very helpful; we were nearly at it in January. If you do not agree now that means that you are going to use again the "Liberum Veto" which shattered the independence of Poland. What does it matter supposing you lose the support of some of the Poles? Think what you will gain in return! Ambassadors will come. The British Ambassador will be with you. The Americans, the greatest military power in the world will have an Ambassador. You *must* do this. If you miss this moment everything will be lost!

Answering this long argument of Prime Minister Churchill, Prime Minister Mikolajczyk said that he had been thinking over all night the questions discussed during yesterday's conference. It follows that the decisions of Poland's problems were taken up at the Teheran Conference, and now the only thing that remains is for the Polish Government to place its signature upon them. The Prime Minister's personal decision is a different question and it is still a different decision of those who collaborate with the Prime Minister and support him. Firstly, we should have to decide to deprive ourselves of the Polish territory, and secondly we should have to agree to join the Committee. Although Stalin declared that he was not interested in the Polish Constitution, there still remains the problem of the independence of the rest of Poland.

CHURCHILL [interrupts]. There are other Powers involved in the settlement.

MIKOLAJCZYK. Should I sign a death sentence against myself?

EDEN. If the formula on the Curzon Line is agreed upon, then it will be possible to gain from Stalin full guarantees of the independence of Poland.

MIKOLAJCZYK. The problem of frontiers is of such a nature that all the Polish people should express their opinion.

CHURCHILL. Had Pilsudski lived, things would have taken a different turn. Although I had no opportunity to meet him, I cherish great respect for his person and I am convinced that "if he had not died, Beck would not have done what he did with the Czechs."

MIKOLAJCZYK, coming back to the frontier question, stated that Stalin declared that the Curzon Line must be the boundary line between Poland and Russia.

CHURCHILL [angrily]. I wash my hands of this business; as far as I am concerned we shall give the whole business up. We are not going to wreck the peace of Europe because of quarrels between Poles. In your obstinacy you do not see what is at stake. It is not in friendship that we shall part. We shall tell the world how unreasonable you are. You will start another war in which twenty-five million lives will be lost. But you don't care.

MIKOLAJCZYK. I know that our fate was sealed in Teheran.

CHURCHILL. It was *saved* in Teheran.

MIKOLAJCZYK. I am not a person completely devoid of patriotic feeling, to give away half of Poland.

CHURCHILL. What do you mean by saying "you are not devoid of patriotic feeling?" Twenty-five years ago *we* reconstituted Poland although in the last war more Poles fought against us than for us. Now again we are preserving you from disappearance, but you will not play ball. You are absolutely crazy.

MIKOLAJCZYK. But this solution does not change anything.

CHURCHILL. Unless you accept the frontier you are out of business forever. The Russians will sweep through your country and your people will be liquidated. You are on the verge of annihilation.

EDEN. Supposing that we get an understanding on the Curzon Line, we will get agreement on all the other things from the Russians. You will get a guarantee from us.

CHURCHILL. Poland will be guaranteed by the three Great Powers and certainly by us. The American Constitution makes it difficult for the President to commit the United States. In any case you are not giving up anything because the Russians are there already.

MIKOLAJCZYK. We are losing everything.

CHURCHILL. The Pripet marshes and five million people. The Ukrainians are not your people. You are saving your own people and enabling us to act with vigor.

MIKOLAJCZYK. Must we sign this if we are going to lose our independence?

CHURCHILL. You have only one thing to do. It would make the greatest difference if you agreed.

MIKOLAJCZYK. Would it not be possible to proclaim that the three Great Powers have decided about the frontiers of Poland without our presence?

CHURCHILL. We will be sick and tired of you if you go on arguing.

EDEN. You could say that in view of the declaration made by the British and Soviet Governments, you accept a *de facto* formula, under protest if you like, and put the blame on us. I quite see the difficulty of saying it of your own volition.

CHURCHILL [coming back to the question of consolidation of the Government with the Committee]. I might get better than fifty-fifty. I think I ought to get 60:40. It is your fault that the Lublin Poles have come into existence. With regard to the frontiers, think what you get in Silesia.

MIKOLAJCZYK explains that the eastern territories do not contain mere marshes and non-arable land. On the contrary, the province of Tarnopol, for instance, has the most fertile soil among all the provinces. On the other hand, Eastern Prussia is a poor country, full of lakes and marshes.

CHURCHILL. If you accept the frontier, the United States will take a great interest in the post-war rehabilitation of Poland and may grant you a big loan after this war. At any rate I will try to get you the best possible solution.

CHURCHILL leaves the room to draw up a declaration.

ROMER. Two months ago Stalin said to us that we can postpone the frontier issue.

EDEN. Stalin is not interested in the Constitution. The only thing he talked about was the Curzon Line. The Russians will drop the other things. We could argue endlessly, everybody stating his case. We could try the other way, first getting an agreement with the Committee.

MIKOLAJCZYK. We lose all authority in Poland if we accept the Curzon Line, and furthermore nothing is said about what we could get from the Germans.

EDEN. I think we could do this, we could take this risk. We could say what you are going to get.

MIKOLAJCZYK. The only way out is: the three Powers announce their decision and we make a formal protest. A government which wants to retain authority with its people cannot give up territory. Stalin put forward two conditions: (1) the Curzon Line, (2) recognition of the Committee.

EDEN. Prime Minister Churchill intends to offer Stalin the Curzon Line in exchange for his concession in matters of the Committee and Constitution. If you reject agreement now, then all people in Poland will rally around the Committee because they will have nothing else to rally around.

MIKOLAJCZYK cites Lenin's utterances on Hungary, according to which the Soviet policy made a mistake in commencing to set up a communist government there. On the contrary, a temporary leftist government should have been admitted, which would have paved the way for the assumption of government by the communists.

EDEN. I quite realize that you cannot say it of your own.

MIKOLAJCZYK. But it may end that we shall have been cut off in the East and shall not have gained anything in the West.

EDEN. We could make a public pronouncement on that matter. There was no binding commitment at Teheran, but only an expression of opinion.

MIKOLAJCZYK explains what President Roosevelt told the Prime Minister on Poland's frontiers in June 1944 in Washington.

EDEN. The British War Cabinet decided over a year ago what their attitude is on that matter.

ROMER. It is the most important thing for Poland to be really on good relations with Russia but they cannot be built upon the Polish people's feeling of being wronged.

CHURCHILL [comes back with the draft of declaration]. Before the draft was read he announced that he would have to phone London to get approval, as well as phone to Washington to get an explanation of the position of the United States before the declaration is signed. Publication at present of what it is intended to take away from the Germans in the East would arouse the German fury and this would cost many human lives. On the other hand if the agreement between Poland and Russia is not reached now, it would also cause victims in human beings.

CHURCHILL then reads the draft of his declaration and says that he intends to declare the following to Stalin: "If I can procure the agreement of the Polish Government to this, will you back it up and support it in the letter and in the spirit?" Churchill speaks further on: "If Stalin's answer is negative or unsatisfactory, and I doubt if it would be, you'll lose nothing, on the contrary you'll go back to London strengthened and will continue to have our support. If, on the other hand, Stalin thinks that it is all right, then I would put off the meeting with the Lublin Poles in the presence of Eden, Molotov, and the representatives of the United States. You are bound to accept the decision of the Great Powers."

MIKOLAJCZYK says that he cannot agree to the word "accept."

CHURCHILL [angrily and with a gesture of impatience]. I take no further interest in you.

MIKOLAJCZYK once again explains the reasons why he cannot express his consent to Churchill's formula.

CHURCHILL. Everything is in the word "accept."

On the question asked by ROMER whether Prime Minister Churchill would agree to cede the British territory, Churchill answers: "I certainly would and be blessed by future generations if I were in your situation. Look, what is the alternative? You are threatened with virtual extinction, you will be effaced as a nation."

At this moment Professor GRABSKI takes the seat near Churchill and expounds him in French his opinion on the solution of the Russo-Polish conflict. He begins with the statement that for thirty years he has been struggling for friendly relations between Poland and Russia. Professor Grabski explains the importance to Poland of Lwow and of the oil fields in particular and concludes with the expression of the view that the public opinion of Poland would not be able to understand and to agree to that paradox that Poland, who first opposed German aggression, would be diminished in her territory after the war.

CHURCHILL [ironically]. Nothing can prevent Poland from declaring war on Russia once she is deprived of support by other Powers * * * What is public opinion? The right to be destroyed * * * I want to save the flower of the Polish nation * * *

CHURCHILL before he leaves addresses Mikolajczyk with sympathy and mentioning the Committee says: "I don't envy you. I took a considerable dislike to them."

The conference concluded a few minutes before two o'clock. The Polish delegation remained at the British Embassy to work on remarks with regard to the English project. These remarks were to be presented to Prime Minister Churchill before his conference with Stalin.

During the one hour break between 2:15 and 3:15 P.M. the Polish delegation was not able to elaborate in writing their reservations as to the British declaration. Ultimately it was agreed that the Polish side could not express their consent for the acceptance of the Curzon Line as a frontier between Poland and Russia and this decision should be conveyed orally to Prime Minister Churchill by Prime Minister Mikolajczyk.[139]

Less than two hours later Mikolajczyk and his companions met with Churchill again.

The Polish delegation arrived at Mr. Churchill's urban residence in Moscow, situated in the Narkomindel's "Osobniak" [private residence, mansion] on Ostrovsky Street, at 3:30 P.M. The forty-minute-long conference, which nobody else attended on the British side, was carried on by Mr. Churchill in a very violent mood.

CHURCHILL started with an announcement that he had not yet received an answer as to the meeting with Stalin. The Soviets replied that Stalin was "out of town" and that really means that Stalin takes a rest in the afternoon—as Mr. Churchill used to do.

Prime Minister MIKOLAJCZYK, answering Premier Churchill's question, informs him that after a renewed consideration he cannot give his consent to the acceptance of the Curzon Line as a frontier for the reasons expounded several times. The Polish Government cannot determine the loss of nearly half of the Polish territory in the east without hearing the opinion of the Polish people, which is decisive for the Government.

CHURCHILL. You are no Government if you are incapable of taking any decision. You are callous people who want to wreck Europe. I shall leave you to your own troubles. You have no sense of responsibility when you want to abandon your people at home, to whose sufferings you are indifferent. You do not care about the future of Europe, you have only your own miserable selfish interest in mind. I will have to call on the other Poles and this Lublin Government may function very well. It will be *the Government*. It is a criminal attempt on your part to wreck, by your "Liberum Veto," agreement between the Allies. It is cowardice on your part.

On the remarks of Mikolajczyk that Churchill may set forth to Stalin his declaration as his project, toward which the Polish Government will confine itself to sheer protest, CHURCHILL replies: "I am not going to worry Mr. Stalin. If you want to conquer Russia we shall leave you to do it. I feel like being in a lunatic asylum. I don't know whether the British Government will continue to recognize you."

CHURCHILL then states with passion that Great Britain is powerless toward Russia. On Mikolajczyk's remark that the Polish Government must secure to itself the right to defend the interests of Poland at the peace conference, CHURCHILL replies: "You are not going to be in a better position at the peace conference. I cannot speak for the American Government. The United States is not represented here."

In the last war more Poles fought against us than for us. In this war what is your contribution to the Allied effort? What did you throw into the common pool? You may withdraw your divisions if you like. You are absolutely incapable of facing facts. Never in my life have I seen such people!

CHURCHILL then cites General Anders' words that "after the Germans' defeat we shall beat the Russians" and remarks with emphasis "You hate the Russians. I know you hate them."

On Minister ROMER's remark that the presence of the Polish delegation here is the best proof that the reproach of hateful feelings of Poles towards Russians and their reluctance to achieve good relations with them is a lie, CHURCHILL reiterates with obstinacy: "You hate the Russians."

ROMER makes a statement that Prime Minister Churchill cannot expect that the Polish delegation can within an hour take a decision determining the Polish consent to cede eastern Poland to Russia, and CHURCHILL reiterates several times with emphasis that he did not at all want to obtain from the Poles decisions of this kind by coercion but only a consent, not binding toward Russia, to accept the Curzon Line as a demarcation line for the future frontier between Poland and the Soviet Union.

MIKOLAJCZYK repeats his request that Churchill in his conference with Stalin should not refer to the Polish declaration as implying a definite acceptance of the British declaration by the Polish side, as it might frustrate the possibility of reaching an agreement. In connection with Churchill's remark that in this situation there is no reason for the Polish delegation to come back to London, Mikolajczyk states that because of the position taken by Churchill, he himself understands very well that the Polish Government will not be able to stay in London any longer.

The conference is interrupted at 4:20 P.M. by Martin, Chief of Churchill's Secretariat, who announces that Marshal Stalin will receive the British Prime Minister at 4:30 P.M. Churchill leaves in haste, almost not saying good-bye. After a while the Polish delegation leaves also.[140]

Upon orders of Anthony Eden, the British Embassy drafted another agreement on Poland, similar to the one produced previously by Churchill. But Mikolajczyk refused to accept it and offered the following counter-proposition referring to the British draft which was handed to Churchill and Eden in Moscow on October 15, 1944.

1. Participation of the United States Government in the Arrangement, if only on the military plane, through General Eisenhower, is highly desirable. If the Arrangement is to be signed in London, on the basis of texts established in Moscow, American participation could be secured in the meantime.

2. To Paragraph 1. Instead of: "Polish Prime Minister and Minister for Foreign Affairs" insert: "Polish Government."

3. To Paragraph 1. Instead of: "Make the following declaration" insert: "reached the following agreement."

4. To Paragraph 2. Instead of: "territory of Poland on the west will include the Free City of Danzig, the regions of East Prussia west and south of Königsberg, Oppeln-Silesia and the lands desired by Poland to the east of the line of the Oder" insert: "the northern and western frontiers of Poland will include the Free City of Danzig, the regions of East Prussia west and south of Königsberg, the Regency of Oppeln in Silesia, and follow the river Oder from the point where it leaves the Regency of Oppeln to its estuary including the town and harbor of Stettin. A map showing the new frontier is enclosed herewith."

5. To Paragraph 2. Instead of: "German populations of the said region shall be repatriated to Germany" insert: "Germans of the said regions shall be removed."

6. To Paragraph 3. Instead of: "The Curzon Line" insert: "the so-called Curzon Line, and in former Eastern Galicia the so-called Line 'B'."

7. To Paragraph 3. Add to last sentence: "Separate Polish-Soviet agreements will regulate the reciprocal transfer and the repatriation of the population of both countries, the release of persons detained, and the restitution of cultural, artistic, and historical values situated in territories to be ceded by Poland to the Soviet Union."

8. To Paragraph 4. Instead of: "It is agreed that a united Polish Government will be set up at once in the territory already liberated by Russian arms" insert: "Upon the signature of the present agreement diplomatic

relations will be re-established between the Soviet Government and the Polish Government in London. The Prime Minister of this Government will thereupon proceed to the territory of Poland already liberated by Russian arms in order to effect the reconstruction of the Government based on the five main political parties, on democratic and anti-fascist lines. This new Government will function until the convocation of a Parliament elected by free and democratic vote, and will at once negotiate the envisaged agreements with the U.S.S.R."

9. To Paragraph 5. Instead of: "durable friendship and mutual aid with a Polish Government established on an anti-fascist and democratic basis" insert: "durable friendship and mutual aid with a Polish Government re-established in their homeland. On their part H.M.G. (and—if possible—the U. S. Government) will guarantee the sovereignty and independence of Poland within her new frontiers."

10. To Paragraph 6. Instead of: "the treaty and relationships established with other United Nations" insert: "the treaties and relationships existing between Poland and other countries."

11. Add: "On the cessation of hostilities all foreign troops will immediately be withdrawn from Polish territories. "

12. Add: "Polish armed forces will take part in the occupation of Germany, especially of her eastern territories to be surrendered to Poland."

13. The prolongation of the Alliance between Great Britain and Poland will be dealt with by an exchange of letters between the respective Prime Ministers.[141]

On October 15 Mikolajczyk again conferred with Churchill and this time was ready to accept the Curzon Line with a condition that Lwow and the oil fields in Galicia remain Polish. Churchill again became furious, shouted, and threatened, which led Mikolajczyk to a very firm and energetic rebuttal of Churchill's position. Churchill canceled the scheduled conference for the afternoon and shouted to Mikolajczyk that "everything between us is finished" and left the room banging the door. Eden wanted to console him. Mikolajczyk also left the room after refusing to shake Eden's hand.[142]

On October 16, reporting to his King, Churchill stated:

The day before yesterday was "All Poles Day." Our lot from London are, as your Majesty knows, decent but feeble, but the delegates from Lublin could hardly have been under any illusions as to our opinion of them. They appeared to me to be purely tools, and recited their parts with well-drilled accuracy. I cross-examined them fairly sharply, and on several points Marshal Stalin backed me up. We shall be wrestling with our (London) Poles all today, and there are some hopes that we may get a settlement. *If not we shall have to hush the matter up and spin it out until after the (American) Presidential election.*[143]

It appears that Churchill was interested primarily in a speedy solution to the problem, regardless of the sacrifices to be paid by the Poles. His main objective in this was the preservation of Allied unity and the removal of the Polish problems from internal American politics. As was noted previously, the Polish Government was particularly careful to avoid getting involved in American politics.

On October 16 Mikolajczyk handed United States Ambassador Harriman the following letter:

Mr. Ambassador:

I learned with shocked surprise from Mr. Molotov's statement at the meeting on October 13 that at the Teheran Conference the representatives of all the three Great Powers had definitely agreed that the so-called Curzon Line should be the frontier between Poland and the Soviet Union.

In this connection, I should like to recall that during the conversations which I had the honor to have with the President in Washington in June 1944, I was told that only Marshal Stalin and Prime Minister Churchill had agreed on the Curzon Line. In particular, the President indicated that the policy of the United States Government was contrary to the settlement of territorial problems before the end of the war. The President said that at the Teheran Conference he had made it clear that he held the view that the Polish-Soviet conflict should not be settled on the basis of the so-called Curzon Line, and he assured me that at the appropriate time he would help Poland to retain Lwow, Drohobycz, and Tarnopol and to obtain East Prussia including Königsberg, and Silesia. On the other hand, the President expressed the view that Marshal Stalin would not give his consent to the return of Wilno to Poland.

I would be most grateful to you, Mr. Ambassador, if you could help to clear up this misunderstanding on a subject of such vital importance to Poland.[144]

In an immediate reply Harriman, visibly embarrassed, stated that Molotov was most disloyal to the President and had misinterpreted his views. Harriman stated that he could not correct Molotov because he was just an observer. He thought that this might create an American-Soviet incident and cost the President a few million votes in the coming election. He further expressed his appreciation for Mikolajczyk's tact in not raising this issue again at the conference.

When Foreign Minister Romer described how difficult the position of the Polish delegation was, owing to the Soviet territorial demands and British pressure, and asked if the Poles could count on some support from the American side, Harriman pointed to the difficulties created for Roosevelt by the pre-election problems and advised the Poles not to overestimate (even later) any possibility of American intervention into territorial disputes in Europe. "But, Poland can count on American defense if the Soviet Union will endanger Polish independence and freedom." He advised the Polish Government to reach an agreement now, because time worked against Poland. Any delay would endanger the position of the Polish Government inside Poland and in the international arena.[145]

After reflecting about Harriman's arguments, Mikolajczyk was certain that he was simply repeating the British line of reasoning.[146]

In spite of Polish resistance, Churchill did not give up hope. On October 16 he drafted the final proposal of a Soviet-Polish agreement which he subsequently showed to Stalin on the same day.

The British and Soviet Governments, upon the conclusion of the discussions at Moscow in October, 1944, between ourselves and with the Polish Government, have reached the following argreement:

Upon the unconditional surrender of Germany, the territory of Poland in the West will include the Free City of Danzig, the regions of East Prussia west and south of Königsberg, the Administrative District of Oppeln Silesia, and the lands desired by Poland to the east of the line of the Oder. It is further agreed that the possession of these territories shall be guaranteed to Poland by the Soviet and British Governments. It is understood that the Germans in the said regions shall be repatriated to Germany and that all Poles in Germany shall at their wish be repatriated to Poland.

In consideration of the foregoing agreement, the Polish Government accepts the Curzon Line as the (÷) line of demarcation (÷) between Poland and the U.S.S.R.

Separate Soviet-Polish agreements will regulate reciprocal transfer and the repatriation of the population of both countries and the release of persons detained. It is agreed that the necessary measures will be taken for the transfer of all persons of both countries desiring to change their allegiance in accordance with their freely expressed wishes.

It is agreed that a Polish Government of national unity (') under Prime Minister Mikolajczyk (') will be set up at once in the territory already liberated by Russian arms.

The Soviet Government takes this occasion of reaffirming their unchanging policy of supporting the establishment, within the territorial limits set forth, of a sovereign, independent Poland, free in every way to manage its own affairs, and its intention to make a treaty of durable friendship and mutual aid with the Polish Government, which it is understood will be established on an anti-fascist and democratic basis.

The treaties and relationships existing between Poland and other countries will be unaffected by this settlement, the parties to which declare again their implacable resolve to wage war against the Nazi tyranny until it has surrendered unconditionally.

Upon getting acquainted with the contents of this proposal, Stalin demanded replacing:

1. (÷)—(÷) with the words: "basis for a frontier"
and
2. (')—(') with the words: "in accordance with the agreement (or

understanding) reached between the Polish Government in London and the Polish Committee of National Liberation in Lublin.[147]

Explaining this to Mikolajczyk, Churchill added that although Stalin eliminated any mention of Mikolajczyk's name, he (Stalin) reassured him that he maintained Mikolajczyk's candidacy without any reservation as the only one acceptable.

Churchill understood that those changes might be unacceptable to the Poles. In such an event nothing else could be done but to return to London without revealing the fiasco of the whole effort and to continue striving for a solution. The British Government promised its support.

Nevertheless, Churchill urged an immediate acceptance of Stalin's corrections, because any delay would bring only harm. Mikolajczyk pointed out that he went quite far to meet the Soviet demands but he could not see how he could accept the Soviet's rigid stand.[148]

On October 17 Mikolajczyk informed Churchill that he had decided to return to London in order to consult with his Cabinet. Before that, he would like to make a final attempt to reach an agreement in a conference between Stalin and himself only, wherein he could clarify the changes and conditions regarding the formation of a new government and its practical function. He would also like to have a similar private meeting with Bierut to discuss the same problems. Mikolajczyk asked for British support in these matters. Churchill expressed his willingness to arrange such meetings.

The same day Mikolajczyk met Bierut for tea at the Grand Hotel. During the conversation Bierut insisted that if Mikolajczyk were to be Premier, he (Bierut) must have 75% of the Cabinet. Mikolajczyk proposed that each of the five Polish parties should be represented. Since his Government in London was a coalition of four political parties he would have a majority composed of personalities not obnoxious to Stalin. The meeting ended in a deadlock.[149]

On October 18 Stalin received Mikolajczyk, and the following conversation took place.

MIKOLAJCZYK. Mr. Marshal. In this historic moment I wish to emphasize once again that your generosity and magnanimity, Mr. Marshal, in the matter of frontiers, may win the heart of the entire Polish nation. (Prime Minister Mikolajczyk discusses at length the necessity of not deciding at present the question of Polish frontiers and he proposes as the only concession the fixation of the demarcation line.)

STALIN. A demarcation line is not a frontier. I firmly insist on immediate settlement of frontiers which as I said before shall follow the Curzon Line. And this Curzon Line was not invented by us but by the allies at that time. It was approved by the Americans, French, and English who were our enemies at that time. We cannot depart from the Curzon Line. If we would make concessions from that line we would be ashamed of it. Therefore, we cannot do it. These territories were always the object of conflicts and struggles between Poles, White Russians and Ukrainians and this must end once and for all. Whoever wants peace must accept this. In addition, the Polish nation will not object to it. Messrs. Bierut and Osobka, representatives of the Lublin Committee, declared that this new frontier was just. Finally, the new frontier line will put an end to mistrust between Poles and Ukrainians. Émigrés in London oppose this frontier, but I do not consider them as the nation. In addition, these émigrés expect a conflict between Russia and England. We need a final frontier.

MIKOLAJCZYK again defended the integrity of the Polish frontier and discussed at length the question of Eastern Galicia, stressing that this part of the Polish Republic was not included in the Curzon Line, mentioning also that it was not a part of Russia before the 1914 War.

STALIN [interrupts]. But Warsaw was within the boundaries of Tsarist Russia.

MIKOLAJCZYK mentions the statement of Lenin that Poland should rise free and independent.

STALIN. We also share this view.

MIKOLAJCZYK once again defends Polish frontiers—.

STALIN. I repeat once more that I cannot agree. And what would the Ukrainians say to it, who fought so valiantly against the Germans and suffered so many losses? In addition, as you know, English and Americans support us in the matter of these frontiers.

MIKOLAJCZYK. As you know, Mr. Marshal, Polish soldiers from eastern territories of Poland fought valiantly against the Germans and what would be my position should I come to them and tell that they have no home and no place to return to?

STALIN. We have already mobilized our citizens in Eastern Galicia and all of them very willingly fought the Germans. Those, however, from among the Ukrainians who cooperated with the Germans were executed as enemies of the United Nations.

MIKOLAJCZYK. How do you, Mr. Marshal, imagine the future foreign policy of Poland? Poland besides friendly relations with Russia is in alliance with Great Britain and France.

STALIN. Of course, besides friendly relations with Soviet Russia, Poland has to maintain friendly relations not only with Great Britain and France but also with the United States, the Czechs, and the Hungarians. The states bordering upon Poland have to live in friendship together, so that if the Germans would provoke an aggression these states would strike at them.

MIKOLAJCZYK. Will Poland take part in the occupation of Germany, together with the Soviet army?

STALIN. If Poland wishes, we will give part of the German territories for occupation.

I wish to emphasize once again that the Polish policy should be independent.

MIKOLAJCZYK. As you know, Mr. Marshal, communists are small in numbers in Poland. Then do you think, Mr. Marshal, that the form of government of Poland will be communist?

STALIN. Of course not. The form of government of Poland should be democratic. Private ownership system and free private economic enterprise should be preserved. Under the control of the State over capitalism, of course. There are no conditions for the communist system in Poland.

MIKOLAJCZYK. If it comes to an understanding in Poland, would it then be possible to count on the friendliness of Russia for the future Polish Government?

STALIN. I do not doubt it.

MIKOLAJCZYK. After liberation from the Germans the people in Poland will want to live a free life, there will be various political parties, of course, and the views will conflict. There will be a free interchange of thought at last.

STALIN. It will be permitted only up to some limits; for the work of the reconstruction of the State and not for a revolt.

MIKOLAJCZYK. Do you think, Mr. Marshal, that the members of the National Democratic Party of western Poland whose representatives always wished friendly collaboration with Russia, will be able to work in Poland?

STALIN. We shall admit all who wish to work in the democratic spirit, both those from the left and those from the right. But we shall not admit those who want under these or other pretenses to come for the purpose of making revolutions. It would be best to discuss with the Committee the matter of returning people from London. As you know, in the course of this war the composition of political parties has been completely changed; there are new people everywhere, people connected with the struggle against the Germans. It should be taken into account. To avoid misunderstanding, we shall not admit even one man who in this or another way is connected with the reactionary elements of Sosnkowski. You should go to Poland, talk with the Committee, and then you will orient yourself. One thing is sure. Political parties created now in Poland wish sincere and friendly collaboration with Russia and they must have their voice.

MIKOLAJCZYK underlines the share of Poland in the war against the Germans, great political significance in Poland of four political parties forming the Government in London, and assures Marshal Stalin that as soon as he returns to London he will endeavor to convince his colleagues in the Cabinet about the necessity of arriving at an understanding with Russia; however, he firmly insists upon postponement of the controversial matters relating to the frontiers to a future time.[150]

After that conference Mikolajczyk informed Churchill and Eden of the results of his talks with Bierut and Stalin.

Churchill expressed a firm determination that Mikolajczyk must have a free hand in choosing the members of a new Cabinet in Poland because only a government so formed could be recognized by the Western democracies.[151]

After this series of frustrating attempts to reach an acceptable compromise, Mikolajczyk flew back to London. Although, as previously stated, Churchill considered the Polish problem to be the main item on his agenda in Moscow he had other issues to discuss with Stalin.

On leaving after this profoundly interesting fortnight, in which we got closer to our Soviet Allies than ever before—or ever since—I had written to Stalin:

"Eden and I have come away from the Soviet Union refreshed and fortified by the discussions which we had with you, Marshal Stalin, and with your colleagues. This memorable meeting in Moscow has shown that there are no matters that cannot be adjusted between us when we meet together in frank and intimate discussion. . . ." [152]

On October 22 Churchill reported all the above to Roosevelt and added:

Mikolajczyk is going to urge upon his London colleagues the Curzon Line, including Lwow, for the Russians. I am hopeful that even in the next fortnight we may get a settlement. If so I will cable you the exact form so that you can say whether you want it published or delayed. [153]

By return wire Roosevelt replied:

I am delighted to learn of your success at Moscow in making progress toward a compromise solution of the Polish problem.

When and if a solution is arrived at I should like to be consulted as to the advisability from this point of view of delaying its publication for about two weeks. You will understand. [154]

The general public was dependent upon the Soviet press for information as to what went on behind the conference doors. For this reason a brief review of the comments provided by the Soviet press will supplement the official records.

On October 12, the day of the arrival of the Polish delegation from London, *Pravda* omitted that fact but instead, in an ostentatious manner, put on its front page a full report of the arrival of Bierut, Morawski, and Zymierski who were received with all honors.

On October 13 *Pravda* and *Izvestia*, on its last pages, had short items about the arrival of "Messrs. Mikolajczyk, Grabski, and Romer." In the same issue *Pravda* and *Izvestia* had a long report from their TASS correspondent about the festivities in Lublin and the speeches by Bierut, Morawski, and Putrament, who attacked Raczkiewicz, Sosnkowski, and their agencies for spreading hatred in Poland. They were accused of pro-German sympathies.

On October 14 *Pravda* and *Izvestia* carried a report of a congress of the Polish Peasant Party held in Zamość and about the telegrams with congratulations sent to Stalin and Zymierski.

On October 15 *Pravda* and *Izvestia* carried articles in connection with the "liberation" of the Western Ukraine with its capital, Lwow.

In its review of international affairs, *Pravda* attacked "Polish reactionary circles" in the United States, accusing them of exploiting the pre-election campaign for their "dirty, anti-Soviet connivings." In this field they had, as *Pravda* asserted, the support of Thomas Dewey, who was particularly attacked for his speech on Pulaski Day.

On October 16 the TASS correspondent reported in *Pravda* that the Anglo-Soviet Parliamentary Committee had, in its bulletin, attacked anti-Soviet propaganda conducted by the Polish Government in London. The same was published in *Izvestia* the next day.

On October 18 *Pravda* carried a highly complimentary story of the "splendid achievements" of the Lublin Committee in restoring normal life in Poland—how cultural, social, and economic life had returned to normal; how factories, bridges, railways, schools, movies, theaters were already rebuilt and functioning.

On October 19 the Soviet press was silent about the Polish question. Only Radio Moscow had information, supplied by the Polpress (Polish press):

> The reason for the arrival in Moscow of the delegation of the Committee of National Liberation was to resume talks with the Polish delegation which had begun in August but were interrupted because of the unwillingness of the London Poles to accept, as a basis for discussion, the Polish Constitution of 1921. On October 13 the delegation of the Lublin Committee had a conference with Stalin, Churchill, etc. At that conference, which was permeated with the spirit of mutual trust and friendship, the delegation of the Committee expressed its readiness to reach an agreement with the representatives from London. The delegation of the Committee stressed its constant and main goal to reach a unification of the Polish nation. On October 16 a meeting took place between Mr. Bierut and Mr. Mikolajczyk which enabled them to deepen their mutual outlook. Mr. Mikolajczyk declared that he wanted to consult his colleagues in London and to obtain authorization to continue negotiations in the nearest future.

On October 20 *Pravda* reprinted an extract from an article published in *Rzeczpospolita* which maintained that Mikolajczyk's first journey to Moscow was connected with the Warsaw uprising and his present visit was connected with the terroristic attacks in Poland which were organized by the London Government.

Just below that reprint was another article which stated that although the terror in Poland was organized by Sosnkowski, Mikolajczyk was really responsible for it. According to *Pravda*, a series of public meetings were held in Lublin where shouts were heard: "Away with Mikolajczyk's Government!" It was alleged that full solidarity existed between the four parties—the Peasant Party, Socialist Party, Democratic Party, and Workers' Party.

On October 21 *Pravda* published a leading article about the results of the negotiations in Moscow.

The importance of the Polish question is not a secret. This problem played an important role in the history of Europe. The birth of the Soviet Union and its policy of peace and international friendship created the necessary conditions for a profitable solution of the Polish problem. The greatest difficulty in the last twenty-five years has been the troublesome policy of Polish reactionaries. Soviet public opinion will be pleased to know that, as a result of detailed discussions, substantial successes towards the solution of the Polish problem were achieved.

For a long time Poland has been a corridor for foreign invaders of our land. Our generation witnessed two invasions by German bandits. It is obvious that the nations of the Soviet Union desire to see that Poland and other countries will cease to serve as a corridor for new attempts of invasion by the Germans. Poland must be free, independent, and democratic and she must abandon her rapacious desire towards Ukrainians and Byelorussians. Only a Poland organized on democratic principles can liberate its people from the oppression of its feudal landlords and then she can give land to the peasants. Such a Poland will be a rock of peace in Europe. For the sake of the creation of such a Poland, negotiations took place with the participation of the Polish Government in exile and the Committee of National Liberation. Discussions about unsolved problems are still going on. *Rzeczpospolita* points out that the first visit of Mikolajczyk in Moscow coincided with the uprising in Warsaw—while the second visit was connected with the organization of terroristic attacks in Poland. Every sensible person understands that such methods will not achieve anything, and if the Government in exile will not abandon these methods the guilt will rest on its shoulders.

The majority of the British press was informing its people that the whole difficulty in reaching an understanding in Moscow was due to quarrels between the Poles in London and the Lublin Committee.

Only the *Daily Herald*, the *Nineteenth Century and After*, the *Tablet Tribune*, and the *Spectator* preserved the traditional British sense of fair play.

On October 13 Mr. Richard Neilson wrote in the *Spectator*:

John Moscow maintains that there are no reasons whatsoever to doubt Stalin's good intentions to establish a free and independent Poland. Everything speaks against this. All Soviet moves from the moment they entered Poland are dangerous to Poland and her people. The Soviet Union arrested those who helped the advance of the Red Army. She deported Polish citizens, established a Lublin Committee—which does not represent anyone except themselves. Yet they defy the Polish Government and accuse it of Hitlerism. But Russia forgets her relations with Hitler from 1939–1941. This Lublin Committee sentences to death General Bor for starting the Warsaw uprising, but it was the Radio of Moscow which kept calling the Poles to rise.

What did the Polish Government do to endanger the Soviet Union? There might not have been a Soviet Union if in 1939 Poland had not taken arms against Hitler. Since that time they have sabotaged the German supply lines leading to Russia quite effectively.

If two years ago England and America had intervened into Soviet-Polish relations, we should not be witnessing this tragic spectacle today. To be silent today is to commit a crime. . . . Did we go through five years of war to discover today that . . . logic, honesty and respect for principles failed us? Some are destroyed by bombs while others are murdered in quiet conference halls. How can we reconstruct the world which should be built on morals and law?

Upon his return from Moscow on October 24, 1944 Mikolajczyk reported to his Cabinet about his negotiations with the Soviets. His conclusions were:

The British are enthusiastic about the results of the negotiations in Moscow, and are optimistic about the chances of reaching an agreement, not only about the Polish problems but also about combined action in the Far East. The Soviets are absolutely determined to get the Curzon Line because the Soviet Union is more important to Churchill and Roosevelt than we are, and Stalin knows that neither of them will support our position. Without their help, we are bound to lose. There are no chances of getting any land east of the Curzon Line. Although the Soviets are somewhat critical of the Lublin Committee, their prestige is involved in establishing that Committee and signing the treaty with them. Inside Poland, people are showing signs of exhaustion and are longing for some solution of this difficult problem.

The British Foreign Office asked us not to reveal the complete fiasco of our negotiations in Moscow. They maintain that we should wait for a development of events. The British pressure on us to make us accept the Curzon Line is not ceasing. There is no chance of having a new war. We should think about the danger that the Red Army may take over the whole of Poland while we may not have any agreement with Moscow or Lublin.[155]

There was no discussion and the meeting was adjourned.

On October 30, at the second meeting of the Cabinet, Mikolajczyk began by saying that any further delay in a decision about the eastern frontier would be catastrophic to Poland. An acceptance now would permit the London Government to go to Poland and prevent a complete communization of the rest of the country.

Future generations will judge us not only by the frontiers which we may or may not secure, but also by the economic and political system which we may help establish in the new Poland.[156]

Then he invited the views of the three other parties represented in his Government. As for himself, he was willing to accept the Curzon Line provided that,

1. It would be in the framework of a general agreement with Russia which would guarantee freedom to the rest of Poland.
2. That Poland would get an effective guarantee from her Allies that territorial compensation in the west and north would be granted her.
3. That Poland should be helped financially to resettle her population from the east.

He concluded by suggesting that a special committee, composed of the chairmen of the four parties represented in the Government plus his Foreign Minister, be created to work out a program for the solution of the problem of whether to accept the Curzon Line and that this should be submitted at the next Cabinet meeting.

Vice-Premier KWAPINSKI stated that Poland's Allies were performing political sabotage against Poland and suggested that nothing should be done until the American election was over.

Minister POPIEL observed that as a result of this war, Poland was going to lose more than Germany would. He was puzzled by the British pressure on the Polish Government and suggested, also, that a decision should be postponed until after the American election, and that the underground organizations in Poland should be consulted.

Minister KOMARNICKI [former university professor] expressed suspicion of the British tactics and pressure, and warned against a hasty acceptance of the Soviet demands.

Minister General KUKIEL [former university professor] warned against going too far west, because undoubtedly at some time after this war the Germans would be asking for a return of those territories. Poland would not be able to count on a Western guarantee or support, so Poland would have to rely on the Soviet Union. This would be obtained only after a substantial political price. He suggested that the possibility should be explored as to what chance there was to appeal to American and British public opinion.

Minister GROSFELD supported Mikolajczyk's reasoning and his proposal.

Minister STANCZYK also supported Mikolajczyk's views.

Minister Rev. KACZYNSKI asked why the Big Powers wanted the signature of the Polish Government in London to a decision about Poland which they had already made.

Foreign Minister ROMER supported the Prime Minister.

Mikolajczyk wound up the meeting without reaching any solution. During the subsequent meeting which took place on November 2, it was decided to establish the proposed committee to work out a tentative plan for a solution.[157]

Subsequently Mikolajczyk reported the results of his negotiations with the Russians to the (Polish) National Unity Council. He summed them up as follows:

We are faced with naked reality. Without the acceptance of the Curzon Line and a recognition [i.e., a recognition based on formal statements rather than the true merits of the case] of the Soviet prestige involved in their support of the Lublin Committee we have no chance of reaching a Polish-Soviet understanding.

What is worse, when it comes to the question of the Polish eastern frontier we are faced with a united Anglo-Soviet front and a passive (as until now) American stand. The impression is that the Soviets do not particularly care to solve their relations with us now. They discussed the problem with us only because of British pressure upon them to do so. I have to state that the whole attitude of the Soviet leaders and the Soviet press towards us during our visit to Moscow was critical.

It is not without significance that:

1. In case we accept the Curzon Line we can get British and Soviet guarantees that Poland will receive East Prussia (except Königsberg), Danzig, Stettin—along the Oder River, and the whole of Silesia. The American stand on this matter is still to be clarified.

2. In case we reach an agreement on the formation of a new Government, the Polish Government would take over the administration of Poland and the Soviet Government would sign a declaration promising noninterference into Polish internal affairs.

3. The possibility would arise as to the signing of a treaty of friendship and mutual respect with the Soviet Government, under which compensation for lost properties, a choice of residence, and the release of the arrested would take place.

4. We would have an opportunity to revise the Polish-British Treaty of Mutual Help of August 25, 1939 and to extend it to the same date as the Anglo-Soviet Treaty of May 26, 1942 which is valid for the next twenty years.

These are not minor things—especially if they take place before the rest of Poland is freed from the German forces; before huge repressions are introduced as the result of the failure of the Lublin Committee. Such an event will cause only bloodshed and we cannot imagine what consequences may follow from it.

I have presented to you the actual state of affairs. I want to declare that I did not undertake any obligations because I was aware of the responsibilities connected with them. I was mindful that the decisions could be taken only by all of us because the future of Poland and her independence depends on it.

Weigh this case in your conscience and remember your responsibility and by your advice show us which road to take in this decisive and historical moment for Poland.[158]

His audience was divided. The right-wing members were against such a far-reaching compromise, because they were of the opinion that the Soviets would not be satisfied with territorial concessions alone. The moderates were convinced that an effort should be made to save what could be saved and they believed that if Poland agreed to territorial concessions and admitted a certain number of the Lublin Poles into its legal Government, the Western Powers would sanction its inviolability.[159]

On October 26, 1944 upon return to London, Churchill informed Mikolajczyk that during his last conference in the Kremlin, Stalin had insisted on a fusion of the Lublin Committee with the Polish Government in London on the basis of 75% of the ministerial portfolios for Lublin and 25% for London—with the provision that Mikolajczyk would be the Prime Minister. Churchill had replied that this was absurd because it would deprive the head of the Government of any influence on policies. He had demanded for Mikolajczyk an effective majority and expressed the definite support of Mikolajczyk by His Majesty's Government. Further, he stated that the British Government would never recognize such a solution. He was certain that it would be possible to get at least a combination of 50:50. Churchill urged the Polish Government to resume negotiations in Moscow as soon as possible and described the Lublin Committee as "bastards, wretched swine," and added, "you would not have them in Poland today if you had listened to my advice and accepted the Curzon Line last January.[160]

Mikolajczyk retorted that the Lublin Committee would not be in Poland now if Churchill and Roosevelt had supported the Polish Government from the beginning—that is, from July 1941. Since they were prepared to sacrifice Polish territorial and political sovereignty for the sake of buying Stalin's friendship, Stalin had taken full advantage of it. Churchill did not share Mikolajczyk's interpretation of the reasons why the communists were taking over the whole of Poland.

The following day, October 27, Churchill reported to the House of Commons about his conferences in Moscow.

The most urgent and burning question was that of Poland, and here again I speak words of hope, and of hope reinforced by confidence.

In this sphere there are two crucial issues. The first is the question of the eastern frontier of Poland and the Curzon Line, as it is called, and the new territories to be added to Poland in the north and west. The second is the relation of the Polish Government with the Lublin National Liberation Committee.

On these two points we held a series of conferences with both parties. We saw them together and separately, and of course were in constant discussion with the heads of the Soviet Government. I had several long talks with Marshal Stalin. The Foreign Secretary was every day working on this and cognate matters with Molotov. Two or three times we all four met together with no one but the interpreters present. I wish I could tell the House that we had reached a solution of these problems. It is certainly not for want of trying. I am quite sure, however, that we have got a great deal nearer to the solution of both.

I hope Mr. Mikolajczyk will soon return to Moscow, and it will be a great disappointment to all sincere friends of Poland if a good arrangement cannot be made which enables him to form a Polish Government on Polish soil—a Government recognized by all the Great Powers concerned and, indeed, by all those Governments of the United Nations which now recognize only the Polish Government in London.

Although I do not underrate the difficulties which remain, it is a comfort to feel that Britain and Soviet Russia and, I do not doubt, the United States, are all firmly agreed to the re-creation of a strong, free, independent, sovereign Poland, loyal to the Allies and friendly to her great neighbor and liberator, Russia.

Speaking more particularly for His Majesty's Government, it is our constant aim that the Polish people, after their suffering and vicissitudes, shall find in Europe an abiding home and resting place which, though it may not entirely coincide with the prewar frontiers of Poland, will nevertheless be adequate for the needs of the Polish nation and will not be inferior in character and quality to what they had previously possessed.

These are critical days, and it would be a great pity if time were wasted in indecisions or protracted negotiations. If the Polish Government had taken the advice we tendered them at the beginning of this year, the additional complication produced by the formation of the Polish National Committee of Lublin would not have arisen, and any prolonged delay in the settlement can only have the effect of increasing the divisions between the Poles in Poland and also of hampering the common action which Poles, Russians, and the rest of the Allies are taking against Germany. Therefore, I hope no time will be lost in continuing these discussions and pressing them to an effective conclusion.[161]

This public pronouncement by Churchill, like several of his previous ones, did not help the Poles a bit; on the contrary, it made their position more difficult.

Prior to Mikolajczyk's journey to Moscow, and even while he was there, the pro-London Poles in America, under the leadership of the President of the Polish Congress in the United States, Karol Rozmarek, were making every effort to enlist the support of President Roosevelt for the Polish case. Their requests to see the President were turned down on the basis of heavy schedules and the poor health of Roosevelt. Only when Rozmarek requested Mayor Kelly of Chicago to help him in this endeavor, did Roosevelt receive Rozmarek on October 19.

Rozmarek urged the President to take a more definite stand on the Polish issue. Roosevelt replied that he could not do so because this might lead to World War III with Russia. Rozmarek did not share this view and pointed out that the President had a powerful weapon in his hand in the form of Lend-Lease. If the President told Stalin firmly that unless he adopted a reasonable attitude towards the Polish Government Lend-Lease would be stopped, this would be sufficient to convince Stalin that America would not permit a new partition of

Poland. Roosevelt assured Rozmarek of his friendship for Poland but did not make any clear promise.[162]

The following day, Rozmarek telegraphed Mikolajczyk as follows:

In view of the fact that the concessions offered by you remained fruitless, I urge you, on behalf of the Polish organizations in America, to defend without further compromise the essential rights of full sovereignty, territorial integrity and the honor of the Polish nation. We earnestly warn you against taking communists into your Cabinet because it would be the beginning of the loss of Polish independence. We assure you of the highest efforts and support for your stand. We believe in the victory of justice and truth.[163]

Although Mikolajczyk shared Rozmarek's fears, he was convinced that only a compromise would now save Polish independence from the NKVD. Because of the West's appeasement of Stalin and their lack of a forthright policy on Poland during the past several years, they had let the initiative fall into Soviet hands. With Soviet troops in control of a large section of Poland and the defeat of Germany almost a certainty, the possibility of using Lend-Lease as a bargaining lever on the Soviets was now fading. In addition, it was clear that the West wanted Stalin to fulfill his commitment in the war in the Pacific and thus could not risk antagonizing him.

A more realistic and informative analysis of the American scene came from Ambassador Ciechanowski.

Up to your departure to Moscow American public opinion, press, radio, and Congress were showing uneasiness and suspicion towards Soviet policies in Europe. They even doubted the chances of collaboration with Russia because of (1) the Soviet behavior in the Balkans, (2) their attitude to the Warsaw uprising, and (3) the peculiar behavior of the Lublin Committee towards the tragedy of Warsaw.

American public opinion has shown an understanding of the puppet nature of the Lublin Committee, its lack of Allied support and the lack of support from the Polish nation. On the other hand, it has confidence in Premier Mikolajczyk who has the support of the nation and is the legal authority in Poland. Without those elements Stalin's policy via Lublin cannot succeed. The development of the talks in Moscow is misleadingly presented by some British and American correspondents, presumably to push the Polish problem out of the elements standing in the way of reaching an agreement between the three Powers.

The anticipation of concessions from the London Poles makes things easier for certain circles over here who want to get rid of the Polish problem, and by so doing, are making things more difficult for those in the administration who, for the sake of expediency, are willing to defend the Polish cause during the next few weeks until the election takes place.

American public opinion is still under the influence of the long conference held between the President and the leadership of the Polish Congress in America. After the visit to the President, Mr. Rozmarek told the press that the Poles in America recognized only the Polish Government in London and stuck to the territorial integrity of Poland, and they would not be bound by any concessions made by the Polish Government under external pressure.[164]

In another confidential message to his Government, Ambassador Ciechanowski reported that on October 8, 1944, during the Pulaski Parade in New York, he spent three hours with Governor Dewey on the reviewing stand, during which Dewey told him that Roosevelt's passive policy towards Poland revolted him and that he, if elected, intended to take a firmer stand against Soviet appetites.

On October 6 and October 20 Ambassador Ciechanowski visited former President Herbert Hoover, whom he had known for eighteen years. Hoover expressed a belief that at Teheran President Roosevelt undertook an obligation towards Stalin to preserve a passive policy towards the Polish question and that he had agreed to the Curzon Line with compensation for Poland in the west. But there was no guarantee about that. As Hoover put it, "Poland was double-crossed" by Stalin and by Roosevelt.

"To my question," wrote Ciechanowski, "what Poland should do," Hoover replied:

The only thing left for you is to appeal to public opinion. The President, the same way as Churchill—for their own political reasons and under the pretext not to spoil the relations between the Allies—demands from you silence and secrecy. You should, on the contrary, bring the whole thing before the American and British public opinion. American public opinion will not fight for the Polish frontier if it will be said that an agreement was reached between you, even if under some pressure. But if it came out into the open that Russia is striving to control Poland, which she is undoubtedly doing, then you will get such indignation and protest from American public opinion between the Atlantic and Pacific Oceans that no American Government could conduct an appeasing policy toward the Soviet Union.

Hoover then added that in view of the danger to the United States rising out of the pro-Soviet policy of the New Deal, such a sobering of public opinion would be a great kindness to the American nation.

Ciechanowski observed that it would be impossible for the Polish Government to do anything like that, because it would be an interference into the internal affairs of the United States. Furthermore, the Polish Government was still hopeful that by direct negotiation the whole problem could be solved. However, should nothing come of it, Poland would be anxious to show that the responsibility for the failure rested on Stalin's shoulders. Hoover said that when the need arose he personally would undertake to launch an appeal to American public opinion in order to enlist its support for Poland.

On October 20, 1944 Ciechanowski had a meeting with John Foster Dulles, during which Dulles promised to exert influence on Dewey in order to reinforce his friendly attitude toward the Polish question. Dulles expressed dissatisfaction with Dewey's promise to Cordell Hull that foreign policy would not be a campaign issue.[165]

This report encouraged but at the same time depressed the Polish Government. At least one major party, it was comforting to know, was aware of the long-range significance of Soviet foreign policy. But Mikolajczyk ruled out any possibility of using the Republican offer of support as a matter of principle.

Another report came from the first counselor of the Polish Embassy in Washington, Minister Kwapiszewski, who suggested sending a special mission to Washington under the official pretext of discussing the post-war economic reconstruction of Poland but actually to establish close contact with that influential group around the President to which Sidney Hillman belonged. He argued that only through his excellent relations with this group had the Soviet Ambassador in Washington secured either support or a passive attitude (whatever the case may be) for the gradual but clever fulfillment of Soviet plans. Therefore, it was obvious, he urged, that once the Polish Government enlisted the sympathy and support of this group, Polish problems would be treated differently by the Soviets, because they could not afford to antagonize that group.[166]

Mikolajczyk was tempted to put the above suggestion into effect, but other matters in London demanded his immediate attention.

6. Reports on American Attitudes toward the Polish Problem

Instead, the Polish Cabinet decided to ask Roosevelt for a definite formulation of his position in regard to the Polish-Soviet dilemma. On October 26 the following telegram was sent to President Roosevelt:

> Mr. President, you probably have heard of the recent transactions at Moscow from Ambassador Harriman, and you know of the great pressure put on us to recognize the Curzon Line as the future frontier between Poland and Russia.
>
> I think I have shown how diligently I have tried to reach a Polish-Russian agreement and how I wish to serve the cause of the Allies and the future peace. I think you appreciate, too, how terrible would be the injury to the Polish nation if, after all the losses it has suffered in this war, it would then be forced to suffer the loss of one-half its territory.

We cannot accept a plan that would deprive Poland of this land, which includes the only oil we have and the potash we need so critically because we are an agricultural nation. If my Government did so agree, we would quickly lose the confidence of the Polish people and the Agreement would, in fact, cause tremendous disagreement.

I tried to persuade Marshal Stalin and Prime Minister Churchill to permit us to retain at least the Lwow area, with its oil and potash, for it is a region that never belonged to Russia. My efforts were in vain.

Before I make my final decision, I would like to know your attitude. I remember your own feelings about our retention of the Lwow area, as expressed at our last meeting. I still cannot believe what Molotov revealed about the secret decisions made by the Big Three at Teheran, in view of the assurances that you gave me at our last meeting.

If Russia takes Lwow and its oil, the production there will represent only about one percent of the total oil production of the U.S.S.R. But it represents nearly one hundred percent of Poland's oil. Our only source of potash is in that same region.

I understand how busy you are. I hope, however, that now when we must make such a tremendous decision, you will take the time to assert your great authority and influence in this matter. I can assure you that for helping us, the Polish nation will be eternally grateful, the cause of the Allies will be aided, and the future development of Europe enhanced.[167]

On October 30 Ambassador Ciechanowski sent a confidential report to Minister Romer about Ambassador Harriman's visit to Washington during which he reported to the President about the Churchill-Stalin-Mikolajczyk conference in Moscow. The concluding part of that report stated:

As far as Polish matters are concerned, I know that Harriman is praising the Prime Minister (Mikolajczyk) very highly—who, as he put it, made a deep impression on him as "a very statesmanlike man and an excellent negotiator." However, my personal friends with whom Harriman talked confidentially about the Polish-Soviet matters convinced me that we have an enemy in him and that we cannot count on his friendly attitude to the Polish problem. I was warned about this from two different unconnected sources.[168]

If this report was true, and in view of Harriman's influential position with the White House, Poland's situation was desperate indeed.

At the same time when the telegram of October 26 was dispatched to Roosevelt, the Polish Foreign Minister sent a separate note to the British Foreign Office asking whether Britain favored advancing Poland's post-war frontier as far as the Oder River and Stettin and whether she was prepared to guarantee the independence and integrity of the new Poland—in a joint declaration with Russia—pending the establishment of a United Nations guarantee.

On November 2 Minister Romer received the following reply from Sir Alexander Cadogan:

Dear Monsieur Romer,

I duly reported to the Prime Minister the conversation which I had with Your Excellency and the Polish Ambassador on October 31, in the course of which you put to me three questions for the consideration of His Majesty's Government.

The Prime Minister, after consultation with the Cabinet, has now directed me to give you the following replies.

You asked in the first place whether, even in the event of the United States Government finding themselves unable to agree to the changes in the western frontier of Poland foreshadowed in the recent conversations in Moscow, His Majesty's Government would still advocate these changes at the Peace Settlement. The answer of His Majesty's Government to this question is in the affirmative.

Secondly, you enquired whether His Majesty's Government were definitely in favor of advancing the Polish frontier up to the line of the Oder, to include the port of Stettin. The answer is that His Majesty's Government do consider that Poland should have the right to extend her territory to this extent.

Finally, you enquired whether His Majesty's Government would guarantee the independence and integrity of the new Poland. To this the answer is that His Majesty's Government are prepared to give such a guarantee jointly with the Soviet Government. If the United States Government could see their way to join also, that would plainly be of the greatest advantage, though His Majesty's Government would not make this a condition of their own guarantee in conjunction with that of the Soviet Government. This Anglo-Soviet guarantee would, in the view of His Majesty's Government, remain valid until effectively merged in the general guarantee which it is hoped may be afforded by the projected world organization.

With regard to what you said in regard to anticipated difficulties in the way of negotiations in Moscow for a reformation of the Polish Government, the Prime Minister observes that the success of these negotiations must depend on a solution of the frontier question. It is impossible to ignore the possibility that agreement might be reached on the frontier question and that it might nevertheless prove impossible to reach agreement on the other matter. That would of course be most unfortunate, but the Polish Government would be in a much better position if negotiations broke down on this point, on which they would have the support of His Majesty's Government and probably of the United States Government, than on the frontier question.[169]

The Poles were dissatisfied with the vagueness of this reply.

Besides the difficulties encountered in the diplomatic field, the Polish Government was swamped with disturbing reports from Poland. Here is a portion of one report which was transmitted by Mikolajczyk to the British Government in order to illustrate how the Soviets were in fact implementing their promise to build a "free and independent Poland."

In August 1944, a Soviet military commission was set up in Lublin to collect proof of alleged anti-Soviet activities by the Home Army and the Polish underground administration. The commission is composed of a considerable number of members and is under the chairmanship of General Bogdanov of the Red Army. The committee includes: The Soviet General Zhukov, representative of the Red Army with the Polish Committee of National Liberation; Colonel Melnikov, Colonel Strelov, Lieutenant Colonel Ivanov, and Captain Godlevsky of Kiev, an NKVD interpreter. Members of the underground military and civilian organizations are placed at the disposal of this commission, which collects material to prove alleged anti-Soviet and "Fascist" activities by the civilian and military organizations working under the Polish Government. Furthermore, certain cases against members of Polish military and civilian underground organizations are investigated by organs of the People's Commissariat for the Interior (NKVD) and by Soviet military prosecutors.

In the light of the above facts there can be no doubt that the Soviet Government is responsible for organizing and carrying out repressions with regard to the Polish Home Army on the territory of the Polish State.

Similar repressions are also applied against officials of the Polish underground administration. In compliance with instructions from the Polish Government, these officials disclosed to the Soviet authorities their identity as Polish civil servants appointed to carry out specified public duties. According to information in possession of the Polish Government, the majority of these officials have been arrested, while the few who have retained their liberty have been forbidden to carry out their duties. It has been definitely ascertained that the delegates of the Polish Government in Lublin, Lwow, Tomaszow Lubelski and the mayor of Biala Podlaska have been placed under arrest.

The cases of the arrested officials of the Polish underground administration are investigated by Soviet military prosecutors and officials of the People's Commissariat for the Interior (NKVD), and the charges brought forward against them are as a rule of a very general nature, like those of "Fascism" and "collaboration with the Germans." These facts are a further proof that the real authority on Polish territory is that of the Soviet administration, whether the territory is recognized by the Soviet Government on the strength of their own decision as forming part of the U.S.S.R. or whether they recognize it as belonging to the Polish State. The responsibility for the state of affairs described above rests in both cases entirely with the Government of the U.S.S.R.

Besides the actions of the Soviet authorities with regard to the soldiers of the Polish Home Army and officials of the Polish underground administration, repressions are also applied to the general Polish public. An instance of these are the mass deportations of many thousands of men, women, and children, carried out with particular ruthlessness in Wilno, Lwow, Kolomyja and the regions of Zloczow, Rzeszow, and Jaroslaw. It is not possible at the present moment to ascertain the category of persons affected nor the real purpose of these arrests and deportations. It appears, however, that they affect primarily members of the families of arrested soldiers of the Polish Home Army and of officials of the underground administration, a procedure entirely in accordance with the principles adopted by Soviet law of responsibility for the deeds of others. Among those deported to Russia there are also technical experts, a fact which seems to indicate that one reason for these deportations is the desire to supplement Soviet cadres of experts. Nevertheless the mass character of the deportations seems, however, to indicate that their main purpose may be the elimination of the Polish population in the affected territories.

Finally, it should be pointed out that the deportations are being carried out just as those of 1939–1941, solely on the strength of an arbitrary decision of the Soviet administrative authorities, viz., that of the People's Commissariat for the Interior (NKVD).

The facts adduced above give only a partial illustration of the position of the Polish population on the territories occupied by the Red Army. They unquestionably constitute a violation of international law and of universally recognized humanitarian principles by the Government of the U.S.S.R.—a violation of particular gravity in view of the fact that it was committed by one member state of the United Nations and affected the citizens of another member state of the United Nations engaged in the struggle against the common enemy.

In bringing the above facts to the notice of the British Government I beg again to recall the note which I had the honor to address to you, Sir, on October 7, and reiterate the Polish Government's confidence that His Majesty's Government will not fail to take all appropriate measures in order to bring about the release of arrested persons and their repatriation to their homes, and to prevent the recurrence of repressions against the members of the Home Army, the Polish underground administration, and the Polish citizens in general.

Without such a radical change in the attitude and the action of the Soviet authorities and of those acting on their behest it would be vain to expect progress towards an understanding between the Polish Government and the Government of the U.S.S.R., however considerable such an understanding may be in the interest of the two countries and in that of all the member states of the United Nations.[170]

Eden did not offer any help and only expressed his sympathy. He drew the attention of the Poles to the fact that the data submitted only emphasized the necessity of reaching a speedy agreement with the Soviets.

Churchill was impatiently awaiting a reply from the London Poles. The Poles in turn were waiting for a clarification of the American position on this matter before they could answer Churchill.

On November 2, 1944 Mikolajczyk, Romer, and Ambassador Raczynski met with Churchill and Sir Alexander Cadogan at Churchill's request to discuss Polish-Soviet problems. Churchill was in an aggressive mood.

CHURCHILL. How long is it since you gentlemen returned from Moscow? About two weeks ago?

ROMER specifies October 22nd.

MIKOLAJCZYK. That is correct. Time is pressing, and the problem before us is enormous.

CHURCHILL. Delay in deciding threatens to nullify the friendly atmosphere created in Moscow.

MIKOLAJCZYK. My Cabinet has asked that in a matter so important to us we consult the American Government. [He reads the preliminary reply received today from President Roosevelt, who indicates that he will soon send a more factual reply.]

CHURCHILL. What practical value has this at present? Will the Polish-Americans vote against President Roosevelt?

MIKOLAJCZYK. There is no fear of that.

CHURCHILL. That is good.

MIKOLAJCZYK. We are concerned, however, with the maintenance of Poland's independence, and unfortunately our concern is not without grounds.

CHURCHILL. It would be better if the negotiations broke down on this very point, in which case you may count on our standing by you. In the matter of the eastern frontier we cannot support you.

MIKOLAJCZYK. If we were to agree to the territorial demands made, our Polish people would accuse us of selling out our independence.

CHURCHILL. If you had followed our counsel in January and accepted the Curzon Line, you would not have had those horrible Lublin Poles in Lublin today!

MIKOLAJCZYK. The most recent examples of Soviet behavior in Iran and Rumania are not encouraging.

CHURCHILL. You had better attend to your own affairs. In the case of Rumania it is another matter, since it concerns recent satellites of Germany, who had attacked Russia. In Greece we have a good chance to take control of the situation. But what is our attitude to be towards the Polish Government, which cannot decide to say either yes or no? It would be better, therefore, if you state clearly that you will never agree to a solution which will not give Lwow to Poland. I will then wash my hands of you! You have really reached the limit!

MIKOLAJCZYK. This is a misunderstanding. Together with the Minister of Foreign Affairs, I endeavoured to influence the Government in this spirit, devoting due attention to all arguments. I admit that we are meeting with very strong reservations when it comes to the solution proposed in Moscow. One can hardly be surprised. Why is Poland, alone among the United Nations, to bear territorial sacrifices, and so soon?

CHURCHILL [restraining his impatience]. All right, then! Let the Lublin Poles continue to hold the leadership of Polish affairs in their hands, since you do not want to take it away from them. Quisling Poles, dirty, filthy brutes, will be at the head of your country! You may continue to sit here, but Russia will not want to talk with you any more. After all, this concerns the third world power! On my part, I did what I could; I explained to Stalin and convinced him of the need of an understanding with

Poland. Today you could again be in Moscow, close to success; instead, you sit here perplexed. I am very sorry.

MIKOLAJCZYK. The difficulty is that even despite our compromising gestures the independence of Poland is not secured.

CHURCHILL. Surely you can say that you recognize the Curzon Line on condition that the independence of Poland shall be respected and guaranteed in the agreement. If this condition should not be possible of realization and the negotiations break down on that, you will not be bound in the matter of frontiers and you will have us behind you—and, also, surely the Americans.

MIKOLAJCZYK. Unfounded rumours are being spread among Poles from the circles around Ambassador Lebedev, that the Soviets await the arrival in Moscow this time not only of members of the Polish Government, but of a delegation sent by it for the purpose of further negotiation on the basis of Soviet territorial concessions, which reach to the east of the Curzon Line. This is a maneuver calculated to obstruct the agreement being reached in Polish circles. In order to frustrate it, I instructed the reply that we are ready to dispatch such a delegation at any moment, should we receive the assurance that the subject of conversations in Moscow with it will be Polish territories to the east of the Curzon Line.

CHURCHILL. That is absurd, pure Utopia! Don't you remember my laborious attempt with Stalin to make it possible for the visit to Moscow for you gentlemen? At present your endeavours will evaporate into thin air; you will lose control over the further development of events. I shall have to tell Stalin that the Polish Government cannot make up its mind. You are returning to the old tradition of Liberum Veto. As far as I am concerned, I shall stop at that and will not follow you. Under those conditions what will Poland's prospects for the future be? Think only of the terrible massacres that await your Underground Movement!

MIKOLAJCZYK. I have quoted to you in confidence the maneuver attributed to the Russians and my reaction to it, which has as its purpose only the unmasking of a diversion, and which should prove that I am not falling for rumours.

CHURCHILL. You yourself know best what Stalin wants and thinks. Unless you give me an answer by today or tomorrow, I shall consider everything finished. Take into consideration what awaits you. I have done everything I could. I shall explain before Parliament. There is indeed no Polish Government if it is unable to decide anything. I know the views of Mr. Mikolajczyk and Mr. Romer, but what of that, when they are unable to put them into effect? Meantime, the Lublin Poles are active and despite everything increase their significance.

MIKOLAJCZYK. I cannot persuade my colleagues of the necessity to accept the heavy conditions made without proper guarantees. The reply of the British Government to our inquiries, which was transmitted to us in the letter from Cadogan, constitutes in that respect not so much assistance as obstacle, because it constitutes a step backward in comparison with the stand formulated in Moscow.

CHURCHILL. You say that our letter is an obstacle? Please consider it, therefore, cancelled as of this moment. I withdraw our proposals.

RACZYNSKI attempts to explain the misunderstanding, but Churchill does not let him finish and continues himself:

I have had enough of this! On leaving Moscow, you mentioned the possibility that your stay in London would not be for more than forty-eight hours before negotiations were renewed. Today, after two weeks have passed, you have made no progress whatsoever. You are all able to bargain about one thing only—the Curzon Line. You had already rejected it in January, and here now are the consequences of this step. Do you perhaps think that the Russian armies have once and for all stopped where they are now, and are unable to move on any further?

MIKOLAJCZYK. Not at all! On the contrary, we anticipate the further advance of the Soviet armies and this is taken into account in our instructions sent to Poland.

CHURCHILL. The result of your attitude, Gentlemen, shall be the unavoidable creation in Poland of a rival Government. I don't condemn you, but you are confused men, who are incapable of saying either yes or no. To us, it will be a relief not to feel bound by anything. I have told Stalin in Moscow that I don't allow the ratio of strength 75 percent to 25 percent in favour of the Committee in the new Polish Government, and I demand at least 50 percent to 50 percent.

MIKOLAJCZYK. Enormous and extremely difficult things are demanded of us. After all, this concerns the transfer of five to six million Poles into the sphere of the new regions of Poland as well as the removal from them of seven million Germans.

CHURCHILL. The main thing is that you find yourself in Lublin as soon as possible. Otherwise regrettable events will take place there which cannot be mended.

CADOGAN. Was our reply of any use to you, Gentlemen?

MIKOLAJCZYK explains the difference which occurred between the Polish Government's formulation of their first question, and that which Cadogan made of this question in his letter to Romer, and the effect thereof on the reply. He points out also the small value for them of a joint British-Soviet guarantee for the safeguard of the independence and territorial integrity of Poland.

CADOGAN. Perhaps I had not formulated precisely the question which Minister Romer had put to me verbally. This is my fault. As to the joint guarantee, I admit that in the event of aggression by Russia on Poland, the British guarantee does not come into play. But in that case, a Soviet aggression would be, however, a clear violation of international obligations by Russia. That alone is already some security.

CHURCHILL. How can you wait helplessly, as though you were paralyzed? You are playing delaying tactics by posing still other new questions to us. We take a lot of trouble to reply to them—and I won't hide from you the fact that it has not become easy for me to convince my colleagues of the necessity of giving you satisfaction—and then, as a result, you pose still further questions to us, because it is all the same to you. I have had enough of that and I withdraw my promises.

[Here follows a discussion and mutual explanations concerning the particular points of questions and answers; it is conducted in a somewhat chaotic manner by all present, and does not lead to any result. It becomes clear only, that Churchill does not have much of an idea of the legal intricacies of Cadogan's letter, and apparently is not familiar with its exact formulation. He stresses only that all the London Government's questions were submitted for consideration by the British Cabinet, as a result of which to each of these questions he personally made a pencilled reply in the affirmative.]

CHURCHILL. If you don't leave for Moscow by tomorrow evening I shall consider everything as finished and shall telegraph Stalin about it. I withdraw our letters containing guarantees. You have brought about the state of affairs that leads to the existence of the Committee of National Liberation.

MIKOLAJCZYK. I cannot agree with that. When Sikorski was at the Kremlin on that very same day was constituted the Union of Polish Patriots out of which afterwards emerged the Committee of National Liberation. And during my trip to Moscow the Soviet Government hastened to sign an agreement with that Committee. Where is the good will there?

CHURCHILL. I personally went to Moscow only for you, only in the interest of Poland. But you care only about your "Liberum Veto" and your extraordinary habits, thanks to which one of the most valiant nations in Europe has in the past fallen into slavery. If you had really wanted to cooperate with Stalin, you could have been in Poland by now in the company of the British and American Ambassadors.

MIKOLAJCZYK. Only because I have not ceased to contemplate this have we not yet said no, although everything induces us to do so.

[CHURCHILL repeats once again the comparison so often used by him of the losses which Poland would have to accept in the east with the much greater benefits which the change of frontiers in the west would bring to her.]

MIKOLAJCZYK. Of all countries, not excluding Germany, Poland is to suffer the greatest territorial sacrifices after this war. How is that to be explained?

CHURCHILL. What did you Gentlemen accomplish in these two weeks? What did you return to London for? The Soviet Government intimates to us now that it will not sit at a joint table with the Polish Government at any international conference and that it shall demand a place at them for the representatives of the Lublin Committee. You will be liquidated step after step, this you will rightly not escape. Have the courage to say: No! I shall repeat it to Stalin.

MIKOLAJCZYK. You know well, that I did everything to bring about an understanding with Russia and have done so with no small risk.

CADOGAN. I am only a humble official and would not wish to exceed my competence by interfering in the discussion. Yet I am concerned to establish what facts we may communicate to Stalin, because since the Moscow Conference we have not made any remarks, not even one word, on Polish matters to him, despite their importance and urgency. If we are therefore to avoid a fundamental change of atmosphere, which would necessarily reflect also on British-Soviet relations, then we must inform him without further delay of the situation. Are we to tell the Russians that the Polish Government cannot agree to the Curzon Line?

MIKOLAJCZYK. At the moment, no.

CHURCHILL. Are you prepared to leave tomorrow evening for Moscow?

MIKOLAJCZYK. No, I could not do it.

CHURCHILL. And the day after tomorrow?

MIKOLAJCZYK. I am not certain of receiving the Polish Government's decision within that limited time. You will understand that we are concerned with the independence of Poland and this is no small matter in the present state of affairs.

CHURCHILL. This is a matter of your undestanding with Bierut. I give you forty-eight hours' time. In the absence of your reply within that time, I shall telegraph to Stalin and let come what may.

MIKOLAJCZYK. The attitude of the British Government does not help to make a decision easier.

CHURCHILL. I shall be glad to withdraw our guarantees given to you.

CADOGAN. We gave in the connection of guarantees more than we usually give. I shall not betray a secret by pointing out that Prime Minister Churchill had yesterday serious difficulties in forcing through the resolution on that matter at a meeting of the War Cabinet.

CHURCHILL. If your attitude is negative, then have the courage to say so. I shall not hesitate to stand up against you. You have fruitlessly wasted two whole weeks in continuous debates without any results! Where does this lead? Today I am telling you for the last time. After tonight I shall not speak to you any more!

MIKOLAJCZYK. Perhaps the fate of Maniu awaits me, but you won't mind that!

CADOGAN. Can you give Stalin any indication of your position, suggest anything? Because in the event of our silence the last chance of agreement will vanish.

CHURCHILL. You have not budged one inch!

MIKOLAJCZYK [refers to the position of President Roosevelt in the Polish question and to the basic divergence between Roosevelt's definition of the situation during his own conversations with the President, which took place in June in Washington, and the interpretation of this given by Molotov at the Moscow Conference.] It is a matter of primary importance to us, which requires clearing up before we undertake a final decision.

CHURCHILL. I had already said I shall still wait forty-eight hours. A further delay would threaten us with incalculable consequences. Again a new campaign of hate shall be let loose by Lublin.

[MIKOLAJCZYK reads the last reports from Poland which inform of the terrible conditions in which disarmed soldiers of the Home Army are held imprisoned near Siedlce.]

CHURCHILL. Only your presence in Poland may bring an end to these horrors.

MIKOLAJCZYK. If you leave to me only forty-eight hours and if I am not to have the opportunity to await the American reply to our questions, then I warn you that the answer which you will receive shall be negative. I am quite certain that if you yourself were a Pole you would not act otherwise.

CHURCHILL. I never shirked a decision nor a responsibility.

MIKOLAJCZYK. The attitude of America is the more important to us, for, in accordance with your own remarks which I heard in Moscow, the material aid with which we are unable to dispense, having to deal with resettlements on such a vast scale and the subsequent rebuilding of economies will depend on America. For after the sacrifices suffered by Poland will she have to pay that by herself also? Out of what?

CHURCHILL again reminds Mikolajczyk of the last demand of the Soviet Government, that at international conferences in which it is to participate the Lublin Committee, not the Polish Government, will be seated. This is most embarrassing in connection with the London Conference on inland communications.

ROMER reminds Churchill that we find ourselves in that respect in company with Swiss and Portuguese "Fascists," as is evident from the absence of Russia at the International Conference of Civilian Airlines in the United States.

CADOGAN explains that with regard to the London Conference mentioned by Churchill, the Foreign Office had made reservations against the attitude taken by the Soviet Government, so that probably this matter shall not have any unpleasant repercussions for the time being.

CHURCHILL. Notwithstanding, the Poles continue to have a hostile attitude towards the Soviets. Was it not madness to appoint Bor after Sosnkowski, if one was concerned to improve the Polish-Soviet relations?

MIKOLAJCZYK. Whas is wrong with Bor? After all, he was the heroic leader of the Warsaw Garrison. Why should we be ashamed of him? I understand why the Soviets attacked him, but I cannot see why you should uphold their point of view. After Sosnkowski was removed, the Soviets attacked Bor; after he was taken prisoner by the Germans, President Raczkiewicz was attacked. Tomorrow the attacks shall be directed against me or whoever replaces me.

CHURCHILL. I like Anders as a valiant soldier, but I remember what he told me: "Today we fight the Germans, tomorrow we shall fight the Russians." But this is an aberration! Don't count on us to help you in that. Do you realize how very much your standing in the world has deteriorated since the beginning of this year?

MIKOLAJCZYK. Not in the moral sense!

CHURCHILL. I am withdrawing my guarantees contained in Cadogan's letter, since you are unable to give me a reply.

CADOGAN. Perhaps Prime Minister Churchill shall agree not to do this yet, because we have learned from Premier Mikolajczyk that he unfortunately received my letter too late to be able to submit it to the Council of Ministers today, consequently the Polish Government had no opportunity whatsoever to become acquainted with this matter. Will it take place tomorrow?

MIKOLAJCZYK. Yes, I shall call a special meeting for that purpose.

[In the conclusion of the discussion it was mentioned on the Polish side, as proof of the enormous existing difficulties, the fact that Stalin deleted from the text of the British proposal the name of Premier Mikolajczyk as the chief of the future Polish Government in Poland; also that the ratio of strength in this Government, which is under the present conditions even with a fifty-fifty proportion, and to which ratio the Lublin Committee does not agree, gives no possibility of governing. The British side explains in the first matter that Stalin gave to Churchill verbal assurance that he accepts and will honor Mikolajczyk as a candidate, and in the second matter that it shall remain a problem for negotiations in Moscow and Lublin, to guarantee a sufficient and permanent majority in the future Government following Premier Mikolajczyk's idea. If it will not be possible to carry this out, an understanding, and together with it, a Polish consent to the Curzon Line, shall not come about, and the whole thing will fall apart on a point on which the Polish Government will be able to count for a continuous support of the British Government, as opposed to the matter of the Polish frontiers in the east.] [171]

When Mikolajczyk reported the substance of this conference with Churchill to his Cabinet, the Ministers were indignant concerning what they regarded as Churchill's arrogant manner, an attitude which was so humiliating to Poland. They were perplexed by Churchill's continuous insistence on their accepting the Soviet demands. After exploring all possible courses of action, they decided to make the following announcement on November 3.

The first demand put before the Polish Government in Moscow as the condition on which Polish-Soviet agreement depends is the ultimate acceptance of the Curzon Line as a basis for a Polish-Soviet frontier.
Considering:
1. That besides the formal and legal nature of the issue, the Polish Government would have to accept definitely and without delay this new Polish frontier in the east, without waiting for the end of the war or the Peace Conference;
2. that, on the other hand, the establishment of the Polish western and northern frontiers would have to wait until the Peace settlement;
3. that the independence, sovereignty, and territorial integrity of Poland in her new frontiers cannot now be guaranteed by the main Allied Powers;
4. that the Government of the United States has not yet had the opportunity to take a stand on these questions;
the Polish Government, although mindful of the urgency of finding an agreement with the Soviet Union, which it desires most earnestly and is determined to keep striving for in the future, cannot at present accept the conditions put forth in Moscow, and therefore, asks again that the whole matter be reconsidered by the Three Allied Powers with the participation of the Polish Government.[172]

This announcement was intended to clarify the Polish position *vis-à-vis* the Soviets and to justify the delay in giving the final answer by the necessity of first knowing Washington's attitude.

Early in November, the American people re-elected Roosevelt for a fourth term as President of the United States.[173]

On November 17, 1944 President Roosevelt replied to Mikolajczyk's note of October 26 as follows:

While I would have preferred to postpone the entire question of this Government's attitude until the general post-war settlement in Europe, I fully realize your urgent desire to receive some indication of the position of the United States Government with the least possible delay. Therefore, I am giving below, in broad outline, the general position of this Government in the hope that it may be of some assistance to you in your difficult task.

1. The United States Government stands unequivocally for a strong, free and independent Polish State, with the untrammeled right of the Polish people to order their internal existence as they see fit.

2. In regard to the future frontiers of Poland, if a mutual agreement on this subject, including the proposed compensaton for Poland from Germany is reached between the Polish, Soviet, and British Governments, this Government would offer no objection. Insofar as the United States guarantee of any specific frontiers is concerned, I am sure you will understand that this Government, in accordance with its traditional policy, cannot give a guarantee for any specific frontiers. As you know, the United States Government is working for the establishment of a world security organization through which the United States, together with the other member states, will assume responsibility for the general security, which of course includes the inviolability of agreed frontiers.

3. If the Polish Government and the Polish people desire, in connection with the new frontiers of the Polish State, to bring about the transfer of national minorities, to and from the territory of Poland, the United States Government will raise no objection and as far as practicable will facilitate such a transfer.[174]

On November 21, 1944 Ambassador Harriman, on his way to Moscow, stopped in London to inform Churchill, Eden, and Mikolajczyk of President Roosevelt's stand on the Polish question. When he met Mikolajczyk on November 22, he stated that, in connection with Roosevelt's letter, he was instructed to ask Stalin, on the President's behalf, to leave Lwow and the oil fields in Galicia to Poland. But he confessed that there did not seem to be any chance of success. He agreed with Mikolajczyk that the question of the eastern frontiers should be dealt with in the frame of the general settlement of Polish independence and the western and northern frontiers.

Mikolajczyk informed Harriman that in view of the fact that the leaders of the three other parties represented in his Government were opposed to the territorial concessions demanded by Russia, he did not see any point in having Harriman press for Lwow and the oil fields. Furthermore, Mikolajczyk stated that because of this deadlock created as a result of Soviet demands, British pressure, America's noncommitment, and the attitude of the three Polish parties, he did not see anything else to do but to resign.[175]

His decision to resign was precipitated by a move of the right-wing element in the Polish National Council to oust its speaker, Professor

Grabski, a staunch supporter of Mikolajczyk's policies. Mikolajczyk interpreted this as an attack on his policies.

On November 24, 1944 Mikolajczyk resigned as Prime Minister. The President of the Polish Republic accepted his resignation.

The following day the British press was unanimous in its praise for Mikolajczyk and its regret that he had departed from the important post from which he had been striving to reach an agreement with Russia and, in so doing, to save the moral face of the Allies.

The most thoughtful appraisal of the Polish problem appeared on November 27, 1944 in the *Scotsman*. It ran as follows:

With the resignation of Mr. Mikolajczyk, the Polish Prime Minister, the prospect of an agreed solution of the Polish-Russian problem has receded sharply. The occasion of his resignation may have been unexpected, but it is the logical outcome of what appears to be an irreconcilable division among the members of the Polish Government. . . .

Critics of Poland will be quick to claim that the present crisis reveals the fundamental disunity of the Poles and their inability to compromise. That is a harsh and unfair judgment. Having suffered, in proportion to her population, more horribly than any other nation in this war, Poland is being asked to make sacrifices greater than those which are to be exacted, apparently, from some enemy nations. She is being asked to do so at a time when her soldiers are performing brilliant feats of arms on the Allied fronts and when her indomitable underground armies are resisting the Germans to the death. In her cruel and tragic dilemma Poland is entitled to the sympathy of her friends. It ill becomes her Allies to be impatient because Poland shows little inclination to acquiesce in self-immolation. If Poland, in the common interest, must display a heroic generosity, the conscience of her Western friends may be less disturbed were Russia to underline her professed desire to see a "free and independent" Poland by herself making a liberal gesture. Equality of sacrifice is a principle that ought to appeal to two nations which have shed their blood as freely and as gallantly as Russia and Poland have done. But with the lapse of time Moscow appears to have hardened its heart.

Before his resignation, Mikolajczyk affirmed in the dispatches sent to the underground government in Poland that:

We consider the necessity of a speedy settlement of Polish-Soviet relations as a problem vital to the existence of the nation and the independence of the State. . . .

The future of Poland will depend in a large measure on your actions, on your finding a common language and—I emphasize this—on your loyalty in cooperating with Russia. The Allies will not be able to help much so long as a Polish-Soviet settlement is not arrived at. . . .[176]

After Mikolajczyk's resignation as Prime Minister, his successor, the Premier Designate, Jan Kwapinski, was unable to form a Cabinet because the Peasant Party and the Christian Democrats refused to join him.

On November 28, 1944 a conversation took place between Mikolajczyk, Romer, Prime Minister Churchill, Minister Eden, and Ambassador O'Malley regarding matters caused by the crisis of Mr. Mikolajczyk's Government.

At 3:00 P.M. we were received in the ante-room at 10 Downing Street by Minister Eden and Ambassador O'Malley.

EDEN inquires about the development of the crisis in the Polish Government. We inform him of the attempt undertaken by Minister Kwapinski yesterday to form for the short period of talks between the political parties, a provisional cabinet composed of the present members, without filling the posts at present left vacant by representatives of the Peasant Party. In view of the refusal of Romer and, later, of Raczynski and others to take part in this cabinet the attempt produced no results and will probably be undertaken later in another form.

EDEN is of the opinion that in the present state of affairs the British side should not undertake any steps which could give the impression that an interference is made in internal Polish affairs. He is somewhat disturbed by the prospect of a lengthy debate on foreign affairs, which is to begin tomorrow in the House of Commons. He would consider it advisable to limit the statements of the British Government on Polish matters, so as not to cause an effect undesirable for Poland. For that reason he will endeavour to reassure the more prominent speakers and asks Minister Romer to act in the same spirit with the friendly Members of the House. He believes that the British press is showing a great restraint and sense in commenting upon the Polish crisis and asks if we have any observations or requests to make on this matter.

ROMER shares in principle Eden's views, suggests however that one should endeavour to correct the unduly critical speculations which occurred in connection with President Roosevelt's reply to Premier Mikolajczyk of the 17th instant. Eden agrees with that and quotes the *Manchester Guardian*, which expresses similar views. Mikolajczyk believes that Roosevelt's letter was even more favorable in actual fact for Poland than we anticipated, particularly in view of verbal explanations given by Harriman.

EDEN, referring to his conversations with Harriman, completely confirms that. In particular he declares that the British Government not only encouraged Harriman to make representation to Stalin on behalf of Roosevelt, favoring Poland's retention of Lwow and the oil basin, but also expressed readiness on their part to support these endeavours, should Harriman consider that it will advance and not injure the cause, for the success of which the British Government is most concerned.

We enter the conference room, in which Churchill awaits us. Greeting him, Mikolajczyk tenders in advance his best wishes for his 70th birthday, which he will celebrate the day after tomorrow. Romer does the same. Churchill returns warm thanks. He looks wonderfully well and is evidently in a good disposition. He invites all present to the conference table, at which we sit as usual: the British and Poles facing each other.

CHURCHILL opens the conversation with a statement that we had acted most correctly and in his opinion the resignation under these circumstances was the only sensible way out.

MIKOLAJCZYK explains, that in view of the conditions created in Teheran, despite the best endeavours and intentions (here Churchill nods), he could not act otherwise, because he had the majority of the Government against him, and had he accepted the views of the majority he could not count on the support of the Western Powers. On departing, Mikolajczyk asks that the British Government, regardless of what men hold the power in Poland, should not cease to act in her interest and avoid acts which eventually may prove obstacles in returning to the present active policy of attempts towards an understanding with Russia.

CHURCHILL is not certain who will now take the helm of the Polish Government. He knows that the task to set it up was given to Mr. Kwapinski and personally he is inclined to assume that despite apparent difficulties he may succeed. On the British side, Polish statehood will naturally not be questioned and the new Government will receive the normal diplomatic privileges, which are enjoyed by foreign governments now in London. But this relationship shall not enjoy the personal confidence which was formerly bestowed on General Sikorski and later on Mr. Mikolajczyk. This will be clearly expressed to the representatives of the new Polish Government if they call on us—continued Churchill—though they may not call at all, realizing that they do not stand on the same political grounds with us. In particular, the special privileges which were not available to the other governments, and which were the result of the personal confidence in General Sikorski and Mr. Mikolajczyk, as for instance the use of their own code in communications with Poland, could no longer be granted.

MIKOLAJCZYK asks that it be remembered that the main issue is Poland and her interests, and not these or other people who are temporarily entrusted with them. In particular, he is most concerned that the aid given to the Underground Movement in Poland be not discontinued, in accordance with the principle that whoever fights the Germans shall be assured of help.

EDEN intercalates that he has already issued the proper instructions as a result of the conversation he had with us yesterday, and asks whether we attach great importance to making it possible for Wincenty Witos and a few other persons to be flown from Poland, for whom a discreet escape from under the German occupation was planned.

MIKOLAJCZYK requests that this be carried out and explains that an early presence in London of Wincenty Witos could contribute greatly to the clearing up of the Polish political situation.

CHURCHILL enquires about the role of Witos in Poland and his personal relations with Mikolajczyk, to which the latter replies.

EDEN promises to issue the necessary instructions at once but adds that to have them carried out will take a few weeks. Referring to his conversation with us yesterday, he asks Churchill whether, in his opinion, the British military mission, whose parachuting in Poland was recently suspended may now be sent to the Polish Underground Movement under German occupation.

MIKOLAJCZYK presses that this be done, supporting our wishes with the argument that the British should have their own sources of information in Poland, where we have nothing to hide from them.

CHURCHILL is disposed in principle to comply with the wishes of Mikolajczyk, and formulates a directive for Eden, that in all current matters, which are not connected with the personal relationship of confidence in Mr. Mikolajczyk, actions are to be consistently carried out as heretofore. Besides—he adds—I do not doubt that, irrespective of the temporary stay of Mr. Mikolajczyk outside the Government, he will continue to maintain the closest contact with us.

MIKOLAJCZYK replies that in his capacity as Chairman of the Peasant Party, he will naturally see to it.

ROMER reminds Eden of his promise to take care of the problem of aid for the civilian population evacuated from Warsaw and dispersed over Poland in terrible misery. We are mainly concerned to get some blockade exemptions in respect of clothing and transfer of currency to Switzerland.

EDEN gives an assurance that he has already taken care of this matter and shall bear it in mind, fully aware of its importance.

CHURCHILL returns to the question of the change in the Polish Government and considers it under the existing conditions as an unavoidable occurrence, purely temporary and perhaps even desirable. He says—One should not hurry now. You gentlemen rest now for two or three weeks. Thereafter Premier Mikolajczyk shall return strengthened to power in a cleaned-up political atmosphere and I am convinced that you shall be able to reach a better agreement with Russia at a cheaper price. Meantime let these gentlemen from Lublin, Morawski and * * * (Romer prompts: Bierut)—yes, Bierut—really, I dislike these men very much—they will loosen their tongues. Then your own return, Gentlemen, to the Government and to negotiations with Russia will constitute a valuable concession.

MIKOLAJCZYK gives the assurance that he will endeavour as far as possible to strive toward a further realization of his policy of reconciliation with Russia, counting upon support of the Western Powers, which is indispensable.

EDEN considers how representatives of His Majesty's Government should deal with the Polish problem during the debate on foreign affairs in the House of Commons.

CHURCHILL believes that statements should be most guarded, pointing out that, despite difficulties, the door still remains open for a Polish-Soviet understanding, to the conclusion of which the British Government, in the interest of unity in the whole Allied camp, lends its patronage. Asked about his opinion in this matter, MIKOLAJCZYK agrees with the need for restraint in making disclosures, asks, however, to stress the point of the recognition of the Polish Government in exile as opposed to the Committee of National Liberation, and to stress strongly the demand for an independent Poland, as one of the essential aims of this war.

CHURCHILL agrees with this entirely.

There follows a warm leavetaking of each other, and taking the opportunity, Mikolajczyk expresses regret that he had sometimes appeared too stubborn, but that this had to be done—he adds—I am still first of all a Pole and you understand that.

EDEN follows us to the door and bidding us good-bye, assures us once more that he shall always be at our disposal whenever we wish.

The whole conversation had taken place in an extremely friendly and relaxed atmosphere.[177]

On November 29 the leader of the Polish Socialist Party, Tomasz Arciszewski, an old, experienced, and courageous fighter in the Underground was appointed Prime Minister. He was an honest patriot who had proved his worth in long, hard, underground struggles against Tsarist Russia, at which time he had collaborated with Lenin (with whom he later parted ways because he could not share Lenin's objectives after the successful October Revolution). Later, during World War II, Arciszewski fought in the Underground Movement in Poland until July 1944 when he was secretly brought to London from Poland.

The Peasant Party did not join his Government in order not to deprive itself of any future opportunity to salvage what might be left of Polish independence; for, realizing that Arciszewski would be unable to make any territorial concessions, they knew that his Government would be completely deprived of Western support and therefore would be impotent so far as Poland was concerned. The foreign press did not approve of Arciszewski or his Government for his firm stand in defense of Polish rights.

Fearing that a considerable number of the members of the Polish National Council (Parliament) were in sympathy with Mikolajczyk's views, President Raczkiewicz dissolved the Council upon the advice of Arciszewski. This unfortunate move did not attract much attention from the Western press. If it had, it would undoubtedly have been exploited to Poland's disadvantage. The dissolution of the National Council was a move reflecting the short tempers of people caught in the web of desperation.

On December 4, 1944 *Pravda*, in its review of international affairs, had this to say about the new Polish Government:

After unsuccessful attempts by Kwapinski to form an exile government, another "socialist," Arciszewski, was pushed forward to do so. As was reported previously, the representatives of the Peasant Party did not join his government.

The London correspondent of the American paper *P.M.* said on December 4, 1945:

The composition of the Arciszewski Government gives an impression of hatred towards the Soviet Union.

For many years Arciszewski was closely associated with Pilsudski's group. Acting in the spirit and according to the plan of that group, Arciszewski attempted to break down and disorganize anti-fascist workers movements in Poland. He is one of the most bitter enemies of the Soviet Union. For this reason exactly President Raczkiewicz designated him as his successor after Sosnkowski was removed.

. . . Kwapinski, the new Minister of Commerce and the Merchant Navy is one of the closest partners of Raczkiewicz and Sosnkowski. He is considered as an uncompromising enemy of the Soviet Union.

Folkierski, the Minister of Cooperational Planning, used to belong to a so-called "Great Poland" camp. He is one of the most extreme nationalists and anti-Semitists.

Berezowski, the Minister of Interior, belongs to the fascistic group of Bielecki, who copies Hitler and his methods.

Professor Kukiel, the Minister of National Defense, is a right-hand man of Sosnkowski. He became famous for his cultivation of the fascist regime in the Polish Army. Kukiel was one of the main organizers of the Hitlerite provocation about Katyn. When that criminal affair was unmasked, Kukiel got the nickname of "Kukiel from Katyn."

Such is the political character of the "Arciszewski Cabinet." The formation of this Government by Arciszewski fully unmasks the dirty game of Polish reactionary exiles. It is absolutely clear that the Polish reactionary group in London has decided to begin an offensive action and has completely broken away from the policy which Mikolajczyk strove to pursue.

These Polish reactionaries, in an impertinent and cynical way, try to provoke not only the Soviet Union but the British and United States Governments, who are accused of refusing to support the territorial demands of the Polish imperialists. . . .

Other American and British papers, with the exception of the *Daily Worker* of both countries, were either completely silent or spoke of the Polish situation in more moderate terms.

On December 15 Churchill made a speech in Parliament about the future frontiers of Poland. He said:

All territorial changes must await the conference at the peace table after victory has been won. But to that principle there is one exception, and that exception is, changes mutually agreed.[178]

Writing about this, Sherwood stated:

As Winant had predicted, the debate on Poland in the House of Commons caused further serious ructions. . . . It conveyed the disturbing suggestion of "secret agreements" among the big powers for the carving up of the small ones, and it revived the ugly accusations against which Roosevelt had been compelled to defend himself time and again ever since the Atlantic Conference.

. . . the following day (December 16) Hopkins cabled Churchill,

"Due to the Greek situation and your statement in Parliament about Poland public opinion has rapidly deteriorated here. . . . Although I do not know what the President and Stettinius may be compelled to say publicly it is quite possible that one or both of them will have to proclaim their determination in unequivocal terms to do everything we can to seek a free world and a secure one."

There was plenty of indignation in Whitehall at the somewhat sanctimonious, holier-than-thou attitude which the United States was assuming toward a situation in which it was undoubtedly concerned but for the solution of which it was taking no responsibility whatsoever.[179]

The new Government was determined to defend the sovereignty of Poland to the last, come what may. Arciszewski expressed his policies towards the Soviet Union as follows:

1. A guarantee of sovereignty and freedom for the new Polish State.
2. The solution of the problem of frontiers.
3. The establishment of a civilian administration on the territories of Poland liberated by the Red Army.
4. The establishment of Polish-Soviet relations.[180]

The majority of Poles in England supported Arciszewski's stand. The British and American Governments were not pleased with this because they did not think that in the face of such support they would be able to force Arciszewski to reach a compromise with the Russians. For the Soviets, this new Polish Government was very convenient because the Western Allies would more readily believe the Soviets when they stated that they were not responsible for the lack of agreement. For all practical purposes the Western Allies ignored the new Government of Poland.

The Soviets thereupon proceeded to make further unilateral arrangements for Poland.

Notes

[1] Poland, *Official Government Documents*, Vol. IV, Doc. 8.
[2] *Ibid.*, Doc. 10.
[3] *Ibid.*, Doc. 13.
[4] *Ibid.*, Docs. 14–17.
[5] *Ibid.*, Doc. 19.
[6] *Ibid.*, Vol. LVI, Doc. 4.
[7] *Ibid.*, Vol. IV, Doc. 32.
[8] *Ibid.*, Vol. LVI, Doc. 6.
[9] *Ibid.*, Doc. 6c.
[10] *Ibid.*, Doc. 7.
[11] *Ibid.*, Doc. 7a.
[12] *Ibid.*, Doc. 52.

[13] *Ibid.*, Doc. 51.

[14] *Ibid.*, Vol. IV, Doc. 37.

[15] *Ibid.*, Vol. LVI, Doc. 31.

[16] *Ibid.*, Doc. 10.

[17] *Ibid.*, Doc. 23.

[18] *Ibid.*

[19] *Ibid.*, Vol. IV, Doc. 40.

[20] *Ibid.*, Doc. 41.

[21] *Ibid.*, Doc. 41a.

[22] *Ibid.*, Doc. 42.

[23] *Ibid.*, Vol. LVI, Doc. 65.

[24] *Ibid.*, Doc. 30.

[25] *Ibid.*, Vol. XLVIII, Doc. 47.

[26] *Ibid.*, Doc. 21.

[27] *Ibid.*, Vol. III, Doc. 98.

[28] *Ibid.*, Doc. 87.

[29] Romuald Traugutt was one of the leaders of the 1863 uprising against Russia. In 1864 he formed the last Polish Revolutionary Government.

[30] The British military attaché declined the invitation to attend the ceremony.

[31] Tadeusz Kosciuszko was the military leader of a Polish insurrection against Russian occupation of Poland. He defeated the Tsarist armies at Raclawice.

[32] Andrzej Witos was the brother of Wincenty Witos, three times former Prime Minister of Poland, and leader of the Peasant Party.

[33] Poland, *Official Government Documents*, Vol. LVI, Doc. 60.

[34] *Ibid.*

[35] *Ibid.*, Docs. 60, 61.

[36] *Ibid.*, Doc. 62.

[37] Stanislaw Mikolajczyk, *The Rape of Poland: Pattern of Soviet Aggression*, New York, Whittlesey House, 1948, p. 55.

[38] *Ibid.*

[39] Poland, *Official Government Documents*, Vol. LVI, Doc. 70.

[40] *Ibid.*, Vol. III, Doc. 104.

[41] *Ibid.*, Vol. LVI, Doc. 79.

[42] *Ibid.*, Vol. III, Doc. 101.

[43] *Ibid.*, Vol. LVI, Doc. 82.

[44] *Ibid.*, Doc. 72.

[45] *Ibid.*, Doc. 83.

[46] *Ibid.*, Doc. 78. (Italics are by the author of the letter.)

[47] *Ibid.*, Vol. III, Doc. 93.

[48] *Ibid.*, Vol. LVI, Doc. 79.

[49] *Ibid.*, Vol. III, Doc. 122.

[50] Ciechanowski, *op. cit.*, pp. 277–282.

[51] *Ibid.*

[52] Poland, *Official Government Documents*, Vol. III, Doc. 123.

[53] *Ibid.*

[54] Personal description of his reactions by Mikolajczyk as told to the author.

[55] Poland, *Official Government Documents*, Vol. III, Doc. 127.

[56] *Ibid.*, Doc. 112.

[57] *Ibid.*, Doc. 112a.

[58] *Ibid.*, Vol. LXXVIII, Doc. 14.

[59] *Ibid.*, Doc. 14a, and a verbal description of this event by M. Mikolajczyk to the author.

[60] *Ibid.*, Docs. 14, 15.

[61] *Ibid.*, Doc. 16.

[62] *Ibid.*, Doc. 19.

[63] *Ibid.*, Vol. XIII, Doc. 2.

[64] *Ibid.*, Doc. 3.

[65] *Ibid.*, Docs. 6–7a.

[66] *Ibid.*, Vol. LXXVIII, Doc. 25.

[67] *Ibid.*, Doc. 26.

[68] *Ibid.*, Vol. XIII, Doc. 7.

[69] *Ibid.*, Vol. LXXVIII, Doc. 35.

[70] *Ibid.*, Vol. CLVI, Doc. 162.

[71] *Ibid.*, Doc. 182.

[72] *Ibid.*

[73] See Appendix 2.

[74] For a better description of these men, see Appendix 2.

[75] Poland, *Official Government Documents*, Vol. VII, Doc. 9.

[76] *Ibid.*, Doc. 10.

[77] *Ibid.*, Vol. LXIV, Doc. 2.

[78] *Ibid.*, Vol. CLVI, Doc. 191.

[79] Great Britain, 182 *Hansard's Parliamentary Debates* (1944), p. 1482.

[80] Poland, *Official Government Documents*, Telegram No. 6, Vol. VII, Doc. 16.

[81] *Ibid.*, Vol. LXIV, Doc. 7.

[82] *Ibid.*, Doc. 7b.

[83] *Ibid.*, Doc. 8.

[84] *Ibid.*, Doc. 10.

[85] Captain Kalugin, the Soviet officer who sent the message for help which Mikolajczyk handed to Stalin, later disappeared. He was presumably liquidated for transmitting this politically inopportune message to Stalin.

[86] Poland, *Official Government Documents*, Vol. LXIV, Doc. 11.

[87] *Ibid.*, Doc. 13.

[88] Winston S. Churchill, *Triumph and Tragedy*, Boston, Houghton Mifflin Company, 1953, pp. 130, 131.

[89] *Ibid.*

[90] Poland, *Official Government Documents*, Vol. CLVI, Doc. 196.

[91] Churchill, *op. cit.*, p. 133.

[92] Poland, *Official Government Documents*, Vol. CLVI, Doc. 197.

[93] *Ibid.*, Doc. 197a.

[94] *Ibid.*, Doc. 198.

[95] Churchill, *op. cit.*, pp. 135–136.

[96] *Ibid.*, pp. 135–136.

[97] *Ibid.*, p. 139.

[98] *Ibid.*, pp. 139–140.

[99] *Ibid.*, p. 140.

[100] *Ibid.*

[101] Cordell Hull, *The Memoirs of Cordell Hull* (2 vols.), New York, The Macmillan Company, 1948, pp. 1445–1447.

[102] Poland, *Official Government Documents*, Vol. CLVI, Doc. 267.

[103] *Ibid.*, Doc. 220.

[104] *Ibid.*, Doc. 221.

[105] Churchill, *op. cit.*, pp. 140–141.

[106] *Ibid.*, p. 140.

Ambassador O'Malley informed Foreign Minister Romer that the person who was most antagonized by Soviet policies was Ernest Bevin who saw the long-range significance of Soviet actions for the Western Powers and therefore repeatedly urged the British Government to take firmer steps to counter these Soviet measures. Poland, *Official Government Documents*, Vol. CLVI, Doc. 225.

[107] Churchill, *op. cit.*, pp. 141–142.

[108] *Ibid.*, pp. 143–144.

[109] *Ibid.*, p. 143.

[110] Poland, *Official Government Documents*, Vol. CLVI, Doc. 229.

[111] *Ibid.*, Vol. CLVI, Doc. 268.

[112] *Ibid.*, Doc. 246.

[113] *Ibid.*, Doc. 243.

[114] *Ibid.*, Doc. 248.

[115] *Ibid.*, Doc. 269.

[116] *Ibid.*, Doc. 267b.

[117] *Ibid.*, Doc. 249.

[118] Churchill, *op. cit.*, pp. 144–145.

[119] Poland, *Official Government Documents*, Vol. CLVI, Doc. 250.

[120] *Ibid.*, Doc. 277.

[121] *Ibid.*, Doc. 280.

[122] *Ibid.*, Doc. 281.

[123] Great Britain, 122 *Hansard's Parliamentary Debates*, CDIII (1944), p. 489.

[124] *Ibid.*, p. 520.

[125] *Ibid.*, pp. 552–553.

[126] *Ibid.*, pp. 556–557.

[127] After long pressure by the Soviets, the British Government insisted that General Sosnkowski be removed. On September 20 Eden attempted to persuade President Raczkiewicz to oust him but without success. Only when the Polish Government learned that Sosnkowski was either originating or tolerating anti-government action in the Polish Armed Forces for the failure of Warsaw did the Polish Cabinet request President Raczkiewicz to dismiss him as Commander-in-Chief. The President complied. Poland, *Official Government Documents*, Vol. CLVI, Doc. 230.

[128] *Ibid.*, Doc. 234.

[129] *Ibid.*, Doc. 274. See Appendix 1.

[130] *Ibid.*, Doc. 275.

[131] Mikolajczyk, *op. cit.*, p. 92.

[132] Churchill, *op. cit.*, p. 208.

[133] *Ibid.*, p. 219.

[134] *Ibid.*, p. 220.

[135] *Ibid.*, p. 227.

[136] Poland, *Official Government Documents*, Vol. VII, Doc. 3.

[137] *Ibid.*, Doc. 4. First edition drafted personally by Churchill in the British Embassy on October 14, 1944.

[138] Churchill, *op. cit.*, p. 235.

[139] Poland, *Official Government Documents*, Vol. VII, Doc. 5.

[140] *Ibid.*, Doc. 6.

[141] *Ibid.*, Doc. 7.

[142] *Ibid.*, Doc. 8.

[143] Churchill, *op. cit.*, p. 239. (Italics mine.)

[144] Poland, *Official Government Documents*, Vol. VII, Doc. 9.

[145] *Ibid.*, Doc. 9a.

[146] *Ibid.*, Doc. 9b.

[147] *Ibid.*, Doc. 10.

[148] *Ibid.*

[149] *Ibid.*, Doc. 11.

[150] *Ibid.*, Doc. 12.

[151] *Ibid.*, Doc. 13.

[152] Churchill, *op. cit.*, pp. 242–243.

[153] *Ibid.*, p. 241.

[154] *Ibid.*, p. 242.

[155] Poland, *Official Government Documents*, Vol. CCXCI, Doc. 302.

[156] *Ibid.*

[157] *Ibid.*, Doc. 302a.

[158] *Ibid.*, Vol. VII, Doc. 11.

[159] *Ibid.*, Doc. 11a.

[160] *Ibid.*, Vol. CCXCI, Doc. 296.

[161] *Ibid.*, Doc. 297.

[162] *Ibid.*, Doc. 294.

[163] *Ibid.*, Doc. 295.

[164] *Ibid.*, Vol. VII, Doc. 15.

[165] *Ibid.*, Vol. CCXCI, Doc. 301.

[166] *Ibid.*, Vol. CLVI, Doc. 289.

[167] *Ibid.*, Vol. CCXCI, Doc. 298.

[168] *Ibid.*, Vol. XXI, Doc. 299.

[169] *Ibid.*, Doc. 301.

[170] *Ibid.*, Doc. 328.

[171] *Ibid.*, Doc. 303.

[172] *Ibid.*, Doc. 304.

[173] According to information provided this author by Professor W. W. Kulski of Syracuse University, who has done some research on the 1944 pre-election campaign, it appears that several weeks before the election the head of the American-Polish organizations, Rozmarek, had promised Governor Thomas E. Dewey that the Poles would support him in his candidacy for the United States presidency. Roosevelt had not planned any tour of the country but immediately before the election was persuaded by Democratic leaders to make an appearance in the major cities. When he arrived at Chicago, various delegations were lined up on the railroad platform. Among them, somewhere in the middle, was Rozmarek with his group. When the doors of the Presidential section of the train were opened, F.D.R. asked to be wheeled to Rozmarek first. Upon approaching him the President stretched forth both his hands and said, "I am delighted to see you again, and I hope that you will support me so that I can see that justice is done to Poland." Rozmarek was touched by the President's gesture and replied, "Yes, Mr. President, we shall stick with you to the end." Dewey was furious that Rozmarek had broken his word.

[174] Poland, *Official Government Documents*, Vol. CCXCI, Doc. 316.

[175] *Ibid.*, Doc. 318.

[176] *Ibid.*, Vol. X, Doc. 46a. The above-entitled documents will henceforth be named: *Mikolajczyk's Private Files.*

[177] *Mikolajczyk's Private Files*, Vol. CCXCI, Doc. 330.

[178] Sherwood, *op. cit.*, p. 842.

[179] *Ibid.*

[180] Sunday *Times*, London, December 17, 1944.

From the Soviet Establishment of the "Provisional Government" to the Allied Recognition of It as the "Provisional Government" of National Unity

December 1944 to June 1945

1. The Formation of the "Provisional Government"

On December 31, 1944 the "Council of National Unity," sitting in Lublin, proclaimed its National Liberation Committee to be the Provisional Government of Poland. Mr. Bierut, the Chairman of the "Council of National Unity" was declared temporary President of liberated Poland. Mr. Osobka-Morawski, the head of the National Liberation Committee was designated Premier and Foreign Minister in the Provisional Government.

Mr. Wladyslaw Gomulka, hitherto the Secretary General of the Polish Workers' Party (communists), was appointed First Deputy Prime Minister.

Mr. Stanislaw Janusz, the Vice-Chairman of the Peasant Party, was made Second Deputy Prime Minister.

General Rola-Zymierski became Minister of National Defense, in addition to being the Commander-in-Chief.

Mr. Jozef Maslanka, the leader of the Peasant Party, became the Minister for Home Affairs.

Mr. Stanislaw Radkiewicz (Workers' Party), became the Minister of Public Security.

Mr. Konstanty Dombrowski (Socialist Party), became the Minister of Finance.

Mr. Edmund Zalewski became Minister of Justice.

Mr. Edward Bertold (Peasant Party), became Minister of Agriculture and Agrarian Reform.

Mr. Wiktor Trojanowski (Socialist Party), became Minister of Public Works.

Mr. Stefan Matuszewski (Secretary General of the Socialist Party), became Minister of Information.

Officially, the Provisional Government consisted of five members from the Socialist and Peasant Parties, four members from the Workers' Party, two members from the Democratic Party, and one "nonparty" army general, but actually all of them were communists or were closely controlled by them.

The policy of the new Government was outlined as follows: The main lines of the resolution issued by the National Committee of Liberation on the previous July, which called for the incorporation of Pomerania, Silesia, and East Prussia into Poland, for broad access to the sea, and for a frontier on the River Oder, were approved. The main objective of their foreign policy was to form a great defensive alliance of the Slav nations, based on an agreement between Poland, Soviet Russia, and Czechoslovakia.[1]

The leadership of the Provisional Government was in the hands of the Workers' Party, which was formed by the Comintern in the winter of 1941-1942 to replace the Polish Communist Party, dissolved in 1937 by the same *Comintern.*

Even prior to this announcement the Soviet Government had been dealing with the National Liberation Committee as the *de facto* authority in the liberated areas of Poland. There was no doubt that this new step was taken with Soviet consent and approval, if not from a direct Soviet order. The Soviets were undoubtedly in a better position to evaluate and to ascertain the moods of the Western Allies than were the Lublin Committee.

This action brought the Polish crisis to a head. Theoretically, Poland now had two governments—one in London and the other in Lublin. The London Government issued, on January 1, 1945, an emphatic protest against the action of the Lublin Committee and declared that it had illegally assumed the title of Provisional Government. This new Government was, however, recognized as the Provisional Government of Poland by the Soviet Union on January 5, 1945 and by Czechoslovakia on January 31, 1945.

Prior to the recognition by the Soviets of the Lublin Committee as the Provisional Government of Poland, Stalin sent a telegram to Roosevelt in which he tried once more to discredit the Polish Government in London and its political representatives in Poland and suggested:

> I have to say frankly that if the Polish Committee of National Liberation will transform itself into a Provisional Polish Government, then, in view of the above-said, the Soviet Government will not have any serious ground for postponement of the question of its recognition. It is necessary to bear in mind that in the strengthening of a pro-Allied and democratic Poland the Soviet Union is interested more than any other Power.[2]
>
> . . . I think that it would be natural, just, and profitable for our common cause if the Governments of the Allied countries as the first step have agreed on an immediate exchange of representatives with the Polish National Committee, so that after a certain time it would be recognized as the lawful Government of Poland after the transformation of the National Committee into a Provisional Government of Poland. Otherwise I am afraid that the confidence of the Polish people in the Allied Powers may weaken. I think that we cannot allow the Polish people to say that we are sacrificing the interests of Poland in favor of the interests of a handful of Polish emigrants in London.[3]

Roosevelt, in the following telegram to Stalin expressed his stand:

> I am disturbed and deeply disappointed over your message of December 27 in regard to Poland, in which you tell me that you cannot see your way clear to hold in abeyance the question of recognizing the Lublin Committee as the Provisional Government of Poland until we have had an opportunity at our meeting to discuss the whole question thoroughly. I would have thought no serious inconvenience would have been caused your Government or your armies if you could have delayed the purely juridical act of recognition for the short period of a month remaining before we meet.
>
> . . . I must tell you with a frankness equal to your own that I see no prospect of this Government's following suit and transferring its recognition from the Government in London to the Lublin Committee in its present form. This is in no sense due to any special ties or feelings for the London (Polish) Government.
>
> . . . If at some future date following the liberation of Poland a provisional government of Poland with popular support is established the attitude of this Government would of course be governed by the decision of the Polish people.
>
> I fully share your view that the departure of M. Mikolajczyk from the Government in London has worsened the situation. I have always felt that M. Mikolajczyk, who, I am convinced, is sincerely desirous of settling all points at issue between the Soviet Union and Poland, is the only Polish

leader in sight who seems to offer the possibility of a genuine solution of the difficult and dangerous Polish question. . . .

. . . I am sending you this message so that you will know the position of this Government in regard to the recognition at the present time of the Lublin Committee as the Provisional Government. I am more than ever convinced that when the three of us get together we can reach a solution of the Polish problem, and I therefore still hope that you can hold in abeyance until then the formal recognition of the Lublin Committee as a Government of Poland. I cannot from a military angle see any great objection to a delay of a month.[4]

Stalin replied to the above:

I greatly regret that I have not been able to convince you of the correctness of the Soviet Government's attitude towards the Polish question. I nevertheless hope that events will convince you that the Polish National Committee has always rendered and will continue to render to the Allies, and in particular to the Red Army, considerable assistance in the struggle against Hitlerite Germany, whereas the *émigré* Government in London assists the Germans by creating disorganization in this struggle.

I naturally fully comprehend your suggestion that the Soviet Government's recognition of the Provisional Government of Poland should be postponed for a month. There is however a circumstance here which makes it impossible for me to fulfill your wish. The position is that as early as December 27 the Presidium of the Supreme Soviet of the U.S.S.R. informed the Poles in reply to an inquiry on the subject that it proposed to recognize the Provisional Government of Poland as soon as the latter was formed. This circumstance makes it impossible for me to fulfill your wish.[5]

On January 4 Stalin informed Churchill directly about his plans.

You are of course already aware of the publication by the Polish National Council in Lublin of the decision to which it has come regarding the transformation of the Polish Committee of National Liberation into the National Provisional Government of the Polish Republic. You are also well aware of our relations with the Polish National Committee, which in our view has already acquired great authority in Poland and is the lawful exponent of the will of the Polish nation. The transformation of the Polish National Committee into a Provisional Government seems to us entirely opportune, especially since Mikolajczyk has ceased to be a member of the *émigré* Polish Government and the latter has thus ceased to possess any semblance of a Government. I consider it impossible to leave Poland without a Government. Accordingly the Soviet Government has consented to recognize the Polish Provisional Government.

I much regret that I was unable completely to convince you of the correctness of the Soviet Government's attitude towards the Polish question. I nevertheless hope that future events will show that our recognition of the Polish Government in Lublin is in the interests of the general Allied cause and will contribute to hasten the defeat of Germany.[6]

According to Churchill:

Further correspondence did not seem to me to be likely to do much good. Only a personal meeting gave hope.[7]

Since Stalin realized that his Western Allies were not determined to oppose his move but were only pleading with him, he decided to proceed with his plan for the recognition of the Lublin Poles. He was not accustomed to paying attention to pious sentiments. Nothing else stood in the way of the realization of his objectives.

On January 2, 1945 the Polish Peasant Party in London, under the leadership of Mikolajczyk, issued the following declaration:

The so-called Polish National Council of Lublin have proclaimed themselves the Parliament of Poland and declared that the Lublin Committee is the Provisional Government of Poland. This in no way alters the actual situation.

The National Council of Lublin was formed on January 1, 1944. Some communist members of the Council (several of whom had spent many years in Russia) declared themselves at that time to be the representatives of Poland; although it was generally known by then that the Underground State of Poland existed.

In this Underground State all the political movements are represented, and it is headed by the Underground Parliament of Poland and the Council of National Unity, known at the beginning of the war as the "Political Representation of the country."

Ever since 1939, when four men (the late Mr. Ratay of the Peasant Party, the late Mr. Niedzialkowski of the Socialist Party, the late Mr. Kwiecinski of the Christian Labor Party, and the late Mr. Debski of the National Party) laid the foundation for the Underground State, continuous warfare has been waged, with great sacrifice, against the Germans. During the whole period, the Vice-Premier, who was the Delegate of the Government abroad, three other Ministers, and the Commander-in-Chief of the Home Army have been carrying out their duties within this Underground State. In the course of these five years, two Delegates of the Government, in turn two successive Commanders-in-Chief of the Home Army, as well as many outstanding leaders and hundreds of thousands of political party members, active in the resistance, officers, and soldiers of the Home Army have paid for this unrelenting struggle against the Germans with their lives, through torture and imprisonment.

All these facts have been ignored by the few men who created the Lublin National Council on January 1, 1944. It was this National Council which appointed the Lublin Committee.

Originally, such men as Andrzej Witos and others were induced to join the Committee with the communists. Later on they disappeared. Although the Lublin Committee acts within Poland, it does not include any of those persons, available locally, who are known to be entitled to represent the main political parties. Nevertheless, allegedly in the name of these political parties, men who have never been known as members of these parties and who are completely unknown to the rank and file, have been introduced into the Committee, appointed from above. Thus communists, changing their colors like chameleons, speak in the name of each of the other political parties.

Such a masquerade will deceive the public as little as the recent gathering of the so-called National Council, which is usurping the rights of a Parliament, and their promotion of the Lublin Committee to the status of a Polish Government.

The Lublin Committee has already usurped the privileges of a Government. It has introduced conscription, issued currency, imposed taxes and so forth. Thus the Committee had assumed the functions which normally lie within the scope of a recognized Government.

A change in the political situation could only occur if the "Lublin Government" were recognized by the Soviet Union, Great Britain, and the United States.

The recognition of this "Government" by the Soviet Union before the next meeting of the representatives of the three major Allied Powers would mean the adoption of a policy of *fait accompli*, which would testify to a serious lack of agreement among the Allied Nations.[8]

It was the general opinion of all Poles in London, including Mikolajczyk and his Party, that if the Western Powers recognized the new "Government" it would signify the approval by those countries of the establishment of a communist Poland; of a Poland standing on the threshold of incorporation into the Soviet Union; of a Poland whose independence and freedom would be obliterated with the consent of the Western Powers.

On January 11, 1945 Mikolajczyk had lunch with Eden, Sir Orme Sargent, and Mr. Allen in the Foreign Office. Eden said that he was being approached from various quarters for assurance that the Polish Government in London would be changed. Furthermore, in view of the approaching conference of the Big Three, Britain would not have any basis upon which to defend Polish interests, because she did not support Arciszewski's Government. Therefore, he said, he thought that an effort should be made to establish a representative Government which the British Government could support, and this would enable her to present the Polish case more firmly at the conference of the Big Three. Eden also added that he was against such proposals of interfering in the internal affairs of the Polish Government because sooner or later it would come out into the open and would make the British position very difficult at the forthcoming "Conference of the Three." Then he asked Mikolajczyk for his opinion on this matter.

Mikolajczyk replied that he still maintained the same position on this question as before. This position was that Britain should not interfere in Polish internal matters. He continued:

I want to ask you if you think the establishment of the Provisional Government in Lublin is the final Soviet step. If so, then I would say that a more representative Government should be established over here because it would improve the Polish position for the Anglo-Americans, and would reinforce the British hand against recognizing the Lublin Government. Although the British Government may not get anything in this matter at the Conference of the Three, it will give you a reason for longer resistance against the recognition of the Lublin Government.

EDEN. Obviously in some not too distant future we will have to recognize the Lublin Provisional Government, and therefore withdraw recognition of the Polish Government in London.

MIKOLAJCZYK. If on the other hand the Soviet Union, despite its recognition of the Lublin Committee has not yet said the final word in the matter, but plans to make a final decision during the Conference of the Three, then it is more important for our foreign policy, as well as yours, to have a well-thought-out plan for a more representative Government here. Such a Government may be more of a hindrance than a help. I know that Mr. Popiel saw President Raczkiewicz and submitted a plan to have a conference of the leaders of the four parties in order to form a coalition Government. I think that the President will go along with that proposal. It all depends on our interpretation of the Soviet stand. What is your opinion, Mr. Eden?

EDEN turned to Sir Orme Sargent and to Mr. Allen and asked them for their opinions. Both thought that Russia had made a final decision and would not retract her action.

EDEN said that he thought this was not so, and asked all present what the British Government should do in this situation.

MIKOLAJCZYK. In my opinion the most important thing is the forthcoming Conference of the Three. In Teheran the Big Three decided on our frontiers, now they will decide on our sovereignty and independence. I am very disturbed because trial balloons have been released which argue that although it is unfortunate, nevertheless there must be some administration in Poland. Therefore, it is necessary to recognize the Lublin Provisional Government and then the Allies will make an effort to see that the Polish nation will have an opportunity to determine its future.

The *Manchester Guardian* came out with just such a thesis. So did Roosevelt. Since the Lublin Government is purely communistic, once it gets entrenched in the saddle with the help of the NKVD, there will not be any chance whatsoever for the Polish nation to freely express its will. It is imperative, therefore, to have a good and effective plan for the Conference of the Three, which should be formed in consultation with the Poles. Then it should be the common plan of both the British and American participants at that Conference.

EDEN. Is there such a plan? Who will submit it to us?

MIKOLAJCZYK. I know that the underground organizations submitted their views on the Polish-Soviet question to the Polish Government. You know that plan because now you read all the messages from Poland first. I know that the Polish Government is preparing such a plan to be submitted to the British and American Governments.

EDEN. The messages from Poland follow your line of policy. Could you not submit such a plan?

MIKOLAJCZYK. I cannot because I know that the Polish Government is preparing it. I can only express my views on it afterwards.

EDEN. But you know I did not receive or meet that Government and I don't intend to do so!

MIKOLAJCZYK. This doesn't matter. You can receive them when they submit that program and you can discuss it with them.

EDEN. But if their program will be unrealistic—based on the principle of delay?

MIKOLAJCZYK. I don't think that the program of the Government can depart from the stand taken by the underground organizations.

Then Mikolajczyk described how the Lublin Committee eliminated all the non-communist members, such as Kotek-Agroszewski, Grubecki, Sommerstein, Drobner, Haneman, Witos, Jedlinski, and General Berling. He said also, that Jedrychouski had informed some people in London that during the Conference of the Three the American and British might be able to persuade Stalin to make changes in the Lublin Government. In such an event Mikolajczyk might become an important personality, and in anticipation of such an event, Lublin had begun to attack him personally. He said, too, that Professor Lange of the University of Chicago was complaining that the Lublin Committee was sending only communists (or completely unknown personalities) to the United States as its representatives, and that as a result of this, the powerful, albeit non-communist, circles in America were cooling off towards Lublin.[9]

On January 20, 1945 Premier Arciszewski in his speech to Poland over the BBC stated:

As a Pole, one of the leaders of the Underground Movement who fought against the German invaders, as a socialist and as Prime Minister of the Polish Government, I am extending my hand to the Soviets in order to establish not a temporary but a permanent understanding and honest friendship between our two countries. I am extending my hand on behalf of the much suffering nation and my Government.

I believe that despite everything that was said and that has happened, such an understanding could be reached.

I am extending my hand and do not believe that it will be pushed aside. The right to true independence for our nation is all that we ask, and that is our program. This right means not that every bayonet shining in glory can dictate who will rule our country. Freedom for us does not mean only liberation from German slavery. To us freedom means individual liberty, the freedom of thought and speech, the freedom of the press, the freedom of public meetings and unions, and the freedom of religion. Freedom also means that our nation will have a government not imposed by force but one created by democratic elections, free from any foreign or domestic pressure.

If these principles are recognized and applied and all the implications executed there is no problem which can stand in our way of achieving Polish-Soviet understanding.[10]

As it turned out, the Soviets were not ready or willing to clasp that outstretched hand.

On January 21 Roosevelt sent Hopkins to London to smooth out American-British relations which had been disturbed since the middle of December. Anglo-American harmony was essential prior to the Yalta Conference. On January 24, 1945 Harry Hopkins held a confidential press conference for American correspondents in London. When asked what the American view on the Curson Line or Oder Line was, Hopkins declined to answer. This later was communicated privately to the Polish authorities,[11] who interpreted this as a dark omen for Poland.

Although everything pointed to the probability that neither Churchill nor Roosevelt would attempt to oppose Stalin's demands concerning Poland, the Poles still wanted to believe, against mounting evidence to the contrary, that both these leaders of democracy, and particularly Roosevelt, would not abandon Poland and that the professed principles of freedom, justice, and the rule of international law would prove stronger than expediency. They wanted to believe that Roosevelt and Churchill would see through Stalin's demands to the subtle and far-reaching design which was aimed not so much against small countries such as Poland, but ultimately against the Western Powers themselves through the control and conquest of the small nations.

On January 22, in order to explain the Polish position once more, the Arciszewski Government sent the following memorandum to Churchill and Roosevelt:

1. The Polish Government assumes that questions concerning Poland will be discussed during the pending meeting of the highest executives of the great Allied Powers. With full confidence in the resolve of the Prime Minister of Great Britain to assure the Allied Polish Republic genuine independence and to guarantee its rights, the Polish Government desires to take advantage of this occasion to state its views as follows:

The Polish Government is of the opinion that territorial questions should be settled after termination of hostilities. In this matter the opinion of the Polish Government coincides with the general principles enunciated by the Governments of Great Britain and the United States of America.

The Polish Government is prepared for a friendly settlement of the Polish-Soviet dispute arising from claims of the U.S.S.R. to eastern territories of the Polish Republic, and it will agree to any method provided for by international law, for a just and equitable settlement of the dispute with participation of both sides. Furthermore, the Polish Government is determined to conclude an alliance with the U.S.S.R., guaranteeing security of both States and to collaborate closely with the Government of the U.S.S.R. within the framework of a universal, international security organization, and within that, of an economic organization of states of central Eastern Europe. However, as Poland, one of the United Nations, made immense sacrifices in material and spiritual values in the common struggle for the freedom of the world, lost nearly one-fifth of her population—killed in battles, massacred in penal camps and ghettos, perished in prisons, in banishment, and in forced-labor camps—the Polish Government cannot be expected to recognize decisions unilaterally arrived at.

2. The Polish Government is convinced that a simultaneous establishment and guarantee of the entire territorial status of the Polish Republic, settlement of the dispute with the U.S.S.R., allocation to Poland of territories situated north and west of her frontiers embracing lands to which she is justly entitled, assurance of her genuine independence and of full rights to organize her internal life in conformity with the will of the Polish nation untrammeled by any foreign intervention, are matters of vital importance, not only to Poland, but also affecting the whole of Europe.

3. If, in spite of the constant endeavours of the Polish Government, the Soviet Government should not agree to an understanding freely arrived at, the Polish Government, desirous of assuring internal peace and liberty to the country, suggests that a military inter-Allied commission be set up, under control of which local Polish administration would discharge its functions until resumption of authority by a legitimate government. The commission would have at their disposal military contingents supplied by powers represented in it. The status of the commission and the principles on which local administration would be based should be elaborated in agreement with the Polish Government. The Polish Government desires to state here that lawful Polish authorities, which were abolished by German occupying power in violation of stipulations of the Fourth Hague Convention of 1907, continued to function underground and should form a basis of administration of the country.

After the return to Poland of supreme state authorities and those of her nationals, who, owing to military events, remain outside the frontiers of the country, elections will be held on the basis of a universal, free, direct, secret, and proportional ballot, which offers all political parties full freedom of electoral activities and all citizens an equal and free right to express their will. The Polish Government will retain its authority until convocation of the Sejm (Parliament), elected in accordance with the aforesaid principles and the formation in Poland of a new legitimate Government.

4. The Polish Government is confident that the Government of Great Britain will not agree to be a party to decisions concerning the Allied Polish Republic arrived at without the participation and consent of the Polish Government. The Polish Government confidently trusts that at the Conference of the great Allied Powers, the British Government will give expression to their resolve not to recognize accomplished facts in Poland, particularly not to recognize a puppet government. Recognition of such a government in Poland would be tantamount to recognition of the abolition of the independence of Poland, in defense of which the present war was begun.[12]

Like many previous official communications to the Western Governments, this memorandum was ignored by its recipients.

On January 25, 1945 prior to the Yalta Conference, Sir Alexander Cadogan asked Mikolajczyk if he would be willing to go to Poland and join the Lublin Government. He admitted, also, that the situation was more complicated than before, but that the British Government was of the opinion that this was only temporary because the first elections would undoubtedly place the communists in the minority.

Mikolajczyk replied that at the present time he did not see any chance of his return to Poland.

It is quite a different matter, when one goes as a Prime Minister than when one goes as a private person without any backing of the two Western Allies. The measure of the Soviet good will must first of all be demonstrated through a conference of the representatives of the four political parties in Poland with the Lublin Committee. I intend to submit on January 26 a memorandum to Mr. Eden to that effect.[13]

Cadogan stated that Mikolajczyk's return would be backed by the complete and firm guarantees of Great Britain and the United States insuring his complete freedom of action as well as his personal safety.

Mikolajczyk replied that despite these promised guarantees he thought that it would be more difficult to receive Soviet permission for the conference of the Poles from London with those from Lublin. Therefore, it would be easier to have a conference between the Lublin people and the representatives of the political parties in Poland, plus the leaders of the Underground Movement. Moreover, the representatives of the Three Powers should sit at such a conference as observers.

Cadogan expressed doubt of the possibility of obtaining Soviet consent to such a proposal. Mikolajczyk asked what the British attitude was towards the memorandum submitted by the Polish Government, and whether the British were going to discuss its contents with the representatives of the Polish Government. Cadogan replied that the British Government was being consistent in its decision not to deal with the Polish Government and then stated that the memorandum was unrealistic and could not, therefore, serve as a basis for Soviet-Polish negotiations.[14]

On January 25, 1945 Mikolajczyk met Charles E. Bohlen, who stated that President Roosevelt had full confidence in Mikolajczyk and that the American Government did not meet with anyone from the Polish Government. They intended to deal with Mikolajczyk alone. Then he stated that the United States Government would insist upon Lwow and the oil fields for Poland at the next Big Three Conference (Yalta) and that they were convinced that the Lublin Government was purely communistic. Consequently, the United States was determined to strive for the independence of Poland and to establish a Government which would include the representatives from all the political parties in Poland (not from abroad). The United States desired to see Mikolajczyk as the Prime Minister of that Government. Then he asked whether the United States should begin negotiations regarding Poland by forcing the Soviet Union to permit Mikolajczyk to return to Poland.

Mikolajczyk replied that it would be sufficient if the United States could convince the Soviet Government to force Bierut to change his treatment of Poles in Poland. It might be more difficult to arrange a meeting between the Lublin and the London Poles. Bierut did not want to meet the leaders in Poland, and for this reason he had ordered their arrest. If Bierut could be compelled to talk to these people, then the London Poles would automatically come into the picture. If he refused to do so, then any newcomer from London would not be a candidate for the Government but for prison. Bohlen ended by admitting that the meeting of the Big Three would be difficult but that he hoped some solution might be found which would secure the independence of Poland.[15]

Mikolajczyk was greatly encouraged by Bohlen's remark that the United States Government was "convinced that the Lublin Government was purely communistic." This admission tended to convince him that the United States would never give its consent to the subjugation of the Polish Nation to communist rule, and for this reason he looked hopefully to the outcome of the forthcoming Big Three Conference.[16]

On January 26, 1945 Eden told Mikolajczyk that the Soviet Government did not want to deal with the Polish Government in London. Mikolajczyk asked if the British Government had discussed the Polish problems with the London Government. Eden replied, "No. Furthermore, neither Prime Minister Churchill nor I have any desire to receive those gentlemen and to discuss their unrealistic memorandum with them."

Mikolajczyk then presented the same view which he had previously outlined to Cadogan and to Bohlen and asked Eden to strive, while at the Big Three Conference, for the relief of Poland from the Bierut-Soviet terror. Eden promised to do so—to try to arrange a conference between the Lublin Government and the representatives of the political parties in Poland. He also stated that the British Government would try to establish the Polish frontiers and to secure the independence of Poland by forming a representative government.

Mikolajczyk said that he believed that the establishment of the Polish frontiers should be done with the participation of the Poles.[17]

On January 28, 1945 the *Sunday Times* published the following article:

Polish circles in London attach great hopes to the meeting of the "Big Three." It is believed that it may result in the present deadlock over their country being broken and new proposals emerging which might be acceptable to all parties.

M. Mikolajczyk has put forward an interesting suggestion in the newspaper *Jutro Polski*. This is that both the London and the Lublin administrations should resign and make way for a new Government formed on a wide political basis.

This idea has been well received in Polish official circles. A Government spokesman said that he was convinced that M. Arciszewski, the Prime Minister, would not raise any objections to such a solution. The present administration was prepared at any time to make place for any Government formed in a legal and constitutional manner.

On the other hand, Soviet circles in London expressed scepticism about the proposal. They do not believe that a solution on these lines would be practicable. They hold that any reconstruction of the Polish Government would have to be based on the fact of the existence of the Provisional Lublin Government and on the Polish Constitution of 1921.

2. The Yalta Conference

The World War in Europe was coming to an end. Western armies were moving steadily into the heart of Germany and freeing the German people from Nazi tyranny, while the Red Army was regrouping in the plains of Poland for its final surge against the other German flank. Following their now established custom, the Big Three decided to meet in Yalta in order first, to synchronize this final military action against Hitler and to map out their plan for the political reorganization of post-war Europe; and second, to coordinate their plans for ending the war in the Far East by the destruction of the Japanese military machine. Among the most disagreeable problems of post-war Europe to be settled by the Big Three was the future of Poland.[18]

As the records show, President Roosevelt opened the discussion of the Polish problem on February 6 by saying, ". . . As I said in Teheran, in general I am in favor of the Curzon Line. Most Poles, like the Chinese, want to save face." This policy statement undoubtedly set the stage for the subsequent treatment of the fate of Poland. Since it was known that at Teheran both Churchill and Stalin were strongly in favor of the Curzon Line as the western frontier of the Soviet Union, this statement of Roosevelt's effectively closed the discussion of the Polish-Soviet border dispute. The President subsequently appealed to Stalin for a "gesture," i.e., to leave Lwow and the oil fields to Poland in order to ease his domestic political situation; but Stalin was not accustomed to honor such appeals. The matter was therefore not pressed any further, and the Big Three addressed themselves to the next problem: the establishment of a permanent Government for Poland.

Roosevelt stressed that the future Government of Poland must be "thoroughly friendly to the Soviet Union for years to come," but that American public opinion was opposed to the recognition of the present Lublin Government on the grounds that it represented only a small portion of the Polish people. He suggested a government embracing the five major parties, and mentioned how impressed he had been with Mikolajczyk. He then threw the question open to discussion.

Churchill began by saying:

> I have made repeated declarations in Parliament in support of the Soviet claims to the Curzon Line, that is to say, leaving Lwow with Soviet Russia. . . . I have always considered that after all Russia has suffered in fighting Germany and after all her efforts in liberating Poland, her claim is one founded not on force but on right. In that position I abide. But, of course, if the mighty power, the Soviet Union, made a gesture suggested by the President, we would heartily acclaim such action.
>
> However, I am more interested in the question of Poland's sovereign independence and freedom than in particular frontier lines.

Then Churchill said that he wanted the Poles to be free and independent in Europe.

> That is an objective which I have always heard Marshal Stalin proclaim with the utmost firmness. . . . However, I do not think that the freedom of Poland could be made to cover hostile designs by any Polish Government, perhaps by intrigue with Germany, against the Soviet.

After reiterating that he wanted a free Poland, he admitted that:

> I have never seen any of the present London Government. We recognize them but have not sought their company, but Mikolajczyk, Romer, and Grabski are men of good sense and we have confidence in them.

He then said that the Big Three should not become divided over the Polish issue and suggested that a provisional or interim government be formed right there at Yalta. This step would insure the stability of Central Europe for years to come.

Stalin, after hearing his Western colleagues, stated that while neither of them had a material interest in Poland, for the Soviet Union it was a matter of security. Therefore it was in the interests of the Soviet

Union to have a strong Poland, free and independent, which could thus block off the traditional invasion route to the Soviet Union from the West.

That is why Russia today is against the Tsarist policy of abolition of Poland. We have completely changed this inhuman policy and started a policy of friendship and independence for Poland. . . .

Then, referring to the Allies' appeals with respect to the Curzon Line modifications, Stalin reminded his colleagues that:

The Curzon Line was invented not by Russians but by foreigners. The Curzon Line of Curzon was made by Curzon, Clemenceau and the Americans in 1918-1919. Russia was not invited and did not participate. This Line was accepted against the will of the Russians on the basis of ethnological data. Lenin opposed it.

Obviously Stalin took a chance that his colleagues would be unfamiliar with the true origin and meaning of the Curzon Line and that they would not be able to check his misrepresentation of the facts effectively. They could not, therefore, present a rational counterargument against Stalin's seemingly patriotic defense of Soviet interests.

Then, with great tactical skill, Stalin maneuvered the discussion to the question of Poland's western frontiers. He presented the Soviet view as favoring the Western Neisse and Oder Rivers as Poland's future boundaries and asked Roosevelt and Churchill to support this claim. Finally, when Stalin turned to the question of the Polish Government, he observed:

The Prime Minister has said that he wants to create a Polish Government here. I am afraid that was a slip of the tongue. Without the participation of Poles we can create no Polish Government. They all say I am a dictator but I have enough democratic feeling not to set up a Polish Government without Poles. It must be with participation of Poles.

Stalin then proceeded to explain why the London Poles could not be invited to such a consultation. They were, he said, proven reactionaries, and the Lublin Poles were unwilling to meet them, except for Grabski and General Zeligowski [both of these men were very old]. Mikolajczyk was specifically unacceptable. Therefore, Stalin offered to call "the Warsaw (i.e., Lublin) Poles" to Yalta or, even better, to Moscow for such a conference. Then, to make his point as vivid as possible, he exploited the generally known difficult relations which existed between Churchill and Roosevelt on the one hand and DeGaulle on the other by saying, "But frankly, the Warsaw Government has as great a democratic basis in Poland as DeGaulle has in France."

Concluding this masterful presentation of the Soviet case, Stalin accused the London Government of deliberately obstructing Soviet military operations against Germany through its agents and, as he put it, the "so-called underground." He contrasted this with the uniformly cooperative attitude of the Lublin Government with the Red Army.

This prompted Churchill to say that the Lublin Government did not represent even one-third of the Polish people, but he went on to add, "Anyone who attacks the Red Army should be punished. . . ." He concluded by saying that the Lublin Government had no right to represent the Polish nation. President Roosevelt did not take part in the discussion, and the meeting adjourned. Further discussion of the problem was referred to the conferences of the respective Foreign Ministers.[19]

After adjournment, however, Roosevelt wrote a letter to Stalin, in which he made three basic points. First, he said that it was of fundamental importance to his political position in the United States that complete unity between the Big Three on all important matters, including Poland, be maintained. Second, he stated that the Lublin Government as now composed was unacceptable to the United States. Third, he suggested bringing to Yalta Bierut and Osobka-Morawski of the Lublin Government and two or three of the following representative Poles from within Poland: Archbishop Sapieha of Krakow, Wincenty Witos, Z. Zulawski, Prof. Buyak, and Prof. S. Kutrzeba. He wanted them to participate in the formation of the new Polish Government, which would no doubt include some leaders from abroad, such as Mikolajczyk, Grabski, and Romer. Should this be successful, Roosevelt did not doubt that the British and American Governments would then recognize this new Polish Government. He added that it goes without saying that any such interim government would be pledged to the holding of free elections in Poland at the earliest possible date.[20]

The next day, February 8, President Roosevelt, as before, resumed the discussion of the topic.

PRESIDENT. I think we should take up the Polish question. When we concluded our meeting yesterday Marshal Stalin had explained his views. I have nothing special to add to what I said yesterday. I think it is particularly important to find a solution of the governmental question. I am not so concerned with frontiers. I am likewise not so concerned on the question of the continuity of the Government. There hasn't really been any Polish Government since 1939. It is entirely in the province of the three of us to help set up a government—something to last until the Polish people can choose. I discard the ideal of continuity. I think we want something new and drastic—like a breath of fresh air. But before we go on with Poland I think Mr. Molotov should report to us, on the meeting of the three Foreign Ministers.

Mr. Molotov then reads his proposals in regard to the Polish question, as follows:

1. It was agreed that the line of Curzon should be the eastern frontier of Poland with a digression from it in some regions of five to eight kilometers in favor of Poland.

2. It was decided that the western frontier of Poland should be traced from the town of Stettin (Polish) and farther to the south along the River Oder and still farther along the River Neisse (western).

3. It was deemed desirable to add to the provisional Polish Government some democratic leaders from Polish *émigré* circles.

(The words "and from inside Poland" were added at the end of this paragraph in the subsequent discussion.)

4. It was regarded desirable that the enlarged Provisional Polish Government should be recognized by the Allied Governments.

5. It was deemed desirable that the Provisional Polish Government, enlarged as was mentioned above in Paragraph 3, should as soon as possible call the population of Poland to the polls for organization by general voting of permanent organs of the Polish Government.

6. V. M. Molotov, Mr. Harriman, and Sir Archibald Clark Kerr were entrusted with the discussion of the question of enlarging the Provisional Polish Government and submitting their proposals to the consideration of the three Governments.

In the subsequent portion of the conference, Stalin informed Roosevelt that he had attempted to locate Bierut and Osobka-Morawski but that they were out of Warsaw and could not be located in time to be of any use for the conference. As to Witos and Sapieha, he said that, "I do not know their addresses," and that there would not be sufficient time to locate them either. Since it is doubtful that Stalin could not, with the known efficiency of the NKVD, have located any of these people immediately, it must be assumed that he preferred to have the meeting held in Moscow at a later date. As Molotov stated during the course of the Conversations, the impossibility of locating these men made it "impossible to try the President's proposal." On this note the question of the consultation of Poles in forming a Polish Government was dropped for the time being.

Churchill now raised the issue of Poland's frontiers along the Oder-Neisse line.

I have always qualified a movement west by the Poles, but say that the Poles should be free to take territory but not more than they wish or can manage. I do not wish to stuff the Polish goose until it dies of German indigestion. I also feel conscious of the large school of thought in England which is shocked by the idea of transferring millions of people by force. Personally I am not shocked but much of the opinion in England is. . . .

Stalin assured Churchill that there would be no more Germans left in those territories after his troops occupied them and that Churchill need have no worries about the mass transfer of populations by force, since the issue would not arise.

CHURCHILL. Then there is the problem of how to handle them in Germany. We have killed six or seven million and probably will kill another million before the end of the war.

STALIN. One or two?

CHURCHILL. Oh, I am not proposing any limitation on them. So there should be room in Germany for some who will need to fill the vacancy. I am not afraid of the problem of the transfer of populations as long as it is in proportion to what the Poles can manage and what can be put in the place of the dead in Germany.

I have only one other comment. It is a reference in Mr. Molotov's plan to the utilization of some democratic leaders from *émigré* circles. Would Marshal Stalin be willing to add "and some within Poland itself." This was also suggested in the President's message.

STALIN. Yes, that is acceptable.

CHURCHILL. Well, I am in agreement with the President's suggestion that we should sleep on this till tomorrow.

STALIN. I likewise find this acceptable.

The meeting is adjourned until 4:00 P.M. tomorrow.

The difficulties connected with the transfer of four or five million Poles to these new territories was not discussed.[21]

On the third day of the discussion of the Polish question, Stalin inquired whether Britain and the United States would withdraw recognition of the Polish Government in London after the establishment of the new interim government in Warsaw; and after he was assured by President Roosevelt that they both would, Stalin further inquired as to what would happen to the property of the London Government. President Roosevelt assured him, "That automatically would go to the new government."

Molotov now attempted to convince the Western Allies that it would be sufficient for all concerned simply to enlarge the present Lublin Government rather than to create a new one. Churchill, however, opposed this.

CHURCHILL. If we accept that each recognize separate Governments it will be this Government on the one hand and the U. S. and British Governments on the other. The consequences would be most lamentable in the world and would stamp the conference as a failure. On the other hand, I take a different view about the basic facts on some of these. According to our information, the present Lublin, now Warsaw, Government does not commend itself to the vast majority of the Polish people. We feel that it is not accepted abroad as representative. If we were to brush away the London Government and lend all our weight to the Lublin Government there would be a world outcry. As far as we can see, the Poles outside Poland would make a united protest. We have an army of 150 thousand Poles who are fighting bravely. That army would not be reconciled to Lublin. It would regard our action in transferring recognition as a betrayal. As Molotov and the Marshal know, I do not agree with the London Government's action. They have been very foolish. But the formal act of transfer of recognition to a new Government would cause the very gravest criticism. It would be said that we have broken altogether with the lawful Government of Poland which we have recognized during the five years of war. It would be said that we have no knowledge of conditions in Poland. We cannot enter the country and must accept the statements of the Lublin Government. Therefore, it would be charged in London that we are forsaking the cause of Poland. Debates would follow in Parliament which would be most painful and embarrassing to unity of the Allies if we were to agree. The proposals of Mr. Molotov do not go nearly far enough. If we give up the Poles in London it should be for a new start on both sides, more or less on equal terms. Before His Majesty's Government could leave its present position on continuing recognition of the London Government we would have to be satisfied that the new Government was fairly representative of the Polish nation. I agree that this can be only a view because we do not know the facts. Our doubts would be removed by elections with full secret ballot and free candidacies to be held in Poland. But it is the transfer before then which is causing so much anxiety to us. That is all I have to say.

MOLOTOV. Perhaps the discussions in Moscow will have a useful result. It is difficult to consider the Polish question without the presence of Poles.

Stalin proceeded to reassure his colleagues that Bierut, Osobka-Morawski, and Rola-Zymierski were all very popular within Poland, and that the Poles were delighted by the fact that their country had been liberated by the Red Army.

The Poles for many years have not liked Russia because Russia took part in three partitions of Poland. But the advance of the Soviet Army and the liberation of Poland from Hitler has completely changed that, the old resentment has completely disappeared. Now there is good will toward Russia. . . . The population is surprised, even astounded, that the people of the London Government do not take any part in this liberation. Members of the Provisional Government are there, but where are the London Poles? These two circumstances produce the fact that the members of the Warsaw Government, though they may not be great men, enjoy great popularity. Can we take account of this fact? We cannot ignore it—the feelings of the Polish people.

Stalin admitted that the Lublin Government was not founded by popular elections.

It is like that of DeGaulle who is also not elected. Who is more popular, DeGaulle or Bierut? We have considered it possible to deal with DeGaulle and make treaties with him. Why not deal with an enlarged Polish Provisional Government. We cannot demand more of Poland than of France. So far the French Government has not carried out any reforms to create enthusiasm. The Polish Government has carried out a great reform which gives it great popularity. If we approve this government without prejudice we can find a solution. . . . It is better to reconstruct than to create a new government. Molotov is right. . . . If we do not talk to them they would accuse us of being occupiers and not liberators.

Neither Churchill nor Roosevelt had any comment to make on Stalin's arguments or the veracity of the facts on which they were based. The President inquired how long a time would elapse before elections could be held, and Stalin replied that it would take a month. [It took exactly two years, to January 1947, before general elections were in fact held in Poland.] Again the matter was referred to the Foreign Ministers, and the meeting was adjourned.

At the meeting of the Foreign Ministers, Molotov insisted that the simplest solution to the Polish question was to expand the existing Lublin Government. Eden opposed this suggestion on the grounds that such a solution would be unacceptable to British public opinion which considered the Lublin Government as unrepresentative, and added that the British Government had an obligation to 150,000 Polish fighting men who were comrades-in-arms on the British side. He therefore wanted to see a settlement which would be acceptable to these soldiers. Stettinius supported Eden. Molotov then attempted to minimize the problem of the popular support of the government by indicating that the Soviet Union considered the elections for a future government to be the most important single matter, and conceded that it might have been a mistake to say that Mikolajczyk was unacceptable to the Lublin Poles. This, he suggested, had to be cleared with the Lublin Government first. Eden agreed with Molotov's observations but expressed fears that if the elections were controlled by the Lublin Government that they would not be free. He thought that the presence of the Western Ambassadors to supervise the elections would remove such doubts. Stettinius agreed and supported Eden. In response, Molotov said:

It might be better to leave out reference to the Allied Ambassadors in Warsaw since this reference would undoubtedly be offensive to the Poles as it would indicate that they, the Poles, were under the control of foreign diplomatic representatives.

This remark undoubtedly fell on sympathetic ears, for there was no argument about it and no such provisions for Allied supervision of elections appeared in the final declaration. The meeting ended with no agreement being reached.

At the next Plenary Session of the three delegations, Molotov expressed Soviet willingness to allow all non-fascist and anti-fascist democratic parties to take part in the elections and to put forward their candidates. Churchill and Roosevelt considered this as proof that considerable progress had been made and expressed hope that the next meeting of the Foreign Ministers would complete the solution of the Polish problem. Churchill appealed to Stalin to allow the Western Ambassadors to supervise the elections, for otherwise the Lublin Government would "win," and to illustrate his point he cited the Egyptian elections as an example. This led Stalin to defend the Poles against comparison with the Egyptians. "I don't believe much in Egyptian elections. It is all rotten corruption there. They buy each other. . . ." After clarifying this point, Churchill stated, "In Parliament I must be able to say that the elections will be held in a fair way. I do not care much about Poles myself." Stalin observed that, "there are some very good people among the Poles; they are good fighters. Of course they fight among themselves, too. I think on both sides there are non-fascist and anti-fascist elements." The President repeated his desire to have a "pure" Polish election, which would be authentic and could not be questioned. This led Molotov to remark that the Lublin Poles should be consulted, because otherwise, ". . . they will feel that it shows a lack of confidence in them." Subsequent discussion did not add anything substantive to the positions already expressed by the participants.[22]

After another meeting of the Foreign Ministers, a communiqué was drafted and agreed upon by all present and issued on February 11, 1945. It read:

> We came to the Crimea conference resolved to settle our differences about Poland. We discussed fully all aspects of the question. We reaffirm our common desire to see established a strong, free, independent and democratic Poland. As a result of our discussion, we have agreed on the conditions in which a new Polish Provisional Government of National Unity may be formed in such a manner as to command recognition by the three major powers.
>
> The agreement reached is as follows:
>
> A new situation has been created in Poland as a result of her complete liberation by the Red Army. This calls for the establishment of a Polish Provisional Government which can be more broadly based than was possible before the recent liberation of western Poland. The Provisional Government which is now functioning in Poland should therefore be recognized on a broader democratic basis with the inclusion of democratic leaders from Poland itself and from Poles abroad. This new Government

should then be called the Polish Provisional Government of National Unity.

M. Molotov, Mr. Harriman, and Sir A. Clark Kerr are authorized as a Commission to consult in the first instance in Moscow with members of the present Provisional Government and with other Polish democratic leaders from within Poland and from abroad, with a view to the reorganization of the present Government along the above lines. This Polish

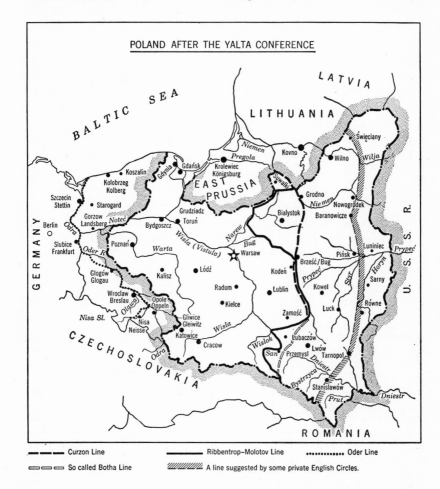

POLAND AFTER THE YALTA CONFERENCE

_____ Curzon Line   Ribbentrop-Molotov Line   ●●●●●●●●●●● Oder Line

⊂⊐⊂⊐⊂⊐ So called Botha Line   ▨▨▨▨▨▨ A line suggested by some private English Circles.

Provisional Government of National Unity shall be pledged to the holding of free and unfettered elections as soon as possible on the basis of universal suffrage and secret ballot. In these elections all democratic and anti-Nazi parties shall have the right to take part and to put forward candidates.

When a Polish Provisional Government of National Unity has been properly formed in conformity with the above, the Government of the U.S.S.R., which now maintains diplomatic relations with the present Provi-

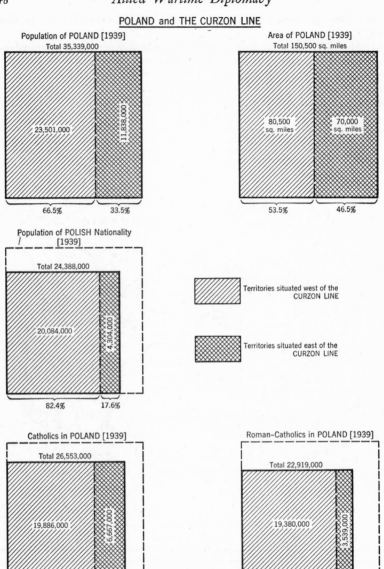

POLAND and THE CURZON LINE

Population of POLAND [1939]
Total 35,339,000

23,501,000   11,838,000

66.5%   33.5%

Area of POLAND [1939]
Total 150,500 sq. miles

80,500 sq. miles   70,000 sq. miles

53.5%   46.5%

Population of POLISH Nationality
[1939]

Total 24,388,000

20,084,000   4,304,000

82.4%   17.6%

Territories situated west of the CURZON LINE

Territories situated east of the CURZON LINE

Catholics in POLAND [1939]

Total 26,553,000

19,886,000   6,667,000

74.9%   25.1%

Roman-Catholics in POLAND [1939]

Total 22,919,000

19,380,000   3,539,000

84.6%   15.4%

sional Government of Poland, and the Government of the United Kingdom and the Government of the United States will establish diplomatic relations with the new Polish Provisional Government of National Unity, and will exchange Ambassadors by whose reports the respective Governments will be kept informed about the situation in Poland.

The three heads of government consider that the eastern frontier of Poland should follow the Curzon Line with digressions from it in some regions of five to eight kilometers in favor of Poland. They recognize that Poland must receive substantial accessions of territory in the north and west.

They feel that the opinion of the new Polish Provisional Government of National Unity should be sought in due course in the extent of these accessions and that the final delimitation of the western frontier of Poland should thereafter await the peace conference.[23]

For the other countries freed from Nazi tyranny, a different declaration was issued.

DECLARATION ON LIBERATED EUROPE

The following declaration has been approved:

The Premier of the Union of Soviet Socialist Republics, the Prime Minister of the United Kingdom, and the President of the United States of America have consulted with each other in the common interests of the peoples of their countries and those of liberated Europe. They jointly declare their mutual agreement to concert during the temporary period of instability in liberated Europe the policies of their three Governments in assisting the peoples liberated from the domination of Nazi Germany and the peoples of the former Axis satellite states of Europe to solve by democratic means their pressing political and economic problems.

The establishment of order in Europe and the rebuilding of national economic life must be achieved by processes which will enable the liberated peoples to destroy the last vestiges of nazism and fascism and to create democratic institutions of their own choice. This is a principle of the Atlantic Charter—the right of all peoples to choose the form of government under which they will live—the restoration of sovereign rights and self-government to those peoples who have been forcibly deprived of them by the aggressor nations.

To foster the conditions in which the liberated peoples may exercise these rights, the three Governments will jointly assist the people in any European liberated state or former Axis satellite state in Europe where in their judgment conditions require (A) to establish conditions of internal peace; (B) to carry out emergency measures for the relief of distressed peoples; (C) to form interim governmental authorities broadly representative of all democratic elements in the population and pledged to the earliest possible establishment through free elections of governments responsive to the will of the people; and (D) to facilitate where necessary the holding of such elections.

The three Governments will consult the other United Nations and provisional authorities or other governments in Europe when matters of direct interest to them are under consideration.

When, in the opinion of the three Governments, conditions in any European liberated state or any former Axis satellite state in Europe make such action necessary, they will immediately consult together on the measures necessary to discharge the joint responsibilities set forth in this declaration.

By this declaration we reaffirm our faith in the principles of the Atlantic Charter, our pledge in the declaration by the United Nations, and our determination to build in cooperation with other peace-loving nations world order under law, dedicated to peace, security, freedom and general well-being of all mankind.

In issuing this declaration, the three powers express the hope that the Provisional Government of the French Republic may be associated with them in the procedure suggested.[24]

The Yalta agreement was hailed by both Roosevelt and Churchill as the best possible settlement, whose execution would mean Poland's freedom and independence.

Moscow interpreted it to mean that the creation of a new Government should be affected only by somewhat expanding the Lublin Government.

Although at that time the Poles did not know how the Yalta Declaration had been conceived and what the exact meaning of the Declaration was, they were shocked, nevertheless, by the joint declaration on Poland. They were deeply hurt that Stalin had managed to persuade Roosevelt and Churchill to ratify Poland's eastern frontier, which in effect was the Ribbentrop-Molotov Line and furthermore had agreed to place the remainder of Poland under communist rule. They were certain of this last effect of the meeting because they were convinced that the fusion of a small fraction of Poles from outside with a communist-dominated administration could not, and would not, weaken communist power. They were surprised that both Western leaders were so ignorant of the communist pattern of behavior.[25]

As the record of Yalta points out, Roosevelt wanted to find a formula to "save the Polish face," and to quiet the disturbed Americans of Polish origin. He seems to have believed that the Soviets would actually carry out their promises to establish a strong, independent Poland, friendly to Russia, and that the main worry of Stalin was to secure a safe rear for his armies.

Churchill, too, wanted to have an independent Poland and he thought that Stalin's promises were genuine with respect to that end. Above all, Churchill wanted to tell the British Parliament that, at Yalta, the Big Three had found the best possible solution to this troublesome dilemma.

Stalin managed to use effectively a number of democratic terms to assure his partners that the Soviets and their Lublin Government were much better friends of the Polish nation than the London Government. He had succeeded in persuading Roosevelt and Churchill that the London Government was not representative and that the Polish nation was at best indifferent to it.[26] Proof of this success was reflected in the fact that in no official communiqué or declaration issued at Yalta was the legal Polish Government in London mentioned even once. Yet this was the Government with whom the Western Allies had official diplomatic relations and under whose command hundreds of thousands of Poles inside and outside of Poland were fighting for the Allied cause.

In terms of broader strategy, Stalin knew that the Western Powers would be anxious to get his commitment against Japan and that the West would be willing to pay the price he exacted.

For Poland, Yalta was a political death warrant. The Poles only regretted that the five years of struggle against the Nazis had been futile. Six and a half million of their citizens had been killed, the country was devastated and impoverished, and, at the end, when all other Western European countries were getting back their independence, the war-time Allies of Poland had decided at Yalta to subjugate the whole Polish nation to another totalitarian system—one which would occupy Poland this time, presumably, for generations. Morally and emotionally, it would have been easier for the Poles to accept a similar decision made by Stalin and Hitler, rather than by Churchill and Roosevelt. They kept asking whether Churchill and Roosevelt had any moral right to make such a decision.[27]

Accordingly, on February 13, 1945 the Polish Government in London denounced the Crimea Conference proposals regarding Poland. It declared that the decisions of the Big Three "cannot be recognized by the Polish Government and cannot bind the Polish people."

Asserting that the decisions were taken without the Polish Government's knowledge and that the method adopted constituted a violation of the letter and spirit of the Atlantic Charter, the statement went on:

The Polish Government will consider the severance of the eastern half of the territory of Poland through the imposition of a Polish-Soviet frontier following along the so-called Curzon Line as a fifth partition of Poland, now accomplished by her Allies.

The intention of the Three Powers to create a "Provisional Polish Government of National Unity" by enlarging the foreign appointed Lublin Committee with persons vaguely described as "democratic leaders from Poland itself and Poles abroad" can only legalize Soviet interference in Polish internal affairs.

So long as the territories of Poland remain under the sole occupation of Soviet troops, a government of that kind will not safeguard for the Polish nation, even in the presence of British and American diplomats, the unfettered right of free expression.

The statement ended by reaffirming the Government's offer to "co-operate in the creation of a government in Poland truly representative of the will of the Polish nation." [28]

The *Daily Herald* on February 14, 1945 stated:

The Polish protest will have little or no effect on the sequence of events. Already work has begun on the preliminaries for forming a new Government. . . .

There is no doubt that M. Mikolajczyk and the Peasant Party leaders will be prepared to cooperate in the new regime, for the "Crimea Plan" is based on M. Mikolajczyk's own suggestions.

This prompted Mikolajczyk to reply in a letter to the Editor, which stated:

I have on many occasions made my views on the settlement of the Polish-Soviet relations publicly known.

The essential aspects of the Polish problem are two-fold: the question of frontiers, and the question of the Government. These are the starting points of all considerations aiming at securing Poland's freedom and independence.

On the frontier question I maintain the view that the Three Great Powers should share the responsibility in the frontier settlement, in which Poland should also participate.

I also maintain the view that by such a settlement the frontiers of Poland in the east as well as the west and north should be fixed simultaneously. Moreover, I have always stated that at least Lwow and the oil fields should remain within Poland.

On the second subject—the question of the Government—I have pronounced myself in public in favor of convening a round-table conference of all leaders of the Polish Underground in Warsaw and of basing the Government in Poland on all democratic elements, and guaranteeing to such a Government the means of unhampered action.

I have never suggested that this should be accomplished by the broadening and reorganization of the so-called Provisional Government in Lublin. One cannot assert, therefore, that the "Crimea Plan" concerning Poland, both on the subject of frontiers and on the subject of the new Government in Poland, is based on my suggestions.[29]

The Soviets were anxious to attack any defensive move made by the Poles in London in order to further discredit them and to destroy their political importance.

On February 18, 1945 the Soviet Home Service in Moscow broadcast the following:

Arciszewski & Co. have certainly struck a very high and a very false note. Mikolajczyk has shown his solidarity with Arciszewski. To keep the musical terminology, the London Poles are acting in unison with Berlin. The Wilhelmstrasse gladly greets the Arciszewski decision not to recognize the Crimea Conference, and his prattle about the Fifth Partition of Poland (reference to Braun von Strumm saying that the Poles in London reacted courageously to the Big Three decisions). Birds of a feather flock together.

The British and United States press speaks with obvious irritation about the opposition of the Polish *émigré* circles.

The London correspondent of *The New York Times* considers that they are seriously trying the patience of the United States and British Governments (reference to Low's cartoon). This caricature gives an exact explanation of things as they are. The Polish reactionaries have placed themselves outside the ranks of the Allied nations. Their song is sung. The inglorious saga of the Polish reactionaries has come to its logical conclusion. The farce has been played. The curtain is about to fall.[30]

All Polish political parties condemned the Yalta decision.

A considerable number of the British were critical of the Polish resistance to the Soviet demands at Yalta.[31]

The treatment of Poland at Yalta had far-reaching effects inside Poland also. On February 13, 1945 the *Dziennik Polski* of Krakow, sponsored by the Polish Provisional Government, published an article entitled, "From the Congress of Vienna to the Teheran Conference," in which it said:

In the minds of some Polish circles Britain was to be the State which would restore Poland's independence. Such reasoning, which magnified the power of Britain out of all proportion and created a political legend, almost a political myth, was very far from corresponding to the realities. This false reasoning was nullified by Soviet Russia, her diplomacy and her Red Army, which has liberated Poland and a considerable part of Europe. Polish political thought must adapt itself to facts and abandon stereotyped reasoning. Such a policy has already led to the disaster of 1939, and must not be allowed to occur again.

The reaction of the British press to Yalta, especially as illustrated by the leading articles of February 14, 1945 in the *Manchester Guardian*, the *News Chronicle*, the *Daily Telegraph*, the *Daily Herald*, the *Daily Express*, and the *Daily Worker*, was one of exultation.

The American press at the same time also greeted the Yalta decision with visible approval, especially the *New York Times*, the *New York Herald Tribune*, and the *Chicago Daily News*. Only a few papers in both countries aired their misgivings about Poland.

The American participants at the Conference fully believed the lofty words of the Declaration and were very pleased with the results of the Conference. At Yalta they felt that they had reached an honorable and equitable solution to the difficult problem of Poland.[32]

Speaking about Yalta to Sherwood, Hopkins said:

We really believed in our hearts that this was the dawn of a new day we had all been praying for and talking about for so many years. We were absolutely certain that we had won the first great victory of the peace—and, by "we," I mean *all* of us, the whole civilized human race. The Russians had proved that they could be reasonable and farseeing and *there wasn't any doubt in the minds of the President or any of us that we could live with them and get along with them peacefully for as far into the future as any of us could imagine.* But I have to make one amendment to that—I think we all had in our minds the reservation that we could not foretell what the results would be if anything should happen to Stalin. We felt sure that we could count on him to be reasonable and sensible and understanding—but we never could be sure who or what might be in back of him there in the Kremlin.[33]

It can hardly be doubted that Hopkins was expressing the views of the American policy makers. Churchill and Roosevelt believed that the Yalta decision on Poland was just. Stalin's feelings about the outcome of Yalta were presumably reflected in the Soviet press, which overflowed with praise for the Yalta communiqué.

Pravda published a special issue devoted to the Conference and said in its editorial that the Yalta Conference had proved that

. . . the alliance of the Three Big Powers possessed not only a historic yesterday and a victorious today, but also a great tomorrow.

Izvestia called the Conference the "greatest political event of current time." [34]

But Stalin did not exhibit a permanent joy and gratitude for his success at Yalta. In a speech on February 23, 1945, on the occasion of the celebration of Red Army Day, he did not mention Yalta even once. He avoided displaying his appreciation, presumably in the fear that the Western Powers would exploit this by asking for similar favors in return. His plan was still only partially realized. An appearance of indifference to the results of the Yalta Conference paid him better dividends than exultation would have. Poland was only a stepping-stone in the fulfillment of Soviet objectives, anyhow. Now that Poland was removed as a cause of diplomatic friction between the Big Allies, an era of "friendly understanding and collaboration" was supposed to follow.

The *Daily Sketch* of February 14, 1945 quoted the conversation of their Moscow correspondent (Alexander Werth) with a Russian member of the Yalta Conference, who is reported to have said:

We are resolved that the Poles are not going to cause friction, still less a breach, between us. They have got to recognize their responsibilities. They have their duties to us. They owe their existence to us, and have got to act accordingly.

On February 13, 1945 Prime Minister Arciszewski sent an appeal to Roosevelt about the Yalta resolutions pertaining to Poland, requesting a clarification of the American attitude towards Poland. On February 16 he received the following telegram from the President, forwarded to him through the American Embassy with the Polish Government.

Your telegram of February 3, 1945. You may be assured that Polish problems were considered with great care and friendliness at our last Crimean Conference. I hope that we all shall be able to work in harmony so as to find the proper solution at the proper time.[35]

The weakness of Roosevelt's reply prompted Arciszewski to present his Government's view of Yalta in unequivocal terms, which he transmitted on February 17 through the same channels to President Roosevelt.

I received your message yesterday, February 16, 1945. I welcome your assurance, Mr. President, that the Polish problems at the Crimean Conference were considered with the greatest care and friendliness, and that you hope to find the proper solution in due time.

At this opportunity I consider it my duty to state that the resolutions of the Crimean Conference, as they were published, have been accepted by all Poles as a new partition of Poland, and as placing her under the Soviet protectorate. Despite everything, the Polish nation is deeply convinced that this is not the final settlement of the Polish problem and it continues to have an unshakeable hope both in your deep sympathies for Poland, Mr. President, and in the conviction that you are a determined defender of the ideals of liberty and justice, in the defense of which American soldiers and Polish soldiers so willingly are giving their lives.[35]

There was no reply from Roosevelt.

After the initial shock brought about by the Yalta decisions receded, the Poles began to appraise their position more realistically. Their reasoning went as follows:

The Big Three Powers are still striving for the complete defeat of Germany, and their moment of success lies in the not too distant future. Undoubtedly the Anglo-Americans will try to secure Soviet participation against Japan.

The Soviets are exploiting the strong position which they gained through their military successes. In a very clever and determined manner they are forcing the Anglo-Americans to make various concessions which will have greater significance in the future than they do now. On the other hand, Soviet concessions to the Western Powers are confined to the promise that they will enter the war against Japan. They preserve a determined appearance to fulfill their obligations in a just and objective manner, which is appreciated by the Western mind.

The Anglo-Americans are determined to avoid any conflict with the Soviets and they see a chance to resolve their differences by compromises on the following issues:

(*a*) The final defeat of Germany and a combined action against Japan.

(*b*) The post-war organization of the world, with the division of the spheres of influence.

(*c*) The establishment of the system of collective security.

The Polish problem, they reasoned, was solved arbitrarily, without the participation of the Poles, which proves that the Western Powers adhered to the Soviet demands. This means that there is no point in hoping that the Polish problem will be reconsidered should a conflict between the main Allies take place. There are no symptoms that such a conflict will occur in the foreseeable future. This conflict can be provoked only by the Soviets; not by the Anglo-Americans. It is also difficult to foresee the final results of such a conflict, should it occur.

The organization of the new Poland was already predetermined and will be carried out according to the Soviet plan, and the Western Powers will have nothing to say about it. Poles should not expect any help in this matter from England or America. Therefore, our plan to rebuild Poland with the political support of the West is futile and out of the question. Poland was forced into the Soviet orbit, and this means that her independence is lost for a very long time. Her possible liberation will be a resultant of the conflict of forces between the East and the West.

Patriotic elements in Poland, which may attempt to resist communization, are bound to lose against the overwhelming power of the communist rulers and will be liquidated. This presents a mortal danger to the Polish Nation. Therefore, although Poland will have to resist sovietization, this must be done intelligently and without too many human sacrifices. In view of the colossal losses in manpower during the war, this is especially imperative if the Polish Nation is to survive.

Poles should not avoid participation in the new organization of the Polish State because this would abandon the whole field of social and political activity to the communists. No help should be expected either from the East or from the West. Only the ingenuity of intelligent patriots can slow down complete annihilation. Polish strength will lie only in unity. Avoidance of responsibility will only multiply the power of the pro-Soviet elements.

Poles should not avoid collaboration with the Soviets, but this should be done in such a way as to benefit Poland. Every Soviet weak point should be exploited to strengthen the Polish cause. No effort should be spared to avoid an aggravation of the situation in Poland.[36]

3. The Allied Attempts to Implement the Yalta Decisions

The next problem was how to implement this realistic appraisal. Not many Poles were willing to risk their personal safety by returning to Poland or to face the possibility of being called "traitors" by those who would remain behind in the West.

The British hope to fulfill the Yalta decision centered around Mikolajczyk—that he would accept it and go to Poland, via Moscow, to join the new Government. The Poles in London were aware of this, too. Some of them attempted to persuade him not to go because it would provide an easy excuse to the British that they had fulfilled their obligations.

After persistent pressure from various sources that he receive General Anders, and after several refusals, Mikolajczyk agreed to see him on February 24, 1945.

Anders pleaded with Mikolajczyk not to go to the Moscow Conference because, as he put it,

. . . if anyone else will go, that will not count. But if you go it will not help but harm the Polish Government. Russia has her imperialistic aim to conquer the whole world and she will not abandon it. Unfortunately, the British do not yet understand this, nor does Churchill. Therefore, there will not be a war now. But war is inevitable even if the British and Americans do not want it. For this reason one should not go to Poland but should strive to prepare the means of receiving the two million Poles from Germany and the several million from Poland who will flee abroad. Soon the Russians will show what they are after, and this will lead to a global conflict, whether the British like it or not. It is unfortunate that President Raczkiewicz and the Polish Government did not accept my proposal to withdraw the Polish Army from the front. This would have been the only dignified and realistic protest against the Crimea Conference. I shall try once more to persuade the President and the Government. I don't know what I should do. Churchill does not agree with my view, but I know that soon a conflict will begin. Next Wednesday I shall see Churchill and will try to discuss with him the future of our Army abroad—how we can keep and preserve it. My subsequent behavior will depend on what kind of assurances I shall get.
Mikolajczyk replied that Anders' reasoning was wrong and fallacious.
One should not condition our Army to the idea that it will never return home, that it has to stay and fight for others on territories outside of Europe when the war in Europe is over. I consider such an eventuality as the most tragic. Last year I was saying to the National Council that it might be that today our soldiers have agitated against me as a "traitor" and would shoot me. But when the war is over in Europe and the same soldiers are ordered to go on fighting in other parts of the world instead of returning home, they will shoot their own officers. For this reason your

policy should be "everybody returns home." We should strive to provide security, freedom, and the proper conditions for a decent life for them. That is my policy. Will I succeed? Only time will tell. Your policy that return is prohibited or that only those who want to can return and that the rest should wait until the whole world will go against Russia is harmful and unpatriotic.

Before leaving, Anders said that he was against those who called Mikolajczyk "traitor," because he knew that Mikolajczyk was a patriot. He repeated his belief that soon, despite British and American wishes the whole world would have to fight Russia.[37]

As this and other records previously quoted show, Mikolajczyk was genuinely interested in showing the Russians that he and his group were ready to cooperate with them on a friendly basis. His desire to help the Polish people forced him to disregard the symptoms whose logic pointed to the fact that the Soviets were bent on a complete domination of Poland. The Western Powers were constantly assuring him that Stalin meant what he said and that England and the United States would support Mikolajczyk if he undertook to join the new Government. He seriously considered what Churchill had said to the Athenians:

Let no one fail in his duty towards his country. Let no one swerve off the high road of truth and honor. Let no one fail to rise to the occasion of this great moment.[38]

Above all, Mikolajczyk knew that someone from the London Poles had to accept the thankless assignment of implementing the Yalta agreement so that the Soviets would be forced to honor their obligations and that everything should be done not to let them find an excuse for not fulfilling them. If they did fulfill them, then the Polish Nation would greatly benefit thereby. If they violated their written promises made at Yalta, the Western Powers could not then say that the London Poles, by refusing to cooperate, had permitted the Russians to enslave the whole of Poland.

Mikolajczyk's task became even more compelling when, on February 27, Churchill spoke about the Yalta decision in regard to Poland.

The Three Powers are agreed that acceptance by the Poles of the provisions on the eastern frontiers, and, so far as can now be ascertained, on the western frontiers, is an essential condition of the establishment and future welfare and security of a strong, independent, homogeneous Polish State. . . . But even more important than the frontiers of Poland, within the limits now disclosed, is the freedom of Poland. The home of the Poles is settled. Are they to be masters in their own house? Are they to be free, as we in Britain and the United States or France are free? Are their sovereignty and their independence to be untrammelled, or are they to become a mere projection of the Soviet State, forced against their will by an armed

minority to adopt a communist or totalitarian system? I am putting the
case in all its bluntness. It is a touchstone far more sensitive and vital than
the drawing of frontier lines. Where does Poland stand? Where do we
all stand on this?

Most solemn declarations have been made by Marshal Stalin and the
Soviet Union that the sovereign independence of Poland is to be maintained, and this decision is now joined in both by Great Britain and the
United States. Here also the World Organization will in due course
assume a measure of responsibility. The Poles will have their future in
their own hands, with the single limitation that they must honestly follow,
in harmony with their Allies, a policy friendly to Russia. That is surely
reasonable. . . .

The agreement provides for consultations, with a view to the establishment in Poland of a new Polish Provisional Government of National
Unity, with which the three major Powers can all enter into diplomatic
relations, instead of some recognizing one Polish Government and the rest
another. . . . His Majesty's Government intend to do all in their power
to ensure that . . . representative Poles of all democratic parties are given
full freedom to come and make their views known.

. . . The impression I brought back from the Crimea, and from all my
other contacts, is that Marshal Stalin and the Soviet leaders wish to live in
honorable friendship and equality with the Western democracies. I feel
also that their word is their bond. I know of no Government which stands
to its obligations, even in its own despite, more solidly than the Russian
Soviet Government. I decline absolutely to embark here on a discussion
about Russian good faith. It is quite evident that these matters touch the
whole future of the world. Sombre indeed would be the fortunes of mankind if some awful schism arose between the Western democracies and the
Russian Soviet Union.[39]

Churchill's assurances to the House of Commons of a fair deal for
Poland brought him unqualified support of his policy. Only a small
group of thirty Members of Parliament felt so strongly that an in-
justice had been done to Poland that they spoke against Churchill.
The Parliamentary Secretary to the Ministry of Town and Country
Planning, Mr. H. G. Strauss, resigned in protest against that policy.[40]

Gradually, the grim reports coming from the British Ambassador in
Moscow had a sobering effect upon Churchill. He was afraid that

. . . once it was seen that we had been deceived and the well-known technique was being applied behind closed doors in Poland, either directly by
the Russians or through their Lublin puppets, a very grave situation in
British public opinion would be reached. . . .

After a fairly promising start Molotov was now refusing to accept any
interpretation of the Crimea proposals except his own extremely rigid and
narrow one. He was attempting to bar practically all our candidates for
the consultations, was taking the line that he must base himself on the
views of Bierut and his gang, and had withdrawn his offer to let us send
observers to Poland. He clearly wanted to make a farce of consulting the

"non-Lublin" Poles—which meant that the new Government of Poland would be merely the existing one dressed up to look more respectable to the ignorant—and also wanted to stop us seeing the liquidations and deportations and all the manoeuvres of setting up a totalitarian regime before elections were held and even before a new Government was installed. If we did not get things right the world would soon see that Mr. Roosevelt and I had underwritten a fraudulent prospectus when we put our signatures to the Crimea settlement.

. . . Far more than Poland was involved. This was the test case between us and the Russians of the meaning of such terms as democracy, sovereignty, independence, representative government, and free and unfettered elections. . . .[41]

Consequently, on March 8, 1945 Churchill dispatched the following message to Roosevelt proposing that he (Churchill) send Stalin a message along the lines set in the message to Roosevelt and hoping that the President would send a similar one.

I am bound to tell you that I should have to make a statement of our failure to Parliament if the Commission in Moscow were not in the end able to agree on the following basis:

(a) M. Molotov appears to be contending that the terms of the Crimea communiqué established for the present Warsaw Administration an absolute right of prior consultation on all points. In the English text the passage of the communiqué in question, which was an American draft, cannot bear this interpretation. M. Molotov's construction therefore cannot be accepted.

(b) All Poles nominated by any of the three Governments shall be accepted for the consultations unless ruled out by unanimous decision of the Commission, and every effort made to produce them before the Commission at the earliest possible moment. The Commission should ensure to the Poles invited facilities for communicating with other Poles whom they wish to consult, whether in Poland or outside, and the right to suggest to the Commission the names of other Poles who should be invited to its proceedings. All Poles appearing before the Commission would naturally enjoy complete freedom of movement and of communication among themselves while in Moscow, and would be at liberty to depart whither they chose upon the conclusion of the consultations. Mr. Molotov has raised objections to inviting M. Mikolajczyk, but his presence would certainly be vital.

(c) The Poles invited for consultations should discuss among themselves with a view to reaching agreement upon the composition of a Government truly representative of the various sections of Polish opinion present before the Commission. The discussions should also cover the question of the exercise of the Presidential functions. The Commission should preside over these discussions in an impartial arbitral capacity.

(d) Pending the conclusion of the Commission's discussions, the Soviet Government should use its utmost influence to prevent the Warsaw Administration from taking any further legal or administrative action of a fundamental character affecting social, constitutional, economic, or political conditions in Poland.

(e) The Soviet Government should make arrangements to enable British and American observers to visit Poland and to report upon conditions there in accordance with the offer spontaneously made by M. Molotov at an earlier stage in the Commission's discussions.

We must not let Poland become a source of disagreement and misunderstanding between our two peoples. For this reason I am sure you will understand how important it is for us to reach an early settlement on the basis of the Yalta decision, and it is because I am confident that you will do your utmost to bring this about that I am now telegraphing to you.[42]

Two days later he sent another message to Roosevelt:

The Lublin Poles may well answer that their Government can alone ensure "the maximum amount of political tranquility inside," that they already represent the great mass of the "democratic forces in Poland," and that they cannot join hands with *émigré* traitors to Poland or Fascist collaborationists and landlords, and so on, according to the usual technique.

Meanwhile we shall not be allowed inside the country or have any means of informing ourselves upon the position. It suits the Soviets very well to have a long period of delay, so that the process of liquidation of elements unfavorable to them or their puppets may run its full course. This would be furthered by our opening out now into proposals of a very undefined character for a political truce between these Polish parties (whose hatreds would eat into live steel) in the spirit and intent of the Crimea decision, and might well imply the abandonment of all clear-cut requests, such as those suggested in my last telegram to you. Therefore I should find it very difficult to join in this project of a political truce.

I have already mentioned to you that the feeling here is very strong. Four Ministers have abstained from the divisions and two have already resigned. I beg therefore that you will give full consideration to my previous telegram.[43]

As before, Poland's tragedy was shaped by the fact that the policies of those two Western leaders and their comprehension of the nature of the Soviet designs were not synchronized. Up to Yalta it was Churchill who had been too anxious to obtain Soviet cooperation against Hitler through the appeasement of Stalin and it was Roosevelt who was upholding the traditional Western moral principles. After Yalta, it was Churchill who first saw the consequences of their mistakes *vis-à-vis* Stalin and who was willing to act energetically to correct them because he detected in them a threat to the security of Great Britain. This time it was Roosevelt who weakened his determination because of a desire not to lose the promised Russian participation in the war against Japan, which by that time became his primary strategic interest. Stalin managed to exploit their difference of interests to the benefit of the Soviet Union.

Churchill was not discouraged by Roosevelt's cautiousness. On March 13 he sent another telegram to the President.

At Yalta also we agreed to take the Russian view of the frontier line. Poland has lost her frontier. Is she now to lose her freedom? That is the question which will undoubtedly have to be fought out in Parliament and in public here. I do not wish to reveal a divergence between the British and the United States Governments, but it would certainly be necessary for me to make it clear that we are in presence of a great failure and an utter breakdown of what was settled at Yalta, but that we British have not the necessary strength to carry the matter further and that the limits of our capacity to act have been reached. The moment that Molotov sees that he has beaten us away from the whole process of consultations among Poles to form a new Government, he will know that we will put up with anything. On the other hand, I believe that combined dogged pressure and persistence along the lines on which we have been working and of my proposed draft message to Stalin would very likely succeed.[44]

Churchill commented thus on the reply received from the President:

This produced a strongly argued reply, which had no doubt been the work of the State Department since my long telegram of March 8 had been received in Washington.[45]

The reply ran as follows:

I cannot but be concerned at the views you expressed in your message of the 13th. I do not understand what you mean by a divergence between our Governments on the Polish negotiations. From our side there is certainly no evidence of any divergence of policy. We have been merely discussing the most effective tactics, and I cannot agree that we are confronted with a breakdown of the Yalta agreement until we have made the effort to overcome the obstacles incurred in the negotiations at Moscow. I also find puzzling your statement that the only definite suggestion in our instructions to (Ambassador) Harriman is for a political truce in Poland. These instructions, of which you have a copy, not only set forth our understanding of the Yalta agreement, but they make the definite point that the Commission itself should agree on the list of Poles to be invited for consultation, and that no one of the three groups from which the reorganized Government is to emerge can dictate which individuals from the other two groups ought to be invited to Moscow. . . . Our chief purpose . . . remains, without giving ground, to get the negotiations moving again, and tackle first of all the point on which they had come to a standstill. I cannot urge upon you too strongly the vital importance of agreeing without further delay on instructions to our Ambassadors so that the negotiations may resume. . . . With this in mind I have examined the points which you propose to submit to Stalin in your message of March 8, and have the following comments to make:
We are in agreement on point (a) that the Warsaw Administration is not entitled to an absolute right of prior consultation on all points, and this is covered in our instructions to Harriman.

I cannot believe that Molotov will accept the proposal contained in point (*b*), that any Pole can be invited unless all three members of the Commission object, and I am opposed to putting forward such a suggestion at this time, as it would in my view almost certainly leave us in a stalemate, which would only redound to the benefit of the Lublin Poles. I also think the demand for freedom of movement and communication would arouse needless discussion at this stage in the negotiations.

On point (*c*) we are agreed that the Poles invited for consultation should discuss the composition of the Government among themselves, with the Commission presiding in an impartial arbitral capacity so far as possible. Harriman has already been instructed to this effect, but feels, and I agree, that this might be pressed later.

I have covered your point (*d*) [about stopping any major changes in Poland] in my previous message, and continue to feel that our approach would be better calculated to achieve the desired result. With reference to point (*e*) [sending in observers], you will recall that this had been agreed to by Molotov, who took fright when Clark Kerr revealed that you were thinking of a large mission. I am willing to include in Averell's instructions the wording you propose in point (*e*).

Please let me know urgently whether you agree that in the light of the foregoing considerations our Ambassadors may proceed with their instructions. . . .[46]

This led Churchill to send a rejoinder in which he elucidated the previous telegrams, but no positive results came from it.

The Soviets, meanwhile, were establishing firm control over Poland and asked that at the forthcoming United Nations Conference in San Francisco Poland be represented only by the Lublin Government. The Western Powers objected to this demand and in retaliation Stalin refused to let Molotov attend it. The problem of how to implement the Yalta decisions remained unsolved.

On March 16, 1945 the United States Chargé d'Affaires in London asked if Mikolajczyk could issue a declaration in which he would comply with Stalin's request to approve the Yalta decisions. This would pave the way to his participation in the Moscow consultations about the expansion of the Lublin Government. Mikolajczyk declined to do so for the following reasons:

On the basis of the statements in the Moscow and Lublin press, it is obvious that the Soviet Union does not intend to implement the decisions of Yalta and everything is being done to avoid fulfilling them. I have a secret report of a conference between Bierut and Osobka-Morawski in Moscow, which states that everything should be done to postpone the realization of the Yalta decisions. In the meantime, certain Polish political leaders should be liquidated while pressure should be put on the others to join the Lublin Government. Should the United Kingdom and the United States press for the fulfillment of the Yalta agreement, the Soviets can say that the Lublin Government is representative and there can be only very small changes. The latest information from Poland about the arrest of prominent political personalities indicates that these instructions from Moscow are being carried out.[47]

A similar request was made of Mikolajczyk by the British Government, and he gave the same reply. The British and the Americans were in a dilemma as to how they should go about implementing the Yalta decisions.

The special Commission which was established in Moscow was composed of the British Ambassador, Sir Archibald Clark Kerr; the American Ambassador, Averell Harriman; and V. M. Molotov, Chairman. Their task was to implement the Yalta decisions. Because of their different interpretations of the terms of the Yalta decision the expected results were not forthcoming. This deadlock could be explained in terms of the subsequent communist attempts to eliminate the participation of the British and the Americans in the settling of the Polish problem.

The communists therefore decided to try to bypass the Commission by approaching Mikolajczyk and his group unofficially and directly in order to persuade him to join the Lublin Government. This would solve the whole issue and render superfluous any attempts at interference by the American and British Governments.

On March 28, 1945 an unofficial representative of the Lublin Committee, Mr. Jagodzinski, sought and arranged a meeting with Professor Grabski, the former speaker of the Polish Parliament in London and a close friend of Mikolajczyk. Through Grabski he wanted to convey certain points to Mikolajczyk.

When Grabski asked about the Inter-Allied Commission of the Three in Moscow (the United States, the United Kingdom, and the U.S.S.R.), Jagodzinski replied as follows:

The Commission of the Three is not important. Actually, it can only accept what the Lublin Government does in expanding the political basis of its Government.

GRABSKI. But the Yalta decisions say something different.

JAGODZINSKI. The Yalta agreement speaks about the expansion of the political basis of the Lublin Government. The British and the Americans are liars. They don't want to realize that there can only be a continuation of the present Lublin Government, with the possible addition of a few other persons. Stalin's prestige is too much involved in support of the present Government, so the Soviet Union will not tolerate any American or British interference into Polish internal affairs. We are completely and permanently united with Russia.

GRABSKI. I have a sense of proportion of the relative power and influence of the United States, the United Kingdom, and the Soviet Union. This is their business. But tell me, who conducts the mass arrests in Poland, the NKVD or the Lublin Committee?

JAGODZINSKI. We do all the arresting, because we have a better information machine than the NKVD. We have to arrest all who are potentially dangerous to the Red Army.

GRABSKI. I know that you have also arrested very respectable citizens, determined supporters of Mikolajczyk's policy of reaching an understanding with Russia. But when war is over, what kind of excuse will you have for further arrests?

JAGODZINSKI. We can always find pretexts. [Becomes excited.] Those dreadful people are sabotaging state authority. They are getting friendly with the Russians but pull out revolvers against us. Those are Poles.

GRABSKI. The Polish nation did not fight so long for freedom against Germans in order to surrender it to a new totalitarian regime. If you think that you can bribe them now with a piece of bread you are mistaken. Above everything else, the Poles desire freedom. If you don't give them that you will have to fight the whole nation, and, if you do that, sooner or later you will lose.

JAGODZINSKI. [Even more excited.] Yes, we have already begun that fight because they fight us. If I could I would execute the whole "Rubens" (G.H.Q. of the Polish Army in London). "Rubens" is sending people to Poland to act against our Government. I have the names and photographs of those who were sent to Poland last week.

GRABSKI. Where did you get that information?

JAGODZINSKI. There are those who take money from both sides. [Here he pulls out a checkbook.] I pay for certain information. . . . Soon we will stop this nonsense. We shall have a new election which will solve everything.

GRABSKI. In Yalta the prestige of the Three Powers was involved in that this election should be really free. Do you think that these Powers will entrust you, who arrest your political opponents, to conduct the elections?

JAGODZINSKI. Must we always look for intermediaries? Would it not be possible to have Mikolajczyk, you, and three others join our Government?

GRABSKI. No responsible person will join you. You will have the majority and if you do not like our arguments, undoubtedly we could be arrested and deported to Kazakhstan or to one of your concentration camps.

Furthermore, we cannot ignore Churchill, Roosevelt, and Stalin. They did not create the "Commission of the Three" for us to ignore it.

JAGODZINSKI. "The Commission of the Three" is only window dressing. Stalin himself will decide all. He in turn has given his complete confidence and support to the Lublin Government.[48]

At this point Grabski decided to end the conversation.

A similar approach was made directly to Mikolajczyk. He, in turn, informed Cadogan that a representative of the Lublin Government had approached him with a proposal of reaching an agreement directly between the London and the Lublin Poles without any Allied intermediaries. He was told by the Lublin Pole that the Soviet Union would never allow any British or American interference in Polish affairs. At the same time, the Lublin Government had approached the political parties in Poland with an invitation for them to go to Moscow, where they would meet Mikolajczyk and subsequently reach an agreement with Moscow. Mikolajczyk expressed the fear that these people in Poland would undoubtedly be subjected to great pressure and that if they did not accept the proposed conditions they might be arrested and accused of sabotage. He suggested that the British Government should be prepared for such an eventuality in order to rescue these people by an appeal to world opinion.

Cadogan replied that the British Government would not allow any *fait accompli* and would obtain the release of these representatives should they be subjected to any blackmail.[49]

All of these deliberations were suddenly overshadowed by the sudden death of President Roosevelt on April 12. His death was mourned by Poles everywhere—inside and outside of Poland. They felt that a great champion of freedom, justice, and the rule of law had departed. The underground authorities in Poland thereupon sent the following telegram of sympathy to the American Nation, addressed to President Truman:

> The Polish nation and its Home underground authorities send the American nation and the family of the late President Roosevelt an expression of their profound sympathy in the blow which has fallen on the American nation and on all the Allied nations. The Polish nation in particular feels this deeply, for a great Statesman has passed from the world, one who did not allow himself to be deceived by the façade behind which a disastrous policy has attempted to hide the real character and desires of the Polish nation. He supported us in our struggle for real freedom and a truly democratic regime. We place the hopes we had centered in him in the hands of the American nation and in those of his worthy successor, Harry Truman.
>
> (signed) THE COUNCIL OF NATIONAL UNITY AND THE
> GOVERNMENT PLENIPOTENTIARY.[50]

Only a few Poles knew anything about Roosevelt's successor. Ambassador Ciechanowski reported that he had had a very pleasant conversation with Truman before Roosevelt's death and that Truman had shown a ready understanding of the Polish situation and had expressed his concern.

> From what he (Truman) told me, I realized that he was apprehensive of Soviet Russia's policies. . . . He impressed me as a man of sincere and direct approach to all problems.[51]

This change of American leadership brought new hope to the Poles that American policies towards Poland would become firm. Many detected significance in his name, which they interpreted to read "true man." As Mr. Truman's subsequent policies towards the Soviet Union showed, the Poles' hopes were not misplaced.

One of the first political acts which Truman performed as President was to send a joint American-British declaration to Stalin about Poland. This declaration suggested Stalin's agreement to the following plan:

You mention the desirability of inviting eight Poles—five from within Poland and three from London—to take part in these first consultations and in your message to the Prime Minister you indicate that Mikolajczyk would be acceptable if he issued a statement in support of the Crimean decision. We, therefore, submit the following proposals for your consideration in order to prevent a breakdown, with all its incalculable consequences, of our endeavors to settle the Polish question. We hope that you will give them your most careful and earnest consideration.

1. That we instruct our representatives on the Commission to extend immediately invitations to the following Polish leaders to come to Moscow to consult: Bierut, Osobka-Morawski, Rola-Zymierski, Bishop Sapieha; one representative Polish political party leader not connected with the present Warsaw Government (if any of the following were agreeable to you they would be agreeable to us: Witos, Zulawski, Chacinski, Jasiukowicz); and from London, Mikolajczyk, Grabski, and Stanczyk.

2. That once the invitations to come for consultation have been issued by the Commission that representatives of Warsaw could arrive first, if desired.

3. That it be agreed that these Polish leaders called for consultation could suggest to the Commission the names of a certain number of other Polish leaders from within Poland or abroad who might be brought in for consultation in order that all major Polish groups be represented in the discussions.

4. We do not feel that we could commit ourselves to any formula for determining the composition of the new Government of National Unity in advance of consultation with the Polish leaders and we do not in any case consider the Yugoslav precedent to be applicable to Poland.

We ask you to read again carefully the American and British message of April 1 since they set forth the larger considerations which we still have very much in mind and to which we must adhere.[52]

Stalin realized that he would have to change his tactics in order to give a new appearance to his interpretation of the Yalta agreements. In the meantime, Churchill began to work on Mikolajczyk in order to persuade him to join the Lublin Government.

On April 15, 1945 Churchill invited Mikolajczyk to Chequers where he gave him to read a telegram from Stalin

. . . in which Stalin complained about Churchill's pressure to have Mikolaj-czyk in the new Government of Poland. Stalin underlined his desire to fulfill the Yalta agreement and therefore was ready to approach the Lublin Government about it and to suggest that they should invite Mikolajczyk. But Mikolajczyk, supported by the British and American Governments, publicly criticizes the Yalta agreement, and is sabotaging it. If Mikolajczyk will make some public declaration to the contrary, Stalin is ready to act in order to have Mikolajczyk invited.[53]

Churchill, therefore, asked Mikolajczyk if it would not be possible for him to issue such a declaration as would express his readiness for friendly Polish-Soviet cooperation and to express his acceptance of the Yalta decisions. He went on to say that

. . . Russia is anxious to have a good relationship with the two Great Powers (the United Kingdom and the United States) because they possess the greatest military and naval force. Those are the arguments which the Soviets respect. We shall not keep twenty million men under arms. We shall not attack Russia. In two years the United States of America will withdraw all its forces from Europe. For this reason, now, when they respect us and are afraid of us, all problems must be solved. . . . Although it is not publicly known, Russia is anxious to get an American loan. Therefore, we have to exploit the situation and move the Polish problem. We cannot wait for the publication of an article by you. A declaration must be made today.[54]

Then Churchill showed Mikolajczyk four telegrams from Eden about his discussion of this problem with Truman, which indicated that Truman was determined to force Stalin to fulfill his obligations with respect to the Yalta agreements.

I am certain, said Churchill, that the Polish question will be solved well. If they do not form a representative government neither Britain nor the United States will recognize it. You cannot be too modest, Mr. Mikolaj-czyk. We have complete confidence in you. Roosevelt had the same feeling about you, and that is why you must be there. If you will be there Great Britain and the United States will support the Polish problem. Otherwise we shall not be involved at all.[55]

Mikolajczyk replied:

I am not so optimistic as you are that the Polish question will be solved well. I am certain that the accusation that I am sabotaging the Yalta deci-sions is only an excuse for a non-fulfillment of those decisions. If I make the declaration that Stalin wants, Poles here will call me a "traitor." The Soviet Union may say that it is too late, and they will try to discredit me. Yet, in spite of this, I shall issue such a declaration, because I want to help Great Britain and the United States to have a basis for their support of our cause. I don't want you, Mr. Churchill, to go to the House of Commons next Thursday and shift the blame on the Poles because of lack of success in this matter. When the interest of my country and the unity of the Allies are involved, the disgrace of one man is insignificant.[56]

Churchill wanted Mikolajczyk's declaration to follow exactly the Yalta text, especially where it referred to the reorganization of the Government. Mikolajczyk objected and proceeded to write his own declaration as he thought best, and explained his reasons for doing so as follows:

I cannot do that. Minister Eden told me that he interprets the Yalta terms to mean that a new Government of Poland is going to be formed. The struggle for the interpretation of the Yalta terms must take place between the Great Powers. If I follow your advice in writing this declaration, it would only make your position and that of the Americans more difficult to win in your struggle with the Soviets about the interpretation of Yalta. I did not recognize the Lublin group as the legal Government previously, and I do not intend to do so now. If the term "Government" is used alone, neither the listener nor the reader will know whether it refers to the reorganization of the Lublin Government or to the London Government.[57]

Churchill accepted Mikolajczyk's logic and his views, and approved the text of his declaration with the remark that it "will put problems on the right track." Although it was Sunday, Churchill immediately ordered his personal secretary to arrange with the BBC and the press that Mikolajczyk's declaration would get full publicity. The text of that declaration read as follows:

Statement by Monsieur Mikolajczyk on the Polish Question

I consider that the close and lasting friendship with Russia is the keystone of future Polish policy within the wider friendship of the United Nations.

To remove all doubt as to my attitude, I wish to declare that I accept the Crimea decision in regard to the future of Poland, its sovereign independent position and the formation of a provisional Government representative of national unity.

I support the decision arrived at in the Crimea that a conference of leading Polish representatives be called with a view to constituting a Government of National Unity as widely and fairly representative of the Polish people as possible, and one which will command recognition by the three major Powers.[57]

Churchill forwarded the declaration to Moscow and Washington. Upon its publication the London Poles became disturbed and angry with Mikolajczyk for what they called a surrender to Soviet and British pressure.

On April 18, 1945 Undersecretary for Foreign Affairs Sir Orme Sargent informed Mikolajczyk that Mr. Churchill had received a reply from Stalin in which Stalin asked if Mikolajczyk's acceptance of the Yalta agreement also meant that he accepted the Curzon Line. "Churchill asks you to permit him to say yes." [58] Mikolajczyk agreed. He stated that he had written an article to his Party organ *Jutro Polski* (Poland's Tomorrow) in which he went a step further towards "the Line."

On previous occasions when Sikorski or Mikolajczyk were on their way to Moscow to settle disputes, and when chances for success looked very promising, the Soviets would destroy those chances for agreement with some unexpected moves. This time was no exception.

In early April the London Government received information that fifteen eminent Polish political leaders, members of the underground organization in Poland, had been arrested by the Soviets.[60] They were:

The Vice Premier of the Polish Government, Jan Jankowski (Labor Party).
Three Ministers of the Polish Government, permanently in Poland, Adam Bien (Peasant Party); Stanislaw Jasiukowicz (National Democratic Party); and Antoni Pajdak (Socialist Party).
The Commander of the former Home Army, General Leopold Okulicki.
The Chairman of the secret Polish Parliament, known as the Council of National Unity, Kazimierz Puzak (Socialist Party).
Eight members of the Council of National Unity, representing the chief political parties in Poland, as follows:
Stanislaw Mierzwa (Peasant Party)
Kazimierz Baginski (Peasant Party)
Josef Chacinski (Labor Party)
Franciszek Urbanski (Labor Party)
Zbigniew Stypulkowski (National Democratic Party)
Kazimierz Kobylanski (National Democratic Party)
Piotr Czernik (National Democratic Party)
Michalowski (National Democratic Party).

The above-mentioned men, who represented a broad coalition of political parties in Poland, were members of the governing, military, and political bodies and for five years directed the Polish Nation's struggle against the German occupants in Poland. They held the general esteem of the Polish people both in Poland and abroad, and the Polish Government had complete confidence in them.

The details regarding the contacting of the Polish representatives by the Soviet military authorities were as follows:

At the end of February, Colonel-General Ivanov, acting in the name of the Commander of the First Byelorussian Front, sent an invitation through intermediaries to Mr. Jan Jankowski, who was both the Vice-Premier of the Polish Government and the Government

Delegate to Poland, to attend a conference to discuss alleged diversionary action by the Home Army in the rear of the Red Army. A similar invitation was sent to General Leopold Okulicki, the former commander of the Home Army, which was dissolved on January 19, 1945. In answer to this invitation, General Okulicki replied that the Home Army had been dissolved by order of the Polish Government, that it had never carried out diversionary action in Poland against the Soviet Armies, and that, on the contrary, up to the very last moment of its existence it had carried out military and sabotage activity against the German Armies and had thus assisted the offensive action of the Red Army.

On the eleventh of March, the persons mentioned above received another invitation, signed by Colonel Pimenov, acting under the order of General Ivanov, to a meeting with Marshal Georgi K. Zhukov. This time the invitation stressed the necessity and importance of such a meeting, which could and should decide matters, a quick solution of which would be hard to reach in any other way. According to Colonel Pimenov, mutual trust and understanding would allow these important matters to be decided and would not lead to an increase of tension. At the same time, Colonel Pimenov, as an officer of the Red Army, guaranteed the personal safety of those invited on their journey to Marshal Zhukov.

The Vice-Premier of the Polish Government accepted the invitation after previous confirmation by Colonel Pimenov as to the authenticity of the invitation and on his renewed assurance that Marshal Zhukov attached great importance to the discussions, the subject of which was to be "the clearing of the atmosphere by the emergence of the Polish political parties and their combining in the general stream of democratic forces in independent Poland." A preliminary discussion was held on March 17, in the course of which the Vice-Premier stated that the Polish political parties, as represented in the Council of National Unity, would gladly reveal themselves and undertake work towards the reconstruction of Poland but that circumstances prevailing in Polish territory had so far not allowed this. The creation of circumstances which would secure the possibility of some political work and the freedom of the citizen depended entirely on the Soviet authorities. Finally, the Vice-Premier asked for information on the following points:

1. Whether Marshal Zhukov was acting with the consent of the Commission of the Three, appointed by the Crimea Conference, or in the name of Commissar Molotov?

2. Why the Commander of the First Byelorussian Front, and not that of the Red Army, had communicated with him?

3. What were the spheres of competence of the NKVD, of the so-called Provisional Lublin Government, and of the political administration of the Commander of the First Byelorussian Front?

At the same time he declared that he would request facilities from General Ivanov to send a delegation to London, in order to consult the Polish Government and the Polish political leaders there and subsequently for them to return to Poland.

Further conversations with Colonel Pimenov were undertaken, with the approval of the Vice-Premier, on March 18, by representatives of the Peasant Party and, on March 20, by those of the National Democratic Party and the Labor Party. It is noted that during conversations with representatives of the National Democratic Party, when concrete questions were put to Colonel Pimenov concerning the competence of the so-called Provisional Lublin Government, he stated that the Lublin Government had to submit itself to the decisions of the Commander of the First Byelorussian Front, which were binding on the Committee.

On March 20 the Vice-Premier received the information that Marshal Zhukov was empowered by the Supreme Command of the Red Army, to which he belonged, to conduct conversations with the Polish political leaders, and that he had ordered an airplane to be put at the disposal of the Vice-Premier in order to facilitate the Polish political leaders' visit to England. On March 21 the Vice-Premier expressed his agreement to the holding of the conference with Marshal Zhukov.

On March 27 the Vice-Premier of the Polish Government, the Commander of the former Home Army, and the Chairman of the Council of National Unity went to Pruszkow, near Warsaw, for the conversations with Marshal Zhukov. Although they did not return that day as expected to the meeting of the Council of National Unity, on March 28 another group of twelve persons went to Pruszkow for the meeting. They included three Ministers of the Home Council of Ministers, eight members of the Council of National Unity, representing the chief Polish political parties, and one interpreter.

None of these men returned from Pruszkow, nor did anyone have news of any of them. It should be added that on March 31, 1945, that is, three days after the disappearance of the above-mentioned political leaders and heads of the Underground Movement in Poland, three men in civilian clothes and one in military uniform arrived by car at the residence of Wincenty Witos, three times Premier of Poland, in Wierzchoslawice, near Tarnow. After a short conversation with the visitors, Mr. Witos was taken off by them in the car to an unknown destination. It appeared from information received that Mr. Witos returned home after a month's absence. During his discussions with the Soviet authorities, who proposed to him that he should join the Lublin Government, Mr. Witos did not see any of the missing Polish political leaders.[61]

All the facts given above, plus the circumstances connected with the contacting of the Soviet authorities by the Polish political leaders and the subsequent disappearance of the Poles, were constantly communicated to the British and American Governments with the request that they should intervene with the Soviet Government to discover what had happened to the missing men.

On May 2 Minister Richard K. Law, in answer to numerous questions put by Members of Parliament in connection with the missing Polish political leaders, stated:

His Majesty's Government has repeatedly pressed the Soviet Government to find out the whereabouts of the above-mentioned eminent Poles. Nevertheless, His Majesty's Ambassador in Moscow has not received any reply to his numerous inquiries. I much regret that I am unable to give the House any assurance as to the safety of those mentioned in the Questions.[62]

On April 12, 1945 the Moscow correspondent of the *Daily Worker*, John Gibbons, sent a dispatch to his paper in which he stated categorically that it was "absolutely untrue that the Polish political and military leaders were in Moscow."

According to a Reuters dispatch, at a press conference held on April 24, a representative of the Lublin Government, on being asked by foreign journalists what had happened to the Polish political leaders who had been invited to a conference by General Ivanov, stated:

We don't know anything about this so-called missing delegation. This question, which we see has been blown up to immense dimensions in the international field, simply does not exist in our country.

Not until forty days after the disappearance of the Polish political leaders did the Soviet Government openly admit the arrest of the Polish political and military chiefs, accusing them of diversionary activity against the Red Army and announcing that they would be brought to trial. In conclusion, it should be pointed out that these men were arrested in territory alleged to be under "Lublin" administration, which showed that the real authority of this territory was in the hands of the executive bodies of the Soviet Union.[63]

With the silencing of these leaders of the democratic parties representing over eighty percent of the Polish people, the Soviets struck another blow at the independence of Poland. Undoubtedly, the reason behind the arrest of these men was to remove them from the political scene of the future Poland and, by trumped-up charges, to discredit them.

On April 22, after the removal of these genuine representatives of Poland, Stalin and Bierut signed a treaty of friendship, mutual assistance, and post-war cooperation.[64] This was in direct violation of the recently signed Yalta agreement, according to which the Lublin Government was only provisional. By this treaty Stalin wanted to acknowledge the permanence of that Government.

The Daily Telegraph of London carried, on May 8, 1945, the following information:

> The Lublin radio, controlled by the Russian-sponsored Polish Government, referring to the arrest of General Okulicki, the Commander-in-Chief of the Polish Home Army, and his fifteen colleagues, stated last night: "Because the criminal activities of Okulicki and his accomplices were also directed against the Polish State, it constituted high treason.
>
> The Provisional Government reserves the right to demand that Okulicki and his accomplices be turned over to the Polish authorities to be indicted in the courts of the Republic."
>
> Mr. Mikolajczyk, the former Polish Prime Minister, announced yesterday that he was preparing an extensive statement concerning the arrests. The arrested Poles, he declares, could not be accused of diversionary acts against the Red Army as they were sincere partisans of a Polish-Soviet understanding.

United behind the Arciszewski Government, the majority of Poles in exile expressed similar views about the innocence of the arrested leaders and of Soviet cruelty.

TASS, the Soviet News Agency, issued the following statement on May 5, 1945 which was broadcast by Radio Moscow:

> According to available information received from fully authoritative sources, TASS is able to state that the group of Poles mentioned in the British press and referred to in the House of Commons is composed of sixteen and not of fifteen people. It is headed by the well-known Polish General Okulicki, about the disappearance of whom the British reports intentionally keep silent in view of the special odiousness of this General.
>
> General Okulicki's group—and especially he himself—are accused of preparing diversionary acts in the rear of the Red Army, as a result of which more than 100 officers and men of the Red Army lost their lives.

This group of sixteen persons did not disappear but was arrested by the military authorities of the Soviet Command, and is now in Moscow pending the investigation of the case.

This group is also accused of organizing and maintaining illegal radio transmitters in the rear of the Soviet Armies, which is against the law. All these men, or some of them, according to the results of the inquiry, will be tried.[65]

When Harriman, in London at the time, asked Mikolajczyk about the validity of these accusations, his reply was as follows:

I reject this accusation of sabotage by the underground organizations. I was prepared for this accusation and even expected the Soviets to say that not just a hundred but a few thousand Soviet officers and men were shot by the Poles. This figure of one hundred shot, even if true, does not prove anything because:

(a) Surely during the fighting certain German units operated behind the Soviet lines until they were liquidated. We know from previous experience that when the German Army is retreating it leaves behind it some agents for special jobs.

(b) In the environment of the life in the underground in any country, a certain amount of criminal element exists, and it acts in an irresponsible way.

(c) It cannot be ruled out that during the arrests and the terror which the communists are perpetuating, certain acts of self-defense undoubtedly took place. I completely reject any assertion of organized sabotage against the Red Army. Our instructions were full of warnings against illegal actions because these would provide an excuse for the Soviets and the Lublin group to introduce political terror and even deportations. I have reports that these instructions were carried out because they reflected the instinct of self-preservation in the nation.[66]

It was obvious that the arrest of the sixteen courageous and patriotic leaders of the Underground had nothing to do with the alleged crimes against the Soviet State but that it was another Soviet tactical move to extort confessions which would incriminate the London Government and its underground organizations in Poland. This was imperative for the communists in order to eliminate potential competition to their absolute rule of Poland.

The discussions about Poland between the Foreign Secretaries of the Three Big Powers in San Francisco did not produce any positive results because of Molotov's evasive attitude.[67]

Upon his return from San Francisco, Eden told Mikolajczyk that he did not think that anything more could have been done with regard to Poland at San Francisco, and that the whole problem would have to be referred back to a new "Big Three Conference" for a final decision. The new Conference would take place very soon, but this was strictly confidential. In the meantime, the Moscow Commission would have to try to make more progress, although the prospects for any real results were very doubtful since it was also probable that any information about the arrest of the sixteen Polish leaders furnished by the Soviets, if it was forthcoming at all, would be insufficient. He had refused to discuss the matter with Molotov in San Francisco any further, he said, since this had become pointless after the disclosure of the arrests and the incomplete and unsatisfactory explanations offered by the Soviets. Eden agreed with Mikolajczyk, who said that in his opinion the arrests were the result of the refusals of the Polish leaders, in defiance of Soviet pressure, to participate in a Government reconstructed without the cooperation of Great Britain and the United States and without at least Mikolajczyk of the London Poles. Furthermore, Mikolajczyk stated that if it had been intended that they be arrested right away, this could have been done in a different and far less conspicuous manner, without giving them the opportunity of communicating with their associates. Eden said that he had expressed a similar opinion openly to Molotov. Molotov maintained that Ivanov had no authority to make any kind of promise to the sixteen Polish leaders. Mikolajczyk then expressed his fear that the next thing the world would hear about the sixteen would be that they had been sentenced on the charges brought up against them and executed.[68]

Meanwhile, the reports from Poland continued to be discouraging. In the absence of any effective opposition the communists were free to do what they pleased. From reliable British sources Mikolajczyk received the following description of the situation in Poland as of May 20, 1945:

The prestige of the "Provisional Government" is still very low. Polish masses, especially in the rural areas, are apathetic. The general feeling prevails that victory over the Germans did not bring freedom to Poland. Young officers in General Zymierski's Army are considered unreliable and for this reason they are watched by the officers of the Red Army and the NKVD. The land reforms did not secure any loyalty to the "Government," because the peasants are deprived of the means to build up their livestock and their implements for soil cultivation. The loudly propagandized resettlement of the population from the east on the western territories is very unpopular, because no one believes that it will be permanent. Every so often fights occur between the elements of the Home Army (A.K.) and the Red Army and Zymierski's Army.

As far as the economic policy is concerned, there is a split in the "Government" between the moderate approach of Minc and the extreme policy symbolized by Gomulka. The former would like to retain small ownership in private hands while making Silesia a self-sufficient unit controlled by the State. On the other hand, Gomulka is for complete communization of Poland along the lines of the Soviet Union, and keeps forecasting that as the October Revolution followed the February one, so will events in Poland follow a similar course. The Soviet Ambassador accredited to the Polish "Government" has supposedly said that the Soviet Union will bring order to the mess, despite the price the Polish nation will have to pay.

The behavior of the Red Army in Poland is outrageous. Industrial installations are stripped and removed to the Soviet Union. Administrative chaos grows because of the confusion as to the power of the "Government" and of the Soviet authorities. People believe that this chaos is purposely fostered by the Soviets. The "triumphant" return of Bierut after signing the treaty in Moscow was confined only to the officials of his Government. It is believed that if Bierut had managed to get even token concessions of independence from Moscow, that the "Government" could then have found some support among the people.

When it comes to the attitude of Poles toward the Anglo-Americans, it is obvious that America is much more popular than Great Britain. This is particularly visible in the Osobka Government and in him especially. The Polish Government in London is still considered a symbol of Polish independence. The popularity of Mikolajczyk among the masses is diminishing and he is gradually being considered as the symbol of Anglo-American interest in Polish affairs.

The arrest of the sixteen Underground political leaders has supposedly passed without making much of an impression, because similar events on a larger scale are taking place every day. It is generally believed that the present state of affairs cannot last long and that either Poland will have to move to the extreme left or else that the Soviet authorities in Poland will have to relax their terror.

The Church is not persecuted and soldiers in Zymierski's Army pray collectively and attend Mass conducted by military chaplains. But in the "Government" itself there are no practicing Catholics and its attitude toward the Vatican is definitely negative.

The food situation is bad. The black market is growing in size.

On May 12 the draft brought new recruits to Zymierski's Army, but its equipment is still poor and incomplete.

About 150,000 people have returned to Warsaw. Now they live in basements. Typhoid is raging. People need medicine. The Polish Red Cross cannot do much good because it is considered an "aristocratic" institution and as such does not have any backing from the "Government."

In May the Lublin Government presented the following declaration of allegiance to the Polish population for signature under pressure:

"I declare that I have not acted and am not acting against the Polish nation and the Polish State; that I agree wholeheartedly with the July manifesto of the Committee of National Liberation, which manifesto is known to me, and that I recognize the Polish Provisional Government in Warsaw as the only legal Government; that I have never collaborated either directly or through intermediaries with any agent of the so-called émigré Government in London, or with any other pro-fascist organization; that I have acted and am acting as a Pole faithful to his country, in proof of which I give the following facts. . . .

I make this declaration in place of an oath, and am prepared to undertake full responsibility for its authenticity." [69]

Through this device, the Security Police were provided with a flexible pretext which they could use to liquidate thousands of innocent people in the future. The Polish Government in London was not in a position to do anything about this.

Returning to Moscow from San Francisco, Harriman stopped in London and saw Mikolajczyk on May 23, 1945. Among other things, he asked what Mikolajczyk thought about the Polish-Soviet problem. The latter replied in the following manner:

I do not believe in the fulfillment of the Yalta agreement by the Russians in either the Allied or Soviet interpretation of its terms. I believe that we are confronted with a long deadlock, which will extend beyond the next meeting of the Big Three and even beyond the conclusion of the war against Japan.

In the strategic plans which the Soviets are preparing, Poland occupies a special place. The main strategic line of the Soviet Union in Europe extends from the Carpathian Mountains and the Sudetenland to the Baltic. Inside this line lie Rumania, Czechoslovakia, and Poland. You may have noticed that Austria and Hungary lie on the other side of this line, and therefore, they represent a secondary problem to the Soviet Union. This is particularly so in view of the fact that Russia is anxious to secure for itself complete influence in Yugoslavia and in the Balkans. Poland, with its flat terrain extending from the Sudeten to the Baltic and with a wide Baltic coast presents a dangerous problem to the Soviet Union, especially since twenty-five million Poles are more than the Czechs, Slovaks, and Rumanians taken together. The spiritual stamina of the Polish nation, and its readiness to sacrifice in defense of freedom is well known. Without a national minority, the united Polish nation presents a formidable problem to the Soviet Union. With the change of its economic structure, with a much more extensive industrialization of the country, and with a certain flexibility of decisions Poland may become a respectable economic and military power. For these reasons Poland now receives special treatment from the Soviet Union. I always tried to avoid a discussion of favorable frontiers, and the independence of external and internal policies, because I knew that the Russians would not agree to that. What I wanted was to preserve a certain amount of freedom so that the Polish nation would survive the worst period which is ahead of us, instead of being deported to and dispersed in the vast territories of the U.S.S.R.

What should be done in this struggle? At the present I believe that Russia will continue the steady sovietization of Poland. This is visible in the undertakings of the Lublin group. I believe they will not succeed. Will they attempt the extermination of the whole nation? I don't think so. We have to counteract, to prevent the Soviet Union from confronting us with irreversible facts. For this reason I made a speech on May 21, 1945.

My main objectives were: From the information which is reaching me from Poland I know that preparations are going on for the election. Instead of a reorganization of the Government which, according to Yalta, was supposed to take place, they intend to confront the world with the appearance of the "nation's will," and in such a way to prevent the Western Powers from interfering in the internal affairs of Poland and to force them to recognize the Government which will be formed as a result of this peculiar election. Therefore, the Soviet Union is constantly creating new difficulties in implementing the Yalta decisions.

I was informed that during the Yalta Conference, when the Western Allies suggested that an election in Poland be supervised by the Allies, Stalin did not object to that suggestion but only observed that the Western Powers could do so only if they were invited by the Polish Government. In the meantime there is no Government in Poland. Everything is being done to prevent a formation of that Government and at the same time all sorts of preparations are going on for the Soviet-style election.

When Stalin stresses that some groups have contact with the Polish people and others do not, it is obvious that the Lublin group will not permit any supervision of the election in Poland by the Western Powers. In such a situation, when the Western Allies cannot secure the fulfillment of the Yalta agreement, they should at least try to prevent the creation of those irreversible facts with which they are constantly confronted. This should be done so that in the future, when conditions are more appropriate, the Yalta agreement can be realized.

For these reasons, I stated in my speech to Poland that the war is over. Let us have an election in Poland. We shall ask the Polish nation what it thinks and desires. But in order to have a free election and because the war is over, the Red Army must leave Poland, and particularly the NKVD. If an election is going to take place there must be freedom of action. Election campaigning and meetings must be permitted to all political parties. If our Allies cannot help us in any other way—although they took upon themselves the burden of establishing a free, sovereign, and independent Poland—let them supervise the election to see that it is free and honest. In the Yalta agreement it was said that elections in Poland must be and will be "free and unfettered," but this term is also used in the Constitution of the U.S.S.R. with regard to elections. It has to be clearly defined what is meant by the term "free elections." In order to avoid a new struggle about the interpretation, I want it to be quite clear. Lublin always maintained that they rest on the Constitution of 1921. I support the reliance on the election procedure of the Constitution of 1921 as a legal basis for a new election in Poland.

I do not think that these conditions will be fulfilled. But I want to use this as a preventive measure against the creation of those accomplished facts. Personally, I do not believe that even a new conference of the Big Three will resolve the Polish problem, because the international atmosphere is not congenial to it.[70]

Harriman did not have any ready answer to Mikolajczyk's proposals. He was preoccupied with the problems of his assignment in the Inter-Allied Commission which was charged with implementing the terms of the Yalta agreement with respect to the formation of the Polish Provisional Government. He therefore asked Mikolajczyk how many Poles from London should be included in the new Government in order to fulfill at least a minimum of the Yalta terms. Mikolajczyk replied:

This problem cannot be considered exclusively in terms of the number of people who may be included in the new Government. The following problems should also be considered:

(1) The necessity to release all those arrested by the communists. Otherwise, it would be very difficult to ask representatives of various parties to join a new Government when their colleagues from the same parties are arrested and accused of sabotage. This is very important, for two reasons: (a) that a proper atmosphere be created, and (b) that those who enter that Government will not be accused by the people of being traitors.

(2) It is necessary to stop further arrests and persecutions in order not to split the nation.

(3) It is imperative to create a head of the State (singular or plural) who could form, or change the Government. Otherwise there is no guarantee that in the absence of such a body any Government cannot be overthrown in the matter of a week. Only the conviction that there is a supreme authority which regulates those matters can give assurance that the basis of the new Government will be firm. Because I don't think that Bierut can be that authority, the question as to who should be arises.

(4) The Government should rest on the coalition of the greatest possible number of parties, in order to protect it against the communist bloc. This also will give it wide popular support.

(5) As far as proportional representation in the new Government is concerned, one should not only keep in mind the number of portfolios allotted to each party from inside and outside the country, but rather the importance of each Ministry. I do not think that it will be easy at all for the communists to give us the Ministry of National Defense. In my opinion one could rank the importance of cabinet positions in the following order:

(a) Premier,
(b) Minister of the Interior,
(c) Minister of National Defense,
(d) Ministers of Trade, Industry, and Agriculture,
(e) Minister of Foreign Affairs.

One should not expect that the Russians will permit complete independence in foreign affairs, and therefore, the Ministry of Foreign Affairs is placed below the others in importance. The Soviets will be most anxious to control the Presidency or the Council of the Presidency, the Ministry of National Defense, and the Ministry of the Interior. These are the key positions. By controlling them the communists will try to enslave the Polish nation.

Harriman ended the conversation by expressing the opinion that although conditions were not favorable for the fulfillment of the Yalta agreement, President Truman and he had a certain amount of hope that they would be implemented somehow.[71]

At this time Truman decided to send Hopkins to Moscow to try, among other outstanding issues, to resolve the deadlock over the Polish question. Hopkins met with Stalin and Molotov on May 26 and brought up the Polish question at that time. He emphasized the growing deterioration of friendliness toward the Soviet Union as evidenced in the change in public opinion, stating that the major cause of this was the apparent inability to implement the Yalta agreement with respect to Poland.

Stalin replied that the reason for the failure on the Polish question was that the Soviet Union desired to have a friendly Poland but that Great Britain wanted to revive the system of *cordon sanitaire* on the Soviet borders.[72]

Hopkins assured Stalin that the United States had no such intentions, whereupon Stalin explained that he was referring only to England, and then primarily to the British conservatives, as the people who did not desire to see a Poland friendly to the Soviet Union. Hopkins stated that the United States would desire a Poland friendly to the Soviet Union and in fact desired to see friendly countries all along the Soviet borders. Stalin replied: if that is so, "we can easily come to terms in regard to Poland."

Hopkins said "he had wished to state frankly and as forcibly as he knew how to Marshal Stalin the importance that he, personally, attached to the present trend of events and that he felt that the situation would get rapidly worse unless we could clear up the Polish matter. He had therefore been glad to hear the Marshal say that he thought the question could be settled."

Marshal Stalin replied that in his opinion it was best to settle it—but not if the British conservatives attempted to revive the *cordon sanitaire*.[73]

It is interesting to note that Stalin blamed the British and especially the conservatives for forcing him to take a defensive step against their hostile intentions. Presumably he felt that an attack upon the conservatives would invoke a sympathetic attitude in the heart of his guest.

Nothing was settled in this meeting, and on May 27 Hopkins raised the Polish issue again by appealing to Stalin to remove the obstacles to the solution of the Polish problem which was, as he put it, not so important *per se* as the fact that it had become "a symbol of our ability to work out problems with the Soviet Union." Stalin thereupon repeated his desire to see a strong and friendly Poland.

He said there was no intention on the part of the Soviet Union to interfere in Poland's internal affairs, that Poland would live under the parliamentary system which is like that of Czechoslovakia, Belgium, and Holland

and that any talk of an intention to sovietize Poland was stupid. He said even the Polish leaders, some of whom were communists, were against the Soviet system since the Polish people did not desire collective farms or other aspects of the Soviet system. In this respect the Polish leaders were right since the Soviet system was not exportable—it must develop from within on the basis of a set of conditions which were not present in Poland. He said that all the Soviet Union wanted was that Poland should not be in the position to open the gates to Germany and in order to prevent this Poland must be strong and democratic.

He then proceeded to justify, in very innocent-sounding terms, the establishment of the Lublin Committee as a means to safeguard the rear of the Red Army, and this the Soviets had to do because the Western Allies had been so slow in reaching an agreement on Poland.

He said it was contrary to Soviet policy to set up Soviet administration on foreign soil since this would look like occupation and be resented by the local inhabitants.

Then Stalin thought that the Warsaw Poles might be willing to offer four ministries (out of a total of twenty) to Poles from the outside. The meeting again ended without any tangible results.[74]

Poland was next discussed on May 30. Hopkins stated that in postwar Poland freedom of speech, freedom of assembly, freedom of movement, and freedom of worship must exist. Stalin agreed with Hopkins, stating that there would be no objections on the part of the Soviet Union but that on the contrary these freedoms would be very welcome. He qualified the full range of their application, however, by saying that they obviously could not be granted to "fascists." Once again Hopkins stressed that a solution was necessary in order to preserve Allied unity, and Stalin again agreed but observed that the British did not seem genuinely anxious to reach a solution. Hopkins doubted the truth of these allegations against the British.[75]

The following day Hopkins raised the question of the sixteen Polish leaders arrested by the Soviets, and asked for their release. Stalin replied that according to his information, all those prisoners were engaged in diversionist activity. He stated that he believed that Churchill had misled the United States in regard to the facts and had made the American Government believe that the statement of the London Polish Government was accurate. Just the opposite was the case. Marshal Stalin stated that he did not intend to have the British manage the affairs of Poland and that this was exactly what they wanted to do. He was inclined to do everything he could to make it easy for Churchill to get out of a bad situation because if and when all the evidence was published, it would look very bad for the British and he did not want to make the situation worse than it was. He stated that the men must be tried, but that they would be treated leniently; and he clearly inferred that he was going to consider at once what could be done in regard to these prisoners that Hopkins was concerned with to clear the matter up.

He said several times that he blamed the British for conniving with the London Poles, and each time I reminded him that we had no desire to support in any way the Polish Government in London. He listened very attentively to everything I said. . . .

Hopkins once more appealed for the release of the arrested men. Stalin once more repeated that they would be tried.[76]

On June 6 Hopkins had his sixth and last meeting with Stalin. Stalin began by ". . . thanking Hopkins for his great assistance in moving forward the Polish question." [77]

Hopkins asked Stalin for permission to send relief in the form of medical supplies for the unfortunate people of Poland through the American Red Cross. He said that the American Red Cross desired to send for this purpose three representatives, headed by Dr. Bowers, to handle the distribution of supplies. Stalin replied that he had no objections but that it would be necessary to obtain the permission of the Polish Provisional Government. This was never granted because the communists suspected the Red Cross of spying.

Stalin's ability to move from a defensive to an offensive position while simultaneously splitting his opponents and playing on the psychological predilections of his adversary were rarely applied so masterfully as in this example.

Writing about this mission to Moscow, Hopkins stated:

One of the difficulties in negotiating the Polish agreement in Moscow was that President Truman had sent me without discussing it in advance with Churchill. Altho, at the time of my departure, he acquainted him with my impending visit to Moscow, no British representative was present at any of my conferences with Stalin and I was in no position to deal directly with Churchill. Fortunately, Clark Kerr, the British Ambassador to Moscow, was an old friend of mine and quite in sympathy with my visit and I am sure he reported very fully to the British Foreign Office and Churchill. And, more than that, he was making recommendations to Churchill urging the British to back us up. I began to hear from Kerr that Churchill was obviously quite disturbed about the whole business but there was not very much he could say because it was probably to his political interest to get agreement on the Polish question before the British elections.[78]

According to Sherwood, in one of his last reflections on American-Soviet relations Hopkins wrote the following:

The thing the American people must look out for is that there is a minority in America who, for a variety of reasons, would just as soon have seen Russia defeated in the war and who said publicly before we got into the war that it did not make any difference which one—Russia or Germany—won. That small, vociferous minority can take advantage of every rift between ourselves and Russia to make trouble between our two countries. There are plenty of people in America who would have been perfectly willing to see our armies go right on through Germany and fight with Russia after Germany was defeated. They represent nobody but themselves and no government worth its salt in control of our country would ever permit that group to influence our official actions.[79]

Apparently Stalin realized from Hopkins' arguments that he would have to enlarge the Lublin Government in order to make it acceptable to the Americans and to the British. Consequently, Molotov became more conciliatory at the subsequent meetings of the Inter-Allied Commission which had been set up to settle the Polish matter. He agreed to invite Mikolajczyk, Professor Grabski, and Mr. Stanczyk from London.

Upon receiving a report from Hopkins about the results of his conversations with Stalin, Truman wrote to Churchill as follows:

I feel that this represents a very encouraging, positive step in the long-drawn-out Polish negotiations, and hope that you will approve the list as agreed to in order that we may get on with this business as soon as possible.

In regard to the arrested Polish leaders, most of whom are apparently charged only with operating illegal radio transmitters, Hopkins is pressing Stalin to grant amnesty to these men in order that consultations may be conducted in the most favorable atmosphere possible.

I hope you will use your influence with Mikolajczyk and urge him to accept. I have asked Hopkins to remain in Moscow at least until I hear from you regarding this matter.[80]

On June 1, 1945 the American Chargé d'Affaires in London, Rudolf E. Schoenfeld, saw Mikolajczyk and handed him a telegram from the State Department which informed him that Hopkins, in his conversation with Stalin, had obtained permission to invite the following persons for a conference in Moscow:

From London: Mr. Mikolajczyk
            Prof. Grabski or Mr. Stanczyk
            Mr. Kolodziej
From Poland: Archbishop Sapieha or Mr. Witos
            Mr. Zulawski
            Prof. Kutrzeba

In addition, Schoenfeld continued, it was agreed, on Stalin's initiative, that the following be invited:

Mr. Kolodziejski

Prof. Adam Krzyzanowski

The telegram said that Hopkins and Harriman were of the opinion that the list reflected Yalta's principles and objectives. President Truman agreed with the view of Hopkins and Harriman and asked Churchill to support it accordingly.

Mr. Schoenfeld asked Mikolajczyk what his attitude was towards this list. Instead of answering immediately, Mikolajczyk asked what had been done to release the sixteen leaders. Schoenfeld replied that Hopkins had tried to get an amnesty for them. Mikolajczyk then said that he would express his opinion about the list on the following day but that he did not think the list was a just interpretation of Yalta's principles and objectives. As far as the arrested leaders were concerned, he said it was dangerous to ask for an amnesty for them. Hopkins, he felt, should have insisted on their release.

Our experience with the Soviet-Polish Treaty of 1941, where the word "amnesty" was used indicates the worst possible consequences. In Soviet legal terminology "amnesty" means a confirmation of guilt and the granting of an "amnesty" does not eliminate the possibility of the further confinement of the person concerned, because he is dangerous to society. The arrest of these people on the basis of trumped-up accusations has eliminated the possibility of using them for the consultations which were provided for by the terms of the Crimea Conference.

Schoenfeld did not know what to answer.[81]

On June 2, 1945 Sir Orme Sargent presented Mikolajczyk with a similar telegram from the British Ambassador Clark Kerr and asked, on behalf of Churchill, to tell him what he thought of it. Mikolajczyk replied that he would accept the invitation only if it was issued by the Commission of Three and not by the Lublin Poles. Furthermore, he asked that Churchill insist that the two omitted parties (the National Democratic Party and the Christian Labor Party) be included and suggested that Rev. Piwowarczyk from Krakow, Popiel from London, and Trabczynski be invited for consultations. Mikolajczyk objected to the invitation of Kolodziej as a representative of the London Poles because he did not represent anyone but himself. He thought that the inclusion of Kutrzeba, Krzyzanowski, and Kolodziej indicated that Moscow had stacked the list with honorable but nonparty people who represented no one. He also asked for the release (not by amnesty) of the arrested leaders. In addition, he requested permission for free communication between London and Moscow for the London Poles, as well as free communication with the non-communist Poles from abroad, while they were in Moscow, and a guarantee that the London group would be free to leave if the Moscow consultations failed.

Sargent said that he would convey Mikolajczyk's views to Churchill. He stressed that in the opinion of the British the consultation was very desirable.[82]

On June 2 Mikolajczyk presented the same answer to Schoenfeld.[83]

On June 6 the Foreign Office informed Mikolajczyk that Churchill accepted Mikolajczyk's views and asked Truman to join him in supporting Mikolajczyk's stand so that both the British and American Ambassadors in Moscow and Hopkins would get the same instructions.[84]

On June 7, 1945 the Foreign Office informed Mikolajczyk that Hopkins could not change Stalin's stand about the sixteen arrested Polish leaders and that it had been decided by the Commission of Three that Mr. Witos, Prof. Kutrzeba, Prof. Krzyzanowski, Mr. Zulawski, and Mr. Kolodziejski would be invited from Poland, while from London Mr. Mikolajczyk, Mr. Stanczyk, and Mr. Zakowski would receive invitations.

After receiving this information, Mikolajczyk said that he would be willing to go to Moscow despite the fact that his conditions were not accepted but that he did not expect a definite solution of the question. He thought that the arrested leaders would not be released before the consultations but that they might be freed as a result of the consultations, or, more specifically, if the Soviet conditions were met by the London Poles. He observed that since the Polish Government in London had announced publicly that no Pole would take part in the consultations until the arrested leaders were freed, Stalin would keep them in prison purposely in order to show a lack of good intention on the part of the London Poles to solve the issue. At the same time, if the London Poles did not accept the invitation to participate, this would provide him with enough time to establish firm control over Poland and to prepare the proper conditions for a Soviet-type election.

Finally, as a last problem, Mikolajczyk drew the attention of Sir Orme Sargent and Mr. Warner, both of whom represented the Foreign Office, to the fact that in Germany 800,000 Ukrainians under the leadership of Bishop Skrypnik, Mr. Melnyk, Mr. Bandura, and Mr. Kujowicz had asked the Polish Government to take them under its protection as Polish citizens. In view of the fact that most of these

Ukrainians had collaborated with the Germans it would be embarrassing politically if some extreme Polish elements in London attempted to exploit this problem politically. It was advisable to stress caution in this matter.[85]

When it became generally known that Mikolajczyk would go to Moscow, the Polish Prime Minister, Arciszewski, visited Mikolajczyk at his residence in Barrie House on June 12, 1945 in order to discuss the future of Poland and Mikolajczyk's decision. He did not question Mikolajczyk's sincerity in trying to settle relations between Poland and Russia during their discussion and, before parting, kissed Mikolajczyk on both cheeks saying, "In your hands lies the future of Poland. You are the only person who can still save it." [86]

On June 14 a conference took place at Mikolajczyk's residence in which the following ex-members of his Cabinet took part: Prof. Kot, Mr. Seyda, Mr. Popiel, Rev. Kaczynski, Mr. Grosfeld, Mr. Stanczyk, Mr. Romer, and Prof. Grabski. All present unanimously supported Mikolajczyk's decision to go to Moscow.[87]

Arciszewski's unexpected demonstration of faith and the complete support of his former colleagues strengthened Mikolajczyk's resolve to try his utmost to save Poland. In the meantime, secret requests were coming in from Poland urging Mikolajczyk to return in order to save the nation from complete and unopposed tyranny.

Mikolajczyk's mission became more complicated and difficult when on June 14 Radio Moscow announced that the investigation of the sixteen arrested leaders had been completed and that they would soon be tried by the Supreme Soviet Military Court.[88]

President Truman saw in that announcement a significant feature of Soviet behavior.

Then came a sudden Moscow announcement that sixteen Polish democratic leaders who had been arrested under outrageous circumstances would now be tried. This was provocative and discouraging. The deliberate timing of events by the U.S.S.R. in order to confront the negotiators with a *fait accompli* at the very outset of discussions was fast becoming part of the habitual pattern of Russian tactics.

I remember other occasions. In 1941, just as Polish Premier Sikorski arrived in Moscow, it was announced suddenly that all Poles of Ukrainian or White Russian descent would be considered Soviet citizens and not Poles. [The reader may remember that Alter and Ehrlich were also arrested and the Union of Polish Patriots established at this time.] [89]

Later when Mikolajczyk was en route from London to Moscow on his first visit after the war, the Lublin Government (Committee) was set up. While he was en route for his second visit, the Lublin Government received formal recognition, and just before Molotov left Moscow to attend the San Francisco conference and to discuss the Polish question with me, the U.S.S.R. signed its twenty-year pact with the Lublin regime. It was all a part of the Russian game.[90]

The Soviet announcement forced Mikolajczyk to revise his decision. On June 15, Mikolajczyk informed the Foreign Office that in view of the fact that the arrested leaders were to be tried by the Soviet Military Court it would be impossible to carry out any consultations, and that he would be unable to take part in them. To him it meant that the Soviets did not intend to permit any real negotiations and that this was the method they had chosen to do it.

Churchill reacted immediately. At 7:00 P.M. of the same day he conferred with Mikolajczyk at 10 Downing Street and advised him that it would be calamitous for Mikolajczyk to refuse to go to Moscow. "You have to put your foot in an open door and should not miss this occasion."

Mikolajczyk replied that he had accepted the invitation but in view of the latest acts performed by Moscow it was now impossible for him to go.

CHURCHILL. You should go and present your conditions. We shall warmly support you. If they will not be accepted you can leave Moscow. We are guaranteeing your complete security. You will have the support in every respect from the two Ambassadors (the American and British).

MIKOLAJCZYK. I cannot count on the two Ambassadors. Mr. Clark Kerr has several times tried to persuade me that the Lublin Poles are decent people, and that they have the complete confidence of people in Poland. Today he is afraid to present my conditions for the consultations.

CHURCHILL. This is nonsense. Those people from Lublin have no support from Poland whatsoever. They need you badly.

MIKOLAJCZYK. No. They need the Red Army and the NKVD badly because otherwise they will be wiped off the earth in any decently conducted election. I cannot do a thing by myself. They do not want anyone else, and especially Witos.[91]

Churchill proceeded to read telegrams from Clark Kerr and Harriman which promised to press for the release of the arrested leaders and to insist on the acceptance of Mikolajczyk's conditions. At the same time they pleaded for Mikolajczyk's acceptance without delay of the invitation. Then Churchill stated that it was because of his efforts and those of President Truman that Mikolajczyk had been invited. Now if he refused, everything would be lost. He continued:

You must realize that behind you stand our two mighty countries with all their resources. We shall not ask for Russian help to finish the war against Japan. We shall finish it by ourselves, although Russia is willing to jump in because she has her interests and appetites in the Far East. Furthermore, Russia is interested in the meeting of the Big Three. It was

Stalin who suggested to me that this meeting take place. Together with Truman we agreed to accept that proposition. For this reason I appeal to you to accept that invitation and go to Moscow. Whatever you will do there, you will have our complete support and our guarantee.

Mikolajczyk, after a lengthy argument with Churchill, agreed.

Because of your insistence I am ready to go. However, you must assure me that the British and American Ambassadors will support me unconditionally in my proposals and that they will give me strong support in my stand.

Churchill said that independently of the results of the coming election, British policy towards Poland would remain unchanged and positive. Churchill assured Mikolajczyk of complete support and asked him to use the facilities of the British Embassy to communicate with him.

During the discussion about the arrested leaders Churchill stated that their forthcoming trial would not mislead anyone. Everyone knew what Soviet political trials meant.[92]

Although all odds seemed to be against him, Mikolajczyk decided to try once more to help his people. Despite Churchill's past performances, Mikolajczyk had a certain affection for him personally.[93]

Before his departure for Moscow, Mikolajczyk was invited to a farewell luncheon by Churchill at Checquers during which Churchill observed, "At last we have managed to open the door a little bit." He urged Mikolajczyk to accept the conditions the Soviets would propose even if they should be unsatisfactory because, in his opinion, the Lublin Government was disliked by the people, and, therefore, "they need you and this is your greatest strength. Once you get hold of the power you will be able to help your country."

In reply, Mikolajczyk said, "I don't think that the Lublin authorities want us. There are two reasons why we have been invited:

1. Russia does not want to be accused of destroying the Yalta decision, and therefore has agreed to arrange this consultation. However, she will undoubtedly put forward such conditions that they will be unacceptable.
2. Because of the feeling in Poland, the Lublin authorities will be willing to add only a few from among us here (London). This makes me rather pessimistic.

Later when Mikolajczyk asked Churchill which Polish Government Britain would recognize, the London or Warsaw, Churchill answered:

The Labor Party is pressing me to liquidate that "rotten Government of Arciszewski." We have come to the conclusion that there is no point in having anything to do with it.

When Mikolajczyk asked about the instructions the British and American Ambassadors in Moscow would receive, Churchill replied:

> Stalin talked about the solution of the Polish problem on a Yugoslavian pattern. That is, fifty-fifty. (Meaning half of the Poles would be from the outside and half from the Lublin group.) This should be profitable and you should remain on speaking terms without breaking up the conference. Democratic nations do not want war and therefore there won't be one.

Before shaking hands in parting, Churchill stated, "We are responsible for your journey. If something should happen to you we shall start fighting." Then, shaking hands with him, Mr. and Mrs. Churchill wept.[94]

The communists were none too happy about Mikolajczyk's decision to come back. They tried to frighten him. A Polish communist in London who had close contact with the Russian Embassy approached him and said:

> You know, Mikolajczyk, you might have an airplane accident on the way to Moscow or even be killed in a traffic accident after you get there. I'd suggest that you remain here.[95]

On June 16, 1945 Mikolajczyk left for Moscow. Upon landing he met the very learned and fearless Prof. Kutrzeba, who had come from Poland for the same consultation. He told Mikolajczyk that the Polish Nation was exhausted. "It prays and hopes that we shall reach some solution over here, because they cannot bear this uncertainty any longer." [96]

Before the negotiations began, the trial of the sixteen leaders was staged. This was after they had been subjected to three months of terror in the Lubianka Prison where all except one (Stypulkowski) had broken down and signed the prefabricated "confessions" of crime against the Soviet Union. The show trial was needed in order to "prove" to the world that the Soviets were justified in arresting them and to "prove" that the London Government was really guilty of all those trumped-up charges.

In this connection the British Ambassador, Clark Kerr, wished to attend the trial but was discouraged by Ambassador Harriman who was of the opinion that it would offend the Soviets and worsen their mutual relations.[97]

The indictment of the leaders read as follows:

> During the German occupation the Polish émigré Government formed in the territories of Poland, Lithuania, and the Western regions of the Ukraine and of Byelorussia an underground military organization named the *Armia Krajowa* (A.K.) (Home Army).

The work of this *illegal* organization, headed by Brigadier General Oku-licki, was directed by Jan Stanislaw Jankowski, who styled himself Presi-dent of the Underground "Council of Ministers" of Poland, and by Minis-ters . . .

At the same time there was created upon Polish territory a so-called *Rada Jednosci Narodowej* (Council of National Unity), *which functioned illegally* and which was headed by Kazimierz Puzak, General Secretary of the Polish Socialist Party (P.P.S.).

The accused Okulicki and the Underground Government had at their disposal armed detachments, supplies of arms and ammunition, radio trans-mitting and radio receiving stations, illegal printing shops and secret head-quarters. . . .

The indictment then enumerated the more specific accusations:

". . . the command of the *Armia Krajowa* and the Underground "Govern-ment" were drawing up plans for military action in a bloc with Germany against the U.S.S.R."

There followed details of alleged plots, instructions from London to organize those plots, terrorist activities, diversions, espionage and the illegal use of radio stations. The evidence consisted of "confessions" made by the defendants and by other imprisoned members of the Home Army.

No justification was offered for the premise which formed the basis of the whole indictment that the Polish Government and everything that it did was illegal. I think, from the Soviet point of view, this was wise. Had they tried to maintain that every act of defense by the Home Army against the Germans in 1939, in 1940–1941, and finally from 1941 onwards, and the creation of the Council of National Unity in western as well as eastern territories of Poland, were illegal, they would have evoked the spectre of Soviet-German collaboration on the ruins of Polish independ-ence as provided for in the treaty of friendship between Hitler and Stalin. The effect of the trial on world opinion would then have been very different.

A characteristic feature of the indictment was that it assumed that all that half of Polish territory which lies to the east of the rivers Bug and San belonged to the Western Soviet Republics of Ukraine, White Russia and Lithuania. Hence any patriotic activities of Poles in those territories were regarded as subversive by the U.S.S.R.[98]

The trial went along according to the Soviet plan. The exhausted and broken men confessed to the crimes attributed to them by their Soviet persecutors. The prosecution had all its "witnesses" available to "prove" the crimes of the arrested. The accused could not provide any witnesses, because it was explained that "transport difficulties" prevented the Soviets from bringing them in time for the trial.

The sentences were as follows:

General Okulicki, ten years in prison;
The Deputy Prime Minister, Jankowski, eight years;

Bien, Jasinkowicz, five years;

Puzak, eighteen months;

Baginski, one year;

Czarnomski, six months;

Pejdak, Mierzwa, Chacinski, Urbanski, Stypulkowski, Kobylanski, Czernik, Michalowski, four months.

Stempler, the interpreter, was not included.[99]

Western reaction to the verdict of the trial was mixed. The *Times* of London, in its editorial of June 22, commented:

Three of the prisoners are acquitted. Most of the rest, with General Okulicki at their head, confessed that they had engaged, as members of the Underground Movement and on the strength of directives received from the Polish Government in London, in various degrees of sabotage directed against the Red Army. Nothing in these confessions will cause surprise to those who have followed with anxiety the increasingly outspoken anti-Russian activities of Polish agents here and elsewhere during the past twelve months.

The *Scotsman* of June 22, stated:

Thus the Soviet purpose appeared to be to discredit those who organized the underground resistance to Germany in Poland and the Polish Government in London, who supported them. There were the usual mysterious confessions which form so startling a feature of Soviet trials. Obviously little reliance can be placed on them. How this purge of Polish patriots—for that is what the trial amounts to—is to secure for Stalin the friendship of Poland must be left to the imagination.

The *Manchester Guardian* in its editorial of June 22 discussed the implications of the Moscow trial and said that each of the great Soviet purges had a political purpose. Not only the last trial of the Polish leaders, but previous trials have had the aim of impressing the Russian people that this trial has been arranged chiefly for the benefit of the Allies, particularly Great Britain, in order to demonstrate why the Soviets refused recognition of the London Government. The *Manchester Guardian* went on to say that whatever one may think of Soviet trials,

it is difficult to read the evidence without concluding that there was a basis of truth in the Russian charges. On their own confession these men regarded the Soviet Union as an enemy and were prepared if the opportunity arose to intrigue and even to act against her. . . . On the other hand, it is not altogether surprising. After all, though the fault is by no means on one side, it cannot honestly be said that Russia has treated Poland particularly well.

The paper recalled the Soviet-German agreement at the outbreak of the war and Molotov's declaration regarding Poland's partition of September 1939.

The Russian treatment of the Poles in her zone was not always as gentle as it might have been and the Red Army's attitude towards the Polish Home Army in 1944 was unnecessarily harsh. . . . One cannot expect a nation to be friendly unless it is treated as a friend. The Soviet Government could now easily afford a more generous policy towards the Home Army and the supporters of the London Government. Such a policy would pay dividends. . . . For if we are expected to learn our lesson from the trial we can fairly ask that the Russians should learn theirs. It is now for the Soviet Union to prove to thousands of Poles simpler and more innocent than Okulicki that it does not threaten Polish independence.

On June 20, 1945 the *Daily Worker* in London stated:

Polish émigrés in London are now officially on record with their definition of "patriotism"—namely, anti-Soviet sabotage, espionage, and murder.

Walter Lippmann wrote in the *New York Herald Tribune* on June 21:

It is impossible to minimize the gravity of the issue which the Soviet Government raised in the public trial of the Polish leaders. The charge is that they were active agents of the movement which was directed by the Polish Government in London and connived at and supported in some Allied quarters to form a hostile coalition in Europe including Germany against the Soviet Union. . . . If the Soviet Government goes through with it this will of course provoke a showdown on the Western fear that Moscow is seeking to expand its domination over all Europe and Eastern Asia. Perhaps it is better to have a showdown now than let the conflicting suspicions become so aggravated that they can never be allayed and the conflicting purposes become so entrenched that they could never be resolved by peaceable means. But in such a showdown there is much at stake and we face the severest test to which British and United States diplomacy has been subjected. . . .

On June 20, 1945 Pertinax wrote in the *New York Times* that although Mikolajczyk and Stanczyk at first thought of making the release of the sixteen Poles a preliminary condition for the acceptance of the invitation, they had been persuaded to drop this demand.

There is some reason to believe that British diplomacy is responsible. Mikolajczyk and Stanczyk are satisfied with the treatment they are receiving in Moscow.

Pertinax concluded that:

Competent observers say that the Russian purpose behind the trial is to show that the Russians are not the men to unguardedly incur the risk of failure which, if it occurred, would surely be ascribed to their interference and machinations by the outside world. The trial is therefore an insurance underwritten against the possibility of final discord in the conference. In practice Mikolajczyk has been notified that if the proceedings end in a deadlock the Underground leaders may have to suffer, and he may be

involved somehow. This indictment contains accusations going back to
the time when Mikolajczyk was at least theoretically responsible for the
happenings in underground Poland. Conversely, if an all-round understanding is reached and a new Polish Government emerges, the defendants
are likely to escape with light sentences of pardon.

Pertinax concluded that the above view was conjectural to some
extent but rested partly on some well-ascertained data.

Finally, on June 22, *The Christian Science Monitor* in its article
"Diplomacy by Trial," said:

It is very awkward, no doubt. The Allies can, if they wish, display
incredulity over the outcome of the trials. But it is doubtful they will
wish to do so. So it looks as if Russia has scored a diplomatic victory in
1945 with methods reminiscent of the Arabian Nights.

Mikolajczyk felt that prior to political negotiations with the Poles
from Lublin and the Inter-Allied Commission composed of Kerr,
Harriman, and Molotov it would be futile to attempt to ask for the
release of the sixteen sentenced leaders.

In his first talk with Bierut he asked forcefully for assurances of
freedom of speech, assembly, press, religion, and release for the arrested members of the Home Army. Moreover, he asked for the
promise that a free election be held as soon as possible and insisted that
the Red Army leave Poland immediately and that the Soviet generals
and other officers in the Polish Army be asked to resign and return to
the U.S.S.R. Bierut would not listen.

On the following day the Lublin Poles managed to persuade Mikolajczyk's companion from London, Stanczyk, to join them as Minister
of Labor and Social Welfare, and in return for this favor he immediately launched an attack on Mikolajczyk. Consequently, Mikolajczyk's bargaining power was diminished. At the end of a whole day
of negotiations a sub-committee, dominated by the communists, was
formed to draft an agreement which would guide the Provisional
Government of National Unity until the election. The following
agreement was produced and accepted:

ARTICLE I

All parties entering the Coalition have full freedom of organizational
work, freedom of assembly, press, and propaganda.

Important decisions are to be arrived at by means of an understanding,
not by majority vote.

The basic foreign policy is friendship, cooperation, and alliance with
democratic states, especially with the Soviet Union, Great Britain, France
and friendship with the United States of America. At the same time it
is based on a Slavonic and anti-German front, having especially in view
an alliance with Czechoslovakia.

Poland will participate in an international organization for peace and security.

The western border of Poland will be fixed as soon as possible.

Elections to the *Sejm* (Parliament) on the basis of universal, equal, direct, and secret ballot, will be made as soon as possible, possibly before the end of 1945.

An amnesty is declared for political prisoners, except national traitors who collaborated with the German invaders.

The Red Army, as well as all other civilian, party, and security organs of foreign powers, will be evacuated.

ARTICLE II

The Peasant Party's participation in the Government should be at least one-third, its candidates to be designated by its competent authorities.

The National Council will be enlarged and the Peasant Party will participate in it in the ratio mentioned above.

Wincenty Witos will be First Vice-President of the National Council and Prof. Stanislaw Grabski its Third Vice-President.

Six members of the Peasant Party will hold Cabinet posts. The Peasant Party will provide a Vice-Premier and Ministers of Public Administration, Agriculture and Agrarian Reform, Education, Posts and Telegraph, Culture and Arts, and Health.

The Presidency of the Supreme Chamber of State Control will be awarded to the Peasant Party.

The Peasant Party will present undersecretaries in Cabinet posts in the ratio of one-third.

The Peasant Party's participation in the diplomatic and consular service will be in a similar ratio.

The Peasant Party is entitled to the Presidency of the State Agricultural Bank and the Central Bank of Agricultural Co-operatives, and Vice-Presidencies in the National Bank, Communal Bank, etc.

The Peasant Party is entitled to a correspondent share in the administration of the Central Co-operative Union *Spolem*, the Co-operative Auditing Union, and other State financial, economic, and cultural institutions.

The Peasant Party will receive an allotment of paper for party publications.

The Peasant Party will take part in the Publication Co-operative.[100]

Molotov immediately proposed that this agreement be accepted by his British and American colleagues. After a short hesitation this was done, with the provision that the American and British recognition would be extended as soon as Warsaw announced the formation of a new Government.

Stalin expressed his feelings and views toward Poland at the end of a dinner which he gave on the occasion of the conclusion of that agreement:

There have been many misunderstandings between Poland and Russia, and much bloodshed. Both sides have made mistakes. But Russia is more responsible, for after all we are a big country. Poles twice took Moscow, and Russians have camped in Warsaw.

Now we sit in friendship. But friendship, true friendship, can be achieved only when certain "old people," let us say, disappear from the horizon, and their suspicions are removed.

Changes in Russia appeared when Russian imperialism disappeared, when the policy of trying to "Russify" other countries was stopped, and when the new Russia was created by the pupils of Lenin. In Poland the sacrifices of the people during the German occupation have brought forth the possibility of changes within Poland and created better grounds for understanding with Soviet Russia.

But I know that in both countries—even here at this table—there are people who have doubts about the real intentions of Russia toward the Poles. These people should observe current events. Then they will find their suspicions have no basis.

Poland is a big country now, backed by Soviet Russia and the Allies. But no country, even the biggest country in the world, can today feel secure with but a single alliance. The Germans can rise again, as they did after World War I, and assume great strength and military power. If this is the case, the Soviet-Polish alliance will not be sufficient. Thus, both nations must have alliances with the West . . . with Great Britain, France, and the United States. (He raised his glass.) I drink a toast to those Allies! [101]

The British Ambassador, Sir Archibald Clark Kerr, delivered two letters to Mikolajczyk, one from Churchill and one from himself.

Churchill's letter read as follows:

How right you were to take the momentous decision you took in my room barely ten days ago. The results that have been achieved seem to me to give the greatest hope of a reconstitution of Polish national power. This can only be through friendship to Russia. The Soviets will, I am sure, appreciate the action on your part as helping them and the Western democracies together. I think you have done very well indeed.[102]

Ambassador Kerr added in his letter:

I should like to take this opportunity to tell You again that You have impelled my admiration for the courage, patience, wisdom, and calm (I could add a dozen words to this list) with which You have conducted the negotiations in Moscow. It is with all my heart that I wish You the best of luck.[103]

At the conclusion of the Moscow meeting, Mikolajczyk held a press conference in which he summed up his plan of work:

We concluded an agreement and we are determined to be loyal to it. We are determined together with all Polish democratic elements to rebuild Poland, to heal her wounds, to work for a free, independent and sovereign Poland. As a free people who love their country, we desire to live in most sincere friendship with the Soviet Union. We want Poland to enter the international arena as a positive partner, as an element of cooperation and unity so she can unite instead of divide democracies which had joined their hands to defeat Hitlerite Germany. Poland will bring in all democratic elements and will base her activities on friendship with the Soviet Union; she will renew her treaties with France and Great Britain; she will maintain her old friendly ties with the United States and will closely cooperate with the Slavic nations and in that way, surely she will contribute to the maintenance of peace.[104]

Lublin Press Agency, Polpress, June 26, 1945.

On his last day in Moscow Mikolajczyk asked Bierut and Osobka-Morawski to make a joint appeal to Stalin to secure the release of the sentenced Polish Underground leaders. Both of them refused. "Furthermore, we do not need those people in Poland." [105]

Persisting in his effort to help these men, Mikolajczyk went to see Molotov and asked him for an appointment with Stalin. Molotov refused by saying that Stalin was too busy but promised to convey Mikolajczyk's plea to secure a pardon for them.[106]

On June 28, the "united" Poles in Moscow flew to Warsaw. The Western leaders were relieved to know that an acceptable solution had finally been found for the unpleasant and difficult Polish problem.

On June 27, Lord Beaverbrook's the *Daily Express* commented:

A splendid easement of post-war Europe's first international problem is the Polish Agreement. It brings great encouragement to all who have worked with patience to reinforce the decisions of the Yalta Conference. Never, never let Russia's own contribution to this most helpful outcome be forgotten. . . . She has shown moderation and Statesmanship of high degree.

The *News Chronicle*, on June 25 commented:

. . . it happily resolved the biggest, and the most critical of the many problems arising from the liquidation of Naziism. . . .

4. Establishment of the "Provisional Government of National Unity" and Liquidation of the Polish Government

On June 28 the make-up of the new Provisional Government of National Unity was announced by Bierut, the President of Poland.

Prime Minister, Edward Osobka-Morawski
First Deputy Premier, Wladyslaw Gomulka
Second Deputy Premier and Minister of Agriculture and Land Reform, Stanislaw Mikolajczyk

The other Ministries were filled as follows:

National Defense, Michal Rola-Zymierski
Foreign Affairs, Wincenty Rzymowski

Public Administration, Wladyslaw Kiernik
Public Security, Stanislaw Radkiewicz
Finance, Konstanty Dabrowski
Industry, Hilary Minc
Reconstruction, Prof. Michal Kaczorowski
Supply and Trade, Dr. Jerzy Sztachelski
Shipping and Foreign Trade, Stefan Jedrychowski
Communications, Jan Rabanowski
Posts and Telegraph, Mieczyslaw Thugutt
Justice, Henryk Swiatkowski
Labor and Social Welfare, Jan Stanczyk
Public Health, Dr. Franciszek Litwin
Education, Czeslaw Wycech
Culture and Arts, Wladyslaw Kowalski
Information, Stefan Matuszewski
Forestry, Stanislaw Tkaczow

Fourteen of the twenty-one were Lublin Poles. Two completely
new Cabinet posts had been arbitrarily added to the Government—the
posts of Jedrychowski, Minister of Shipping and Foreign Trade, and
Stanislaw Tkaczow, Minister of Forestry. Both men were communists.
Tkaczow's power arrogated most of Mikolajczyk's authority as
Minister of Agriculture and Land Reform. Mikolajczyk protested in
vain.[107]

Thereafter, personal threats and intimidations began to be directed
at Mikolajczyk to discourage him from pursuing independent action.
But for almost two years he was not to be frightened. Anti-communist
Poles greeted him enthusiastically. They saw in him a symbol of
freedom and a token of the West's determination to see that Poland
would be free. His presence in Poland encouraged his compatriots to
express their feelings. But the communists were equally determined
not to allow them to slip out of their control. Arrests, various forms
of terror, and even murders were immediately applied against Mikolajczyk's followers. Their resistance to communization was the more
gallant and daring because their struggle was becoming hopeless in
the face of Western aloofness and the new casualties that were being
added to those who had fallen under the recent Nazi and Soviet
invasions. But this was the price that the Polish Nation had to pay
for the optimistic belief of the democracies that the communists might
be persuaded to act in a democratic manner.

Meanwhile, the new Government was awaiting official recognition,
which came promptly.

At Truman's request this (the Provisional Government) was recognized
by both Britain and the United States on July 5.[108]

It was announced in Warsaw on July 6, 1945 at 2:00 A.M. that in an official note President Truman had recognized the new Polish Provisional Government and that an exchange of Ambassadors would take place immediately. The United States appointed Mr. Arthur Bliss Lane as its Ambassador in Warsaw.

At the same time a similar note was received from Churchill and announced to the public. The British Government appointed Mr. Robert Hankey as its Chargé d'Affaires until a new Ambassador was appointed.[109] This recognition was of tremendous importance to the communist regime and it was a final blow to the hopes of the London Government.

Ambassador Ciechanowski recorded the form which the United States Government used to withdraw its recognition from the Constitutional Government of Poland.

On Thursday, July 5, at 2:00 P.M., President Truman's statement granting recognition to the "Provisional Polish Government" was broadcast on the radio, and appeared in the early afternoon editions of the press. Two hours later Durbrow telephoned to tell me that I would shortly receive an official note from the Secretary of State.

At 6:15 P.M. I received this final official note signed by the Honorable James F. Byrnes.

"The Secretary of State presents his compliments to His Excellency the Polish Ambassador and has the honor to quote below for the information of the Embassy the text of a public statement the President is to make at 7:00 P.M., Eastern War Time, today:

'It is with great satisfaction that I announce that effective today as of 7:00 P.M. Eastern War Time the Government of the United States has established diplomatic relations with the newly formed Polish Provisional Government of National Unity now established at Warsaw. The establishment of this Government is an important and positive step in fulfilling the decisions regarding Poland reached at Yalta and signed on February 11, 1945.

The new Polish Provisional Government of National Unity has informed me in a written communication that it has recognized in their entirety the decisions of the Crimea Conference on the Polish question. The new Government has thereby confirmed its intention to carry out the provisions of the Crimea decision with respect to the holding of elections.

Mr. Arthur Bliss Lane, whom I have chosen as United States Ambassador to Poland, will proceed to Warsaw as soon as possible, accompanied by his staff.'

For the further information of the Embassy, there is quoted below the substance of a communication the American Chargé d'Affaires *ad interim* near the Polish Government in London has been instructed to deliver to the Polish Foreign Minister:

'Since the Government of the United States of America has, in conformity with the decisions of the Crimea Conference, decided to recognize effective at 7:00 P.M. Eastern War Time, July 5, the new Polish Provisional Government of National Unity as the Government of the Republic of Poland, I have the honor to inform Your Excellency that the Mission of the American Embassy near the Polish Government in Exile in London will terminate as of that time.'

The Secretary of State, as can be appreciated, will not be able in the circumstances to transact official business with His Excellency the Polish Ambassador after the effective date of the recognition of the new Polish Provisional Government of National Unity.[110]

Churchill decided to give twenty-four hours' notice to the Polish Government in London that the British Government would withdraw its recognition.

The President of the Polish Republic, Wladyslaw Raczkiewicz, issued the following official Declaration to the Polish Nation:

I remain at my post in accordance with both the provisions of the Constitution now in force, and, I think, in accordance with the will of an immense majority of the Polish people. I am confident that this decision of mine will be understood throughout the world by all those who hold freedom, justice, and law in higher esteem and regard than brute force or the temporary victory of violence. It will be the duty of citizens of the Polish Republic, so grievously suffering under so many blows, to see to it that the great traditions of our national culture should not be lost, that our links with our past should not be severed, that our ideals of freedom are not betrayed; it will be their duty to maintain their allegiance to the lawful authorities of the Polish Republic and not to weaken in their strivings for the restoration to the Polish Republic of its rights and for the place due to it among the free nations of the world. We are living through a period of great dangers and difficulties for our nation and our State, but I firmly believe that Almighty God will bless our efforts and will cause Poland to emerge from this new ordeal victorious, secure, and with her rights undiminished.[111]

All the members of the Cabinet and other high officials, including President Raczkiewicz, who previously enjoyed diplomatic privileges now had to register personally at a British alien office near Piccadilly Circus. The line was long and the procedure slow enough to humiliate these former Allies, now aliens in a foreign land.

While previously, the terrorized Polish nation hoped that its Western Allies would hear them through the London Government and would use their influence to protect them, from this time onwards they took it for granted that the Western Allies would be deaf to their sufferings. There was no one to turn to for help.

Notes

[1] *Mikolajczyk's Private Files*, Vol. CCXCI, Doc. 359.

[2] Winston S. Churchill, *Triumph and Tragedy*, p. 333.

[3] *Ibid.*, p. 334.

[4] *Ibid.*, pp. 334–335.

[5] *Ibid.*, pp. 335–336.

[6] *Ibid.*, pp. 336–337.

[7] *Ibid.*, p. 337.

[8] *Mikolajczyk's Private Files*, Vol. CCXCI, Doc. 360.

[9] *Ibid.*, Doc. 367.

[10] *Ibid.*, Doc. 372a.

[11] *Ibid.*, Doc. 376.

[12] Mikolajczyk, *The Rape of Poland: Pattern of Soviet Aggression*, New York and Toronto, Whittlesey House, McGraw-Hill Book Company, Inc., 1948, pp. 289–291.

[13] *Mikolajczyk's Private Files*, Vol. CCXCI, Doc. 377.

[14] *Ibid.*, Vol. XLIII, Doc. 3.

[15] *Ibid.*, Doc. 5.

[16] *Ibid.*, Vol. XLIII, Doc. 5a.

[17] *Ibid.*, Doc. 6.

[18] Although Churchill in his memoirs and Sherwood in his biography of Hopkins have reproduced certain excerpts from the Yalta Conference, the most complete official records of the Yalta proceedings are to be found in the State Department text reprinted in a special supplement of *The New York Times* of March 17, 1955, pp. 47L–78L.

[19] *The New York Times*, March 17, 1955, p. 60L.

[20] *Ibid.*, p. 60L.

[21] *Ibid.*, p. 62L.

[22] *Ibid.*, p. 73L.

[23] *Ibid.*, p. 77L. See also, Robert E. Sherwood, *Roosevelt and Hopkins*, New York, Harper & Brothers, 1948, pp. 850–869 and Churchill, *op. cit.*, pp. 365–387.

[24] *The New York Times*, March 17, 1955, p. 77L.

[25] *Mikolajczyk's Private Files*, Vol. CCXCI, Doc. 401.

[26] Since there was no other way to establish that the London Government actually did have popular support in Poland, it may be of interest to cite the following news report, which testifies to the loyalty of the Underground to the London Government, as reported by Raymond Daniell in *The New York Times* on May 6, 1944.

"Some American sources here are inclined to regard the exiled Government's claims to underground support as somewhat inflated and to question whether it could depend upon the continued loyalty of the Polish people if the Germans were driven from their country and a representative Government of their own people was established.

"In this connection an incident that occurred last week is interesting. Certain high Polish officials were telling equally high British officials of the speed and efficiency with which they were able to maintain contact with the Underground. Some skepticism was expressed and the Polish leaders were challenged to prove the point in a practical way. There were certain bridges leading to Lwow, it was said, that for military reasons had to be destroyed. It was suggested that the Polish Government here could demonstrate its influence in occupied Poland by arranging to have those bridges destroyed. Orders were issued, and two days before the time limit agreed upon, word came that the bridges had been blown up.

"The news that the bridges had been destroyed was released by British, not Polish sources."

[27] *Mikolajczyk's Private Files,* Vol. CCXCI, Doc. 403.

[28] *Ibid.,* Doc. 398.

[29] *The Daily Herald,* London, February 16, 1945.

[30] *Polish Telegraphic Agency,* February 19, 1945.

[31] At a social occasion in London, prominent British conservatives asked Dr. Matthew Fryde, a counselor to the Polish Prime Minister: "Why cannot you Poles get along with the Russians? What is the matter with you?" Dr. Fryde, one of Poland's most brilliant lawyers, answered as follows: "I could illustrate my point by asking you why you can't get along with the Irish, but it wouldn't answer your question." Then he said:

"You see, I am a Jew, and I am fully aware of what Hitler has done to my people. But if I were going to be shot either in Berlin or in Moscow, and if I had a choice as to where I preferred this to happen, I would say that I preferred to be shot in Berlin."

At this point the British were very puzzled. So Fryde continued:

"If I were shot in Berlin, Goebbels would say that it was because I am a Jew, and that would be true. Or he would say that I was a Polish patriot, and that too would be true. Or else he would say that I am against Hitler, the Nazis, and any form of totalitarianism. This would all be true. But if I were shot in Moscow, the Soviets would say that I was an enemy of the people. Or they would say that I was a reactionary, or that I was a Nazi or American spy. All of this would not be true. I have a son at Oxford, and I should like him to know why I had been shot."

The British switched the subject of the conversation.

Dr. Fryde himself narrated this event to the author. It is relevant to mention that, being a most brilliant and learned scholar, he was scheduled to be appointed a Professor at Warsaw University before World War II. Because of his racial origin and the existing lack of tolerance he was turned down.

[32] Sherwood, *op. cit.,* p. 804.

[33] *Ibid.,* p. 870. For Khrushchev's opinion of Stalin see "The Crimes of the Stalin Era," *The New Leader,* New York, 1956.

[34] Quoted in the *New York Herald Tribune,* February 14, 1945.

[35] *Mikolajczyk's Private Files,* Vol. X, Doc. 50.

[36] *Ibid.,* Vol. CCXCI, Docs. 404–408.

[37] *Ibid.,* Vol. XLIII, Doc. 12.

[38] Churchill, *op. cit.,* p. 396.

[39] *Ibid.,* pp. 400–401.

[40] *Ibid.,* pp. 401–402.

[41] *Ibid.,* pp. 421–422.

[42] *Ibid.,* pp. 422–423.

[43] *Ibid.,* pp. 423–424.

[44] *Ibid.,* p. 426.

[45] *Ibid.*

[46] *Ibid.*, pp. 426–427.

[47] *Mikolajczyk's Private Files*, Vol. X, Doc. 17.

[48] *Ibid.*, Doc. 28.

[49] *Ibid.*, Vol. XLIII, Doc. 30.

[50] *Ibid.*, Vol. LII, Doc. 81.

[51] Jan Ciechanowski, *Defeat in Victory*, Garden City, New York, Doubleday & Company, Inc., 1947, pp. 365–366.

[52] Harry S. Truman, *Year of Decisions*, Vol. I, New York, Doubleday & Company, Inc., 1955, p. 39.

[53] *Mikolajczyk's Private Files*, Vol. X, Doc. 47.

[54] *Ibid.*

[55] *Ibid.*

[56] *Ibid.*

[57] *Ibid.*

[58] *Ibid.*, Doc. 48.

[59] *Ibid.*, Doc. 50.

[60] For a first-hand and brilliant account of these acts and their sequence, see Z. Stypulkowski, *Invitation to Moscow*, London, Thames and Hudson, 1951.

[61] *Mikolajczyk's Private Files*, Vol. X, Doc. 52.

[62] *Ibid.*, Doc. 53.

[63] *Ibid.*, Doc. 54.

[64] *Ibid.*, Doc. 49.

[65] Quoted in the *Sunday Times*, London, May 6, 1945.

[66] *Mikolajczyk's Private Files*, Vol. X, Doc. 80.

[67] Stalin reversed his decision about Molotov's attendance at San Francisco.

[68] *Mikolajczyk's Private Files*, Vol. XLIII, Doc. 77.

[69] *Ibid.*, Vol. LII, Doc. 79.

[70] *Ibid.*, Vol. X, Docs. 75–76.

[71] *Ibid.*, Vol. XLIII, Doc. 73.

[72] Sherwood, *op. cit.*, p. 890.

[73] *Ibid.*

[74] *Ibid.*, pp. 898–901.

[75] *Ibid.*, pp. 905–907.

[76] *Ibid.*, pp. 909–910.

[77] *Ibid.*, p. 910.

[78] *Ibid.*, p. 913.

[79] *Ibid.*, p. 923.

[80] Churchill, *op. cit.*, pp. 581–582.

[81] *Mikolajczyk's Private Files*, Vol. XLIII, Doc. 78.

[82] *Ibid.*, Vol. XLIII, Doc. 80.

[83] *Ibid.*, Doc. 81.

[84] *Ibid.*, Doc. 87.

[85] *Ibid.*, Doc. 88.

[86] *Ibid.*, Doc. 118.

[87] *Ibid.*, Doc. 95.

[88] *Ibid.*, Doc. 96.

[89] See page 98.

[90] Truman, *op. cit.*, p. 320.

[91] *Mikolajczyk's Private Files*, Vol. XLIII, Doc. 97.

[92] *Ibid.*, Doc. 98.
[93] This information is based on Mr. Mikolajczyk's conversations with the author.
[94] *Mikolajczyk's Private Files*, Vol. LII, Doc. 2.
[95] Mikolajczyk, *op. cit.*, p. 120.
[96] *Mikolajczyk's Private Files*, Vol. LII, Doc. 3.
[97] *Ibid.*, Doc. 5.
[98] Z. Stypulkowski, *Invitation to Moscow*, London, Thames and Hudson, 1951, pp. 313–314.
[99] *Ibid.*, p. 333.
[100] *Mikolajczyk's Private Files*, Vol. XII, Doc. 4.
[101] *Ibid.*, Doc. 5.
[102] *Ibid.*, Vol. LII, Doc. 32.
[103] *Ibid.*, Doc. 31.
[104] *Ibid.*, Vol. XII, Doc. 7.
[105] *Ibid.*, Vol. XII, Doc. 6.
[106] *Ibid.*
[107] *Ibid.*, Vol. CII, Doc. 96.
[108] Churchill, *op. cit.*, p. 583.
[109] *Mikolajczyk's Private Files*, Vol. LII, Doc. 72.
[110] Ciechanowski, *op. cit.*, pp. 387–388.
[111] *Mikolajczyk's Private Files*, Vol. LII, Doc. 73.

From the Potsdam Conference to the Elections

July 17, 1945 to October 20, 1947

1. The Potsdam Conference

The new Government centered its attention on the preparation of its case for the western frontier to be drawn along the Oder and Neisse Rivers. At this point, the Poles and the Soviets were in agreement to push Polish frontiers west. Only their motives were different. While the Poles, independent of political affiliations, were anxious to regain western territories which had once belonged to the Polish Kingdom, the Soviets were supporting them in their desire in order to advance their own sphere of influence and control to the west. Furthermore, the Soviets were undoubtedly realistic enough to foresee that the Western Powers would not be so anxious to support the Polish claim against Germany, in the expectation that a democratic Germany would be a stronghold against communist pressure from the east.

This meant that only the Soviet Union would support Polish demands and, by doing so, would "prove" to the Poles that the Western Powers were oriented towards Germany while the Soviet Union was the only friend on whom Poles would or could rely. In addition, and from a long-range point of view, the Soviets undoubtedly realized that Polish fears of German efforts to regain these territories would virtually assure Poland's orientation toward Moscow rather than to the West. For the Soviets this was an extremely convenient situation to be exploited for their own purposes.

On July 17, the Big Three met at Potsdam. On the second day of the Conference, Stalin asked for an immediate transfer to the Provisional Government of Poland, "of all stocks, assets and all other property belonging to Poland" which was still at the disposal of the Polish Government in London. Furthermore, he asked that all Polish armed forces, including the Navy and the Merchant Marine be transferred to the new Government.[1]

Churchill explained that there were about twenty million pounds in gold in London and Canada which had been frozen by the British. In order to unfreeze this the establishment of normal diplomatic channels for such a transaction were required. Therefore, he invited the new Polish Government to send an Ambassador to London as soon as possible to take over the Embassy and proceed with normal business. As he put it, "the sooner the better." [2]

As to the Polish armed forces, Churchill resisted Stalin's demands by recalling their gallantry during the fighting and stated that the British Government could not force these men to go back to Poland if they did not wish to go. He assured Stalin

that our policy was to persuade as many as possible, not only of the soldiers but also of the civilian employees of the late Polish Government, to go back to their country. But we must have a little time to get over difficulties.[3]

Stalin agreed with Churchill's point of view and said he appreciated his problems. Then Stalin continued:

The London Polish Government still existed. They had means of continuing their activities in the press and elsewhere, and they had their agents. This made a bad impression on all the Allies.[4]

Undoubtedly Stalin would have been glad to relieve the Allies of this thankless burden in his customary manner. Churchill said there was nothing that could be done about it and added:

. . . We had to be careful about the Polish Army, for if the situation was mishandled there might be a mutiny. I asked Stalin to put his trust and confidence in His Majesty's Government and give us reasonable time. In return everything possible should be done to make Poland an encouraging place for Poles to go back to. Mr. Truman declared that he saw no fundamental difference between us.[5]

Stalin suggested that the whole subject should be referred to the Foreign Secretaries. Churchill and Truman agreed.[6]

On July 21, during the fifth meeting of the Big Three, the Soviet delegation insisted that Poland's western frontier should run along the Oder River, leaving Stettin on the Polish side, and then along the Western Neisse to Czechoslovakia. Churchill and Truman argued that this had to be left until the Peace Conference. Stalin replied that he needed a friendly administration on these territories and "since the Germans fled from that area" only Poles remained to plow the land.[7]

Churchill and Truman were concerned with the economic problem and undoubtedly also with the future strategic importance of Germany and did not want to yield to Stalin, who suggested that Germans would be able to buy food from Poland. The Western Allies argued that they could not harm Germany. To that Stalin replied:

It was better to make difficulties for Germans than for Poles, and the less industry in Germany the more markets for Britain.[8]

The following day the Big Three still could not reconcile their differences. Churchill suggested that an invitation be extended to the Poles to come to the Conference and present their case to the Foreign Ministers. Stalin and the President agreed and so Truman, as presiding officer, issued an invitation to the Poles.[9]

The first hearing of the Provisional Government of National Unity before the three Foreign Ministers, Eden, Byrnes, and Molotov, took place on July 24, 1945. The Polish side was represented by President Bierut, Mikolajczyk, Rzymowski, Grabski, Gomulka, Modzelewski, Zymierski, and Stanczyk. They unanimously asked for all territories east of the Oder and east of the Western Neisse Rivers.

Byrnes, as Chairman of the meeting, stated that the final decision in this matter would be made by the Peace Conference and informed the Poles that they would have to wait until that time.

At this point, Molotov rose to the defense of the Polish claims.

I consider the question of the Polish frontiers to be of historical significance, because its implications are not only important to Poland and to her neighbors but also to the whole of Europe. The solution of the Polish eastern frontiers at the Crimea Conference was a result of an agreement between two neighbors—Poland and Soviet Russia. The Western part of the Ukraine and Byelorussia was given to us by Poland. Therefore, we feel particularly obligated toward Poland in regard to her western frontiers. Here I am not saying anything new to the representatives of Great Britain, the United States, or Poland. I am obliged to support the Polish request because justice demands it. The Soviet Union considers that the Polish striving to place their border on the Oder, including Stettin, and Neisse is just and timely. On the basis of justice the Germans should lose those territories in favor of Poland. In international relations this means stopping German aggression. At the same time it means the rebirth of the Polish nation. A reborn Poland will be a bastion of peace in Europe. Germany will be weakened, while Poland will become strong, not only for the present but for the future. All Poles will be gathered in one State. A truly democratic Poland reborn within those frontiers will be homogeneous in the economic sense also. For those reasons the Soviet delegation hopes that the Polish request will meet with understanding. We are particularly anxious to help Poland because we are her neighbors and we have specific obligations towards her.

Byrnes did not want the Soviet Union to claim the sole monopoly of good intentions towards Poland; therefore, he added: "Although the United States is not a neighbor of Poland she was always a great friend of Poland." Mr. Eden concluded that "England had declared war in defense of Poland," and Mikolajczyk was delighted to be among friends.[10]

When the same delegation met in Babelsberg, Churchill began by repeating Eden's remark:

England declared war in defense of Poland. For this reason we are interested in Poland. If Poles were not going to be free we would have to admit that this war was lost.

Then he went on to say:

We are not going to support your request for the western frontier. We were talking about the Oder Line but now you are asking for more. I think this is a misunderstanding. You are showing too great appetites. . . . You are asking for twenty-five percent of German territory with a population of between eight and nine million Germans, while from your eastern territories you have to resettle four million of Poles. For this reason we have to tell you that we shall not give our blessings to your demands.[11]

The Poles attempted to sway Churchill from his stand, but they did not succeed. They were gradually becoming aware that Churchill's defense of Germany was based on the realization that it was an integral part of the defense of the British Isles.

After the meeting with Churchill the Warsaw delegation was received by President Truman. When they began to present their demands for the western frontier, the President interrupted and said that according to the Yalta decisions the question of the Polish western frontiers had to wait until the Peace Conference and that the Potsdam Conference could not be preoccupied with the solution of that problem. Mr. Truman took that occasion to inform them that the United States Government, and he specifically, would not take part in a policy of unilaterally accomplished moves. Bierut attempted to explain that Poles had to take over the administration of those territories because they were left uninhabited, but the President told him that the conference must come to an end because a meeting of the Big Three had been scheduled.

Mikolajczyk joined in, saying that, as a result of the Crimea Conference, which had decided the Polish eastern frontiers, the Polish Provisional Government of National Unity was faced with the necessity of finding a home for more than four million Poles from the territories east of the Curzon Line; that they had to be settled somewhere; and that there was room for them in the western territories. Therefore, he asked President Truman for advice on how to legalize the action without a unilateral act. The President then informed Mikolajczyk that he would study the solution of that problem. When parting, the President showed particular friendliness toward Mikolajczyk and told him how President Roosevelt had always spoken of him very warmly and with respect.

Eden explained to Mikolajczyk that President Truman was unusually irritated by Bierut and his followers because he did not believe that the Polish delegation reflected his concept of democracy and that, therefore, he had a prejudice against them.[12]

On July 27 Stalin gave a banquet for the Warsaw delegation. During the banquet Professor Grabski proposed a toast to the Slavic nations, which would not follow the path of Tsarist Panslavism but would march along the road of mutual cooperation of free, independent and sovereign nations under the leadership of Stalin. Stalin replied that he did not agree with one point of Professor Grabski's remarks, namely,

A Slav cannot be subordinated to someone else's leadership. Therefore, cooperation between the Slavic nations must be based on full sovereignty and independence. For this reason our cooperation must be as between equals. I do not qualify for the leadership of the Slavs.[13]

When Prime Minister Osobka-Morawski spoke about the necessity of unifying the differences in his Government, Stalin interrupted and said:

You have to maintain a coalition. The existing differences of view cannot be eliminated. They are there and they will have to be there because each party naturally will try to expand its influence, and they have a right to do so.[14]

As the subsequent behavior of the Warsaw communists indicated, these liberal-minded remarks of Stalin were directed to Mikolajczyk and Grabski in order to allay their fears of Soviet domination of Poland.

After a few days of recess necessitated by the departure of the

British delegation to London to face the outcome of the elections, the new British Prime Minister, Clement Attlee, and his Foreign Secretary, Ernest Bevin, attempted to interrogate the Warsaw delegation in order to determine whether they deserved British support in their territorial demands.

On being asked when they proposed to hold the free election in Poland which was envisaged by the Yalta Agreement, Bierut replied:

We cannot make any commitments, especially here in this company, because it would interfere with our democratic principles. Such a question can be considered only by the Polish people in accordance with the opinion of the political parties and social organizations. We are only representatives and not individuals who can freely undertake this sort of obligation. That kind of obligation, imposed on us from outside by any of our Allies, independently of how anxiously we would want to live in friendship with them and in spite of our great respect for them, would endanger our national dignity. How could we, a nation of twenty-six million people permit any outsider to guarantee our democratic principles? This will be done by ourselves. It seems to me that these questions should not be the subject of today's discussion. The Polish nation has a very high level of social culture and during its long history was able to fight for its rights. Today also it can force, even overthrow, any government which will stand in its way. We would like to appeal to the British Government, for which we and the Polish nation have deep respect, to treat the Polish nation and its democratic intentions with greater respect and confidence.[15]

This answer visibly irritated Bevin, and after prolonged and tedious arguments he warned Bierut that unless the Warsaw Government gave a clear-cut answer to several questions, that the British Government would be unable to vote in favor of the Polish territorial demands. As a result of this sobering argument, Bierut promised:

1. To hold a free and unfettered election in the early part of 1946, on the basis of universal suffrage and the secret ballot, in which all democratic and anti-Nazi parties would have the right to take part and to put forward candidates;
2. To guarantee the freedom of the press;
3. To guarantee the freedom of religion;
4. To guarantee the safety and security of all Poles abroad who may return home to Poland.[16]

On July 30, the Big Three announced their decision about the "Western Frontier of Poland" which was proposed by the United States and adopted by the British and Soviet Governments.

In conformity with the agreement on Poland reached at the Crimean Conference the three Heads of Government have sought the opinion of the Polish Provisional Government of National Unity in regard to the accession of territory in the north and west which Poland should receive.

The President of Poland and members of the Polish Provisional Government of National Unity have been received at the Conference and have fully presented their views. The three Heads of Government reaffirm their opinion that the final delimitation of the western frontier of Poland should await the peace settlement.

The three Heads of Government agree that, pending the final determination of Poland's western frontier, the former German territories east of a line running from the Baltic Sea through Swinemunde, and thence along the Oder River to the confluence of the Western Neisse River and along the Western Neisse to the Czechoslovak frontier, including that portion of East Prussia not placed under the administration of the Union of Soviet Socialist Republics in accordance with the understanding reached at this Conference and including the area of the former Free City of Danzig, shall be under the administration of the Polish State and for such purposes should not be considered as part of the Soviet zone of occupation in Germany.[17]

The Poles were delighted to have the West's consent to continue to occupy lands between the Western and Eastern Neisse Rivers that were already under their control and which the peace conference, they hoped, would finally legalize as Polish territory. There were no disputes over the rest of the former German territories now included in Poland.

On July 31, 1945 the Big Three announced a *Statement on the Polish Question.*

We have taken note with pleasure of the agreement reached among the representative Poles from Poland and abroad which has made possible the formation, in accordance with the decisions reached at the Crimea Conference, of a Polish Provisional Government of National Unity recognized by the Three Powers. The establishment by the British and United States Governments of diplomatic relations with the Polish Provisional Government has resulted in the withdrawal of their recognition from the former Polish Government in London, which no longer exists.

The British and United States Governments have taken measures to protect the interest of the Polish Provisional Government as the recognized Government of the Polish State in the property belonging to the Polish State located on their territory and under their control, whatever the form of this property may be. They have further taken measures to prevent alienation to third parties of such property. All proper facilities will be given to the Polish Provisional Government for the exercise of the ordinary legal remedies for the recovery of any property of the Polish State which may have been wrongfully alienated.

The Three Powers are anxious to assist the Polish Provisional Government in facilitating the return to Poland as soon as practicable of all Poles abroad who wish to go, including members of the Polish Armed Forces and the Merchant Marine. They expect that those Poles who return home shall be accorded personal rights and rights of property on the same basis as all Polish citizens.

The Three Powers note that the Polish Provisional Government, in conformity with the Crimea Decision, has agreed to the holding of free and unfettered elections as soon as possible on the basis of universal suffrage and the secret ballot in which all democratic and anti-Nazi parties shall have the right to take part and to put forward candidates, and that representatives of the Allied press shall enjoy full freedom to report to the world upon the developments in Poland before and during the elections.[18]

The communists were pleased with the results of the Conference. They were determined to exploit those aspects of the Potsdam Conference which were convenient to them and to ignore those which bound them to a free election and other pledges.

2. The Fate of the Exiled Poles

In accordance with the Potsdam Statement on the Polish Question, the British Government began to urge Poles, both military and civilian, to return home. Every Pole received a printed appeal from the British Government signed by Foreign Minister Bevin. The Warsaw regime was also issuing appeals to Poles outside to return home. The decision for the exiled Poles was most difficult. While everyone was anxious to return home after five years of war to join his nearest relatives and to help rebuild the ruined country, most of them feared that if they did so they would, sooner or later, be watched, terrorized, and even arrested. On the other hand, the life of an exile was not too promising, especially for those without a trade or a profession. Emigration to other lands was difficult. For example, the United States quota for Poles was 6,500 a year. Britain was already overcrowded. As the days went by the situation became more and more difficult. Nostalgia for home became stronger. The communist appeals began making inroads on distressed minds. Eventually, about 40% of the intelligentsia and about 10% of the others decided to return to Poland, come what may. It was significant that the supposed beneficiaries of the communist system chose not to accept the benefits.

One of the leaders of the Polish intelligentsia was Ksawery Pruszynski, a writer and political commentator whose position and outlook in Poland were similar to Walter Lippmann's in the United States. He came from an aristocratic family of eastern Poland. From 1941 to 1942 he had been a Cultural and Press Attaché in the Polish Embassy in the Soviet Union. From the time of the Allied landing in Normandy until the Western armies reached Germany he was a front gunner in the tank under this writer's command in the First Polish Armored Division. He was a brave officer, who wanted to go through the battles not only to do his share in defeating the common enemy, but also to be able to describe what went on in the minds and hearts of the men who were fighting against the Nazis. After several narrow escapes his tank was hit by a shell from a German Tiger and burst into flames. Two other members of the crew were killed and he himself was wounded in eighteen places. After long months in the hospital the communists began to court him to return home to "help his people." They needed a few respectable names to add dignity to their unknown personalities. After a long inner struggle Pruszynski decided to go back to Poland. When asked what his reasons were for his decision, he gave this lengthy but rather significant reply which was representative of the way most Polish intellectuals were thinking at the time.[20]

I am not a communist. I love freedom and democracy. I have done everything possible to secure it for post-war Poland. I fought against the undemocratic regime in pre-war Poland. From my experiences in Russia I know what is awaiting Poland now. Like every other Pole I trusted England and America; I believed that they would not permit Red slavery to take over Poland in place of the brown tyrants. Poland by herself could not do so. I trusted every word which came from the lips of Churchill and Roosevelt. I wanted to believe in every slogan which they advanced. It soothed my tormented soul. I had a vision of a better, a just and democratic Poland and Europe because I thought that those two outstanding leaders in the struggle against fascism would not permit communism to replace it. But I was deeply shocked and disillusioned by what they did, not only to Poland but to other small nations, and to the principles of justice and international morality. Their Periclean gift, which everyone admires, helped them to camouflage their hypocrisy and to betray those who trusted them. They have defeated Hitler and Mussolini, but Stalin has snatched the victory from their hands. They wanted to save their men from further bloodshed, but the children of those men will have to give their lives to correct these mistakes or will have to live in constant fear if they do not want to accept the yoke of Bolshevik rule over them.

Poles cannot blame them too much. After all, they were not Poland's leaders. They had to look after the interests of their own countries and peoples. But they were too short-sighted. Unintentionally, they helped Stalin spread his power and chain Eastern Europe to the chariot of his power. Those people will have to work and fight for Russia, and they will do so. It is the duty of statesmen to foresee events and not just to comment on them *post mortem.*

Tired Englishmen and Americans did not want to believe that their leaders were wrong; that this war was lost in the long run. Roosevelt was sick and so can be partly excused. But Churchill has no excuse for his blunders. No one can reverse the historical process which they put into action. Churchill and Roosevelt wanted to buy peace for their nations by selling the small Eastern European nations to communism. This was the method of feeding a crocodile. In time he will ask for their skins, too. Who will trust the Anglo-Americans in the future? Who of their potential allies in future conflicts can be sure that when it is profitable for the British or the Americans, they will not abandon them for the sake of appeasing Moscow?

We knew what to expect from Stalin and for this reason we tried to the end to hang on to our Western Allies. In the end they approved Stalin's demands. It is so bitter to be betrayed by your friends, and more difficult to accept than to have to reconcile yourself to the same treachery when it comes from your enemies.

Apparently the Anglo-Americans have two moralities—one for home consumption and the other for export. Democracy can survive only if moral principles are fused with political performances. Neither Teheran nor Yalta indicate that they were. If harm is done to an individual in any moderately civilized society one can appeal to the police or to a court and, relatively speaking, justice will be done. But when a nation is condemned to slavery by the decision of a few individuals, where can you look for justice?

If Poland is to survive, Poles have to learn a lesson from this war, which was so costly to them. Neither England nor America are interested in Poland—they never were and never will be—because of Poland's geographical position. Those hypocritical sentiments expressed by Churchill and Roosevelt have to be analyzed in terms of their ulterior motives. Churchill repeated so many times that Britain went to war because Polish independence was endangered. But I want to ask how many shots were fired by British soldiers in September 1939, when the Polish nation was dying? None. Britain went to war because she knew that Hitler was aiming at her, and she needed time before the Nazi armies would turn against her. Poles can say that over 1,800 Polish pilots lost their lives in the Battle of Britain; that Polish sailors died in defense of this Island. You can find graves of Polish men all over Europe and North Africa. But what is the result of their supreme sacrifice? Over 40,000 soldiers were killed and 20,000 wounded on the Western Front, and 6,000,000 Poles have perished in Poland. And what did Poland gain by it? Nothing. She is sentenced to a slow death under another totalitarian power.

It is not of Poland's choosing that she is cast into Soviet hands. She cannot go on fighting indefinitely, because eventually there would be a country without people. Poles will have to adjust themselves to Russia and forget the West. I am going there not because I love the Soviet Union but only to try to persuade the Russians not to treat harshly my unfortunate nation. Maybe I shall help my people. The older generation will die out. The new will be brought up in a different spirit. They shall not feel the pain of transition. The life of a nation is not measured in terms of one generation. If Poles change, this may be better for them, because it seems that the Russians are going to expand even further since the Western people are afraid to die.

The Western World looks always with a feeling of superiority on the Slavs. Poles can barely be accepted by them as equals; individuals, yes, but not the nation as a whole. The Soviets, at least, look upon the Poles as equals—look at Rokossovsky, Vyshinsky, etc. Is there any Pole in the

West who was admitted into higher echelons? You may object to the morals of those men serving the Russians, but where is Western morality? Expediency is at a premium. You will see that soon after this war the Anglo-American politicians will be anxious to delegate the re-organization of Europe to Germans, because they don't want to be bothered with that task themselves. This surely will push other Eastern and Southern European nations into Soviet arms, because those who suffered from Germany do not believe that so much cruelty and the murder of over twenty million Europeans and Jews was committed by Hitler and Himmler alone. Nations are not changed according to the whims of detached politicians who look at the problem of humanity in a manipulative manner. If the communists are clever enough they will exploit this unfortunate tendency to their advantage.

The sooner Poles accept their tragic fate the better it will be for them. They have to reduce the dangerous effect of communist rule over their national life by collaborating with them. In order to survive Poland must learn her lesson from the present event. If war arises between the East and the West, and Poles are on the Western side and the West wins, we know what they can expect. They were on the Western side this time. If the West loses, we know what Poles have to expect from the Soviets! But, if Poles are on the Eastern side and the East wins, Poland may get something from Russia. If Russia loses, the Poles don't need to be afraid because the West does not know how to punish its enemies.

I am convinced that this line of reasoning will condition the political behavior of most European nations and others who may be caught in a future struggle between the Soviet Union and the United States—if the American people ever have enough courage to fight for their professed beliefs, which undoubtedly will be endangered. I do not think that they would, because they love their comfort and will not be willing to risk death. Together with the British, who are their political masterminds (as the Americans have never liberated themselves in the field of foreign policy from British leadership in spite of the American Revolution), they may try through underground activities to harass the captive countries in the belief that this will shake off the communist yoke. This would be a criminal adventure because it would only push unarmed and desperate people against the communist bayonets, into prisons, execution squads, and concentration camps; and would also provide a pretext for the communists to liquidate the best that is left in Poland.

Undoubtedly many Polish ex-politicians who remain outside would be willing to give their support and blessing to such plans, though this they would do only because they had lost touch with reality in the captive country and because it would provide them with a job. If such a thing ever happens it would be highly immoral; that one who is unwilling to die should put another to do so for him.

I am too old to start a new life in some other country. I must go back and serve my country and my people as best I can by collaborating with the occupiers. And when the time comes to end this life I shall be certain that my bones will be laid for their eternal rest in the soil I love so much.[21]

He returned to become a Minister Plenipotentiary of the Government. Two years later he was killed in a mysterious accident.

Others went home determined not to be involved in any political action in the belief that they would be forgiven their wartime association with London. Soon after their arrival most of them were quietly arrested and put into a new concentration camp in the vicinity of Hrubieszow, only to be subsequently deported to Russia. They could not be trusted, because it was believed that they had been politically "infected" in the West.[22]

The majority of the Poles in exile decided to remain in the West. They were either afraid of communism or were unwilling to compromise certain principles. By this they meant that one cannot serve the oppressor of one's country. They could not forgive the Soviets for Katyn, for the betrayal of the Warsaw uprising, and for the large-scale deportations of innocent people. They had to overcome the pain they felt of never being able to see their loved ones again or to work and live in the country of their forefathers and their childhood. Suspecting the imperialistic aims of Russia, they hoped that sooner or later a clash between the West and the East would take place. Although they were hurt by the decision taken at Yalta, they understood that the West was afraid of Russia and that it believed it could buy peace by satisfying the Soviet demands.

From the contacts with the soldiers and people of the Western democracies they had gained a firm belief in the basic goodness of their nature. They were convinced that the moral principles of the democracies, though temporarily abandoned, would eventually win. Consequently, they decided to "go West," to begin a new life, and when the time came for the "inevitable" conflict they would take part in it and then return home to bring back the experience of democratic life and freedom to their country.

They dispersed to North and South America, to Africa, Australia, New Zealand, and any Western country which was willing to open its hospitable doors to give them shelter.[23]

3. The Communists Tighten Their Control Over Poland

In the meantime, the Provisional Government of National Unity began to consolidate its power and to strengthen its ties with the Soviet Union.

As a gesture to the democratic elements, the communists agreed to release 200,000 members of the Polish Underground Army who had been arrested prior to its disbanding on April 19 and the members of the underground political organizations which had disbanded in the middle of July. The officers, however, were kept in prison as they were regarded as a dangerous element.

It was agreed that those persons who had resided east of the Curzon Line and who could prove beyond any doubt that they were of Polish origin would be transferred to the territories taken over from Germany, and that their personal losses in the east would be compensated for in western Poland. For all practical purposes, religious affiliations were the main criteria which guided the Soviets in deciding who, among those willing to be repatriated, were to be sent to the west. The Roman Catholics were repatriated, while those who belonged to the Orthodox Church were retained in their old places. Many White Russians and Ukrainians preferred to move west under the pretext that they were Catholics.[24] Only a small number, however, managed to evade Soviet scrutiny. Over four million persons were transferred into the western territory of Poland. Here they found that the Russians had stripped it of its factories, railroads, homes, and livestock and had transported everything they could to the Soviet Union.

Since Poland was predominantly an agricultural country, her national recovery depended on the ability of peasants to produce enough food not only for its own hungry population but for export as well. This had to be done quickly and in as great a volume as possible in order to buy other necessary products from either the West or from Russia. In this respect a very grave situation existed as a result of the five years of war.

On August 5, 1945 the Polish Ministry of Agriculture established the war losses in agriculture as follows. These were valued in *zlotys*, one *zloty* corresponding to twenty cents.

Horses	1,383,000	value	273,000,000.
Cows	4,394,000	value	763,000,000.
Pigs	3,784,000	value	424,000,000.
Sheep	880,000	value	20,000,000.
Buildings		value	1,500,000,000.
Farm machinery		value	500,000,000.
Orchards and agricultural industry		value	200,000,000.
Domestic implements		value	200,000,000.
Crop losses		value	8,900,000,000.
Total			12,780,000,000.

Approximate losses of agricultural stock behind the Curzon Line were as follows:

Horses	1,393,000	value	274,000,000.
Cows	4,147,000	value	711,000,000.
Pigs	2,650,000	value	301,000,000.
Sheep	2,283,000	value	52,000,000.
Buildings		value	5,992,000,000.
Farm machinery		value	1,997,000,000.
Total			9,327,000,000.

The total losses of all livestock and farm equipment from all territories would thus be 22,107,000,000 zlotys, or $4,421,400,000.[25] Taking into consideration the general poverty of the country, it can readily be seen that a four billion dollar loss in the agricultural economy was a major disaster.

The Poles hoped to remedy this situation by using the expected reparations from Germany, though the terms and amounts of these reparations had to be transacted, according to the Potsdam agreement, through the Soviet Union. The necessity of settling this matter with the Soviets was due to a provision of the Official Potsdam Declaration which stated that, "The U.S.S.R. undertakes to settle the reparation claims of Poland from its own share of reparations." [26]

On August 15, 1945 Bierut, Osobka-Morawski, and Mikolajczyk went to Moscow and met Molotov and Vyshinsky in the Narkomindel to discuss the problem of reparations.

Mikolajczyk began by asking if it would be possible for Poland to increase her share in reparations to be received from the Soviet occupied zone of Germany from 15% to 20%. Molotov replied, "No."

MIKOLAJCZYK. Did the Allied Conference foresee any compensation for the German citizen who will be resettled from the eastern German territories to the west?

MOLOTOV. No, never. There were precedents. After the Franco-German war, the German citizens were expelled from the disputed territory without any compensation.

MIKOLAJCZYK. What kind of methods are going to be used in collecting reparations? In the Potsdam protocol it is said that during the first six months a complete inventory will be taken of all stocks. Would you agree to the establishment of a mixed Soviet-Polish Commission to take such an inventory in order to avoid any misunderstanding?

MOLOTOV. Yes.

Here Morawski interrupted to say that he was against such a proposal because it indicated a lack of confidence in the Soviet authorities. Bierut remarked that he was in favor of Mikolajczyk's proposal. Molotov not only refused to share with Poland the ten billion dollars' worth of reparations which the Soviets were going to take from Germany, but also "persuaded" the members of the Polish Provisional Government that Poland deliver twelve millon tons of coal annually to the Soviet Union as long as the Red Army remained in occupation of Germany. He offered to pay one dollar and twenty-five cents for a ton, while Denmark and Sweden were willing to pay sixteen dollars per ton. Mikolajczyk's objections that this would not cover even the cost of production were brushed aside.[27]

Furthermore, switching the subject of discussion, Molotov revealed to Mikolajczyk that the problem of the eastern Polish frontier was settled in the Soviet-Lublin agreement signed by Osobka-Morawski and Molotov on July 25, 1944. This was prior to Mikolajczyk's first visit to Stalin as the legal Prime Minister of the London Government and prior to the Soviet recognition of the Lublin Committee. It appears that it was part of the price which the Lublin group had to pay for being recognized as the potential rulers of Poland. By this agreement also, the northern and southern ends of the Curzon Line went much deeper westward than the British had anticipated, thus depriving Poland of its only oil fields. Naturally, that agreement was irrevocable.[28] In a speedy manner the Presidium of the Supreme Soviet had ratified this.

After the Polish failure to get any share of Soviet reparations and after the edification of Mikolajczyk concerning the origins of the settlement of the Polish-Soviet frontiers, the Warsaw delegation was abruptly told to return home.

Mikolajczyk realized that since the frontiers of Poland had been settled the only hope left was the chance of restoring Poland's independence which lay in the organization of a strong opposition which might win in the promised elections. The Peasant Party, of which he was Vice-Chairman, was definitely the largest in Poland and was willing to oppose the communists. But the communists were quick to paralyze his plans by organizing their version of the Peasant Party. Many of its members believed that it was the genuine pre-war Party. When they discovered what had happened and were anxious to join the true Peasant Party, led by the old and respected Witos, they were threatened by the Security Police not to do so. This forced Witos and Mikolajczyk to change the name of the party to the Polish Peasant Party in order to distinguish it from the communist-sponsored Peasant Party and to ask the communists to grant them pledges and other democratic privileges to which the opposition were entitled under the terms of the Moscow agreement. This action intensified communist vigilance. As a warning to the other leaders of the Polish Peasant Party, Wladyslaw Kojder, a member of the executive committee of the Polish Peasant Party and a courageous critic of the Secret Police, was taken away from his home and murdered. The Party itself, and especially Mikolajczyk, were accused, in a flood of leaflets, of selling Poland to foreign capitalists.[29]

While the communists were determined to paralyze Mikolajczyk's activities inside Poland, they were clever enough to exploit his contacts in the West. Poland needed economic help from the outside very badly. The Soviets could not supply the required items. Only the United States could do so. Therefore, in October 1945 Mikolajczyk was sent to Quebec to attend the first meeting of the United Nations Food and Agricultural Organization and was elected a member of its Executive Committee. On his way home he had a talk with President Truman and Secretary Byrnes, which resulted in substantial UNRRA aid to Poland.[30]

Upon his return to Poland he found that further terror and murder of the members of his party by the Security Police had taken place. After long and persistent pressure upon the communists, the Polish Peasant Party was granted permission to publish three newspapers— two weeklies, *Piast* and *Chlopski Sztandar*, and one daily, *Gazeta Ludowa*—although these were severely censored.

The communists decided to eliminate the Peasant influence in the *Sejm* (Parliament) where, according to the Moscow agreement, Mikolajczyk's group was to have one-third of the 435 seats. Instead, the communists offered the Peasant Party only thirty seats instead of the 145 they were entitled to. This led to a walk-out of the Polish Peasant Party from the Sejm. In January 1946, Bierut offered the Polish Peasant Party fifty-two seats which they accepted in order to insure that the proposed "legislation" would be checked by the opposition. Being a small minority, they could not defeat the bills which, among other things, nationalized printing shops and those private enterprises which employed more than fifty workers.[31]

On January 19, 1946 the Polish Peasant Party had its first congress in Warsaw which unanimously elected Mikolajczyk to succeed Witos, recently deceased and passed a resolution calling upon the Government to terminate immediately the prevailing terror, to abolish the Ministry of the Security Police, and to place the police under the Ministry of Interior instead. Moreover, it asked for the abolition of the Ministry of Propaganda, which had become an instrument of communist indoctrination, and speedy elections as well as the establishment of freedom under the rule of law and not of the Communist Party.

In reply, the Security Police intensified the terror over members of the Polish Peasant Party. Numerous murders were committed in various parts of Poland. Peasants were warned not to join their Party. Thirty-six district organizations of the P.P.P. were dissolved by the Government. All meetings of the peasants were forbidden. The main headquarters of the Party in Warsaw was raided by the Security Police, the records seized, the interior demolished, and the clerks arrested. During the terroristic interrogation, they were asked to serve as spies. A great number of peasant dwellings were burned by the Security Police.

The communists ignored the protests of the Peasant leaders. They wanted to break the backbone of the Polish opposition before the election, promised at Potsdam, took place. When the resistance of the patriots mounted in strength, the communists attempted to evade the election altogether by staging a cunningly contrived Referendum in order to present its results to the Western Powers as "proof" of the unanimity of the Polish Nation on the major issues and therefore to eliminate the necessity for holding an election. The Polish Peasant Party decided to take part in the Referendum only after the Government promised to hold the election in the autumn of 1946.[32]

The questions submitted to the people for decision were as follows:

1. Are you in favor of the abolition of the Senate? [33]
2. Are you in favor of making permanent, through the future Constitution, the economic system instituted by the land reform and nationalization of the basic industries, with the maintenance of the rights of private enterprise?
3. Are you in favor of the Polish western frontiers as fixed on the Baltic and on the Oder and Neisse?

The Polish Peasant Party decided to vote "Yes" on the second and third questions and "No" on the first in order to show the power of opposition. On the whole, they were against retaining the Upper House of Parliament because it was superfluous. When the opposition made its decision public, the communists resorted to another wave of terror and arrests which did not break the determination of the peasants. Actually, all other patriotic elements joined the peasants as the only patriotic party in Poland.

The Referendum took place on June 30, 1946. The true results of the Referendum to question number one were "No"—83.54%, "Yes" —16.46%. The communists were embarrassed and afraid of Moscow. For ten days there was no official announcement of the results and when it finally came it stated that 32% had voted "No" and 68% "Yes." [34]

The Polish Peasant Party protested, producing evidence that the Referendum was distorted. It cited examples of packed voting lists, false entries, and the arrest of over 1,000 of the members of the opposition. This protest, like all previous ones, was ignored.[35]

In order to divert the attention of the West from the results of the Referendum, the Security Police staged a Jewish pogrom (massacre) in Kielce, where over eighty Jews were murdered or wounded. This was widely publicized, and Gomulka accused the Polish Peasant Party of staging the massacre as revenge for the lost Referendum, while Osobka-Morawski accused Cardinal Hlond of provoking the people to the murder of the Jews.[36]

Fortunately, other Jews who escaped their executors revealed the real culprits to the foreign press. The communists overcame this embarrassing development by finding scapegoats among local communists and making them responsible for the crime.

Mikolajczyk realized that all his protests were without effect, so he decided to hold a press conference for the American, British, Russian, and French correspondents, during which he read a prepared statement giving details as to how the Referendum had been forged and stating the true results. Then followed a period of questions and answers.

Q. Did the Polish Peasant Party attempt to publish its results?

A. Yes, but this was immediately censored.

Q. Was an attempt made to publish your protests?

A. Yes, and this also was censored.

Q. What are your Party's plans for the forthcoming elections?

A. Let me first say that we received thousands of letters after the Referendum, all expressing the deepest regret and indignation over the fraud. The percentage of voters was high because people wanted to express their will legally. Now they ask us if we will be able to secure an honest election, in view of what happened at the Referendum. Many say that unless they can be assured of an honest election they will not go to the polls.

To provide an honest election each Commission will have to be representative of all parties. Legal guarantees must be found to secure all persons from terror. Armed men must be removed from polling places. The Polish Peasant Party must receive guarantees of its freedom of action, particularly with reference to meetings, censorship, allotment of paper, an increased issue of periodicals, and the right to use the radio.

I might add that many of the letters received after the Referendum urged us to secure from the Big Three Powers a guarantee that the elections will follow the line agreed to in Yalta.

Q. Is what you outline the program of the Polish Peasant Party or the will of the nation?

A. This is the voice of simple people, written from the heart. The parliamentary fraction of our Party will advance proposals for legal security from abuses committed in the Referendum. We hope to avoid a repetition.

Q. How many Commission members were there from the Polish Peasant Party during the Referendum?

A. There were about fourteen thousand Commissions spread through the country that day, totalling about seventy thousand members. We had been guaranteed a one-third representation on such boards. But only about three thousand Polish Peasant Party members were permitted to serve on the day in question.[37]

The Western press printed the results of this press conference. The communists were furious and called Mikolajczyk a traitor.

On August 19 the British and American Governments sent a strong protest to the Warsaw regime condemning the communist practices and asked for a free and democratic election with all rights for the opposition, as envisaged in the Potsdam Agreement.

In reply, Bierut instructed his Ambassadors to deliver a vigorous rebuttal to the Americans and the British, accusing them of infringing upon the sovereign and internal rights of Poland.[38]

4. Preparation for and Execution of the Elections of January 1947

On August 28, the Warsaw communists were called to Moscow where they were given instructions by Stalin on how to secure the "proper results" from the forthcoming elections, and were impressed with the necessity of ignoring Western "interference" into their internal affairs. Mikolajczyk and his Party were going to be liquidated if they did not join the Government bloc which would give them 25% of the seats in the Sejm. They would otherwise be branded as enemies of the people, reactionaries, etc., in order to be discredited at home and abroad.[39]

The political position of Mikolajczyk and the Polish Peasant Party was aggravated by a policy statement of the American Secretary of State. On September 16, 1946 Secretary Byrnes made a speech in Stuttgart in which he declared that the decision about eastern German territories at the Potsdam Conference had been unilaterally interpreted by Stalin to mean that the Oder-Neisse Line was the permanent Polish western frontier. He assured his German audience that it was not permanent.[40]

From the point of view of the democratic elements in Poland, the Western Powers could not have committed a worse blunder. It was only a year after Germany had surrendered, but as the communists interpreted Byrnes's speech, the American Government was already supporting Germany against Poland. Mikolajczyk's political assets diminished considerably as a result of this speech, because he was the one who symbolized Western support to the Poles. After Byrnes's speech they realized that Western support meant nothing. The communists, on the other hand, were delighted by this turn of events which convinced many Poles that the only "friend" they had was the Soviet Union. They proceeded to exploit this situation swiftly.

Throughout Poland powerful demonstrations by the population take place against the questioning by Byrnes of the inviolability of Poland's frontiers.[41]

The communists coupled Byrnes's speech with that of Churchill, delivered at Fulton, Missouri on March 3, in which he said that Poland made "enormous and wrongful inroads upon Germany." [42]

On September 20, 1946 President Bierut, in a speech delivered at a meeting of the National Home Council, denounced the attacks of Byrnes and Churchill

. . . on our western frontiers. Generalissimo Joseph Stalin declares that the Soviet Union regards Poland's western frontiers as final.[43]

At that time Mikolajczyk was in Copenhagen attending a meeting of the United Nations Food and Agricultural Organization. At a press conference in Copenhagen he protested against the implications of Byrnes's speech, pointing out that this would deprive the people expelled from the east of food and shelter. Moreover, he explained that, since the Western leaders took part in the decision to deprive five million Poles east of the Curzon Line of their homes, they should at least be as concerned with the fate of the homeless Poles as they were with that of the expelled Germans. "Where would those people go?" he asked.[44]

This press conference was widely publicized in the West but it was purposely not reported in the Polish papers.

Vice-Premier Gomulka organized a huge mob in Warsaw which gathered in front of the American Embassy to protest Byrnes's speech. Then the demonstrators were directed towards the headquarters of the Polish Peasant Party, which they proceeded to demolish. They destroyed all the equipment, the files, and the printing presses. Mikolajczyk and his Party press, which were not allowed to publish any protest against Byrnes's speech, were accused of being "pro-Hitlerite and opposed to the Western frontier." [45]

Furthermore, the communists said, the ruling circles of the United States believed that by means of economic and diplomatic pressure they would succeed in handing power in Poland to people of Mikolajczyk's brand, of whom representatives of the United States Government spoke and wrote as "their men."

. . . in her peaceful activities Poland faced obstacles which resulted above all from the conspiracy of the imperialists wanting to restore in Poland the rule of capitalists and semi-feudal landlords, to turn her again into a plaything in their hands and a source of immense profits. It was American imperialism that proved to be the most determined antagonist of People's Poland, an antagonist trying from the very first day of her existence by all means to block the way to her development.[46]

Having "established" Mikolajczyk's "guilt," the communists renewed their vigorous and extensive terrorizing campaign against his Party and nipped in the bud the re-establishment of the Christian Labor Party of Karol Popiel, whose free existence was provided for by the Moscow agreement. Peasants were murdered and their property confiscated. Still other peasants were arrested. Farms were burned. District offices of the Party were closed or destroyed. District organizations of the peasants were dissolved. The chief editor of the only peasant daily, the *Gazeta Ludowa*, and several of his men were arrested. Pressure was put on the peasants to join the Government bloc or face complete annihilation as a political organization. The Polish Peasant Party refused to surrender.

Instead Mikolajczyk sent Stalin a memorandum requesting intervention to stop these abuses of power; and then, when a reply was not forthcoming, he sent the same memorandum to the three Ambassadors of the United States, the United Kingdom, and the U.S.S.R. In this he stated that, as of December 1, 1946, twenty-two members of the Supreme Council, seven members of provisional executive committees, one hundred forty-nine members of district committees, six hundred seventy members of local executive committees, and scores of thousands of regular members of the Polish Peasant Party were in prison. A list of the names of those people was included as well as the details of the methods used by the communists to destroy the opposition.[47]

In its reply of January 5, 1947, the United States Government sent the following note to the Warsaw regime, as well as to London and Moscow.

The United States Government is especially perturbed by the increasingly frequent reports of repressive measures which the Polish Provisional Government has seen fit to employ against those democratic elements in Poland which have not aligned themselves with the Bloc parties.

According to information reaching this Government from various authoritative sources, these repressive activities have increased in intensity to the point where, if they do not cease immediately, there is little likelihood that elections can be held in accordance with the terms of the Potsdam Agreement, which call for free and unfettered elections on the basis of universal suffrage and secret ballot in which all democratic and anti-Nazi parties shall have the right to take part and put forward candidates.

On December 18, 1946 M. Mikolajczyk addressed a communication to the United States Ambassador in Warsaw in which he called attention to the reprehensible methods employed by the Provisional Government in denying freedom of political action to the Polish Peasant Party. . . . Authoritative reports from other quarters in Poland serve to substantiate the charges brought by M. Mikolajczyk.

What is involved here is the sanctity of international agreements, a principle upon which depends the establishment and maintenance of peace and the reign of justice under law. The obligations with respect to the Polish elections which the United States Government assumed at Yalta and reiterated at Potsdam together with the Soviet and British Governments, provide for the conduct of free and unfettered elections of the type and in the manner described above. . . . For this reason, it is the United States Government's view that it is both a duty and a right for all three Powers who are parties to the Yalta and Potsdam Agreements to call to the attention of the Polish Government the failure of that Government to perform its obligations.

The United States Government feels that it would be failing in its duty if it did not make further efforts prior to the elections to ameliorate the conditions under which certain democratic elements of the Polish population are now struggling to take their rightful part in the national elections. It intends, therefore, in the immediate future again to approach the Polish Government with a reminder of its obligations and to call upon it to provide these conditions of security which will enable all democratic and anti-Nazi parties to take full part in the elections.[48]

Angered by this note, the communists in Warsaw and in Moscow, in separate but almost identical replies, accused the United States of interference in the internal affairs of Poland and charged that America had obtained its information solely from "anti-democratic elements" in Poland. The communists were confident that the West's support of Mikolajczyk and the democratic elements would be limited to paper protests and could, therefore, be ignored.

In order to bring further discredit upon Mikolajczyk and his Party, they staged several "show" trials of his followers, during which "evidence" was provided to "prove" that the United States Embassy and the British Ambassador, Cavendish Bentinck, were involved in activities hostile to the Polish State. On the basis of these trials, innocent people were executed in order to "prove" that the American and British Governments had no right to interfere in Polish affairs.[49] Other trials were confined to providing "evidence" that Mikolajczyk and the entire leadership of the Polish Peasant Party were acting in the interest of Western foreign powers and that, therefore, they were betraying the Polish people. All "proofs" were obtained by extraordinarily severe terrorization of the victims selected by the Security

Police. All of these intimidations were intended to minimize the effectiveness of the opposition in the forthcoming elections. Every conceivable form of chicanery, blackmail, terror, arrest, and murder known to the Security Police and to the NKVD was applied to break the determination of the peasants to vote for a free Poland. All "legal" electoral devices were used to prevent the Polish Peasant Party from registering its candidates, from distributing its literature and from presenting its case to the people.[50] Over seven thousand members of district and local organizations, as well as the provisional executive committees of the Polish Peasant Party were put in prison by the Security Police.[51]

The Soviet General Korczyc, the Chief of Staff of the Polish Army, issued the following order to specially selected military units as to how to liquidate the Polish Peasant Party.

You should inform the broad masses of peasants that in the fight which is going on in Poland and which seeks to establish firmly the freedom, independence and democratic form of Poland, the Polish Army, the iron hand of the People's Poland, marches in the first line.

You should improve the conditions of security in our country and show to all who are open to the advice of the fascist underground (and to their legal supporters—the P.P.P.) the strength of our Government and of the Democratic Front.

You are obliged to counteract actively the hostile underground propaganda and the propaganda of the Polish Peasant Party which supports the bandits. You must penetrate in your action to the most remote hamlets and villages and bring to them the truth about democratic Poland.

The task of the Defense-Propaganda groups is not the hunting of armed gangs. . . . Commanders must study the political conditions along the route of operations. They must study carefully what is the strength and influence of the Polish Peasant Party in each locality, prepare a list of all outstanding political leaders, and mark the more active leaders of the P.P.P. in the locality and watch their activities.

The cost of military quarters for the groups, and their food, will be secured from the farmers of the locality, the local mayor or chairman of the local council.

Upon arriving in a new area commands should contact the local administration and make an immediate investigation of political conditions. After securing food and quarters, mass meetings of the village or area must be scheduled. Knowledge of the influence of the P.P.P. is especially important. Inquiries must be made about the strength of the party in the area, how its members behave in the local cooperatives, how they carry on their duties. Their personal lives and business transactions must be searched, also their association with the distribution of such UNRRA supplies as reached the area.

Dates of local mass meetings should be fixed in consultation with the mayor. Soldiers should be used to inform the people. Clergymen must be told to announce the dates and sites of meetings. Demobilized soldiers in the appointed area must be advised to cooperate and take part in the campaign.

Announcements should carry the names of local leaders, several of whom should be secured to speak in a favorable manner. If a meeting fails because of the absence of the people another must be scheduled and steps taken to secure proper attendance. The defense group must take part in the meeting, but not in loose formation. It must be in military formation and stationed close to the entrance of the assembly hall or other site.

Agendas of all meetings will include (1) Opening speech of the commander, followed by a speech of a local leader (2) Question period (3) Resolution condemning the P.P.P., and closing.

The P.P.P. must be attacked along these lines: Members do not pay taxes or offer public rehabilitation services; they support the underground gangs; they soon will be liquidated by the Government. The question period must be very short. Organizers must prevent discussion or any effort to turn the questions into a line sympathetic to the P.P.P. If a questioner becomes too brave and asks undesirable questions he must be immediately attacked as an instigator, provocator and hostile towards the Government and the State.

Propaganda material should be carefully distributed. The pamphlet "Soldier's Word" should be handed generously to each farmer and he must be warned that this is a military book and cannot be destroyed. Posters must be placed on the walls of P.P.P. members' dwellings. The owner must be present while the posting takes place, his name must be noted and he must be warned that he is personally responsible for its safekeeping.

Soldiers are not permitted to walk alone, but in groups. Their instructions in the political fight must be continuous. The people of each area must be told that the group will come again to test their political consciousness and knowledge. Attitudes of teachers, priests, local mayors and P.P.P. leaders must be forwarded in memoranda at frequent periods.[52]

Other instructions were issued to the military garrison of Praga, a suburb of Warsaw, which stated:

You are authorized to make arrests and executions of Peasant Party members. You must seize their party cards, and you may take other personal effects. You must at all times charge that Mikolajczyk is pro-German and a traitor. The Polish Peasant Party must be thoroughly terrorized before election time. Mass meetings must be forced to promise to vote for the bloc. It must be made apparent that the party and its supporters will be exterminated immediately after the elections.[53]

Various magazines and papers printed for soldiers were full of unfounded accusations against the Polish Peasant Party, the United States, and Great Britain. They intended to remove any scruples the soldiers might have had in carrying out their orders to destroy the Polish Peasant Party. The peasants were equally determined to resist all forms of pressure and terror.[54] The instinct of self-preservation and five years of experience under the German occupation were of the greatest assistance in carrying out this new task.

On January 18, 1947 Mikolajczyk delivered the second note of protest against the Warsaw regime to the Soviet, American, and British Ambassadors in which he supplied evidence of the reign of terror and all other illegal communist methods. He charged that over one hundred thousand of his Party men were under arrest.

Since the prisons were already overcrowded, the communists had herded these people, many of whom were women, into open fields, surrounded them with barbed wire, and kept them there. It was January, the coldest month of the year, with the temperature below 0° C, yet these stalwart people refused to betray their democratic ideals when they were asked to withdraw their support of the Peasant Party.

The same day Mikolajczyk repeated all his information at a press conference which he summoned especially for this purpose. No mention of this press conference, however, appeared in the Polish communist-controlled press.[55]

On the following day communist-style elections were held all over Poland.[56] Only thirty-six witnesses of the Peasant Party were allowed to be present during the counting of the ballots in 5,200 polling places. In those thirty-six polling places the Polish Peasant Party officially gained between 65% and 85% of the majority of the votes, which the communists were bound to recognize.

On January 28, 1947 the communists published the results. Out of a total electorate of 12,701,056 voters, 11,413,618 cast their votes. The published results were as follows.[57]

Government Bloc	394 seats
Polish Peasant Party	28 seats
Christian Labor Party	12 seats
PSL, New Liberation Party	7 seats
Catholic Progressive Party	3 seats
Total	444 seats

The Polish Peasant Party once more filed a protest with the Government. All instances where violations of the electoral law had occurred were verified by dates, places, and names of the guilty, as well as by the testimony of witnesses. Immediately afterwards, all of these witnesses were arrested by the Security Police under the *ad hoc* fabricated pretext that they were "enemies of the Polish people."[58]

Consequently Mikolajczyk submitted a detailed memorandum on the "free and unfettered elections" to the American and British Ambassadors. Soon after, both these Governments registered their disapproval of the communist methods in conducting the elections and said that they "cannot consider that the provisions of the Yalta and Potsdam Agreements have been fulfilled." [59]

By that time the Warsaw communists were firmly in power and had learned to ignore paper protests from the West.

The United States Ambassador to Poland, Arthur Bliss Lane, a dedicated friend of the Polish people, could not reconcile himself with the ineffectual manner in which his Government attempted to enforce the Yalta and Potsdam Agreements. In a protest against this policy, he submitted the following letter of resignation to President Truman.[60]

My reasons for asking you to relieve me of the post with which I was entrusted by you and by President Roosevelt are the following: My principal duty in Poland, outside of the protection of American interests, was under the terms of the Yalta decision, to report to my Government regarding conditions in Poland in connection with the elections which were held on January 19, 1947. As you know, these elections were not "free and unfettered" as the Polish Provisional Government of National Unity had previously pledged, in keeping with the Yalta and Potsdam agreements. Quite the contrary, the pre-election period was characterized by coercion, intimidation and violence—thus rendering the elections a farce and indicating on the part of the Polish Government a cynical disregard of its international obligations.

Under the circumstances I feel that I can do far more for the cause of relations between the peoples of the United States and Poland if I should revert to the status of a private citizen and thus be enabled to speak and write openly, without being hampered by diplomatic convention, regarding the present tragedy of Poland.[61]

Truman accepted Lane's resignation and appointed Stanton Griffis to succeed him. Since communist violations of the Yalta and Potsdam Agreements had not resulted in a United States refusal to recognize the new Polish Government or even in a break in diplomatic relations with them, the Warsaw regime presumably interpreted the change of ambassadors to mean that, while the United States did not approve of the communist implementation of Yalta and Potsdam, nevertheless the United States would not do very much about it. Consequently, they continued to reinforce their power, undeterred by any fear of outside intervention.

5. The Aftermath

At the opening session of the new Sejm, Bierut was elected President of the Polish People's Republic by a vote of 408 to 25. The next move was the establishment of a so-called "Small Constitution," as an "interim law" before the new Constitution was drafted. Under the terms of the "Small Constitution" the "Council of State" was created which was composed of the President, the Speaker, three Deputies, and three other individuals chosen by the Sejm. Their power was absolute and therefore superior even to that of the communist-controlled Sejm. They could make any decision or initiate any laws, and the Sejm was bound to obey and support them. Mikolajczyk and his supporters resigned from the Government, and their small group in the Sejm furiously and indefatigably attacked the totalitarian measures in the hope that foreign correspondents present in the Sejm galleries would take notice of what was going on. Through them the Polish Peasant Party intended to appeal to the conscience of the West. But the Western Powers were not interested in getting involved in any further difficulties with the Soviet Union. Indeed, the British Government saw fit to invite Judge Kazimierz Bzowski, who had been in charge of the recent election, to England together with three other lawyers who had helped him in falsifying the election returns. This was a shock to the Polish people.[62]

This British indifference to the methods with which the communists decided to fulfill their Yalta and Potsdam obligations may be partly explained by the following incident. Early in February, 1947 Richard K. Law, the former Minister of State in Churchill's Cabinet, addressed the students of Reading University in England on the international situation. During the discussion one of the British listeners asked him what would have been the attitude of the Conservative Government, if it had been in power, towards the recent election in Eastern Europe (meaning Poland). In answer Law stated:

> The wartime Coalition Government in general, and the Conservatives in particular, were and are of the opinion that the Eastern European nations are not mature politically to govern themselves, so we were always of the opinion that Eastern Europe should be under the Soviet sphere of influence while Western Europe, including Germany, should be under ours.

When this writer asked the speaker if by his answer he meant to imply that the Soviets were more mature politically than Eastern Europe and that Holland, Denmark, Belgium, France, and other Western European nations were incapable of self-rule, Mr. Law was slightly embarrassed.

In April 1947 the communists changed their tactics. The Minister of the Security Police, Radkiewicz, addressing his police and the communists in Lodz and other places, told them:

> . . . there will be a war with the West. It will be won by the U.S.S.R. Of that there must be no doubt. Therefore, first, we must indoctrinate the

people of Poland for that war. They must be told that American capitalists want to rule the world and because they fear the economic collapse of the United States and that in order to avert such a catastrophe they have forced their Government into a policy of world-wide imperialism, a war will result.

In Poland we must quietly prepare for that war by liquidating the Peasant Party and the remnants of independent thought in the Socialist Party. We trust the top Socialist leaders. They are our men. But the dissenting rank and file must be crushed. Polish youth must be prepared and trained. . . .[63]

This standard communist technique of justifying their more stern measures by referring to a possible war which the actions of the communist bloc were actually provoking, proved to be effective.

The Security Police proceeded to apply these instructions against the peasants, the Church, and the youth of the nation. The unarmed nation had to face 230,000 Security policemen, who were divided as follows: 90,000 were spread all over the country in special police stations; 100,000 were in formal military units; and 40,000 were plain-clothesmen. There also were 120,000 of the so-called O.R.M.O., or "Voluntary Police," who cooperated with the Security Police. In addition to the above, 300,000 men of the Red Army and 200,000 of the Polish Army were stationed in Poland at that time. Together with the NKVD they took part in remolding the national character of the Polish people. The members of the Communist Party served as spies and denunciators. In spite of these formidable obstacles, patriotic elements did not give up the struggle, although their available strength was not up to their great courage.

On October 18 Mikolajczyk learned from reliable sources that he and three other members of the Sejm would be deprived of parliamentary immunity at the opening session of the Parliament on October 20 and that a military court in Warsaw had already been instructed to try them and sentence them to death. The communists accused Mikolajczyk of being a Western agent.[64]

Fearing that his execution would lead to a possible mass slaughter, Mikolajczyk decided to escape to the free world. The United States Ambassador, Stanton Griffis, provided help which made that escape successful.[65]

As former Ambassador to Poland Stanton Griffis put it,

The story of Mikolajczyk stands out as a light in the communist darkness. . . .

Had he not escaped the country he would not be alive today. It will be remembered that it was Mikolajczyk who apparently, in the minds of both the United States and Great Britain, was meant to be the catalytic agent between Russia, the Lublin Government and the Polish Exile Government in London. . . . . Mikolajczyk fought hard for his Party and to obtain voting control of the Government, but the famous "free elections" of January 1947 substantially ended any hope of power which the Peasant Party had and Mikolajczyk was relegated to a minor ministry, and finally to an obscure though active position in the Parliament. . . .

During the last three quarters of 1947 a series of political trials were conducted involving about 100 alleged members of the underground secret organizations who had been arrested in 1946 and early 1947. Charges invariably involved treason, espionage for "foreign powers," and collusion with Mikolajczyk and the Peasant Party. Defendants were uniformly convicted and death sentences were pronounced in a majority of instances. . . .

Puppet pro-communist leaders immediately moved in to control his organization, the Peasant Party, and its newspapers and October 20, 1947, substantially marked the end of legal or organized opposition to the Government in Poland.[66]

The last gigantic effort of the Polish Nation to free itself from tyranny had failed. Much new blood had soaked into the soil. The bodies of courageous people covered the mournful Polish landscape with a mass of new graves.

The question arises: Was all this necessary? In terms of subsequent developments it was not. Nothing had been achieved and the price had been high. But, to be fair to these people, the future was unknown at that time.

Mikolajczyk's courageous attempt to help his people had failed, but some sacrifice had been warranted. Having only the fault of over-confidence in the integrity of others, he had trusted Western leaders when they said that Poland would not be abandoned in the face of communist aggression. The Polish nation believed that his personal courage was based on his conviction and knowledge that in the crucial moment England and America would come to the rescue—not only of Mikolajczyk but of a brave nation facing impending slavery. Like Mikolajczyk, they could not believe that they would be left alone to struggle with the antagonistic despots, well trained in the art of terror.

When Mikolajczyk arrived in London, the other Poles who had not trusted the communist promises pointed out to him that they, and not he, had been right, and in their bitterness, they branded him a traitor.[67] However, they did not realize that Mikolajczyk's mission was needed in order to prove that they were right and that the Western Powers were wrong in the belief that a compromise could be reached with the communists. The Polish Nation and Mikolajczyk proved that good will and a sincere desire to live in friendship with the communists had been on their side. If Mikolajczyk had not gone back and made that attempt, undoubtedly the apologists for Soviet policies, or the misinformed, would have said that it was the fault of the London Poles that the communists had taken over Poland.

Churchill arranged for Mikolajczyk to address a private meeting of the members of the House of Commons. In introducing him, Churchill remarked, "I never thought that I would see M. Mikolajczyk alive again."

After describing the events which had led to the complete subordination of Poland to communist dictatorship, Mikolajczyk observed:

One of the factors which eased the Western conscience in settling the future of Poland directly with the Soviets was the assumption that the Poles did not know exactly what democracy meant. Gentlemen, you know from your own correspondents who were in Poland during the elections how courageously the Polish nation defied communist threats, intimidation, arrests and torture in order to try to secure freedom for herself. I ask you: How many people in the Western democracies would have done as much if they had found themselves in a similar position, where their freedom was in mortal danger?

The members of the House of Commons responded by giving him a warm ovation.[68]

In Mikolajczyk's escape from Poland, the communists found another pretext with which they could "justify" their complete liquidation of political opposition. Once this was accomplished Poland became completely subordinated to the Soviet Union.

By and large, the individuals who are selected by the Soviets to rule the Polish Nation are those whose past renders them vulnerable to immediate removal or liquidation. This situation makes them completely dependent on their Soviet superiors, and their willingness and anxiety to serve the Soviet Union to save their own skins is one of the most powerful means by which the Soviet Union can perpetuate its rule over a nation which wants to be free.[69] This is the upshot of what the Soviets meant when they referred to a "free, strong, and friendly Poland."

Thus a nation which, without quite enjoying the Western brand of democracy, nevertheless made the supreme sacrifice that she might more fully establish it, was abandoned by her Allies and engulfed in the tyranny of communism.

Churchill himself wrote:

So far only dust and ashes had been gathered, and these are all that remain to us today of Polish national freedom.[70]

And to the Polish nation, the sweat of the exploited, the tears of the betrayed, and the blood of the slain patriots became the chief harvest of its unmerited enslavement.

Notes

[1] Winston S. Churchill, *Triumph and Tragedy*, p. 651.

[2] *Ibid.*

[3] *Ibid.*, p. 652.

[4] *Ibid.*, p. 653.

[5] *Ibid.*

[6] Harry S. Truman, *Year of Decisions*, Garden City, New York, Doubleday & Company, Inc., 1955, p. 366.

[7] Churchill, *op. cit.*, p. 655. Also, Truman, *op. cit.*, pp. 367, 368.

[8] Churchill, *loc. cit.*, p. 658.

[9] Churchill, *loc. cit.*, p. 661. Also, Truman, *op. cit.*, p. 373.

[10] *Mikolajczyk's Private Files*, Vol. CXV, Doc. 1.

[11] *Ibid.*, Doc. 2.

[12] *Ibid.*, Doc. 2a.

[13] *Ibid.*, Doc. 3.

[14] *Ibid.*

[15] *Ibid.*, Doc. 4.

[16] *Ibid.*, Doc. 5.

[17] *Ibid.*, Doc. 7.

[18] *Ibid.*, Doc. 10.

[19] See *Nowa Polska* (New Poland Monthly), Tom. III, Londyn, Wrzesien, 1944, pp. 564–586.
Also, *Ibid.*, Listopad 1944, pp. 721–740.

[20] S. Balinski, A. Slonimski (who later became head of the Polish delegation to UNESCO), K. Estreicher (who was appointed Professor at the University of Krakow), M. Pruszynski (who was appointed as Cultural Attaché to the Polish Embassy in Rome), and J. Winiewicz (who later was appointed as Ambassador to the United States).

[21] Bearing in mind the example of Margrave Wielopolski (1803–1874) who, during the Tsarist occupation of Poland sacrificed himself for a similar cause, Pruszynski wrote the above as his political testament, and, before going to Poland, left it with this author to be delivered at an appropriate time to his children if anything should happen to him.

[22] Jozef Swiatlo, *Inside Story of Bezpieka* (Security Police) *and the Communist Party*, No. 21–22, New York, Radio Free Europe, 1954, to be found in the files of the Political Adviser of Radio Free Europe.

[23] It must be stated that the official attitude of the British Government toward those Poles who, in spite of British pressure to return to Poland, decided to remain in Britain was very correct. Those who had served in the armed forces were offered British citizenship and were helped in resettlement.

[24] *Mikolajczyk's Private Files*, Vol. CXV, Doc. 12.

[25] *Ibid.*, Vol. CII, Doc. 4a.

[26] *Ibid.*, Doc. 4.

[27] *Ibid.*, Doc. 5. For a detailed account of these negotiations see Mikolajczyk, *op. cit.*, pp. 140–142.

[28] *Mikolajczyk's Private Files*, Vol. CII, Doc. 7.

[29] *Ibid.*

[30] *Ibid.*, Docs. 8–9.

[31] *Ibid.*, Doc. 12.

[32] *Ibid.*, Doc. 14.

[33] Upper House of Parliament.

[34] *Mikolajczyk's Private Files*, Vol. CII, Docs. 15–25. For a summary account of the methods by which the Referendum was staged see Mikolajczyk, *op. cit.*, pp. 161–179.

[35] *Mikolajczyk's Private Files*, Vol. CII, Docs. 26–30.

[36] *Ibid.*, Doc. 32.

[37] *Ibid.*, Doc. 31.

[38] *Ibid.*, Doc. 32.

[39] *Ibid.*, Doc. 34.

[40] Poland, Ministry for Foreign Affairs of the Polish People's Republic, *Documents on the Hostile Policy of the United States Government towards People's Poland*, Warsaw, 1953, p. 13.

[41] *Ibid.*, p. 12.

[42] *Ibid.*, p. 11.

[43] *Ibid.*, p. 13.

[44] *Mikolajczyk's Private Files*, Vol. CII, Doc. 35.

[45] *Ibid.*, Docs. 36–37.

[46] Poland, Ministry for Foreign Affairs of the Polish People's Republic, *Documents on the Hostile Policy of the United States Government towards People's Poland*, Warsaw, 1953, p. 6.

[47] *Mikolajczyk's Private Files*, Vol. CII, Docs. 37–43.

[48] *Ibid.*, Doc. 46.

[49] *Ibid.*, Doc. 38.

[50] Mikolajczyk, *op. cit.*, pp. 181–202.

[51] *Mikolajczyk's Private Files*, Vol. CII, Docs. 39–43.

[52] *Ibid.*, Doc. 44.

[53] *Ibid.*, Doc. 51.

[54] *Faked Elections in Poland*, As Reported by Foreign Observers, A. Bregman (ed.), London, The Polish Freedom Movement, 1947; *The Polish Elections*, British Joint Committee for Polish Affairs, London, 1947; Duchess of Athol, *Polish Elections: The Background*, London, The British League for European Freedom, 1947.

[55] *Mikolajczyk's Private Files*, Vol. CII, Doc. 52.

[56] See Appendix 3.

[57] *Mikolajczyk's Private Files*, Vol. CII, Doc. 55. For a first-hand account of the methods used in conducting the elections see Appendix III.

[58] *Ibid.*, Docs. 60–62.

[59] *Ibid.*, Docs. 63–65.

[60] Subsequently, Mr. Lane described his experiences in Poland in a book, *I Saw Poland Betrayed*, Indianapolis, Bobbs-Merrill Company, 1948.

[61] *Faked Elections in Poland*, p. 61.

[62] *Mikolajczyk's Private Files*, Vol. CII, Doc. 67.

[63] *Ibid.*, Vol. CII, Doc. 69.

[64] *Przyczyny Ucieczki Mikolajczyka,* Poznan, Wielkopolska Ksiagarnia Wydawnicza, 1947.

[65] Stanton Griffis, *Lying in State,* Garden City, New York, Doubleday & Company, Inc., 1952, pp. 170–175.

[66] *Ibid.,* pp. 197–198.

[67] One of the minor politicians in the Polish Peasant Party, Stefan Korbonski, writing about this problem stated that Mikolajczyk should have stayed in Poland and been killed.

"This may even be politically profitable. It would open the eyes of the West to what is going on in Poland. The former Polish Premier and Vice Premier in jail or even before the execution squad! This would shake the conscience of the world. But we from the Council of the Polish Peasant Party should find ourselves abroad."

Stefan Korbonski, *W Imieniu Kremla* (In the Name of the Kremlin), Instytut Literacki, Paryz 1956, p. 313.

[68] *Mikolajczyk's Private Files,* Vol. CII, Doc. 76.

[69] See Appendix 4.

[70] Churchill, *op. cit.,* p. 584.

Conclusion

As the foregoing study and subsequent events have shown, the Soviet conquest of Poland was one of the preliminary objectives in the Soviet attempt to establish communist control over all Europe. This plan was nothing new in the history of Soviet foreign policy; indeed, it was among the earliest and most consistent of communist objectives and was explicitly stated to be such. The Soviets' ambition to achieve a communist Europe is as old as the existence of the Soviet Union.

The first attempt to conquer Poland, which stood on their way to Western Europe, had failed in 1920. That bitter experience convinced the rulers in the Kremlin that revolutionary forces in Poland were not powerful enough to fulfill what their orthodox Marxism taught them to be "historically inevitable." The "exploited masses" of Poland did not support Soviet efforts to "liberate" them from their "oppressors"; instead, they most vehemently opposed these Soviet policies. As a result of this and similar experiences in Hungary, Germany, and China, the Soviets were compelled to re-evaluate the effectiveness of the communist-led "proletarian" revolution as a means to expand Soviet power, and they concluded that it would be more realistic to build up the strength of the Soviet State and to use it as the primary instrument to extend communist control over the world. But to do this required time. In order to gain the time necessary to build economic and military strength, they concluded a series of non-aggression and friendship treaties with various European countries, but primarily with their immediate neighbors, of which Poland was one.

By signing the Treaty of Riga in 1921, which ended the Soviet-Polish War, the Soviet Union not only repudiated the Curzon Line as an "unjust frontier" to Poland but publicly stated that the Riga Treaty was more beneficial to the Soviet Union than to Poland. Moreover, the Treaty of Riga implemented Paragraph 3 of Decree No. 698, issued on August 8, 1918 by the Council of Peoples' Commissars, which repudiated the previous partitions of Poland and "recognized the rights of the Polish nation to independence and unity." (See Chapter 2.)

On July 25, 1932 a pact of non-aggression between the Soviet Union and Poland was signed in Moscow. In this pact, both signatories renounced the use of war as an instrument of national policy in their mutual relationships. On May 5, 1934, in the midst of the years when Hitler's policies were beginning to endanger the peace of Europe, this pact was extended to December 31, 1945.

As Soviet behavior has shown, however, Soviet adherence to international treaties is based on expediency. They honor their obligations only as long as they serve Soviet purposes and, in fact, all of the treaties mentioned above were violated by the Soviet Union when it seemed to their advantage to do so.

Once the Soviets realized that by coaxing Hitler to unleash his armies against the West they could benefit from this war, they silenced their criticisms of fascism, rejected Western offers of alliance, and helped plunge Europe into World War II. Although at that time the Soviets could not have foreseen the outcome of Hitler's adventure, they took a calculated risk in precipitating it, nevertheless, and watched the trend of events carefully in order to be able to exploit any weaknesses on either side. Undoubtedly they were aware that they would be welcome as allies of the West, and this awareness broadened their margin of safety in dictating their conditions for "neutrality" with Hitler. The Molotov-Ribbentrop Pact gave the Soviet Union twenty-two months to prepare their own armed forces for combat on either side. It also ceded them territories from Finland, all three Baltic States, Eastern Poland, Northern Bukovina, and Bessarabia.

Having acquired Eastern Poland by force when Poland was engaged in a mortal struggle against the Nazi invader, the Soviets attempted to "legalize" this seizure by staging a "plebiscite." Conducted in the well-known communist fashion, the "elections" were manipulated so as to indicate that the conquered population, in unequivocal terms, had expressed its enthusiastic desire to be incorporated into the

Union of Soviet Socialist Republics. The Soviets graciously complied with the results of this travesty and incorporated the territories into the U.S.S.R. This was another clear-cut violation of the *very* international law to which they themselves claimed to subscribe.

Under the protection of the Red Army, the Soviets made the maximum use of the NKVD and local communists to arrest, deport, and murder local Polish patriots and those whom they considered as potential leaders of the opposition to Soviet rule. These actions signified that the Soviet Union intended to retain these territories regardless of what would happen to the rest of Poland in the course of the war.

When the Nazi-Soviet Pact was terminated in the same way in which the Soviets terminated their own alliances when they ceased to be useful, the Polish Government extended its hand in friendship to the Soviet Union in order to strengthen Allied unity. The Poles wanted to re-establish diplomatic relations on the basis of the Riga Treaty. Although in mortal danger from the rapidly advancing Wehrmacht, the Soviets refused to include any reference to that treaty in their rapprochement with the Poles. Despite the fact that the Soviet Union, in order to survive, was forced to change its allies, its determination to retain the territories acquired as a result of its deal with Hitler never faltered. The Soviet Union was the only state which was able to benefit from its friendship with both the Nazis and the West in World War II. This was the fruit of a foreign policy masterfully calculated to bring the Soviet Union on the stronger side irrespective of previous obligations or of orthodox ideology.

The British, in their anxiety to preserve the appearance of Allied unity, forced the Polish Government to accept Soviet terms despite the fact that these terms omitted any reference to Poland's post-war frontiers. At the same time, the British stated publicly that they did not recognize any territorial changes made after August 1939. The Poles interpreted this to mean that the British were guaranteeing the Polish eastern frontier. This interpretation proved to be wrong.

From the documents cited in the foregoing pages, it is clear that the Soviets were aware of the British attitude toward the Soviet-Polish border dispute and therefore did not see any reason to modify their firm stand.

After the signing of the Soviet-Polish Treaty of 1941, the Soviets never implemented its terms. Within less than four months of signing this treaty, the Soviets established the Union of Polish Patriots in Saratov; on December 31, 1944 this group was transformed into the Lublin Committee and a year later it became the Polish Government of National Unity. This development was possible because the Soviets were aware of British pressure on the Polish Government to comply with the constantly multiplying Soviet demands and *faits accomplis* which the Poles were forced to accept in order not to weaken the Soviet stake in the Western Alliance.

The diplomatic strategy and tactics used toward Poland passed through several phases after the signing of the treaty of 1941. Anxious to extend their control over Eastern Europe and to shorten their borderline with the West, they first concentrated their diplomatic attack on the Polish frontier question.

After enlisting British and American support for this program, they proceeded to undermine the power of the Polish Government, accusing it of hostility toward the Soviet Union and of harboring anti-Soviet elements within its councils. This led to a direct Soviet interference in the question of what should be the composition of the Polish Government. When the Poles rejected these demands, the Soviets achieved their objective by inducing the British Government to exert pressure upon the Poles. By being able to convince the British of the justice of their accusations, the Soviets managed to make the Polish Government appear guilty in the eyes of the other Western Allies and were thus able to discredit it. Once this was achieved, Soviet diplomacy could with impunity heap on the London Government all manner of accusations and blame for the Soviet-Polish dispute. In the third phase, the tactics of Soviet foreign policy were directed toward dividing Polish political leaders and political parties from each other, alienating the armed forces from the Polish Government, and undermining the support which Polish settlements abroad gave the London Government. Finally, the advance of the Red Army into Poland enabled the Soviets to destroy the underground military and political organizations which were the ultimate source of power of the London Government and to impose upon the Polish nation a tightly organized network of control, consisting of the Secret Police, the Communist Party, and the Soviet-sponsored Army as the principal elements. This, coupled with Soviet diplomatic maneuvers to deprive the Polish Government of British and American support, effectively reduced to insignificance the diplomatic effectiveness and prestige of the Polish Government.

The success of these tactics was greatly aided by the mistaken assumption of the British that post-war Europe would be organized according to the theory of the balance of power. The British tacitly acknowledged the Soviet Union as the dominant state of Eastern Europe in return for its presumed willingness to recognize a similar position for Britain in Western Europe. The United States, being relatively uninterested in European politics, did not object to this clearly developing pattern of diplomacy. This was the background for the Teheran and the Yalta Conferences.

Anticipating Stalin's position on Poland and wishing to secure his support for other mutual problems of the Allies, Churchill opened the discussion of the Polish question at Teheran by throwing the support of the British Government behind Soviet demands for the Curzon Line as the new Soviet-Polish frontier. Stalin readily accepted the British support, and Roosevelt did not object. The Soviets interpreted Roosevelt's silence to mean support for their claims. Thus, the Polish-Soviet frontier dispute was settled at Teheran in the Soviets' favor without previous consultation with the duly elected representatives of the Polish Nation.

At Yalta, the Big Three determined the political future of the now truncated Poland without so much as consulting the Polish Government. This was done as a result of the two Western Allies agreeing to recognize the Soviet-controlled Lublin Government after the addition of four Poles from abroad to the cabinet of that government. Churchill and Roosevelt chose to trust in Stalin's promises to establish a "strong, free, and democratic Poland" and decided to ignore his previous record in his dealings with Poland. This record included the deportation of Poles to Russia, the liquidation of numerous Polish patriots, the Katyn Massacre, the deliberate abandonment of the Warsaw insurgents and their pitiless immolation to the Germans, the execution of numerous members of the Home Army, the intimidation of the Polish nation through NKVD terror, and the continued demonstration of bad faith on the part of the Soviets in their dealings with Poland. Against such a background, it is difficult to understand how Churchill and Roosevelt could believe in Stalin's promises to carry out the terms of the agreement, for both Churchill and Roosevelt had unrestricted access to the Soviet record. The enslavement of Poland was the price the Western Powers had to pay for their belief that Soviet verbal promises could be trusted.

It has been argued that if the Yalta Agreement had been carried out by the Soviets, there would not have been any betrayal of democratic principles and that the countries which are now under Soviet control would still be free. This argument is indefensible, at least in the case of Poland. Once the Soviets had established their own brand of government inside Poland, it was obvious that it would have to be subservient to Soviet purposes, which were clearly defined in communist writings well before either Teheran or Yalta, as were Hitler's objectives in *Mein Kampf*. From the Soviets' agreement to give 25% of the cabinet posts to the "Poles from abroad" in a cabinet controlled by the communists, one could not expect that this minority could alter the character of the government even if the communists did adhere to the principles of majority rule. The Lublin Government's determination to stay in power would in any case have induced them to falsify the promised elections in order to give "legal" sanction to their seizure of power. It appears that the Yalta decision with respect to Poland was based on a complete disregard of twenty-eight years of Soviet practices. As Professor Sidney Hook observed, "Had Roosevelt and Churchill and their advisers been better informed of them they would have been better prepared for the Soviet strategy of the Cold War." [1]

The record shows that it was primarily Churchill and Eden and secondarily Roosevelt and his advisers who, by their negative attitude toward the Polish Government, encouraged Stalin to be uncompromising in his demands with respect to Poland. Then, for the sake of "larger" questions of military strategy and Allied unity, they acceded to Stalin's demands and agreed to his terms of settlement of the Soviet-Polish dispute.

For Churchill and Roosevelt this meant the establishment of a somewhat smaller but free Poland through genuinely free elections, whereas for Stalin it meant the liquidation of a free Poland and the creation of a Soviet satellite. Since the Western Powers did not then or subsequently show any determination to enforce their interpretation of the Yalta Agreement, the Soviets proceeded to exploit this laissez faire policy to their own advantage. This unwillingness of the Western leaders to distinguish between the professed intentions of the Soviets and their actual goals contributed to the enslavement of Poland, a faithful ally of the West and an eastern outpost of Western civilization.

Although the actual conquest of Poland was performed by the Red Army and the NKVD, this was only the final step of a carefully prepared and skillfully executed move of Soviet foreign policy in general, and its diplomacy in particular. It would be an over-simplification, however, to attribute the conquest of Poland exclusively to the capacities and efforts of the Soviet Union, although by their effective use of the various arms of their foreign policy the Soviets undoubtedly must be rated as the primary cause. A major contributing factor was Allied acquiescence in Soviet acts, which Soviet diplomacy was able to win by means of a cunning verbal camouflage which deceived the Western Powers and concealed the U.S.S.R.'s real objectives.

This Western consent was necessary to the success of their planned conquest, for without it the Soviet Union alone did not have the power to enforce their *faits accomplis*. Had Britain and the United States reacted firmly to Soviet violations of the Yalta and Potsdam Agreements, as Truman was later to do in the case of Greece and Turkey, it is probable, in view of the then United States monopoly of the A-bomb, that the Soviets would not have risked war with the West. That being the case, the Soviet Union would have had no choice but to comply with Western insistence on genuinely free elections throughout Eastern Europe. As it turned out, Eastern Europe lay in a zone of indifference for the Western Allies. When the Soviet Union enslaved the Polish nation through a falsified election, the Western Powers confined the discharge of their Yalta obligations to the issuing of protestations. This ineffectual reaction finally sealed the Soviet control of Poland.

Since in a democracy the ultimate approval or disapproval of any significant step of foreign policy depends on an aroused public opinion, it may be asked how this policy towards Eastern Europe in general, and Poland in particular, could have escaped public condemnation in Britain and in America. It appears that the public in the Western democracies had been so thoroughly conditioned by Allied propaganda to think of the Soviets not only as gallant fighters on the battlefield, but also as a genuine, if somewhat peculiar, type of democratic society, that the tide of opinion so mightily whipped up could not suddenly reverse its momentum on discovering the despotism behind the mask of cooperation. Exhausted by war and not directly affected by the abuses of Soviet totalitarianism, they reacted largely with apathy and weariness. Since their comprehension was blunted by an incomplete view of the true nature of the new Soviet aggression, they did not realize that it was ultimately aimed at them.

Throughout the war and immediately thereafter both the Western Governments and their people were blinded by the Soviet contribution to the defeat of Hitler in the titanic struggle on the eastern battlefields. This feeling of gratitude led them to forget the cruelty of the Soviet leadership both towards their own people and towards their immediate neighbors. Thus the Allies overlooked the Polish contribution to the common struggle, viewing the Polish share as involving a few ground divisions or a couple of air wings supporting the British and therefore not of first-rate importance.

An objective observer of World War II, disregarding for a moment the Atlantic Charter and the Four Freedoms—as the Big Three did in their post-war settlement of Europe—might ask himself:

What would have been the outcome of World War II if the Poles, instead of rejecting the persistent German invitations to join them in their war of conquest, had accepted? If sixty Polish divisions had been equipped with German tanks and aircraft, and together with Hitler's armies had been used in 1939 either against the West or the Soviet Union, there is little doubt that Hitler would have succeeded in conquering Europe before Britain, France, and the Soviet Union could have armed themselves. Would Poland have suffered more from such a decision than she did from her alliance with the West? Presumably not. The Polish decision to resist the Nazi demands and to forfeit the rewards of Nazi promises gave Britain, France, and the Soviet Union eight precious months to prepare to defend themselves before Hitler recuperated from the Polish War and reorganized his armies. Although Great Britain and France had declared war on Hitler, they did not attempt to help Poland either through direct or indirect action against Hitler. Consequently, it was Poland who stood alone against the might of the Nazi Armies in defense of the values of Western civilization.

From the point of view of Polish survival, it might have been a kindness to Poland on the part of Great Britain and France had they *not* declared war on Germany. This might have compelled the Polish leadership to reappraise its decision to resist Hitler. Had such a reappraisal taken place and had Poland surrendered earlier, the Western Allies would have been faced with a more complicated and difficult situation. The determination of Poles to resist the Nazis in 1939 and their subsequent contribution to the common effort (400,000 men in the Home Army, 250,000 soldiers fighting in the West) put the Polish share in the ultimate military victory far above the estimation of what they actually received from their Allies. Even on the basis of this purely military calculation, leaving ethics aside for the moment, Poland deserved far better than what she actually received from her more fortunately situated Allies.

In his final attempt to justify Western policy towards Poland and in his customary accusations against the legal Polish Government, Churchill attempted to blame it for the Polish tragedy, arguing that had the Polish Government made territorial concessions to the Soviet Union early enough, it could have salvaged the political and social future of what was left of Poland. However, the fate of Czechoslovakia contradicts Churchill's conclusions. In spite of the genuine desire of two outstanding democrats of Eastern Europe, i.e., President Eduard Beneš and Foreign Minister Jan Masaryk, to live in friendship with the Soviet Union, their country was forced to share the fate of other Eastern European nations.

In the case of Poland, the Soviets argued that because of her "fascistic elements," her landlords, her hostile attitude towards the Soviet Union, her control of the non-Polish minorities, and because the Polish plains constituted an avenue of attack on the Soviet Union by aggressors from the West, Poland had to be remolded into a neighbor "friendly" towards her Eastern Ally.

These rationalizations for the Soviet conquest of Poland were not applicable to Czechoslovakia. Surely this peaceful, democratic, and mountainous nation did not endanger the security of the Soviet Union. The long and persistent efforts of Beneš to establish a friendly relationship with the Soviets counted for nothing as far as the strategic and imperialistic aims of the Soviet State were concerned. When the opportune moment arrived, the Soviets conquered Czechoslovakia as they did other Eastern European countries. Thus, there is no justification in holding the Polish Government responsible for the situation which permitted the communists to seize their country. The record is clear that the real or alleged shortcomings of the Soviet Union's neighbors are not primary or even significant reasons for the Soviets' determination to incorporate them into the communist system at an appropriate time.

As Professor Merle Fainsod correctly observed:

> The outward projection and expansion of Soviet power constitute a primary goal. . . . In this struggle, political and military weapons are treated as interchangeable. The choice of weapon depends on time, place, and circumstance. If military force promises to be decisive, there is no inhibition against its employment. The only operative limits which the Soviet leadership recognizes are the capabilities at its disposal and its own estimate of the risks involved in each act of expansion.[2]

Thus the original dogma of Marxist literature, that a proletarian revolution is the midwife of the destruction of "oppressive capitalism," has been replaced by the strategy and tactics of Soviet foreign policy, backed by the overwhelming power of the Red Army and the NKVD. What they were unable to accomplish in 1920 through attempts to incite popular revolutions among the Polish masses they achieved in the course of the Second World War through a masterful application of the elements of foreign policy. The establishment of control over Poland has extended their strategic area *vis-à-vis* the West. This may serve as a preliminary step in their persistent but tactically diversified endeavor to overturn the Western democracies—the major remaining obstacle in their path on the road to world domination.

Notes

[1] Sidney Hook, *Marx and the Marxists*, Princeton, New Jersey, D. Van Nostrand Company, Inc., 1955, p. 3.

[2] Merle Fainsod, *How Russia Is Ruled*, Cambridge, Massachusetts, Harvard University Press, 1953, p. 286.

1

Appendix

Among numerous eye-witness accounts of Soviet rule in eastern Poland, the following one is typical. Its selection and insertion into the records quoted below was dictated by their editors' high regard for the abilities of its author, Dr. Wladyslaw Wielhorski, *docent* of the University of Wilno and Director of its School of Political Science. The report describes Soviet rule in Wilno (Vilna) and covers the period from August 12, 1940 to June 23, 1941.

1. *Introductory remarks:* I am illustrating the nature of Soviet-Polish relations exclusively by my own observations and experiences and by those of my few reliable friend-companions from prison. I omitted every other story which could not be verified as absolutely reliable.
2. What were the criteria which the NKVD used in selecting people for arrest?

It was the desire of the Soviet Union to eliminate from social life all those individuals who were active, politically or ideologically, or those who could become so if conditions became favorable. The Soviet authorities decided to separate the actual or the potential leaders from the rest. For this reason, the local collaborators of the NKVD prepared lists of the potential victims, but this was ineptly done. It is for this reason that some of the actual or potential leaders were left out while people of mistaken identity were arrested, as well as those who for personal reasons were denounced by the confidants of the NKVD.

The actual "guilt" of the arrested was measured by the spirit and letter of the Soviet penal criminal code. Almost any paragraph at random of that code was used against the arrested in order to preserve the appearance of legal detention.

During the actual interrogation each prisoner was asked to describe the political activity of all his friends, acquaintances, and those whom he knew even long ago. It was irrelevant whether or not those people were involved in an action which even remotely carried an anti-Soviet stigma. These testimonies and confessions were to serve as evidence for further arrests of Polish citizens. The second reason for these confessions was to determine the guilt and punishment of the interrogated individual.

Between July 1940 and June 1941 several thousand people went through Wilno's prison, Lukiszki, before they were deported to Russia. About two-thirds of these were Poles, the others were Jews and Byelorussians. The most wanted people were members of the Polish Socialist Party and the Right Wing "Ozon." The first step of terror was gradual starvation. This was used to weaken the psychological resistance of those imprisoned. No one who was undergoing interrogation was allowed to receive any food parcels from outside. Only when the accused received his sentence was he permitted to get one food parcel a week from outside. In practice, this did not last long because the sentenced man was shortly thereafter taken away to Russia to serve his term.

According to medical doctors imprisoned, the daily ration in the autumn of 1940 consisted of 1,500 calories. The interrogations consumed most of the energy derived from that. Gradually, the weakened individuals were unable to function normally and developed a semi-coma state. After five or six months of such conditions, permission was given to purchase food from the prison canteen. As a rule, however, this was too late.

From the beginning of the interrogation, the accused was not allowed to take the half hour walk in fresh air which was provided by the prison regulations. According to that, this exercise could be suspended for a maximum of two weeks as punishment for the most severe offense. The cells of the prison had five or six times as many inmates as was prescribed by official instructions. Lack of exercise, foul air, and starvation weakened the interned. Sicknesses of heart, blood, and respiratory organs became normal phenomena. After several months most of the inmates were unable to walk into the interrogation room. For the final three to six weeks of interrogation the inmates were moved into 100 cells built in the basement of the Appeals Courthouse, where the NKVD had its headquarters. Those cells were extremely damp and were almost hermetically sealed from the outside. They had very tight iron doors and three sets of glass in each window. Only twice a day, when buckets of excrement were removed, did a little fresh air enter the cells. All physiological functions had to be performed inside. The moisture and foul air were responsible for the swelling of legs.

The brutality against the interrogated was an additional factor in breaking the health and spirit of those resisting. The accused was often kept in the interrogation room for several days without being permitted to sleep, take food or water, or to relieve himself. Dr. Wielhorski reported that he knew of cases when such treatment lasted for six days without interruption. The accused had to sit up straight. Whenever he fainted or fell asleep he was awakened with cold water or with the butts of rifles. Spitting at the face and slaps were a lighter form of torture. Beating on the head and genitals was the more severe punishment. This was applied by the interrogating judge when he decided that the accused was on the verge of a breakdown, so that the provoked shock might finally convince the delinquent to say what he was expected to say. The beating was applied at different stages of the interrogation according to the judge's appraisal of the given inmate. Women underwent the same treatment, together with the use of the most vulgar words to be found in the rich Russian vocabulary. Weeks later such inmates were unable to walk or to sit and were covered with bruises. In the cases where the most stubborn resistance was encountered the judge read to the accused a verdict of the "council of interrogating judges" sentencing him to death. At the same time he observed that if the accused confessed his guilt, the verdict would be changed. This also proved to be ineffective in most cases.

The human spirit was stronger than the methods of terror. The resistance of the accused did not depend on his degree of intelligence, education, profession, age, sex, or state of health. It was found, however, that people who earned their living through physical work (peasants, workers, or craftsmen) did show more resistance to the brutality and terror than did the intelligentsia. It was seldom that the persecutors were able to achieve their objectives. The victims became more hard and determined. Their spirit achieved unbelievable heights, and they became fearless of death. The behavior of the victims depended greatly on the moral stamina of the comrades in the cell. Often one morally strong individual was able to uplift nineteen others in the cell.

Dr. Wielhorski went through nine cells within one year. This gave him the opportunity to meet hundreds of colleagues and friends. At the beginning of the confinement the NKVD did not intend to shift people around, but later it became indispensable to inject provocateurs into each cell and this was possible only through the reshuffling of the inmates. The provocateurs began their work on the weakest (physically or psychologically) inmates to break their resistance. The other part of their assignment consisted in identifying the strongest one who provided encouragement for the weak ones. Their presence confused the others in distinguishing who was strong and who was the provocateur.

As a result of this elaborate scheme some inmates lost their minds, others developed epilepsy, still others, like Professor Kempista of Wilno University hung themselves by means of a towel. A few cut their veins and still others committed suicide in various ways. Some attempted suicide in order to get to the hospital where food and treatment were better. Even the strongest were so badly shaken that their behavior became deranged. The mentally sick were left in the cells in order to spread disorder and to exert mental pressure on the others. Corpses of those who died were left in the cells for several days to remind those who were alive that their struggle was pointless. Those sick of tuberculosis, cancer, heart disease, etc. were not treated. Their suffering was a part of their punishment.

Of the inmates about 5% were women, and another 5% consisted of students between fourteen and eighteen years of age.

After five or six months of interrogation and torture, the accused was sentenced, usually under the provisions of paragraph 58 of the Soviet Criminal Law, which is concerned with membership in a secret organization attempting to harm the U.S.S.R. through spying, propaganda or armed acts. The accused was informed of his sentence (*post facto*) in the office of the prosecuting judge. Most inmates were sentenced to labor camps for from five to eight or ten years, usually between three to fifteen years.

Sentences of death were frequently passed. The sentenced persons were then placed in separate cells especially isolated. They were able to appeal the sentence but there is no way of knowing exactly how many sentences were commuted—if any. Executions were constantly carried out in the basement.

On June 22, 1941 all prisoners were taken into the U.S.S.R. At the same time, the Lithuanian citizens who were used as supplementary guards were arrested and deported also, so that no evidence of the crimes would remain. The inmates were put into two trains, each containing twenty cattle cars. Each boxcar was 20 square meters in size. Out of the four little windows in each, three were firmly blocked off, and the fourth had iron bars. Between forty-five and fifty inmates were pushed into each of the wagons. The temperature was above 30° C. (One-fourth of the prisoners in the wagons consisted of criminals from another prison which was also evacuated. These took over "command of the wagons and created hell.") Doors were locked and conditions became unbearable. On July 3 the transport reached the prison in Gorky. During those eleven days each inmate received two and one-half kilograms of bread and a little water in three instalments. About 20% of the inmates died during the transport mainly because of the heat and the lack of water. Another 5% or 10% perished upon reaching the new prison.[1]

Notes

[1] Poland, *Official Government Documents*, Vol. II, Doc. 3.

Appendix

On July 23, 1944 the Moscow radio broadcast the news that an executive organ had been created by the so-called Home National Council under the name of "Polish Committee of National Liberation."

This same broadcast stated that the Committee consisted of thirteen departments. Given below is a list of these departments, with the names of those appointed at their head, together with the information on them available at the time.

1. *Edward Boleslaw Osobka-Morawski, Chairman of the Committee and Head of the Department of Foreign Affairs*

Before the war was an administrator of a housing cooperative in Warsaw: member of the local branch of the Polish Socialist Party. At present member of the PPR (Polish Workers' Party)—a communist organization in Poland. Has so far played no part in political life.

2. *Andrzej Witos, Vice-Chairman of the Committee, Head of the Agricultural Department*

Brother of the former Polish Premier Wincenty Witos. Left the Peasant Party in 1928 and joined the Government Bloc. In February 1940, deported from Poland to the interior of the U.S.S.R. and sentenced to death under Article 58 of the Soviet Penal Code. The sentence was not carried out because of the "amnesty" resulting from the Soviet-Polish Agreement. Before his release Witos was forced to sign a declaration that he would collaborate with the NKVD. In April 1944, Witos was appointed Deputy

Chairman of the Union of Polish Patriots, probably because of the great authority enjoyed by his brother.

3. *Wanda Wasilewska-Korneychuk, Vice Chairman of the Committee*

Member of the Supreme Soviet of the U.S.S.R. and Colonel of the Red Army. Wife of Alexander Korneychuk, until recently Foreign Minister of the Ukrainian S.S.R. Before the war a journalist with pronounced communist views. She joined the Ukrainian Communist Party in November 1939, and obtained U.S.S.R. citizenship. Chairman of the Union of Polish Patriots in Moscow and editor of its press organ, *Free Poland.*

Korneychuk is her third husband. Her first husband died before the outbreak of the war; her second, a Pole of the name Bogatko, was shot by the NKVD in Lwow.

4. *General Michal Rola-Zymierski, Head of the Department of National Defense*

His real name is Lyzminski. He assumed the name of Rola-Zymierski during the last war. In the late twenties he was reduced to the ranks by sentence of court-martial, dismissed from the Army and sentenced to five years imprisonment for a fraudulent transaction in a gas-mask factory working for the Army. At the time of this fraudulent action he was Deputy Minister of War. Discharged from prison, he entered commerce. Until taking up his present position in the Committee nothing known of his political activities.

5. *General Zygmunt Berling, Deputy Head of the Department of National Defense*

Lieutenant Colonel of the Polish Army. In 1940 a prisoner of war in the U.S.S.R. There he was contacted by the NKVD and signed a declaration of loyalty to the Soviet Union. Later he organized a group of nineteen officers who in 1940 were transferred by the NKVD to a villa near Moscow, where a course for Polish political officers of the Red Army was held. After the conclusion of the Soviet-Polish Agreement in 1941, he joined the Polish Army in Russia. When the Polish Army left the U.S.S.R. in 1942 he deserted from the Army and remained in the Soviet Union. For his desertion he was reduced to the ranks by court-martial and dismissed from the Polish Army. In the middle of 1943 he began to organize Polish units in Russia and received rapid promotion from the Soviet authorities. He now holds the rank of Lieutenant General, is Commander of Polish units in Russia and a member of the Presidium of the Union of Polish Patriots.

6. *Stanislaw Kotek-Agruszewski, Head of the Department of Public Administration*

No details available. Member of the PPR. Unknown in politics.

7. *Jan Stefan Haneman, Head of the Department of National Economy*

Before the war a bank clerk in Lodz, member of an atheist organization with communist tendencies. Played no part in politics.

8. *Janusz Czeckowski, Head of the Department of Justice*

No details available. Member of the communist organization in Poland. Name unknown in Polish politics.

9. *Stanislaw Radkiewicz, Head of the Department of Public Security*

Lawyer. Since July 16, 1944 member of the Presidium of the Union of Polish Patriots. Name unknown in Polish politics.

10. *Boleslaw Drobner, Head of the Department of Labor, Social Welfare, and Health*

Member of the Polish Socialist Party which he reportedly left to organize an independent Socialist Workers' Party with communist tendencies. In 1934–1935 expelled from the Polish Socialist Party; subsequently he was arrested as an organizer of strikes and sentenced to two years of imprisonment. In 1940 deported into the interior of the U.S.S.R. From April 1944 a member of the Presidium of the Union of Polish Patriots.

11. *Jan Michal Grubecki, Head of the Department of Transport, Posts, and Telegraphs*

Civil engineer. Since July 16, 1944 a member of the Presidium of the Union of Polish Patriots.

12. *Emil Sommerstein, Head of the Department of War Reparations*

Member of the parliamentary Zionists' Club. Holds moderate views, voted in favor of the 1935 Constitution together with his Party. Arrested in 1939 he served a long sentence in Russian prisons. Released as a result of the efforts of the Polish Embassy in the U.S.S.R. Since April 1944, member of the Presidium of the Union of Polish Patriots.

13. *Stanislaw Skrzeszowski, Head of the Department of Education*

Before the war a lecturer in the Pedagogical Institute in Krakow. Played no part in Polish politics. At present member of the Presidium of the Union of Polish Patriots.

14. *Wincenty Rzymowski, Head of the Department of Culture and Fine Arts*

Writer and prominent journalist of the "Kurjer Poranny," a Government newspaper in Warsaw. Was formerly a member of the Polish Academy of Literature. Before the war he published a book in which parts were found to have been plagiarized from a book written by Bertrand Russell. For this reason, he had to resign from the Academy.

15. *Stefan Jedrychowski, Head of the Department of Propaganda and Information*

Member of the Supreme Council of the Lithuanian SSR. Lawyer, well-known before the war for his communist activities in Wilno. At present member of the Presidium of the Union of Polish Patriots.

At the same time a Supreme Military Command has been created consisting of General Rola-Zymierski, General Zygmunt Berling, and General Alexander Zawadzki.

The latter was a Colonel in the Frontier Forces of the NKVD and commanded a sector on the border of Manchuria. In 1936 he was dismissed from the Communist Party and shortly afterwards arrested and sentenced to ten years imprisonment. In December 1943 he was assigned to the "Kosciuszko Division" and six months later was promoted to the rank of Major-General and Deputy to General Berling.

Thus it can be seen that of the fifteen members of the Committee, nine are at the same time members of the Presidium of the Union of Polish Patriots in Moscow, and four members of the communist organization in occupied Poland known as the Polish Workers' Party. At least two-thirds of the Committee are communists. Only two or three of the members have played a certain, though a very modest, part in politics; the rest are completely unknown and took no part in the public life of Poland.

Finally, two members of the Committee are members of the Supreme Soviet of the U.S.S.R.[1]

Notes

[1] Poland, *Official Government Documents*, Vol. CLVI, Doc. 184.

Appendix

One of the high-ranking officers of the Polish Security Police, Jozef Swiatlo, who later defected to the West, gave this writer the following description of the "elections" in Poland:

Before anybody is elected or, as it is termed, "chosen" as a member of Party authorities or as a delegate to the meetings, as a deputy to the Sejm, or as a councilor to the National Council, the Tenth Department of the Security Police[1] must express its opinion about every individual candidate. I emphasize that this refers to all Party functionaries, delegates to the meetings of deputies and councilors except for the members of the Politburo. The Tenth Department is presented by the Party with a list of candidates whom they wish to have and who later will be elected, and is told: "Check what you have in your files." Then the Tenth Department checks all names with their own security files and the courts' conviction registers. After that, it fills out for each individual candidate an extremely detailed questionnaire. That type of questionnaire and its contents was prepared by the Tenth Department and accepted by Antoni Alster, Chief of the organization section of the Central Committee of P.Z.P.R. (Polish United Workers Party), an old communist. The demand for this questionnaire is so great that Radkiewicz (the Minister of the Security Police) gave instructions to the secret printing establishment of the Ministry of Security, which is located in Mokotowski Prison, to print several thousand of those questionnaires. Everything is included in that questionnaire: Starting from the candidate's birth, the period of his eventual studies, social work, private life, political past, governmental work, till the very moment of his becoming a councilor, deputy, delegate to a meeting, or member of the Party Executive. In the questionnaire there are details concerning his family, whether and with whom he carries on correspondence, whether he is going abroad and how he behaves. Briefly every candidate is described completely and there is not a single factor which we would not examine thoroughly. The questionnaire of each individual candidate starts to be filled on the proper regional level. The candidates proposed by the Party are divided by groups of five to ten people. To each group a special U.B. (Security Police) functionary is assigned, who works on them according to the questionnaire and is obliged to examine their past in a most thorough way. The second investigation is carried on by the Tenth Department. It is a tremendous task. To perform that work two or three functionaries from each regional Security Office are recalled to Warsaw. The workers from the Central Office are assigned to these functionaries but they are especially responsible for candidates from their own districts.

If, after such a thorough investigation, results are satisfactory, only then will the so-called Party masses "choose" a particular person as their candidate to the Party Executive, as their delegate, or the nation will "choose" him for the post of a deputy or councilor. If we reject him, then it is certain that "the nation will never present him" as its candidate. Occasionally Bierut himself intervenes in such a matter, but only in cases when criminal offenses are involved, never when the candidate's Party or political past is questioned. I remember such a case during the election to the Sejm in 1952, when a certain Karasiewicz or Karasinski was a candidate as a deputy. I don't recall his exact name right now. When the Party presented his photo and published his life story, a young girl reported to this Security Office at Czestochowa and declared: "How is it possible that the same Karasiewicz who killed my father and was tried and sentenced for six years, now will be a deputy?" The poor girl, seeking justice in People's Poland, did not realize that the Party knew that before choosing him as its candidate. Then we did a summary and presented it to "Comrade Tomasz" (Bierut). We received instructions from Bierut to investigate to what extent the whole affair had been publicized. We made an investigation and found that the whole case was not well known among the population of Czestochowa, as Karasiewicz did not live there before the war. Then Bierut decided: "Let them choose him." Bierut did not see anything improper in the fact that a candidate for the post of a deputy was a murderer. Finally, Karasiewicz—or Karasinski, the exact name I don't recall— a murderer, sentenced for six years to prison, became a deputy to the Sejm.

This method of selecting the candidates was only one of the tasks of the Security Police. Another was to make sure that the candidates were elected. Reporting on this aspect of Security Police activity, Swiatlo went on to say:

I was a member of a Special Central Commission to Falsify the Elections in Poland. This was not its official name, but it served only this objective. It was established by the Political Bureau of the Central Committee of the Polish United Workers Party long before organizing the elections to the Sejm. I know how the election returns in 1947 were faked, and therefore I decisively state that these elections to the Sejm and all other elections in Poland have been falsified by the Party and the Government. The Political Bureau as well as the Ministry of Security have no doubt whatsoever as to the sentiments of the people and how they behave. And therefore we knew perfectly well that the vast majority of the people hated the Party and the men who seized power. In the Political Bureau no one has the slightest doubt that the communists can not win the elections in Poland without cheating.

In 1947 the Party laid stress on the selection of the members of the election commissions. People, mostly from Lodz and Katowice, whom the Central Committee could absolutely trust, were sent to the various districts. The second category of the members of the electoral commissions was composed of regular agents of the Security Office and consequently of people who, by reason of their functions, were obliged to blind obedience. In the respective districts instructions for them were different and depended on the calculations of so-called election mathematicians. They were confidence men of the Central Committee specially sent to each district. One of their duties was to forecast how many votes were to come from the polls, how many valid, how many invalid, and how many votes were to be cast for a given list, so that the returns could be according to the wishes of the Party. Moreover, each candidate from the so-called "democratic list" had to sign an undated declaration beforehand, about resigning his seat. These declarations were filed in the Central Committee. In this way the Central Committee held each deputy under its strong control and could blackmail him. In case of insubordination, the signed declaration was made public. Thus each deputy from each list could in practice be immediately recalled by order of the Central Committee of the Communist Party.[2]

Notes

[1] According to Swiatlo, "The Tenth Department safeguards the purity of Party ranks. It is, in the full meaning of the term, the counter-intelligence of the Party, directed against all Party deviations, especially against rightist, nationalist, and Trotskyist factions. It is the best proof that those factions exist. The Department is also responsible for fighting foreign espionage and the influence of the pre-war Military Intelligence; for processing the activity of the pre-war police and its informers; for collecting material concerning the informers and the collaborators of the Gestapo during the occupation. In order to facilitate its activities, the Tenth Department has an Investigation Department at its disposal, its own section in Mokotowski Prison, and other villa prisons—among others, Miedzeszyn near Warsaw." *Loc. cit., Inside Story of Bezpieka,* New York, Radio Free Europe, 1954.

[2] Swiatlo, *loc. cit.*

Appendix

The most authoritative information as to how Poland was ruled since Mikolajczyk left is provided by Jozef Swiatlo. According to Swiatlo:

Poland is ruled only and exclusively by Moscow. It is necessary to distinguish between two channels. The first is the Soviet channel—the Kremlin, or, in other words, the Politburo of the Soviet Party, Soviet advisers in Poland, in the Warsaw Ministry of Security, and the Soviet Ambassador. That is how the situation looks from the Soviet side, whence come the decisions and instructions. On a lower level there is the so-called Polish channel to which belong Bierut and the Politburo, Rokossovski, and the Ministry of Security. That is the executive level.

The general political line is decided in Moscow at the conferences, in which some other members of the Soviet Party Politburo participate. Crucial decisions are made there concerning changes in policy. To obtain those instructions Bierut always goes personally to Moscow. Most often he takes some other members of the Warsaw Politburo with him, especially when it is known in advance that the new instructions will have to be executed on the local Polish level by Ochab, Mazur, or somebody else. It often happens that Berman says to "Comrade Tomasz" (Bierut), "This time you should take Ochab, as he has not been to Moscow for a long time." Anyway, Bierut is always the only person who receives the essential political instructions in Moscow, but that refers only to political matters. The military instructions concerning army assignments and plans are obtained by Rokossovski directly from the Soviet army headquarters. Most often Bierut is not familiar with military directives. In Warsaw, Rokossovski is not active in political life. Very often he does not participate in the meetings of the Politburo; he simply does not come. On the other hand he almost never informs Bierut of his military matters. This way political and military instructions come through separate channels and in Poland they do not merge either. As a matter of fact it is possible to assert that Soviet control on the Polish executive level is unnecessary. Bierut and his collaborators are always so well trained that they fulfill Moscow orders even more fervently than is needed and often they go far ahead in guessing Moscow's wishes and intentions.

Nevertheless the entire Polish political and economic life is held in a hard, iron grip which is concentrated in the Ministry of Security. That rigid control is executed by a group of the so-called Soviet advisers who are headed by General Lalin. Those advisers receive instructions directly from Moscow, and supervise the performance of political and economic assignments designed for Warsaw. The Ministry of Security is organized in a way which gives it the chance to control all phases of life in Poland. Having such an arrangement in operation, the function of the Soviet Ambassador in Warsaw is limited to the reporting of the existing situation. Right now the Soviet Ambassador is almost exclusively a diplomat who is not intervening in Polish problems because it is simply not necessary. There are others who perform those functions. Only sporadically does the Soviet Ambassador present some additional suggestions. But he does this always in a very delicate way. The Warsaw regime is very sensitive in that respect. On the other hand, Moscow wishes to retain in their diplomatic relations the appearance of Warsaw's independence. That was one of the reasons why Bierut and the Politburo achieved Lebedev's recall, as he was very aggressive and brutal.

The Soviet Union is extremely careful to hide from the Polish people the true wheels of government in Poland. They want the people to believe that the Polish Government, as well as the Polish Communist Party, are truly independent and sovereign, directed only by the wishes and interests of the Polish people. That is why in such parts of public life as the economy, politics, and so forth, where large masses participate, there is no direct Soviet interference, no Soviet agent—of course, only on the surface.

The Soviets use two methods to control Poland; one political, the other through the MVD (the Ministry of Public Security of the U.S.S.R.). The political bureau of the Central Committee of the U.S.S.R., usually known as the political bureau, is the direct superior of the political bureau of the Communist Party in Poland.

Within the Polish Communist Party, you have departments all of which coincide with or correspond to all ministries in the Polish Government, as well as to the most important activities in public life, such as transport, religious activity, economic, and so forth.

Any chief of any department in the Polish political party is the superior authority of the respective ministry in the Government. So, the chief of the economic division in the party is of a higher rank than the Minister of National Economy.

Since that is so, the party is really the directing and controlling body in Poland.

Now, independently of this first line of dependence on the Soviet Union through the party apparatus, there is a second channel of control which goes from the Soviet MGB (Ministry of State Security)[1] to the Ministry of Public Security in Poland.

In the Ministry of Public Security there are departments which are responsible for every activity of public life, and for every ministry in the Government. Soviet advisers or controllers work through the Ministry of Public Security. So, externally, as far as the masses are concerned, nobody sees the Soviet controllers, called "advisers."

The Polish Government is controlled directly by the party. The party is controlled by the Ministry of Public Security.

SOVIET CONTROL OF POLAND

SOVIET UNION

Political Bureau of the Central Committee of U.S.S.R.	M.V.D. Ministry of Internal Security U.S.S.R.	
Communist Party of Soviet Union		

POLAND

	Political Bureau of Central Committee of Poland	M.B.P. Ministry of Public Security Poland
	Polish Communist Party (P.Z.P.R.—United Workers Party)	
Central Committee	P.Z.P.R. Polish Communist Party	Security of Communist Party Members
Regional Committee City Committee County Committee Cell Committee	Other Political Parties Subversive Elements Ministry of Foreign Affairs	Internal Security Political Parties Subversive Elements
	Economic Trade—commerce agriculture heavy & light industries	Security of Regime's Economy System
	Transport railroad—air lines highways—maritime	Security of Regime's Transport System
	Religious Affairs Church—Clergy	Security of Religious Affairs
		Foreign Intelligence

The Ministry of Public Security, in every department, has a Soviet adviser who, of course, is directly controlled and ordered by the Soviet authorities. However, the populace does not see these Soviet advisers.

With such a structure the Soviet Union does not need to have its own representatives (controllers) in the Polish administration, in the Polish Government, or in the Polish public organizations. It is sufficient for them to control the Polish Security apparatus.

Consequently, no one can be appointed as a member of the Polish Central Committee of the Polish Communist Party, and no one can receive any higher position in the Government without the prior approval of the Soviet authorities, since all such people must first receive a security clearance through the Ministry of Public Security. Of course, the Soviet Union grants its approval to such a nomination only if it is absolutely sure that the man will serve Soviet interests primarily. As far as the Polish Government is concerned, it is but a figurehead in Polish political life.[2]

Notes

[1] This Ministry was subsequently reorganized in 1954 from the Ministry of State Security (MGB) to the Committee on State Security (KGB), currently headed by General Ivan Serov. (Author)

[2] Swiatlo, *loc. cit.*, No. 13.

5

Appendix

CONCLUSIONS OF THE SPECIAL COMMISSION INVESTIGATING
THE CIRCUMSTANCES OF THE SHOOTING OF POLISH
PRISONERS BY THE GERMANS IN THE KATYN FOREST

This report was published in January 1944 and the full text in
English appeared in a special supplement to *Soviet War News*.

From all the material at the disposal of the Special Commission, namely
evidence given by over 100 witnesses questioned, data supplied by the
medico-legal experts, documents and material evidence found in the graves
in the Katyn Forest, the following conclusions emerge with irrefutable
clarity:

(1) The Polish prisoners of war who were in the three camps west of
Smolensk, and employed on road building before the outbreak of war,
remained there after the German invaders reached Smolensk, until September 1941, inclusive.

(2) In the Katyn Forest, in the autumn of 1941, the German occupation
authorities carried out mass shootings of Polish prisoners of war from the
above-named camps.

(3) The mass shootings of Polish prisoners of war in the Katyn Forest
was carried out by a German military organization hiding behind the
conventional name "H.Q. of the 537th Engineering Battalion," which consisted of Ober-leutnant Arnes, his assistant Ober-leutnant Rekst, and Lieutenant Hott.

(4) In connection with the deterioration of the general military and
political situation for Germany at the beginning of the year 1943, the German occupation authorities, with provocational aims, took a number of

steps in order to ascribe their own crimes to the organs of the Soviet Power, calculating on setting Russians and Poles at loggerheads.

(5) With this aim, (*a*) the German-Fascist invaders, using persuasion, attempts at bribery, threats and barbarous torture, tried to find witnesses among Soviet citizens, from whom they tried to extort false evidence alleging that the Polish prisoners of war had been shot by the organs of Soviet Power in the spring of 1940; (*b*) the German occupation authorities in the spring of 1943 brought in from other districts bodies of Polish war prisoners whom they had shot and put them into the open graves in the Katyn Forest, calculating on covering up the traces of their own crimes, and on increasing the number of "victims of Bolshevik atrocities" in the Katyn Forest; (*c*) preparing for their provocation, the German occupation authorities started opening the graves in the Katyn Forest, in order to take out documents and material evidence which exposed them, using for this work about 500 Russian prisoners of war who were shot by the Germans after the work was completed.

(6) It has been established beyond doubt from the evidence of the medico-legal experts, that (*a*) the time of the shooting was the autumn of 1941; (*b*) in shooting the Polish war prisoners the German hangmen applied the same method of pistol shots in the back of the head as they applied in the mass execution of Soviet citizens in other towns, e.g., Orel, Voronezh, Krasnodar and Smolensk itself.

(7) The conclusions drawn from the evidence given by witnesses, and from the findings of the medico-legal experts on the shooting of Polish war prisoners by the Germans in the autumn of 1941, are completely confirmed by the material evidence and documents excavated from the Katyn graves.

(8) In shooting the Polish war prisoners in the Katyn Forest, the German-Fascist invaders consistently carried out their policy of physical extermination of the Slav peoples.

SIGNED:

Chairman of the Commission, Academician Burdenko.
Members:
Academician Alexei Tolstoy.
The Metropolitan Nikolai.
Chairman of the All-Slav Committee, Lieutenant-General Gundorov.
Chairman of the Executive Committee of the Union of the Red Cross and Red Crescent Societies, Kolesnikov.
People's Commissar for Education of the Russian S.F.S.R., Academician Potemkin.
Chief of the Central Medical Administration of the Red Army, Colonel-General Smirnov.
Chairman of the Smolensk Regional Executive Committee, Melnikov
Smolensk, 24 January 1944.[1]

Notes

[1] S. Konovalov (ed.), *Russo-Polish Relations,* Princeton, Princeton University Press, 1945, pp. 92–94.

Bibliography

DOCUMENTS

Degras, Jane (ed.), *Soviet Documents on Foreign Policy* (3 vols.), London, Oxford University Press, 1951–1953.

Great Britain, 122 *Hansard's Parliamentary Debates*, CDIII, September 28, 1944.

International Military Tribunal, *Indictment of the German War Criminals Presented to the International Tribunal at Nürnberg:* Count Three—War Crimes Section (c), Murder and Ill-Treatment of Prisoners of War, Section 2.

Mikolajczyk, Stanislaw, *Private Files*, Vols. X, XII, XLIII, LII, CII, CXV, CCXCI. This list does not include all volumes consulted. Only those cited in the text are listed.

Poland, Ministry of Foreign Affairs of the Polish People's Republic, *Documents on the Hostile Policy of the United States Government towards People's Poland*, Warsaw, 1953.

Poland, Ministry of Foreign Affairs, *The Polish White Book*, Official Documents Concerning Polish-German and Polish-Soviet Relations, 1933–1939, published by authority of the Polish Government, London and Melbourne, Hutchinson & Company (publishers), Ltd.

Poland, *The Eastern Provinces of Poland*, Polish Ministry of Preparatory Work Concerning the Peace Conference, London, 1944.

Poland, *Polish-Soviet Relations 1918–1943*, published by the Polish Embassy in Washington, 1943.

Poland, *Official Government Documents*, Vols. II, III, IV, V, VII, X, XII, XIII, XV, XVII, XXI, XLIII, L, LII, LVI, LXIV, LXVIII, CII, CXV, CLVI, CLXI, CCXCI. This list does not include all volumes consulted. Only those cited in the text are listed.

Polska (Poland), *Przyczyny Ucieczki Mikolajczyka. Zatajony Dokument. Rewe-*

lacyjne Zeznania (Reasons for Mikolajczyk's Escape. Secret Document. Revealing Testimonies), Poznan, Wielkopolska Ksiagarnia Wydawnicza, 1947.

Sukiennicki, Wiktor, *Report on the Massacre of Polish Officers in Katyn Wood: Facts and Documents*, London, Kolins, 1946.

U.S. Department of State, *Nazi-Soviet Relations, 1939–1941,* Documents from the Archives of the German Foreign Office, edited by Raymond James Sontag and James Stuart Beddie, 1948.

U.S. Department of State, *Official Record of the Yalta Conference,* New York, *The New York Times,* March 17, 1955.

U.S. House of Representatives, *The Strategy and Tactics of World Communism,* Report No. 619, 80th Congress, 2nd Session, 1948.

U.S.S.R., *Constitution of the U.S.S.R. 1936,* New York, International Publishers, 1937.

U.S.S.R., Ministry of Foreign Affairs of the U.S.S.R., *Documents and Material Relating to the Eve of the Second World War,* November 1937–1938, from the Archives of the German Ministry of Foreign Affairs, printed in the U.S.S.R.

BOOKS

Anders, Wladyslaw, *An Army in Exile: The Story of the Second Polish Corps,* London, Macmillan & Company, 1951.

Bardoux, Jacques, *De Paris a Spa, La Bataille Diplomatique Pour la Paix Française* (From Paris to Spa, The Diplomatic Battle for the Peace of France), Paris, F. Alcan, 1921.

Beneš, Eduard, *Memoirs,* Boston, Houghton Mifflin Company, 1954.

Bilainkin, G., *Maisky: Ten Years Ambassador,* London, Allen and Unwin, 1944.

Bonnet, Georges, *Défense de la Paix: De Washington ou Quai d'Orsay* (Defense of Peace: From Washington to the Quai d'Orsay), Geneva, Bournin, 1946.

Buell, R., *Poland, Key to Europe,* 3rd edition, New York, Knopf, 1939.

Byrnes, James F., *Speaking Frankly,* New York and London, Harper & Brothers, 1947.

Carr, E. H., *The Bolshevik Revolution, 1917–1923* (3 vols.), New York, The Macmillan Company, 1951–1953.

Chamberlin, W. H., *The Russian Revolution, 1917–1921* (2 vols.), New York, The Macmillan Company, 1935.

Churchill, Winston S., *The Aftermath, The World Crisis, 1918–1928,* New York, Charles Scribner's Sons, 1929.

—— *The Second World War,* Houghton Mifflin Company, 1948–1953.

—— *The Gathering Storm,* Boston, Houghton Mifflin Company, 1948.

—— *Their Finest Hour,* Boston, Houghton Mifflin Company, 1949.

—— *The Grand Alliance,* Boston, Houghton Mifflin Company, 1951.

—— *The Hinge of Fate,* Boston, Houghton Mifflin Company, 1950.

—— *Closing the Ring,* Boston, Houghton Mifflin Company, 1951.

—— *Triumph and Tragedy,* Boston, Houghton Mifflin Company, 1953.

Ciechanowski, Jan, *Defeat in Victory,* Garden City, New York, Doubleday & Company, Inc., 1947.

Clausewitz, Karl von, *La Campagne de 1812 en Russie* (The Campaign of 1812 in Russia), trans. M. Gegouen, Paris, R. Chapelot et Cie., 1900.

Clemenceau, G., *Grandeur and Misery of Victory,* New York, Harcourt, Brace and Company, 1930.

Czapski, Jozef, *What Happened in Katyn*, Newport, Rhode Island, United States Naval War College, Department of Intelligence, 1950.

—— *Wspomnienia Starobielskie* (Memories of Starobielsk), Wyd. 2. (Nakladem Oddzialu Kultury i Prasy 2go Korpusu), 1945.

Czarski, Z., *Od Borysowa do Rygi* (From Borysow to Riga), Warszawa, Drukiarnia Polska, 1930.

Dallin, David J., and Boris I. Nicolaevsky, *Forced Labor in Soviet Russia*, New Haven, Yale University Press, 1947.

Dallin, David J., *Soviet Russia's Foreign Policy 1939–1942*, New Haven, Yale University Press, 1942.

Dangerfield, Elma, *Beyond the Urals*, London, British League for European Freedom, 1946.
   This book deals with the persecution and deportation of over a million citizens from Poland by the Soviet authorities during September 1939—June 1941.

Davies, Joseph E., *Mission to Moscow*, New York, Pocket Book Edition, Inc., 1941.

Dennett, Raymond and Joseph Johnson (ed.), *Negotiating with the Russians*, Boston, World Peace Foundation, 1951.

Fainsod, Merle, *How Russia Is Ruled*, Cambridge, Harvard University Press, 1953.

Fisher, Louis, *Soviets in World Affairs* (2 vols.), Princeton, Princeton University Press, 1952.

Fisher, Ruth, *Stalin and German Communism*, Cambridge, Harvard University Press, 1948.

Gliksman, J., *Tell the West*, New York, Greshman Press, 1948.
   A first-hand account of Soviet labor camps by one of the victims.

Goebbels, Joseph, *The Goebbels Diaries*, Introduction and Notes by Louis P. Lochner, Garden City, New York, Doubleday & Company, Inc., 1948.

Griffis, Stanton, *Lying in State*, Garden City, New York, Doubleday & Company, Inc., 1952.
   An account of events in People's Poland by a United States ambassador.

Gurian, Waldemar (ed.), *The Soviet Union: Background, Idelogy, Reality*, Notre Dame, Indiana, University of Notre Dame Press, 1951.

—— *Soviet Imperialism: Its Origins and Tactics*, Notre Dame, Indiana, University of Notre Dame Press, 1953.

Hazard, John (ed.), *Soviet Legal Philosophy*, trans. Hugh W. Babb, Cambridge, Harvard University Press, 1951.

Henderson, H. W., *An Outline of Polish-Soviet Relations*, Perth, Scotland, The Munro Press, Ltd.

Hook, Sidney, *Marx and the Marxists: The Ambiguous Legacy*, Princeton, New York, D. Van Nostrand Company, Inc., 1955.

Hull, Cordell, *The Memoirs of Cordell Hull*, New York, The Macmillan Company, 1948.

Hunt, Carew R. N., *The Theory and Practice of Communism*, New and revised edition, New York, The Macmillan Company, 1951.

Karski, Jan (pseud.), *Story of a Secret State*, Boston, Houghton Mifflin Company, 1943.
   A first-hand account of the organization and function of the Polish Underground.

Kohn, Hans, *Pan-Slavism, Its History and Ideology*, Notre Dame, Indiana, University of Notre Dame Press, 1953.

Konovalov, S. (ed.), *Russo-Polish Relations*, Princeton, Princeton University Press, 1945.
This book upholds the Soviet claim to eastern Poland.
Korbonski, Stefan, *W Imieniu Rzeczypospolitej* . . . (In the Name of the Republic), Paryz, Instytut Literacki, 1954.
Korovin, E. A., *Mezhdunarodnoe Pravo Na Sovremennom Etape* (International Law at the Present Stage), Moscow, 1946.
Kot, Stanislaw, *Listy z Rosji do Gen. Sikorskiego* (Letters from Russia to General Sikorski), London, St. Martin's Printers, 1956.
Kumaniecki, Kazimierz Wladyslaw, *Odbudowa Panstwowosci Polskiej, Najwazniejsze Dokumenty 1912–Styczen 1924* (The Reconstruction of Polish Statehood, The Most Important Documents 1912–January 1924), Krakow, Ksiegarnia Powszechna, 1924.
Lane, Arthur Bliss, *I Saw Poland Betrayed*, Indianapolis, Bobbs-Merrill Company, 1948.
Langer, William Leonard and S. E. Gleason, *Undeclared War 1940–1941*, New York, Harper & Brothers, 1953.
Lansing, Robert, *The Big Four and Others of the Peace Conference*, Boston, Houghton Mifflin Company, 1929.
Lenin, V. I., *Marxism*, London, Modern Books, Ltd., 1929.
Lenin, V. I., *Imperialism, The Highest State of Capitalism*, Moscow, Foreign Languages Publishing House, 1940.
——— *Socialism and War*, Moscow, Foreign Languages Publishing House, 1950.
——— *The State and Revolution*, New York, International Publishers, 1932.
——— *Two Tactics of Social Democracy in the Democratic Revolution*, New York, International Publishers, 1935.
——— *Sochineniya* (Works) (35 vols.), 4th edition, *Gosudarstvennoe Izdatel'stvo Politicheskoi Literatury*, Moscow, 1941–1951.
Leninism, Selected Writings, New York, International Publishers, 1945.
Lloyd George, David, *The Truth About the Peace Treaties* (2 vols.), London, V. Gollancz, Ltd., 1938.
——— *War Memoirs of David Lloyd George* (6 vols.), Boston, Little Brown and Company, 1933–1937.
Mackiewicz, S., *Colonel Beck and His Policy*, London, Eyre and Spottiswood, 1944.
Marx, Karl and Friedrich Engels, *The Russian Menace to Europe*, edited by Paul W. Blacstock and Bert F. Hoselitz, Glencoe, Illinois; The Free Press, 1952.
Mehnert, Klaus, *Stalin Versus Marx*, London, George Allen and Unwin, Ltd., 1952.
Mikolajczyk, Stanislaw, *The Rape of Poland: Pattern of Soviet Aggression*, New York and Toronto, Whittlesey House, McGraw-Hill Book Company, Inc., 1948.
Moore, Barrington, *Soviet Politics: The Dilemma of Power; the Role of Ideas in Social Change*, Cambridge, Harvard University Press, 1950.
Neumann, William L., *Making the Peace 1941–1945*, Washington, Foundation for Foreign Affairs, 1950.
A very critical appraisal of Roosevelt's and Churchill's policies.
Paris Peace Conference, 1919–1920, *Traktat Pokoju Miedzy Mocarstwami Sprzymierzonemi i Stowarzyszonemi a Niemcami*, Podpisany w Wersalu 28 Czerwca 1919 (Peace Treaty Between Allied and Associated Nations and Germany, Signed in Versailles 28 June 1919), Warsaw, 1919.

Paris Peace Conference, 1919–1920, *Proposal of the Russian Political Conference in Paris to the Peace Conference on the Question of the Nationalities in Russia,* Paris, 1919.

Potemkin, V. P. (ed.), *Istoria Diplomatii* (The History of Diplomacy) (3 vols.), Moscow, 1941–1945.

Ross, M., *A History of Soviet Foreign Policy,* New York, Workers Library Publishers, 1940.

Schwarz, Solomon M., *The Jews in the Soviet Union,* Syracuse, Syracuse University Press, 1951.

Scott, J., *Duel for Europe,* Boston, Houghton Mifflin Company, 1942.

Seton-Watson, Hugh, *From Lenin to Malenkov,* New York, F. A. Praeger, 1953.

Sherwood, Robert E., *Roosevelt and Hopkins,* New York, Harper & Brothers, 1948.

Shotwell, James T. and Max M. Lasernon, *Poland and Russia 1919–1945,* New York, King's Crown Press, published for the Carnegie Endowment for International Peace.

The significance of this book lies in the fact that it provides a rationale for the fourth partition of Poland.

Stalin, Joseph, *Theory and Practice of Leninism,* London, published by the Communist Party of Great Britain, 1926.

—— *Leninism,* New York, International Publishers, 1928.

—— *The Great Patriotic War of the Soviet Union,* New York, International Publishers, 1945.

—— *Marxism and the National Question,* New York, International Publishers, 1942.

—— *Dialectical and Historical Materialism,* Moscow, Foreign Languages Publishing House, 1951.

—— *For Peaceful Co-existence—Post-war Interviews,* New York, International Publishers, 1951.

Stettinius, Edward R., Jr., *Roosevelt and the Russians: The Yalta Conference,* New York, Doubleday & Company, Inc., 1949.

Stewart, George, *The White Armies of Russia,* New York, The Macmillan Company, 1933.

Stypulkowski, Z., *Invitation to Moscow,* London, Thames and Hudson, 1951.

Taracouzio, T. A., *The Soviet Union and International Law,* New York, The Macmillan Company, 1935.

—— *War and Peace in Soviet Diplomacy,* New York, The Macmillan Company, 1940.

Temperley, *A History of the Peace Conference of Paris,* edited by H. W. V. Temperley (6 vols.), London, H. Frowde, Hodder and Stoughton, 1920–1924.

Timasheff, Nicholas S., *The Great Retreat,* New York, E. P. Dutton & Company, 1946.

Toynbee, Arnold and Frank T. Ashton-Gwatkin (ed.), *The World in March 1939,* London, Oxford University Press, Royal Institute of International Affairs, 1952.

Tommasini, Francesco, *La Resurrezione della Polonia* (The Rebirth of Poland), Milano, 1925 Odrodzenie Polski, Warszawa, Nak. F. Hoesicka, 1928.

Trotsky, Leon, *The Revolution Betrayed. What Is the Soviet Union and Where Is It Going?* Translated by Max Eastman, Garden City, New York, Doubleday & Company, Inc., 1937.

Truman, Harry S., *Year of Decisions,* Garden City, New York, Doubleday & Company, Inc., 1955.
Umiastowski, R., *Russia and the Polish Republic, 1918–1941,* London, Aquafondata, 1945.
U.S.S.R., *Strategy and Tactics of the Proletarian Revolution,* New York, International Publishers, 1946.
Vyshinsky, Andrei Y., *The Law of the Soviet State,* translated by Hough W. Babb, New York, The Macmillan Company, 1948.
Willkie, Wendell L., *One World,* New York, Simon and Schuster, 1943.
Zhukov, E. M., *Sovetskii Souz v Borbe za Sovobodii i Nezavisimost Narodov* (The Soviet Union in a Struggle for the Freedom and Independence of Nations), Moscow, 1947.

PAMPHLETS

Duchess of Athol, *Polish Elections: The Background,* London, The British League for European Freedom, 1947.
Bregman, A. (ed.), *Faked Elections in Poland as Reported by Foreign Observers,* London, The Polish Freedom Movement "Independence and Democracy," 1947.
British Joint Committee for Polish Affairs, *The Polish Elections 19th January 1947,* Newton, Montgomeryshire, Montgomeryshire Printing Company, Ltd., 1947.
Foreign Affairs, Dexter, Byron, *Clausewitz and Soviet Strategy,* XXIX, No. 1, October, 1950.
Great Britain, *Report on the Crimea Conference, 11 February, 1945,* London, printed and published by His Majesty's Stationary Office, 1945.
Journal of Central European Affairs, April 1949, D. Dallin, *The Month of Decision, July 22–August 22, 1939.*
Molotov, V. M., *Stalin and Stalin's Leadership,* Moscow, Foreign Languages Publishing House, 1950.
——, *Speeches and Statements made at the Moscow Session of the Council of Foreign Ministers, 1947,* London, published by "Soviet News," 1947.
News from Behind the Iron Curtain. The Swiatlo Story, IV. No. 3, New York, Free Europe Press, Free Europe Committee, Inc., March, 1955.
Nowa Polska (New Poland, Monthly), Tom. III, Londyn, Wrzesien, 1944.
Sovetskoe Gosudarstvo i Pravo (Soviet State and Law), Moscow.
Swiatlo, Jozef, *Inside Story of Bezpieka,* New York, Radio Free Europe, 1954.
U.S.S.R., The Soviet Embassy, *Information Bulletin,* Washington, 1946.

Note: This bibliography does not include names of the various newspapers cited in the text or those consulted.

Index